FOURTH EDITION

EFFECTIVE PROJECT MANAGEMENT

JAMES P. CLEMENTS
Towson University

•

JACK GIDO
Penn State University

Australia • Brazil • Japan • Korea • Mexico • Singapore • Spain • United Kingdom • United States

Effective Project Management, Fourth Edition

James P. Clements and Jack Gido

VP/Editorial Director:
Jack W. Calhoun

Editor-in-Chief:
Alex von Rosenberg

Senior Acquisitions Editor:
Charles McCormick, Jr.

Senior Developmental Editor:
Laura Bofinger

Marketing Coordinator:
Suellen Ruttkay

Marketing Manager:
Bryant Chrzan

Production Technology Analyst:
Adam Grafa

Content Project Manager:
Jacquelyn K Featherly

Technology Project Manager:
Robin Browning

Editorial Assistant:
Bryn Lathrop

Senior Manufacturing Coordinator:
Diane Gibbons

Production House/Compositor:
Integra

Senior Art Director:
Stacy Jenkins Shirley

Internal Designer:
Lou Ann Thesing

Cover Image:
© Brand X Pictures, Inc.

For product information and technology assistance, contact us at **Cengage Learning Customer & Sales Support, 1-800-354-9706**

For permission to use material from this text or product, submit all requests online at **www.cengage.com/permissions** Further permissions questions can be emailed to **permissionrequest@cengage.com**

Library of Congress Control Number: 2008923299
International Student Edition Package 13: 978-0-324-65889-7
International Student Edition Package 10: 0-324-65889-3

Cengage Learning International Offices

Asia
cengageasia.com
tel: (65) 6410 1200

Australia/New Zealand
cengage.com.au
tel: (61) 3 9685 4111

Brazil
cengage.com.br
tel: (011) 3665 9900

India
cengage.co.in
tel: (91) 11 30484837/38

Latin America
cengage.com.mx
tel: +52 (55) 1500 6000

UK/Europe/Middle East/Africa
cengage.co.uk
tel: (44) 207 067 2500

Represented in Canada by Nelson Education, Ltd.
nelson.com
tel: (416) 752 9100 / (800) 668 0671

For product information: **international.cengage.com**
Visit your local office: **international.cengage.com/regions**
Visit our corporate website: **cengage.com**

Printed in Canada
2 3 4 5 6 7 12 11 10 09

To Beth, Tyler, Hannah, Maggie, and Grace for bringing me so much joy and happiness. I love you all very much!

J.P.C.

To my wonderful family: my wife, Rosemary; our sons, Steve and Jeff; our "daughters", Teresa and Wendy; and our marvelous grandchildren, Matthew, Alex, Allison, Meghan, and Sophie.

J.G.

Brief Contents

Contents

Part 3

Preface

We'll start digging from this side of the mountain. You and your gang start digging from the other side. When we meet in the middle, we will have made a tunnel. And if we don't meet, we will have made two tunnels!

OUR APPROACH

Project management is more than merely parceling out work assignments to individuals and hoping that they will somehow accomplish a desired result. In fact, projects that could have been successful often fail because of such take-it-for-granted approaches. Individuals need hard information and real skills to work successfully in a project environment and to accomplish project objectives. *Effective Project Management* was written to equip its users with both—by explaining concepts and techniques and by using numerous examples to show how they can be skillfully applied.

Although the focus of the book is squarely on the practical things readers absolutely need to know to thrive in project environments, the book does not forsake objective learning; it simply challenges readers to think critically about project management principles and to apply them within the context of the real world. We capture lessons learned from years of managing projects, teaching project management, and writing extensively about it.

Effective Project Management is intended for students as well as for working professionals and volunteers. The book is designed to present the essential skills readers need to make effective contributions and to have an immediate impact on the accomplishment of projects in which they are involved. Thus, it supports business and industry's lifelong learning programs, which develop and train employees to succeed on interdisciplinary and cross-functional teams, and it sends students into the workforce with marketable skills.

Effective Project Management is written for everyone involved in projects, not just project managers. Projects with good or even great project managers still may not succeed, as the best efforts of all involved are essential. All the people on the project team must have the knowledge and skills to work effectively together in a project environment. People do not become project managers by reading books; they become project managers by first being effective project team members. This book provides the foundation individuals need to be effective members of project teams and thereby boosts everyone's potential to rise to the challenge of managing teams and projects.

The book is written in an easy-to-understand, straightforward style with a minimum number of technical terms. Readers acquire project management terminology gradually as they read the text. The text does not use complex mathematical theories or algorithms to describe scheduling techniques, nor does it include highly technical projects as examples. An overtly technical approach can create a barrier to learning for individuals who lack deep understanding of advanced mathematics or technical backgrounds. Our book includes a broad range of easily understood examples based on projects encountered in everyday situations. For example, real-world applications include conducting a market survey, building an information system, and organizing a town festival. The mathematics is purposely kept simple. Separate appendixes are provided for those readers who want more in-depth coverage of probability considerations and time–cost trade-offs.

DISTINCTIVE FEATURES

Effective Project Management has many distinctive features to enhance learning and build skills.

Real-World Vignettes Each chapter contains two real-world vignettes that illustrate the topics in the chapter. These vignettes not only reinforce chapter concepts, but also draw readers into the discussion and pique their interest in applications of project management.

Chapter Outlines Each chapter opens with an outline of the key topics that will be covered. These outlines clarify expectations and allow readers to see the flow of information at a glance.

Examples and Applications Real-world examples and applications are diffused throughout this text, ensuring that specific, relevant, and compelling illustrations are never far from view.

Global Considerations A globe icon in the margin of the text serves as a flag to students that the material is pertinent to global project management involving international team members, vendors, or clients.

Graphics and Figures Numerous exhibits appear in the text to illustrate important points and project management tools.

Reinforce Your Learning Questions Brief questions appear alongside the text to ensure that readers retain key concepts and that the fundamentals are not ignored. These in-the-margin questions "pop up" throughout the text to provide positive reinforcement and serve as an in-text study guide.

Critical Success Factors Each chapter contains a concise list of the important factors that project managers and team members need to know in order to help make their projects a success.

Chapter Summaries At the end of each chapter is a concise summary of the material presented in the chapter—a final distillation of core concepts.

Review Questions and Problems Each chapter has a set of questions and problems that first test and then apply chapter concepts.

Internet Exercises Each chapter has a set of exercises that ask readers to search websites for information on various project management topics. These exercises invite learners to explore real world applications of project management in an on-line, hands-on manner. Students can go to **international.cengage.com** for updated web addresses pertinent to each Internet Exercise, as well as for a list of useful professional project management websites referenced in the appendices.

Case Studies End-of-chapter case studies provide critical-thinking scenarios for either individual or group analysis. Variety in case format ensures that all learners can relate to the problems presented. The cases are fun and are intended to spark interesting debates. By fostering discussion of various viewpoints, the cases provide opportunities for participants to expand their thinking about how to operate successfully when differing views arise in the work environment. Thus students gain valuable insight into what teamwork is all about.

Project Management Software An appendix discusses the use of project management software as a tool in the planning and control of projects. Common features of project management software systems are discussed, along with selection criteria.

Microsoft Project New examples of how to use and apply Microsoft Project are included in Part 2 of this book. A plethora of screen displays, inputs, and reports are included.

Project Management Organizations A list of project management organizations worldwide is provided in an appendix for those individuals who want to contact these organizations about professional development, access to periodicals and other publications, or career opportunities.

ORGANIZATION

Effective Project Management is divided into three parts:

- Part 1, The Life of a Project, covers project management concepts, needs identification, proposed solutions, and implementing the project.
- Part 2, Project Planning and Control, covers planning, scheduling, schedule control, resource considerations, and cost planning and performance.
- Part 3, People: The Key to Project Success, discusses the project manager, the project team, types of project organizations, and project communication and documentation.

Part 1 consists of four chapters. Chapter 1, Project Management Concepts, covers the definition of a project and its attributes, the key constraints within which a project must be managed, how a project is "born," the life of a project, the steps in the project management process, examples of projects, the implications of global project management, and the benefits of project management. Chapter 2, Needs Identification, includes identifying needs and selecting projects, developing a request for proposal, and the proposal solicitation process. Chapter 3, Proposed Solutions, deals with building effective relationships with customers and partners, proposal marketing strategies, the bid/no-bid decision, development of winning proposals, the proposal preparation process, pricing considerations, evaluation of proposals, types of contracts, and measuring success of proposal efforts. Chapter 4, The Project, discusses the elements involved in establishing a project plan, managing risk, the steps in the project control process, and actions that should be taken when a project is terminated.

Part 2 contains five chapters. Chapter 5, Planning, discusses clearly defining the project objective, developing a work breakdown structure, assigning responsibilities and defining detailed activities, developing a network diagram, and utilizing the systems development life cycle for information system development projects. Chapter 6, Scheduling, covers estimating activity durations, calculating earliest and latest start and finish times for each activity, determining slack, and identifying the critical path of activities. This chapter also includes a special appendix on probability considerations. Chapter 7, Schedule Control, deals with the steps in the project control process, the effects of actual schedule performance on the project schedule, incorporating project changes into the schedule, calculating an updated project schedule, and approaches to controlling the project schedule. This chapter also includes a special appendix on the time–cost trade-off. Chapter 8, Resource Considerations, includes taking resource constraints into account when developing a project plan, determining the planned resource utilization for a project, leveling the use of resources within the required time frame for a project, and determining the shortest project schedule when the number of available resources is limited. Chapter 9, Cost Planning and Performance, covers items to be considered when estimating the project cost, preparation of a baseline budget, cumulating actual costs, determining the earned value of work actually performed, analyzing cost performance, calculating a forecast for the project cost at completion, approaches to controlling costs, and managing cash flow.

Part 3 includes four chapters. Chapter 10, The Project Manager, discusses the responsibilities of the project manager, the skills needed to manage projects successfully and ways to develop those skills, approaches to effective delegation, and how the project manager can manage and control changes to the project. Chapter 11, The Project Team, covers the development and growth of teams, characteristics of effective project teams and barriers to effectiveness, team building, valuing team diversity, ethical issues, sources of conflict during the project and approaches to handling conflict, problem solving, and effective time management. Chapter 12, Project Communication and Documentation, includes personal communications, effective listening, types of project meetings and suggestions for productive meetings, formal project presentations and suggestions for effective presentations, project reports and suggestions for preparing useful reports, project documentation and keeping track of changes, and collaborative communication tools. Chapter 13, Types of Project Organizations, deals with the characteristics, advantages, and disadvantages of the functional, project, and matrix organization structures.

The book includes a special appendix devoted to project management software, which discusses the common features of project management software systems, criteria for selecting a software package, and advantages of and concerns about using project management software. Other appendixes provide a list of project management organizations around the globe, project management websites, and project management acronyms. Finally, the book includes references for each chapter, answers to the Reinforce Your Learning questions, and a glossary.

SUPPORT MATERIALS

A comprehensive set of support materials is available for *Effective Project Management* on international.cengage.com. These materials are designed to guide the instructor and to minimize class preparation time.

The materials include:

- a sample syllabus
- a set of learning objectives for each chapter
- suggested teaching methods for each chapter
- lecture outlines for each chapter
- answers to the end-of-chapter questions

- a comprehensive test bank of true/false, multiple-choice, and problem-solving exercises for each chapter
- PowerPoint slides for each chapter
- PowerPoint slides of figures and tables for each chapter.

ACKNOWLEDGMENTS

We would like to acknowledge the individuals who helped with the publication of this book. Jason Oakman did a meticulous job in preparing the graphics, Dr. Bob Hammell did a wonderful job creating the Microsoft Project screen shots, and Dr. Gloria Chou, Amber Bailey, and Jordan Plumhoff who all did a great job tracking down and summarizing the real-world vignettes and updating the websites and references. We offer special appreciation to Wes Donahue and Beth McLaughlin of Penn State University for providing support materials and suggestions. We want to thank all the members of the project team at South-Western College Publishing, who helped turn our vision into reality and contributed to the successful completion of this project. Special recognition goes to Charles McCormick Jr., Senior Acquisitions Editor, Laura Bofinger, Senior Developmental Editor, Jacquelyn Featherly, Content Project Manager, and Menaka Gupta, Project Manager at Integra Software Services.

We are grateful to the following reviwers of the first three editions for their valuable comments that enhanced the text:

Fred K. Augustine, Jr.
Stetson University

Charles Bilbrey
James Madison University

Vicki Blanchard
Gibbs College of Boston

Victoria Buenger
Texas A&M University

Thomas Bute
Humboldt State University

Tim Butler
Wayne State University

John H. Cable
University of Maryland

David T. Cadden
Quinnipiac University

Craig Cowles
Bridgewater State College

Sam DeWald
Penn State University

Ike Ehie
Southeast Missouri State University

James Ford
Ford Consulting Associates

Philip Gisi
DePaul University

Bhushan L. Kapoor
California State University, Fullerton

Barbara Kelley
St Joseph's University

Laurie J. Kirsch
University of Pittsburgh

Brian M. Kleiner
Virginia Tech

Shawn Krest
Genesee Community College

Richard E. Kust
California State University, Fullerton

Mary Jo Maffei
MQ Associates

William Milz
Northeast Wisconsin Technical College

David Moore
Colorado School of Mines

William A. Moylan
Eastern Michigan University

John Olson
DePaul University

Shrikant S. Panwalkar
Purdue University

Fariborz Y. Partovi
Drexel University

Joseph A. Phillips
DeVry University

Tim Ralston
Bellevue Community College

H. Dan Reid
University of New Hampshire

Eltgad Roces
Penn State University

Carl. R. Schultz
University of New Mexico

Wade H. Shaw
Florida Institute of Technology

Kevin P. Shea
Baker University

Dr. Yosef S. Sherif
California State University, Fullerton

William R. Sherrard
San Diego State University

Anne Marie Smith
La Salle University

Christy Strbiak
New Mexico State University

Fredrick A. Tribble
California State University, Long Beach

We would also like to recognize the important contributions of the following reviewers for providing constructive comments for advancing this fourth edition:

Kwasi Amoako-Gyampah
University of North Carolina at Greensboro

Ed Arnheiter
Rensselaer Polytechnic Institute—Hartford

Mehmet Barut
Wichita State University

Dr. Dorothy Brandt
Brazosport College

David E. Clapp
Florida Institute of Technology

Mike Ensby
Clarkson University

Charlene A. Dykman, Ph.D.
University of St. Thomas – Houston

Darryl S. Habeck
Milwaukee Area Technical College

Mamoon M. Hammad
The George Washington University

Joan E. Hoopes, Ph.D
Marist College

Margaret Huron
Lone Star College – North Harris

Lois M. Lemke
Northeast Wisconsin Technical College

Ardeshir Lohrasbi
University of Illinois—Springfield

Nicoleta Maghear
Hampton University

Reza Maleki
North Dakota State University

David M. Marion
Ferris State University

James Marlatt, PMP
University of Colorado

Kirsten Mast
Albertson College of Idaho

Dr. Philip F. Musa
The University of Alabama at Birmingham

Carl Nelson
Polytechnic University

Hameed G. Nezhad, Ph.D.
Metropolitan State University

Tony B. Noble
Mohave Community College

Reed E. Pendleton
DeVry University—Fremont

Pedro M. Reyes
Baylor University

P.K. Shukla
Chapman University

A. P. Skudzinskas
Towson University—Maryland

Taverekere Srikantaiah
Dominican University

Jimmy C. Stallings
Webster University

Anthony P. Trippe
Rochester Institute of Technology

We would like to acknowledge all the individuals with whom we worked on projects and all the people who participated in our many project management seminars. They provided a learning environment for testing the practical lessons included in this book.

There are those who make things happen,
those who let things happen, and
those who wonder what happened.

We hope that *Effective Project Management* will help readers/learners have an enjoyable, exciting, and successful experience as they grow through their future project endeavors and that it will be the catalyst for helping them make things happen.

James P. Clements
Jack Gido

About the authors

James P. Clements is the Provost and Vice President for Academic Affairs and the Robert W. Deutsch Distinguished Professor of Information Technology at Towson University. He previously held positions as Vice President for Economic and Community Outreach, executive director of the Center for Applied Information Technology, and Chair of the Department of Computer and Information Sciences at Towson University. He holds an M.S. and a Ph.D. in operations analysis from the University of Maryland Baltimore County, an M.S. in computer science from Johns Hopkins University, and a B.S. in computer science from the University of Maryland Baltimore County. He has published and presented more than 50 papers on various project management and information systems topics. During the past 20 years, he has served as a consultant to numerous industry and business groups. Dr. Clements is also a four-time winner of the Faculty Member of the Year Award given by students at Towson University.

Jack Gido is former director of Economic and Workforce Development and prior director of PENNTAP, the Pennsylvania Technical Assistance Program, at Penn State University. He previously held dual positions as manager of the Industrial Technology Extension Service for the New York Science and Technology Foundation and as deputy director of the Industrial Effectiveness Program at the New York State Department of Economic Development. His 20 years of industrial management experience includes management of productivity improvement and manufacturing technology programs for General Electric and Mechanical Technology, Inc. He received a B.S. in electrical engineering from Penn State University and an M.B.A. from the University of Pittsburgh. He has authored two other books on project management and teaches workshops on project management. Jack is a member of the Project Management Institute and was president of the Upstate New York chapter.

FOURTH EDITION

EFFECTIVE PROJECT MANAGEMENT

JAMES P. CLEMENTS
Towson University

JACK GIDO
Penn State University

PART

The Life of a Project

CHAPTERS

1 Project Management Concepts

Provides an overview of project management concepts, the project life cycle, and the steps in the project management process.

2 Needs Identification

Discusses identifying needs and soliciting proposals, the first phase of the project life cycle.

3 Proposed Solutions

Explains the development of proposals for addressing a need or solving a problem, the second phase of the project life cycle.

4 The Project

Discusses the implementation of the proposed solution, the third phase of the project life cycle, including what is involved in planning and controlling the project. It also covers what should be done in the termination phase of the project life cycle.

The chapters in Part 1 introduce the concepts of project management and the project life cycle. A project is an endeavor to accomplish a specific objective through a unique set of interrelated tasks and the effective utilization of resources. It has a well-defined objective stated in terms of scope, schedule, and cost. Projects are "born" when a need is identified by the customer—the people or the organization willing to provide funds to have the need satisfied.

The first phase of the project life cycle involves the identification of a need, problem, or opportunity and can result in the customer's requesting proposals from individuals, a project team, or organizations (contractors) to address the identified need or solve the problem. The second phase of the project life cycle is the development of a proposed solution to the need or problem. This phase results in the submission of a proposal to the customer by one or more individuals or organizations. The third phase of the project life cycle is the implementation of the proposed solution. This phase, which is referred to as performing the project, results in accomplishment of the project objective, leaving the customer satisfied that the full scope of work was completed in a quality manner, within budget, and on time. The final phase of the project life cycle is terminating the project.

Project management involves the process of first establishing a plan and then implementing that plan to accomplish the project objective. Taking the time to develop a well-thought-out plan is critical to the successful accomplishment of any project. Once the project starts, the project management process involves monitoring progress to ensure that everything is going according to plan. The key to effective project control is measuring actual progress and comparing it to planned progress on a timely and regular basis and taking corrective action immediately, if necessary.

The ultimate benefit of implementing project management techniques is having a satisfied customer — whether you are the customer of your own project or a business (contractor) being paid by a customer to perform a project. Completing the full scope of work of the project in a quality manner, on time, and within budget provides a great feeling of satisfaction. When projects are successful, everybody wins!

© Comstock Images/Jupiter Images

CHAPTER 1

Project Management Concepts

Attributes of a Project

Project Life Cycle

The Project Management Process

Global Project Management

Benefits of Project Management

Summary

Questions

Internet Exercises

Case Study #1 E-Commerce for a Small Supermarket

- Case Questions
- Group Activity
- Optional Activity

Case Study #2 A Not-for-Profit Organization

- Case Questions
- Group Activity

Real World PROJECT MANAGEMENT

Irish Agency Halts Work on Two SAP Application Projects

In October of 2005, two controversial SAP AG ERP system rollouts were halted in Ireland. The halting of these projects, valued at more than $380 million, ignited a political firestorm in Ireland. New York–based consulting firm Deloitte & Touche LLP was the contractor hired to implement both projects.

The Irish Health Service Executive (HSE), an oversight committee for Ireland's national health department, suspended work on the Personnel, Payroll and Related Systems (PPARS) project. The project was started 10 years ago to handle payroll functions for 120,000 employees.

It was halted on October 6 after numerous and widespread errors that were attributed to the implementation of the software were found at the major pilot site, St. James Hospital in Dublin. Problems were also identified in other regional installations in operations that employ over 37,000 department workers. One employee, for example, was accidentally paid $1.2 million.

In addition, HSE ceased work on another, unrelated health department project, the Financial Information Systems Project (FISP), which was designed to build a single financial and materials management system to support current and best practices. It was designed to replace a mismatch of legacy systems and processes. About $36 million had been spent on that project and it was expected to cost a total of $203 million to complete.

Critics in Parliament referred to the projects as examples of mismanagement and waste. A spokesman for Edna Kenny, the leader of Irish opposition party Fine Gael, stated, "It's like a case study in how not to run a project." The PPARS application has been described as the most complex human resources, time management, and payroll system ever to be implemented in Ireland.

The PPARS project was initially launched in 1995. The budget was set at $10.7 million and the project schedule was set at three years. After 10 years, the project cost had skyrocketed to $180 million before the project was scrapped. For this price, Kenny reported, the agency could have built a "brand new 600-bed hospital." HSE publicly reported that they did not realize the complexity of the older payroll system until the PPARS project was well underway.

Behind the success or failure of these projects and numerous others lies a critical component—project management. Projects such as these require serious planning, scheduling, organization, teamwork, communication, and leadership—all of which will be discussed in detail in this book.

By mastering these concepts you will greatly improve your chances of avoiding the pitfalls of the projects discussed above, while increasing your chances of success.

Songini, M., "Irish Agency Halts Work on Two SAP Application Projects," *Computerworld*, October 17, 2005.

This chapter presents an overview of project management concepts. You will become familiar with

- the definition of a project and its attributes
- the key constraints within which a project must be managed
- how a project is "born"
- the life of a project
- the steps involved in the project management process
- the implications of global project management
- the benefits of project management

ATTRIBUTES OF A PROJECT

A **project** is an endeavor to accomplish a specific objective through a unique set of interrelated tasks and the effective utilization of resources. The following attributes help define a project:

- A project has a well-defined **objective**—an expected result or product. The objective of a project is usually defined in terms of *scope, schedule*, and *cost*. For example, the objective of a project might be to introduce to the market—in 10 months and within a budget of $500,000—a new food preparation appliance that meets certain predefined performance specifications. Furthermore, it is expected that the work scope will be accomplished in a *quality manner* and to the *customer's satisfaction*.
- A project is carried out through a series of *interdependent tasks*—that is, a number of nonrepetitive tasks that need to be accomplished in a certain sequence in order to achieve the project objective.
- A project utilizes various *resources* to carry out the tasks. Such resources can include different people, organizations, equipment, materials, and facilities. For example, a wedding is a project that may involve resources such as a caterer, a florist, a limousine, and a reception hall.
- A project has a *specific time frame*, or finite life span. It has a start time and a date by which the objective must be accomplished. For example, the refurbishing of an elementary school might have to be completed between June 20 and August 20.
- A project may be a *unique* or *one-time endeavor*. Some projects, like designing and building a space station, are unique because they have never before been attempted. Other projects, such as developing a new product, building a house, or planning a wedding, are unique because of the customization they require. For example, a wedding can be a simple, informal occasion, with a few friends in a chapel, or a spectacular event staged for a prince.
- A project has a customer. The **customer** is the entity that provides the funds necessary to accomplish the project. It can be a person, an organization, or a partnership of two or more people or organizations. When a contractor builds a customized home for a couple, the couple is the customer funding the project. When a company receives funds from the government to develop a robotic device for handling radioactive material, the customer is the government agency. When a company provides funds

for a team of its employees to upgrade the firm's management information system, the term *customer* takes on a broader definition, including not only the project funder (the company's management) but also other stakeholders, such as the people who will be the end users of the information system. The person managing the project and the project team must successfully accomplish the project objective to satisfy the customer(s).

- Finally, a project involves a *degree of uncertainty*. Before a project is started, a plan is prepared based on certain assumptions and estimates. It is important to document these assumptions, because they will influence the development of the project budget, schedule, and work scope. A project is based on a unique set of tasks and estimates of how long each task should take, various resources and assumptions about the availability and capability of those resources, and estimates of the costs associated with the resources. This combination of assumptions and estimates causes a degree of uncertainty that the project objective will be completely accomplished. For example, the project scope may be accomplished by the target date, but the final cost may be much higher than anticipated because of low initial estimates for the cost of certain resources. As the project proceeds, some of the assumptions will be refined or replaced with factual information. For example, once the conceptual design of a company's annual report is finalized, the amount of time and effort needed to complete the detailed design and printing can be better estimated.

The following are some examples of projects:

Reinforce Your Learning

1. What are some attributes of a project?

Staging a theatrical production
Developing and introducing a new product
Planning a wedding
Designing and implementing a computer system
Issuing a new $1.00 coin
Modernizing a factory
Consolidating two manufacturing plants
Converting a basement to a family room
Hosting a conference
Designing and producing a brochure
Executing an environmental cleanup of a contaminated site
Holding a high school reunion
Building a shopping mall
Performing a series of surgeries on an accident victim
Putting on a centennial celebration
Rebuilding a town after a natural disaster
Hosting a dinner for 20 relatives
Designing a business internship program for high school students
Building a tree house

Reinforce Your Learning

2. Identify five projects in which you have been involved during your lifetime.

The successful accomplishment of the project objective is usually constrained by four factors: *scope, cost, schedule*, and *customer satisfaction* (see Figure 1.1).

FIGURE 1.1 ***Factors Constraining Project Success***

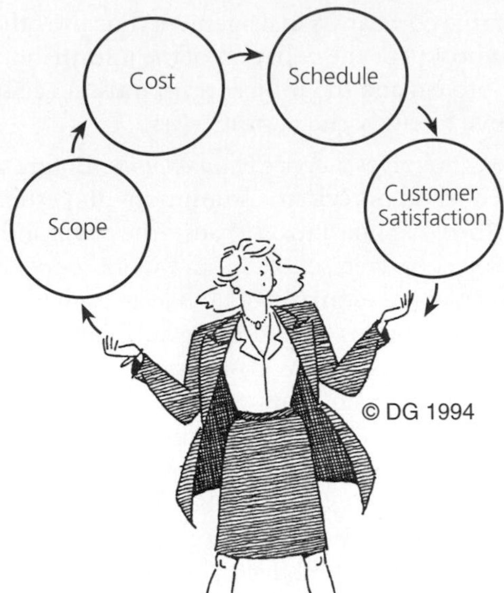

Courtesy of Dynamic Graphics, Inc.

The scope of a project—also known as the **project scope** or the **work scope**—is all the work that must be done in order to satisfy the customer that the **deliverables** (the tangible product or items to be provided) *meet the requirements or acceptance criteria agreed upon at the onset of the project*. For example, the project scope might be all of the work involved in clearing the land, building a house, and landscaping to the specifications agreed upon by the contractor and the buyer. The customer expects the work scope to be accomplished in a quality manner. For example, in a house-building project, the customer expects the workmanship to be of the highest quality. Completing the work scope but leaving windows that are difficult to open and close, faucets that leak, or a landscape full of rocks will result in an unsatisfied customer.

The **cost** of a project is the amount the customer has agreed to pay for acceptable project deliverables. The project cost is based on a budget that includes an estimate of the costs associated with the various resources that will be used to accomplish the project. It might include the salaries of people who will work on the project, materials and supplies, rental of equipment or facilities, and the fees of subcontractors or consultants who will perform some of the project tasks. For example, if the project is a wedding, budgeted items might include flowers, gown, tuxedo, caterer, cake, limousine rental, photographer, and so on.

The **schedule** for a project is the timetable that specifies when each activity should start and finish. The project objective usually states the time by which the project scope must be completed in terms of a specific date agreed upon by the customer and the individual or organization performing the work. It might be the date when a town's centennial celebration will take place or the date by which you want to complete the addition of a family room to your home.

The objective of any project is to complete the scope of work within budget by a certain time to the customer's satisfaction. To help assure the achievement of this objective, *it is important to develop a plan before the start of the project; this plan should include all the work tasks, associated costs, and estimates of the time necessary to complete them.* The lack of such a plan increases the risk of failing to accomplish the full project scope within budget and on schedule.

Once a project is started, unforeseen circumstances may jeopardize the achievement of the project objective with respect to scope, cost, or schedule.

Reinforce Your Learning

3. What are four factors that constrain the achievement of a project objective?

- The cost of some of the materials may be higher than originally estimated.
- Inclement weather may cause a delay.
- Additional redesign and modifications to a sophisticated piece of automated machinery may be required to get it to meet the performance specifications.

The challenge to the project manager is to prevent, anticipate, or overcome such circumstances in order to complete the project scope on schedule, within budget, and to the customer's satisfaction. *Good planning and communication* are essential to prevent problems from occurring or to minimize their impact on the achievement of the project objective when they do occur. The project manager needs to be proactive in planning and communicating and provide leadership to the project team to accomplish the project objective.

Ultimately, the responsibility of the project manager is to make sure the customer is satisfied. This goes beyond just completing the project scope within budget and on schedule or asking the customer at the end of the project if he or she is satisfied. It requires ongoing communication with the customer to keep the customer informed and to determine whether expectations have changed. Regularly scheduled meetings or progress reports, frequent phone discussions, and e-mail are examples of ways to accomplish such communications. Customer satisfaction means involving the customer as a partner in the successful outcome of the project through active participation during the project. The project manager must be aware of the degree of customer satisfaction throughout the project. By maintaining regular communication with the customer, the project manager demonstrates to the customer that he or she is genuinely concerned about the expectations of the customer; it also prevents unpleasant surprises later.

PROJECT LIFE CYCLE

Figure 1.2 shows the four phases of the **project life cycle** and the relative amount of effort and time devoted to each phase. As the project moves through its life cycle, different organizations, individuals, and resources play dominant roles.

Projects are "born" when a need is identified by the *customer*—the people or the organization willing to provide funds to have the need satisfied. For example, for a growing family, the need may be for a larger house, whereas for a company the problem may be a high scrap rate from its manufacturing process that makes its costs higher and production times longer than those of its competitors. The customer first must identify the need or problem. Sometimes the problem is identified quickly, as in the case of a disaster such as an earthquake or explosion. In other situations, it may take months for a customer to clearly identify a need, gather data on the problem, and define certain requirements that must be met by the person, project team, or contractor who will solve the problem.

FIGURE 1.2 *Project Life Cycle Effort*

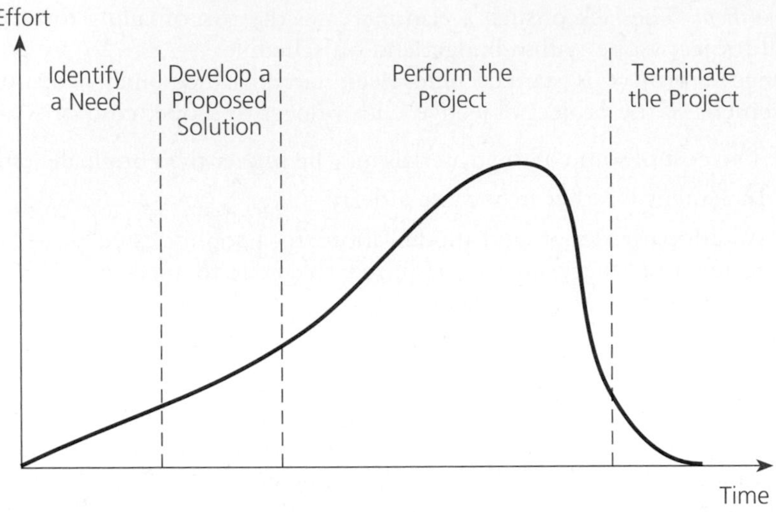

This *first phase* of the project life cycle involves the identification of a need, problem, or opportunity and can result in the customer's requesting proposals from individuals, a project team, or organizations (contractors) to address the identified need or solve the problem. The need and requirements are usually written up by the customer in a document called a **request for proposal (RFP)**. Through the RFP, the customer asks individuals or contractors to submit proposals on how they might solve the problem, along with the associated cost and schedule. A couple who need a new house may spend time identifying requirements for the house—size, style, number of rooms, location, maximum amount they want to spend, and date by which they would like to move in. They may then write down these requirements and ask several contractors to provide house plans and cost estimates. A company that has identified a need to upgrade its computer system might document its requirements in an RFP and send it to several computer consulting firms.

Not all situations involve a formal RFP, however. Needs often are defined informally during a meeting or discussion among a group of individuals. Some of the individuals may then volunteer or be asked to prepare a proposal to determine whether a project should be undertaken to address the need. Such a scenario might be played out when the management of a hospital wants to establish an on-site day care center for the children of its employees. The management team or a specific manager may write down the requirements in a document and give it to an internal project team, which in turn will submit a proposal for how to establish the center. In this case, the contractor is the hospital's own internal project team, and the customer is the hospital's manager or, possibly, board of directors. It is important to define the right need. For example, is the need to provide an on-site day care center, or is it to provide child care for the children of the hospital's employees? Is "on-site" necessarily part of the need?

The *second phase* of the project life cycle is the development of a proposed solution to the need or problem. This phase results in the submission of a **proposal** to the customer by one or more individuals or organizations (contractors) who would like to have the customer pay them to implement the proposed solution. In this phase, the contractor effort is dominant. Contractors interested in responding to the RFP may spend several weeks developing approaches to solving the problem, estimating the types and amounts of resources that would be needed as well as the time it would take to design and implement the proposed solution. Each contractor documents this information in a written proposal. All of the contractors submit their proposals to the customer. For example, several contractors may submit proposals to a customer to develop and implement an automated invoicing and collection system. After the customer evaluates the submissions and selects the winning proposal, the customer and the winning contractor negotiate and sign a **contract** (agreement). In many situations, a request for proposal may not involve soliciting competitive proposals from external contractors. A company's own internal project team may develop a proposal in response to a management-defined need or request. In this case, the project would be performed by the company's own employees rather than outsourcing it to an external contractor.

The *third phase* of the project life cycle is the implementation of the proposed solution. This phase begins after the customer decides which of the proposed solutions will best fulfill the need and an agreement is reached between the customer and the individual or contractor who submitted the proposal. This phase, referred to as performing the project, involves doing the detailed planning for the project and then implementing that plan to accomplish the project objective. During the course of performing the project, different types of resources will be utilized. For example, if the project is to design and construct an office building, the project effort might first involve a few architects and engineers in developing the building plans. Then, as construction gets under way, the resources needed will substantially increase to include steelworkers, carpenters, electricians, painters, and the like. The project will wind down after the building is finished, and a smaller number of different workers will finish up the landscaping and final interior touches. This phase results in the accomplishment of the project objective, leaving the customer satisfied that the full scope of the work was completed in a quality manner, within budget, and on time. For example, the third phase is complete when a contractor has completed the design and installation of a customized automation system that satisfactorily passes performance tests and is accepted by the customer or when an internal project team within a company has completed a project, in response to a management request, which consolidated two of its facilities into one.

The *final phase* of the project life cycle is terminating the project. When a project is completed, certain close-out activities need to be performed, such as confirming that all deliverables have been provided to and accepted by the customer, that all payments have been collected, and that all invoices have been paid. An important task during this phase is evaluating performance of the project in order to learn what could be improved if a similar project were to be carried out in the future. This phase should include obtaining feedback from the customer to determine the level of the customer's satisfaction and whether the project met the customer's expectations. Also, feedback should be obtained from the project team in the form of recommendations for improving performance of projects in the future.

Project life cycles vary in length from a few weeks to several years, depending on the content, complexity, and magnitude of the project. What's more, not all projects formally go through all four phases of the project life cycle. If a group

Reinforce Your Learning

4. Match the phases of the project life cycle, in the column on the top, with the descriptions, in the column on the bottom:

__ First phase
__ Second phase
__ Third phase
__ Fourth phase

A. Developing the proposed solution
B. Implementing the proposed solution
C. Identifying the need or problem
D. Terminating the project

of community volunteers decide that they want to use their own time, talents, and resources to organize a food drive for the homeless, they may get right into phase 3—planning the event and carrying it out. The first two phases of the life cycle would not be relevant to such a project. Likewise, if a company's general manager determines that changing the layout of equipment in the factory will increase efficiency, she might simply instruct the manufacturing manager to initiate such a project and to implement it using the company's own people. In this case, there would be no written request for proposal from external contractors.

In other situations, such as a home remodeling project for which a contractor will likely be hired, a customer may go through the first two phases of the project life cycle in a less structured, more informal manner. He may not write down all of the requirements and ask several contractors for estimates. Rather, he may call a contractor who has done satisfactory work for him or for a neighbor in the past, explain what he wants done, and ask the contractor to provide some sketches and a cost estimate.

In general, the project life cycle is followed in a more formal and structured manner when a project is conducted in a business setting. It tends to be less formal when a project is carried out by a private individual or volunteers.

THE PROJECT MANAGEMENT PROCESS

Succinctly, the project management process means *planning the work and then working the plan*. A coaching staff may spend hours preparing unique plans for a game; the team then executes the plans to try to meet the objective—victory. Similarly, project management involves a process of first *establishing a plan* and then *implementing that plan* to accomplish the project objective.

The front-end effort in managing a project must be focused on establishing a baseline plan that provides a roadmap for how the project scope will be accomplished on time and within budget. This planning effort includes the following steps:

1. *Clearly define the project objective.* The definition must be agreed upon by the customer and the individual or organization who will perform the project.
2. *Divide and subdivide the project scope into major "pieces," or* ***work packages***. Although major projects may seem overwhelming when viewed as a whole, one way to conquer even the most monumental endeavor is to break it down. A **work breakdown structure (WBS)** is a hierarchical tree of work elements or items accomplished or produced by the project team during the project. The work breakdown structure usually identifies the organization or individual responsible for each work package. Figure 1.3 is an example of a work breakdown structure. (Work breakdown structures will be discussed further in Chapter 5.)
3. *Define the specific activities that need to be performed for each work package in order to accomplish the project objective.*
4. *Graphically portray the activities in the form of a* ***network diagram***. This diagram shows the necessary sequence and interdependencies of activities to achieve the project objective. Figure 1.4 is an example of a network diagram. (Network diagrams will be discussed further in Chapter 5.)

Real World **PROJECT MANAGEMENT**

Maine's Medical Mistake

In January 2005, Maine introduced a new web-based Maine Medicaid Claims System designed to process $1.5 billion in annual Medicare claims and payments. The new program cost $25 million and was referred to as a more secure, faster system that would track costs better and provide more accurate information on the status of claims. In a matter of days following the implementation of the new system, Craig Hitchings, director of information technology for the state of Maine's Department of Human Services (DHS), knew something was seriously wrong.

From the beginning, there was an unusually high rate of rejected claims being reported, but Hitchings assumed these rejected claims could be attributed to providers entering the wrong codes on the new electronic claims forms. Hundreds of calls began to pour in from doctors, dentists, health clinics, and nursing homes to the department's Bureau of Medical Services, which runs the Medicaid program. These health care providers were angry because their claims were not being paid.

The new system had placed most of these rejected claims in a "suspended" file for forms that were suspected to contain errors. This glitch left tens of thousands of claims, totaling millions of dollars, in limbo.

Hitchings' team of 15 IT staffers and four dozen employees from CNSI (the contractor hired to develop the system) were working 12-hour days to attempt to write software fixes and quickly perform adjustments. Hitchings knew project management guidelines were being ignored because of the short staffing and hasty repairs and adjustments being performed.

By the end of March, 300,000 claims had reached the suspended bin and the state was falling further behind in its capacity to process them. By the end of the summer that number rose to nearly 650,000. Since their bills were considered unpaid, some of Maine's 262,000 Medicaid recipients were being turned away from doctors' offices. Some dentists and therapists were forced to shut down their businesses; other physicians had to take out loans in order to stay open.

Since the new system's implementation, it has cost the state of Maine almost $30 million. In December 2005, the commissioner of the DHS, who oversaw the project, resigned. Additionally, Maine was not in compliance with the Health Insurance Portability and Accountability Act (HIPAA).

Since then, state IT officials claim they have fixed most of the bugs in the system and that it is now processing 85% of the claims. They are also able to look back and determine why this project went wrong. First, the vendor hired, CNSI, had no experience in developing Medicaid systems. Additionally, the vendor decided to build a new and unproven technology platform for the system as opposed to simply integrating a web-based portal with back-end legacy systems. The system also had no backup in case something went wrong. In addition, prior to implementation sufficient amount of end-to-end testing and training were not conducted.

Clearly, the system's problems resulted from poor project management and poor communication between staff, contractors, and business users. Most notably, the cost of the project was more than 50% higher than the original projection. According to Dick Thompson, the then head of procurement and now the CIO for the state of Maine, "It was clear that we were missing any sort of basic management of this project and were in complete defensive mode."

Holmes, A., "Maine's Medical Mistake," *CIO* magazine, April 15, 2006.

5. *Make a* ***time estimate*** *for how long it will take to complete each activity.* It is also necessary to determine which types of resources and how many of each resource are needed for each activity to be completed within the estimated duration.

FIGURE 1.3 ***Work Breakdown Structure***

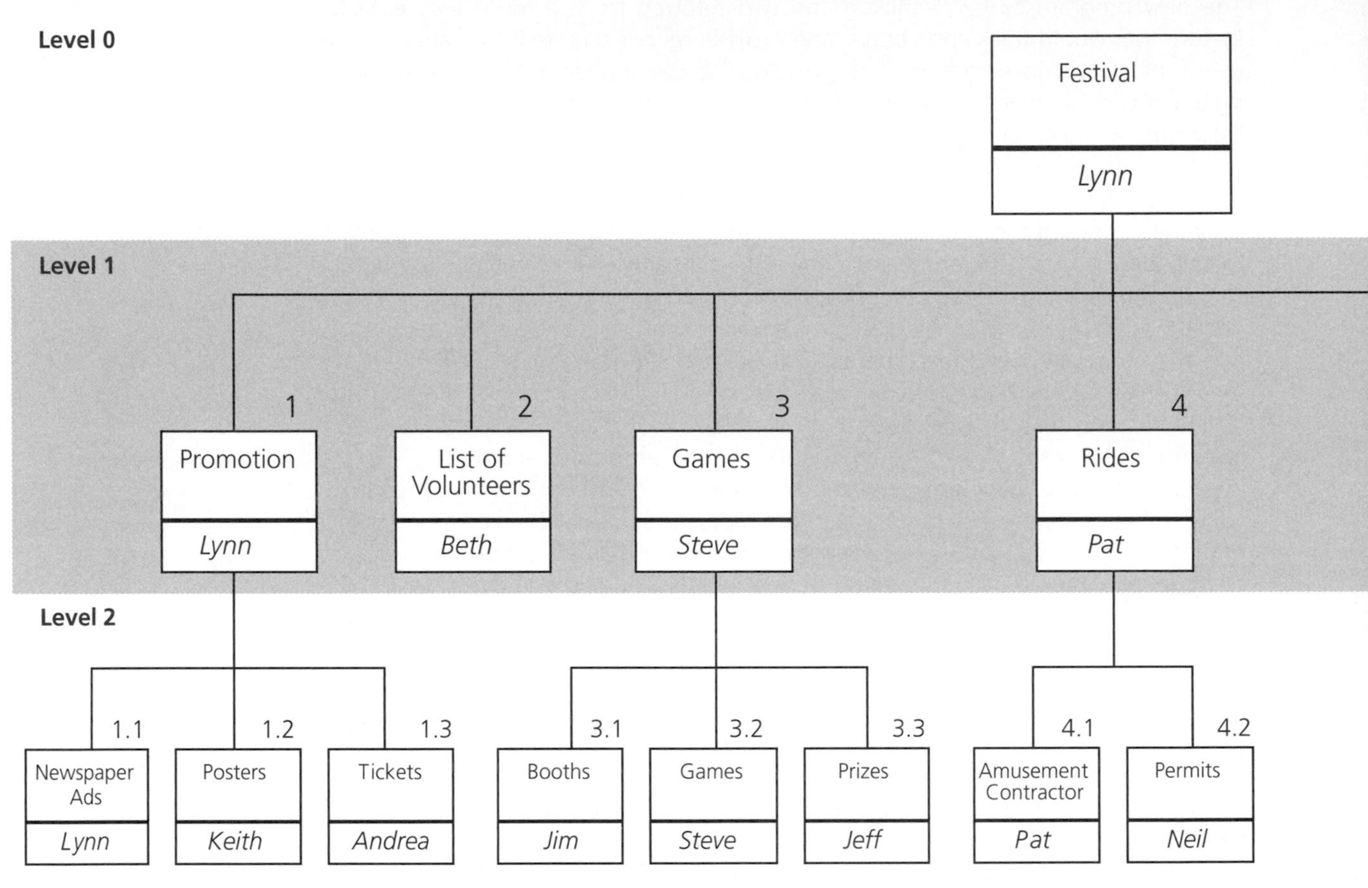

6. *Make a* ***cost estimate*** *for each activity.* The cost is based on the types and quantities of resources required for each activity.
7. *Calculate a project schedule and budget to determine whether the project can be completed within the required time, with the allotted funds, and with the available*

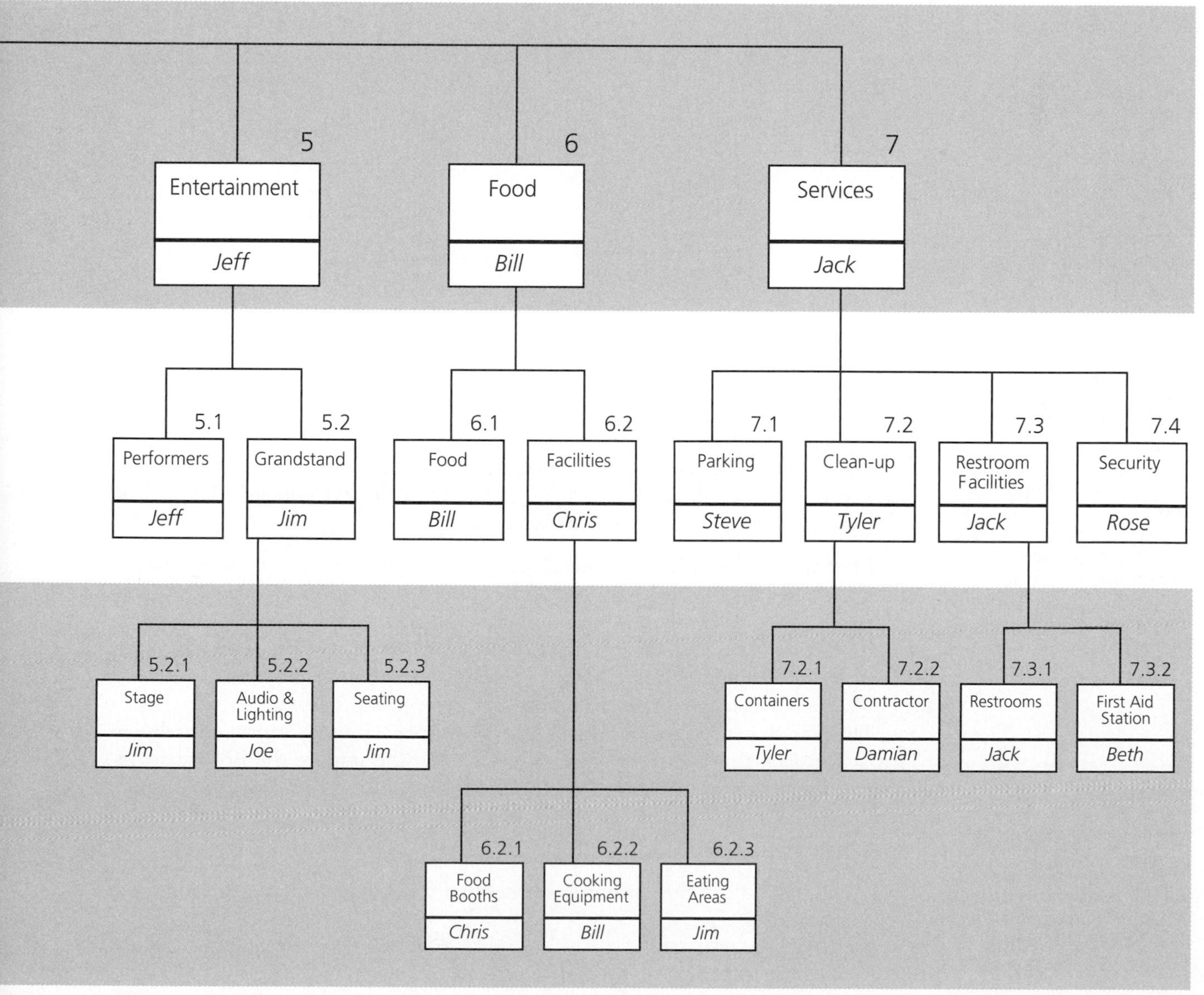

FIGURE 1.4 *Network Diagram*

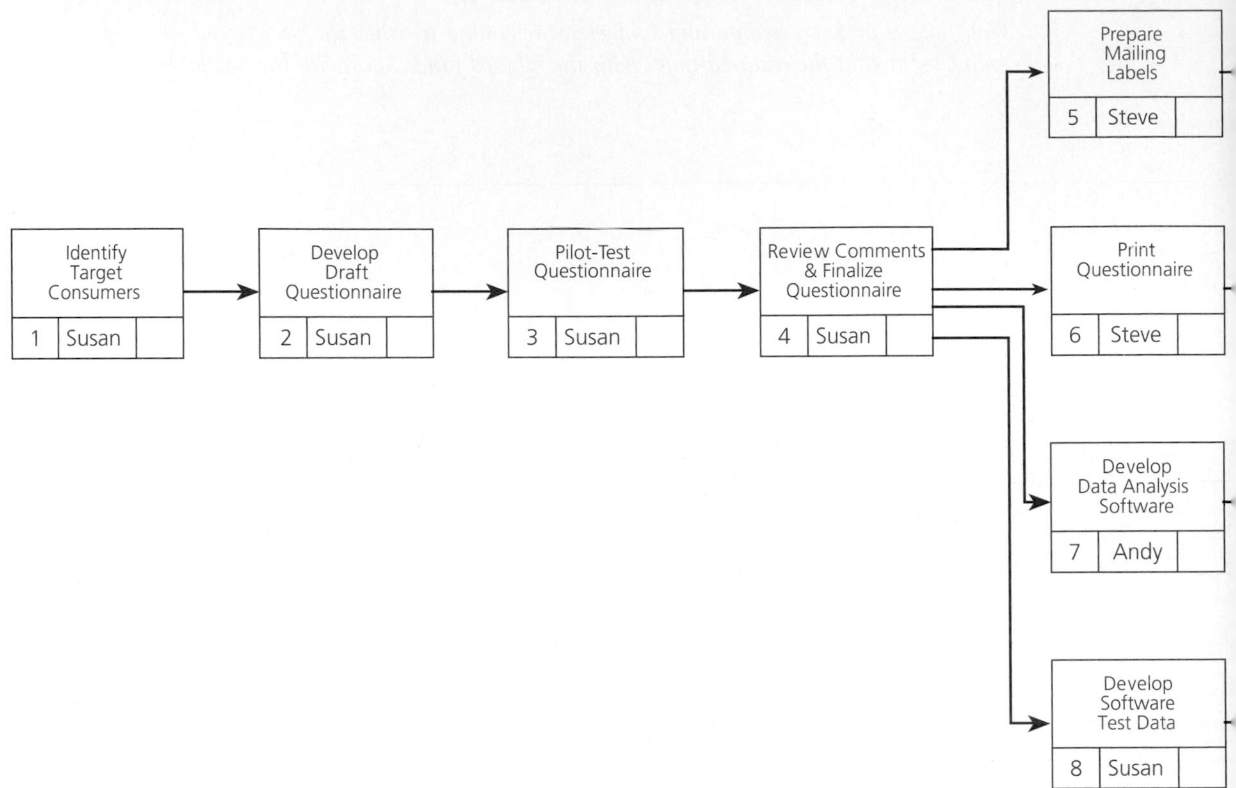

Reinforce Your Learning

5. The project ________ must be agreed upon by the ________ and the individual or organization who will ________ the project.

resources. If not, adjustments must be made to the project scope, activity time estimates, or resource assignments until an achievable, realistic **baseline plan** (a roadmap for accomplishing the project scope on time and within budget) can be established. Figure 1.5 shows an example of a project schedule, and Figure 1.6 illustrates a project budget. (These will be covered in Chapters 6 through 9.)

Planning determines what needs to be done, who will do it, how long it will take, and how much it will cost. The result of this effort is a baseline plan. Taking the time to develop a well-thought-out plan is critical to the successful accomplishment of any project. Many projects have overrun their budgets, missed their completion dates, or only partially met their requirements because there was no viable baseline plan before the project was started.

The baseline plan for a project can be displayed in graphical or tabular format for each time period (week, month) from the start of the project to its completion. (Plans are discussed and illustrated in Part 2.) Information should include

Reinforce Your Learning

6. The front-end effort of managing a project involves establishing a ________ ________.

- the start and completion dates for each activity
- the amounts of the various resources that will be needed during each time period
- the budget for each time period, as well as the cumulative budget from the start of the project through each time period

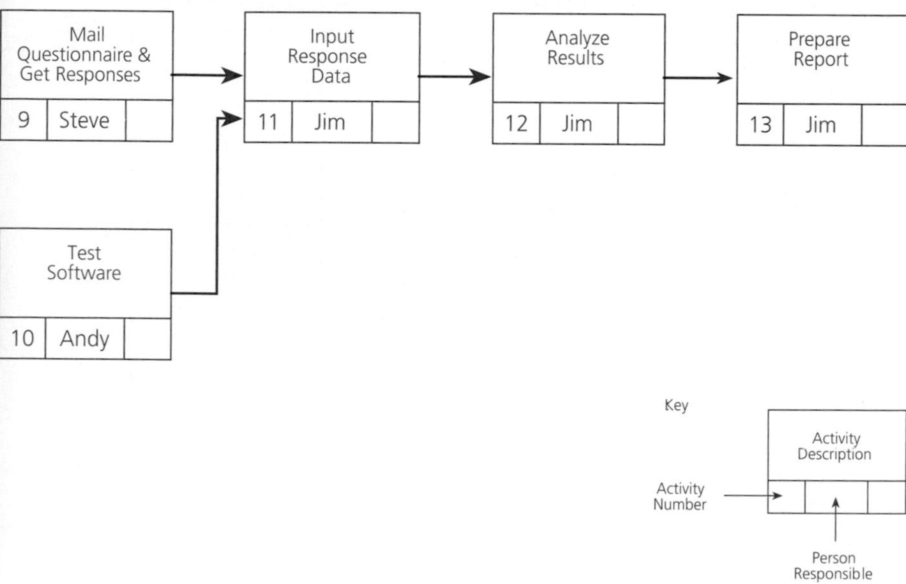

Once a baseline plan has been established, it must be implemented. This involves performing the work according to the plan and controlling the work so that the project scope is achieved within the budget and schedule, to the customer's satisfaction.

Once the project starts, it is necessary to monitor progress to ensure that everything is going according to plan. At this stage, the project management process involves measuring actual progress and comparing it to planned progress. To measure actual progress, it is important to keep track of which activities have actually been started or completed, when they were started or completed, and how much money has been spent or committed. If, at any time during the project, comparison of actual progress to planned progress reveals that the project is behind schedule, overrunning the budget, or not meeting the technical specifications, corrective action must be taken to get the project back on track.

Before a decision is made to implement corrective action, it may be necessary to evaluate several alternative actions to make sure the corrective action will bring the project back within the scope, time, and budget constraints of the objective. Be aware, for instance, that adding resources to make up time and get back on schedule may result in overrunning the planned budget. If a project gets too far out of control, it may be difficult to achieve the project objective without sacrificing the scope, budget, schedule, or quality.

The key to effective project control is measuring actual progress and comparing it to planned progress on a timely and regular basis and taking corrective

Reinforce Your Learning

7. Implementing the baseline plan for a project involves __________ the work according to the plan and __________ the work so that the project scope is achieved within the __________ and __________ to the customer's __________.

FIGURE 1.5 *Project Schedule Consumer Market Study Project*

Consumer Market Study Project

	Activity	Respon.	Dur. Estim.	Earliest		Latest		Total Slack	
				Start	Finish	Start	Finish		
1	Identify Target Consumers	Susan	3	0	3	–8	–5	–8	
2	Develop Draft Questionnaire	Susan	10	3	13	–5	5	–8	
3	Pilot-Test Questionnaire	Susan	20	13	33	5	25	–8	
4	Review Comments & Finalize Questionnaire	Susan	5	33	38	25	30	–8	
5	Prepare Mailing Labels	Steve	2	38	40	38	40	0	
6	Print Questionnaire	Steve	10	38	48	30	40	–8	
7	Develop Data Analysis Software	Andy	12	38	50	88	100	50	
8	Develop Software Test Data	Susan	2	38	40	98	100	60	
9	Mail Questionnaire & Get Responses	Steve	65	48	113	40	105	–8	
10	Test Software	Andy	5	50	55	100	105	50	
11	Input Response Data	Jim	7	113	120	105	112	–8	
12	Analyze Results	Jim	8	120	128	112	120	–8	
13	Prepare Report	Jim	10	128	138	120	130	–8	

action immediately, if necessary. Hoping that a problem will go away without corrective intervention is naive. Based on actual progress, it is possible to forecast a schedule and budget for completion of the project. If these parameters are beyond the limits of the project objective, corrective actions need to be implemented at once.

Attempting to perform a project without first establishing a baseline plan is foolhardy. It is like starting a vacation without a roadmap, itinerary, and budget. You may land up in the middle of nowhere—out of money and out of time!

GLOBAL PROJECT MANAGEMENT

Globalization adds a unique dimension to managing projects. It changes the dynamics of the project and adds a layer of complexity which can adversely affect the project outcome if the project participants are not aware of what they might encounter regarding cultural differences and multinational economic transactions. For example, there could be a project contractual outsourcing requirement to spend a percentage of the project budget on wages and materials

FIGURE 1.6 *Cumulative Budgeted Cost Curve*

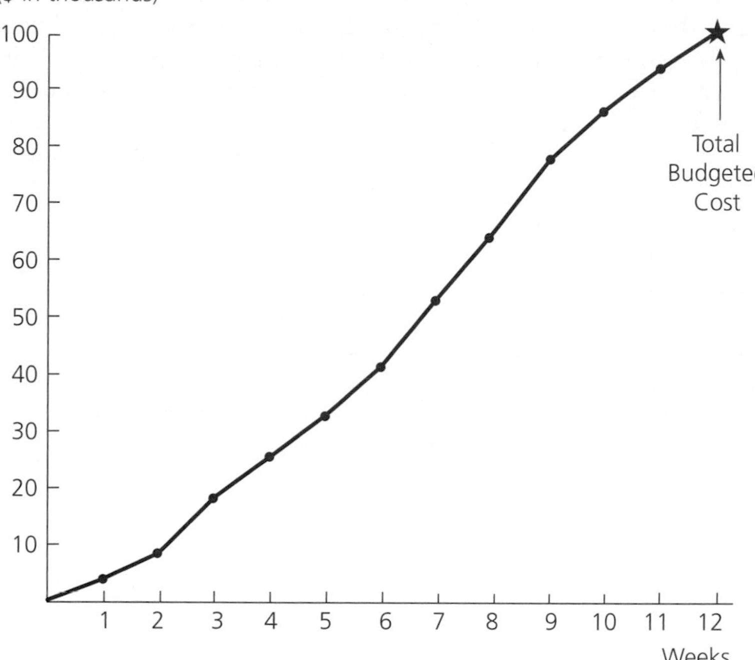

in the customer's country by employing indigenous labor to perform certain project tasks and using in-country suppliers for project materials. Factors external to the project itself, or to the project or customer organizations, can create a dynamic and perhaps unstable environment over the life of the project, introduce sources of risk, and affect the success of the project. Such influencing factors can include:

- currency fluctuations and exchange rates
- country-specific work codes and regulations, such as hours per day, holidays, and religious observances
- interdependence of economies
- corporate joint ventures and partnerships creating entities with a presence and facilities in multiple countries
- political relations between countries
- availability of high-demand workforce skills

Large international events, such as the Olympics or rebuilding a region after a natural disaster, require multilingual project teams. Global projects can be multinational and multilingual, with participants located in various countries and who speak different languages. These aspects can create barriers to communication, team development, and project performance.

Global project management requires an additional set of competencies. It is helpful for the project manager and team to have foreign language skills and also knowledge and understanding of other countries and cultures, as well as geography, world history, and international economics (currencies, exchange rates, export/import transactions, etc.). There is a need to have awareness and understanding of the culture and customs (meal times, eye contact, possible differing roles of men and women, dress codes, religious practices, lines of authority, communication protocol, etc.) and etiquette (for example, in some countries crossing your legs when sitting is considered an insult, or shaking hands or touching someone of the opposite sex is frowned upon) of the countries of the various project participants (project team, customer, subcontractors, and suppliers). It is also vital to have an awareness of the geopolitical environment of the countries of the various project participants, in particular the country of the customer, or where the project is being delivered or implemented.

Technology (for example, computers, Internet access) enables project participants to be just a mouse-click away, despite being thousands of miles apart physically. It also helps to reduce the impact that time zone differences between the locations of various project participants can have on project communication. One way to facilitate communication in multilingual project teams could be to utilize software that translates e-mails and documents between the languages of the various project participants.

Globalization and the Internet have also brought new opportunities for firms, as seen in multisourcing project work elements to more different competitive participants worldwide as well as in purchasing materials and services from suppliers in multiple countries around the globe.

Cultural awareness and sensitivity are not only important but imperative for successful global project management. Learning and understanding the culture and customs of other project participants demonstrates respect, helps build trust, aids in developing an effective project team, and is critical for successful global project management.

See sections on "Valuing Team Diversity" in Chapter 11 and "Collaborative Communication Tools" in Chapter 12 for additional related information. Also see Appendix B for a list of project management organizations around the globe.

Reinforce Your Learning

8. ______________ ______________ and sensitivity are not only important but ______________ for successful ______________ project management.

BENEFITS OF PROJECT MANAGEMENT

The ultimate benefit of implementing project management techniques is having a *satisfied customer*—whether you are the customer of your own project, such as remodeling your basement, or a business (contractor) being paid by a customer to perform a project. Completing the full project scope in a quality manner, on time, and within budget provides a great feeling of satisfaction. For a contractor, it could lead to additional business from the same customer in the future or to business from new customers referred by previously satisfied customers.

Critical Success FACTORS

- Planning and communication are critical to successful project management. They prevent problems from occurring or minimize their impact on the achievement of the project objective when they do occur.
- Taking the time to develop a well-thought-out plan before the start of the project is critical to the successful accomplishment of any project.
- A project must have a well-defined objective—an expected result or product, defined in terms of scope, schedule, and cost, and agreed upon by the customer.
- Involve the customer as a partner in the successful outcome of the project through active participation during the project.
- Achieving customer satisfaction requires ongoing communication with the customer to keep the customer informed and to determine whether expectations have changed.
- The key to effective project control is measuring actual progress and comparing it to planned progress on a timely and regular basis and taking corrective action immediately, if necessary.
- After the conclusion of a project, the project performance should be evaluated to learn what could be improved if a similar project were to be done in the future. Feedback should be obtained from the customer and the project team.
- Learning and understanding the culture and customs of other project participants will demonstrate respect, help build trust, aid in developing an effective project team, and is critical for successful global project management.

"Hey! Great for the customer, but what about me? What's in it for me?" If you are the project manager, you have the satisfaction of knowing you led a successful project effort. You also have enhanced your reputation as a project manager and positioned yourself for expanded career opportunities. If you are a member of a project team that successfully accomplished a project, you feel the satisfaction of being on a winning team. You not only contributed to the project's success, but also probably expanded your knowledge and enhanced your skills along the way. If you choose to remain an individual contributor, you will be able to make a greater contribution to future, more complicated projects. If you are interested in eventually managing projects, you will be in a position to take on additional project responsibilities. When projects are successful, everybody wins!

SUMMARY

A project is an endeavor to accomplish a specific objective through a unique set of interrelated tasks and the effective utilization of resources. It has a clearly defined objective stated in terms of scope, schedule, and cost. The responsibility of the project manager is to make sure that the project objective is accomplished and that the work scope is completed in a quality manner, within budget, and on time, to the customer's satisfaction.

The first phase of the project life cycle involves the identification of a need, problem, or opportunity and can result in the customer's requesting proposals from individuals, a project team, or organizations (contractors) to address an identified need or solve a problem. The second phase of the project life cycle is the development of a proposed solution to the need or problem. This phase results in the submission of a proposal to the customer by one or more individuals or contractors or the project team. The third phase of the project life cycle is the implementation of the proposed solution. This phase, which is referred to as performing the project, results in accomplishment of the project objective, leaving the customer satisfied that the work scope was completed in a quality manner, within budget, and on time. The final phase of the project life cycle is terminating the project, which includes evaluating the execution of the project in order to enhance work on future projects.

Project management involves a process of first establishing a plan and then implementing that plan to accomplish the project objective. This planning effort includes clearly defining objectives, dividing and subdividing the project scope into major "pieces" called work packages, defining the specific activities that need to be performed for each work package, graphically portraying the activities in the form of a network diagram, estimating how long each activity will take to complete, defining the types of resources and how many of each resource are needed for each activity, estimating the cost of each activity, and calculating a project schedule and budget.

Taking the time to develop a well-thought-out plan is critical to the successful accomplishment of any project. Once the project starts, project management involves monitoring the progress to ensure that everything is going according to plan. The key to effective project control is measuring actual progress and comparing it to planned progress on a timely and regular basis and taking corrective action immediately, if necessary.

Globalization changes the dynamics of a project and adds a layer of complexity which can adversely affect the project outcome if the project participants are not aware of what they might encounter regarding cultural differences and multinational economic transactions. Factors external to the project itself, or to the project or customer organizations, can create a dynamic and perhaps unstable environment over the life of the project, introduce sources of risk, and affect the success of the projects. Global projects can be multinational and multilingual, with participants located in various countries and who speak different languages. Technology (for example, computers, Internet access) enables project participants to be just a mouse-click away, despite being thousands of miles apart physically. Global project management requires an additional set of competencies. Cultural awareness and sensitivity are not only important but imperative for successful global project management. Learning and understanding the culture and customs of other project participants demonstrates respect, helps build trust, aids in developing an effective project team, and is critical for successful global project management.

The ultimate benefit of implementing project management techniques is having a satisfied customer—whether you are the customer of your own project or a business (contractor) being paid by a customer to perform a project. Completing the full project scope in a quality manner, on time, and within budget provides a great feeling of satisfaction to everyone involved in the project.

QUESTIONS

1. Define the term *project objective* and give some examples.
2. Define *project.*
3. What role does a customer have during the project life cycle? Why is it important to satisfy the customer?
4. List some examples of resources that are used on a project.
5. Define *scope, schedule, cost,* and *customer satisfaction.* Why are these considered to be constraints?
6. What aspects of a project might involve some degree of uncertainty? Why?
7. List and describe the steps required to develop a baseline plan.
8. List and describe the main phases of the project life cycle.
9. Describe how a global project can be more complex than a project performed within just one country. How might these elements affect the successful outcome of the global project?
10. Why must a manager monitor the progress of a project? What can be done if a project is not proceeding according to plan?
11. Consider a project in which you are currently involved or in which you have recently been involved.
    a. Describe the objectives, scope, schedule, cost, and any assumptions made.
    b. Where are you in the project life cycle?
    c. Does this project have a baseline plan? If yes, describe it. If not, create it.
    d. Are you or is anyone else monitoring the progress of the project? If so, how? If not, how could you do so?
    e. Describe some unexpected circumstances that could jeopardize the success of the project.
    f. Describe the anticipated benefits of the project.
12. List some benefits of using project management techniques.

INTERNET EXERCISES

For the website addresses of the organizations mentioned in these exercises, go to "Internet Exercises" at the book's companion website at **international.cengage.com**. It is suggested that you save this website in your "Favorites" for easy access in the future.

1. Do several additional web searches by adding, after the words "project management," some of the key words listed in this chapter. For example, search for "project management objectives," "project management life cycle," "project management process," "project management work breakdown structures," and so on. What did you find?
2. Using your favorite web search engine perform a search for "project management." Explore at least five of the links that your search produces. Give the web address for each site and describe what it contains.
3. PMI is an international organization with chapters worldwide. Search for PMI Global Congresses. Describe what you find, including upcoming international conferences. Also, explore the link for your local PMI chapter. Print out the information for PMI chapters in your local area. In addition, explore the link for Resources. Browse through the Virtual Library, Research, Publications, and Standards links. *PM Network*, *PMI Today*, and the *Project Management Journal* are excellent sources of project management information published by PMI. Select an article that interests you, locate it in the library or online, and provide a one-page summary.
4. Executive Planet™ provides valuable tips on business etiquette, customs, and protocol for doing business worldwide. Go to the organization's website and explore the business culture guides for three different countries. Summarize key points regarding etiquette and customs for each of the three countries.
5. Since it was founded in 1969, the Project Management Institute (PMI) has grown to over 250,000 members in more than 160 countries. The Pennsylvania-based PMI is, by far, the leading nonprofit professional association in the area of project management. It establishes standards, sponsors seminars, develops educational programs, has a professional certification program, and publishes *Project Management Journal* and *PM Network*. Check out the PMI website for information regarding memberships, certification, education, and publications. Describe the benefits of having a membership. Apply for membership online if you are interested (student rates are available).

E-Commerce for a Small Supermarket

CASE STUDY 1

Matt and Grace own a small supermarket in a rural town with a large and growing elderly population. Because of their remote location, they don't have any competition from the large chain stores. A small private liberal arts college, with about 1,500 students, is also located in the town.

"I think we need a website for our store," Matt tells Grace.

"Why?" asks Grace.

"Everybody has one. It's the wave of the future," responds Matt.

"I'm still not clear, Matt. What would be on our website?" Grace asks.

"Well, for one thing we could have a picture of our market with me and you standing in front of it," says Matt.

"What else?" asks Grace.

Matt answers, "Ah, maybe people could look up stuff and order it through the website. Yeah, those college kids would think that's great; they're into using computers all the time. That will increase our business. They'll buy food from our store rather than the pizza and burgers they always eat or get delivered from Sam's Sub Shop. And those people who live in the senior citizens apartments would use it too. I heard they're teaching them how to use computers. And maybe we can even set up a delivery service."

"Hold on," says Grace. "Those college students get pizza and subs from Sam's at all hours of the night. Long after we're closed. And I think the senior citizens enjoy getting out. They have a van that brings some of them here each day to shop; and they really don't buy much anyway. And how will they pay for what they order through the website? I'm all for keeping up with things, but I'm not sure this makes sense for our little supermarket, Matt. What would we be trying to accomplish with a website?"

"I just explained it to you, Grace. It's the way all businesses are going. We either keep up with things or we'll be out of business," replies Matt.

"Does this have anything to do with that Chamber of Commerce meeting you went to in Big Falls last week, where you said they had some consultant talking about e-business or something?" asks Grace. "Yeah, maybe," Matt says. "I think I'll give him a call and tell him to stop by and tell him what I want."

"How much is all this going to cost us, Matt?" asks Grace. "I think we need to think about this some more. You know we are probably going to have to pave the parking lot this summer."

Matt answers, "Don't worry. It'll all work out. Trust me. Our business will increase so much, it'll pay for itself in no time. Besides, it can't cost that much; this consultant probably does these kinds of projects all the time."

CASE QUESTIONS

1. What are the needs that have been identified?
2. What is the project objective?
3. What are some things Matt and Grace should do before they talk with the consultant?
4. What should the consultant tell Matt and Grace?

GROUP ACTIVITY

Select two course participants to use this case script to role-play Matt and Grace in front of the class. Then divide the course participants into groups of three or four to discuss the case questions. Each group must choose a spokesperson to present its responses to the entire class.

OPTIONAL ACTIVITY

Have each course participant contact a business that went "online" and ask the business what led it to that decision and if the project met its initial expectations.

CASE STUDY 2

A Not-for-Profit Organization

The officers of the student community service organization—which collects and buys food and distributes it to people in need—of a local college are having their February meeting. Sitting in the meeting room are Beth Smith, the organization's president, and two officers, Rosemary Olsen, vice president, and Steve Andrews, volunteer coordinator. Beth announces, "Our funds are almost exhausted. The demands on the food bank have been increasing. We need to figure out how to get more funds."

"We need to have a fundraising project," responds Rosemary.

Steve suggests, "Can't we ask the city government if they can increase their allocation of funds to us?"

"They're strained. They may even cut our allocation next year," replies Beth.

"How much do we need to get us through this year?" asks Rosemary.

"About $10,000," answers Beth, "and we are going to start needing that money in about two months."

"We need a lot of things besides money. We need more volunteers, more space for storage, and more food donations," says Steve.

"Well, I guess we can make that all part of the fund-raising project. This is going to be fun!" says Rosemary excitedly.

"This project is growing. We'll never get it done in time," Beth says.

Rosemary responds, "We'll figure it out and get it done. We always do."

"Is a project what we need? What are we going to do next year—another project?" asks Steve. "Besides, we're having a hard time getting volunteers anyway. Maybe we need to think about how we can operate with less funds. For example, how can we get more food donations on a regular basis so we won't have to buy as much food?"

Rosemary jumps in. "Great idea! You can work on that while we also try to raise funds. We can't leave any stone unturned."

"Time out," says Beth. "These are all very good ideas, but we have limited funds and volunteers and a growing demand. We need to do something now to make sure we don't have to close our doors in two months. I think we all agree we need to undertake some type of initiative. But I'm not sure we all agree on the objective."

CASE QUESTIONS

1. What are the needs that have been identified?
2. What is the project objective?
3. What assumptions, if any, should be made regarding the project to be undertaken?
4. What are the risks involved in the project?

GROUP ACTIVITY

Contact a local not-for-profit organization in your community. Tell them that you are interested in learning about their operations. Ask them to describe a project that they are currently working on. What are the objectives? The constraints? The resources?

If possible, have your team contribute a few hours to the project. Through this process you will be helping someone in need and learning about a real-world project at the same time. Prepare a report summarizing the project and what you learned from this experience.

© Bilderlounge/Jupiter Images

CHAPTER 2

Needs Identification

Real World PROJECT MANAGEMENT

Successful Messaging Services in Poland

Polska Telefonia Cyfrowa (PTC) is Poland's leading wireless services provider, and maintains Era, the largest mobile network in Poland. Era serves more than seven million subscribers and has almost 37 percent share of the total Polish market.

PTC consists of 24 dealers and a direct sales force of 105 business advisors. Several years ago, it introduced Eranet (a basic e-mail service for Era) powered by Sun Internet Mail Server (SIMS), which is equipped with short messaging service (SMS) applications. The messaging system is designed to notify mobile subscribers by cell phone text messages when they have new e-mail. PTC decided to expand its offerings to customers by delivering two-way SMS services. With the enhanced SMS services, subscribers would be able to manage their e-mail inboxes more conveniently than before.

A detailed needs assessment was a key to this successful initiative. Sun Services helped to map out all of the requirements for the Eranet project from the beginning and remained involved at every stage. Sun's involvement included project management; evaluation of hardware and software needs; architectural design; implementation of the new infrastructure; migration to the new mail server; skills assessment and training; and ongoing support. Sun Services developed use cases, broke the project into smaller chunks, and applied an iterative development process in order to minimize risks involved in the engagement, while increasing speed to the market.

Since PTC intended to grow its subscriber base and e-mail volume quickly, solutions needed to consider security, scalability, and availability. Sun consultants developed an implementation plan that first determined needs and then designed effective solutions. The plan was introduced slowly and seamlessly to avoid inconvenience to users. The project was completed in just 12 months, which was nearly 50 percent earlier than anticipated. Sun consultants also developed a new SMS gateway for integration of Java 2 Platform, Enterprise Edition (J2EE) technology-compliant applications for SMS messaging.

With the implementation of the new Sun e-mail software, PTC was able to grow its subscriber base by approximately 80 percent in one year, with the anticipation of further growth. This will enable the company to achieve 100 percent payback on the new messaging infrastructure in only two years. The PTC introduced a trial subscription program, which provides more information to the company about customers' usage and is now 1.5 times more productive in yielding paid subscribers. Finally, the messaging system allowed network offerings to have higher availability and lower costs of maintenance and management, and to add new functionality more easily.

Sun Microsystems, "Sun Helps Polish Telecom Maintain Market Leadership with Messaging Migration Solution," www.sun.com/software/customers, July 23, 2007.

Recall that the project life cycle consists of four phases: identifying needs, proposing a solution, performing the project, and terminating the project. This chapter focuses on needs identification, the first phase of the project life cycle (see Figure 2.1). You will become familiar with

- identifying needs and selecting projects
- developing a request for proposal
- the proposal solicitation process

NEEDS IDENTIFICATION

Needs identification is the initial phase of the project life cycle. It starts with the recognition of a need, problem, or opportunity and ends with the issuance of a request for proposal (RFP). The customer identifies a need, a problem, or an opportunity for a better way of doing something and therefore sees some benefit to undertaking a project that will result in an improvement or advantage over the existing condition.

For example, suppose a company's management recognizes that the time the company takes to issue invoices and collect payments from its customers is too long. Furthermore, the fact that company payment records are not up to date has caused second invoices to be sent to customers who have already paid, thus upsetting some good customers. Also, as business increases, more clerical staff must be added to process the additional invoices and payments, and more file cabinets must be purchased to store the growing amount of paperwork. Management recognizes several problems and opportunities for improvement, so it develops an RFP asking contractors to submit proposals for implementing an automated billing and collection system. In a different scenario, the company's management might request a proposal from an in-house individual or project team rather than from an external contractor.

FIGURE 2.1 ***Project Life Cycle***

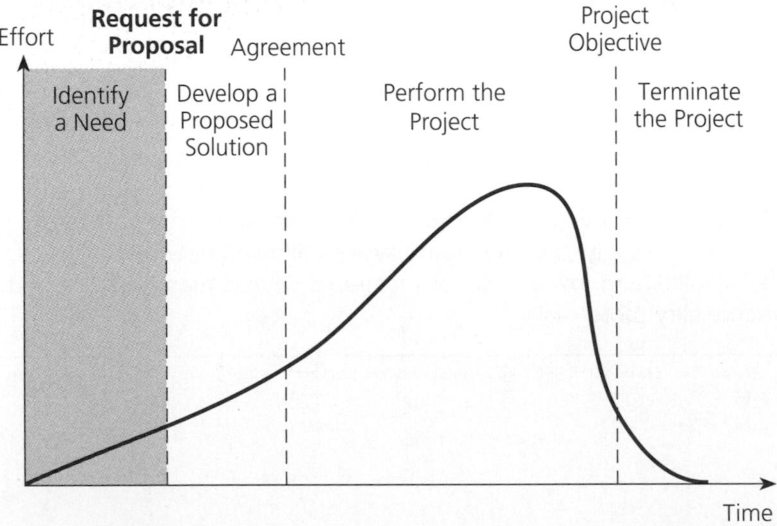

Before a request for proposal is prepared, the customer must clearly define the problem or need. This may mean gathering data about the magnitude of the problem. For example, if a business thinks the scrap rate or reject rate from one of its manufacturing processes is too high, it may need to gather data regarding the actual rate and its impact on costs and cycle times. It is important to try to quantify the problem so as to determine whether the expected benefits from implementing a solution outweigh the costs or consequences of conducting the project and, if so, by how much.

Once the magnitude of the benefit or improvement has been estimated, the customer can determine the budget for a project to implement an improvement. For example, if a business estimates that it could save $100,000 a year by reducing its scrap rate from 5 percent to 1 percent, it might be willing to pay a one-time cost of $200,000 for new automated production equipment, thus breaking even after two years of operation. However, the business may not be willing to spend $500,000 for a solution. Businesses have a limited amount of funds available and, therefore, usually want to spend those funds on projects that will provide the greatest return on investment or overall benefit. Even in a nonbusiness example, such as staging a town's Fourth of July celebration, there is usually a budget within which the project must be accomplished.

There are often situations where a company has identified several needs but has limited funds and people available to pursue projects to address all of those needs. In such cases, the company must go through a decision-making process to select those needs that, when met, will result in the greatest overall benefit.

Reinforce Your Learning

1. The initial phase of the project life cycle is

____

______________________.

It starts with the recognition of a need or opportunity and ends with the issuance of a

____

____

______________________.

PROJECT SELECTION

Project selection involves evaluating various needs or opportunities, and then deciding which of these should move forward as a project to be implemented. The benefits and consequences, advantages and disadvantages, plusses and minuses of each opportunity need to be considered and evaluated. They can be both quantitative and qualitative, tangible and intangible. Quantitative benefits could be financial, such as an increase in sales or a reduction in costs. There also may be intangible benefits associated with an opportunity, such as improving the company's public image or employee morale. On the other hand, there are quantitative consequences associated with each opportunity, such as the cost required to implement the project or disruption to work throughput while the project is being implemented. Some consequences may be less tangible, such as legal barriers or reaction from a particular advocacy group.

Reinforce Your Learning

2. Project selection involves

____

various needs or opportunities, and then

____

which of those should move forward as a

______________________.

The steps in project selection are as follows:

1. *Develop a set of criteria against which the opportunity will be evaluated.* These criteria will probably include both quantitative and qualitative factors. For example, if a pharmaceutical company is considering opportunities involving the development and introduction of several new products, it might evaluate each opportunity against the following criteria:
   - Alignment with company goals
   - Anticipated sales volume
   - Increase in market share

Reinforce Your Learning

3. Benefits and consequences can be both

____

and tangible or qualitative and

______________________.

- Establishment of new markets
- Anticipated retail price
- Investment required
- Estimated manufacturing cost per unit
- Technology development required
- Return on investment
- Human resources impact
- Public reaction
- Competitors' reaction
- Expected time frame
- Regulatory approval

Sometimes the opportunities and needs may not all be similar, such as several alternative new products. They could be very different and all compete for a company's resources. One may be to put a new roof on the factory, another to implement a new information system, and a third to develop a new product to replace one that is outdated and for which sales are rapidly declining.

2. *List assumptions* that will be used as the basis for each opportunity. For example, if one opportunity is to build an on-site day care center for children and elderly relatives of company employees, one assumption might be that the company would be able to obtain a bank loan to build such a center.
3. *Gather data and information for each opportunity* to help ensure an intelligent decision regarding project selection. For example, it may be necessary to gather some preliminary financial estimates associated with each opportunity, such as estimated revenue projections and implementation and operating costs. These costs may then be analyzed using certain mathematically based financial models so they can be compared on an equal basis. Such financial or economic models can include methodologies used to calculate simple payback, discounted cash flow, net present value, internal rate of return, return on investment, or life cycle costs associated with each opportunity being considered.

   In addition to gathering hard data, it may also be necessary to obtain other information regarding each opportunity. This could include getting information from various stakeholders who would be affected by the opportunity. These could be employees, consumers, or community residents, depending on the specific opportunity. Methods of gathering this information could include surveys, focus groups, interviews, or analysis of available reports. For example, if the opportunities being considered have to do with introducing several alternative food preparation products into the market, it may be valuable to conduct some focus groups with consumers to determine their needs and preferences. In the case of building an on-site day care center, it may be worthwhile to survey employees to determine how many employees would use the day care center for children or elderly relatives, and how often (all day, second shift, before or after school), ages of children, the health care needs of elderly relatives, and so forth.
4. *Evaluate each opportunity against the criteria.* Once all the data and information has been collected, analyzed, and summarized for each opportunity,

it should be given to all the individuals who are responsible for performing the evaluation. It is beneficial to have several individuals involved in the evaluation and selection decision in order to get various viewpoints. Each person on the evaluation and selection team or committee should have a different background and experiences to bring to the decision-making process. There may be someone from marketing who knows consumer preferences; someone from finance who knows costs and the company's financial condition; someone from production who understands what process and equipment changes may be needed; someone from research and development who can provide expertise on how much additional technology development may be required; and someone from human resources to represent any impact on the workforce or the community.

Although it may take longer and be more stressful to gain group consensus on project selection and priorities, it will most likely be a better quality decision than if the decision is made by just one individual. Acceptance of the decision will also be greater.

One approach to the evaluation and selection process would be to have the evaluation and selection committee meet to develop a set of evaluation criteria. They may also develop some type of rating system (such as High-Medium-Low, 1 to 5, 1 to 10) against which to rate each opportunity against each criterion. Then each committee member should be provided with any data and information that has been collected, analyzed, and summarized. Before the entire committee meets, each member can individually assess the benefits and consequences, advantages and disadvantages of each opportunity against the evaluation criteria. This will give each member sufficient time for thoughtful preparation prior to a meeting of the entire committee.

It is advisable to develop a project evaluation form listing the criteria with space for comments and a rating box for each criterion. Each evaluation and selection committee member could then complete a form for each opportunity prior to coming to a meeting of the entire committee.

In most cases the project selection will be based on a combination of quantitative evaluation and what each person feels in her or his "gut" based on experience. Although the final decision may be the responsibility of the company owner, president, or department head, having a well-understood evaluation and selection process and a well rounded committee will increase the chances of making the best decision that will result in the greatest overall benefit.

Reinforce Your Learning

4. What are the four steps in the project selection process?

Once the decision has been made regarding which opportunity or opportunities to pursue, the next step is to prepare a request for proposal if it is expected that a contractor or consultant will be hired to perform the project. If the project is going to be carried out by an in-house project team, then a document should be prepared outlining the project requirements in a form similar to what would be included in an RFP.

PREPARING A REQUEST FOR PROPOSAL

The purpose of preparing a request for proposal is to state, comprehensively and in detail, what is required, from the customer's point of view, to address the identified need. A good RFP allows contractors or a project team to understand what the customer expects so that they can prepare a thorough proposal that will satisfy the customer's requirements at a realistic price. For example, an RFP that simply requests contractors to submit a proposal for building a house is not specific enough. Contractors could not even begin to prepare proposals without information about the kind of house that is wanted. An RFP should be comprehensive and provide sufficiently detailed information so that a contractor or project team can prepare an intelligent proposal that is responsive to the customer's needs. A sample RFP is shown in Figure 2.2.

Reinforce Your Learning

5. What is the purpose of a request for proposal?

It should be noted that in many situations a formal RFP may not be prepared; instead, the need is communicated informally—and sometimes orally rather than in writing. This is often the case when the project will be implemented by a firm's internal staff rather than outsourcing it to an external contractor. For example, if a company needs to change the layout of its manufacturing facility to make room for new production equipment that has to be incorporated into the production flow, the manufacturing manager may simply ask one of the supervisors to put together a proposal for "what it's going to take to reconfigure the production line."

Following are some guidelines for drafting a formal request for proposal to external contractors:

1. *An RFP* must provide a ***statement of work (SOW).*** An SOW deals with the scope of the project, outlining the tasks or work elements the customer wants the contractor or project team to perform. For example, if the RFP is for a house, the contractor needs to know whether he should design and build the entire house, build it according to the customer's design, or include finishing the basement and installing the carpeting. If a customer needs a marketing brochure, the RFP must state whether the contractor is to design the brochure or design, print, and mail it.
2. *The RFP must* include the ***customer requirements,*** which define *specifications and attributes*. Requirements cover size, quantity, color, weight, speed, and other physical or operational parameters the contractor's proposed solution must satisfy. For the marketing brochure, the requirements might be for a trifold self-mailer, printed on card stock in two colors, with a print run of 10,000. Requirements for the house might include an overall size of 3,000 square feet with four bedrooms, two baths, a two-car garage, central air conditioning, and a fireplace.

   Some requirements address performance. If the RFP is for an automated billing and collection system, performance requirements might include the capacity to process 12,000 transactions a day and provisions for special functions such as consolidated multiple invoices for individual customers and automatically generated second invoices for payments not received within 30 days of the initial invoice.

   Such performance requirements may also be used as acceptance criteria by the customer. For example, the project contractor will have to run tests on the automated billing and collection system to prove to the customer that it meets the performance requirements before the customer accepts the system and makes the final payment to the contractor.
3. *The RFP should state what* ***deliverables*** *the customer expects the contractor or project team to provide*. Deliverables are the tangible items that the contractor is to supply. With the brochure example, the only deliverable might be 10,000 copies of the brochure. With the billing and collection system, the contractor may be expected to supply the hardware (computers), software

FIGURE 2.2 ***Request for Proposal***

February 1st

To Whom It May Concern:

AJACKS Information Services Company is seeking proposals from contractors with relevant experience to conduct a market survey of the technical information needs of manufacturing firms nationwide. The objectives of this project are

1. To determine the technical information needs of manufacturing firms nationwide, and
2. To recommend approaches to promote the purchase and utilization of AJACKS Information Services by such firms.

This project must provide adequate information for AJACKS Information Services Company to determine

- Future information products or services, and
- The best methods for delivering these products or services to its customers.

The contents of this request for proposal are to be considered confidential information.

1. **Statement of Work**

   The contractor will perform the following tasks:

   Task 1: Identify Technical Information Needs of Manufacturing Firms

   Conduct a survey of manufacturing firms nationwide to determine their specific needs for external (to their firms) technical information. The assessment should determine the various specific types of technical information needed and the frequency with which each type of information is needed.

   Task 2: Determine the Best Approaches to Promote the Purchase and Utilization of AJACKS Information Services by Businesses

   The survey should include an identification of the firms' perceptions of the most effective direct and indirect marketing approaches that influence the firms' decisions to both purchase and utilize specific services or products, in particular, information services.

2. **Requirements**

   The survey should determine the various specific types of technical information needed and the frequency with which each type of information is needed.

   The survey should identify the current sources for the various types of technical information that are used by manufacturing firms, their frequency of use, and the firms' perception of the value (benefit, cost, accuracy, timeliness) of each source. It should determine the various methods the firms currently use to access these sources of information. The survey should determine the average and range of funds (both internal to the firm and external fees) that firms currently expend for obtaining the various types of technical information.

   The assessment must provide sufficient detail to permit demand-driven product planning by AJACKS Information Services Company. Therefore, it must include: (1) the information content most frequently needed by firms; (2) the applications for which the firms use the information; (3) the persons (title, skill level) responsible for both accessing and utilizing the information; and (4) the channels that firms use to access the various types of information.

   AJACKS Information Services Company is interested in developing and delivering products and services that are valued by the users (manufacturing firms). With these interests in mind, the contractor must generate information about which firms (as distinguished by size, sector, location, or other important factors) may benefit most from information products and services or represent the most appropriate markets for such products and services.

   The contractor should determine the size of the market for the various types of technical information and determine the market sensitivity to price, timeliness, accuracy, and delivery mechanisms for such information.

   The survey methodology should include both focus groups and mail surveys.

   The focus groups should be categorized by major manufacturing sectors and by multisector firm size (large, medium, small).

FIGURE 2.2 *Request for Proposal (Continued)*

Based on the results from the focus groups, a draft mail survey questionnaire should be developed and pre-tested on representative firms. This survey instrument should be finalized after sufficient pre-testing.

The contractor should provide a sampling design for the mail survey that is stratified by sector and firm size, is representative of the entire population of manufacturing firms, and is sufficiently large to present the survey results for each stratum at the 90 percent confidence level.

3. **Deliverables**

A. A detailed report of the results of Task 1 must be prepared that identifies and analyzes the results for all respondents and also provides detailed analyses (1) for each sector and (2) by firm size. The contractor must provide an electronic copy and twenty (20) hardcopies of the report. The database of the survey responses used in the analysis must be delivered in a format suitable for further analysis by AJACKS Information Services Company.

B. Based on the analysis of Tasks 1 and 2, provide a detailed report of recommendations of the most effective approaches, and associated costs, to promoting technical information services to manufacturing firms with the objective of getting such firms to purchase and use such services. Discuss any differences in approaches based on sector or size of business. The contractor must provide an electronic copy and twenty (20) hardcopies of the report.

C. Status reports on project progress must be e-mailed to AJACKS Information Services Company on the 15th and 30th of each month. Reports should be brief and focus on progress compared to the contractor's original plan and schedule. These reports should cover activities, milestones achieved, plans for the next month, obstacles encountered or anticipated, and hours and dollars expended. For any work items where progress is behind schedule, a plan must be proposed to complete the project within the original schedule and budget.

4. **Items Supplied by AJACKS Information Services Company**

AJACKS will provide the contractor with detailed information about its current information services and products as well as statistical information regarding its current customer base.

5. **Approvals Required**

The contractor must obtain the approval of AJACKS for the final version of the survey instrument before it is implemented.

6. **Type of Contract**

The contract will be for a fixed price for all of the work the contractor proposes to meet all the requirements of this request for proposal.

7. **Due Date**

The contractor must submit an electronic copy and five (5) hardcopies of the proposal to AJACKS Information Services Company on or before February 28th.

8. **Schedule**

AJACKS Information Services Company expects to select a contractor by March 30th. The required period of performance of this project is six months, from May 1st to October 30th. All deliverables must be provided to AJACKS on or before October 30th.

9. **Payment Terms**

AJACKS Information Services Company will make payments to the contractor according to the following schedule:

- One-third of total amount when project is shown to be one-third complete
- One-third of total amount when project is shown to be two-thirds complete
- One-third of total amount when AJACKS Information Services Company is satisfied that the project is 100 percent complete and that the contractor has fulfilled all contractual obligations

FIGURE 2.2 *Request for Proposal (Continued)*

10. Proposal Contents

As a minimum, the contractor's proposal must include the following:

A. Approach

A discussion that indicates the contractor clearly understands the request for proposal and what is expected. Also, a detailed discussion of the contractor's approach to conducting the project and a detailed description of each task and how it will be accomplished.

B. Deliverables

A description of each deliverable the contractor will provide.

C. Schedule

A bar chart or network diagram showing the weekly schedule of the detailed tasks to be performed in order to complete the project by the required project finish date.

D. Experience

A discussion of recent similar projects the contractor has performed, including customer names, addresses, and phone numbers.

E. Staffing

The names and detailed resumes of the specific individuals who will be assigned to work on the project and highlights of their experience on similar projects.

F. Costs

The total fixed price must be stated and supported by a detailed breakdown of hours and an hourly cost rate for each person who will be assigned to the project. Additionally, an itemized list of all direct expenses must be included.

11. Proposal Evaluation Criteria

AJACKS Information Services Company will evaluate all contractor proposals according to the following criteria:

A. Approach (30%)

The approach and methodology the contractor proposes to conduct the survey and analyze the results.

B. Experience (30%)

The experience of the contractor and the staff assigned to the project in performing similar projects.

C. Price (30%)

The fixed price of the contractor's proposal.

D. Schedule (10%)

The detail and overall duration of the contractor's proposed schedule to complete the project on or before the required project finish date.

(disks, as well as certain printouts), operator manuals, and training sessions. Deliverables could also include periodic progress reports or a final report that the customer requires the contractor to provide.

4. *The RFP should list any customer-supplied items.* For example, the RFP might state that the customer will supply a copy of its logo for use on the brochure. If the RFP is for a piece of automated equipment for testing electronic circuit boards, it may state that the customer will provide a certain quantity of the boards for the contractor to use during factory testing of the equipment before it is shipped to the customer.

5. *The RFP might state the approvals required by the customer.* For example, the housing customer may want to review and approve the plans before construction is started. The brochure customer may want to review and approve the brochure's layout before printing is started.
6. *Some RFPs mention the type of contract the customer intends to use.* It could be fixed-price, in which case the customer will pay the contractor a fixed amount regardless of how much the work actually costs the contractor. (The contractor accepts the risk of taking a loss.) Or the contract might be for time and materials. In this case, the customer will pay the contractor whatever the actual costs are. For example, if the RFP is to remodel a basement, the RFP might state that the contractor will be paid for the hours expended and the cost of materials.
7. *An RFP might state the payment terms the customer intends to use.* For example, the brochure customer may intend to make one payment at the end of the project. On the other hand, the customer for the house may specify progress payments, based on a percentage of the total price, that are made as certain milestones are accomplished—25 percent when the foundation is complete, another 25 percent when the framing is complete, and so on, until the entire project is finished.
8. *The RFP should state the required schedule for completion of the project.* It might state simply that the house must be completed within six months, or it might include a more detailed schedule. For example, the billing and collection system must be designed and developed and a design review meeting conducted within four months of the start of the project; then, the system must be installed and tested within four months of the design review; and, finally, the contractor must provide all system documentation and operator training within one month of the system's installation.
9. *The RFP should provide instructions for the format and content of the contractor proposals.* If the customer is going to compare and evaluate proposals from several contractors, it is important that they be consistent in format and content so that a fair evaluation can be made. Instructions might state the maximum number of pages, the number of details the customer wants the contractor to show regarding the costs, and other specifications.
10. *The RFP should indicate the* ***due date*** *by which the customer expects potential contractors to submit proposals.* Customers want to receive all proposals by a certain date so that they can compare and evaluate them at the same time. For example, a customer may give potential contractors 30 calendar days from the time the RFP is formally issued to submit a proposal. Customers usually state in the RFP that any proposals submitted after the due date will not be accepted for consideration, because it would be unfair to give some contractors extra time.
11. *An RFP may include the* ***evaluation criteria***. These are the criteria that the customer will use to evaluate proposals from competing contractors in order to select the one to perform the project. Criteria might include the following:
    a. The contractor's experience with similar projects. How recently has the contractor completed similar projects? Were they completed within budget and on schedule? Were the customers satisfied?
    b. The technical approach proposed by the contractor. What type and configuration of computer hardware will be used? What is the

Real World PROJECT MANAGEMENT

Red Light, Green Light

Catherine Aczel Boivie joined Pacific Blue Cross in 2003 as the Vice President of Information Technology. She made it her goal to use project management guidelines and a new reporting structure to keep her IT department aligned with her company's business goals. When she began, she and the CEO agreed on two principles: (1) Technology has no value alone, and (2) technology management needs to focus on enabling business as opposed to operations.

In large companies, like Pacific Blue Cross, it is common for these general and self-evident tenants to be swept under the rug. Boivie believed this was occurring when she started working at Pacific Blue Cross. She made it her personal mission to turn the IT department into a business enabler.

Pacific Blue Cross created a Balanced Scorecard that displays and measures the organization's performance from the following six perspectives: qualitative, quantitative, infrastructure, clients, people, and community-related goals. Each project must now be aligned and justified in terms of how it supports the goals explained in the Scorecard. This must be done during the needs identification phase of each project.

After compiling a list of all projects currently in progress, Boivie introduced the project management office (PMO) function. The PMO is designed to oversee all projects (of more than one-month duration at their organization) through all stages, from the business case to a post-implementation review. The PMO consists of managers, project managers, and contract managers, who conduct three half-day workshops for personnel involved in the projects. These workshops are followed by coaching sessions for project managers. Finally, all project management processes are made available online to create a shared knowledge base.

A report she called the Traffic Light was implemented to allow the PMO to regularly report project status to IT management, executive committees, and the board of directors. The report lists each project with a brief description, schedule, current stage, and a status comment. A red, yellow, or green symbol is found next to the project to illustrate whether it's on time, budget, and scope. The Traffic Light reports are posted on the company's intranet to allow all employees to follow the project's progress.

During Boivie's second year at Pacific Blue Cross, she introduced a gating process to govern her projects. The gates are as follows:

— Gate 1—The executive sponsor introduces the project concept to the executive committee. The executive committee then gives each project a thumbs-up or thumbs-down. If the committee approves, the project moves on to Gate 2.

— Gate 2—A detailed cost-benefit analysis of the project is presented by the sponsor. If the project passes, it moves on to Gate 3.

— Gate 3—A detailed business case is formulated.

— Gate 4—This gate is designed for projects that cost more than $1 million or have a very high level of complexity. Here, projects are reviewed at the executive level.

— Gate 5—Involves a post-implementation review.

This governance process allows everyone to see how projects are approved and prioritized. In addition, projects can be evaluated in terms of how they enable the company's business goals.

Finally, a change review board was implemented to review all change requests and prioritize how the proposed changes enable the business. When Boivie began working at Pacific Blue Cross, the IT department was swamped with 700 change requests. The review board allowed the company to determine the changes that are the most pressing and if any changes overlap.

While her company still faces a number of challenges, Boivie is confident that the project management processes she put in place will help ensure that each project is focused on advancing business goals, and can be completed on time and within budget!

Boivie, C., "Red Light, Green Light," *CIO Magazine*, June 15, 2006.

design approach for the database? Which software language will be used for developing the management information system?

c. The schedule. Will the contractor be able to meet or beat the required schedule?

d. The costs. If the estimate is based on time and materials, are the costs reasonable? Have any items been left out? Does it appear that the contractor has submitted a low cost estimate but will add costs after the project is under way, resulting in final costs that are much higher than the original estimate?

Reinforce Your Learning

6. What are some elements that may be included in a request for proposal?

12. *In rare cases an RFP will indicate the funds the customer has available to spend on the project.* Usually, the customer expects contractors to submit a proposal that meets the requirements in the RFP at the most reasonable cost. In some situations, however, it may be helpful for the customer to indicate a "ballpark" amount to be spent. For example, stating in the RFP that the cost of building the house should be about $300,000 would be helpful. Contractors can then submit proposals that are appropriate to that level of funding, rather than submitting proposals for houses that cost far more than the customer has available. Otherwise, all the contractors might submit proposals with prices much higher than the available funding, and the disappointed customer will have to ask all the contractors to resubmit proposals for a less expensive house.

Additional examples of Requests for Proposals can be found by using a search engine to search the web for "Request for Proposals."

SOLICITING PROPOSALS

Once the RFP has been prepared, the customer solicits proposals by notifying potential contractors that the RFP is available. One way for customers to do this is by identifying a selected group of contractors in advance and sending each of them a copy of the RFP. For example, a customer who has prepared an RFP for designing and building a customized piece of automated testing equipment might send it to several well-known companies (contractors) that specialize in producing such equipment. Another approach to soliciting potential contractors

Critical Success FACTORS

- The need must be clearly defined before preparing a request for proposal (RFP).
- When selecting a project from among several needs or opportunities, the decision should be based on which project will provide the greatest overall benefits compared to its costs and possible consequences.
- Having a well-understood evaluation and selection process and a well-rounded committee will increase the chances of making the best project selection decision.
- A good RFP allows contractors or a project team to understand what the customer expects so they can prepare a thorough proposal that is responsive to the customer's needs and requirements.
- A request for proposal should include a statement of work, customer requirements, expected deliverables, and the criteria by which the customer will evaluate proposals.
- An RFP should provide instructions for the format and content of contractor proposals so the customer will be able to make a consistent and fair comparison and evaluation of all the proposals.
- Customers must be careful not to provide information to only some of the contractors because it would give these contractors an unfair competitive advantage in preparing their proposals.

is for the customer to advertise in certain business newspapers and on websites that the RFP is available and give instructions on how interested contractors can obtain or download a copy. For example, federal government organizations advertise their RFPs in the *Commerce Business Daily*, as well as posting them on the agency's website.

Business customers and contractors consider the RFP/proposal process to be a competitive situation. Customers should be careful not to provide one or more of the contractors with information that is not provided to all interested contractors. Therefore, during the proposal development phase, customers may not want to answer questions from individual contractors who are preparing proposals for fear of giving those contractors an unfair competitive advantage over other contractors who do not have the same information. Business or government customers may hold a bidders' meeting to explain the RFP and answer questions from interested contractors.

Reinforce Your Learning

7. Care should be taken not to provide ____________ to only some of the ____________ that is not provided to all interested contractors because it would give some of them an ____________ ____________ ____________.

As a final note, we should repeat that *not all project life cycles include the preparation of a written request for proposal and subsequent proposals from contractors.* Some endeavors move right from defining what needs to be done into the project phase of the life cycle, where the project is planned and performed to satisfy the need. This process bypasses the RFP and proposal steps. For instance, when a company decides to initiate and implement a project to meet a certain need or solve a particular problem, it may use its own staff and project team rather than external contractors. Or when a group of volunteers decides to put on a countywide week-long arts festival, the volunteers may elect to do all the work themselves. When an accident victim requires a series of reconstructive surgeries, a team of surgeons may determine what needs to be done and then plan and perform a series of operations spanning several years. In all these examples, requests for proposal or proposals from contractors would not be appropriate.

There are other projects in which requirements are not written down in a formal RFP, but are communicated to several providers or suppliers (contractors). For example, in planning a wedding, the bride and groom may define their requirements for the reception, dinner, flowers, and other items and then shop around to select the suppliers that most closely match their requirements and budget.

Although projects can be businesslike or informal, they all start with the identification of a need, problem, or opportunity and then proceed to the customer's defining (in writing or orally) the scope, requirements, budget, and schedule for what is to be accomplished.

SUMMARY

Needs identification is the initial phase of the project life cycle. The customer identifies a need, a problem, or an opportunity for a better way of doing something. The need and associated requirements are usually written down by the customer in a document called a request for proposal (RFP).

Before a request for proposal is prepared, the customer must clearly define the problem or need. This may mean gathering data about the magnitude of the problem. It is important that the customer try to quantify the problem so as to determine whether the expected benefits from implementing a solution outweigh the costs or consequences of conducting the project.

There will be situations where several needs or opportunities have been identified but there are limited funds or resources available to pursue all of them. Project selection involves evaluating various needs and opportunities, and then deciding which of those should move forward as a project to be implemented. The steps in project selection are: developing a set of criteria against which the opportunity will be evaluated; listing assumptions about each opportunity; gathering data and information about each opportunity; and evaluating each opportunity against the criteria. Having a well-understood evaluation process and a well-rounded evaluation and selection committee will increase the chances of making the best decision that will result in the greatest overall benefit.

The purpose of preparing a request for proposal is to state, comprehensively and in detail, what is required, from the customer's point of view, to address the identified need. A good RFP allows contractors or a project team to understand what the customer expects so that they can prepare a thorough proposal that will satisfy the customer's requirements at a realistic price.

RFPs may contain a statement of work; customer requirements for physical or operational parameters, such as size, quantity, color, weight, and speed; deliverables the customer expects the contractor to provide; a list of any customer-supplied items; any approvals required by the customer; the type of contract the customer intends to use; the payment terms; the required schedule for completion of the project; instructions for the format and content of the contractor proposals; the due date by which the customer expects potential contractors to submit proposals; and criteria by which the proposals will be evaluated.

Once the RFP has been prepared, the customer solicits proposals by notifying potential contractors that the RFP is available. Business customers and contractors consider the RFP/proposal process to be a competitive situation. Customers should be careful not to provide one or more contractors with information that is not provided to all interested contractors.

Not all project life cycles include the preparation of a written request for proposal and subsequent proposals from contractors. Some endeavors move right from defining the need into the project phase of the life cycle.

QUESTIONS

1. Describe a situation in your life in which you performed needs identification.
2. Why is it important to do a thorough and detailed job of needs identification?
3. Describe how a business selects which projects to work on when there are numerous projects that could be done.
4. Why is it important to select the right project before you begin working?
5. Give examples of situations in which an individual might develop a request for proposal.
6. Give examples of situations in which a business might develop a request for proposal.
7. What should be contained in a statement of work?
8. Why is it important for a business to try to quantify the expected benefits of implementing a solution to a problem?
9. Why would an RFP state the approvals that will be required during the project? Give some examples.
10. What is meant by customer requirements? Why must they be precise?
11. Develop an RFP for a real-world project such as landscaping the grounds surrounding a nearby business office, building a deck for your house, or holding a big graduation celebration. Be creative in specifying your needs. Feel free to come up with unique ideas for the RFP.
12. Why would a customer give contractors instructions in the RFP to submit their proposals according to a standard format?

INTERNET EXERCISES

For the website addresses of the organizations mentioned in these exercises, go to "Internet Exercises" at the book's companion website at **international.cengage.com**. It is suggested that you save this website in your "Favorites" for easy access in the future.

In order to answer the following questions, perform a search for "Requests for Proposals" using your favorite search engine.

1. Based on the results of your search, find an RFP that has been posted on the web. What company developed the RFP and what are they looking to accomplish?
2. Evaluate the effectiveness of this RFP based on information you have studied in this chapter. Discuss the strengths and weaknesses of the RFP. Are there any items missing from the RFP that should have been included?
3. Download the RFP, and based on what you learned in this chapter, revise it. Highlight the areas you revised. What makes your revised RFP better than the original?

4. Perform a web search for software systems that can help you develop an RFP. Provide the web address and a brief summary for three of the systems you found. Download a demo copy of at least one, if possible.
5. Locate a website that provides suggestions for developing RFPs. Compare and contrast this with what was presented in the chapter.

CASE STUDY 1

Transportation Improvements

Polk County is the largest, yet one of the most sparsely populated, counties in the state. It has a fairly mountainous terrain. The lakes and forests provide great fishing and hunting for many of its residents as well as for people from outside the county. It gets some pretty rough winters. It has the highest unemployment rate in the state. Both the average age of its population and the percentage of people over age 65 are substantially higher than the state statistics.

Mainville, located on the eastern side of the county, is the county seat. With a population of 15,000, it is the largest town in the county. Many of the people in Mainville work for the hospital, for the town school system, for the town government, or at the Big John's superstore that is on the outskirts of town just beyond the town limits. The largest employer in the county is a state correctional facility for female offenders located in the southwestern part of the county.

The county is governed by an elected three-member board of commissioners. They receive a minimal stipend for serving on the board. The current members are Commissioners Thomas, Richardson, and Harold. None of them are from Mainville; they all are from more remote parts of the county. They don't want much to do with Mainville, other than traveling there once a week for the commissioners' meeting at the county office building. Both Commissioners Thomas and Harold are retired. Commissioner Richardson lives on the western edge of the county and is a foreman at Ye Olde Saw Mill in the adjacent western county.

JR is the supervisor of the county Transportation Department; he lives in Mainville. Most of the department's budget is used to clear and salt the roads during the long winters, and for minimal maintenance. Until about five years ago, the county Transportation Department would get a special allocation of state funds, thanks to the state Senator Joe Smoozer, who was from Mainville. Twenty years before Joe had been supervisor of the county Transportation Department, then was elected to the state senate. JR had worked for Joe at the Transportation Department, and they became good friends. After years of being reelected, Joe gained enough seniority in the state senate to be named head of its Transportation Committee. Through that position, he was able to make sure that each year Polk County got a special allocation of state funds for its Transportation Department. However, Joe passed away about five years before, and the special allocation stopped. The new state senator representing Polk County is focused on economic development for the county, not on transportation.

Without the special state allocation, the county roads have gotten progressively worse. JR is concerned. He knows there are several critical projects that must be done. However, with his budget, he is worried that he may not even be able to do one of them. The county commissioners will make the final decision. He also knows that the commissioners will not be willing to raise the tax rate to pay for such projects. However, they may reallocate some funds from another department's budget.

One project is at the entrance to the Big John's superstore that opened three years before. The store is off a two-lane highway. Everyone seems to shop at the store because there aren't any shopping malls in the county. The traffic on the highway has increased substantially in the past three years. The store entrance is at the base of a hill so it is difficult for cars traveling in one direction to see cars in the opposite direction until they come over the crest. As a result, people making a left turn into the store entrance need to be careful of cars coming over the crest in the opposite direction. There have been a number of accidents at this spot since the store opened. JR knows that either the road needs to be widened to add a turn lane or a traffic light needs to be installed.

JR approached the manager of the store about possibly paying for the improvements to the highway in front of the store entrance. However, the manager said that the store was already a good community citizen; it had created jobs for people, kept its prices low, gave discounts to senior citizens, and donated a percentage of its sales receipts to various charities and fund-raisers in the county. As a result, he said the store was barely making a profit. If it didn't make a profit, corporate headquarters would close it down, and a lot of people would be put out of work. (By the way, Commissioner Thomas' wife works part-time at the store.) Although the store manager sympathized with JR, he said the store could not pay for adding a turn lane to the highway. Concern about the increase in the number of accidents has been raised by several residents at the commissioners' meetings in the past, but nothing has been done. The commissioners just said that the people must be more careful. However, several months ago, one person was very seriously injured. JR knows that if something isn't done, someone will be killed there eventually.

A second project is to widen and repair Elk Mountain Road in the northwest part of the county. Many people use the road to go to the lakes on Elk Mountain and for hunting. JR can't remember the last time the road was paved or fixed in any way. Rough winters have left it filled with potholes. After each winter the potholes get larger and deeper and there are more of them. Because of the unemployment in the county, recently independent loggers from the county have started using the road to go up to Elk Mountain to clear trees and bring the logs to several sawmills. The logging trucks are causing the road to deteriorate at an even faster rate. One of the mills getting the logs is Ye Olde Saw Mill in the adjacent county, where Commissioner Richardson is foreman. Both Commissioners Thomas and Richardson know the worsening conditions of Elk Mountain Road; after all, they use it frequently for going hunting and fishing on Elk Mountain. They also get an earful of complaints from many of their friends who use the road.

Finally, County Route 1045 is the main road to the state correctional facility in the southwestern part of the county. It is a two-lane road, just like all the other roads in the county. Near the prison, the road has a bridge that goes over Crockett Creek. Four years before, the bridge barely passed state inspection. At the time, JR was told that the bridge needed to be substantially upgraded by the next scheduled inspection, or it might not pass, and the bridge would have to be closed. That inspection is scheduled for next year. After the winter thaw, the water in Crockett Creek can get pretty high and flow pretty fast. People have voiced their concern about the bridge washing out. If that happened, traffic would need to be rerouted nearly 15 miles for most of the people who work at the prison.

At one commissioners' meeting last year, Commissioner Thomas said to wait until the bridge washed out; then maybe the state would give the county some money to build a new one. Besides, all those people who worked at the prison were state employees anyway and made a lot of money compared to retired people who have to live on a fixed income. That raised the ire of Commissioner Harold, whose daughter is a correctional officer at the prison, and he and Commissioner Thomas got into a shouting match at the meeting.

It is now June, and the commissioners will be reviewing the county Transportation Department's budget for next year at the September 15 commissioners' meeting. JR is worried that unless he presents a good case for which project should be given priority, the commissioners will probably not provide an increase in his budget for any of them. He fears that all three of the projects are disasters waiting to happen.

Zachary is a civil engineering student at the state university going into his senior year. He is from Mainville and is working at the county Transportation Department for the summer. It is June 15 when JR asks Zachary to help him pull together some information on the three projects by August 15, before Zachary goes back to school. JR can then be prepared for the commissioners' September 15 budget review meeting.

Because Zachary has lived in Mainville all his life, he is somewhat familiar with the three situations, although he has never given them much thought. However, the more he thought about it, he realized he had a personal connection to each of them.

That serious accident in front of Big John's superstore several months ago—the person who was seriously hurt was Peggy Sue Suite, one of Zachary's best friends from high school. She was going to turn left into the store entrance when she was struck from behind by a pickup truck that hit a patch of ice and couldn't stop in time. She is still in rehabilitation and wears a neck brace.

Last hunting season, Zachary was driving up Elk Mountain in his old clunker of a car. The week before, he had just wired up the muffler to the frame because the bracket fell off. He didn't do the greatest job of it, and the muffler and tail pipe hung pretty low to the ground. The next week when he was driving up Elk Mountain Road, he was almost run off the road by a logging truck coming down the mountain that seemed to enjoy the advantage it had over Zachary's smaller car. Zachary hit a huge pothole and ripped the muffler and tail pipe off his car. Although he was mad at the truck driver and the loggers who were tearing up the road, Zachary was just glad he wasn't hurt and his car didn't get sideswiped.

Zachary's brother is a correctional officer at the prison. Zachary heard him say more than once that it was just a matter of time until the Crockett Creek bridge collapsed or washed out. He swears he can feel it shake and sway when he goes over it. He said he hopes that he or his girlfriend (Commissioner Harold's daughter) aren't on it when it happens.

"Why don't the commissioners just give you the money for all three projects?" Zachary asked JR.

"I wish it was that simple," replied JR. "They don't want to raise taxes, and even if they did, we are a poor county and the people probably wouldn't have the money to pay any more taxes anyway. They also have other budgets to think about besides just the Transportation Department. I'm sure all the other county departments would like more money too."

"Zachary, I'm hoping that some of what you learned at that university is going to help you put together what I need—a priority ranking of the three projects and the information on each one to back it up. I know the commissioners are going to ask a lot of questions, and I need to be prepared. If we're lucky, they'll approve the project we recommend. If we don't have a good story to help them with a decision, they may just argue about it and deadlock with no decision. And we won't get any money for any of the projects. Yep, I think this will give you an opportunity to get a different kind of education than you get at the university. Why don't we get together next week and you can give me your ideas about how you'll tackle this? This may be a bigger job than you think. I want you to work on it full-time for the next two months. This is very important, and I want you to do a thorough job."

CASE QUESTIONS

1. What criteria should Zachary use to evaluate the projects?
2. What assumptions should he make?
3. What data and information should he gather, and how should he go about gathering the data and information?
4. After he has evaluated each project against the evaluation criteria, how should he decide the priority of the three projects?

GROUP ACTIVITY

Ask each course participant to individually answer the first case question. Then, divide the course participants into groups of three or four to discuss the case questions. Each group must select a spokesperson to present its answers to the entire class.

A Midsize Pharmaceutical Company

CASE STUDY 2

Jennifer Childs is the owner and Chief Executive Officer of a midsize global pharmaceutical company with sales offices or manufacturing plants in eight countries. At an October staff meeting she tells her managers that company profits for the year are expected to be $2,000,000 more than anticipated. She tells them she would like to reinvest this additional profit by funding projects within the company that will either increase sales or reduce costs. She asks her three key managers to get together to develop a prioritized list of potential projects and then to meet with her to "sell" her on their ideas. She mentions that they should not assume the funds will be divided equally among the three of them. She also mentions that she is willing to put all of the funds into just one project if it seems appropriate.

Julie Chen, manager of product development, has had a team of scientists working on a new prescription drug. This effort has been taking much longer than expected. She is worried that larger firms are working on a similar prescription drug and that these firms might get it to the marketplace first. Her team has not made any major breakthroughs yet, and some tests are not producing the expected results. She knows this is a risky project but feels that she can't stop it now. Julie believes the company's long-term growth depends on this new drug, which can be sold worldwide. She has tried to be optimistic at staff meetings about progress on this development project, but she knows that Jennifer is growing impatient and that her peers believe she should have terminated the project after the initial tests were less than promising. Julie would like to use the additional funds to accelerate the development project. She would hire a highly respected scientist from a larger firm and buy more sophisticated laboratory equipment.

Tyler Ripken, manager of production at the firm's largest and oldest manufacturing facility, has been with the company only six months. His early observation is that the production flow is very inefficient. He believes this is the result of poor planning when additions were made to the plant over the years as the company grew. Tyler would like to form several employee teams to implement a better layout of the equipment in the plant. He thinks this would increase plant capacity while reducing costs. When Tyler mentions this idea to some of his supervisors, they remind him that when Jennifer's father ran the business, Jennifer was in charge of production, and she was responsible for the design of the current plant layout. They also remind Tyler that Jennifer is not a fan of using employee teams. She believes production employees are paid to do their jobs, and she expects her managers to be the ones to come up with and implement new ideas.

Jeff Matthews, manager of operations, is responsible for the company's computers and information systems as well as its accounting operations. Jeff believes that the company's computer systems are outdated, and as the business has grown with locations worldwide, the older computer equipment has been unable to handle the volume of transactions. He thinks that a new computer system could keep better track of customer orders, reduce customer complaints, and issue more timely invoices, thus improving cash flow. The employees in Jeff's operation joke about their outdated computer systems and put pressure on Jeff to buy newer equipment. Jennifer has told Jeff in the past that she is not interested in spending money on new computers just for the sake of having the latest equipment, especially if the current system is working all right. She had suggested that Jeff look into hiring an outside service to do the accounting operations and reduce his own staff. Jeff would like to use this year's excess profits to buy new computers and to hire a computer programmer to upgrade the software to run on the new computers. He feels that this would be cost-effective.

After Jennifer's October staff meeting, Joe Sanchez, manager of marketing, stops by Jennifer's office. He says that although he has not been asked to come up with project ideas for the extra profits, his feeling is that she should forget this project nonsense and just give him a larger budget to hire more sales representatives in several additional countries. "That would increase sales faster than anything else," Joe tells her. "And besides, that's what your father would have done!" Joe is counting on disagreements among the other three managers in establishing priorities. He hopes that if Jennifer sees a lack of consensus, she might give him funds to hire the additional sales representatives.

CASE QUESTIONS

1. How should Jennifer go about making her decision?
2. What kind of additional data or information should she collect?

3. What exactly should Jennifer require the others to submit in the way of proposals?
4. What do you think Jennifer should do with the $2,000,000? In explaining your answer, address the concerns and positions of Julie, Tyler, Jeff, and Joe.

GROUP ACTIVITY

Select five course participants to play the roles of Jennifer, Julie, Tyler, Jeff, and Joe. While Jennifer and Joe leave the room, have Julie, Tyler, and Jeff role-play (preferably in front of the remaining course participants) a meeting in which they discuss their proposed projects and develop a prioritized list to "sell" to Jennifer.

After Jennifer and Joe reenter the room, have all five participants role-play (preferably in front of the class) a meeting with Jennifer in which Julie, Tyler, and Jeff try to sell her on the prioritized list of projects and Joe promotes his agenda.

Discuss what took place. What positions did the players take? How was the final decision made? What was the final decision?

© Comstock Images/Jupiter Images

CHAPTER 3

Proposed Solutions

Real World PROJECT MANAGEMENT

Renovating the Baltimore Arena

In 1962, Baltimore, Maryland, unveiled the Baltimore Civic Center, a 13,000-person capacity arena located in the heart of downtown. It was reopened after renovations in 1986, and renamed the "Baltimore Arena." In its over 40-year history, the arena has hosted many notorious performers and events including the likes of The Beatles, Elvis Presley, Frank Sinatra, and a 1966 speech given by Dr. Martin Luther King Jr.

In 2003, 1st Mariner Bank purchased the rights to the Baltimore Arena, and renamed it the "1st Mariner Arena." More recently, the arena has been the home of the MLS indoor soccer team the Baltimore Blast, Ringling Bros. and Barnum & Bailey Circus, World Wrestling Entertainment, and the Miss USA Pageant. The arena has served the downtown community well, and is credited as the cornerstone of Inner Harbor redevelopment during the 1980s. The arena hosts an estimated 800,000 guests and 120 events a year. However, it is increasingly clear that it is outdated, and as the *Baltimore Sun* quoted, has "served its useful life."

In 2004, the Maryland Stadium Authority began soliciting proposals to build a new indoor sports and concert arena in downtown Baltimore. With this new project, the city hopes to stay on top of technological changes in order to attract minor league sports teams and exceptional performers. As of November 2007, seven prominent developers have submitted proposals. The proposed plans differ on many factors, including location, cost, and size.

One major debate is whether or not the new arena should be built on the current site. This would require the arena to be shut down for a minimum of two years, and many fear that this would cause Baltimore to lose several events for good. Struever Bros. Eccles & Rouse and Capital Venture Group LLC are looking at several locations; however, they acknowledge that the current location is ideal and capitalizes upon the vibrancy of downtown. However, another developer, Edward Hale, of the Hale Properties LLC and Greenberg Gibbons Commercial Corp. team, is also the owner of the Baltimore Blast Soccer team. He is proposing to build the new arena across the city in order to preserve the team's current space. Yet, finding a new location for such a large project is not easy in the already crowded city, and with this comes issues such as parking and accessibility to public transportation.

Cormony Development LLC, Harrison Development LLC, and Team 52 Development LLC are proposing to build the new arena in between the city's football and baseball stadiums, creating one large event area that has excellent accessibility to parking and public transportation. Their project also includes office buildings, retail stores, and a sports complex. However, several developers see this project as a way to revitalize an up-and-coming part of the city. Turner Development Group proposes to build the arena in South Baltimore, an area where they are already planning on creating office, residential, retail, and hotel space. They feel that the arena would "enliven" the nightlife in that area.

Another unresolved debate is the size of the new arena. The Maryland Stadium Authority proposed a 15,000–16,000-seat arena, which assumes that Baltimore will never be able to attract a major league basketball or hockey franchise, which would require an arena of at least 17,000 seats. Many developers feel that is it not prudent to rule out this option, and are proposing arenas of major-league size.

The Baltimore Development Corporation will ultimately decide the fate of the new Baltimore Arena, and they have a hard decision ahead of them. With so many diverse proposals, they will have many factors to take into account. One thing that is certain, however, is that the future of attracting exceptional events in downtown Baltimore looks exciting.

Kiehl, S., "New Ballgame: The BDC Entertains Ideas for a Sports and Concert Facility to Replace 1st Mariner Arena", *Sun Paper*, November 14, 2007.

Kiehl, S., "Group Wants Arena Site Near M&T," *Sun Paper*, November 18, 2007.

The development of proposed solutions by interested contractors or by the customer's internal project team in response to a customer's request for proposal is the second phase of the project life cycle. This chapter covers this phase, which starts when the RFP becomes available at the conclusion of the needs identification phase and ends when an agreement is reached with the person, organization, or contractor selected to implement the proposed solution (see Figure 3.1). You will become familiar with

- building relationships with customers and partners
- proposal marketing strategies and the bid/no-bid decision
- the development of winning proposals
- the proposal preparation process and the elements that may be included in a proposal
- pricing considerations
- the evaluation of proposals
- types of contracts between the customer and the contractor
- measuring success of proposal efforts

FIGURE 3.1 ***Project Life Cycle***

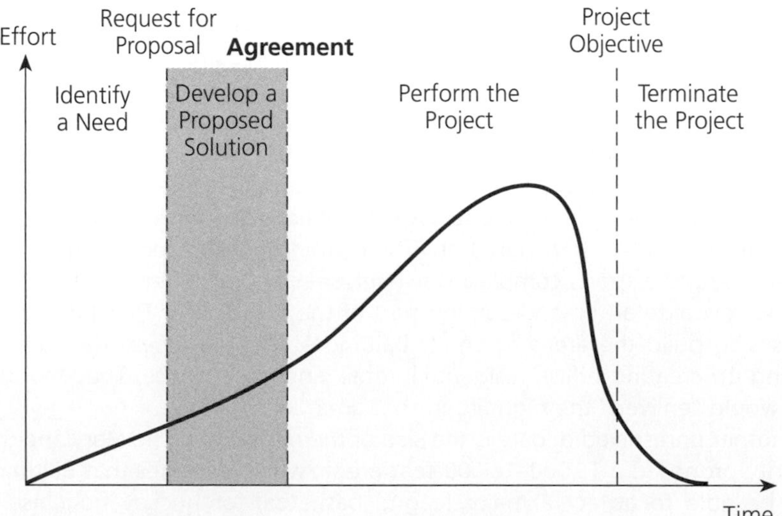

In many situations a request for proposal does not involve soliciting competitive proposals from external contractors. For example, suppose company management sees a need to develop new marketing materials (brochures, DVDs, sample CDs of software) or to reconfigure the office layout. Management may ask an individual or team to prepare a proposal that defines what should be done, what company resources would be needed, how much it would cost, and how long it would take. Once the individual or team has prepared the proposal, management can decide whether to go forward with the project, maybe modifying it in the process. Once a decision is made to go forward, the project proceeds directly to the third phase of the project life cycle: creating a detailed plan for the project and then implementing that plan to accomplish the project objective.

The second phase of the project life cycle may be completely bypassed for certain endeavors. Examples would include a project that one or two individuals do by themselves, such as remodeling their basement into a family room, or a project carried out by a volunteer group, such as organizing a fund-raising charity event, or a series of complex reconstructive surgeries performed by a medical team. In such situations, there is neither a request for proposal nor an actual proposal; rather, after the need is identified, the project moves right into the planning and implementation phase of the project life cycle.

BUILDING RELATIONSHIPS WITH CUSTOMERS AND PARTNERS

Customers (clients) and partner organizations prefer to work with people they know and can trust.

Relationships establish the foundation for successful funding and contract opportunities. Relationship building requires being proactive and engaged. Relationship building, in many ways, is a contact sport. It requires getting out of the office and having face-to-face contacts. It cannot be done as effectively through e-mail or phone conversations. For example, if you were soliciting proposals from several contractors for a house you want them to build, would you make a final decision of which contractor to select based solely on e-mail exchanges and phone conversations? Probably not. You would want to meet the contractors face-to-face.

Contractors should get to know people in potential customer organizations on a personal basis. Relationship building necessitates being a good listener and a good learner. When you are with clients, ask questions and listen. Make the discussion about them, not about you. You learn more from listening than from telling. Try to learn some personal information about them—where they are from, their career and prior work assignments, where they may have gone to college, their hobbies or interests, their family, etc.—without seeming intrusive. Look for things that you may have in common: do you know people from the same city, do you have common interests (sports, gardening, children on sports teams, etc.), or did you attend the same university as they did? You can store this information for later recall in future encounters with them. Start every dialogue by showing a personal interest and make a personal inquiry such as, "How is your daughter's soccer team doing?" or "How is your mother recovering from her hip surgery?" Show a genuine interest; they will be impressed or flattered that you remembered. Make the client feel good. Empathize with their issues whether they are business or personal. Look for opportunities to congratulate or console them. If they just got married, had a baby, or had a death in their family, send them a card with a handwritten note. If

Reinforce Your Learning

1. ____________ establish the foundation for successful funding and contract ____________.

Reinforce Your Learning

2. Relationship building requires being ____________ and ____________.

you know that a client has a particular personal or business interest, such as mountain climbing, collecting antiques, the American civil war, or a technology such as digital media or biofuels, send her any articles you may come across, along with a handwritten note stating, "I thought this might be of interest to you." The personal touch is special and endearing. In addition, sending an e-mail with a link to an article on a website could also be a nice gesture.

Contacts with potential clients should be frequent and not just when there is a current opportunity for funding or just before they will be issuing a Request for Proposal (RFP).Whenever you are in the city where the client is located, plan ahead to schedule a lunch with the client, or perhaps just stop by their office to say "Hello." If you stop by for an impromptu visit and the client isn't available, make sure you leave your business card and a note to let them know that you stopped by to see him or her. During these lunches or brief encounters don't just talk all business. You can discuss personal interests that you have in common, such as specific sports, recent vacations, current news events, etc. However, you may want to avoid some topics such as politics that could lead to strong disagreements, unless you get to know the client's views better.

During contacts, don't focus on discussing potential contract opportunities. If you talk too much business or ask too many questions about upcoming RFPs or funding opportunities, the client will know you are just trying to pry information from them. When business is discussed, try to listen and understand the client's needs and determine if you or your organization can help the client achieve their goals and be successful. After meeting with a client, always express your appreciation and thank them for making the time to meet with you. You may want to follow up with a brief e-mail thanking them. Offer to provide any help or information they may need, or extend an invitation to them to visit you and your organization's office. Leave the door open for continuing the dialogue and developing a stronger relationship with them.

Establishing and building trust is key to developing effective and successful relationships with clients and partners. One way to foster this is to always keep your word; be reliable and responsive. If you tell a client that you will send them particular information by the end of the week, make sure you do it.

Reinforce Your Learning

3. Establishing and building ________________ is key to developing ________________ and successful ________________.

Ethical behavior in dealing with clients and partners is also imperative for building trust. Nothing can sour a business relationship faster than doing or saying something that the client may perceive as unethical. In encounters with clients and partners, don't do anything that would give the impression that you are trying to get away with something or acting shady or underhanded. Don't exaggerate or stretch the truth. Be fair and always do the right thing. Don't be nosey or try to pry insider or confidential information from them. For example, don't ask a client about the detailed budget for a recent contract that the client awarded to one of your competitors. Similarly, if the client asks you for information that is confidential, you should tell her that you can't divulge it; they will respect you for being honest and truthful, and it will build their trust in you. Don't pass along gossip, rumors, or hearsay and then tell the client that they should keep it confidential or that they shouldn't tell anyone else. You are asking them to do something that you yourself could not do—keep a secret—and they will lose trust in you. Also do not make negative comments about other people or organizations, even if the client does; don't join the feeding frenzy.

The first impression you make on a client is pivotal to developing a continuing and fruitful relationship. It is important to control your emotions and be tactful and not confrontational in discussions with clients. Don't make quick knee-jerk responses that you may regret later. It is better to sleep on a contradictory issue and provide a more thoughtful response the next day. Learn to guide the conversations with the client by knowing when to keep quiet, when not to respond, when to give your opinion or not to give it prematurely, and when to change the topic of discussion. If you prematurely respond to a client's comment before she is finished with it, your response can be totally off-base from where she was going with her comments. Also be careful and sensitive to making, or responding to, comments or jokes that may be inappropriate. For example, telling a joke about a person of a certain religious faith or about a person with a certain disability, or an off-color remark about the opposite gender may strike a discord with the client and could end the relationship and close your firm out of future business opportunities with that client.

Maintain a positive and can-do attitude in your dealings with clients and partners. Don't be negative and dwell on why things won't work or can't be done. Rather, try to suggest creative approaches of how things can be done. Clients want to work with people who can solve problems, not with those who merely identify them.

Build credibility based on performance. Don't just say you can deliver; prove it. Go the extra mile, make the extra effort, and exceed expectations.

Always put the client first. Clients want to be confident that any projects they do with the contractor will be successful, will involve a good working relationship with the contractor, and will help the client achieve their business goals.

It is advisable not to rely on a good relationship with just one individual in a client or partner organization, but rather to build relationships with several key people in a client or partner organization since key individuals may leave and others become more influential.

Building effective and successful relationships takes time and work; it doesn't happen overnight.

Reinforce Your Learning

4. Building effective and successful relationships takes

____

and

______________________.

PRE-RFP/PROPOSAL MARKETING

Contractors whose livelihood depends on creating winning proposals in response to business or government RFPs should not wait until formal RFP solicitations are announced by customers before starting to develop proposals. Rather, such contractors need to develop relationships with potential customers long before the customers prepare requests for proposal.

Contractors should maintain frequent contacts with past and current customers and initiate contacts with potential customers. During these contacts, contractors should help customers identify areas in which they might benefit from the implementation of projects that address needs, problems, or opportunities. Working closely with a potential customer puts a contractor in a better position to be selected eventually as the winning contractor when the customer does issue an RFP. A contractor who is familiar with a customer's needs, requirements, and expectations can prepare a more clearly focused proposal in response to the customer's RFP. These pre-RFP or pre-proposal efforts by a contractor are considered marketing or business development and are performed at no cost to the customer. The payoff to the contractor for these efforts is expected to come later—when the contractor is selected as the winning contractor in response to the customer's RFP.

Reinforce Your Learning

5. Contractors need to

____

____

with potential customers

____

customers prepare an RFP.

During this pre-RFP/proposal activity, the contractor should learn as much as possible about the customer's needs, problems, and decision making process. The contractor should ask the customer for information, data, and documentation about the identified need or problem. The contractor may then develop some pre-proposal concepts or approaches and present them to or review them with the customer. By getting the customer's reactions to such concepts, the contractor can begin to understand and clarify what the customer expects, as well as develop a responsive and favorable image in the eyes of the customer. The contractor may invite the customer to visit another of the contractor's customers who had a similar need or problem for which the contractor proposed and implemented a successful solution. Such a visit can enhance the contractor's reputation with the customer.

In some cases, the contractor may prepare an *unsolicited proposal* and present it to the customer. If the customer is confident that the proposal will solve the problem at a reasonable cost, the customer may simply negotiate a contract with the contractor to implement the proposal, thus eliminating the preparation of an RFP and the subsequent competitive proposal process. By doing a good job in pre-RFP/proposal marketing, the contractor may obtain a contract from a customer without having to compete with other contractors.

Whether the goal is winning a competitive RFP or obtaining a noncompetitive contract from a customer, *a contractor's pre-RFP/proposal efforts are crucial to establishing the foundation for eventually winning a contract from the customer to perform the project.*

Reinforce Your Learning

6. What is the outcome of a successful pre-RFP/proposal marketing effort?

BID/NO-BID DECISION

Because the development and preparation of a proposal takes time and can be costly, contractors interested in submitting a proposal in response to an RFP must be realistic about the probability of being selected as the winning contractor. Evaluating whether to go forward with the preparation of a proposal is sometimes referred to as the bid/no-bid decision. Some factors that a contractor might consider in making a **bid/no-bid decision** are the following:

1. *Competition.* Which other contractors might also submit a proposal in response to the RFP? Do any of these contractors have a competitive advantage, because of either pre-RFP marketing efforts or their previous work for or reputation with the customer?
2. *Risk.* Is there a risk that the project will be unsuccessful—technically or financially? For example, are there too many uncertainties regarding the technological feasibility of developing an integrated electronic circuit that will meet the customer's requirements? Or, does the customer want contractors to submit a proposal based on a fixed-price contract for a project that involves a research and development effort with only a 50 percent chance of technical success?
3. *Mission.* Is the proposed project consistent with the contractor's business mission? For example, if a contractor's business is to develop and implement automated systems for business-oriented applications, such as accounting, order tracking, or financial reporting, developing an automated system for monitoring, testing, and controlling a chemical process for a pharmaceutical company would not be within this contractor's business mission.
4. *Extension of capabilities.* Would the proposed project provide the contractor with an opportunity to extend and enhance its capabilities? For example, if a contractor has been providing automated inventory control systems to individual food markets, an RFP to provide an integrated inventory control system for a supermarket chain of 10 stores might provide the

contractor with an opportunity to extend its capabilities and expand its business to a larger customer base.

5. *Reputation.* Has the contractor successfully completed projects for the same customer in the past, or were there problems that left the customer dissatisfied? Has the contractor unsuccessfully bid on RFPs from the customer in the past?
6. *Customer funds.* Does the customer really have funds available to go forward with the project? Or is the customer on a "fishing expedition"—issuing an RFP although unsure whether the project will ever be funded? A customer may issue an RFP with the best of intentions but do so prematurely, anticipating that the board of directors will approve funding. However, if the company is having financial difficulties, the board may decide to postpone the project indefinitely, even after proposals have been received from interested contractors. Good pre-RFP marketing by the contractor will help to determine the viability of a project. Contractors should not spend time responding to RFPs by developing proposals for projects that probably will not be funded.
7. *Proposal resources.* Are appropriate resources available to prepare a quality proposal? It is not enough for a contractor to just prepare a proposal. It is imperative that the proposal be of sufficient quality to have a good chance of winning. To prepare a quality proposal, a contractor must have the appropriate people—that is, resources—to work on it. If the contractor's organization does not have the right resources available to prepare a quality proposal, the contractor should make arrangements to secure other resources to ensure the best possible proposal. A contractor should not use inappropriate resources to prepare a proposal just for the sake of submitting a proposal. Submitting a poor quality proposal can leave the customer with a negative impression, which can hurt the contractor's chances of winning future contracts from that customer.
8. *Project resources.* Are appropriate resources available to perform the project if the contractor is selected as the winner? Contractors need to be sure that the appropriate individuals within their organization will be available to work on the project. If, after being awarded the contract, the contractor discovers that the team must be made up of individuals other than those originally planned for the project, the chances of successfully completing the project may diminish. The result could be a dissatisfied customer who will not ask the contractor to respond to future RFPs. If a contractor is not sure that it has the resources to perform the project, it must have a plan for securing the resources needed to perform the project successfully (such as hiring new people, or outsourcing some work elements to subcontractors, or partnering with other contractors).

Reinforce Your Learning

7. What are some factors that a contractor should consider when deciding whether to respond to an RFP?

Contractors need to be realistic about their ability to prepare proposals and about the probability of winning the contract. The proposal selection process is competitive—the customer will select one winner from among competing proposals. For a contractor, success is winning the contract, not merely submitting a proposal. Submitting a lot of nonwinning proposals in response to RFPs can hurt a contractor's reputation. So, although it is often the right thing to do, sometimes the hardest thing for a contractor to do is to decide to *no-bid* an RFP.

Reinforce Your Learning

8. Contractors need to be ______________ about their ability to prepare proposals and about the ______________ of winning the contract.

Figure 3.2 is an example of a bid/no-bid checklist that a contractor might use in deciding whether to submit a proposal in response to a request for proposal. Such a checklist might be used by the decision makers in the contractor's

FIGURE 3.2 *Bid/No-Bid Checklist*

Bid/No-Bid Checklist

Project Title: Supervisory Training Program

Customer: ACE Manufacturing, Inc. Due Date: 5/31

Score each factor as High, Medium, or Low

Factor	Score	Comments
1. Competition	H	Local university has been providing most of the training to ACE in the past
2. Risk	L	Requirements in RFP are well defined
3. Consistent with our mission	H	Training is our business
4. Opportunity to extend our capabilities	H	Some tasks require videoconferencing, which we haven't done before
5. Reputation with customer	L	Have not done any training for ACE before
6. Availability of funds	H	ACE has funds budgeted to implement the training
7. Resources available to prepare quality proposal	M	Lynn will have to reschedule her vacation. Will probably need to work over Memorial Day weekend to finish proposal
8. Resources available to perform project	M	Will have to hire subcontractors for several specific training topics

Our advantages, strengths, or distinct capabilities:

- Good track record in supervisory training—we have many repeat customers
- More flexible than local university in meeting ACE's need for on-site training during 2nd and 3rd shift operations

Our weaknesses:

- Most of our customers have been in the service sector, such as hospitals. ACE is a manufacturer
- President of ACE is a graduate of local university and a large contributor to it

organization to reach a consensus. The checklist in Figure 3.2 illustrates the consensus of key individuals from a training consulting firm. It summarizes their deliberations over whether to bid on an RFP from Ace Manufacturing, Inc., to conduct a substantial supervisory training program for employees at seven plant locations nationwide. Do you think they should submit a proposal to Ace?

DEVELOPING A WINNING PROPOSAL

It is important to remember that *the proposal process is competitive.* A customer uses a request for proposal to solicit competing proposals from contractors. Each contractor, therefore, must keep in mind that its proposal will be competing with other contractors' proposals to be selected by the customer as the winner. Submitting a proposal that meets the customer's statement of work and requirements in the RFP is not sufficient to guarantee selection as the winning contractor. Many or all of the proposals will likely meet the requirements. The customer will select the one that it expects will provide the best value.

A proposal is a selling document; it is not a technical report. In the proposal the contractor must convince the customer that the contractor

- understands what the customer is looking for
- can carry out the proposed project
- will provide the greatest value to the customer
- is the best contractor to solve the problem
- will capitalize on its successful experience with previous related projects
- will do the work professionally
- will achieve the intended results
- will complete the project within budget and on schedule
- will satisfy the customer

Reinforce Your Learning

9. The proposal process is a ______________ process. A proposal is a ______________ document.

In the proposal the contractor must highlight the unique factors that differentiate it from competing contractors. The contractor proposal must emphasize the benefits to the customer if the customer selects the contractor to perform the project.

Key partners and subcontractors can complement a contractor's expertise. Identifying and including appropriate partners or subcontractors to perform specific key tasks on a proposed project can provide a significant competitive advantage, especially if those organizations have specific technical expertise that is crucial to the project, or have an excellent reputation, or perhaps already have good credibilty with the customer.

Reinforce Your Learning

10. In a proposal, the contractor must highlight the ______________ factors that ______________ it from ______________ proposals.

Proposals should be written in a simple, concise manner; they should not be wordy or redundant. They should use terminology with which the customer is familiar and avoid abbreviations, acronyms, jargon, and other words that the customer may not know or understand. Simple illustrations and graphics should be used when possible. Overly complex illustrations should be avoided; several simple graphics will likely be easier for the customer to understand than one complicated graphic. When a point is made or an approach or concept proposed, it should be supported with logic, rationale, or data. Proposals must specifically address the customer's requirements as laid out in the RFP. Proposals written in generalities will cause the customer to question whether the contractor really understands what needs to be done and how to do it. For example, suppose one of the requirements in a customer's RFP is that a specialized piece of machinery be designed to produce 20 parts per minute. A contractor proposal stating that "the machine to be designed will in fact produce 20 parts per minute" is more convincing than one stating that "the machinery will be designed to produce the maximum number of parts per minute." The customer will be doubtful about the latter statement, because maximum could be something less than 20 parts per minute.

Finally, proposals must be realistic, in terms of the proposed scope, cost, and schedule, in the eyes of the customer. Proposals that promise too much or are overly optimistic may seem unbelievable and again raise doubt about whether the contractor understands what needs to be done and how to do it.

PROPOSAL PREPARATION

The preparation of a proposal can be a straightforward task performed by one person, or it can be a resource-intensive effort requiring a team of organizations and individuals with various expertise and skills. In the simple case of designing and printing an annual report, an experienced commercial printer (the contractor), after meeting with the customer regarding the requirements, may be able to prepare a proposal within a short period of time without involving other individuals. However, in the case where a government agency has issued an RFP for a multimillion-dollar project to design and construct a new regional rapid transit system, each interested contractor may have to assemble a team of many individuals, subcontractors, or partners to help develop the proposal. In such situations the contractor may designate a *proposal manager* who coordinates the efforts of the proposal team to ensure that a consistent, comprehensive proposal is prepared by the due date stated in the RFP.

Developing a comprehensive proposal for a large project should be treated as a project in itself; thus, the proposal manager needs to meet with the proposal team to develop a schedule for completing the proposal by the customer's due date. The schedule should include the dates by which various individuals will have drafts of their assigned portions of the proposal, dates for conducting reviews with appropriate people on the proposal team, and the date on which the proposal will be finalized. The proposal schedule must allow time for review and approval by management within the contractor's organization. Time must also be provided for preparing any graphic illustrations, typing, copying, and delivery of the proposal to the customer, who may be hundreds of miles away from the contractor.

Proposals in response to RFPs for very large technical projects can be multivolume documents that include engineering drawings and hundreds of pages of text. And, yes, such proposals are often due within 30 calendar days of the RFP's issuance! Contractors who bid on such large projects usually do pre-RFP marketing, and so they may have a draft proposal prepared before the customer even issues a formal RFP. In such cases, during the 30-day response period, the contractor can first revise the draft proposal to incorporate any unanticipated requirements and then use any remaining time to "package" a first-class professional proposal.

Customers do not pay contractors to prepare proposals. Contractors absorb such costs as normal marketing costs of doing business, in anticipation of winning contracts and making profits on them.

As stated previously, a proposal is a selling document, not a technical report. It may consist of several pages or several volumes, containing hundreds of pages, illustrations, and tabulations. A proposal should contain sufficient detail to convince the customer that the contractor will provide the best value to the customer. Too much detail in a proposal, however, may overwhelm the customer and needlessly increase the proposal preparation costs for the contractor.

PROPOSAL CONTENTS

Proposals are often organized into three sections: technical, management, and cost. For large proposals, these could comprise three separate volumes. The amount of detail the contractor includes will depend on the complexity of the project and the contents of the RFP. Some RFPs state that contractor proposals that exceed a certain number of pages won't be accepted by the customer. After all, customers are anxious to do an expeditious evaluation of all proposals submitted, and they may not have the time to review a large number of voluminous proposals.

Reinforce Your Learning

11. A proposal should address three topics or contain three sections. What are they?

Technical Section

The objective of the technical section of the contractor proposal is to *convince the customer that the contractor understands the need or problem and can provide the least risky and most beneficial solution.* The technical section should contain the following elements:

1. *Understanding of the problem.* The contractor should state its understanding of the customer's problem or need in its own words. The contractor should not merely restate the problem statement that appears in the customer's RFP. This first part of the technical section must show the customer that the contractor thoroughly understands the problem to be solved or the need to be addressed and establish the basis for the solution proposed later in the technical section. The contractor may want to describe, in narrative or graphic form, the customer's current condition. For example, if the problem is a high reject rate from a manufacturing process, the contractor may want to incorporate a flowchart of the customer's current manufacturing process that indicates where the rejects are occurring and what other problems they may be causing, such as production bottlenecks. Customers will feel more confident working with a contractor who they believe really understands their problem.
2. *Proposed approach or solution.* Some problems lend themselves to a specific proposed solution—for example, an RFP to reconfigure a large office to accommodate 10 percent more people. Other problems, however, do not. A problem may require that an analysis and development task be conducted as part of the proposed project before a specific solution can be described in detail. In such cases, the contractor proposal must describe the approach or methodology that would be used in developing the solution. For example, if an RFP is for a specialized noncontact inspection system to measure certain characteristics of a complexly shaped product made of an advanced material, it would be unrealistic for the customer to expect the

contractors to design such a system as part of the proposal itself; rather, such engineering design and development would be done as part of the proposed project. However, in the proposal, the contractor must convince the customer that the approach proposed for designing, developing, and building such a system is logical and realistic and would lead to the contractor's supplying a system that would successfully meet the customer's requirements.

This part of the technical section might contain the following:

a. A description of how the contractor would collect, analyze, and evaluate data and information about the problem.
b. Methods that would be used by the contractor to evaluate alternative solutions or further develop the proposed solution to the problem. This portion could include a discussion of various experiments, tests, or physical or computer models the contractor would use or has used on similar projects.
c. The rationale for the proposed approach or solution. This rationale could be based on experiments previously conducted by the contractor, the contractor's experience in solving similar problems, or a unique patented technology the contractor would use to solve the problem.
d. Confirmation that the proposed solution or approach would meet each of the physical, operational, and performance requirements stated in the customer's RFP. For example, if the RFP for the design and construction of a day care center states that certain furnishings must be at a specific height to accommodate children under 48 inches tall, the proposal must state that the contractor will meet that requirement. Not addressing each of the customer's requirements will raise doubt in the customer's mind about the proposed solution and could hurt a contractor's chances of winning the contract, especially if competing contractors' proposals state that they will meet the requirements.

Reinforce Your Learning

12. What is the objective of the technical section of a proposal?

If the contractor cannot meet a specific customer requirement, that fact should be stated in the contractor proposal. A variation from specified requirements is known as an **exception**. For each exception taken to a customer requirement, the contractor should explain why the requirement will not or cannot be met and propose an alternative. Although contractors should avoid taking exceptions to customer requirements, there may be circumstances where an exception is appropriate. For example, if the customer requires an electric heating system for an office building, the contractor may take exception and show in the proposal that the initial and operating costs for a natural gas heating system would be less expensive for the customer. However, the customer may have very good reasons beyond cost for requiring an electric heating system and may reject proposals that take exception to that requirement.

3. *Benefits to the customer.* The contractor should state how the proposed solution or approach would benefit the customer. Benefits could be quantitative or qualitative and could include cost savings; reduced processing time; reduced inventory; better customer service; less scrap,

rejects, or errors; improved safety conditions; more timely information; and reduced maintenance. This portion of the proposal should help convince the customer of the value of the proposed approach compared with proposals the customer may receive from other competing contractors.

Management Section

The objective of the management section of the contractor proposal is to *convince the customer that the contractor can do the proposed work (the project) and achieve the intended results.* The management section should contain the following elements:

1. *Description of work tasks.* The contractor should define the major tasks that will be performed in carrying out the project and provide a brief description of what each major task includes. The contractor should not merely restate the statement of work that may be included in the customer's RFP. The proposal need not include a lengthy list of detailed activities; such an activity list would be developed during the initial planning effort of the project phase, after the contract has been awarded.
2. *Deliverables.* The contractor should include a list of all deliverables (tangible products or items) that will be provided during the project, such as reports, drawings, manuals, and equipment.
3. *Project schedule.* The contractor should provide a schedule for performing the major tasks required to complete the project. The schedule must show that the contractor can complete the project within the time frame stated in the RFP. The task schedule can be given in any one of several formats: a list of tasks with their estimated start and completion dates; a bar chart, often called a *Gantt chart* (covered in Chapter 5), with the estimated duration of each task represented by a bar along a horizontal timeline; or a network diagram in which the tasks are portrayed graphically, showing the sequence of and interdependencies among the tasks.

   In addition to the major tasks, the schedule might include dates for other key events such as important review meetings, customer approval activities, and completion of deliverable items such as progress reports, drawings, manuals, or equipment.
4. *Project organization.* The contractor should describe how the work and resources will be organized to perform the project. For large projects involving many people and subcontractors or partners, it may be appropriate to include an organization chart (covered in Chapter 13), which gives the major project functions along with the name of the specific individual who will be assigned responsibility for each function. Resumes of the key people who will be assigned to the project should be included to convince the customer that their significant related experience will be brought to bear to ensure the project's success. In addition to or in place of an organization chart, the contractor may include a responsibility matrix (covered in Chapter 5) that lists the major project tasks and the name of the person, organization, or subcontractor responsible for the achievement of each task.

5. *Related experience.* To help convince the customer that the contractor can do the project, the contractor should provide a list of similar projects it has completed. The contractor should briefly describe each past project and explain how the experience from that project will be helpful in successfully performing the proposed project. The contract dollar value of each project should also be provided to give the customer a sense of the contractor's ability to manage projects the size of the proposed one. The probability of a contractor's winning a contract for a six-figure project is not very high if all its previous related experience is on $20,000 projects. For each previous similar project, the contractor might want to include the name, title, and phone number of an individual the current customer could contact to check on the contractor's performance. Reference letters from satisfied customers might also be included. This type of information will be particularly helpful if the contractor has a strong performance record.

   Additionally, if key tasks are proposed to be outsourced to subcontractors or partners, the relevant experience of those organizations should also be stated, including why they were selected to be part of the proposed project team. Resumes of their key people might also be included.

Reinforce Your Learning

13. What is the objective of the management section of a proposal?

6. *Equipment and facilities.* Some projects require the contractor to use or have access to unique equipment such as computers, software, manufacturing equipment, or testing facilities. In these cases, the contractor may want to provide a list of the equipment and special facilities it has, in order to convince the customer that it has the necessary resources.

Cost Section

Reinforce Your Learning

14. What is the objective of the cost section of a proposal?

The objective of the cost section of the contractor proposal is to *convince the customer that the contractor's price for the proposed project is realistic and reasonable.* In some cases, the customer may want only the bottom line total cost of the project. Some customers also want to see the costs of optional items. For example, a couple who is asking several contractors for proposals for building a house may be looking for the total cost plus costs of options such as landscaping, a deck, a finished basement, a built-in swimming pool, and a fence around the backyard. Government agency RFPs usually require contractors to provide a detailed breakdown of the various costs.

The cost section usually consists of tabulations of the contractor's estimated costs of elements such as the following:

1. *Labor.* This portion gives the estimated costs of the various classifications of people who are expected to work on the project. It might include the estimated hours and hourly rate for each person or classification, such as senior engineer, designer, machinist, or programmer. The estimated hours must be realistic. If they are too high and have too much "fat" in them, the total estimated costs may be higher than what the customer is willing to pay. On the other hand, if the estimated hours are too low, the contractor may lose money on the project. The hourly rate is usually

based on the annual salary for each person or the average annual salary for each classification plus an additional percentage to cover employee fringe benefits (health insurance, retirement, and so forth). These salaries are then divided by the number of normal work hours in a year (for example, 40 hours a week times 52 weeks equals 2,080 hours) to determine the hourly labor rate for each person or classification.

2. *Materials.* This portion gives the cost of materials the contractor needs to purchase for the project. For example, the cost of materials for a remodeling project might include lumber, new windows, electrical and plumbing supplies, and carpeting.
3. *Subcontractors and consultants.* When contractors do not have the expertise or resources to do certain project tasks, they may outsource some of the work to subcontractors or consultants to perform those tasks. For example, a project to make over a church basement into a day care center might require that the contractor hire a subcontractor to remove any asbestos and a consultant to provide advice on state regulations and codes for day care facilities. The contractor usually asks the subcontractors and consultants to submit a proposal of work scope and cost for their tasks. The contractor then includes these costs in the overall cost of the project.
4. *Equipment and facilities rental.* Sometimes the contractor will have to rent special equipment, tools, or facilities solely for the project.
5. *Travel.* If travel (other than local travel) is required during the project, the costs of travel (such as air fare), lodging (hotel rooms), and meals need to be included. The contractor must first estimate the number and duration of trips. For example, if the customer is a government agency in Washington, DC, and the contractor is in California, the costs associated with travel to Washington for review meetings with the customer need to be included.
6. *Documentation.* Some customers want the contractor to show separately the costs associated with the project documentation deliverables. This would be the cost of printing manuals, drawings, or reports or the cost of producing DVDs.
7. *Overhead.* Contractors will add a percentage to costs in items 1 through 6 to cover their normal **overhead**—the **indirect costs** of doing business, such as insurance, depreciation, accounting, general management, marketing, and human resources. Of course, in informal projects, such as organization of a town celebration by volunteers, such overhead costs are not applicable.
8. *Escalation.* For large projects that are expected to take several years to complete, the contractor needs to include the costs of escalation in wage rates and materials costs over the length of the project. For example, for a three-year project, the contractor may want to anticipate a 4 percent wage increase in each of the final two years of the project. If the same project requires that the contractor purchase most of the materials during the third year, the current materials cost estimates may need to be increased by a certain percentage to cover the expected cost of the materials at the time they will be purchased.

Reinforce Your Learning

15. What elements might each of the three sections of a proposal contain?

9. *Contingency.* **Contingency**, or **management reserve**, is an amount the contractor may want to include to cover the unexpected—items that have been overlooked or tasks that may have to be redone because they might not work the first time.
10. *Fee or profit.* Items 1 through 9 are costs. The contractor must now add an amount for its fee or profit. The total cost plus the profit is the contractor's price for the proposed project.

It is good practice to have the person who will be responsible for the costs associated with the work make the cost estimates. This generates a commitment from the responsible person and prevents any bias that might result from having one person make all the cost estimates for the entire project. In large projects involving several hundred people, it is not practical to have every person provide cost estimates. In such cases, each organization or subcontractor involved may designate an experienced individual to make the cost estimates for which that organization or subcontractor will be responsible. If a contractor or organization has performed similar projects in the past and has kept records of the actual costs for various items, these historical data can be used as guides in estimating costs for the proposed project.

Cost estimates should be aggressive yet realistic. They should not be so heavily "padded" that they include contingency funds for every conceivable thing that might come up or go wrong. If cost estimates are overly conservative, the total estimated cost for the project is likely to be more than the customer is willing to pay—and higher than that of competing contractors. On the other hand, if cost estimates are overly optimistic and some unexpected expenditures arise, the contractor is likely to either lose money (on a fixed-price contract) or have to suffer the embarrassment of going back to the customer to request additional funds to cover cost overruns.

PRICING CONSIDERATIONS

When contractors prepare a proposal, they are generally competing with other contractors to win a contract. Therefore, they need to be careful not to overprice the proposed project, or the customer may select a lower-priced contractor. However, contractors must be equally careful not to underprice the proposed project; otherwise, they may lose money rather than making a profit or may have to request additional funds from the customer, which could be embarrassing and hurt the contractor's reputation.

The contractor must consider the following items when determining the price for the proposed project:

1. *Reliability of the cost estimates.* Does the contractor have confidence that the total cost of the proposed project is complete and accurate? The contractor should take the time to think through the project and estimate costs at a high level of detail, rather than making a ballpark estimate. Ideally the costs should be based on a recent similar project or, in the case of materials cost estimates, on current price lists, catalogues, or quotations. It may be advisable to ask experienced individuals or specialists to help estimate the labor effort. In general, the more detailed the cost estimates, the better.

2. *Risk.* If the proposed project involves an endeavor that has not been undertaken before, such as a research and development project to come up with a drug to control a disease, it may be necessary to include a large amount of contingency, or management reserve, funds.
3. *Value of the project to the contractor.* There may be situations in which the contractor is willing to live with a tight or low price. For example, if the contractor doesn't have many other projects, it may need to lay off workers unless new contracts are obtained. In such a case, the contractor may include only a very small fee to increase the chances of winning the contract and avoid having to lay off people. Another example of a project that may be particularly valuable to the contractor is a project that provides an opportunity to extend capabilities or expand into new types of projects. A building contractor who has been doing only remodeling projects may want to get into building complete homes and may be willing to make a low profit in order to gain entry into the market and establish a reputation.
4. *Customer's budget.* A contractor who knows how much money the customer has budgeted for a project should not submit a price that exceeds what the customer has available. This is where good pre-RFP marketing is important. By helping a potential customer identify a need or submitting unsolicited proposals with cost estimates, a contractor can help the customer determine a budget for the project. Then, if the customer issues a competitive RFP (and doesn't disclose the amount budgeted for the project), the contractor with the customer budget "intelligence" information may be in a better position to submit a proposal with an acceptable price than are contractors who have not done similar homework.
5. *Competition.* If many contractors are expected to submit proposals in response to a customer RFP or if some competing contractors are hungry for work, it may be necessary to submit a price that includes only a small profit to increase the chances of winning the contract.

Reinforce Your Learning

16. What are some items a contractor needs to consider when determining a price for a proposed project?

PROPOSAL SUBMISSION AND FOLLOW-UP

The customer's RFP will usually provide instructions regarding the due date by which proposals must be submitted and the name and address of the person to whom the proposals should be submitted. Some customers want the contractor to provide an electronic copy and/or several hardcopies of the proposal because the proposal will be distributed to various individuals within the customer's organization for review and evaluation. From the customer's point of view, it is easier and less costly to have the contractor make the necessary copies. This is especially true for large projects, where proposals may be several hundred pages long and may include large drawings or color graphics. Government agencies are very strict about having proposals submitted on time; those submitted late will not be accepted—and the contractor's efforts will have been wasted. Rather than trust the mail, some contractors hand-deliver proposals to ensure that they arrive on time. Other contractors have been known to send two sets of proposals by different express mail services to ensure that at least one set arrives at its destination on time. Such precautions are usually taken for multimillion-dollar projects or when thousands of hours have been spent in pre-RFP marketing and proposal preparation. Customers may request that proposals be submitted only electronically. This approach can save both the customer and bidding contractors time and costs associated with printing, mailing, and distribution.

Contractors must continue to be proactive even after the proposal is submitted. The contractor should call the customer to confirm that the proposal was received. After several days, the contractor should contact the customer again and ask whether the customer has any questions or needs clarification of anything in the proposal. Such follow-up needs to be done in a professional manner in order to make a favorable impression on the customer. If the contractor appears aggressive rather than responsive, the customer may view the contractor as an intrusive element trying to influence the proposal evaluation process. A contractor must always consider whether and how aggressively other competing contractors are following up with the customer after proposals have been submitted.

Reinforce Your Learning

17. Contractors must continue to be

____

even after the proposal is submitted.

Industrial and, especially, government customers usually do not respond to attempted follow-up communications from contractors so that no contractor gains an unfair advantage in influencing the proposal evaluation process. Such customers will initiate any needed communications. The contact will generally be in the form of a written list of specific questions that need to be answered or points that need to be clarified about a particular contractor's proposal. A written response from the contractor is required by a certain date.

CUSTOMER EVALUATION OF PROPOSALS

Customers evaluate contractors' proposals in many different ways. Some customers first look at the prices of the various proposals and select, for example, only the three lowest-priced proposals for further evaluation. Other customers initially screen out those proposals with prices above their budget or those whose technical section doesn't meet all the requirements stated in the RFP. Other customers, especially on large projects, create a proposal review team that uses a scorecard to determine whether each proposal meets all requirements in the RFP and to rate the proposal against predefined evaluation criteria.

Figure 3.3 illustrates a proposal evaluation scorecard. This scorecard was used by AJACKS Information Services Company to review contractor proposals submitted in response to the request for proposal in Chapter 2 (Figure 2.2). It is an evaluation of a proposal from Galaxy Market Research, Inc., one of five contractors that submitted proposals to AJACKS. Each person on the customer's proposal evaluation team completes a scorecard for each of the contractor proposals. These scorecards are then used by the proposal evaluation team to reach a consensus on which contractor, if any, to select as the winner. The scorecards are not the sole mechanism for evaluating proposals and selecting the winner. They are usually used as input to the decision-making process.

Sometimes the technical and management proposals are evaluated first, without consideration of cost. Those proposals with the highest points on the technical/management review are then evaluated for their costs. The customer weighs the technical/management merit against the costs to determine which proposal offers the best value.

FIGURE 3.3 *Proposal Evaluation Scorecard*

AJACKS Information Services Company
Proposal Evaluation

Project Title: Technical Information Needs of Manufacturers

Contractor: Galaxy Market Research Inc.

Score all criteria on a scale from 1 (low) to 10 (high)

Evaluation Criteria	Weight A	Score B	Points AxB	Comments
1. Approach	30	4	120	Shallow description of methodology
2. Experience	30	3	90	Little experience with manufacturing firms
3. Price	30	9	270	Lowest price bid Supported by details
4. Schedule	10	5	50	Schedule is overly optimistic
Total	100		530	

Advantages of this proposal:

- This is the lowest price proposal received. It appears the salaries of Galaxy's staff are low compared to those of other proposers.

Concerns about this proposal:

- Galaxy may not fully comprehend the requirements.
- Low salaries in its budget may reflect low levels of experience of the staff Galaxy plans to use.
- Optimistic schedule (3 months) to complete project may indicate Galaxy doesn't fully comprehend the work scope.

Some of the criteria that might be used by customers in evaluating contractor proposals include the following:

- Compliance with the customer's statement of work and requirements in the request for proposal.
- Contractor's understanding of the customer's problem or need.
- Soundness and practicality of the contractor's proposed approach to solving the problem.
- Contractor's experience and success with similar projects.
- The experience of key individuals who will be assigned to work on the project.
- Management capability, including the contractor's ability to plan and control the project to ensure that the work scope is completed within budget and on schedule.
- Realism of the contractor's schedule. Is it realistic considering the resources the contractor plans to assign to the project? Does it meet the customer's schedule as stated in the RFP? How detailed is the schedule?
- Price. Customers may evaluate not only the contractor's total price for the project but also the detailed costs in the cost section of the proposal. Customers are concerned about the reasonableness, realism, and completeness of the contractor's costs. Did the contractor use sound cost-estimating methodology? Are the labor hours, classifications, and rates appropriate for the type of project? Were any items left out? The customer wants to be sure that a contractor isn't "lowballing" the price to win the contract, expecting to come back to the customer for additional funds if the project overruns its proposed cost. It is unethical and may be illegal for contractors to intentionally lowball their price.

In some instances, especially when a large number of proposals are received, the proposal evaluation process will produce a short list of proposals the customer considers to be acceptable and of good value. The customer may then ask each of these contractors to give an oral presentation of its proposal. This provides a final opportunity for each contractor to convince the customer that its proposal will provide the best value. The customer may also ask each of these contractors to submit a **best and final offer (BAFO)**. This gives the contractor one last chance to reduce its price and possibly win the contract. However, the customer usually requires the contractor to provide a written rationale for any cost reductions to make sure that they are reasonable. The contractor, for instance, might review the people to be assigned to the project and determine that for some tasks individuals with lower labor cost rates could be used, or the contractor might decide that some travel could be eliminated or trips combined to reduce costs.

Once the customer has selected the winning contractor, the contractor is informed that it is the winner, subject to successful negotiation of a contract.

TYPES OF CONTRACTS

Just because the contractor has been selected as the winner doesn't mean the contractor can start doing the work. Before the project can proceed, a contract must be signed between the customer and the contractor—the final step in this second phase of the life cycle.

***Real World* PROJECT MANAGEMENT**

Enterprise Application Suites Fading Out

FleetBoston is a $13.3 billion dollar company that provides financial services. In 2002, FleetBoston Financial decided it wanted to automate the process of identifying potential customers for new products, so they sent out an RFP. The company received two proposals for the project. CRM giant Siebel Systems presented one proposal. Siebel Systems had previously sold Fleet millions of dollars in software licenses in 2000. The other proposal came from MarketSoft, a smaller vendor, whose product focuses on the type of lead management that Fleet was seeking. Even though Fleet had numerous unused Siebel licenses, they decided to pursue MarketSoft's more targeted product, utilizing a best-of-breed management resolution.

Ann Christensen, the former executive vice president of customer and sales management in Fleet's consumer banking group, lead the team who made the decision. The evaluation was based upon functionality, cost, speed of implementation, and a few other factors. "We found that Siebel had, as you would expect, a broader set of functionality than we needed and didn't nearly go as deep as we needed," Christensen explained. In other words, in the eyes of the evaluation committee, the MarketSoft proposal offered more flexibility, deeper functionality, and a better price.

Through the proposal review, Christensen discovered that the bank would have to upgrade the entire organization to Siebel 7.0 in order to use the vendor's lead management tool. Since Fleet had customized an earlier release of the system, they realized that this proposal would make the upgrade a very time-consuming and very expensive proposition. The proposal from MarketSoft, on the other hand, required a much more direct approach, with minimal steps required to achieve the objective.

In addition, Christensen pointed out that she was searching for a solution that had fewer risks and a quicker return on investment. The proposal from MarketSoft that was chosen ended up costing Fleet just a little more than a million dollars, which was significantly lower than the estimate of the other proposal. Furthermore, the MarketSoft product required fewer changes to the current business process and had the potential to pay for itself within one year. This came at a time when Fleet was hurting financially as revenue was down 27 percent and profits were down 76 percent.

Just as MarketSoft discovered that a quality proposal with a strong technical section, management section, and a competitive cost section—as described in this chapter—can help an organization win substantial contracts, Fleet discovered that a thorough review of proposals can help save an organization significant amounts of money!

Overby, S., "Enterprise Application Suites Fading Out," *CIO Magazine*, February 15, 2003.

A contract is a vehicle for establishing good customer–contractor communications and arriving at a mutual understanding and clear expectations to ensure project success. It is an agreement between the contractor, who agrees to provide a product or service (deliverables), and the customer, who agrees to pay the contractor a certain amount in return. The contract must clearly spell out the deliverables the contractor is expected to provide. For example, a contract will state that the project result will meet certain specifications or that certain documentation will be provided. The contract must also state the terms by which the customer will make payments to the contractor. There are basically two types of contracts: fixed-price and cost-reimbursement.

Fixed-Price Contracts

In a **fixed-price contract**, the customer and the contractor agree on a price for the proposed work. The price remains fixed unless the customer and the contractor agree on changes. This type of contract provides low risk for the customer, because the customer will not pay more than the fixed price, regardless of how much the project actually costs the contractor. However, a fixed-price contract is high risk for the contractor, because if the cost of completing the project is more than originally planned, the contractor will make a lower profit than anticipated or may even lose money.

A contractor bidding on a fixed-price project must develop accurate and complete cost estimates and include sufficient contingency costs. However, the contractor needs to be careful not to overprice the proposed project, or a competing contractor with a lower price may be selected.

Fixed-price contracts are most appropriate for projects that are well defined and entail little risk. Examples include the construction of a standard model house or the design and production of a brochure for which the customer has provided detailed specifications regarding format, content, photos, color, number of pages, and number of copies.

Reinforce Your Learning

18. A contractor bidding on a fixed-price contract must develop ______________ and ______________ cost estimates and include sufficient ______________ costs.

Cost-Reimbursement Contracts

In a **cost-reimbursement contract**, the customer agrees to pay the contractor for all actual costs (labor, materials, and so forth), regardless of amount, plus some agreed-upon profit. This type of contract is high risk for the customer, because contractor costs can overrun the proposed price—as when a car repair service provides an estimate for repairing a transmission but presents a final bill that is higher than the original estimate. In cost-reimbursement contracts, the customer usually requires that, throughout the project, the contractor regularly compare actual expenditures with the proposed budget and reforecast cost at-completion, comparing it with the original proposed price. This allows the customer to take action if it looks as if the project will overrun the original proposed budget costs. This type of contract is low risk for the contractor, because all costs will be reimbursed by the customer. The contractor cannot lose money on this type of contract. However, if the contractor's costs do overrun the proposed budget, the contractor's reputation will be hurt, in turn reducing the contractor's chances of winning contracts in the future.

Cost-reimbursement contracts are most appropriate for projects that involve risk. Examples include the development of a new robotics device to assist during surgery or the environmental cleanup of a contaminated site.

Reinforce Your Learning

19. Write the word low or high in each box, depending on the degree of risk for the customer and contractor associated with each type of contract.

	Customer	Contractor
Fixed price		
Cost reimbursement		

CONTRACT PROVISIONS

The following are some miscellaneous provisions that may be included in project contracts:

1. *Misrepresentation of costs.* States that it is illegal for the contractor to overstate the hours or costs expended on the project.
2. *Notice of cost overruns or schedule delays.* Outlines the circumstances under which the contractor must notify the customer immediately of any actual or anticipated cost overruns or schedule delays, submitting in writing both the reason and a plan for corrective action to get the costs back within budget or the schedule back on track.
3. *Approval of subcontractor.* Indicates when the contractor needs to obtain advance approval from the customer before hiring a subcontractor to perform a project task.
4. *Customer-furnished equipment or information.* Lists the items (such as parts for conducting tests) that the customer will provide to the contractor throughout the project and the dates by which the customer will make these items available. This provision protects the contractor from incurring schedule slippage caused by delays in the customer's furnishing information, parts, or other items.
5. *Patents.* Covers ownership of patents that may result from conducting the project.
6. *Disclosure of proprietary information.* Prohibits one party from disclosing to anyone else or using for any purpose other than work on the project confidential information, technologies, or processes utilized by the other party during the project.
7. *International considerations.* Specifies accommodations that must be made for customers from other countries. Contracts for projects that are done for a foreign customer or are conducted in part in a foreign country may require the contractor to make certain accommodations, such as

   - observing certain holidays or work rules
   - spending a certain percentage of the contract costs for labor or materials within the customer's country
   - providing project documentation, such as manuals and reports, in the customer's language
8. *Termination.* States the conditions under which the customer can terminate the contract, such as nonperformance by the contractor.
9. *Terms of payment.* Addresses the basis on which the customer will make payments to the contractor. Some types of payments are
   - monthly payments, based on actual costs incurred by the contractor
   - equal monthly or quarterly payments, based on the expected overall duration of the project schedule
   - percentages of the total contract amount, paid when the contractor completes pre-defined milestones
   - single payment at completion of the project

Critical Success FACTORS

- Customers and partner organizations prefer to work with people they know and can trust. Relationships establish the foundation for successful funding and contract opportunities.
- Establishing and building trust is key to developing effective and successful relationships with clients and partners.
- The first impression one makes on a client is pivitol to developing a continuing and fruitful relationship.
- Pre-RFP/proposal efforts are crucial to establishing the foundation for eventually winning a contract from the customer.
- Do not wait until formal RFP solicitations are announced by customers before starting to develop proposals. Rather, develop relationships with potential customers long before they prepare their RFPs.
- Working closely with a potential customer puts a contractor in a better position to be selected as the winning contractor. Learn as much as possible about the customer's needs, problems, and decision-making process during the pre-RFP/proposal marketing.
- Becoming familiar with the customer's needs, requirements, and expectations will help in preparing a more clearly focused proposal.
- Be realistic about the ability to prepare a quality proposal and about the probability of winning the contract. It is not enough to just prepare a proposal; rather, the proposal must be of sufficient quality to have a chance of winning.
- A proposal is a selling document, not a technical report. It should be written in a simple, concise manner and should use terminology with which the customer is familiar.
- In a proposal, it is important to highlight the unique factors that differentiate it from competitors' proposals.
- Proposals must be realistic. Proposals that promise too much or are overly optimistic may be unbelievable to customers, and raise doubt about whether the contractor understands what needs to be done or how to do it.
- When bidding on a fixed-price project, the contractor must develop accurate and complete cost estimates, and include sufficient contingency costs.

In some cases, such as when the contractor needs to purchase a significant amount of materials and supplies during the early stages of the project, the customer provides an initial down payment at the start of the contract.

10. *Bonus/penalty payments*. Some contracts have a bonus provision, whereby the customer will pay the contractor a bonus if the project is completed ahead of schedule or exceeds other customer performance requirements. On the other hand, some contracts include a penalty provision, whereby the customer can reduce the final payment to the contractor if the project is not completed on schedule or if performance requirements

are not met. Some of these penalties can be substantial, such as 1 percent of the total contract price for each week the project extends beyond the required project completion date, up to a maximum of 10 percent. A 10-week schedule overrun could wipe out the contractor's profit and cause a loss.

11. *Changes.* Covers the procedure for proposing, approving, and implementing changes to the project scope or schedule. Changes can be initiated by the customer or be proposed by the contractor. Some changes may necessitate a change in price (increase or decrease); others may not. All changes must be documented and approved by the customer before they are incorporated into the project. Customers usually want the contractor to provide a price estimate, along with an indication of the schedule impact, for a proposed change before they will allow the contractor to implement the change. If a contractor makes changes without the customer's approval or with only oral approval from someone in the customer's organization who may not be authorized to give it, the contractor runs the risk of being unable to collect payment for the work associated with the changes made.

MEASURING SUCCESS

Contractors measure the success of their proposal efforts by the number of times their proposals are selected by customers and/or by the total dollar value of their proposals that are selected. A measure that is often used is known as the **win ratio**. This measurement is the percentage of the number of proposals a contractor won out of the total number of proposals the contractor submitted to various customers over a particular time period. An alternative method of determining the win ratio is to base it on the total dollar value of proposals that the contractor won as a percentage of the total dollar value of all the proposals the contractor submitted to various customers during a specific time period. The former approach gives equal weight to all proposals, whereas the later approach gives more weight to proposals with larger dollar amounts. For example, assume a contractor submits four different proposals to four different customers in a particular month; for amounts of $120,000, $50,000, $250,000, and $80,000; however, only one of their proposals, the one valued at $250,000, was selected by a client. The contractor's win ratio based on the number of proposals submitted is 0.25 or 25 percent (1 of 4), but their win ratio based on dollar value is 50 percent ($250,000 of $500,000).

Some contractors have a strategy of submitting proposals in response to as many RFPs as they can with the hope that they will eventually win their fair share. Their philosophy is that if they don't submit a proposal, then they don't have any chance to win, but by submitting more proposals, they increase their chances of winning more contracts. Other contractors are more selective in submitting proposals; they respond to only those RFPs where they think they have a better than average chance of winning the contract. These contractors seriously consider the bid/no-bid decision process in responding to RFPs and submit fewer proposals but attempt to have a high win ratio.

Reinforce Your Learning

20. A measure used to determine the success of proposal efforts is known as the

____

____________________.

SUMMARY

The development of proposed solutions by interested contractors or by the customer's internal project team is the second phase of the project life cycle. This phase starts when the RFP becomes available at the conclusion of the needs identification phase and ends when an agreement is reached with the person, organization, or contractor selected to implement the proposed solution.

Customers (clients) and partner organizations prefer to work with people they know and can trust. Relationships establish the foundation for successful funding and contract opportunities. Relationship building requires being proactive and engaged. Establishing and building trust is key to developing effective and successful relationships with clients and partners. Ethical behavior in dealing with clients and partners is also imperative for building trust. The first impression one makes on a client is pivotal to developing a continuing and fruitful relationship. Building effective and successful relationships takes time and work.

Contractors should develop relationships with potential customers long before they prepare requests for proposal. Contractors should maintain frequent contacts with past and current customers and initiate contacts with potential customers. During these contacts, contractors should help customers identify areas in which the customers might benefit from the implementation of projects that address needs, problems, or opportunities. These pre-RFP/proposal efforts are crucial to establishing the foundation for eventually winning a contract from the customer.

Because the development and preparation of a proposal takes time and money, contractors interested in submitting a proposal in response to an RFP must be realistic about the probability of being selected as the winning contractor. Evaluating whether to go forward with the preparation of a proposal is sometimes referred to as the bid/no-bid decision. Some factors that a contractor might consider in making a bid/no-bid decision are the competition, the risk, its business mission, the ability to extend its capabilities, its reputation with the customer, the availability of customer funds, and the availability of resources for the proposal and the project.

It is important to remember that the proposal process is competitive and that the proposal is a selling document that should be written in a simple, concise manner. In the proposal the contractor must highlight the unique factors that differentiate it from competing contractors. The contractor proposal must also emphasize the benefits to the customer if the customer selects the contractor to perform the project. The customer will select the contractor that it expects will provide the best value.

Proposals are often organized into three sections: technical, management, and cost. The objective of the technical section of the contractor proposal is to convince the customer that the contractor understands the need or problem and can provide the least risky and most beneficial solution. The technical section should show an understanding of the problem, a proposed approach or solution, and the benefits to the customer. The objective of the management section of the contractor proposal is to convince the customer that the contractor can do the proposed work and achieve the intended results. The management section should contain a description of work tasks, a list of deliverables, a project schedule, a description of the organization of the project, a synopsis of related experience, and a list of any special equipment and facilities the contractor has. The objective of the cost section of the contractor proposal is to convince the customer that the contractor's price for the proposed project is realistic and reasonable. The cost section usually consists of tabulations of the contractor's estimated costs of such elements as labor, materials, subcontractors and consultants, equipment and facilities rental, travel, documentation, overhead, escalation, contingency, and a fee or profit.

When contractors prepare proposals, they are generally competing with other contractors to win a contract. Therefore, they must consider the reliability of the cost estimates, the risk, the value of the project to the contractor, the customer's budget, and the competition when determining the price for the proposed project.

Customers evaluate contractors' proposals in many different ways. Sometimes the technical and management proposals are evaluated first, without consideration of cost. Those proposals with the highest points on the technical/management review are then evaluated for their costs. The customer weighs the technical/management merit against the costs to determine which proposal offers the best value. Some of the criteria that might be used by customers in evaluating contractor proposals include compliance with the customer's statement of work, the contractor's understanding of the customer's problem or need, the soundness and practicality of the contractor's proposed solution to the project, the contractor's experience and success with similar projects, the experience of key individuals who will be assigned to work on the project, the contractor's ability to plan and control the project, the realism of the contractor's schedule, and the price.

Once the customer has selected the winning contractor, the contractor is informed that it is the winner, subject to successful negotiation of a contract. A contract is an agreement between the contractor, who agrees to provide a product or service (deliverables), and the customer, who agrees to pay the contractor a certain amount in return.

There are basically two types of contracts: fixed-price and cost reimbursement. In a fixed-price contract, the customer and the contractor agree on a price for the proposed work. The price remains fixed unless the customer and the contractor agree on changes. This type of contract provides low risk for the customer and high risk for the contractor. In a cost-reimbursement contract, the customer agrees to pay the contractor for all actual costs (labor, materials, and so forth), regardless of amount, plus some agreed-upon profit. This type of contract provides high risk for the customer, because contractor costs can overrun the proposed price, and low risk for the contractor.

A contract may include miscellaneous provisions covering misrepresentation of costs, notice of cost overruns or schedule delays, approvals for any subcontractors, customer-furnished equipment or information, patent ownership, disclosure of proprietary information, international considerations, termination, terms of payment, bonuses or penalties, and procedures for making changes.

Contractors measure the success of their proposal efforts by the number of times their proposals are selected by customers and/or by the total dollar value of their proposals that are selected. A measure that is often used is known as the win ratio.

QUESTIONS

1. Describe what is meant by pre-RFP/proposal marketing. Why should contractors do it?
2. Describe why building relationships with customers and partners is important. How is this accomplished?
3. Define *proposal*, and describe the purpose of a proposal. In addition, list the three major sections of a proposal and the purpose and elements of each.
4. Discuss why contractors must make bid/no-bid decisions and the factors involved in making these decisions. Give an example of when a contractor should bid and when a contractor should not bid.
5. Should a contractor try to contact a customer after a proposal has been submitted? Why or why not?
6. What factors must be considered when a contractor develops the proposal price? Why is this not an easy task?
7. Should the lowest-priced proposal always be selected as the winner? Why or why not? Give examples.
8. How do customers evaluate proposals? What factors might they consider?
9. Give examples of some miscellaneous provisions that might be found in a contract.
10. Describe two different types of contracts, when each should be used, and the risks associated with each.
11. Develop a complete proposal in response to the RFP you created for question 12 at the end of Chapter 2.
12. Describe two methods for measuring the effectiveness of your proposal efforts.

INTERNET EXERCISES

For the website addresses of the organizations mentioned in these exercises, go to "Internet Exercises" at the book's companion website at **international.cengage.com**. It is suggested that you save this website in your "Favorites" for easy access in the future.

To answer the following questions, perform a web search for sample proposals using your favorite search engine.

1. Based on the results of your search, find a sample proposal that has been posted on the web. What company or organization developed the proposal and what objective were they looking to accomplish?
2. Evaluate the effectiveness of this proposal based on information you have studied in this chapter. Discuss the strengths and weaknesses of the proposal. Are there any items missing from the proposal that should have been included?
3. Based on what you have learned in this chapter, download the proposal and revise it. Highlight the areas you revised. What makes your revised proposal better than the original?

4. Locate a website that provides suggestions for developing effective proposals. Compare and contrast this with what was presented in the chapter.
5. Explore and describe at least three software packages that can help you write effective proposals. What features do these packages provide? Download a demo copy of at least one, if possible.

New Manufacturing Facility in China

CASE STUDY 1

At its January 15 meeting, the Board of Directors of Omega Consolidated Industries made a decision to build a new manufacturing facility in China and approved funding up to $180 million for construction and start-up activities. It wants the new facility completed within two years from the date that a contractor is selected to design and build the facility. Omega is a worldwide corporation with its headquarters in London.

The Board asked I.M. Uno, Omega's president, to assign a team to develop a Request for Proposal (RFP) and solicit proposals from contractors to design and build the facility, including installation of all production equipment, offices, and an integrated information system. The team would also be responsible for monitoring the performance of the selected contractor to ensure the contractor fulfills all contractual requirements and performance specifications.

Ms. Uno selected four members of her management team:

- Alysha Robinson, who will be the plant manager of the new facility
- Jim Stewart, Chief Financial Officer
- Olga Frederick, Vice President of Engineering
- Willie Hackett, Procurement Manager

The team chose Alysha as their team leader. By April 30 they developed a comprehensive RFP that included:

- A statement of work describing the major tasks that the contractor must complete, as well as the performance specifications for the production capacity of the facility,
- A requirement that the contractor complete the project within 24 months after a contract is signed,
- Criteria by which the team would evaluate proposals:
  - Related Experience 30 points
  - Cost 30 points
  - Schedule 15 points
  - Innovative Design 25 points
- The contract would be a fixed-price contract.

The RFP did *not* state how much funding Omega had available for the project.

On May 15 the team announced the RFP in various trade publications and websites and required that interested contractors submit a proposal no later than June 30.

On June 30, the Omega team received three proposals:

1. J&J Inc., an American firm, submitted a proposal for $150 million. However, they stated that they would require 30 months to complete the project.
2. ROBETH Construction Company of Ireland submitted a proposal for $175 million. They had built several other facilities for Omega in the past and felt they had a good relationship with Ms. Uno, Jim Stewart, and Olga Frederick's predecessor who recently left Omega to become president at one of Omega's competitors that is also considering building a facility in China.
3. Kangaroo Architects and Engineers of Australia submitted a proposal for $200 million. Although Kangaroo had never done a project for Omega, they are one of the largest contractors in the world, have designed and built many and various types of facilities, and have a great reputation for innovative concepts, such as "green" environmentally friendly designs, and for building award-winning showcase facilities. They had built facilities for several of Omega's competitors.

The team was disappointed that they received only three proposals; they had expected at least eight.

On July 5, a fourth proposal was received from Asia General Contractors, a company based in China. The proposal was for $160 million. They had built many facilities in China for other global corporations and stated that they have good knowledge of many credible trade subcontractors in China that would be needed to build the facility. They also stated that they could complete the project in 20 months.

The team scheduled a meeting for July 15 to discuss the proposals, and, as a team, to score each of the proposals with respect to the evaluation criteria. That provided the team members with two weeks to individually read the proposals and develop their individual comments about each proposal, but they agreed not to individually score the proposals prior to the July 15 meeting.

At the July 15 meeting, Alysha opened the meeting and stated, "I like the proposal from Kangaroo because it would provide a showcase state-of-the-art facility."

Jim interrupted her, "Their proposal is for more than the Board has allocated for this project, I don't think we should consider them any further. In my mind they are out."

Alysha responded, "Even though it would require some additional funding than the Board had originally approved, I feel confident that I can persuade I.M. and the Board to approve the additional amount required."

Jim said, "I like the proposal from ROBETH. We have worked with them in the past during my thirty years here at Omega, and their proposal cost is just about what the Board has allocated, and I know a lot of the people at ROBETH."

Olga mentioned, "I have only been here at Omega for less than a year, but I took it upon myself to review the final reports of the previous projects that ROBETH did for Omega and found that ROBETH missed their proposed schedules on most of the projects or that some of the production systems never met all the performance specifications." She continued, "I am also concerned about ROBETH's continuing relationship with my predecessor who is now president at one of our major competitors and the potential conflict of interest if they would also be the contractor selected by our competitor to build the plant they are considering in China. They might use some of our proprietary processes in their design for our competitor's facility. I think it would be too risky to use them."

She continued, "I think the proposal from Asia General Contractors should be seriously considered even though it arrived a few days after the required due date."

Willie spoke up. "I strongly disagree. It would be unfair to the other three contractors."

Olga replied, "I think it is our job to select the contractor that will provide the best value and not be concerned about some silly rules about being a few days late; who cares? Besides they state that they can complete the project in 20 months, which means we will get the facility fully operational sooner than with any of the other contractors. And that means more products out the door sooner, more revenues and cash flow earlier, and should give us a better return on our investment, right Jim?"

After everyone's initial comments, Alysha stated, "Okay, I guess we have to score these four proposals against the evaluation criteria."

Jim interrupted, "You mean three proposals."

Olga spoke up loudly, "I think she said the four proposals, not three. Let's not get bogged down in bureaucratic games, we have an important decision to make."

I.M. Uno is expecting the team to recommend a contractor to her by July 31 so she can review it and present it to the Board of Directors at their August 15 meeting.

CASE QUESTIONS

1. Is there anything the team should have done when they received only three proposals by June 30?
2. Should the team consider the proposal from Asia General Contractors? Why?
3. After sharing their individual comments at the start of the July 15 meeting, how should the team proceed with the rest of the meeting and any follow-up?
4. How could the selection process have been improved? Is there anything the Board, I.M. Uno, Alysha or the team could have done differently?

GROUP ACTIVITY

Divide the course participants into teams of three or four to discuss this case and decide which contractor should be selected to design and build the new manufacturing facility in China. Each team must provide reasons for its decision. Have each team select a spokesperson to present its decision and reasons for that decision to the entire class.

Medical Information Systems

CASE STUDY 2

Maggie Pressman, Paul Goldberg, and Steve Youngblood are equal partners in their own consulting business, which specializes in designing and installing computer-based information systems for physicians. These systems usually include patient records, prescriptions, billings, and medical insurance processing. In some cases, the physician customers have a manual system and want to computerize it; in other situations, they have an existing computer system that needs to be upgraded and enhanced.

In most cases, the consulting firm purchases the necessary hardware as well as some packaged software. They add some of their own customized software to meet the specific requirements of the physician, and they install the complete, integrated system. They also provide training for the employees in the physician's office. The cost of most of these projects ranges from $10,000 to $40,000, depending on the amount of hardware needed. Most physicians are willing to spend such amounts rather than hire an additional office person to keep up with the ever-increasing paperwork.

Dr. Houser, one of the physicians for whom Paul had done a project in the past, left her private practice to join a large regional medical practice. This organization has six offices throughout the region, with an average of eight physicians in each office. Two of the offices also include a pharmacy. The organization employs a total of 200 people. Dr. Houser contacted Paul and asked if his consulting firm would be interested in submitting a proposal to upgrade the information system for this entire regional medical practice. The project will include integrating the six offices and two pharmacies into one system; the physicians will eventually hire an information systems person to oversee the operation of the system. Presently each office has its own system.

Dr. Houser tells Paul that some of the other physicians have patients who work for large consulting firms they think could do the job. She says that a team of representatives from the six offices and two pharmacies, with the help of the organization's purchasing manager, has prepared a request for proposal. The proposals are due in two weeks. The RFP was issued two weeks ago to the larger consulting firms, which are already working on their proposals. The purchasing manager was not familiar with Paul's consulting firm, and that is why he didn't receive a copy of the RFP.

Dr. Houser tells Paul that she's sorry she can't talk to him more about this, but she hasn't been involved like some of the other physicians, who discussed ideas with their patients who work at the larger consulting firms *before* the RFP was issued. Dr. Houser says that she will have the purchasing manager send Paul the RFP if he is interested and will be able to submit a proposal within two weeks.

"Sure," Paul says, "I'll drive over this afternoon and pick it up!" He asks if she knows how much money the medical practice has allocated for the project, but she doesn't. Paul picks up the RFP and makes copies for Maggie and Steve. Paul is enthusiastic about the opportunity when he meets with them. "If we do this project, it will propel us into a whole new business arena," Paul tells them. "This is the big break we've been waiting for!" he shouts.

Maggie moans, "This couldn't have come at a worse time. I'm working on three projects for other physicians, and they're all hounding me to finish up. In fact, one of them is not very satisfied. He said that if I don't finish his project in two weeks, he doesn't want it and won't recommend us to other physicians. I'm working 16 hours a day to keep up. I'm just overcommitted. I agree with you, Paul, it is a great opportunity, but I'm afraid I won't be able to spend any time helping with the proposal."

Steve wonders out loud, "Preparing the proposal is one thing, but can we do the project? I think we have the expertise among the three of us to do such a project, but this is a really big project, and we have other customers, too."

Paul replies, "We can hire more people. I have a few friends who would probably want some part-time work. We can do it! If we don't go after projects like this, we'll always be a small firm, each of us working 12-hour days for peanuts. And these small jobs for individual offices aren't going to last forever.

Someday they'll all be computerized, and we'll be out of business. What do we have to lose by submitting a proposal? We can't win if we don't submit one!"

CASE QUESTIONS

1. Why didn't this team receive the RFP at the same time the larger consulting firms did?
2. Why is this team being considered as a candidate to submit a proposal?
3. Develop a bid/no bid checklist to help determine if they should submit a proposal.
4. What should Maggie, Paul, and Steve do? In explaining your answer, address the concerns of each of the three team members.

GROUP ACTIVITY

Divide the course participants into teams of three or four to discuss the case and decide whether the consulting firm should submit a proposal. Each team must provide reasons for its decision. Have each team choose a spokesperson to present its decision and reasons for that decision to the entire class.

© Comstock Images/Jupiter Images

CHAPTER 4

The Project

Real World PROJECT MANAGEMENT

IBM Pitches a New Global Risk Management Strategy

IBM has a long, successful history of producing hardware and software, and managing large, complex projects for major international organizations. They are also well aware of the fact that a large percentage of projects, especially in the IT field, exceed their budgets, are not completed on time, and often do not deliver the required set of objectives that are expected from the project. Many times, project managers and project teams do not properly deal with inherent risks that should have been defined and planned for before the project started.

In order to help with these problems, IBM recently unveiled a new IT governance and risk management strategy to help global enterprise customers better plan, better integrate, and reduce unexpected expenses for security and compliance projects. Other security and segment leaders, such as Symantec and McAfee, are also retooling their marketing strategies to tap into the risk management side of the project management process. IBM contends that it will help companies craft more intelligent top-down strategies to help save time and money, while more closely coordinating project efforts.

A key element of this risk management strategy is for customers to utilize IT products and processes that can be applied to multiple issues rather than to individual problems. IBM intends to change the way companies view IT problems in more general terms, as opposed to specific and isolated issues. In the utilization of this process, companies may additionally begin planning products and budgets more closely along lines of organizationwide risk and governance. The types of standards IBM is integrating into its global risk management strategy encompass a well-defined set of best practices.

IT companies are struggling to deal with the backlash from the persistent flow of new demands, and the risks, related to compliance and security especially when dealing with global projects. Chris Lovejoy, director of governance risk management strategy at IBM, said, "CIOs are looking at this from the perspective of dealing with new threats and regulations, and there is always pressure from business to improve quality of services; IT is having a hard time prioritizing where it will focus limited resources." IBM's Business of IT Dashboard is a bundle of asset management services that are designed to help companies assess their strengths and weaknesses in critical areas of IT risk management.

Industry analysts say that the most significant difference between IBM's governance and risk management strategy and those utilized by its security rivals is that IBM is aiming its efforts at a broader view of business operations and technologies. "Both McAfee and Symantec are focused on security risks and business continuity, with IBM it's more about governance and global risk management backed with real IT process and service delivery considerations," said Michael Rasmussen, analyst with Forrester Research.

Just as IBM has realized that risk management is a major consideration in the project management process, many organizations are now realizing the same fact. In order for projects to be successful in the project planning phase, we must identify risks, assess their impact, properly plan a response, and monitor those risks throughout the project!

Hines, M., "IBM Pitches Risk Management Strategy," *InfoWorld*, May 15, 2007.

FIGURE 4.1 *Project Life Cycle*

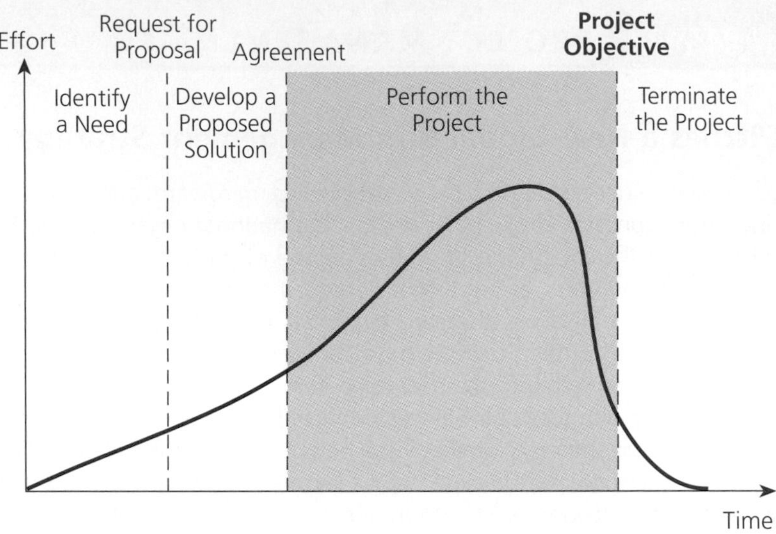

Performing, or doing, the project—implementing the proposed solution—is the third phase of the project life cycle shown in Figure 4.1. This phase starts after a contract or agreement is drawn up between the customer and the contractor or project team, and it ends when the project objective is accomplished and the customer is satisfied that the work has been completed in a quality manner, within budget, and on time. The fourth and final phase of the project life cycle involves terminating the project. This chapter discusses these final two phases of the project life cycle. You will become familiar with

- the elements involved in establishing a project plan
- identifying and assessing risks
- the steps in the project control process
- actions that should be taken when a project is terminated

PLANNING THE PROJECT

The third phase of the project life cycle has two parts: doing the detailed planning for the project and then implementing that plan to accomplish the project objective. Before jumping in and starting the project itself, the contractor or project team must take sufficient time to plan the project properly. It is necessary to lay out a roadmap, or game plan, that shows how the project tasks will be accomplished within budget and on schedule. Trying to perform a project without a plan is like attempting to assemble a child's bicycle without first reading the instructions. Individuals who think planning is unnecessary or a waste of time invariably need to find time later on to redo things. It is important to *plan the work, then work the plan*. Otherwise, chaos and frustration will result, and the risk of project failure will be higher.

Reinforce Your Learning

1. What are the two parts of the project phase of the life cycle?

The planning part of the project phase involves expanding the plan, schedule, and budget in the proposal into much greater detail. The time and expense required to do such detailed planning are not usually warranted during the proposal (second) phase of the life cycle. Detailed planning involves the same steps as the front-end planning discussed in Chapter 1:

1. *Clearly define the project objective.* The definition must be agreed upon by the customer and the individual or organization who will perform the project.
2. *Divide and subdivide the project scope into major "pieces," or work packages.* Although major projects may seem overwhelming when viewed as a whole, one way to conquer even the most monumental endeavor is to break it down. A work breakdown structure is a hierarchical tree of work elements or items accomplished or produced by the project team during the project. The work breakdown structure usually identifies the organization or individual responsible for each work package. (Work breakdown structures will be discussed further in Chapter 5.)
3. *Define the specific activities that need to be performed for each work package in order to accomplish the project objective.*
4. *Graphically portray the activities in the form of a network diagram.* This diagram shows the sequence and interdependencies of activities needed to achieve the project objective. (Network diagrams will be discussed further in Chapter 5.)
5. *Make a time estimate for how long it will take to complete each activity.* It is also necessary to determine the types of resources and how many of each resource are needed for each activity to be completed within the estimated duration.
6. *Make a cost estimate for each activity.* The cost is based on the types and quantities of resources required for each activity.
7. *Calculate a project schedule and budget to determine whether the project can be accomplished within the required time, with the allotted funds, and with the available resources.* If not, adjustments must be made to the project scope, activity time estimates, or resource assignments until an achievable, realistic baseline plan (a roadmap for accomplishing the project scope on time and within budget) can be established.

Reinforce Your Learning

2. The first part of the project phase of the life cycle involves establishing a

____

________________.

Planning determines what needs to be done, who will do it, how long it will take, and how much it will cost. The result of this effort is a baseline plan. Taking the time to develop a well-thought-out plan is critical to the successful accomplishment of any project. Many projects have overrun their budgets, missed their completion dates, or only partially satisfied their technical specifications because there was no viable baseline plan in place before they were started.

It is important that the people who will be involved in performing the project also participate in planning the work. They are usually the most knowledgeable about which detailed activities need to be done. Also, by participating in the planning of the work, these individuals become committed to accomplishing it according to the plan. Participation builds commitment.

Reinforce Your Learning

3. Planning determines:

____

needs to be done;

____

will do it; how

____

it will take; and how much it will

________________.

MANAGING RISK

As mentioned in Chapter 1, one attribute of a project is it involves a degree of uncertainty. Such uncertainty can impact the outcome of a project. There are events that may occur during a project that can have an adverse effect on the success of the project. ***Risk*** is the possibility that an unwanted circumstance will occur that can result in some loss. **Risk management** involves identifying, assessing, and responding to project risks in order to minimize the likelihood and impact of the consequences of adverse events on the achievement of the project objective. Addressing risks proactively will increase the chances of achieving the project objective. Waiting for unfavorable events to occur and then reacting to them can result in panic and costly responses. Managing risk includes taking action to prevent or minimize the chances of occurrence or the impact of such unfavorable events.

Reinforce Your Learning

4. Risk management involves ____________, ____________ and ____________ to project risks to minimize the ____________ and ____________ of the ____________ of adverse events on the achievement of the project ____________.

Some level of risk planning should be done during the proposal phase of the project life cycle to make sure, for example, that a contractor understands the risks involved with bidding on a proposed project. With knowledge of potential risks, the contractor can include contingency or management reserve amounts in the bid price. On the other hand, if the risks seem too great, the contractor may decide to not bid on a proposed project, as discussed in the "Bid/No-Bid Decision" section in Chapter 3. Subsequently, more detailed risk planning should be done at the start of a project.

A project manager cannot be risk averse. She must accept that risk is a part of project management and has to address it head-on. Furthermore, the project manager needs to set the tone for encouraging open and timely discussion of risks among the project team.

Risk Identification

Risk identification includes determining which risks may adversely affect the project objective and what the consequences of each risk might be if they occur.

The most common approach to identifying the sources of risks is brainstorming. (The *brainstorming* technique is discussed in Chapter 11.) The project manager should involve key project team members in identifying potential sources of risk—things that could happen that would negatively impact achieving the project objective. Each member of the project team can bring his or her experience and insight to help develop a comprehensive list of possible sources of risk. How many risks should be identified? A team can go overboard and come up with hundreds of possible risks. For example, there is a chance that every activity can take longer than planned or cost more than budgeted, and there are highly unlikely risks such as "what if our building is destroyed by fire during the project?" Common sense and reasonableness must prevail when identifying risks. The risks should be those that are somewhat likely to occur and can have a significant negative impact on successfully achieving the project objective.

Another source that can be helpful in identifying possible risks is historical information from past projects. If postproject evaluations (discussed later in this chapter) were done on completed projects, they could be a good source for identifying possible risks, as well as information on how to address such risks if they occur again.

Examples of specific risks are:

- Incorporating advanced technology in a new product.
- Performance requirements for taking measurements 10 times faster than can be done currently.
- Technological advances that could make the originally selected technology obsolete before the project is completed.

- First-time use of new robotic equipment for a rare and complex surgical procedure.
- Availability of labor force of certain craftspeople when needed because of a strong local economy and low unemployment rate.
- Encountering more than expected rock formations when excavating.
- Excessive number of revisions to a website design before it is acceptable to the customer.
- Labor strike may occur during the peak of a construction project.
- Severe weather (early snow) may hit during the construction phase of a facility expansion.
- Bank may not approve full amount of the loan for the project.
- Significant price escalation for rare fire retardant coating material.
- Patient may hemorrhage during surgery.
- Sufficient vaccine may not be available to meet emergency needs.
- New product may not pass certification tests.
- Longer than anticipated delivery of key subassembly from overseas supplier.
- Customer will not provide sample parts for testing when needed.
- Rain on the days of a weekend town festival.

For each risk that is identified, the potential consequence should be listed. Such consequences could include schedule delays, substantial additional expenditures, not meeting technical requirements, or adversely affecting customer satisfaction.

Risk Assessment

Assessing each risk involves determining the likelihood that the risk event will occur and the degree of impact the event will have on the project objective. Both of these factors can be assigned a rating of High, Medium, or Low. The project manager, in consultation with appropriate team members who are most knowledgeable about the potential risk, should determine a rating for each risk. Historical data from prior similar projects can also be helpful. For example, if severe weather is a risk, historical daily weather data or consultation with a weather forecasting service may be useful.

Based on the potential likelihood of occurrence and potential impact, the risks can then be prioritized. For example, those with the highest likelihood of occurrence and impact can be given more serious consideration in developing a response plan.

A tool for assessing risk is a **risk assessment matrix** as shown in Figure 4.2.

Reinforce Your Learning

5. Risk response planning involves developing an

____

to reduce the impact or likelihood of each risk, establishing a

____

for when to implement the actions, and assigning

____

to individuals for implementing each response plan.

Risk Response Planning

Risk response planning involves developing an action plan to reduce the impact or likelihood of each risk, establishing a trigger point for when to implement the actions to address each risk, and assigning responsibility to specific individuals for implementing each response plan.

A risk response plan can be to *avoid* the risk, *mitigate* the risk, or *accept* the risk. Avoidance means to eliminate the risk by choosing a different course of

FIGURE 4.2 ***Risk Assessment Matrix***

Risk	Consequence	Chance of Occurrence (L, M, H)	Impact (L, M, H)	Action Trigger	Responsibility	Response Plan
Rain on Day of Event	• Low attendance • Incur financial loss	M	H	Weather forecast two days before event	Laura	• Reserve indoor space now • Recruit extra volunteers to work around the clock to set up indoors • Develop detailed plan
Road Construction	• Reduced attendance • Reduced revenue	H	H	Highway Dept. publishes construction schedule	Allison	• Identify alternate routes • Have signs made • Post signs along all routes • Announce in news media.

action. Examples of avoiding risk would be to decide to use conventional technology rather than advanced state-of-the-art technology in a new product, or deciding to hold a weekend festival indoors to avoid the possibility of a rainout. Mitigating the risk involves taking action to reduce the likelihood that the risk event will occur or reducing the potential impact. For example, reducing the risk of multiple redesigns of a customer's website might require reviewing other sample designs with the client earlier in the project. Accepting a risk can include either accepting the consequence in circumstances where the likelihood of occurrence and potential impact is low, and then dealing with it if and when it occurs, or it can mean developing a contingency plan to execute if a risk event with high probability occurs.

6. A

____

____

is a predefined set of actions that would be implemented if the risk event occurs.

A **contingency plan** is a predefined set of actions that would be implemented if the risk event occurs. Most contingency plans require the expenditure of additional funds for using additional resources, working overtime, paying for expedited shipments, purchasing additional materials, unexpected price escalations, and so forth. Project prices and budgets should include a contingency or management reserve to pay for additional expenses of implementing contingency plans.

A risk response plan must include a trigger point or warning flag for when to implement the action plan for each risk. A trigger point for when to purchase a rare material may be if the current price increases more than 5 percent above the amount budgeted for purchasing the material. The trigger point for deciding to incorporate advanced technology in a new product may be the completion of an engineering feasibility study. Another example would be to authorize overtime if the project falls behind schedule by more than 5 percent of the remaining project duration.

Risk Monitoring

Risk monitoring involves regularly reviewing the risk management matrix throughout the project. During the project, it is important to evaluate all risks to determine if there are any changes to the likelihood of occurrence or the potential impact of any of the risks. These factors can determine if a particular risk has increased in priority for attention or if the risk has diminished in importance. Furthermore, new risks maybe identified that were not considered as a risk earlier in the project, but now need to be added to the risk assessment matrix. For example, early tests for a prototype of a new product indicate the product may now not meet the original performance specifications. Another situation may be that due to previous delays in the design phase, the construction phase of a facility expansion in now scheduled to take place in the middle of the hurricane season. During a project the customer may approve changes to the project work scope, schedule, or budget that could also affect the assessment of previously defined risks or result in the identification of new risks.

The agenda for project status review meetings (see Chapter 12) should include an item for risk assessment. Particular attention should be given to reviewing the trigger points for each risk to determine if any risk response plans are on the verge of having to be implemented.

PERFORMING THE PROJECT

Once the baseline plan has been developed, project work can proceed. The project team, led by the project manager, will implement the plan and perform the activities, or work elements, in accordance with the plan. The pace of project activity will increase as more and various resources become involved in performing the project tasks. For a project to put on a town festival, the major work elements might include the following:

1. Preparing promotions—newspaper advertisements, posters, tickets, and so forth.
2. Selecting volunteers.
3. Organizing games, including constructing booths and acquiring prizes.
4. Contracting for amusement rides and obtaining the necessary permits.
5. Identifying performers to entertain and constructing the grandstand stage.
6. Arranging for food, including making the food and building concession stands.
7. Organizing all the support services, such as parking, cleanup, security, and restroom facilities.

For the more technical project of designing, building, and installing a specialized automated high-speed packaging machine in the customer's factory, major work elements might include the following:

1. Developing both preliminary and detailed designs, including preparation of specifications, drawings, flowcharts, and a list of materials.
2. Preparing plans for testing of the components, subsystems, and system by the contractor, both before shipping the equipment to the customer's plant and after it has been installed at the customer's plant, to ensure that the equipment meets the customer's requirements. The customer may want to review and approve the test plans before the start of testing.

3. Conducting design review meetings, both internally and with the customer. Based on these design review meetings, the customer may initiate or approve changes to the original proposal. These changes could have an impact on the scope, schedule, and price. The customer may need to amend the contract, and the contractor may have to do some replanning of the project to incorporate any changes.
4. Ordering materials and parts.
5. Fabricating components and parts.
6. Writing and testing software.
7. Assembling and testing hardware, including testing components, assembling components into subassemblies, testing subassemblies, assembling subassemblies into the system, and testing the entire hardware system.
8. Integrating hardware and software and testing the system. Customer representatives may want to witness and document the test results to ensure that they meet the contract specifications.
9. Preparing installation requirements, such as floor plans and utility requirements (electrical, plumbing, and so forth), and identifying which items the customer will be responsible for during installation.
10. Preparing training materials (manuals, videotapes, computer simulations) to train the customer to operate and maintain the new equipment.
11. Shipping the equipment to the customer's factory and installing it.
12. Conducting training for the customer.
13. Conducting final acceptance tests to show that the equipment meets all of the customer's specified requirements.

CONTROLLING THE PROJECT

While the project work is being performed, it is necessary to monitor progress to ensure that everything is going according to plan. This involves measuring actual progress and comparing it to planned progress. To measure actual progress, it is important to keep track of which activities have actually been started and completed, when they were started and completed, and how much money has been spent or committed. If, at any time during the project, comparison of actual progress to planned progress reveals that the project is behind schedule, overrunning the budget, or not meeting the technical specifications, corrective action must be taken to get the project back on track. (Corrective action is discussed further in Part 2.)

Before a decision is made to implement corrective action, it may be necessary to evaluate several alternative actions to make sure the corrective action will bring the project back within the scope, time, and budget constraints of the objective. Be aware, for instance, that adding resources to make up time and get back on schedule may result in overrunning the planned budget. If a project gets too far out of control, it may be difficult to achieve the project objective without sacrificing the scope, budget, schedule, or quality.

The key to effective **project control** is measuring actual progress and comparing it to planned progress on a timely and regular basis and taking corrective action immediately, if necessary. Hoping that a problem will go away without corrective intervention is naive. The earlier a problem is identified and corrected, the better. Based on actual progress, it is possible to forecast a schedule and budget for completion of the project. If these parameters are beyond the limits of the project objective, corrective actions need to be implemented at once.

The **project control process** involves regularly gathering data on project performance, comparing actual performance to planned performance, and taking corrective actions if actual performance is behind planned performance. This process must occur regularly throughout the project.

Figure 4.3 illustrates the steps in the project control process. It starts with establishing a baseline plan that shows how the project scope (tasks) will be accomplished on time (schedule) and within budget (resources, costs). Once this baseline plan is agreed upon by the customer and the contractor or project team, the project can start.

FIGURE 4.3 ***Project Control Process***

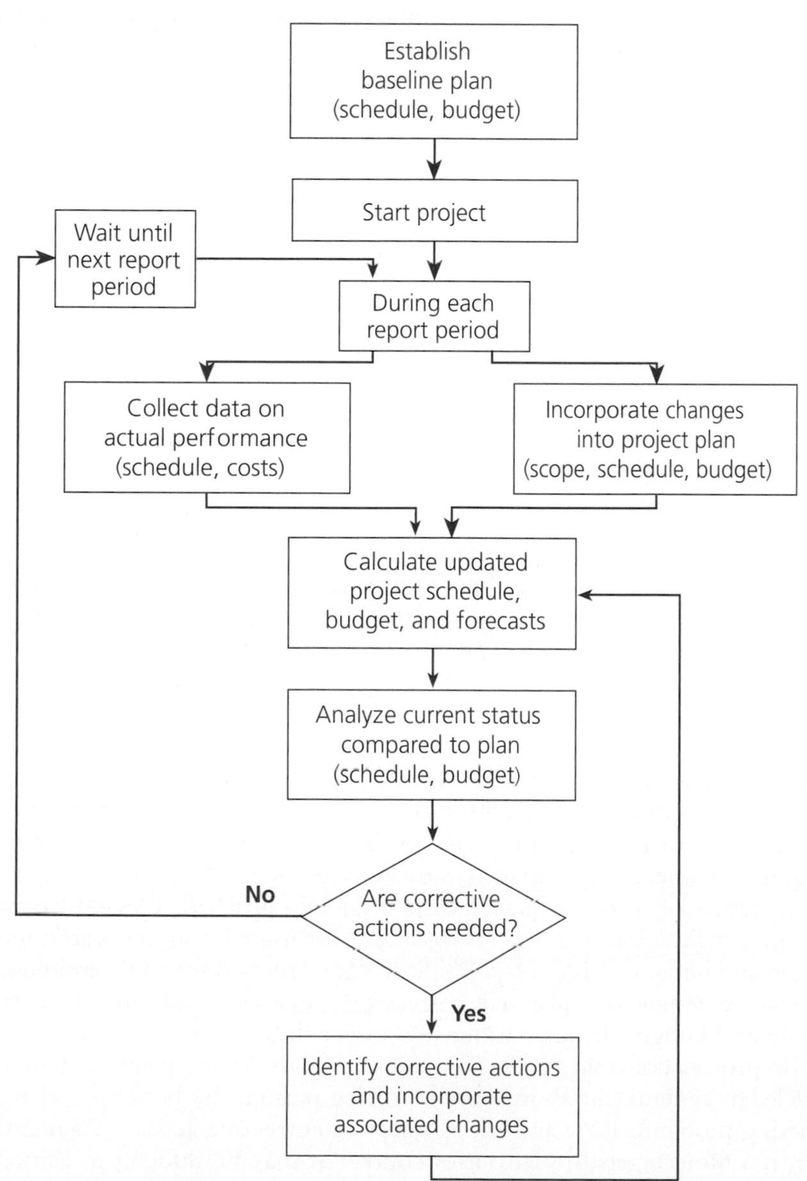

A regular **reporting period** should be established for comparing actual progress with planned progress. Reporting may be daily, weekly, biweekly, or monthly, depending on the complexity or overall duration of the project. If a project is expected to have an overall duration of a month, the reporting period might be as short as a day. On the other hand, if a project is expected to run five years, the reporting period might be a month.

During each reporting period two kinds of data or information need to be collected:

1. *Data on actual performance*. This includes
   - the actual time that activities were started and finished
   - the actual costs expended and committed
2. *Information on any changes to the project scope, schedule, and budget*. These changes could be initiated by the customer or the project team, or they could be the result of an unanticipated occurrence such as a natural disaster, a labor strike, or the resignation of a key project team member.

It should be noted that once changes are incorporated into the plan and agreed on by the customer, a new baseline plan has to be established. The scope, schedule, and budget of the new baseline plan may be different from those of the original baseline plan.

Reinforce Your Learning

7. What are the two kinds of data or information that need to be collected during each reporting period?

It is crucial that the data and information discussed above be collected in a timely manner and used to calculate an updated project schedule and budget. For example, if project reporting is done monthly, data and information should be obtained as late as possible in that monthly period so that when an updated schedule and budget are calculated, they are based on the latest possible information. In other words, a project manager should not gather data at the beginning of the month and then wait until the end of the month to use it to calculate an updated schedule and budget, because the data will be outdated and may cause incorrect decisions to be made about the project status and corrective actions.

Once an updated schedule and budget have been calculated, they need to be compared to the baseline schedule and budget and analyzed for variances to determine whether the project is ahead of or behind schedule and under or over budget. If the project status is okay, no corrective actions are needed; the status will be analyzed again for the next reporting period.

If it is determined that corrective actions are necessary, however, decisions must be made regarding how to revise the schedule or the budget. These decisions often mean a trade-off involving time, cost, and scope. For example, reducing the duration of an activity may require either increasing costs to pay for more resources or reducing the scope of the task (and possibly not meeting the customer's technical requirements). Similarly, reducing project costs may require using materials of a lower quality than originally planned. Once a decision is made on which corrective actions to take, they must be incorporated into the schedule and budget. It is necessary to calculate a revised schedule and budget to determine whether the planned corrective measures result in an acceptable schedule and budget. If not, further revisions will be needed.

The project control process continues throughout the project phase of the life cycle. In general, the shorter the reporting period, the better the chances of identifying problems early and taking effective corrective actions. As mentioned earlier, if a project gets too far out of control, it may be difficult to achieve the project objective without sacrificing the scope, budget, schedule, or quality. There may be situations in which it is wise to increase the frequency of reporting until the project is back on track. For example, if a five-year project with monthly reporting is endangered by a slipping schedule or an increasing budget overrun, it may be prudent to reduce the reporting period to one week in order to monitor the project and the impact of corrective actions more closely.

The project control process is an important and necessary part of performing the project. Just establishing a sound baseline plan is not sufficient, because even the best-laid plans don't always work out. *Project management is a proactive approach to controlling a project,* to ensure that the project objective is achieved even when things don't go according to plan.

This third phase of the life cycle ends when the customer is satisfied that the requirements have been met and the project objective has been accomplished.

Reinforce Your Learning

8. In addition to establishing a baseline plan, it is also necessary to ____________ the project proactively to ensure that the project ____________ is achieved and the customer is ____________.

TERMINATING THE PROJECT

The fourth and final phase of the project life cycle is terminating the project. It starts after the project work has been completed, as shown in Figure 4.4, and includes various actions to close out the project properly.

The purpose of properly terminating a project is to learn from the experience gained on the project in order to improve performance on future projects. Therefore, the activities associated with terminating the project should be identified and included in the project's baseline plan—they should not be done merely as spontaneous afterthoughts. These activities might include organizing and filing project documents, receiving and making final payments, and conducting post project evaluation meetings within both the contractor's and the customer's organizations.

FIGURE 4.4 ***Project Life Cycle***

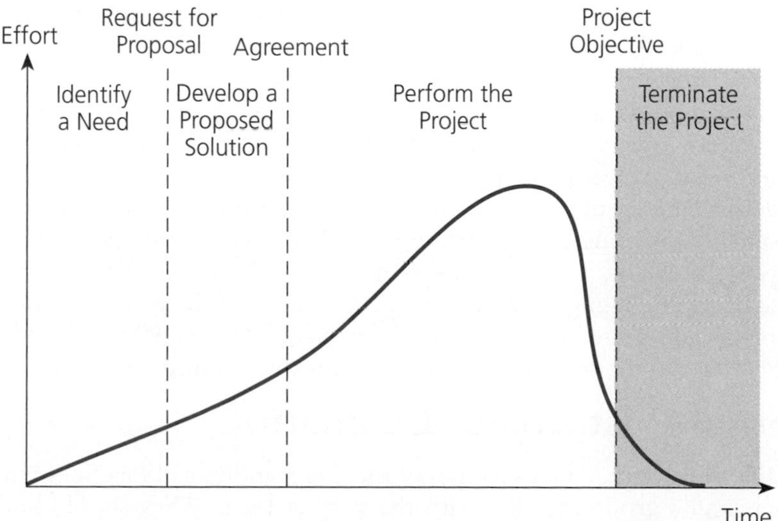

Reinforce Your Learning

9. What is the purpose of properly terminating a project?

The termination phase starts when performance of the project is completed and the result is accepted by the customer. In some situations, this might be a somewhat formal event in which an automated system satisfies a set of criteria or passes tests that were stated in the contract. Other projects, such as a weekend of homecoming activities at a university, are completed merely with the passage of time.

When a contractor completes a project for a customer, the contractor must verify that all the agreed-upon deliverables were, in fact, provided. Such deliverables might include training or procedures manuals, drawings, flowcharts, equipment, software, brochures, reports, and data. During project termination, the contractor or organization that performed the project should ensure that copies of appropriate project-related documentation are properly organized and filed so that they can be readily retrieved for use in the future, if necessary. In the future, the contractor may want to use some actual cost and schedule information from this completed project to help develop the schedule and cost estimates for a proposed project. Or, if the project involved, say, staging an arts festival, the project team should organize all its documentation—including suggestions for improving aspects of the festival—for use by the project team that will do the festival the following year.

Another activity that must be performed during the termination phase is assuring that all payments have been collected from the customer. Many contracts include a progress payment clause, which states that the customer will make the final payment at the completion of the project. In some cases, the final payment is a high percentage (e.g., 25 percent) of the total project price. Similarly, it should be verified that all payments have been made to any subcontractors or consultants and for any purchased materials or items. Once all payments have been received and made, the project "books," or accounting records, can be closed, and a financial analysis of the project can be made, in which actual costs are compared to the project budget.

During the project termination phase, the project manager should prepare a written performance evaluation of each member of the project team and mention how each has expanded her or his knowledge as a result of the project assignment, as well as what areas she or he needs to develop further. If a project team member does not report directly to the project manager within the company's organizational structure, the project manager should provide a copy of the performance evaluation to the person's immediate supervisor.

Finally, no successful project should end without some type of celebration. This can range from an informal pizza party after work to a more formal event, with speakers from the customer's organization and awards or certificates of recognition for project participants.

Another important activity during the termination phase is holding postproject evaluation meetings. These meetings should be conducted internally, within the organization that performed the project, as well as with the customer. The purpose of such meetings is to evaluate performance of the project, to determine whether the anticipated benefits from the project were actually achieved, and to identify what can be done to improve performance on future projects.

Internal Postproject Evaluation

Internally, there should be two types of meetings: individual meetings with team members and a group meeting with the project team. They should be held as

Real World PROJECT MANAGEMENT

UC Berkeley's Success Story

After 40 years of accumulated technology legacy, UC Berkeley decided to pack up and move its data center. The move was to impact more than 40,000 members of the UC Berkeley community who depended on the systems. This was the challenge that the Information Systems and Technology (IST) staff faced in planning the move from Evans Hall to a newly constructed world-class data center.

Eight years ago, Evans Hall was recognized as needing seismic retrofitting based on data developed following an earthquake in Kobe, Japan. UC Berkeley and the IST staff had to decide whether to retrofit the existing space, move its location off-campus, or build a completely new data center from scratch. A hybrid-type approach was chosen, and a space was identified where a building was planned for development. Construction had not yet begun on this site, which allowed the Capital Projects team, architects, and IST workers to change the building design to accommodate the needs of the data center.

The first step in the design project was to ensure a successful move. A detailed evaluation plan was developed that explained the needs of the current data center, as well as the projected needs. It was also critical that the space was flexible enough to handle legacy systems and any new technology and computers that might be installed in the future. A full assessment of more than 300 servers enabled architects and system planners to create a data center design that would allow connecting with the old data center and also allow room for growth.

Representatives from key constituency groups on the campus met to determine the plan and detailed scheduling in terms of a window of downtime for the data center. Since Berkeley is so diverse, it was extremely difficult for all parties to agree upon dates. Finally, the agreed-upon transition was to take place between the end of the fiscal year and the start of the next fiscal year. This schedule worked around summer class sessions but unfortunately allowed for very little flexibility.

Outside consultants provided a detailed analysis of each of the thousands of pieces of infrastructure. The infrastructure was divided into categories: moving, replacing, or retiring. Each system was assigned a category and an assessment of risk, and the likelihood of success was determined. The team had to determine whether each individual option was possible, probable, or mandatory and its specific risk. At the end of this process, the team was able to identify 50 subprojects to be completed in less than 10 months.

In preparation, select servers, disk storage, and tape environments were arranged for replacement, while others were prepared for moving. Extremely old and intricate equipment that would have required expensive vendor-managed move plans were not moved to avoid additional costs and risks. Instead, new and easy to assemble equipment was utilized in those cases. To avoid problems in the restoration of the system, a new mandatory change management process was implemented. This tightly controlled any changes that were to occur.

Affinity groups were formed to determine which systems or networks depended on other systems in order to run successfully. This was one of the most complex phases of the process. The teams also developed scripts for shutting down, restarting, testing, and commissioning each system to be moved. Approximately, 30 people per shift were scheduled to help with the move to keep downtime to a minimum.

Months of advanced planning and design had paid off, and the project was successfully completed ahead of the scheduled time frame and within budget!! Hundreds of servers, applications, devices, and network connections were successfully moved to the new state-of-the-art data center. The project was completed with amazing precision and accuracy based on successful project management principles and an incredibly talented and dedicated team!

Waggener, S., "UC Berkeley's Data Center Success Story," *IST Publication UC Berkeley*, http://istpub.berkeley.edu, October 1, 2004.

soon as possible after the completion of the project, and they should be announced in advance so that people can be prepared.

The project manager should have an individual meeting with each of the team members. These meetings allow team members to give their personal impressions of performance of the project and what can be done better on future projects. Such individual meetings allow people to speak openly, without the constraints of a group meeting.

For example, they can mention any problems in working relationships with other team members. Of course, the project manager must assure team members that any such disclosures will be kept confidential. Once the individual meetings with team members are complete, the project manager can identify common issues brought up in those meetings. With this information, the project manager can then develop an agenda for a group meeting with the entire project team.

Reinforce Your Learning

10. What are the two types of internal post-project evaluation meetings the project manager should have?

At the group meeting with the project team, the project manager should discuss what happened during performance of the project and identify specific recommendations for improvement. A sample agenda for such a postproject evaluation team meeting is shown in Figure 4.5.

Following are some topics that might be discussed under each of the agenda items:

1. *Technical performance*. How did the final scope of the work compare to the scope of the work at the start of the project? Were there many changes to the work scope? Were the changes handled properly in terms of approvals and documentation? What impact did the changes have on project costs and schedule? Was the work scope totally completed? Were the project work and deliverables completed in a quality manner, and did they meet the expectations of the customer?
2. *Cost performance*. How did the final project costs compare with the original project budget and with the final project budget, which included any relevant changes in project scope? If there was a fixed-price contract, was it profitable, or did the project organization lose money? If there was a cost-reimbursement contract, was the project completed within the customer's budget? Were there any particular work packages that overran or underran their budgets by more than 10 percent? If so, why? What were the causes of any cost overruns? Were the cost estimates realistic?
3. *Schedule performance*. How did the actual project schedule compare with the original schedule? If the project was late, what were the causes? How was performance on the schedule associated with each work package? Were the activity duration estimates realistic?

FIGURE 4.5 ***Post-Project Evaluation Team Meeting Agenda***

POST-PROJECT EVALUATION
Team Meeting

Agenda

1. Technical performance
   Work scope
   Quality
   Managing changes
2. Cost performance
3. Schedule performance
4. Project planning and control
5. Risk management
6. Customer relationships
7. Team relationships
8. Communications
9. Problem identification and resolution
10. Lessons learned
11. Recommendations for future projects

4. *Project planning and control.* Was the project planned in sufficient detail? Were the plans updated in a timely manner to incorporate changes? Was actual performance compared with planned performance on a regular basis? Were data on actual performance accurate and collected in a timely manner? Was the planning and control system used on a regular basis by the project team? Was it used for decision making?
5. *Risk management.* Was the project outcome impacted by the occurrence of any unexpected events? If so, were they identified in the risk plan? Were the high probability risks adequately identified at the beginning of the project? Were there any risks that should have been, but were not, identified at the beginning of the project? What risks were identified during the project that were not identified at the beginning, and why weren't they identified at the beginning? For identified risks that occurred, were the response or contingency plans adequate? Were there unexpected events that occurred for which there were no response plans?
6. *Customer relationships.* Was every effort made to make the customer a participant in the success of the project? Was the customer asked on a regular basis about the level of satisfaction with the progress of the project? Were there regularly scheduled face-to-face meetings with

the customer? Was the customer informed of potential problems in a timely manner and asked to participate in the problem-solving process?

7. *Team relationships.* Was there a "team" feeling and a commitment to the success of the project? Were there any conditions that impeded teamwork?
8. *Communications.* Was the team kept informed of the project status and potential problems in a timely manner? Was the project environment conducive to open, honest, and timely communications? Were project meetings productive? Were written communications within the team and with the customer sufficient, insufficient, or overburdening?
9. *Problem identification and resolution.* Were mechanisms in place for team members to identify potential problems early? Was problem solving done in a thorough, rational manner?
10. *Lessons learned.* What worked and what didn't? What particular things were done well on the project that helped the project and should be done on other projects? What things were done that hindered the project and should be eliminated or changed on future projects? If there would be an opportunity to start over and do this project again, what should be done differently?
11. *Recommendations.* Based on the team's discussion and evaluation of the above items, what specific recommendations can be made to help improve performance on future projects?

After the evaluation meeting, the project manager should issue a brief written report to management with a summary of project performance and recommendations.

Customer Feedback

Just as important as the internal meeting is a postproject evaluation meeting with the customer. The purposes of this meeting should be to determine whether the project provided the customer with the anticipated benefits, to assess the level of customer satisfaction, and to obtain any feedback that would be helpful in future business relationships with this customer or with other customers. Meeting participants should include the project manager, key project team members, and key representatives of the customer's organization who were involved with the project. The project manager should schedule the meeting for a time when the customer is in a position to really say whether the project met expectations and achieved the anticipated benefits. In the case of a project to develop an eight-page color brochure for a customer, a meeting can be held shortly after the final printed brochure is given to the customer, because the customer will know immediately whether the brochure met expectations. However, in the case of a project that supplied a customer with a specialized automated assembly machine expected to reduce the product defect rate from 10 percent to 2 percent, it could be several months after the machine is installed before the customer can verify whether the defect rate was reduced. This time may be needed for the operators to learn how to operate the equipment properly or for the company to verify a reduction in returned merchandise.

Reinforce Your Learning

11. List three reasons for having a post-project evaluation meeting with the customer.

Ideally, the contractor should sit down with the customer and ask open-ended questions. This provides an opportunity for customers not only to express their level of satisfaction but also to provide detailed comments about the parts of the project with which they were satisfied or dissatisfied. These comments will not come as a surprise if the project manager has been continually monitoring the level of customer satisfaction throughout the project. If the customer is satisfied with the project, the contractor or organization that performed the project is presented with several opportunities.

First, the contractor should ask the customer about any other projects the contractor could do—perhaps without going through a competitive RFP process. If the customer is satisfied with a brochure, for instance, the contractor should ask if any other brochures, annual reports, or marketing materials are needed. Likewise, if the customer is satisfied with an automated assembly machine, the contractor should ask whether other parts of the manufacturing process need to be studied for additional productivity improvements.

Second, the contractor should ask permission to use the customer as a reference with potential customers. The contractor may even want to feature the customer in a brochure, maybe with a picture and a quote stating how satisfied the customer was with the contractor's performance. Another way to capitalize on the success of a project is for the contractor to write up a news story about the project in collaboration with the customer and issue it as a press release to the appropriate newspapers and other media.

Another way to get feedback from the customer regarding satisfaction with the results of the project is through a postproject customer evaluation survey, as shown in Figure 4.6. The project manager gives this survey form to the customer and, possibly, other project stakeholders to complete and return. For large projects, several individuals in the customer's organization may contribute to formulating the responses.

When there are multiple customers or end users of the results of a project, it may be difficult to get feedback from them. For example, after a volunteer group organizes a week-long town festival, how does it get feedback from the people who attended about their level of satisfaction and their suggestions for improving next year's event? Or consider a project in which a new software product was developed. The immediate customer is the company's product manager, but the true customers are the people who eventually purchase the software. The product manager may be satisfied with the resultant product, but how does the project team determine whether the end users are satisfied? In both of these cases—the town festival and the new software product—the project team may use some type of survey or focus group to obtain feedback from the end users.

Early Project Termination

There may be circumstances that require a project to be terminated before it is completed. For example, suppose a company is working on a research and development project with an advanced material that has certain properties at extremely low temperatures. After some development work and testing, it is determined that further development of the material could cost much more and take far longer than originally thought. If the company decides that the

FIGURE 4.6 *Post-Project Customer Evaluation Survey*

Post-Project Customer Evaluation Survey

Please complete this brief survey to help us evaluate and improve our project management performance. If more space is needed for responses, please attach additional pages.

Project Title: ____________________

	Degree of Satisfaction									
	Low									High
1. Completeness of Work Scope	1	2	3	4	5	6	7	8	9	10
Comments ____________________										
2. Quality of Work	1	2	3	4	5	6	7	8	9	10
Comments ____________________										
3. Schedule Performance	1	2	3	4	5	6	7	8	9	10
Comments ____________________										
4. Budget Performance	1	2	3	4	5	6	7	8	9	10
Comments ____________________										
5. Communications	1	2	3	4	5	6	7	8	9	10
Comments ____________________										
6. Customer Relations	1	2	3	4	5	6	7	8	9	10
Comments ____________________										
7. Overall Performance	1	2	3	4	5	6	7	8	9	10
Comments ____________________										

What **benefits** did you _____ actually realize or _____ anticipate as a result of this project?

A. Quantitative Benefits

B. Qualitative Benefits

Suggestions on how we can improve our performance on future projects:

Name: ____________________ Date: __________

Critical Success FACTORS

- It is important to develop a plan before the start of the project. Taking the time to develop a well-thought-out plan is critical to the successful accomplishment of the project.
- Participation builds commitment. The people who will be involved in performing the project must participate in planning the work.
- Identify risks before the project starts that have a high likelihood of occurrence and/or may have a high impact on the project outcome.
- Develop contingency plans during the project planning process for addressing major risks.
- Schedule regular, face-to-face meetings with the customer.
- Regularly ask the customer about the level of satisfaction with the progress of the project.
- Keep the customer and project team informed of the project status and potential problems in a timely manner.
- The key to effective project control is measuring actual progress and comparing it to planned progress on a timely and regular basis and taking corrective action immediately, if necessary.
- After the conclusion of a project, the project performance should be evaluated to learn what could be improved if a similar project were to be done in the future. Feedback should be obtained from the customer and the project team.

probability that further expenditures on the project will yield a successful outcome is low, the project will be stopped, even though the company has several million dollars invested in it. Another circumstance that can cause a project to be terminated early is a change in a company's financial situation—for example, if a company's sales are going down or if the company is acquired by another company.

Projects also can be terminated by the customer because of dissatisfaction. For example, if the buyers of a house are not satisfied with the quality of the contractor's work or are frustrated with schedule delays, they may terminate the agreement with the contractor and hire another contractor to finish the project. Similarly, if the government is funding the design and production of new military aircraft and project costs begin to overrun the budget significantly, the government may terminate the contract.

Having a project terminated early by a dissatisfied customer can really hurt a contractor's business. The contractor may incur a financial loss due to early termination and may have to lay off some of the employees who were working on the project. More important, the contractor's reputation may be tarnished. There will likely be no future business from the dissatisfied customer, and a tarnished reputation could make it difficult for the contractor to obtain business from other customers. One way to avoid early termination of a project due to customer dissatisfaction is to monitor the level of customer satisfaction continually throughout the project and take corrective action at the first hint of any dissatisfaction.

Reinforce Your Learning

12. For a contractor, what are two potential consequences of having a project terminated early by a dissatisfied customer?

SUMMARY

Performing, or doing, the project—implementing the proposed solution—is the third phase of the project life cycle. This phase starts after a contract or agreement is drawn up between the customer and the contractor or project team, and it ends when the project objective is accomplished and the customer is satisfied that the work has been completed in a quality manner, within budget, and on time.

This third phase has two parts: doing the detailed planning for the project and then implementing that plan to accomplish the project objective. It is necessary to develop a plan that shows how the project tasks will be accomplished within budget and on schedule. Planning determines what needs to be done, who will do it, how long it will take, and how much it will cost. The result of the planning effort is a baseline plan for performing the project. It is important that the people who will be involved in performing the project also participate in planning the work. Participation builds commitment. Once a plan has been established, the project team, led by the project manager, implements the plan.

Risk management involves identifying, assessing, and responding to project risks in order to minimize the likelihood and impact of the consequences of adverse events on the achievement of the project objective. Risk identification includes determining which risks may adversely affect the project objective and what the consequences of each risk might be if they occur. Assessing each risk involves determining the likelihood that the risk event will occur and the degree of impact the event will have on the project objective. Risk response planning involves developing an action plan to reduce the impact or likelihood of each risk, establishing a trigger point for when to implement the actions to address each risk, and assigning responsibility to specific individuals for implementing each response plan. During the project, it is important to evaluate all risks to determine if there are any changes to the likelihood of occurrence or the potential impact of any of the risks; also, new risks maybe identified that were not considered as a risk earlier in the project.

While the project work is being performed by the project team, it is necessary to monitor progress to ensure that everything is going according to plan. The project control process involves regularly gathering data on project performance, comparing actual performance to planned performance, and taking corrective actions if actual performance is behind planned performance. Project management is a proactive approach to controlling a project, to ensure that the project objective is achieved even when things don't go according to plan. The fourth and final phase of the project life cycle is terminating the project. It starts after the project work has been completed. The purpose of this phase is to learn from the experience gained on the project in order to improve performance on future projects. Post-project evaluation activities include both individual meetings with team members and a group meeting with the project team. It is also important to meet with the customer to assess the level of customer satisfaction and determine whether the project provided the customer with the anticipated benefits. Projects may be terminated before completion for various reasons. They may be terminated by the customer because of dissatisfaction. This can result in a financial loss and tarnish the reputation of the contractor or organization performing the project. One way to avoid early termination due to customer dissatisfaction is to monitor the level of customer satisfaction continually throughout the project and take corrective action at the first hint of any dissatisfaction.

QUESTIONS

1. Describe why planning is so important, and list the steps involved in detailed planning.
2. Which phase of the life cycle involves performing the project? When can this phase be started?
3. Describe what might be involved in actually performing a project. List the activities that must be performed for a project on which you are currently working.
4. Think about a project on which you are currently working or have recently worked on. Describe the planning that you did before you started.
5. Describe the project control process. Discuss how it can be applied to a project on which you are currently working or one you have recently worked on.
6. Why is it important to control a project after it has started? How is this done? What can be done if the actual progress on a project doesn't match the expected progress?
7. Describe what needs to be done to manage risk on a project. When should this be done? How can a risk assessment matrix help in this process?
8. Why should a project have a well-defined reporting period? During each reporting period, what kinds of data need to be collected?
9. Discuss the internal postproject evaluation process and the two types of meetings involved.
10. Discuss what needs to be done as part of terminating a project. Why are these activities important?
11. Why are some projects terminated before they are completed? When would it be wise to do so?
12. What are some ways you can obtain feedback from a customer after a project has been completed? How would you use this information?

INTERNET EXERCISES

For the website addresses of the organizations mentioned in these exercises, go to "Internet Exercises" at the book's companion website at **international.cengage.com**. It is suggested that you save this website in your "Favorites" for easy access in the future.

1. Search the web for a project that was completed successfully. Write a three-page summary of the project, including the critical factors that made this project a success. Search the web for a project that was not completed successfully. Write a three-page summary of the project, including the reasons why you think this project failed.
2. Search the web for risk management software. Download a trial version if one is available. Write a two-page summary of the functions available in the software package. How does this compare to what was discussed in this chapter?

3. Search the web for post-project evaluations. Try to find a write-up of a project that was completed. Evaluate the strengths and weaknesses of the post-project review.
4. Search the web for project management standards. Provide a list of the standards that you find. Describe three that you feel are the most important.
5. Search the web and your library for project management journals. Provide a list of these journals and some of their recent articles. If possible, request a free sample from one or more of these journals.

CASE STUDY 1

Factory Expansion Project

Jacob Clemson is the owner of Digitsig, Inc., a growing Canadian electronics company. The company has been receiving orders from customers worldwide and sales have been expanding rapidly. The factory is now working three shifts and is at capacity. Jacob had to lease additional space in a building several miles away. He knows he must expand his factory to keep up with growing demand, to increase efficiency, and to reduce the costs associated with trucking materials and product back and forth between his factory and the building he is leasing. The cost of the lease was very high because there just wasn't much good available space in the area, and Jacob was desperate to get additional space right away, or he would not be able to keep up with demand and customers would go to his competitors.

Jacob met Andy Gibson, part-owner of AG Contractors, at a recent business networking event. He told Andy about his expansion needs. Andy said, "We can do that for you, Mr. Clemson. We've done many similar projects. As you may know, business is booming in the region, and getting a contractor won't be easy. But, it could be lucky we met because we are just finishing up another project and could probably get working on yours if we can get an agreement soon. I've got four other proposals pending, and if they come in we won't be able to handle any other projects. And like I said, I understand all the other contractors are just as busy. It sounds like you really need to start on this factory expansion right away, and I think we can help you out."

Jacob became worried that he might not be able to get another contractor, and he didn't want to waste any more time. So he signed a contract with AG Contractors, for what he thought was a reasonable price, to design and build the expansion to his factory. The expansion space would be used primarily for inventory storage of incoming materials and finished goods. He agreed to a bonus clause in the contract to pay AG Contractors a 10 percent bonus if they completed the building in 12 months rather than the 15 months Andy told him it would normally take.

It is now 14 months later. Andy Gibson and Gerri Penk, a recently hired project manager for AG Contractors, walked into Jacob Clemson's office. The receptionist asked, "May I help you?"

Andy asked, "Is Jacob in?"

"Yes, he is. Do you have an appointment?" responded the receptionist. Andy hurried by the receptionist, saying, "I don't need one. This will only take a minute." A surprised Gerri followed after him. He knocked on Mr. Clemson's door once, opened it, and walked in without waiting for a response.

Astonished, Jacob Clemson looked up and said, "I'm right in the middle of this important . . ."

Andy interrupted. "This will only take a minute. I just wanted to say that we got your factory expansion project completed on time and within budget. We finished in 12 months, just like I knew we, I mean, like I hoped we would. I had to kick butt with some of our subcontractors, but that's the way it goes in this business. Sometimes you've got to be an SOB to get the job done. I'm sure you're the same way, Jacob, or you wouldn't be where you're at."

Jacob Clemson spoke up. "Well, there were some problems . . ."

But Andy interrupted again. "In a big project like this there are always problems, and some people's feathers get ruffled. But that always happens. Don't be concerned about that. In the end it all worked out. I thought maybe we could go to lunch to celebrate, but we have another meeting across town. Give me a call sometime, and maybe we can get together and see if I can help you with any other projects you might have." Andy then turned and quickly left Jacob's office, walking right past Gerri, who ran to catch up with him.

As they left, Jacob was somewhat stunned and became furious. He thought to himself, "Another project? Over my dead body. An SOB? What kind of person does he think I am? Getting the project done on time and within budget—does he think that is all that it's about? This project was a nightmare. It finished up costing about 50 percent more than AG's original price because of all the changes they came back with. They never asked, never listened, never told me what was going on, and never returned my phone calls. What a bunch of jerks! I'll never do business with them again."

As Andy and Gerri walked to Andy's car, he told Gerri, "There you go, another satisfied AG customer. And a pretty naive one too [chuckled Andy]. I knew we could get the project done in 12 months. But I knew he was desperate, and I told him it would take 15 months, and then got him to agree to a bonus payment if we got it done in 12 months."

Gerri asked, "Andy, isn't that unethical?"

"Hey, business is booming for Digitsig, they have plenty of money. Besides, it's his problem for waiting so long before deciding on doing the expansion anyway. He was lucky we helped him out of a bind. But I've got to tell you, Gerri, I wondered why he was building all that warehouse space for inventory when most other businesses are going to just-in-time deliveries. But I wasn't about to tell him that. It's amazing he's in business at all. Oh, well, you'll find out it's a dog-eat-dog world out there, Gerri."

Gerri responded, "Andy, I got a sense that maybe Mr. Clemson wasn't totally satisfied. I mean he really didn't say he was."

"He didn't say he wasn't either," snapped Andy. "Besides, he never seemed interested in the project, he never asked to have any meetings, and when I tried to schedule a meeting, he was too busy. And then his payments were always late—like he was anal or something. Believe me, he's tickled with what AG did. He was desperate to get the project done, and we did it for him—on time and within budget. And made a bunch of money on the project. So we both came out winners."

"In fact, I'll use old Jacob as a reference with the new customer we'll be meeting this afternoon to review their RFP. Customers always ask for references from previous projects, but quite frankly, they hardly ever call them."

"Hey, Gerri, you'll learn that you've got to focus on the next customer and not worry about the old ones. It works, believe me, or I wouldn't be driving this

Porsche. Maybe they didn't teach you that in MBA school Gerri, but I learned from the school of hard knocks when I took this business over from my father. He was well liked in the community, and I'm just following in his footsteps."

CASE QUESTIONS

1. What should Andy Gibson have done differently in his meeting with Jacob Clemson in Jacob's office?
2. What are some things Andy could have done differently from his initial contact with Mr. Clemson and during the project?
3. What are some things Jacob could have done differently from the time he met Andy Gibson initially and during the project?
4. What should Gerri do?

GROUP ACTIVITY

Divide the course participants into groups of three or four to develop responses to the case questions. Each group must choose a spokesperson to present its responses to the entire class.

CASE STUDY 2

Student Fund-Raising Project

In September at its initial meeting of the academic year, the Council of Fraternities and Sororities (CFS) at Mount Clement University decided to organize a project to raise funds to help upgrade the pediatric intensive care unit at the local hospital. The CFS consists of representatives from each of the 24 fraternities and sororities. There were 15 representatives at the meeting.

Although the Council members who were at the meeting expressed enthusiasm for such an endeavor, they also raised some concerns, including:

- What kind of project should we do?
- When would be the best time of the year to do it?
- Do we have a goal for how much money we should try to raise?
- How should we assign responsibilities to all the fraternities and sororities?
- What about the Council members who aren't at the meeting? What if they don't support the idea?
- Are we going to need any money at the beginning to get things going and pay for things like advertising and other things?
- Do we need any kind of approvals?

Hannah said, "This is getting complicated. There are a lot of questions and unknowns."

Marcus added, "What if we don't raise a lot of money? That will be embarrassing, especially if we have to do a lot of work."

Teresa responded, "Sure it may be a lot of work, but we have a lot of people in our fraternities and sororities who we can get to help."

Cathy said, "Maybe we should try to identify what the risks may be, then see if we still think we can do it?"

Meghan said, "I'm not going to stand on corners with a can collecting money."

Wendy added, "Me either, but there are a lot of other things we can do to raise money that could be fun for all the students."

"Maybe even get the community to come too. That will help us raise more money than just from students," added Sophie.

Suli spoke up, "I'm willing to chair a planning committee. Who else wants to be on it? We'll meet here tomorrow at 5:00. I'll send an e-mail to the CFS members who aren't here, inviting them to come. We are going big time and are going to raise a lot of money. Hey, there are risks in anything we do, but they'll work out. We got to have a can-do attitude."

CASE QUESTIONS

1. What would you recommend for the next possible steps?
2. Identify three potential projects to raise funds for the hospital pediatric intensive care unit.
3. Select one of the three projects and identify four risks that could jeopardize the success of the project.
4. Develop a response plan for how each of the four risks can either be avoided or mitigated.

GROUP ACTIVITY

Divide the course participants into teams of three or four. Have them:

- Brainstorm a list of eight possible projects to raise funds for the hospital.
- Agree on one of the eight projects.
- For the selected project, identify six risks that could jeopardize the success of the project.
- Develop a response plan for how each of the six risks can either be avoided or mitigated.

Have each team select a spokesperson to present their responses to the entire class.

Project Planning and Control

PART 2

CHAPTERS

5 Planning

Covers determining what activities need to be done, who will be responsible for them, and in what sequence they will be carried out.

6 Scheduling

Deals with estimating the durations for all activities and developing a detailed project schedule that states when each activity should start and finish.

7 Schedule Control

Discusses monitoring the progress of the project and replanning and updating the project schedule if necessary.

8 Resource Considerations

Explains the incorporation of resource requirements and constraints into the project plan and schedule.

9 Cost Planning and Performance

Includes estimating project costs, developing a project budget, analyzing project cost performance, and forecasting total costs at project completion.

The chapters in Part 2 address techniques for planning and controlling a project in order to achieve the project objective successfully. Planning determines *what* needs to be done, *who* will do it, *how long* it will take, and *how much* it will cost. Taking the time to develop a well-thought-out plan is critical to the successful accomplishment of the project objective. Developing a detailed plan includes: (1) defining the specific activities needed to perform the project and assigning responsibility for each; (2) determining the sequence in which those activities must be accomplished; (3) estimating the time and resources that will be needed for each activity; and (4) preparing a project schedule and budget. Many projects have overrun their budgets, missed their completion dates, or only partially met their technical specifications because no viable plan was created before the project was started. To avoid this, you must *plan the work, then work the plan.*

Once a plan has been established, it must be implemented. This means performing the work according to the plan and controlling the work so that the project scope is accomplished within budget and on schedule. Once the project starts, it's necessary to monitor progress to ensure that everything is going according to the plan. This involves measuring actual progress and comparing it to planned progress. If, at any time, the project is not proceeding according to plan, corrective action must be taken and replanning must be done. The key to effective project control is comparing actual progress with the plan on a timely and regular basis and taking any needed corrective action immediately.

© Brand X Pictures/Jupiter Images

CHAPTER 5

Planning

Real World PROJECT MANAGEMENT

Norfolk County, U.K., Launches a Massive Project

Norfolk County, U.K., a sparsely populated county in England, realized that they were paying the price for a lack of the latest broadband services. The county, located just 109.4 miles (176 kilometers) outside of London, was suffering because its lack of broadband services made it less attractive to new residents and businesses. Many municipalities and counties in England had been starting to regard broadband technology to be as critical as other pieces of infrastructure, such as roads or water and sewer systems. Kurt Frary, integration authority at Norfolk County Council, was concerned about falling behind in the technology arena in comparison to the rest of the country.

Norfolk County, UK, had a few wireless hot spots at coffee shops and hotels; however, users were expected to pay between $9 and $11 per hour to use the technology, and the range was very limited. The Norfolk County Council formed a steering committee to explore the possibility of making broadband capabilities widely available. The county realized that it couldn't fund such a large-scale project but luckily, the East of England Development Agency (EEDA) wanted to fund a broadband project that would demonstrate new and innovative technology. The steering committee decided that a wireless city would best meet the requirement outlined by EEDA. This decision would eventually result in a project that would allow Norfolk County to stake a claim as the largest free community wireless network in the UK.

The EEDA granted Norfolk County $2.05 million dollars to fund the Norfolk Open Link project in December 2004. The Norfolk County Council planned to establish broadband capabilities in the urban areas first and then expand the network to some rural regions. The network requirements were that it should:

1. be easy to use
2. increase the efficiency of public-sector operations (i.e. universities, hospitals)
3. help small businesses with day-to-day operations; and
4. support free public network services.

In November 2005, Norfolk County awarded the deployment contract to Synetrix, a systems integrator located in Staffordshire, UK. The project team was initially assigned the responsibility of creating a communications plan to define the project's brand and message; create a website; and manage the media and relationships with the stakeholders.

The entire project timeline spanned from December 2004 to a projected end date of April 2008. Clear milestones were defined, including defining the project requirements; writing the RFP; selecting the winning contractor; designing the network; testing the network; launching the initial network publicly; and then rolling the network out to rural areas.

A large challenge for the project team was securing more than 200 aerial locations (such as lampposts and buildings) needed for network communication support on street structures. This required altering some streetlights to accommodate the new equipment and running numerous desktop exercises to ensure the effectiveness of the procedure.

The initial phase of the project covered a 2.5-mile radius around Norwich, where the city hall is located. Once the entire network is fully deployed, approximately 9.3 square miles will be covered. The network build-out is divided into three phases: (1) bringing connectivity to the city center; (2) expanding to regions supporting major businesses; and (3) deploying up to 28 hot spots in rural locations.

To date, the team has used weekly conference calls and/or face-to-face meetings to enhance communications and to monitor the progress of the project. Monthly presentations to key stakeholders were also scheduled. In addition, a web-based project document repository was established to allow the project team members and stakeholders to have access to relevant project information. The goal was to have a coordinated, consistent, and proactive approach to handling all project communications.

The early results of the project look very promising! All of the advanced planning appears to be paying off. The project is on schedule and within budget. Currently, the network is still in the pilot phase but small businesses have already reported an increase in efficiency and reduced costs. More than 13,000 individuals used the network in the first four weeks. In addition, the network successfully supports wireless cameras for traffic monitoring and information kiosks. Mr. Frary stated, "Early indicators are that it's so popular that it's going to be difficult to turn it off if we ever have to."

Mentrup, L., "Broad Appeal," *PM Network*, December 2006.

This chapter describes techniques used to plan the work elements and activities that need to be carried out in order to accomplish a project. You will become familiar with

- clearly defining the project objective
- developing a work breakdown structure
- developing a network diagram
- utilizing a project management methodology called the systems development life cycle for information systems development projects

Planning is the systematic arrangement of tasks to accomplish an objective. The plan lays out what needs to be accomplished and how it is to be accomplished. The plan becomes a benchmark against which actual progress can be compared; then, if deviations occur, corrective action can be taken.

It is important that the people who will be involved in performing the work are also involved in planning the work. They are usually the most knowledgeable about what detailed activities need to be done and how long each should take. By participating in the planning of the work, individuals will become committed to accomplishing it according to the plan and within the schedule and budget. *Participation builds commitment.* In large, with multiyear projects that include hundreds or even thousands of people, it's not possible to involve everyone in the initial planning. As the project progresses, however, it may be possible to involve many of these individuals in developing more detailed plans.

PROJECT OBJECTIVE

The first step in the planning process is to define the project objective—the expected result or end product. The objective must be clearly defined and agreed upon by the customer and the organization or contractor that will perform the project. The objective must be clear, attainable, specific, and measurable. Achievement of the project objective must be easily recognizable by both the customer and the contractor. The objective is the target—the tangible end product that the project team must deliver.

For a project, the objective is usually defined in terms of scope, schedule, and cost—it requires completing the work within budget by a certain time. For example, the objective of a project might be to "introduce to the market in 10 months and within a budget of $2 million a new electronic household cooking product, which meets certain predefined performance specifications." Another example is to "produce a four-color, 16-page, back-to-school merchandise catalogue and mail it by July 31 to all targeted potential customers in the county, within a budget of $40,000."

Reinforce Your Learning

1. For a project, the objective is usually defined in terms of

______________,
______________,
and
______________.

A project objective such as "complete the house" is too ambiguous, because the customer and the contractor may have different views of what is meant by "complete." A better objective is to "complete the house by May 31 in accordance with the floor plans and specifications dated October 15 and within a budget of $150,000." The specifications and floor plans provide the details as to the scope of the work that the contractor agreed to perform. Therefore, no arguments should arise about whether the landscaping and carpeting were to be included or about the size of the entrance door, the color of paint in the bedrooms, or the style of lighting fixtures. All of these should have been spelled out in the specifications.

Ideally, the project objective should be clear and concise at the beginning of the project. However, sometimes the project objective needs to be modified as the project proceeds. The project manager and the client must agree on all changes to the initial project objective. Any such changes might affect the work scope, completion date, and final cost.

Reinforce Your Learning

2. State the project objective for a project you are currently working on (or have recently worked on).

WORK BREAKDOWN STRUCTURE

Once the project objective has been defined, the next step is to determine what work elements, or activities, need to be performed to accomplish it. This requires developing a list of all the activities. There are two approaches to preparing such a list. One is to have the project team "brainstorm" the list of activities. This approach is suitable for small projects; however, for larger, more complex projects, it's difficult to develop a comprehensive list of activities without forgetting some items. For such projects, creating a **work breakdown structure (WBS)** is a better approach.

Reinforce Your Learning

3. What is a work breakdown structure?

The WBS breaks a project down into manageable pieces, or items, to help ensure that all of the work elements needed to complete the project work scope are identified. It's a hierarchical tree of end items that will be accomplished or produced by the project team during the project. The accomplishment or production of all of these items constitutes completion of the project work scope. An example of a WBS for a town festival is shown in Figure 5.1.

FIGURE 5.1 ***Work Breakdown Structure for Festival Project***

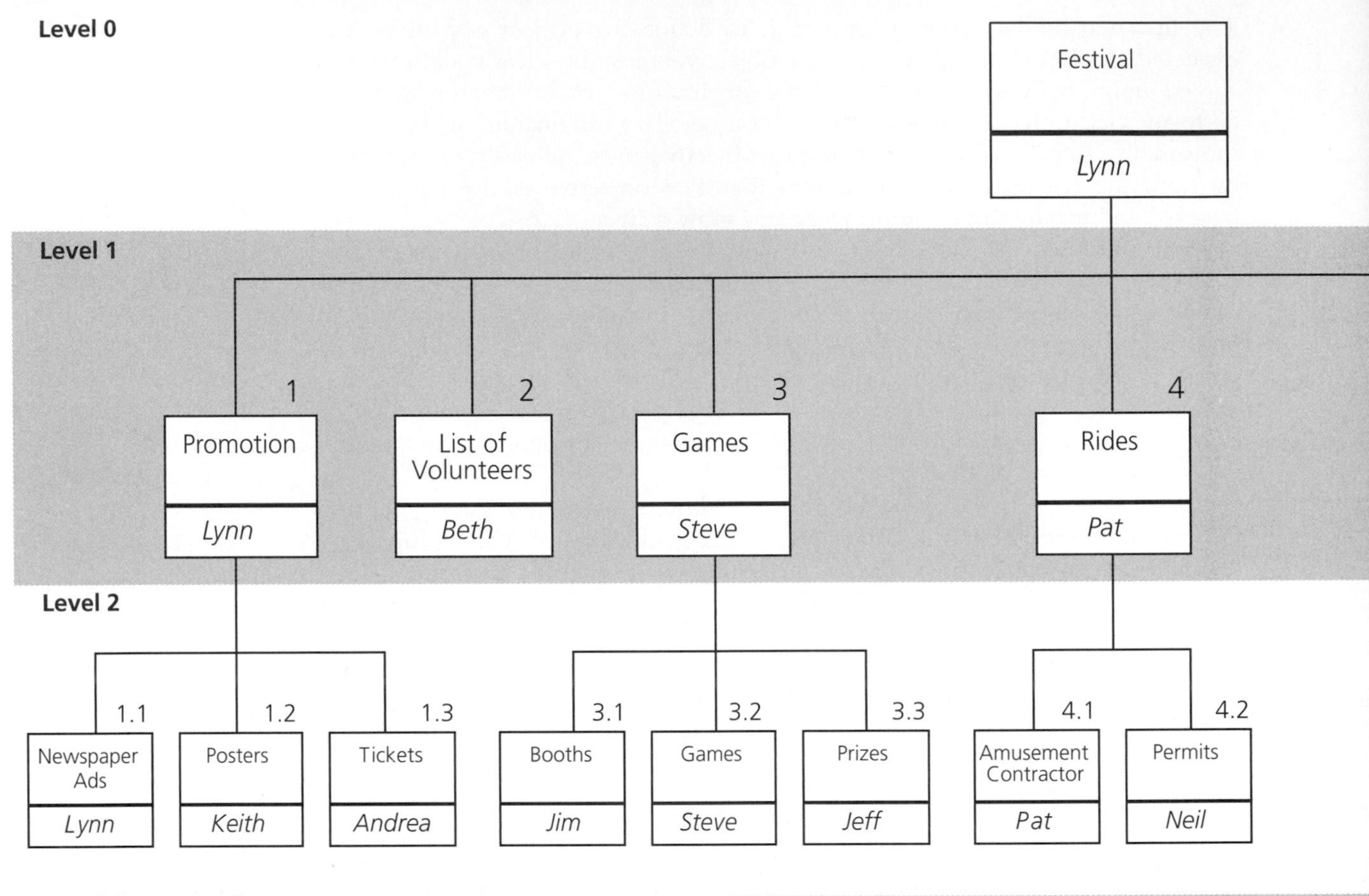

Reinforce Your Learning

4. The lowest-level work item for any given branch of the work breakdown structure is called a

____
____________________.

The graphic structure subdivides the project into smaller pieces called **work items**. Not all branches of the WBS have to be broken down to the same level. The lowest-level item of any one branch is called a **work package**. Most work packages shown in Figure 5.1 are at the second level,

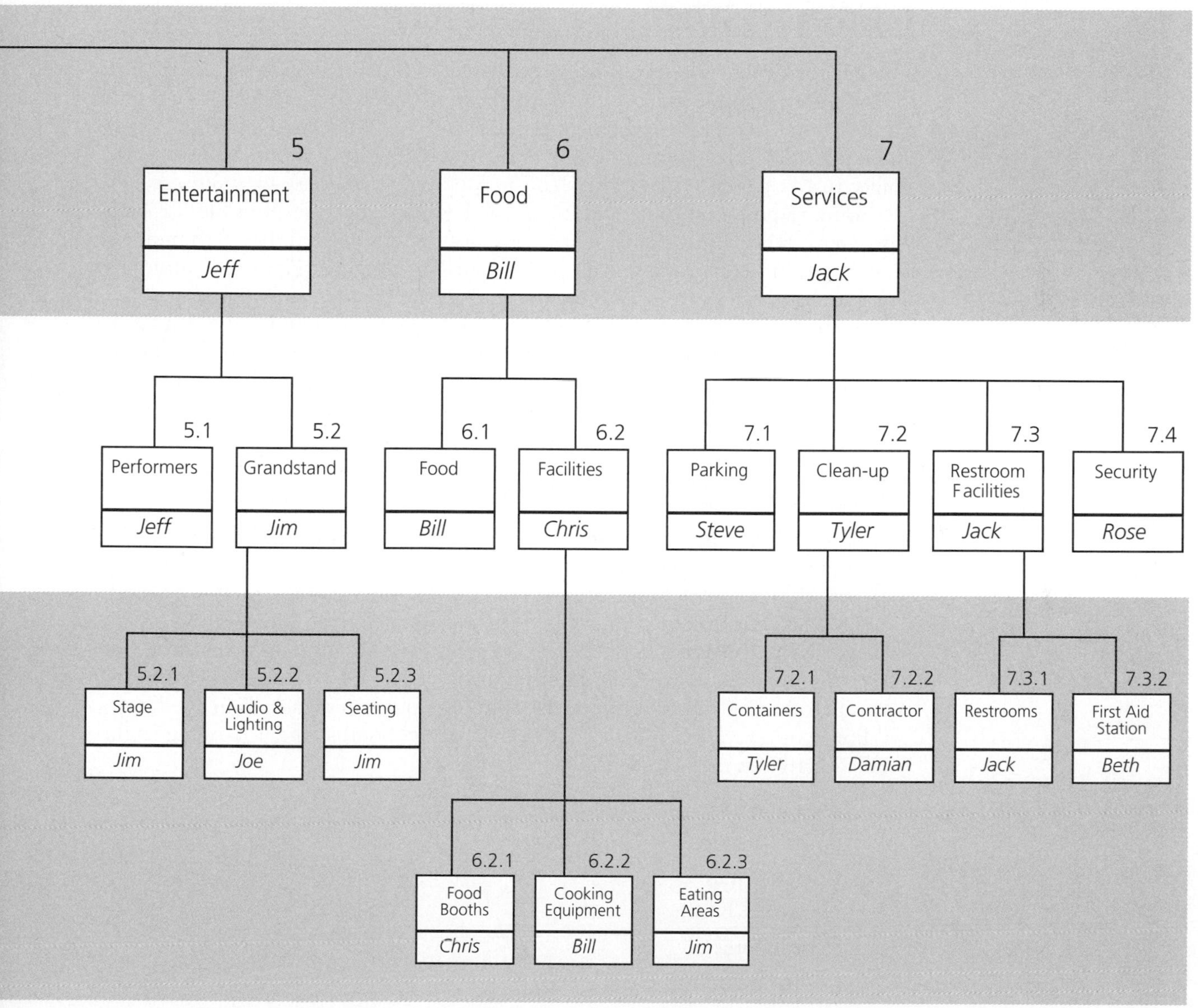

but four work items are further divided into a more detailed third level; one work item (List of Volunteers) is not broken down beyond the first level. The WBS usually indicates the organization or individual responsible for each work item.

The criteria for deciding how much detail or how many levels to put in the WBS are (1) the level at which a single individual or organization can be assigned responsibility and accountability for accomplishing the work package and (2) the level at which you want to control the budget and monitor and collect cost data during the project. There is not a single correct WBS for any project. For example, two different project teams might develop somewhat different WBSs for the same project.

RESPONSIBILITY MATRIX

The **responsibility matrix** is a method used to display, in tabular format, the individuals responsible for accomplishing the work items in the WBS. It's a useful tool because it emphasizes who is responsible for each work item and shows each individual's role in supporting the overall project. Figure 5.2 shows the responsibility matrix associated with the WBS in Figure 5.1 for the festival project.

Reinforce Your Learning

5. A responsibility matrix shows which individual is responsible for accomplishing each

____

____

in the work breakdown structure.

Some responsibility matrices use an *X* to show who is responsible for each work item; others use a *P* to designate primary responsibility and an *S* to indicate support responsibility for a specific work item. For example, Figure 5.2 indicates that Jim has primary responsibility for the game booths, with Chris and Joe supporting this effort. It is a good idea to show only one individual as the lead, or primary, person responsible for each work item. Designating two individuals as cochairpersons increases the risk that certain work will "fall through the cracks" because each person assumes that the other person is going to do it.

DEFINING ACTIVITIES

As noted earlier, a list of specific, detailed activities necessary to accomplish the overall project can be generated through team brainstorming, especially for small projects. However, for projects in which a work breakdown structure is used, individual activities can be defined by the person or team responsible for each work package. An **activity** is a defined piece of work that consumes time. It does not necessarily require the expenditure of effort by people—for example, waiting for concrete to harden can take several days but does not require any human effort.

For work package 3.1 in Figure 5.1, game booths, the following eight detailed activities may be identified:

Design booths
Specify materials
Buy materials
Construct booths
Paint booths
Dismantle booths
Move booths to festival site and reassemble
Dismantle booths and move to storage

When all the detailed activities have been defined for each of the work packages, the next step is to graphically portray them in a network diagram that shows the appropriate sequence and interrelationships needed to accomplish the overall project work scope.

FIGURE 5.2 ***Responsibility Matrix for Festival Project***

WBS Item	Work Item	Andrea	Beth	Bill	Chris	Damian	Jack	Jeff	Jim	Joe	Keith	Lynn	Neil	Pat	Rose	Steve	Tyler
	Festival		S	S			S	S				**P**		S		S	
1	**Promotion**	S									S	**P**					
1.1	Newspaper Ads											**P**					
1.2	Posters										**P**						
1.3	Tickets	**P**	S									S					
2	**List of Volunteers**		**P**						S						S		
3	**Games**							S	S							**P**	
3.1	Booths				S				**P**	S							
3.2	Games														S	**P**	
3.3	Prizes							**P**							S		
4	**Rides**												S	**P**			
4.1	Amusement Contractor													**P**			
4.2	Permits												**P**	S			
5	**Entertainment**							**P**	S	S							
5.1	Performers					S		**P**									
5.2	Grandstand								**P**	S							
5.2.1	Stage								**P**	S							
5.2.2	Audio & Lighting									**P**							
5.2.3	Seating					S			**P**								
6	**Food**			**P**	S												
6.1	Food			**P**											S		
6.2	Facilities			S	**P**				S								
6.2.1	Food Booths				**P**				S	S							
6.2.2	Cooking Equipment			**P**													
6.2.3	Eating Areas								**P**						S		
7	**Services**						**P**								S	S	S
7.1	Parking															**P**	
7.2	Clean-up					S											**P**
7.2.1	Containers																**P**
7.2.2	Contractor					**P**											
7.3	Restroom Facilities		S				**P**										
7.3.1	Restrooms						**P**										
7.3.2	First Aid Stations		**P**														
7.4	Security					S				S					**P**		

KEY: **P** = Primary responsibility; S = Support responsibility.

Real World PROJECT MANAGEMENT

Johns Hopkins Hospital's $252M Cost Overrun

Johns Hopkins Hospital is respected as one of the world's best medical care providers. People travel great lengths to visit Johns Hopkins Hospital in order to be seen by their world-renowned doctors. They have a wonderful history of saving lives and making a positive difference in the lives of many people. However, like many organizations, Johns Hopkins faces the challenge of bringing its projects in on time and on budget.

A current project that includes plans to build two new clinical towers (which will house 530 new beds) and plans to renovate their East Baltimore campus is now $252 million dollars over budget and two years behind schedule! The budget was originally set at a billion dollars, with a completion date of October 2014. Johns Hopkins is now hoping that without any additional cost overruns or schedule delays it can bring the project to completion by October 2016.

On the 5th of December, the hospital filed an application with the Maryland Health Care Commission seeking the state's approval for the new proposed schedule and budget. Unfortunately, this is the second time on this project that Johns Hopkins had to notify the state of cost overruns and schedule delays. The first time Johns Hopkins requested an extension, just a year-and-a-half earlier, they projected that they were eight months behind schedule and $190M over budget. According to the *Baltimore Business Journal*, Johns Hopkins cited significantly increased supply costs and a serious lack of skilled laborers as the major causes for the problems with the project.

In addition to the Johns Hopkins project, more than a dozen other hospital construction projects are planned or under way in the Greater Baltimore area. Several of these projects are significant is size and range from a projected cost of $200M to $400M. In addition, due to the Base Realignment and Closure (BRAC) process, which is bringing thousands of new jobs to the state, numerous other multimillion-dollar construction projects are underway at Aberdeen Proving Ground (APG) and Fort George G. Meade—both locations being within 30 miles of Baltimore.

All of the construction activity in the region is causing materials and laborers to be in high demand and more expensive. According to Sally MacConnell, vice president of facilities for Johns Hopkins Hospital, "We are in an unprecedented time of construction inflation. The marketplace is very busy and our project is very large."

The Johns Hopkins project is financed through their capital campaign, operating revenues, and numerous bonds. In order to help pay for the cost overrun, the hospital plans to ask the state agency that sets hospital rates to increase the rates its patients pay in order to generate more revenue. In addition, Johns Hopkins will have to turn to its donors to help raise significant funds. On the positive side, Johns Hopkins officials stated that they have now forged a new agreement with the builders to lock in an overall maximum price for the project. Any costs above that price would be absorbed by the builders, not the hospital.

Running a project of this size is not an easy task. It takes effective planning, scheduling, communications, coordination, tracking, leadership, and teamwork to be successful. And with that, hopefully, mistakes of this magnitude will be avoided!

Schultz, S., "Hopkins Project Delayed, Over Budget," *Baltimore Business Journal*, December 24, 2007.

DEVELOPING THE NETWORK PLAN

Network planning is a technique that is helpful in planning, scheduling, and controlling projects that consist of many interrelated activities.

Two network planning techniques, **program evaluation and review technique (PERT)** and the **critical path method (CPM)**, were developed in the 1950s. Since that time, other forms of network planning, such as the **precedence diagramming method (PDM)** and the **graphical evaluation and review technique (GERT)**, have been developed. All of these fall under the general category of network planning techniques, because they all make use of a **network diagram** to show the sequential flow and interrelationships of activities.

In the past, there were distinguishable methodological differences between PERT and CPM. Today, however, when most people refer to a CPM diagram or PERT chart, they mean a generic network diagram. See Figures 5.8 and 5.9 (discussed later in this chapter) for examples of network diagrams for a project to conduct a consumer market study; Figure 5.14 is an example of a project to develop a web-based reporting system.

Network planning techniques are often compared with a somewhat more familiar tool known as a **Gantt chart** (sometimes called a **bar chart**). This is an older planning and scheduling tool, developed in the early 1900s; however, it remains very popular today, mainly because of its simplicity.

The Gantt chart combines the two functions of planning and scheduling. Figure 5.3 shows a Gantt chart for a consumer market study. Activities are listed down the left-hand side, and a time scale is shown along the bottom. The estimated duration for each activity is indicated by a line or bar spanning the period during which the activity is expected to be accomplished. Columns that indicate who is responsible for each task can be added to the chart.

With Gantt charts, the scheduling of activities occurs simultaneously with their planning. The person drawing the activity lines or bars must be aware of the interrelationships of the activities—that is, which activities must be finished before others can start and which activities can be performed concurrently. One of the major drawbacks to the traditional Gantt chart is that it does not graphically display the interrelationships of activities. Therefore, it's not obvious which activities will be affected when a given activity is delayed. However, most project management software packages can produce Gantt charts that display the interdependencies among tasks by using connecting arrows.

Because planning and scheduling are done simultaneously in a traditional Gantt chart, it is cumbersome to make changes to the plan manually. This is especially true if an activity at the beginning of the project is delayed and thus many of the remaining lines or bars have to be redrawn. Network techniques, on the other hand, separate the planning and scheduling functions. A network diagram is the result, or output, of the planning function and is not drawn to a time scale.

From this diagram a schedule is developed (this topic will be covered in detail in the next chapter). Separating the two functions makes it much easier to revise a plan and calculate an updated schedule.

FIGURE 5.3 ***Gantt Chart for Consumer Market Study Project***

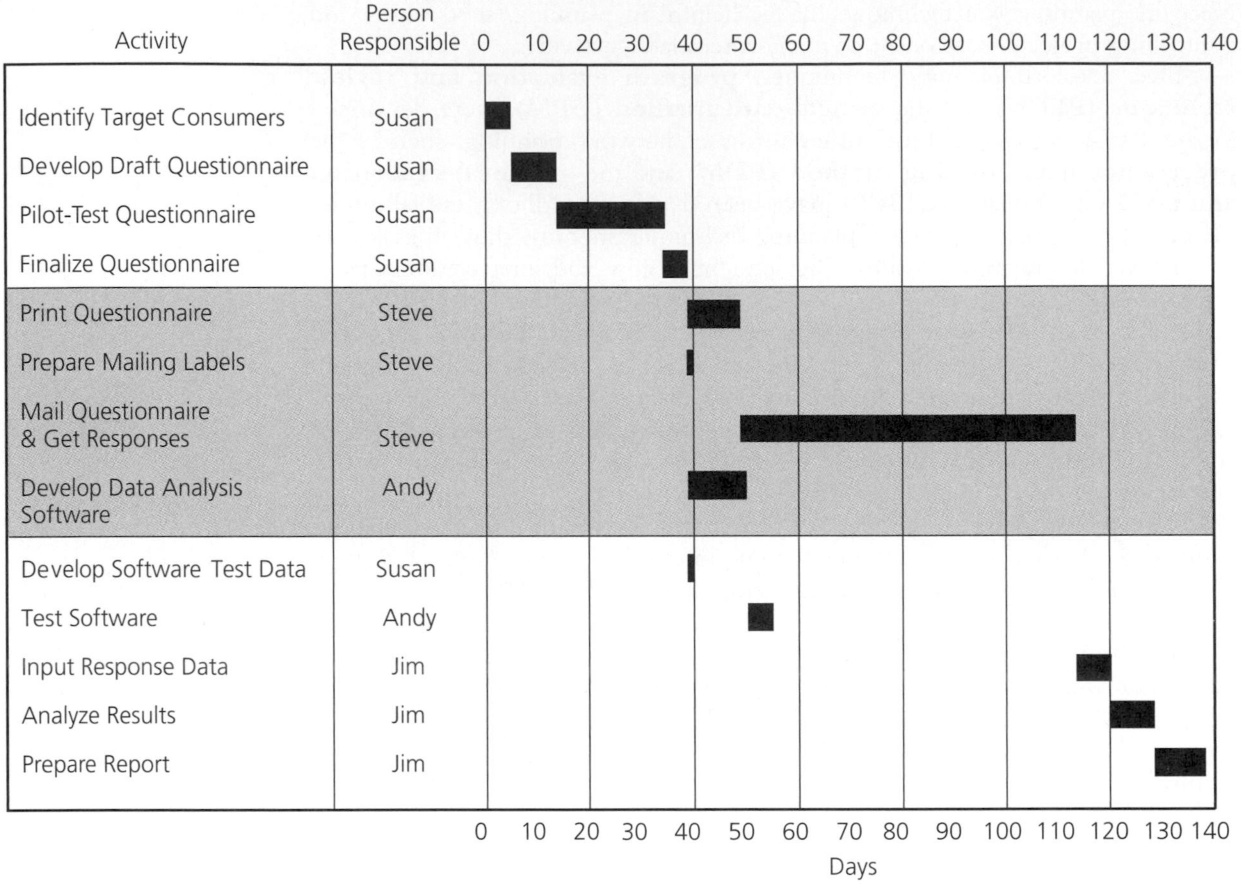

Activity
Person Responsible
0 10 20 30 40 50 60 70 80 90 100 110 120 130 140
Identify Target Consumers
Susan
Develop Draft Questionnaire
Susan
Pilot-Test Questionnaire
Susan
Finalize Questionnaire
Susan
Print Questionnaire
Steve
Prepare Mailing Labels
Steve
Mail Questionnaire & Get Responses
Steve
Develop Data Analysis Software
Andy
Develop Software Test Data
Susan
Test Software
Andy
Input Response Data
Jim
Analyze Results
Jim
Prepare Report
Jim
0 10 20 30 40 50 60 70 80 90 100 110 120 130 140
Days

Network Principles

Reinforce Your Learning

6. Identify two formats for drawing a network diagram.

There are a few basic principles that must be understood and followed in preparing a network diagram. There are also different formats that can be used in drawing the diagram. One format is **activity in the box (AIB)**, also known as activity on the node (AON). Another format is **activity on the arrow (AOA)**.

ACTIVITY IN THE BOX (AIB)

In the AIB format, each activity is represented by a box in the network diagram, and the description of the activity is written within the box, as shown below.

Get Volunteers
7

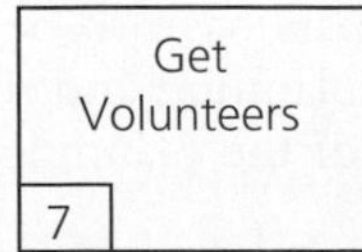

Activities consume time, and their description usually starts with a verb. Each activity is represented by one and only one box. In addition, each box is assigned a *unique* activity number. In the above example, the activity "Get Volunteers" has been given activity number 7.

Activities have a **precedential relationship**—that is, they are linked in a precedential order to show which activities must be finished before others can start. Arrows linking the activity boxes show the direction of precedence. *An activity cannot start until all of the preceding activities that are linked to it by arrows have been finished.*

Certain activities have to be done in serial order. For example, as shown below, only after "Wash Car" is finished can "Dry Car" start.

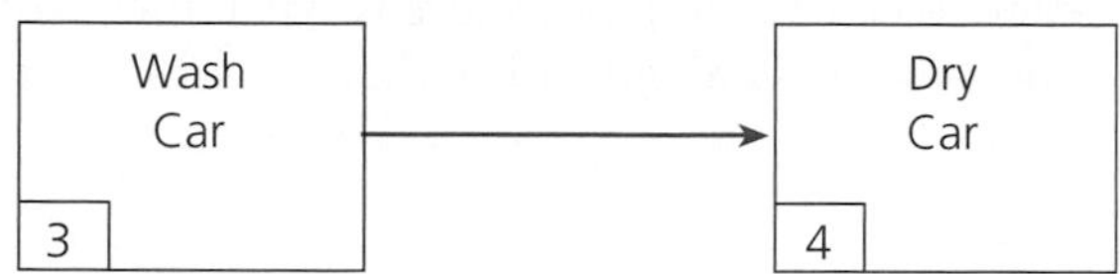

Some activities may be done concurrently. For example, as shown below, "Get Volunteers" and "Buy Materials" can be done concurrently; when they are *both* finished, "Construct Booth" can start. Similarly, when "Paint Booth" is finished, *both* "Dismantle Booth" and "Clean Up" can start and be worked on concurrently.

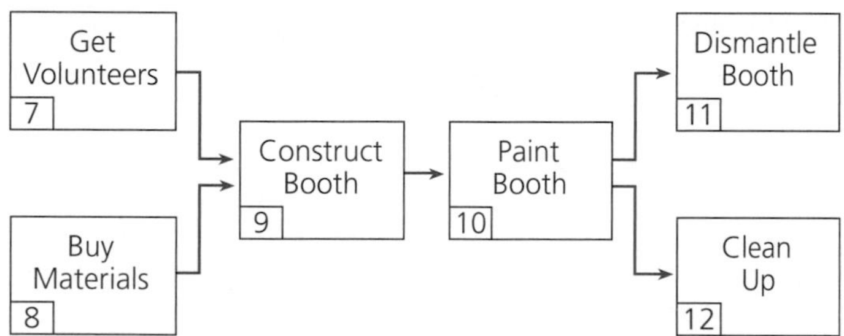

ACTIVITY ON THE ARROW (AOA)

In the AOA format, an activity is represented by an arrow in the network diagram, and the activity description is written above the arrow, as shown below.

Each activity is represented by one and only one arrow. The tail of the arrow designates the start of the activity, and the head of the arrow represents the completion of the activity. The length and slope of the arrow are in no way indicative of the activity's duration or importance (unlike the situation in the Gantt chart, in which the length of the line or bar indicates the duration of the activity).

In the AOA format, activities are linked by circles called **events**. An event represents the finish of activities entering into it and the start of activities going out of it. In the AOA format, each event—not each activity—is assigned a unique number. For example, the activities shown below, "Wash Car" and "Dry Car," have a serial relationship and are linked together by event 2. Event 2 represents the completion of "Wash Car" and the start of "Dry Car."

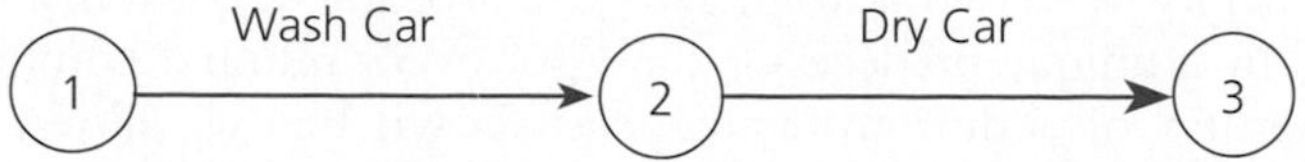

Reinforce Your Learning

7. Activities are linked in a ______________ order to show which activities must be ______________ before others can be ______________.

Reinforce Your Learning

8. In the activity-on-the-arrow format for drawing a network diagram, activities are linked together by circles called ______________.

The event at the beginning (tail of the arrow) of the activity is known as the activity's **predecessor event**, and the event at the end (head of the arrow) of the activity is known as the activity's **successor event**. For the activity "Wash Car," the predecessor event is 1 and the successor event is 2; for the activity "Dry Car," the predecessor event is 2 and the successor event is 3.

All activities going into an event (circle) must be finished before any activities leading from that event can start. For example, as shown below, the activities "Get Volunteers" and "Buy Materials" can be done concurrently, but only when they are *both* finished can the activity "Construct Booth" start. Similarly, when "Paint Booth" is finished, *both* "Dismantle Booth" and "Clean Up" can start and be worked on concurrently.

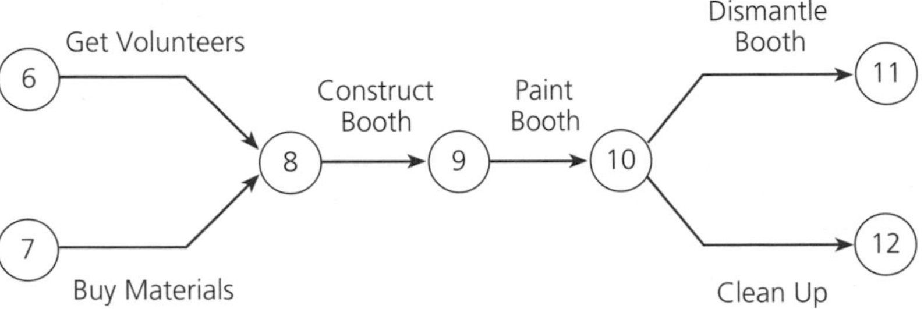

DUMMY ACTIVITIES

In the activity-on-the-arrow format, there is a special type of activity known as a **dummy activity**, which consumes zero time and is represented by a dashed arrow in the network diagram. Dummy activities, which are used only with the activity-on-the-arrow format, are needed for two reasons: to help in the unique identification of activities and to show certain precedential relationships that otherwise could not be shown.

In drawing an activity-on-the-arrow network diagram, there are two basic rules with regard to the unique identification of activities:

1. Each event (circle) in the network diagram must have a unique event number—that is, no two events in the network diagram can have the same event number.
2. Each activity must have a unique combination of predecessor and successor event numbers.

Activities A and B below both have the predecessor-successor event number combination 1–2. This is not allowed in an AOA network diagram, because if someone referred to activity 1–2, you would not know whether activity A or activity B was being discussed.

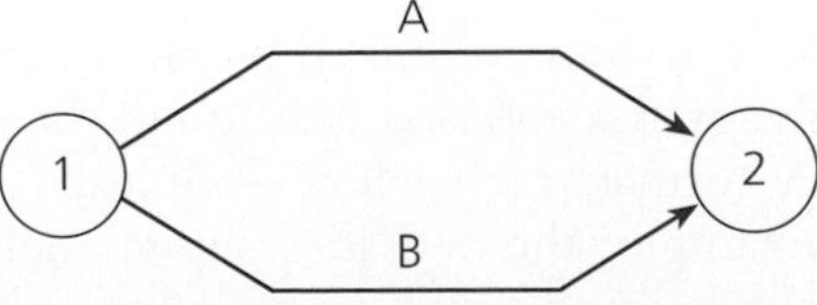

If computer software is used to calculate a project schedule based on an activity-on-the-arrow network diagram, it will probably require that each activity be identified by a unique predecessor-successor event number combination.

The insertion of a dummy activity, as shown below, allows activities A and B to have unique predecessor–successor event number combinations.

In (a), activity A is referred to as 1–3 and activity B as 1–2. Similarly, in (b), activity A is referred to as 1–2 and activity B as 1–3. Both approaches are acceptable ways of dealing with this situation.

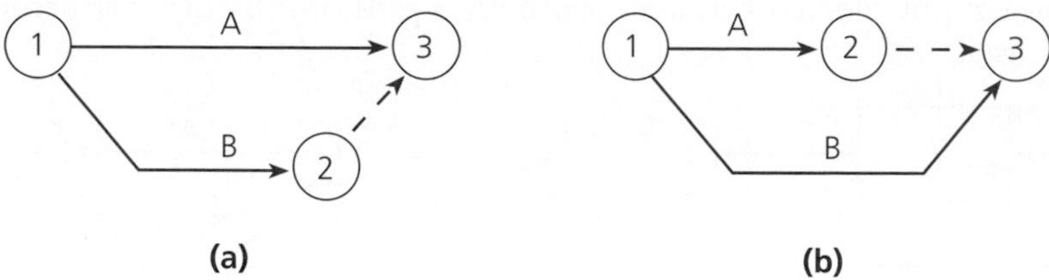

Let's consider an example of a case in which a dummy activity must be used to show precedential relationships that otherwise could not be shown. The situation is as follows:

- Activities A and B can be done concurrently.
- When activity A is finished, activity C can start.
- When both activity A and activity B are finished, activity D can start.

To portray this logic a dummy activity must be used, as shown below.

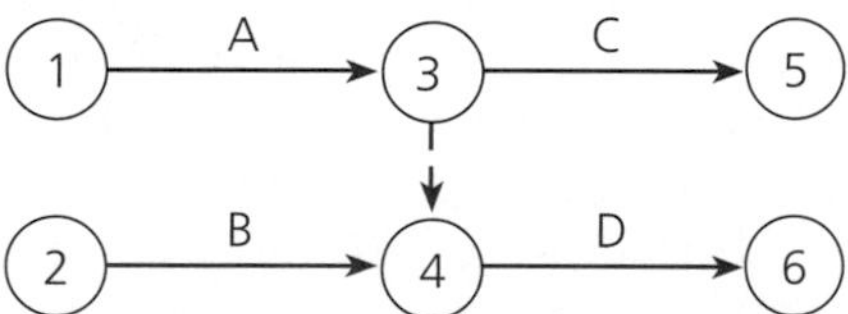

The dummy activity 3–4 in a sense extends activity A to show that, in addition to being necessary in order to start activity C, its finish is also needed (along with the finish of activity B) in order to start activity D.

The format shown below is incorrect because it indicates that activities A and B must both be finished in order for activities C and D to start, when, in fact, only activity A (not A and B) must be finished in order for activity C to start.

Reinforce Your Learning

9. Dummy activities are used only when the ________________ format is used for drawing a network diagram. Dummy activities are shown using a ________________ ________________.

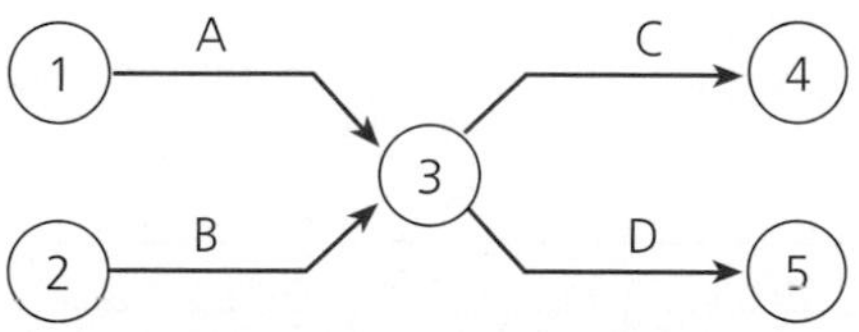

An advantage of the activity-in-the-box format is that the logic can be shown without the use of dummy activities. For example, below is the AIB format for the relationship shown above; no dummy activity is needed.

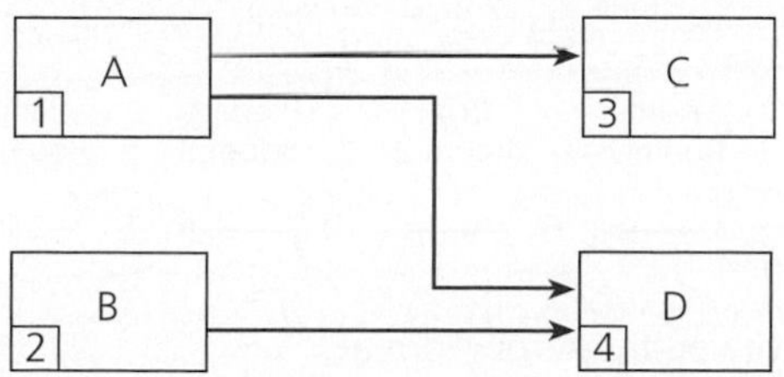

LOOPS

Shown below in AIB and AOA formats is an illogical relationship among activities known as a *loop*. In preparing a network diagram, drawing activities in a loop is not allowed because it portrays a path of activities that perpetually repeats itself.

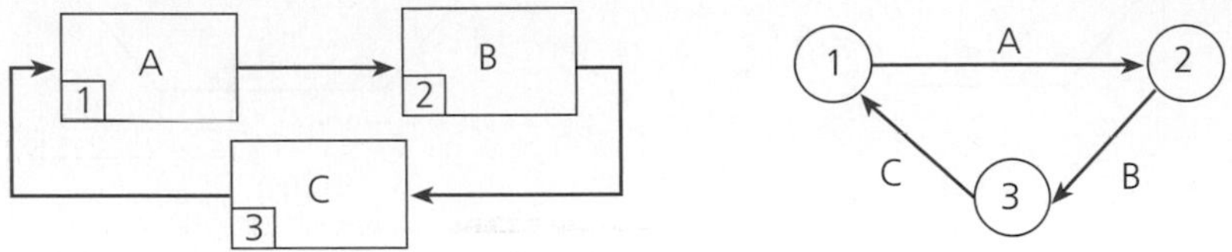

LADDERING

Some projects have a set of activities that are repeated several times. For example, consider a project involving the painting of three rooms. Painting each room requires (1) preparing the room to be painted, (2) painting the ceiling and walls, and (3) painting the trim. Assume that three experts will be available—one to do the preparation, one to paint the ceilings and walls, and one to do the trim.

It may seem logical to draw a network diagram for the project as shown in Figure 5.4 or 5.5. However, Figure 5.4 indicates that all the activities must be done in serial order, which means that at any one time only one person is working while two other people are waiting. Figure 5.5, on the other hand, indicates that all three rooms can be done concurrently, which is not possible because only one expert is available for each type of activity.

Figure 5.6 shows a technique known as **laddering**, which can be used to diagram this project. It indicates that each expert, after finishing one room, can start working on the next room. This approach will allow the project to be completed in the shortest possible time while making the best use of available resources (the experts).

FIGURE 5.4 ***Activities Performed Serially***

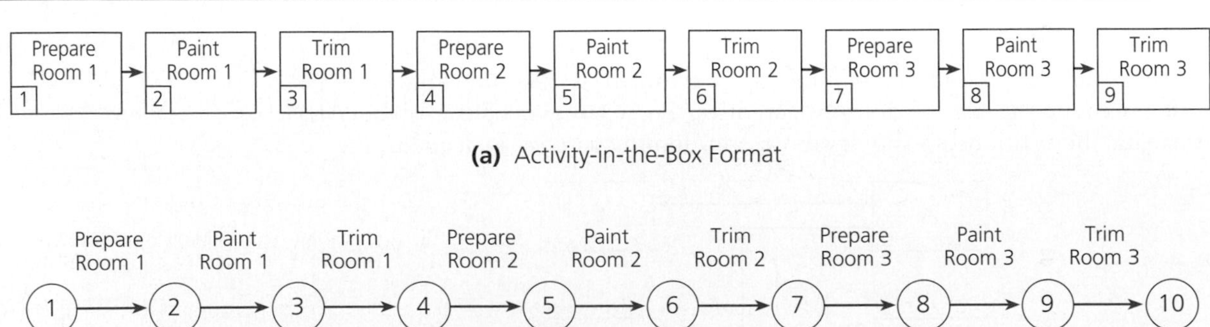

(a) Activity-in-the-Box Format

(b) Activity-on-the-Arrow Format

FIGURE 5.5 ***Activities Performed Concurrently***

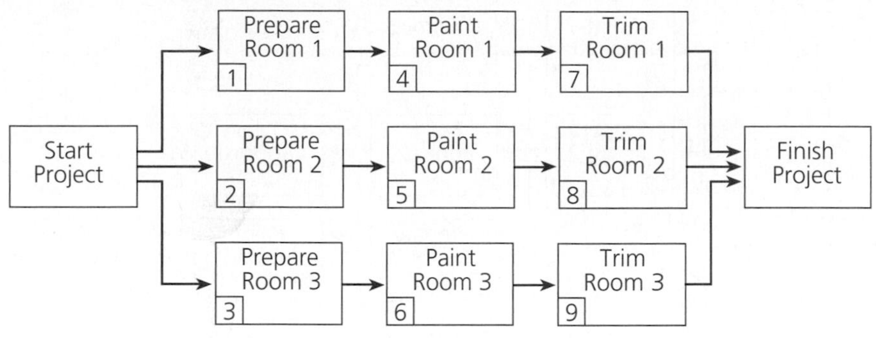

(a) Activity-in-the-Box Format

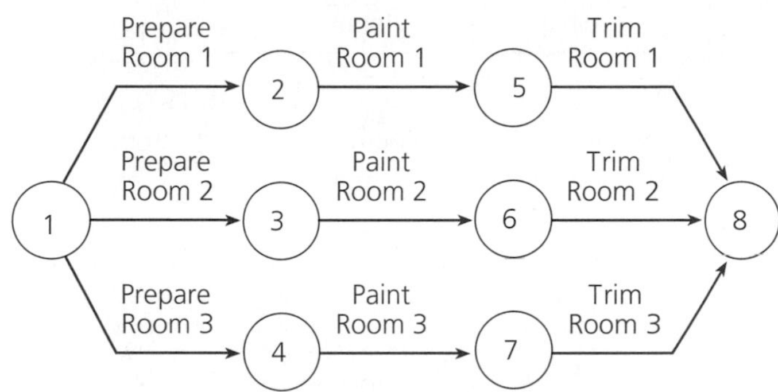

(b) Activity-on-the-Arrow Format

Preparing the Network Diagram

Given a list of activities and knowledge of network principles, you can prepare a network diagram. First, select the format to be used—activity in the box or activity on the arrow. Next, start drawing the activities in their logical precedential order, as the project should progress from initiation to completion. When deciding on the sequence in which the activities should be drawn to show their logical precedential relationship to one another, you should ask the following three questions regarding each individual activity:

1. Which activities must be finished *immediately* before this activity can be started?
2. Which activities can be done concurrently with this activity?
3. Which activities cannot be started until this activity is finished?

By answering these questions for each activity, you should be able to draw a network diagram that portrays the interrelationships and sequence of activities needed to accomplish the project work scope.

The entire network diagram should flow from left to right, although some arrows may flow from right to left to prevent the overall diagram from becoming too long. Unlike the Gantt chart, the network diagram is *not* drawn to a time

FIGURE 5.6 *Laddering*

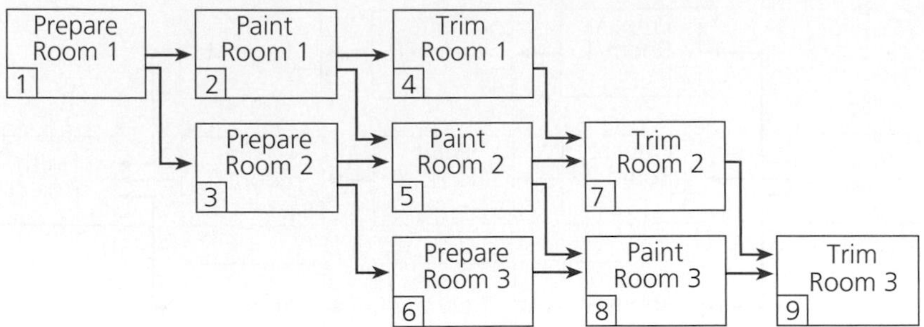

(a) Activity-in-the-Box Format

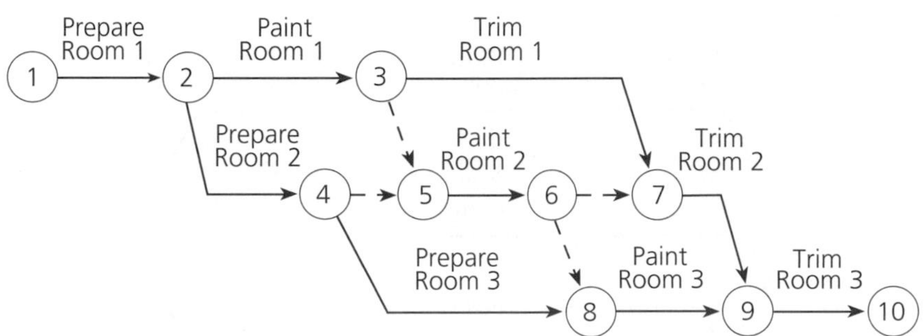

(b) Activity-on-the-Arrow Format

scale. It is easier to visualize the entire project if the network diagram can be drawn to fit on a large sheet of paper. If the network is very large, however, it may require multiple pages. In such cases, it may be necessary to create a reference system or set of symbols to show the linkages between activities on different pages.

When initially drawing the network diagram for a project, don't be too concerned about drawing it neatly. It's better to sketch out a rough draft of the diagram and make sure the logical relationships among the activities are correct. Then, go back later and draw a neater diagram (or have the computer generate the diagram if you are using project management software).

The following guidelines should be considered in deciding how detailed (in terms of number of activities) a network diagram for a project should be:

1. If a work breakdown structure has been prepared for the project, then activities should be identified for each work package. For example, Figure 5.7 shows a WBS for a project involving a consumer market study and the activities that have been identified for each work package.
2. It may be preferable to draw a summary-level network first and then expand it to a more detailed network. A *summary network* contains a small number of higher-level activities rather than a large number of detailed activities. In some cases, a summary network may suffice for use throughout a project.
3. The level of detail may be determined by certain obvious interface or transfer points:

FIGURE 5.7 ***Work Breakdown Structure for Consumer Market Study Project***

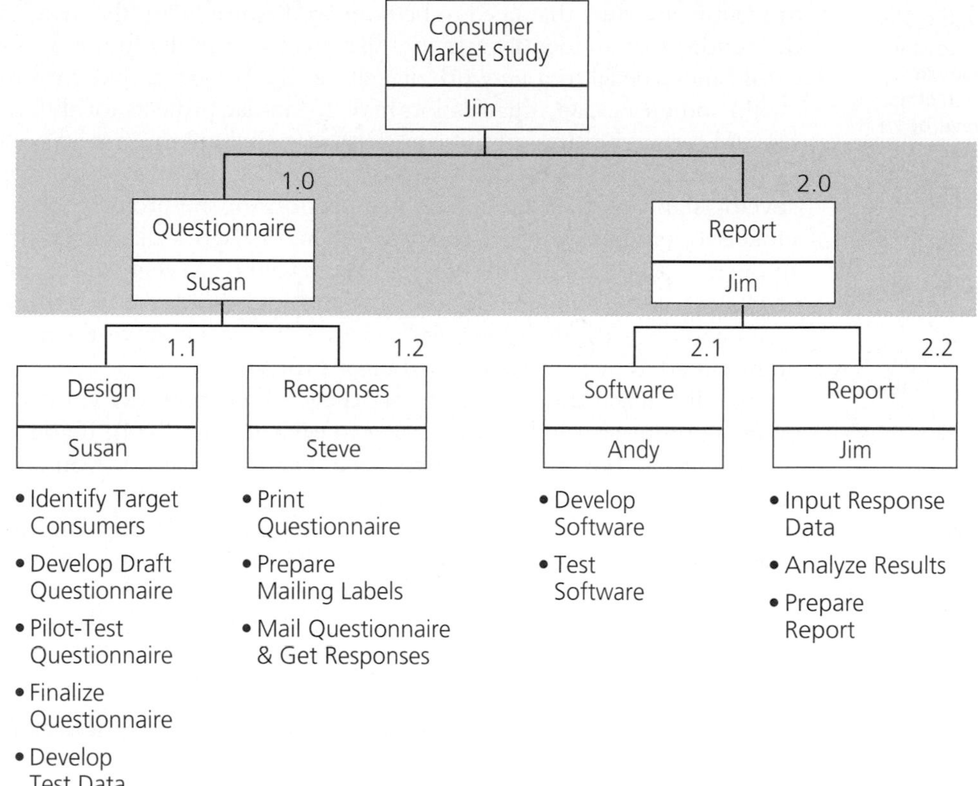

- If there is a change in responsibility—that is, a different person or organization takes over responsibility for continuing the work—it should define the end of one activity and the start of other activities. For example, if one person is responsible for building an item and another person is responsible for packaging it, these should be two separate activities.
- If there is a tangible, deliverable output or product as a result of an activity, it should define the end of one activity and the start of other activities. Some examples of outputs include a report, a drawing, the shipment of a piece of equipment, and the design of computer software. In the case of a brochure, the production of a draft brochure should be defined as the end of one activity; another activity, perhaps "Approve Draft Brochure," would follow.

4. Activities should not be longer in estimated duration than the time intervals at which actual project progress will be reviewed and compared to planned progress. For example, if the project is a three-year endeavor and the project team plans to review project progress monthly, then the network should contain no activities with estimated durations greater than 30 days. If there are activities with longer estimated durations, they should be broken up into more detailed activities with durations of 30 days or less.

Reinforce Your Learning

10. Refer to Figure 5.8.
    a. When "Prepare Mailing Labels" and "Print Questionnaire" are finished, what activity can be started?
    b. In order to start "Input Response Data," which activities must have been finished immediately beforehand?

Reinforce Your Learning

11. Refer to Figure 5.9.
    a. In order to start "Test Software," which activities must have been completed immediately beforehand?
    b. True or false: Once "Print Questionnaire" is finished, "Mail Questionnaire & Get Responses" can start immediately.

Whatever the level of detail used in the initial network diagram, some activities may be broken down further as the project progresses. It's always easier to identify activities that need to be done in the near term (the next several weeks or months) than to identify activities that are a year in the future. It is not unusual to add more detail to a network diagram as the project moves forward.

In some cases, an organization may do similar projects for different customers, and certain portions of these projects may include the same types of activities in the same logical precedential relationships. If so, it may be worthwhile to develop standard *subnetworks* for these portions of the projects. Having standard subnetworks can save effort and time when a network diagram is developed for an overall project. Standard subnetworks should be developed for those portions of projects for which the logical relationships among the activities have been well established through historical practice. These subnetworks may, of course, be modified as necessary for a particular project.

Finally, when the entire network diagram has been drawn, it's necessary to assign a unique activity number either to each activity (box), if you are using the activity-in-the-box format, or to each event (circle), if you are using the activity-on-the-arrow format.

Figures 5.8 and 5.9 show complete network diagrams for the consumer market study project in the AIB and AOA formats, respectively. Notice the addition of the person responsible on these diagrams.

The choice between the activity-in-the-box format and the activity-on-the-arrow format is a matter of personal preference. Both formats use a network

FIGURE 5.8 ***Network Diagram for Consumer Market Study Project (Activity-in-the-Box Format)***

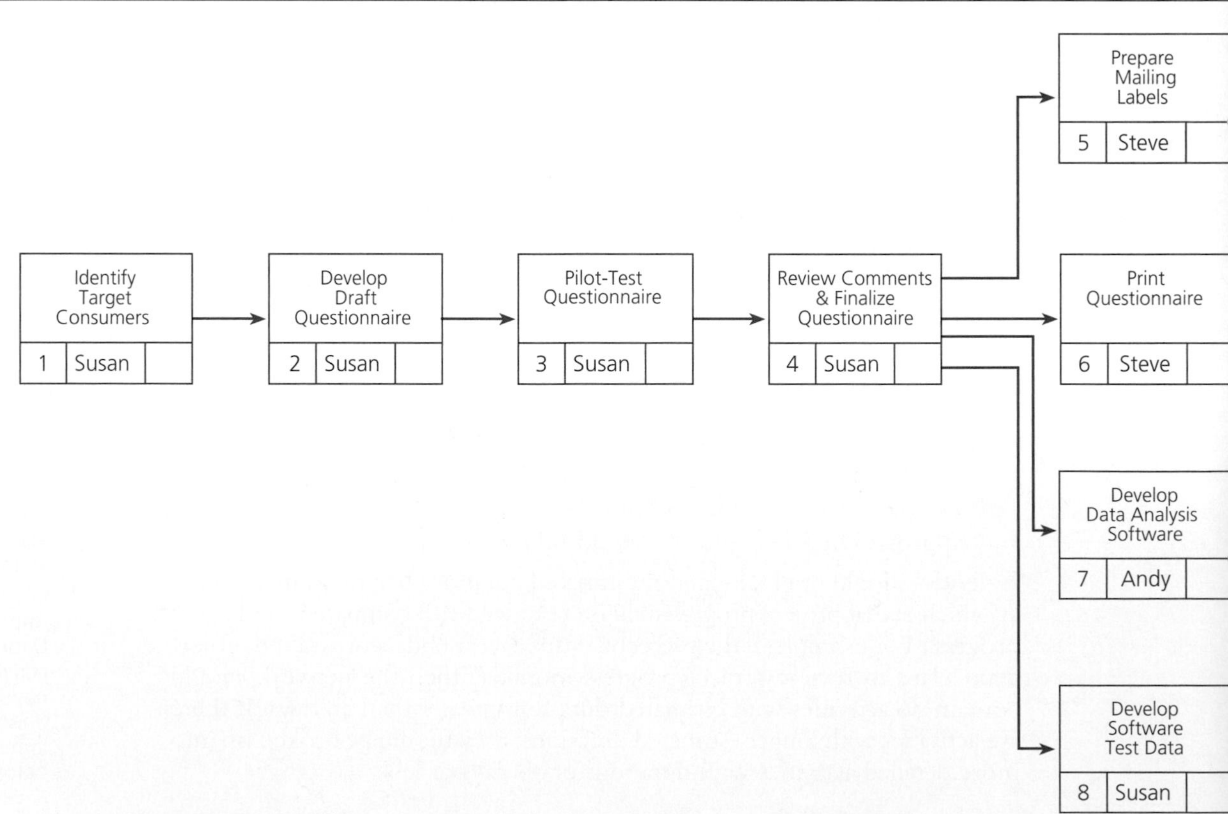

based on precedential relationships. The network is a roadmap that displays how all the activities fit together to accomplish the project work scope. It also is a communication tool for the project team because it shows who is responsible for each activity and how that person's work ties into the overall project.

PLANNING FOR INFORMATION SYSTEMS DEVELOPMENT

Because of the rapidly increasing number of information technology-related projects that are being undertaken, it seems appropriate to include a section in each of the next few chapters on project management practices in information systems development. An **information system (IS)** is a computer-based system that accepts data as input, processes the data, and produces useful information for users. Information systems include computerized order entry systems, e-commerce systems, automatic teller machines, and billing, payroll, and inventory systems. The development of an IS is a challenging process that requires extensive planning and control to ensure that the system meets user requirements and is finished on time and within budget.

A project management planning tool, or methodology, called the **systems development life cycle (SDLC)** is often used to help plan, execute, and control IS development projects. The SDLC consists of a set of phases or steps that need to be completed over the course of a development project. Many

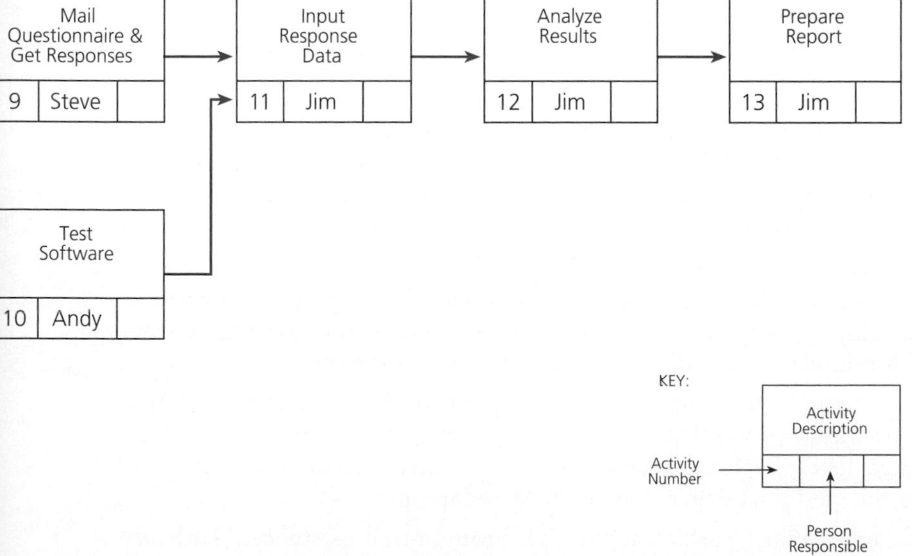

FIGURE 5.9 ***Network Diagram for Consumer Market Study Project (Activity-on-the-Arrow Format)***

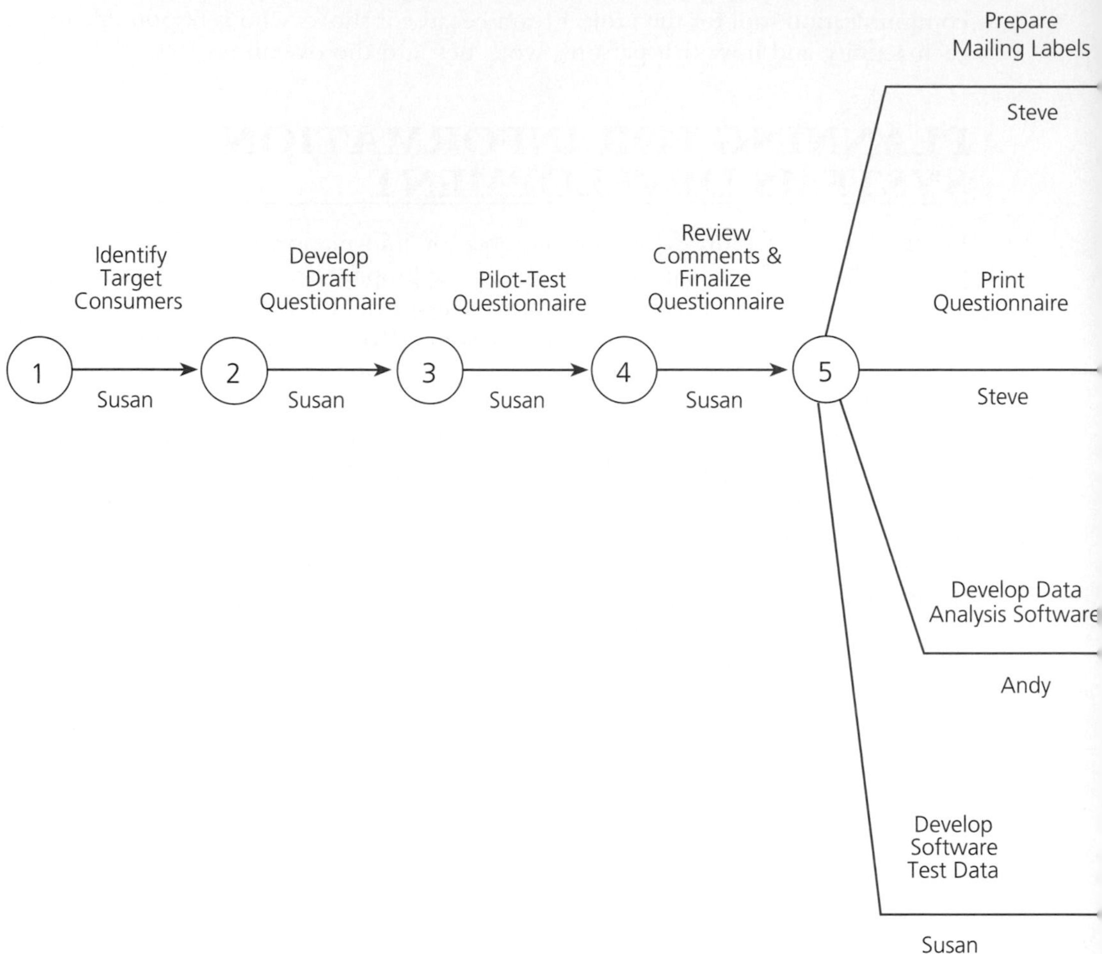

people view the SDLC as a classic problem-solving approach. It consists of the following steps:

1. *Problem definition.* Data are gathered and analyzed, and problems and opportunities are clearly defined. Technical, economic, operational, and other feasibility factors are defined and studied to determine, at least initially, whether the IS can be successfully developed and used.
2. *System analysis.* The development team defines the scope of the system to be developed, interviews potential users, studies the existing system (which might be manual), and defines user requirements.
3. *System design.* Several alternative conceptual designs are produced that describe input, processing, output, hardware, software, and the database at a high level. Each of these alternatives is then evaluated, and the best one is selected for further design and development.
4. *System development.* The actual system is brought into existence. Hardware is purchased, and software is either purchased, customized, or developed.

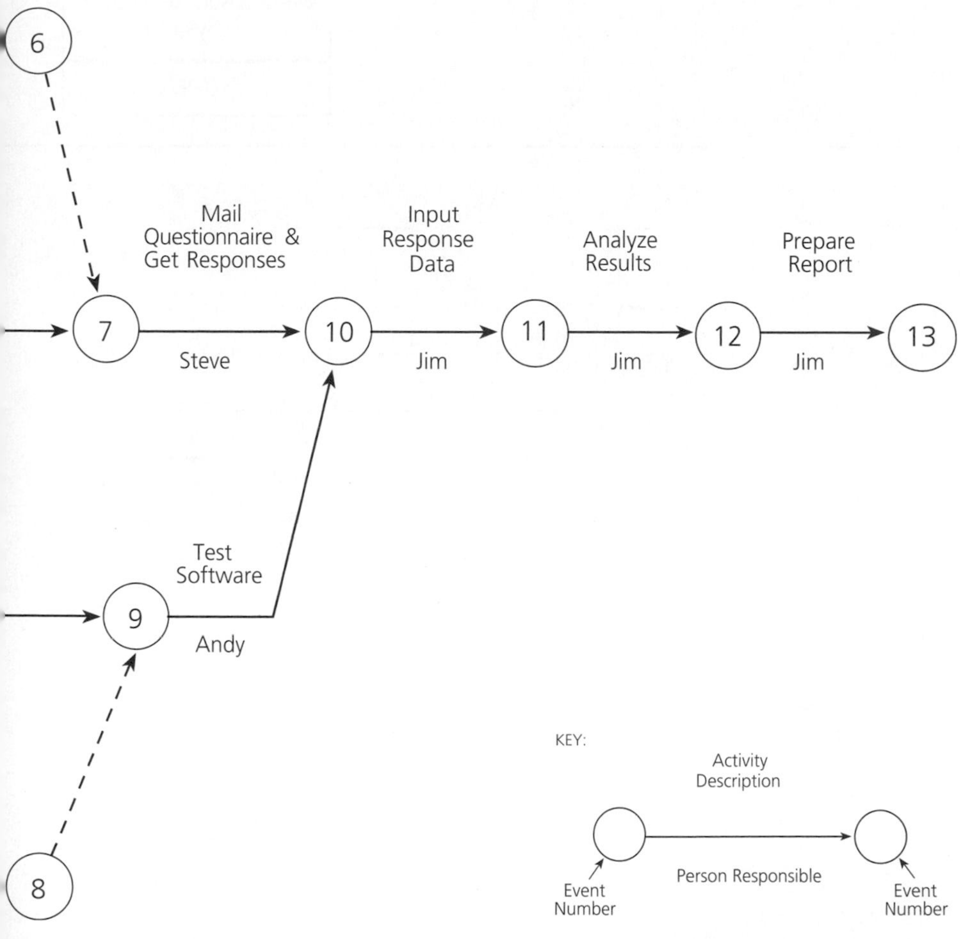

Databases, input screens, system reports, telecommunication networks, security controls, and other features are also developed.

5. *System testing*. After individual modules within the system have been developed, testing can begin. Testing involves looking for logical errors, database errors, errors of omission, security errors, and other problems that might prevent the system from being successful. After the individual modules are tested and problems are corrected, the entire system is tested. Once the users and the developers are convinced that the system is error-free, the system can be implemented.
6. *System implementation*. The existing system is replaced with the new, improved system, and users are trained. Several methodologies exist for converting from the existing system to the new system with minimal interruption to the users.

The SDLC concludes with implementation of the system. The system life cycle itself continues with a formal review of the development process after the system is up and running, and then continues with maintenance, modifications, and enhancements to the system.

FIGURE 5.10 *Work Breakdown Structure for Web-Based Reporting System Project*

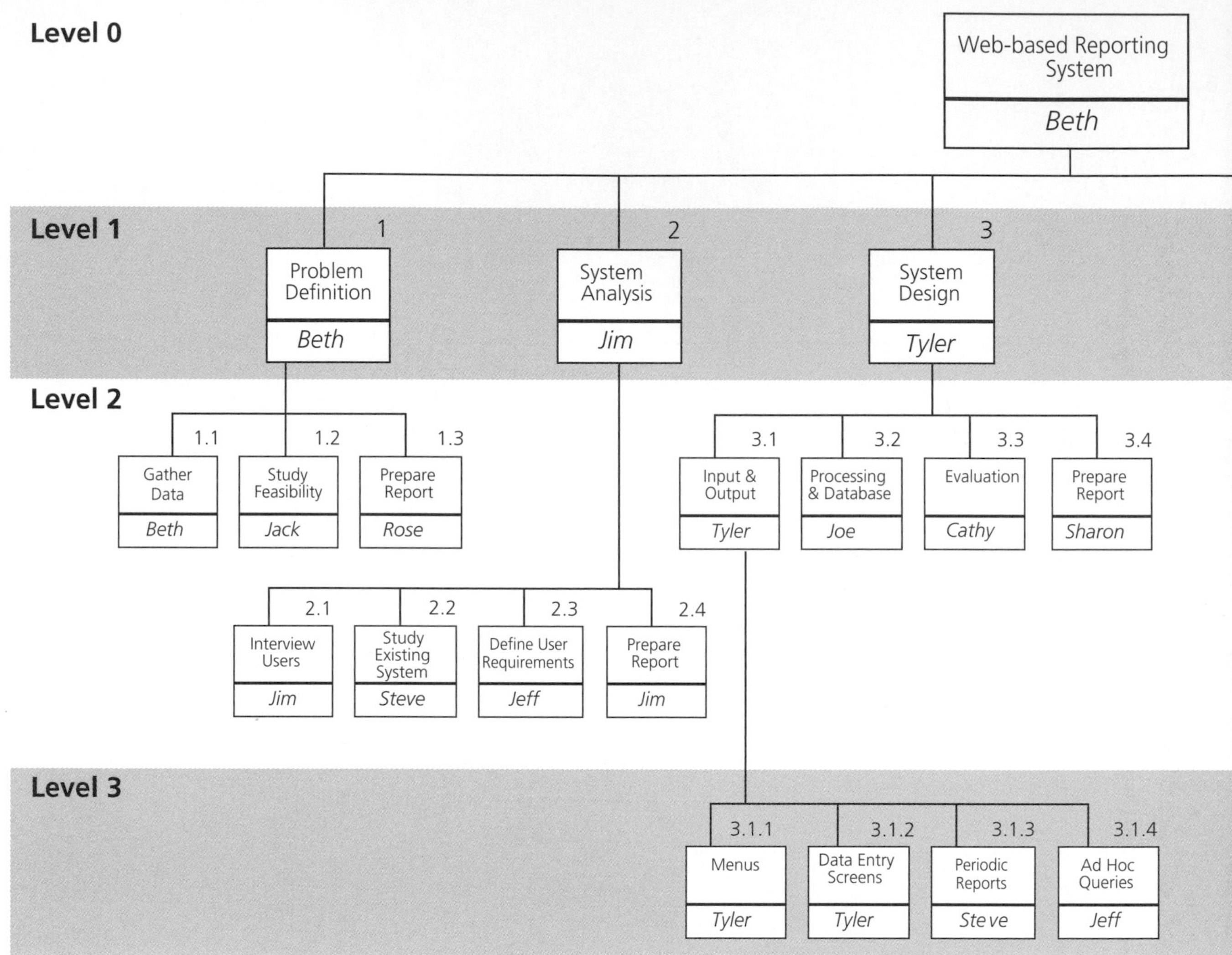

An IS Example: Internet Applications Development for ABC Office Designs

A corporation called ABC Office Designs has a large of number of sales representatives who sell office furniture to major corporations. Each sales representative is assigned to a specific state, and each state is part of one of four regions in the country. To enable management to monitor the number and amount of sales for each representative, for each state, and for each region, ABC has decided to build a web-based information system that will track prices, inventory, and the competition.

The IS Department within the corporation has assigned Beth Smith to be the project manager of the Web-based Reporting System development project. With the help of her staff, Beth identified all of the major tasks that need to be accomplished and developed the work breakdown structure shown in Figure 5.10. Notice that the WBS follows the SDLC. At level 1, the major tasks are

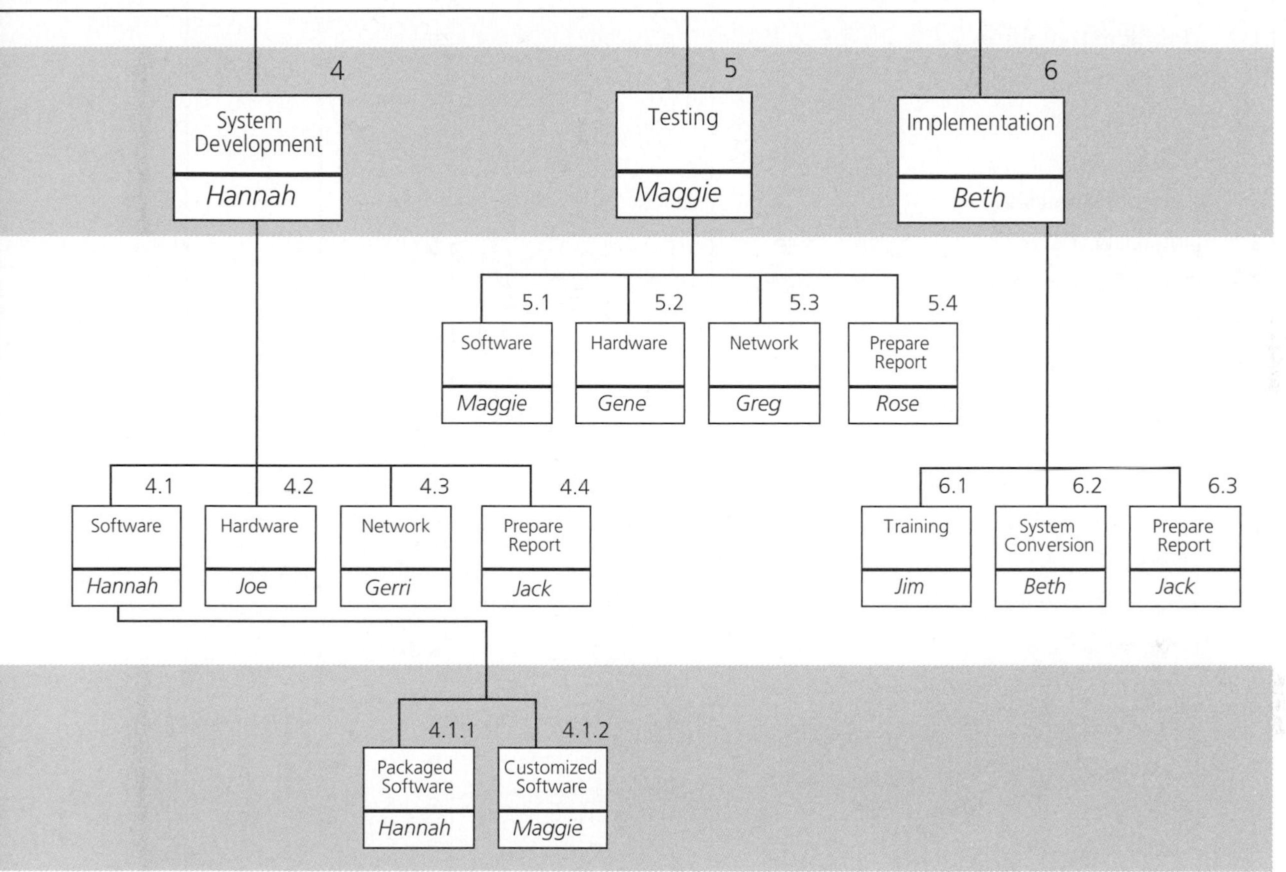

problem definition, analysis, design, development, testing, and implementation. Each of these tasks is further broken down into level 2 tasks, and a few are broken down further into level 3 tasks.

After the project team developed the WBS, the responsibility matrix shown in Figure 5.11 was developed. Notice that this table reflects all of the activities shown in the WBS. In addition, it shows who has primary responsibility and secondary responsibility for each task.

After each task was assigned to team members, the project manager put together a Gantt chart of the major tasks to be accomplished. The Gantt chart is shown in Figure 5.12. Notice that the Gantt chart provides a clear visual representation of the activities to be performed and the time frame in which each will be done. The project manager has allocated 5 days for problem definition, 10 days for system analysis, 10 days for system design, 15 days for system development, 8 days for system testing, and 5 days for system implementation. The project, as shown, needs to be completed within 50 days.

FIGURE 5.11 *Responsibility Matrix for Web-Based Reporting System Project*

WBS Item	Work Item	Beth	Jim	Jack	Rose	Steve	Jeff	Tyler	Cathy	Sharon	Hannah	Joe	Gerri	Maggie	Gene	Greg
	Web-based Reporting System	**P**	S					S			S			S		
1	**Problem Definition**	**P**		S	S											
1.1	Gather Data	**P**	S										S			
1.2	Study Feasibility			**P**		S	S		S	S						
1.3	Prepare Report	S			**P**											
2	**System Analysis**		**P**			S	S									
2.1	Interview Users		**P**		S						S			S		
2.2	Study Existing System					**P**										
2.3	Define User Requirements						**P**									
2.4	Prepare Report		**P**													
3	**System Design**							**P**	S	S		S				
3.1	Input & Output					S	S	**P**								
3.1.1	Menus		S					**P**								
3.1.2	Data Entry		S					**P**								
3.1.3	Periodic Reports					**P**	S						S			
3.1.4	Ad Hoc Questions					S	**P**						S			
3.2	Processing Database											**P**			S	S
3.3	Evaluation	S	S	S					**P**							
3.4	Prepare Report									**P**	S					
4	**System Development**			S							**P**	S	S			
4.1	Software										**P**	S	S	S		
4.1.1	Packaging										**P**	S	S	S		
4.1.2	Customize Software											S	S	**P**		
4.2	Hardware							S				**P**				
4.3	Network												**P**			
4.4	Prepare Report			**P**												
5	**Testing**				S									**P**	S	S
5.1	Software					S	S							**P**		
5.2	Hardware											S	S		**P**	
5.3	Network								S		S					**P**
5.4	Prepare Report				**P**									S	S	S
6	**Implementation**	**P**	S	S												
6.1	Training		**P**								S		S			
6.2	System Conversion	**P**									S		S			
6.3	Prepare Report	S	S	**P**												

KEY: **P** = Primary responsibility; S = Support responsibility.

FIGURE 5.12 *Gantt Chart for Web-Based Reporting System Project*

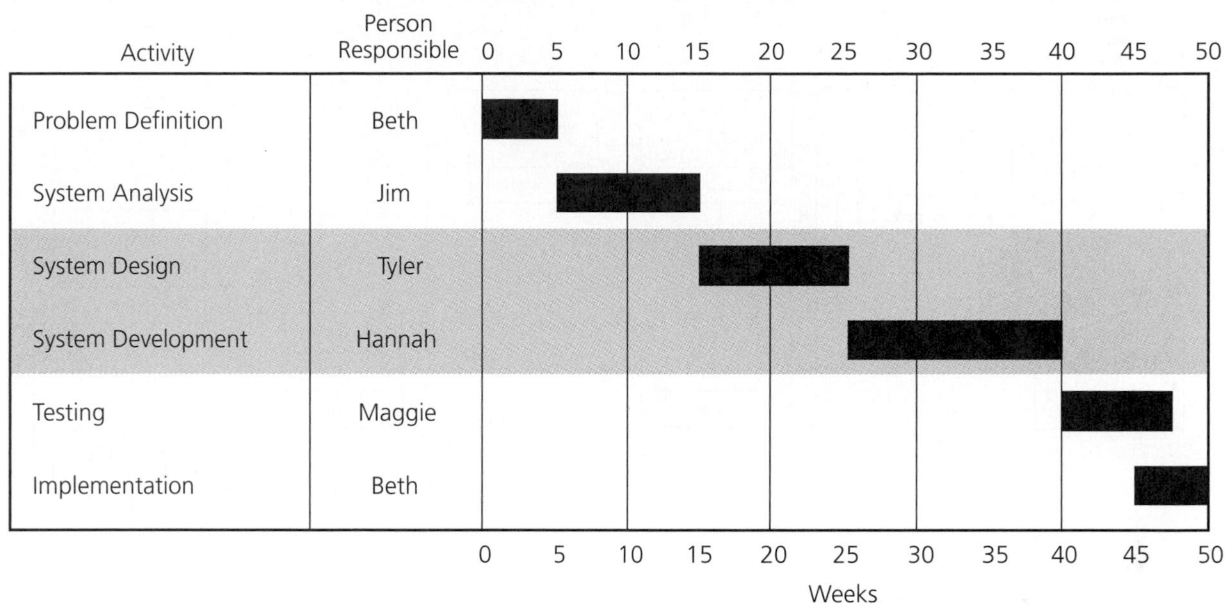

FIGURE 5.13 *List of Activities and Immediate Predecessors*

Web-based Reporting System Project

Activity	**Immediate Predecessors**
1. Gather Data	—
2. Study Feasibility	—
3. Prepare Problem Definition Report	1, 2
4. Interview Users	3
5. Study Existing System	3
6. Define User Requirements	4
7. Prepare System Analysis Report	5, 6
8. Input & Output	7
9. Processing & Database	7
10. Evaluation	8, 9
11. Prepare System Design Report	10
12. Software Development	11
13. Hardware Development	11
14. Network Development	11
15. Prepare System Development Report	12, 13, 14
16. Software Testing	15
17. Hardware Testing	15
18. Network Testing	15
19. Prepare Testing Report	16, 17, 18
20. Training	19
21. System Conversion	19
22. Prepare Implementation Report	20, 21

FIGURE 5.14 *Network Diagram for Web-Based Reporting System Project (Activity-in-the-Box Format)*

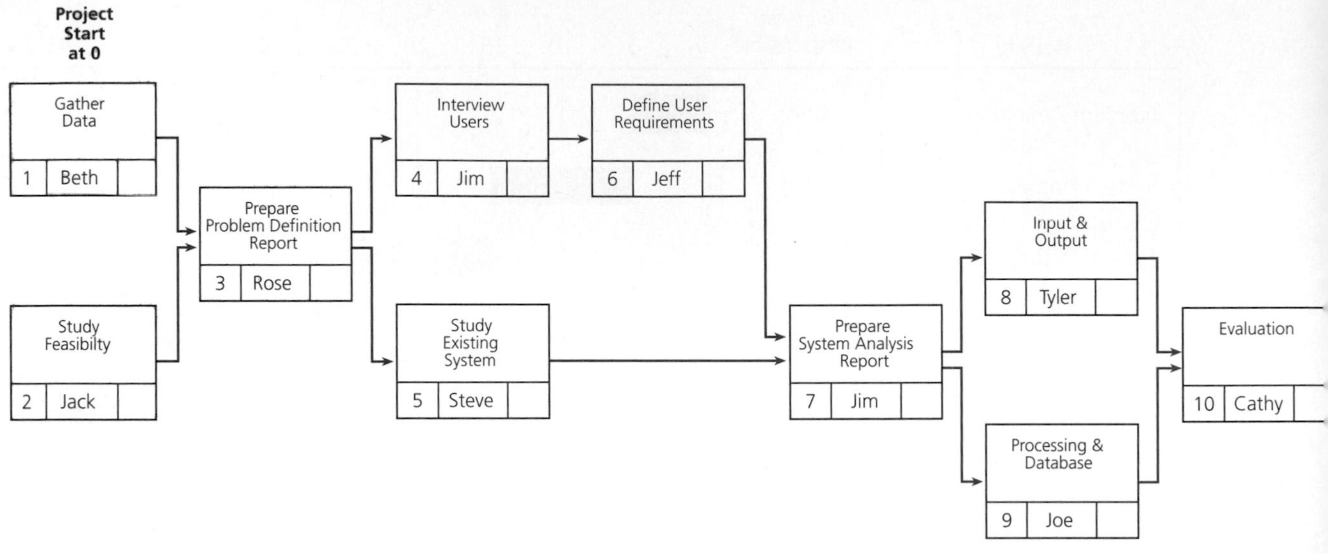

After completing the Gantt chart, the project manager felt that it was important to develop a network diagram to show the interdependencies that exist among tasks. Before Beth did this, however, she and the project team created a list of all tasks to be done, with the immediate predecessor for each task listed to the right of the task, as shown in Figure 5.13. Notice that before "Prepare Problem Definition Report" can start, both "Gather Data" and "Study Feasibility" must be finished. Similarly, before "Prepare System Analysis Report" can start, both "Study Existing System" and "Determine User Requirements" must be completed.

With this list Beth then prepared the network diagram using the activity-in-the-box format as shown in Figure 5.14.

PROJECT MANAGEMENT SOFTWARE

A wide variety of affordable project management software packages are available for purchase. These packages allow the project manager and the project team to plan and control projects in a completely interactive mode. See Appendix A at the end of the book for a thorough discussion of project management software.

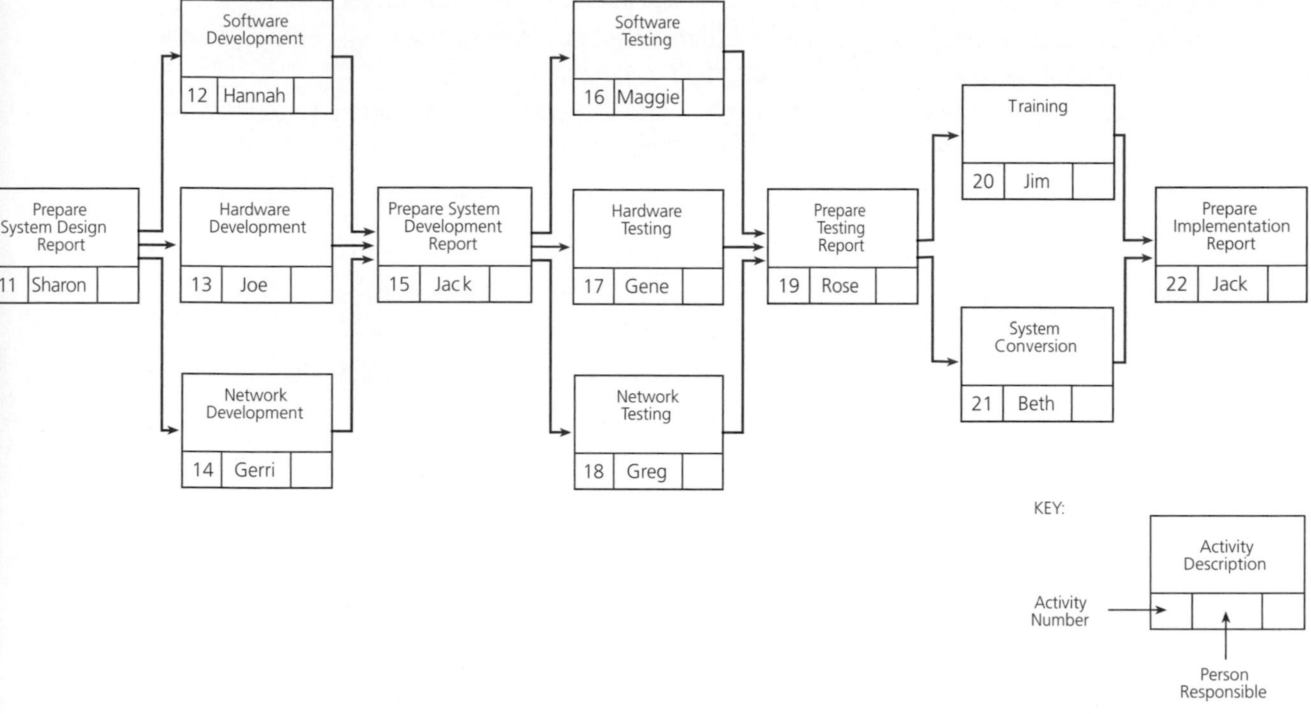

Common features of project management software allow the user to

- create lists of tasks with their estimated durations
- establish interdependencies among tasks
- work with a variety of time scales, including hours, days, weeks, months, and years
- handle certain constraints—for example, a task cannot start before a certain date, a task must be started by a certain date, labor unions allow no more than two people to work on the weekends
- track team members, including their pay rates, hours worked thus far on a project, and upcoming vacation dates
- incorporate company holidays, weekends, and team member vacation days into calendaring systems
- handle shifts of workers (day, evening, night)
- monitor and forecast budgets
- look for conflicts—for example, overallocated resources and time conflicts
- generate a wide variety of reports
- interface with other software packages such as spreadsheets and databases
- sort information in a variety of ways—for example, by project, by team member, or by work package

Critical Success FACTORS

- It is important to develop a plan before the start of the project. Taking the time to develop a well-thought-out plan is critical to the successful accomplishment of any project.
- Participation builds commitment. By participating in the planning of the work, individuals will become committed to accomplishing it according to the plan.
- The project objective must be clear, attainable, specific, measurable, and agreed upon by the customer and the organization that will perform the project.

- handle multiple projects
- work online and respond quickly to changes in schedule, budget, or personnel
- compare actual costs with budgeted costs
- display data in a variety of ways, including both Gantt charts and network diagrams

Note: As mentioned earlier, most project management software has the ability to provide Gantt charts that display the interdependencies among tasks by connecting tasks and their predecessors by lines with arrowheads. The network diagrams most commonly displayed with project management software use the activity-in-the-box format. The user can move back and forth between the Gantt charts and the network diagrams with a click of the mouse.

SUMMARY

Planning is the systematic arrangement of tasks to accomplish an objective. The plan lays out what needs to be accomplished and how it is to be accomplished. The plan becomes a benchmark against which actual progress can be compared; then, if deviations occur, corrective action can be taken.

The first step in the planning process is to define the project objective—the expected result or end product. The project objective is usually defined in terms of scope, schedule, and cost. The objective must be clearly defined and agreed upon by the customer and the organization or contractor that will perform the project.

Once the project objective has been defined, the next step is to determine which work elements, or activities, need to be performed to accomplish it. This requires developing a list of all the activities.

The work breakdown structure (WBS) breaks a project down into manageable pieces, or items, to help ensure that all of the work elements needed to complete the project work scope are identified. It's a hierarchical tree of end items that will be accomplished or produced by the project team during the project. It usually indicates the organization or individual responsible for each work item.

A responsibility matrix is often developed to display, in tabular format, the individuals responsible for accomplishing the work items in the WBS. It's a useful tool because it emphasizes who is responsible for each work item and shows each individual's role in supporting the overall project.

Finally, network planning is a technique that is helpful in planning, scheduling, and controlling projects that consist of many interrelated activities. In addition, it is also useful for communicating information about projects. There are several different network plan formats that can be used; the two most popular are activity in the box (AIB) and activity on the arrow (AOA).

In the activity-in-the-box format, each activity is represented by a box in the network diagram, and the description of the activity is written within the box. In the activity-on-the-arrow format, each activity is represented by an arrow in the network diagram, and the activity description is written above the arrow.

After a list of activities has been created, a network diagram can be prepared. When deciding on the sequence in which the activities should be drawn to show their logical precedential relationship to one another, you must determine (1) which activities must be finished immediately before a given activity can be started, (2) which activities can be done concurrently, and (3) which activities cannot be started until prior activities are finished.

Project planning is a critical activity in developing an information system (IS). A project management planning tool, or methodology, called the systems development life cycle (SDLC) is often used to help plan, execute, and control IS development projects. The SDLC consists of a set of phases or steps: problem definition, system analysis, system design, system development, system testing, and system implementation. All of these need to be completed over the course of a development project.

Numerous project management software packages are available to help project managers plan, track, and control projects in a completely interactive way.

QUESTIONS

1. What is meant by *planning a project?* What does this encompass? Who should be involved in planning the work?
2. What is meant by the term *project objective?* What might happen if a project objective is not clearly written? Give three examples of clearly written project objectives.
3. What is a work breakdown structure? What is a *responsibility matrix?* How are they related?
4. What is an activity? Does it always require human effort? Refer to Figure 5.1. Provide a detailed list of activities needed to accomplish work package 3.3. Do the same for work package 4.2.
5. What is meant by the terms *predecessor event* and *successor event?*
6. Refer to Figure 5.9. What activities must be accomplished before "Input Response Data" can start? What activities can start after "Review Comments & Finalize Questionnaire" has finished? List two activities that can be done concurrently.
7. When would you use laddering in a network diagram? Give an example, different from the one provided in the chapter, and draw the

corresponding network diagram in both the activity-in-the-box and the activity-on-the-arrow formats.

8. Why would you recommend project management software to someone involved in project management? What features and benefits does it provide?
9. Draw a network diagram representing the following logic: as the project starts, activities A and B can be performed concurrently. When activity A is finished, activities C and D can start. When activity B is finished, activities E and F can start. When activities D and E are finished, activity G can start. The project is complete when activities C, F, and G are finished. Use both the activity-in-the-box and the activity-on-the-arrow formats.
10. Draw a network diagram representing the following information: the project starts with three activities, A, B, and C, which can be done concurrently. When A is finished, D can start; when B is finished, F can start; when B and D are finished, E can start. The project is complete when C, E, and F are finished. Use both the activity-in-the-box and the activity-on-the-arrow formats.
11. Draw a network diagram that represents the following IS development task list. Use both the activity-in-the-box and the activity-on-the-arrow formats.

Activity	**Immediate Predecessor**
1. Problem Definition	—
2. Study Current System	1
3. Define User Requirements	1
4. Logical System Design	3
5. Physical System Design	2
6. System Development	4, 5
7. System Testing	6
8. Convert Database	4, 5
9. System Conversion	7, 8

12. Find as many errors as you can in the following network diagram:

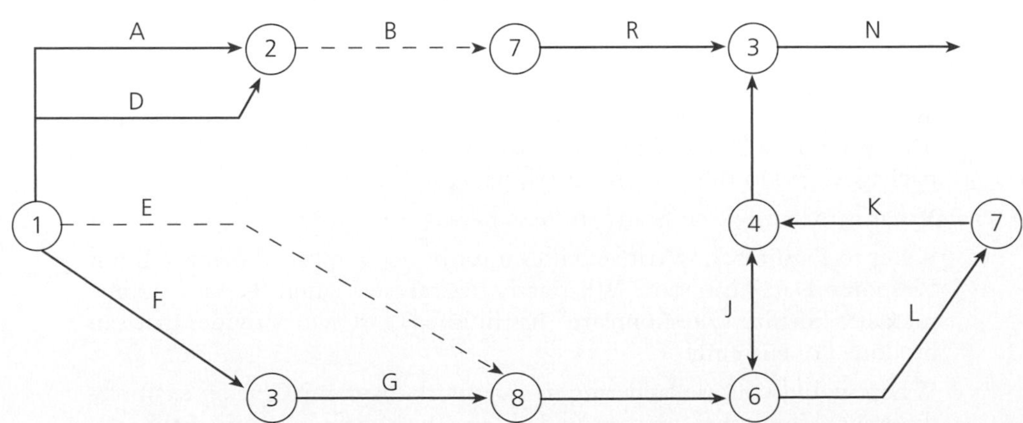

INTERNET EXERCISES

For the website addresses of the organizations mentioned in these exercises, go to "Internet Exercises" at the book's companion website at **international.cengage.com.** It is suggested that you save this website in your "Favorites" for easy access in the future.

1. Search the web for project planning tools and describe at least three sites that you find.
2. Visit the website of the International Project Management Association (IPMA). Explore the site to learn more about certifications, memberships, publications, awards, events, and educational opportunities.
3. Look at the IPMA link called "Young Crew." Young Crew is a key component to IPMA's strategy for nurturing the project management leaders of tomorrow. Describe what you found.
4. The *International Journal of Project Management* is an IPMA publication. Go to the journal's home page or go to the website of Elsevier Science Direct and search for the journal. Click on the "Free Tables of Contents and Abstracts" link. Print out a list of articles from the current edition.
5. Within the "Free Tables of Contents and Abstracts" link perform a quick search using the keyword "Planning." Provide a list of what you found. Next, click on "View Related Articles" and describe what you found.

A Not-for-Profit Medical Research Center

CASE STUDY 1

You are Alexis, the director of external affairs for a national not-for-profit medical research center that does research on diseases related to aging. The center's work depends on funding from multiple sources, including the general public, individual estates, and grants from corporations, foundations, and the federal government.

Your department prepares an annual report of the center's accomplishments and financial status for the board of directors. It is mostly text with a few charts and tables, all black and white, with a simple cover. It is voluminous and pretty dry reading. It is inexpensive to produce other than the effort to pull together the content, which requires time to request and expedite information from the center's other departments.

At the last board meeting, the board members suggested the annual report be "upscaled" into a document that could be used for marketing and promotional purposes. They want you to mail the next annual report to the center's various stakeholders, past donors, and targeted high-potential future donors. The board feels that such a document is needed to get the center "in the same league" with other large not-for-profit organizations with which it feels it competes for donations and funds. The board feels that the annual report could be used to inform these stakeholders about the advances the center is making in its research efforts and its strong fiscal management for effectively using the funding and donations it receives.

You will need to produce a shorter, simpler, easy-to-read annual report that shows the benefits of the center's research and the impact on people's lives. You will include pictures from various hospitals, clinics and long-term care facilities that are using the results of the center's research. You also will include testimonials from patients and families who have benefited from the center's research. The report must be "eye-catching." It needs to be multi-color, contain a lot of pictures and easy-to-understand graphics, and be written in a style that can be understood by the average adult potential donor.

This is a significant undertaking for your department, which includes three other staff members. You will have to contract out some of the activities and may have to travel to several medical facilities around the country to take photos and get testimonials. You will also need to put the design, printing, and distribution out to bid to various contractors to submit proposals and prices to you. You estimate that approximately five million copies need to be printed and mailed.

It is now April 1. The board asks you to come to its next meeting on May 15 to present a detailed plan, schedule, and budget for how you will complete the project. The board wants the annual report "in the mail" by November 15, so potential donors will receive it around the holiday season when they may be in a "giving mood." The center's fiscal year ends September 30 and its financial statements should be available by October 15. However, the nonfinancial information for the report can start to be pulled together right after the May 15 board meeting.

Fortunately, you are taking a project management course in the evenings at the local university and see this as an opportunity to apply what you have been learning. You know that this is a big project and that the board has high expectations. You want to be sure you meet their expectations, and get them to approve the budget that you will need for this project. However, they will only do that if they are confident that you have a detailed plan for how you will get it all done. You and your staff have six weeks to prepare a plan for you to present to the Board on May 15. If approved, you will have six months, from May 15 to November 15, to implement the plan and complete the project.

Your staff consists of Grace, a marketing specialist; Levi, a writer/editor; and Lakysha, a staff assistant whose hobby is photography (she is going to college part-time in the evenings to earn a degree in photojournalism, and has won several local photography contests).

CASE QUESTIONS

You and your team need to prepare a plan to present to the board that includes:

1. The project objective and a list of your assumptions about the project
2. A work breakdown structure and a responsibility matrix
3. A list of the activities that need to be performed to accomplish the project objective
4. A network diagram (using the activity-in-the-box format) showing the interrelationships of all the activities.

Note: This case study will continue in Chapters 6 through 9, where your team will be asked to develop duration estimates for each activity, a project schedule, and a project budget, so save the results of your work.

GROUP ACTIVITY

Divide the course participants into groups of four, with the people in each group assuming the role of Alexis, Grace, Levi, or Lakysha. Then prepare the four items listed above.

Note: This case study will continue in Chapters 6 through 9, so save the results of your work.

The Wedding

CASE STUDY 2

Tony and Peggy Sue graduated from a university in Texas last May. She received a degree in elementary education, and he graduated from the culinary school. They both now work in the Dallas area. Peggy Sue teaches, and Tony is a chef at a resort hotel restaurant.

It is Christmas Day and Tony asks Peggy Sue to get marry him. She excitedly accepts. They set a wedding date of June 30.

Tony is from New York City. He is the only son of "Big Tony" and Carmella. He is known as "Little Tony" to his family. He has three younger sisters, none of whom are yet married. The family owns a restaurant called Big Tony's, of course, and all four children have worked in the restaurant since they were young. They have a large extended family with many relatives, most of whom live in New York City. They also have many friends in the neighborhood.

Peggy Sue is from Cornfield, Nebraska. She is the youngest of four sisters. She and her sisters worked on the family farm when they were young. Her father passed away several years ago. Her mother, Mildred, now lives alone in the family farmhouse and leases the farmland to a neighboring farmer. Peggy Sue's sisters all married local guys and all live in Cornfield. All of their weddings were small (about 50 people), simple and pretty much the same. Mildred has the wedding plans down to almost a standard operating procedure—9:00 A.M. ceremony at the small church, followed by a buffet brunch in the church hall, and that's about it. They really couldn't afford much more elaborate weddings because the income from the farm had been pretty meager. Peggy Sue's sisters didn't go to college, and she had to take out loans to pay for her college expenses.

Tony and Peggy Sue decide to call home and announce the good news about their engagement and the forthcoming wedding.

Tony calls home and tells his mom, Carmella, the news. She replies, "That's great, honey! I've been waiting for this day. I can't believe my little baby is getting married. I'm so excited. We're going to have the biggest, best wedding ever. All our friends and family will come to celebrate. We'll probably have 300 people. And of course we'll have the reception at our restaurant; the banquet room should be big enough. I'll tell your cousin Vinnie that you want him to be best man. You grew up together, although you haven't seen much of each other since you went off to college in Texas. I'll call Aunt Lucy as soon as we're done talking and tell her that we want her little Maria and Teresa to be flower girls and little Nicky to be ring bearer. And, oh, I almost forgot the most important thing—your sisters, they'll all be bridesmaids. I already know what color their gowns will be—a deep rose; they'll be gorgeous. And sweetie, I didn't ask your papa yet, but I know he'll agree with me—on Monday I'm going to call my friend Francine, the travel agent, and get two tickets for you for a two-week honeymoon in Italy. You've never been there, and you must go. It will be a gift from your papa and me. And tell Peggy Lee or Peggy Susie or whatever congratulations. We are so happy for both of you. It's your wedding, and I don't want to interfere. I'll just be here to help. You know what I'm saying. So, my little Tony, whatever you want me to do, you just tell me. And one more thing, I'll see Father Frank after Mass on Sunday and tell him to mark his calendar already for a two o'clock ceremony on June 30. Goodbye, my big boy. I'll tell Papa you called. And I can't wait to start telling everybody to get ready to party on June 30."

Peggy Sue also calls her mom to tell her the news about the upcoming wedding. Mildred responds, "That's wonderful, dear. I'm glad you're finally getting married. You waited so long with going off to college and everything. I'll start getting everything ready. I know how to do this in my sleep by now. I'll mention it to Reverend Johnson after Sunday service. I'll tell your sisters to expect to be bridesmaids again in keeping with the family tradition. I guess Holley will be the Matron of Honor; it's her turn. By the way she's expecting her third child probably right around the same time as your wedding, but I don't think that will matter. Well, I guess pretty soon you'll be having babies of your own like all your sisters. I'm glad you are finally settling down. You should really be thinking about moving back home now that you are done with college. I saw Emma Miller, your second grade teacher, at the grocery store the other day. She told me she is retiring. I told her you would be excited to hear that and probably want to apply for her job."

"She said she didn't think they would have too many people applying so you would have a good chance. You could move in with me. The house is so big and lonely. There is plenty of room, and I can help you watch your babies. And your boyfriend Tony—isn't he a cook or something? I'm sure he could probably get a job at the diner in town. Oh dear, I'm so happy. I've been praying that you would come back ever since you left. I'll tell all your sisters the news when they all come over for family dinner tonight. It won't be long before we're all together again. Goodbye, my dear, and you be careful in that big city."

Tony and Peggy Sue start discussing their wedding. They decide they want a big wedding—with their families and friends, including a lot of their college friends. They want an outdoor ceremony and outdoor reception including plenty of food, music, and dancing into the night. They're not sure how much it will cost, though, and realize Peggy Sue's mother cannot afford to pay for the wedding, so they will have to pay for it themselves. Both Tony and Peggy Sue have college loans to pay back, but they hope that the money gifts they get from the wedding guests will be enough to pay for the wedding expenses and maybe have some left over for a honeymoon.

It is now New Year's Day and Tony and Peggy Sue decide to sit down and start laying out the detailed plan of all the things they need to do to get ready for their wedding.

CASE QUESTIONS

1. Make a list of assumptions that will be used as the basis for planning the wedding.
2. Make a list of activities that need to be done between now and the wedding day.

3. For each activity, identify the person (Tony, Peggy Sue, etc.) who will be responsible for seeing that the activity is accomplished.
4. Using the list of activities, develop a network diagram (using the activity-in-the-box format) showing the interrelationships of all the activities.

Note: This case study will continue in Chapters 6 through 9, where your group will be asked to develop duration estimates for each activity, a project schedule, and a project budget, so save the results of your work.

GROUP ACTIVITY

Divide the course participants into groups of three or four and answer the questions listed above.

And no, it is not acceptable to assume that Tony and Peggy Sue will just elope, no matter how tempting that may be!

Note: This case study will continue in Chapters 6 through 9, so save the results of your work.

Microsoft Project

APPENDIX

Microsoft Project is the most widely used project management software system in the business environment today. It is powerful, easy to use, and available at a very reasonable price. ***A free trial version is included with new copies of this text***. In this appendix we will briefly discuss how Microsoft Project can be used to support the techniques discussed in this chapter based on the consumer market study example.

Becoming oriented with the Microsoft Project 2007 environment: Open Microsoft Project 2007. Notice the Gantt Chart View in the main workspace. If you don't see this view, on the View menu click Gantt Chart. Above the main workspace are the Standard Toolbar, Formatting Toolbar, and the Project Guide Toolbar. If any of these toolbars are hidden, on the View menu, point to Toolbars and select the toolbars from the list. To the left of the main workspace is a narrow Task Pane, which begins with the Getting Started Task Pane and contains links to Microsoft Office Online, a list of the previously opened Microsoft Project files, and the option to begin a New Project. If this Task Pane is hidden, on the View menu, point to Toolbars and select Task Pane from the list. You can move the Task Pane so that it sits to the left or the right of the main workspace.

Visit Microsoft Office Online for online tutorials and more: If you haven't already explored Microsoft Office Online, set aside some time to do so. There you will find tutorials, tips, templates, news, and other valuable information about Microsoft Project 2007. The link to Microsoft Office Online is provided in the Getting Started Task Pane.

Let's begin building the Consumer Market Study Project: On the File menu, click New to begin a new project. Then from the Task Pane on the left, select Blank Project.

About the Project Guide: You may choose to use the Project Guide which will appear in the Task Pane. The Project Guide will provide the basic steps you need in the four areas of your project:

Area 1—Tasks

Area 2—Resources

Area 3—Track

Area 4—Report

These Areas are listed in the Project Guide Toolbar at the top. Click on each Area on the Project Guide Toolbar to see the corresponding guide in the Task Pane. If you don't see this toolbar, on the View menu, point to Toolbar, and click on Project Guide. The Project Guide is a helpful tool for building your first project. However, not all the steps in these Microsoft Project exercises are included in the Project Guide, so the instructions provided in this book will assume that you are not using the Project Guide.

First, set some properties to describe the project file. On the File menu, click on Properties to enter "Consumer Market Study" as the Project Title as shown in Figure 5A.1. You can enter other information, such as Subject, Author, Manager, Company, and other related comments. Click on OK to save and close the Project Properties window.

FIGURE 5A.1 ***Project Properties***

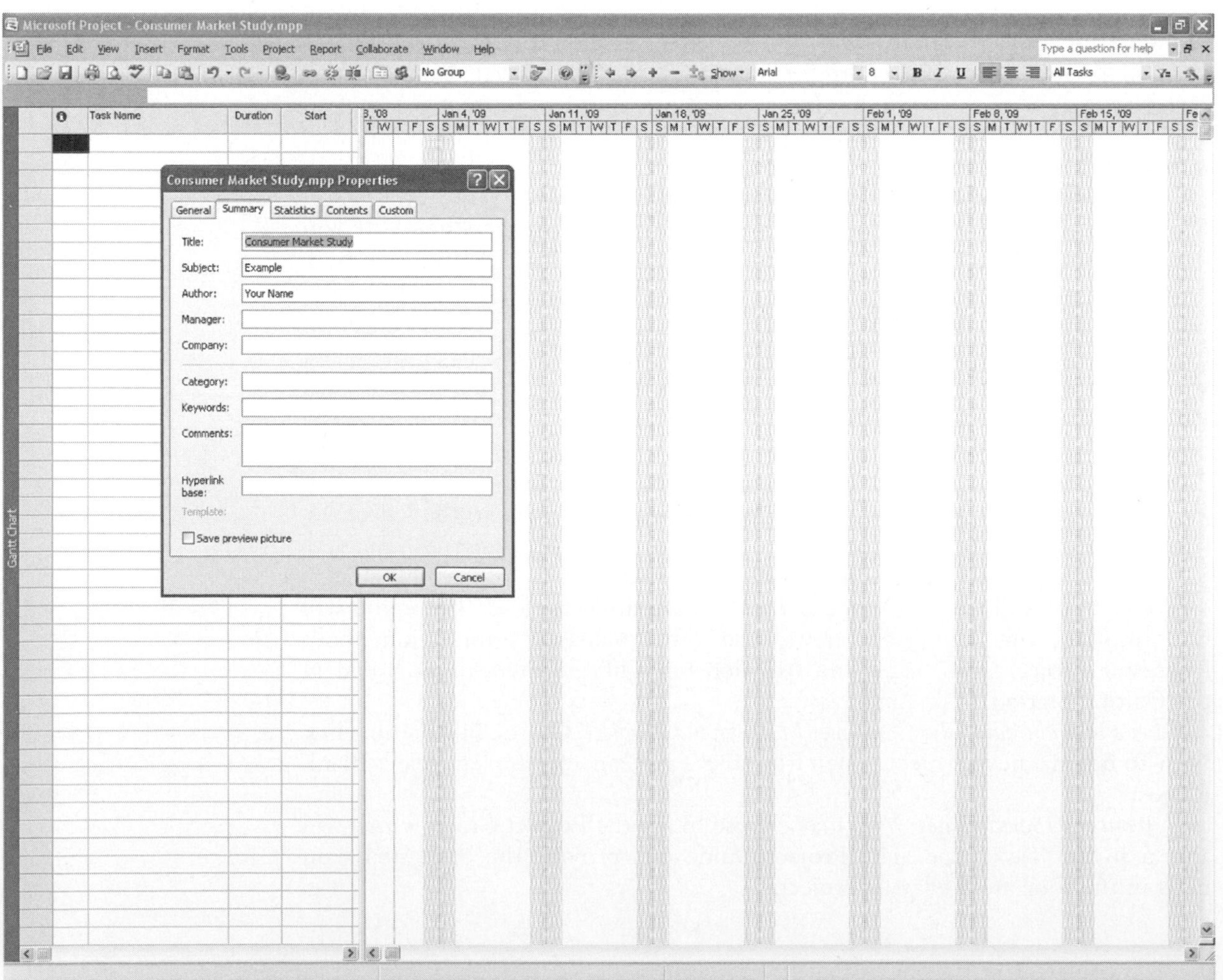

FIGURE 5A.2 ***Project Information***

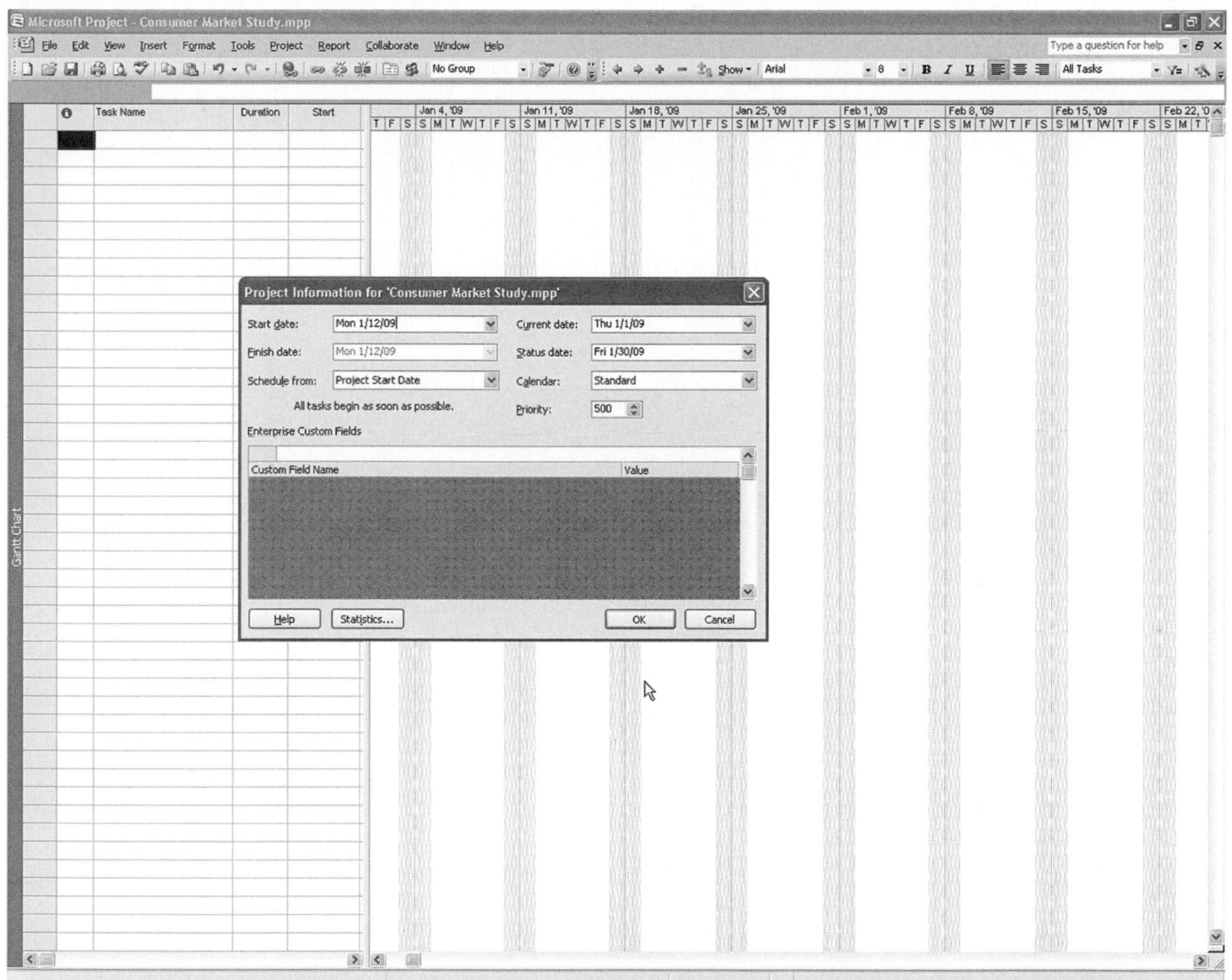

You also first need to enter time-related information so that the software can automatically build project schedules and calculate costs.

On the Project menu, click on Project Information to view the Project Information window, and enter the Start date: Mon 1/12/09, as in Figure 5A.2. Click on OK to close the Project Information Window.

Next, on the Tools menu, click on Change Working Time. Select or enter the following data:

1. For: Standard (Project Calendar) in selection box.
2. Find the January 2009 calendar, click on January 19 and click the Exceptions tab.
3. Type a descriptive name for the exception, such as Holiday, and then click in the Start field (this will set the start and finish times for the exception as the selected day).
4. Click Details
5. Under Set working times for these exceptions, select Nonworking, then click OK.

FIGURE 5A.3 ***Tasks—Task Names, Duration, and Start and Finish Dates***

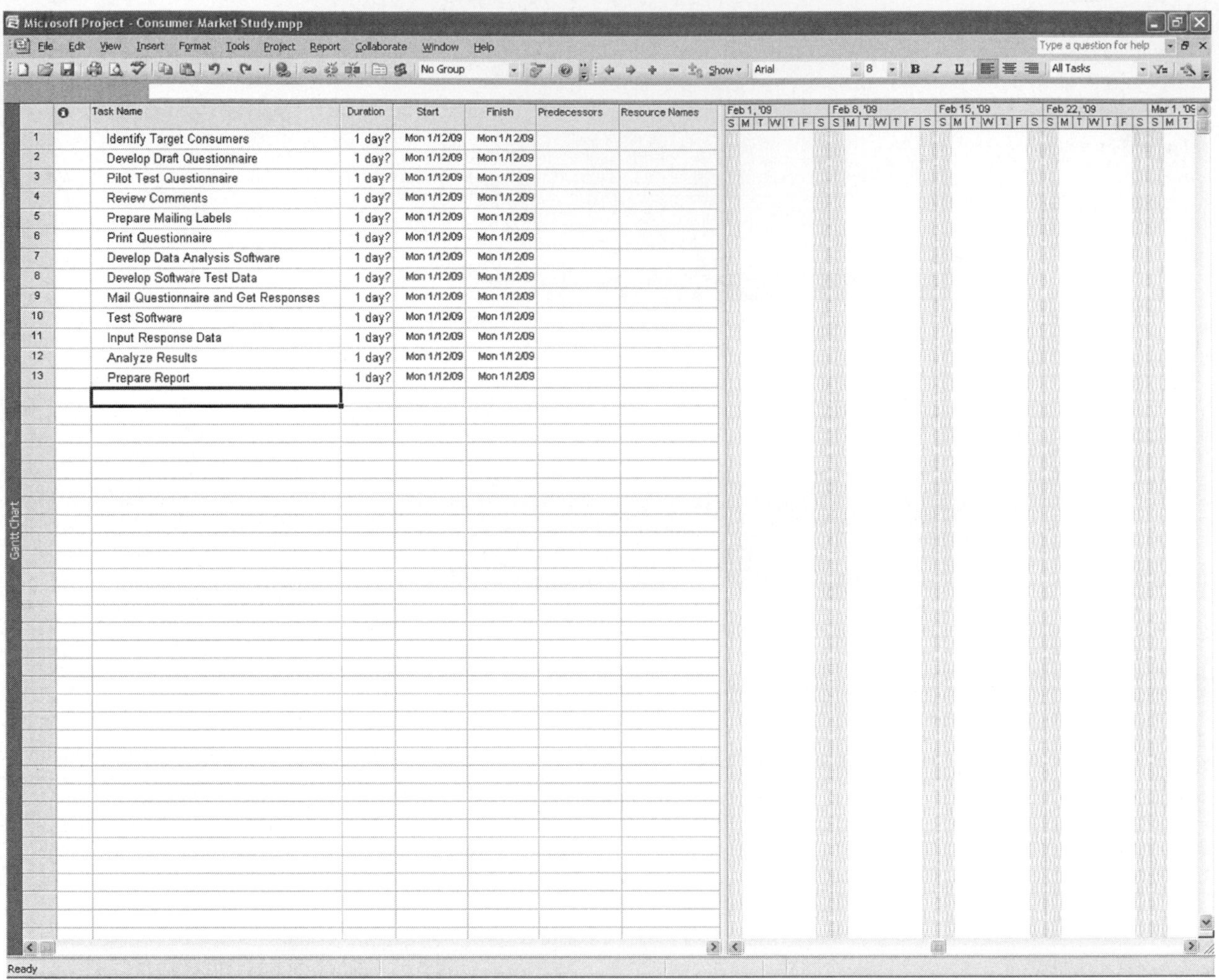

	Task Name	Duration	Start	Finish	Predecessors	Resource Names
1	Identify Target Consumers	1 day?	Mon 1/12/09	Mon 1/12/09		
2	Develop Draft Questionnaire	1 day?	Mon 1/12/09	Mon 1/12/09		
3	Pilot Test Questionnaire	1 day?	Mon 1/12/09	Mon 1/12/09		
4	Review Comments	1 day?	Mon 1/12/09	Mon 1/12/09		
5	Prepare Mailing Labels	1 day?	Mon 1/12/09	Mon 1/12/09		
6	Print Questionnaire	1 day?	Mon 1/12/09	Mon 1/12/09		
7	Develop Data Analysis Software	1 day?	Mon 1/12/09	Mon 1/12/09		
8	Develop Software Test Data	1 day?	Mon 1/12/09	Mon 1/12/09		
9	Mail Questionnaire and Get Responses	1 day?	Mon 1/12/09	Mon 1/12/09		
10	Test Software	1 day?	Mon 1/12/09	Mon 1/12/09		
11	Input Response Data	1 day?	Mon 1/12/09	Mon 1/12/09		
12	Analyze Results	1 day?	Mon 1/12/09	Mon 1/12/09		
13	Prepare Report	1 day?	Mon 1/12/09	Mon 1/12/09		

6. Click on Options to set the following standard work times:
   Hours per day = 8
   Hours per week = 40
   Days per month = 20
   Click OK to close the Options window
7. Click OK to close the Change Working Time Tool

Now, you should see the Gantt Chart View with the Entry Table on your screen. Here you will enter task names into the Task Name Column. Please refer to Figure 5A.3 for task names to enter. After you enter a task name, notice the default duration, 1 Day, is automatically entered, along with start and finish dates. Leave these as the default values for now. You can easily create subsets of tasks. In the Formatting Toolbar at the top, you should see 2 green arrows. You can use these arrows to create subtasks and to bring a task to a higher level of organization. Try these out, even though you will not need to create subtasks for this exercise.

FIGURE 5A.4 ***Tasks—Adding Predecessor Data***

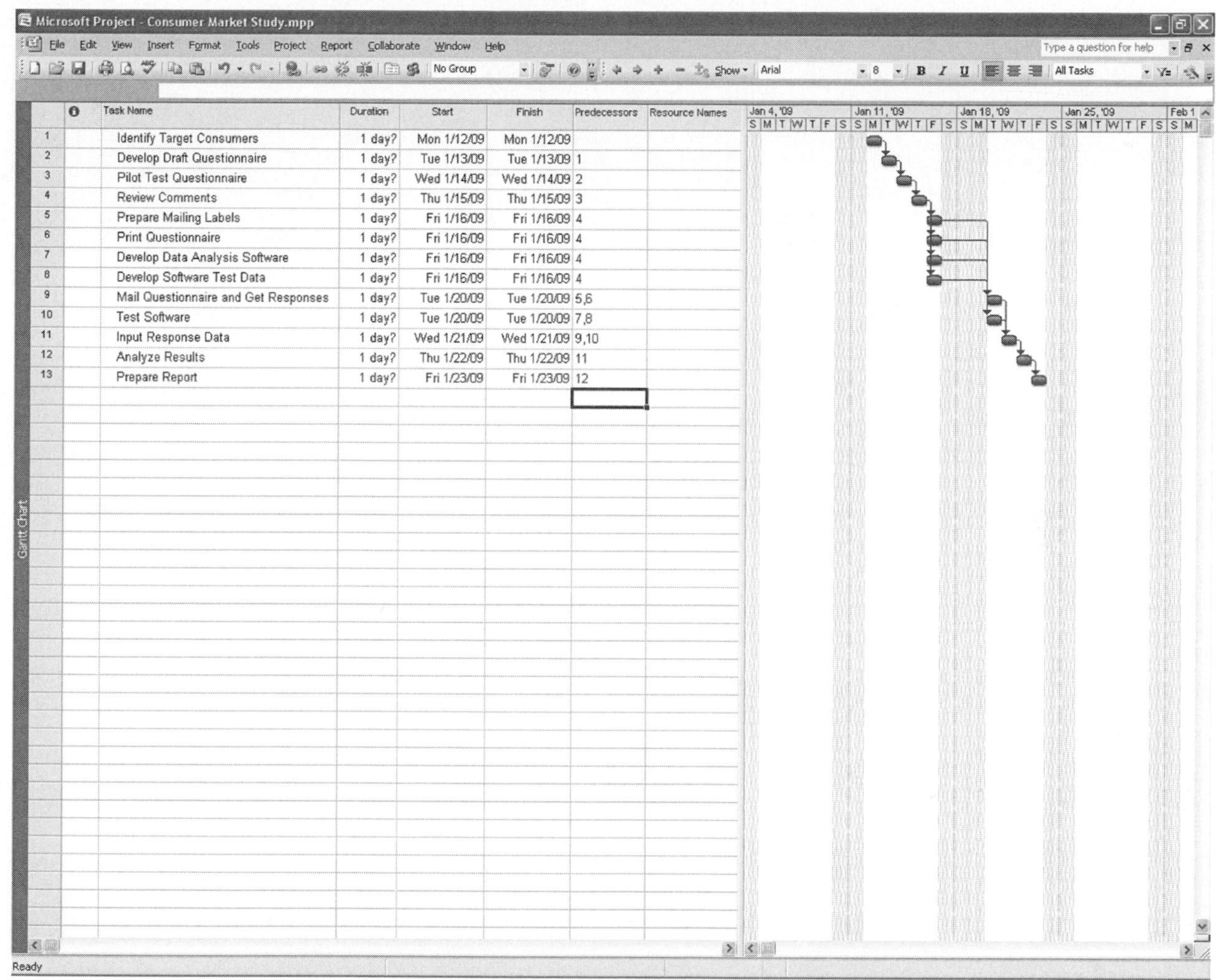

	Task Name	Duration	Start	Finish	Predecessors	Resource Names
1	Identify Target Consumers	1 day?	Mon 1/12/09	Mon 1/12/09		
2	Develop Draft Questionnaire	1 day?	Tue 1/13/09	Tue 1/13/09	1	
3	Pilot Test Questionnaire	1 day?	Wed 1/14/09	Wed 1/14/09	2	
4	Review Comments	1 day?	Thu 1/15/09	Thu 1/15/09	3	
5	Prepare Mailing Labels	1 day?	Fri 1/16/09	Fri 1/16/09	4	
6	Print Questionnaire	1 day?	Fri 1/16/09	Fri 1/16/09	4	
7	Develop Data Analysis Software	1 day?	Fri 1/16/09	Fri 1/16/09	4	
8	Develop Software Test Data	1 day?	Fri 1/16/09	Fri 1/16/09	4	
9	Mail Questionnaire and Get Responses	1 day?	Tue 1/20/09	Tue 1/20/09	5,6	
10	Test Software	1 day?	Tue 1/20/09	Tue 1/20/09	7,8	
11	Input Response Data	1 day?	Wed 1/21/09	Wed 1/21/09	9,10	
12	Analyze Results	1 day?	Thu 1/22/09	Thu 1/22/09	11	
13	Prepare Report	1 day?	Fri 1/23/09	Fri 1/23/09	12	

For each task that is entered, you can add additional details by adding Task Notes. Right-click on a task name to select Task Notes from the Menu. This screen allows you to enter additional information about each task.

Next, you will enter the predecessor data directly into the Predecessor column to show dependencies among the tasks. Please see Figure 5A.4 for this data. For example, Task 1 is the predecessor for Task 2, or in other words, Task 2 is dependent on the completion of Task 1

The Consumer Market Study project team consists of Susan, Steve, Andy, and Jim. Enter these names onto the Resource Sheet, where all team members are listed with his or her corresponding pay rate. On the View menu, click on Resource Sheet. Populate the Resource sheet with the names of the team members: Susan, Steve, Andy, and Jim. You can enter other information such as initials to use, hourly rate, and overtime rate.

Next, you can show who will perform each task that you just listed. On the View menu, click on Gantt Chart and for each task, assign a person to

FIGURE 5A.5 *Resources*

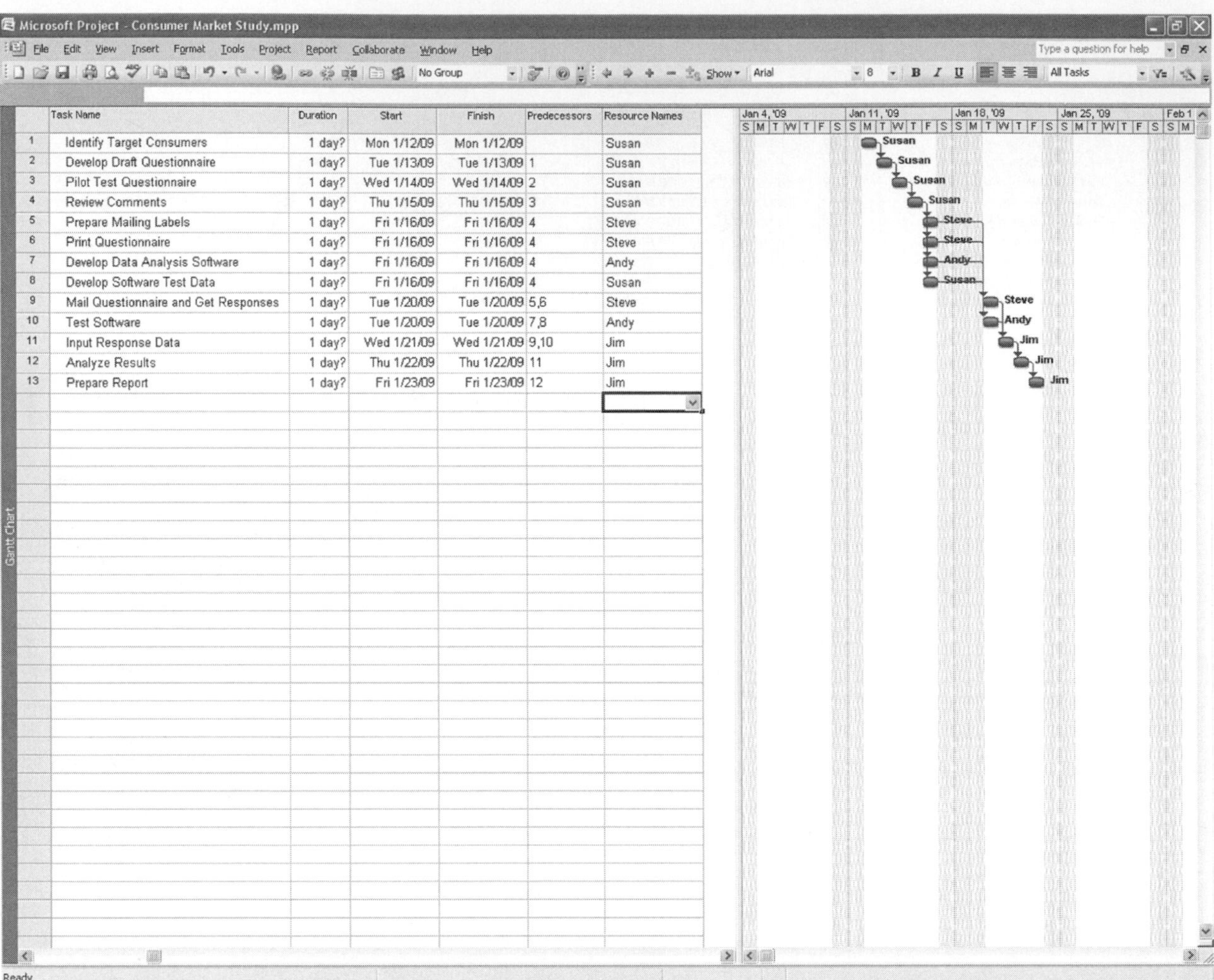

	Task Name	Duration	Start	Finish	Predecessors	Resource Names
1	Identify Target Consumers	1 day?	Mon 1/12/09	Mon 1/12/09		Susan
2	Develop Draft Questionnaire	1 day?	Tue 1/13/09	Tue 1/13/09	1	Susan
3	Pilot Test Questionnaire	1 day?	Wed 1/14/09	Wed 1/14/09	2	Susan
4	Review Comments	1 day?	Thu 1/15/09	Thu 1/15/09	3	Susan
5	Prepare Mailing Labels	1 day?	Fri 1/16/09	Fri 1/16/09	4	Steve
6	Print Questionnaire	1 day?	Fri 1/16/09	Fri 1/16/09	4	Steve
7	Develop Data Analysis Software	1 day?	Fri 1/16/09	Fri 1/16/09	4	Andy
8	Develop Software Test Data	1 day?	Fri 1/16/09	Fri 1/16/09	4	Susan
9	Mail Questionnaire and Get Responses	1 day?	Tue 1/20/09	Tue 1/20/09	5,6	Steve
10	Test Software	1 day?	Tue 1/20/09	Tue 1/20/09	7,8	Andy
11	Input Response Data	1 day?	Wed 1/21/09	Wed 1/21/09	9,10	Jim
12	Analyze Results	1 day?	Thu 1/22/09	Thu 1/22/09	11	Jim
13	Prepare Report	1 day?	Fri 1/23/09	Fri 1/23/09	12	Jim

that task in the Resource Names column. The names from the Resource Sheet can be selected from the provided drop-down box in the Resource Names column. Please refer to Figure 5A.5 for name–task assignments in this exercise. Notice the Gantt Chart is automatically generated on the right side of the screen.

For each task you can see all the detailed information related to that task by right-clicking on the task name and then clicking on Task Information from the menu.

To view the PERT diagram shown in Figure 5A.6, on the View menu, click on Network Diagram. This network diagram is equivalent to the activity-in-a-box format discussed in this chapter. You can also create a less detailed PERT diagram through the View menu—click on More Views and click on Relationship Diagram. To return to the default view, on the View menu, click on Gantt Chart.

FIGURE 5A.6 *The Network Diagram*

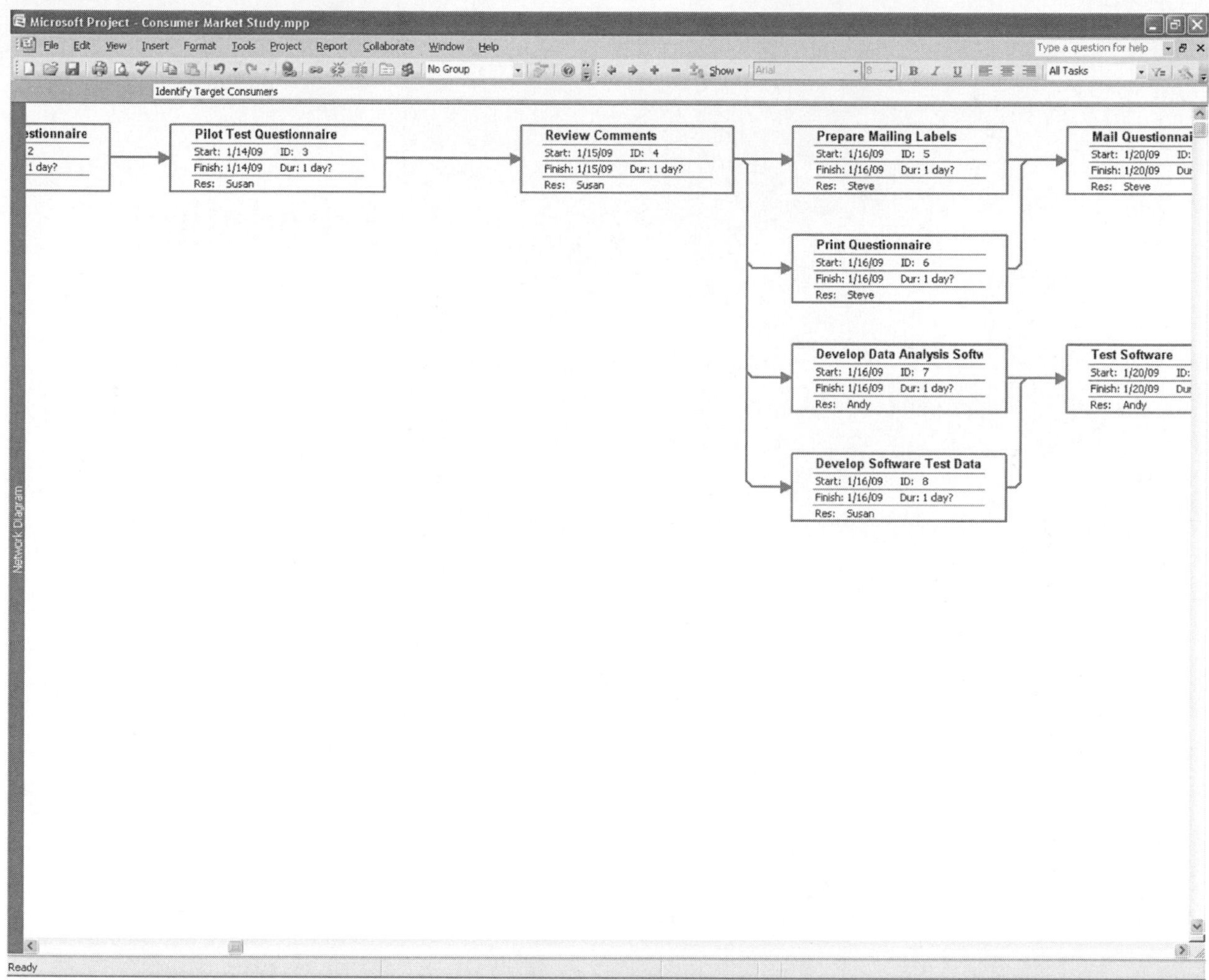

To save your project information, on the File menu, click on Save As. Saving a project with a baseline plan before the project starts is highly recommended so you can compare actual progress versus planned progress once the project has started.

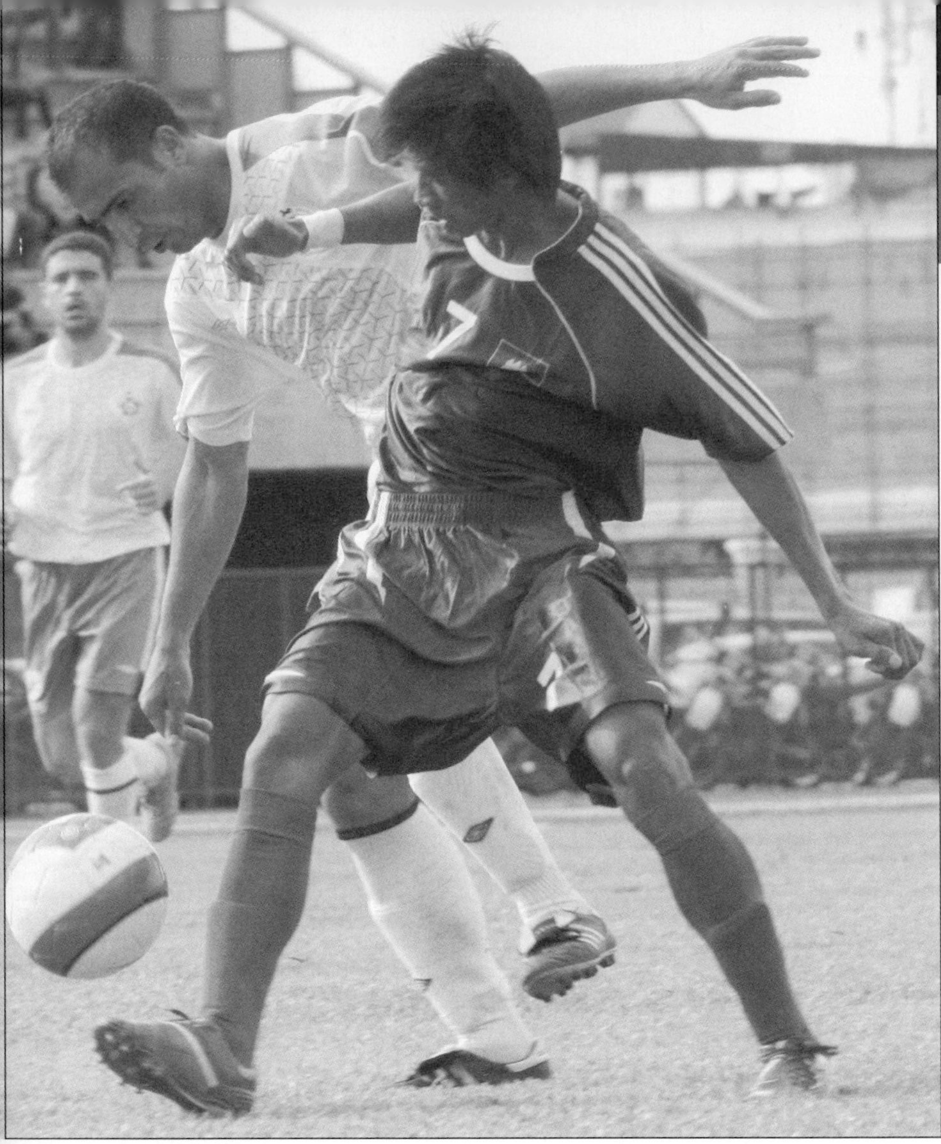

© AP Photo/Heng Sinith

CHAPTER

6

Scheduling

Real World PROJECT MANAGEMENT

The World Cup Tournament

South Africa is the host country for the Fédération Internationale de Football Association (FIFA) World Cup tournament in 2010, one of the biggest sporting events in the world. The tournament consists of 32 teams from around the globe. In order to run the tournament, the host country must complete many information technology and construction projects in preparation for the estimated three million fans who will attend.

In addition, it is estimated that 30 billion people will be watching the tournament on television. According to FIFA president Joseph "Sepp" Blatter, the World Cup is the association's "project number one," and Danny Jordan, the CEO of the 2010 Bid Company, believes the World Cup has become a "project" of the nation!

In preparation for the tournament, the South African government is projected to invest more than R400 billion on infrastructure projects. Additionally, between R2 billion and R5 billion will be spent on information and communication technology projects, including wireless and e-ticketing projects. Recently at the Connect IT: Joburg 2010 conference, it was announced that broadband and wireless hot spots will be implemented in Durban by 2010 and that the needed upgrades in South Africa will extend far beyond those made for the tournament.

Large investments will be made to ensure all transit systems (passenger rail, taxis, buses, and road networks) form an effective public transport network that will be used for the next 50 to 100 years. This project has been divided into two phases, with the first phase to be completed before the games in 2010. The project team has created a comprehensive document management system to demonstrate work-flows and provide real-time reports on project status. The overall transportation project is extremely complex, with more than 30,000 activities defined for the early stages and potentially more than 65,000 interlinked activities with multiple critical paths for the entire project.

Another huge project is the expansion and improvement at the O.R. Tambo International Airport in Johannesburg. Projects are in the works to increase the capacity of the central terminal, expand the international arrival and departure areas, and build a new multistory car park. The airport needed to be upgraded for more passenger growth regardless of the World Cup. Since securing the bid for the tournament, project schedules have been reassessed and the completion date for the central terminal building has been moved up to 2009. The revised schedules are tight, but officials believe they still have sufficient time to deal with any minor adjustments that might be necessary.

In addition to all of the above, the South African government has earmarked $1.1 billion for new and renovated stadiums to hold the games of the World Cup. Johannesburg's 95,000-seat Soccer City, the venue that will host the opening and closing matches, is currently being revamped. Contractors maintain that the Soccer City upgrades will be completed ahead of the October 2009 schedule. Four other arenas—Ellis Park in Johannesburg, Loftus Versfeld in Tshwane, Royal Bafokeng in Rustenburg, and Free State Stadium in Bloemfontein—will also undergo major renovations before the tournament.

Unfortunately, according to the Associated Press, there are reports of schedule delays and budget overruns that have resulted in concerns about the 2010 World Cup tournament. According to Johan Venter, the project administrations manager working for the government team, there have been some complications to the overall project and there is a sense of urgency to get things done. He is quoted as saying, "Many people do not fully understand the details of project management as a specific entity—such as detailed work breakdown structures and critical paths." Clearly this has been an issue. However, project schedules have been revised and officials remain optimistic.

If the project teams get the job done and the games go on as scheduled, although it will be the players in the World Cup who receive the glory, it will be the project managers and their teams who made it all possible!

Kent, S., "Game Plan," *PM Network*, August 2007.

Chapter 5 dealt with determining which activities need to be done and in what sequence in order to accomplish a project objective. The result was a plan in the form of a network diagram that graphically portrayed activities in the appropriate interdependent sequence to accomplish the project work scope. When network planning techniques are used, the scheduling function depends on the planning function. A **schedule** is a timetable for a plan and, therefore, cannot be established until the plan has been developed. In this chapter, we will establish a schedule for the plan. You will become familiar with

- estimating the duration for each activity
- establishing the estimated start time and required completion time for the overall project
- calculating the earliest times at which each activity can start and finish, based on the project's estimated start time
- calculating the latest times by which each activity must start and finish in order to complete the project by its required completion time
- determining the amount of positive or negative slack between the time each activity can start or finish and the time it must start or finish
- identifying the critical (longest) path of activities

ACTIVITY DURATION ESTIMATES

The first step in establishing a project schedule is to estimate how long each activity will take, from the time it is started until the time it is finished. This **duration estimate** for each activity must be the *total elapsed time*—the time for the work to be done plus any associated waiting time. In Figure 6.1, for example, the duration estimate for activity 1, "Varnish Floors," is five days, which includes both the time to varnish the floors and the waiting time for the varnish to dry.

Reinforce Your Learning

1. True or false: The duration estimate for an activity should include the time required to perform the work plus any associated waiting time.

The activity's duration estimate is usually shown in the lower right-hand corner of the box in the activity-in-the-box format of network diagrams. It's shown below the arrow in the activity-on-the arrow format (see Figure 6.2).

It's a good practice to have the person who will be responsible for performing a particular activity make the duration estimate for that activity. This

FIGURE 6.1 ***Activity Duration Estimate (Activity-in-the-Box Format)***

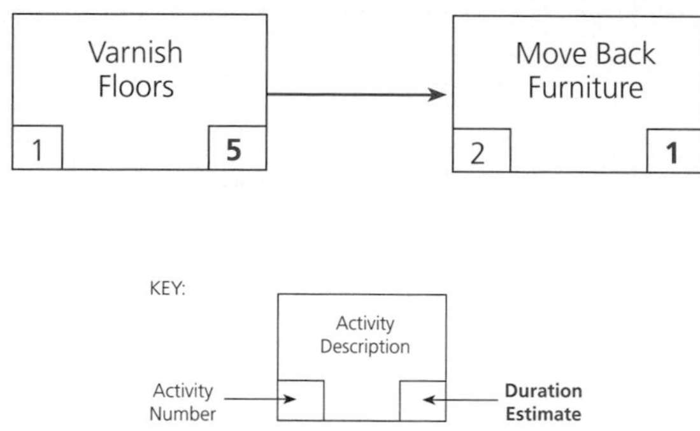

FIGURE 6.2 ***Activity Duration Estimate (Activity-on-the-Arrow Format)***

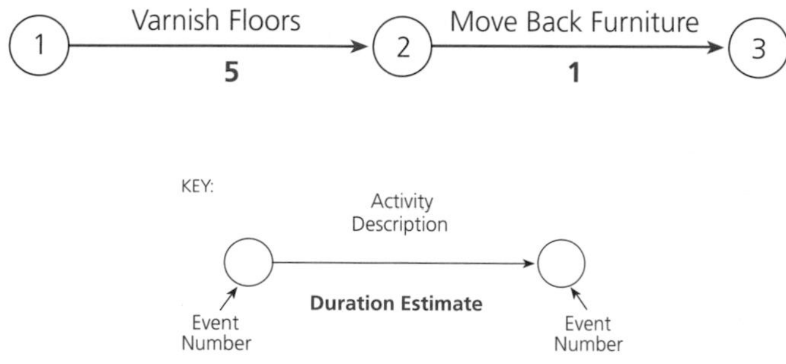

generates a commitment from that person and avoids any bias that may be introduced by having one person make the duration estimates for all of the activities. In some cases, though—such as for large projects that involve several hundred people performing various activities over several years—it may not be practical to have each person provide activity duration estimates at the beginning of the project. Rather, each organization or subcontractor responsible for a group or type of activities may designate an experienced individual to make the duration estimates for all the activities for which the organization or subcontractor is responsible. If an organization or subcontractor has performed similar projects in the past and has kept records of how long specific activities actually took, these historical data can be used as a guide in estimating activity durations for future projects.

An activity's duration estimate must be based on the quantity of resources expected to be used on the activity. The estimate should be aggressive, yet realistic. It should not include time for a lot of things that could possibly go wrong. Nor should it be too optimistically short. It is generally better to be somewhat aggressive and estimate a duration for an activity at five days, say, and then actually finish it in six days, than to be overly conservative and estimate a duration at 10 days and then actually take 10 days. People sometimes perform to expectations—if an activity is estimated to take 10 days, their effort will expand to fill the whole 10 days allotted, even if the activity could have been performed in a shorter time.

FIGURE 6.3 ***Network Diagram for Consumer Market Study Project, Showing Duration Estimates (Activity-in-the-Box Format)***

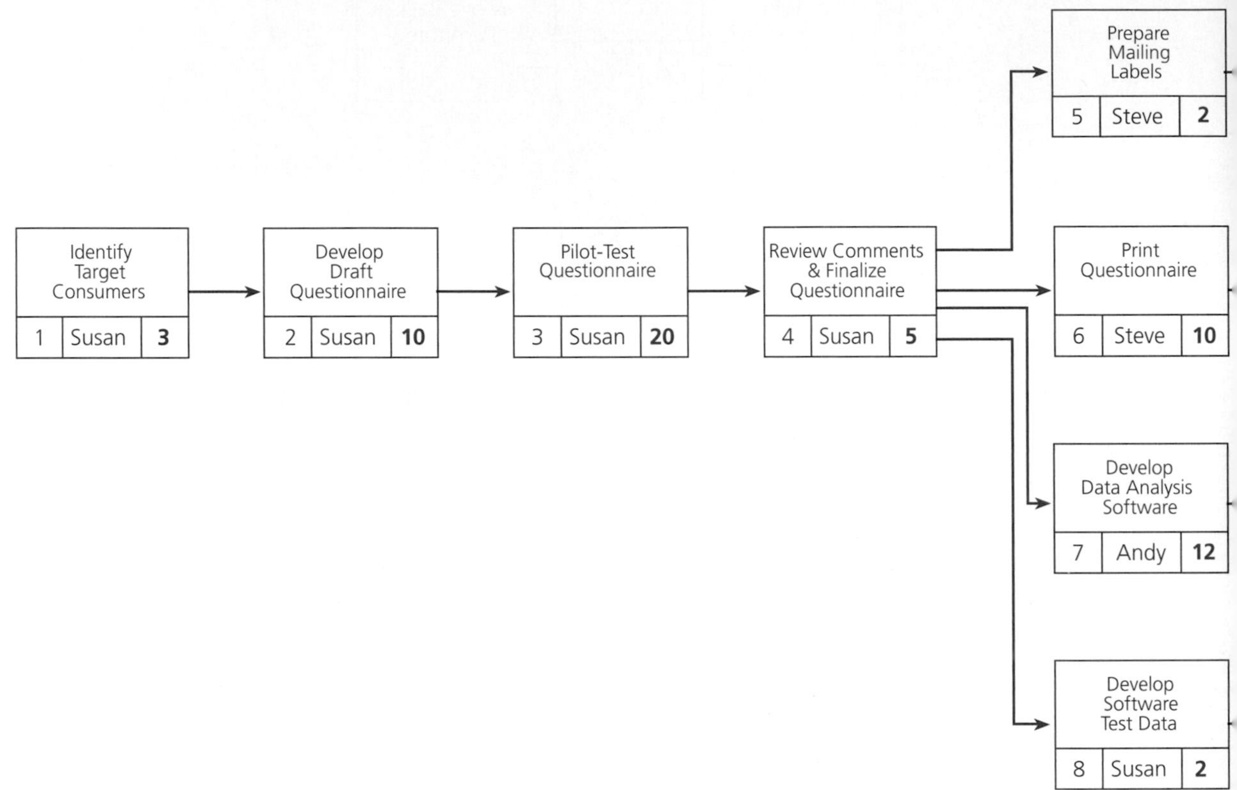

Playing the game of inflating duration estimates in anticipation of the project manager's negotiating shorter durations is not a good practice. Nor is padding estimates with the vision of becoming a hero when the activities are completed in less time than estimated.

Throughout the performance of the project, some activities will take longer than their estimated duration, others will be done in less time than their estimated duration, and a few may conform to the duration estimates exactly. Over the life of a project that involves many activities, such delays and accelerations will tend to cancel one another out. For example, one activity may take two weeks longer than originally estimated, but this delay may be offset by two other activities that are each done a week sooner than originally estimated.

Figures 6.3 and 6.4 show network diagrams for a consumer market study in the AIB and AOA formats, respectively, with the duration estimates in days for each activity. A consistent time base, such as hours or days or weeks, should be used for all the activity duration estimates in a network diagram. Note that in the AOA format it is not necessary to give a duration estimate for dummy activities, because by definition their duration is 0.

With projects for which there is a high degree of uncertainty about the activity duration estimates, it is possible to use three duration estimates: an optimistic, a pessimistic, and a most likely. For a discussion of this technique, see the Appendix 1 at the end of this chapter.

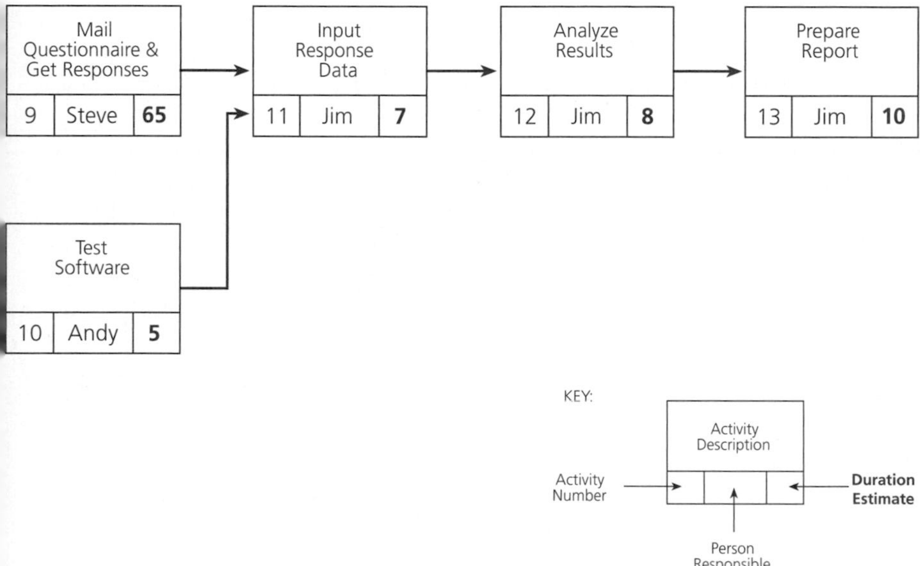

PROJECT START AND FINISH TIMES

In order to establish a basis from which to calculate a schedule using the duration estimates for the activities, it's necessary to select an **estimated start time** and a **required completion time** for the overall project. These two times (or dates) define the overall window, or envelope, of time in which the project must be completed.

The project's required completion time is normally part of the project objective and stated in the contract. In some cases, both estimated start time and required completion time are stated, as in "The project will not start before June 1 and must be completed by September 30." In other cases, the customer specifies only the date by which the project must be completed.

The contractor, however, may not want to commit to completing the project by a specific date until the customer has approved the contract. In such cases the contract may state, "The project will be completed within 90 days of the signing of the contract." Here the overall project time is stated in terms of a cycle time (90 days) rather than in terms of specific calendar dates.

Assume that the consumer market study project shown in Figures 6.3 and 6.4 must be completed in 130 working days. If we define the project's estimated start time as 0, its required completion time is day 130.

Reinforce Your Learning

2. The overall window of time in which a project must be completed is defined by its

____

____________________ time and

____

____________________ time.

FIGURE 6.4 ***Network Diagram for Consumer Market Study Project, Showing Duration Estimates (Activity-on-the-Arrow Format)***

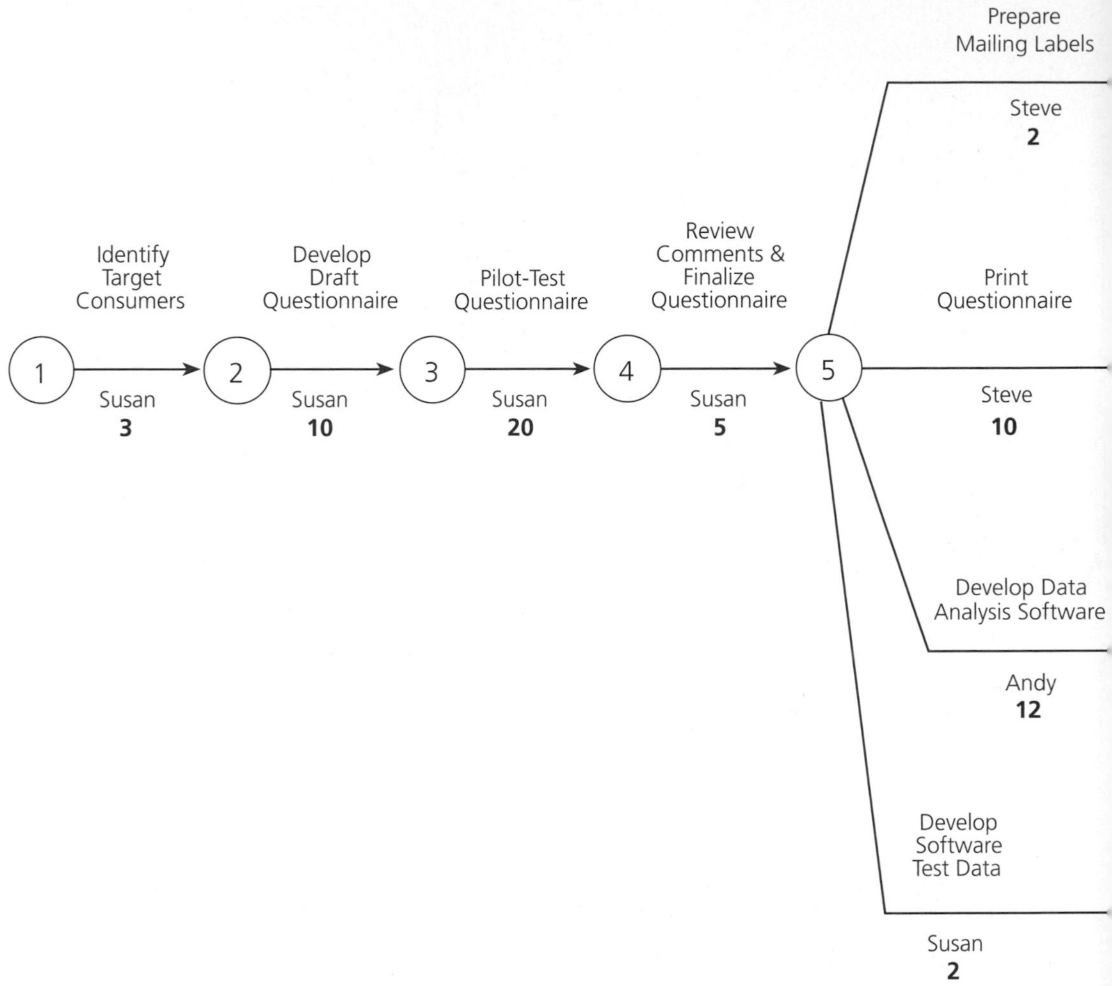

SCHEDULE CALCULATIONS

Once you have an estimated duration for each activity in the network and an overall window of time in which the project must be completed, you must determine (based on durations and precedential sequence) whether the activities can be done by the required completion time. To determine this, you can calculate a project schedule that provides a timetable for each activity and shows

1. the earliest times (or dates) at which each activity can start and finish, based on the project's estimated start time (or date)
2. the latest times (or dates) by which each activity must start and finish in order to complete the project by its required completion time (or date)

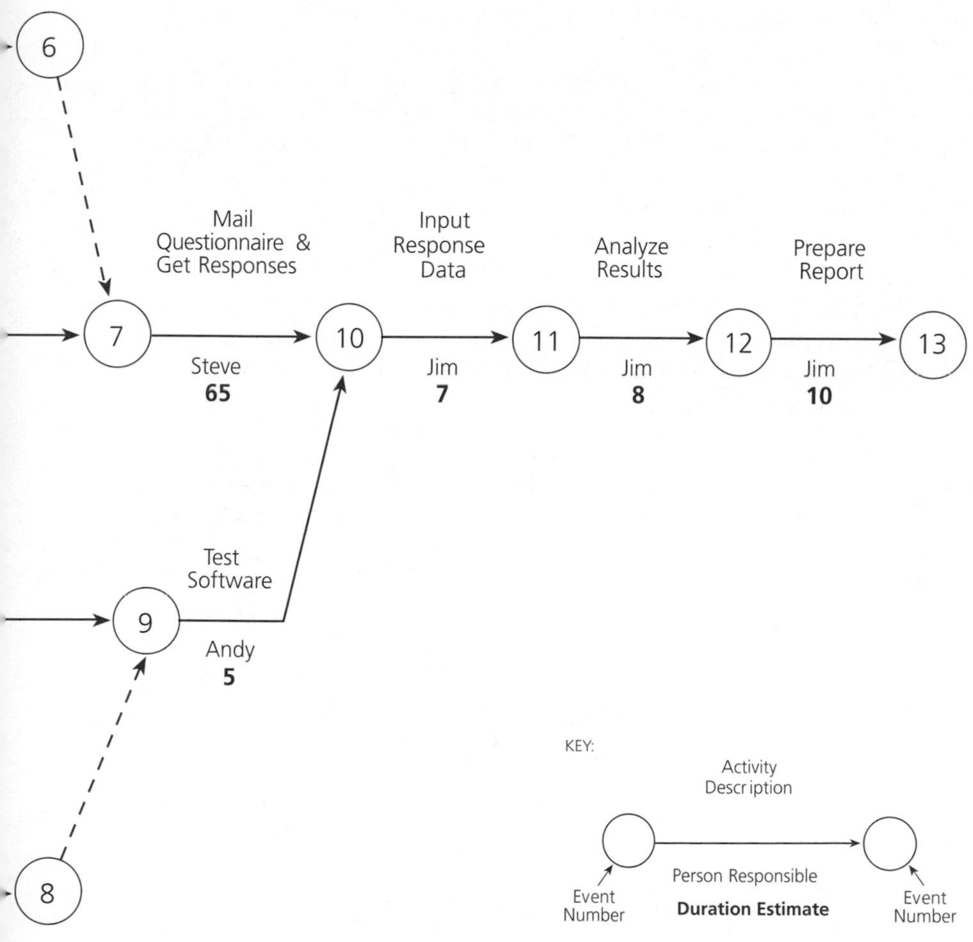

Earliest Start and Finish Times

Given an estimated duration for each activity in the network and using the project's estimated start time as a reference, you can calculate the following two times for each activity:

1. **Earliest start time (ES)** is the earliest time at which a particular activity can begin, calculated on the basis of the project's estimated start time and the duration estimates for preceding activities.
2. **Earliest finish time (EF)** is the earliest time by which a particular activity can be completed, calculated by adding the activity's duration estimate to the activity's earliest start time:

$$EF = ES + \text{Duration Estimate}$$

Reinforce Your Learning

3. What is the equation for calculating an activity's earliest finish time?

Reinforce Your Learning

4. The earliest start and earliest finish times for activities are determined by calculating

____

through the network diagram

The ES and EF times are determined by calculating *forward*—that is, by working through the network diagram from the beginning of the project to the end of the project. There is one rule that must be followed in making these forward calculations.

Rule 1: The earliest start time for a particular activity must be the same as or later than the latest of all the earliest finish times of all the activities leading directly into that particular activity.

Figure 6.5 shows three activities leading directly into "Dress Rehearsal." "Practice Skit" has an EF of day 5, "Make Costumes" has an EF of day 10, and "Make Props" has an EF of day 4. "Dress Rehearsal" cannot start until all three of these activities are finished, so the latest of the EFs for these three activities determines the ES for "Dress Rehearsal." The latest of the three EFs is day 10—the earliest finish time for "Make Costumes." Therefore, "Dress Rehearsal" cannot start any earlier than day 10. That is, its ES must be day 10 or later. Even though "Practice Skit" and "Make Props" may finish sooner than "Make Costumes," "Dress Rehearsal" cannot start because the network logic indicates that *all three activities* must be finished before "Dress Rehearsal" can start.

FIGURE 6.5 *Earliest Start Times*

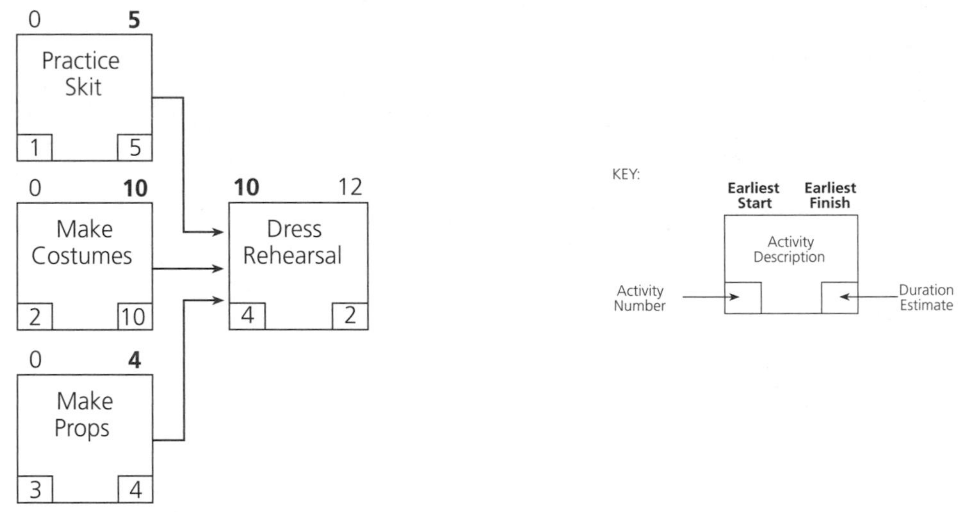

(a) Activity-in-the-Box Format

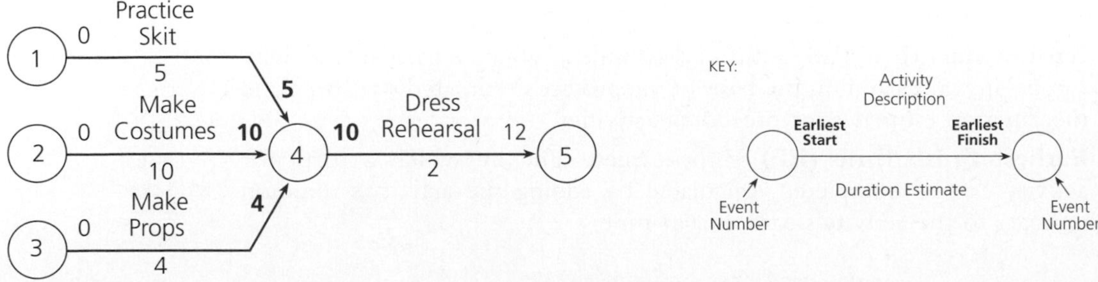

(b) Activity-on-the-Arrow Format

Figures 6.6 and 6.7 show the forward calculations for the consumer market study project. The project's estimated start time is 0. Therefore, the earliest "Identify Target Consumers" can start is time 0, and the earliest it can finish is 3 days later (because its estimated duration is 3 days). When "Identify Target Consumers" is finished on day 3, "Develop Draft Questionnaire" can start. It has a duration of 10 days, so its ES is day 3 and its EF is day 13. The calculations of ES and EF for subsequent activities are done similarly, continuing forward through the network diagram.

Reinforce Your Learning

5. Refer to Figures 6.6 and 6.7. What are the earliest start and earliest finish times for "Pilot-Test Questionnaire"?

Look for a moment at "Test Software." It has an ES of day 50 because, according to Rule 1, it cannot start until the two activities leading directly into it are finished. "Develop Data Analysis Software" doesn't finish until day 50, and "Develop Software Test Data" doesn't finish until day 40. Because "Test Software" cannot start until both of these are finished, "Test Software" cannot start until day 50.

As a further illustration of Rule 1, refer once more to Figures 6.6 and 6.7. In order to start "Mail Questionnaire & Get Responses," the two activities immediately preceding it, "Prepare Mailing Labels" and "Print Questionnaire," must be finished. The EF of "Prepare Mailing Labels" is day 40, and the EF of "Print Questionnaire" is day 48. According to Rule 1, it is the later of the two EFs, which is day 48, that determines the ES of "Mail Questionnaire & Get Responses."

If you continue calculating the ES and the EF for each remaining activity in the network diagram in Figures 6.6 and 6.7, you'll see that the very last activity, "Prepare Final Report," has an EF of day 138. That is 8 days beyond the project's required completion time of 130 days. At this point, we know there's a problem.

It should be noted that although the ES and EF times for each activity are shown on the network diagrams in Figures 6.6 and 6.7, this is *not* normally the case. Rather, the ES and EF times (and the LS and LF times, explained in the following section) are listed in a separate schedule table, like the one in Figure 6.8. Separating the schedule table from the network logic diagram makes it easier to generate revised and updated schedules (perhaps using project management software), without continually making changes to the ES, EF, LS, and LF times on the network diagram itself.

Reinforce Your Learning

6. What determines a particular activity's earliest start time?

Latest Start and Finish Times

Given a duration estimate for each activity in the network and using the project's required completion time as a reference, you can calculate the following two times for each activity:

1. **Latest finish time (LF)** is the latest time by which a particular activity must be completed in order for the entire project to be finished by its required completion time, calculated on the basis of the project's required completion time and the duration estimates for succeeding activities.
2. **Latest start time (LS)** is the latest time by which a particular activity must be started in order for the entire project to be finished by its required completion time, calculated by subtracting the activity's duration estimate from the activity's latest finish time:

$$LS = LF - \text{Duration Estimate}$$

The LF and LS times are determined by calculating *backward*—that is, by working through the network diagram from the end of the project to the

FIGURE 6.6 *Network Diagram for Consumer Market Study Project, Showing Earliest Start and Finish Times (Activity-in-the-Box Format)*

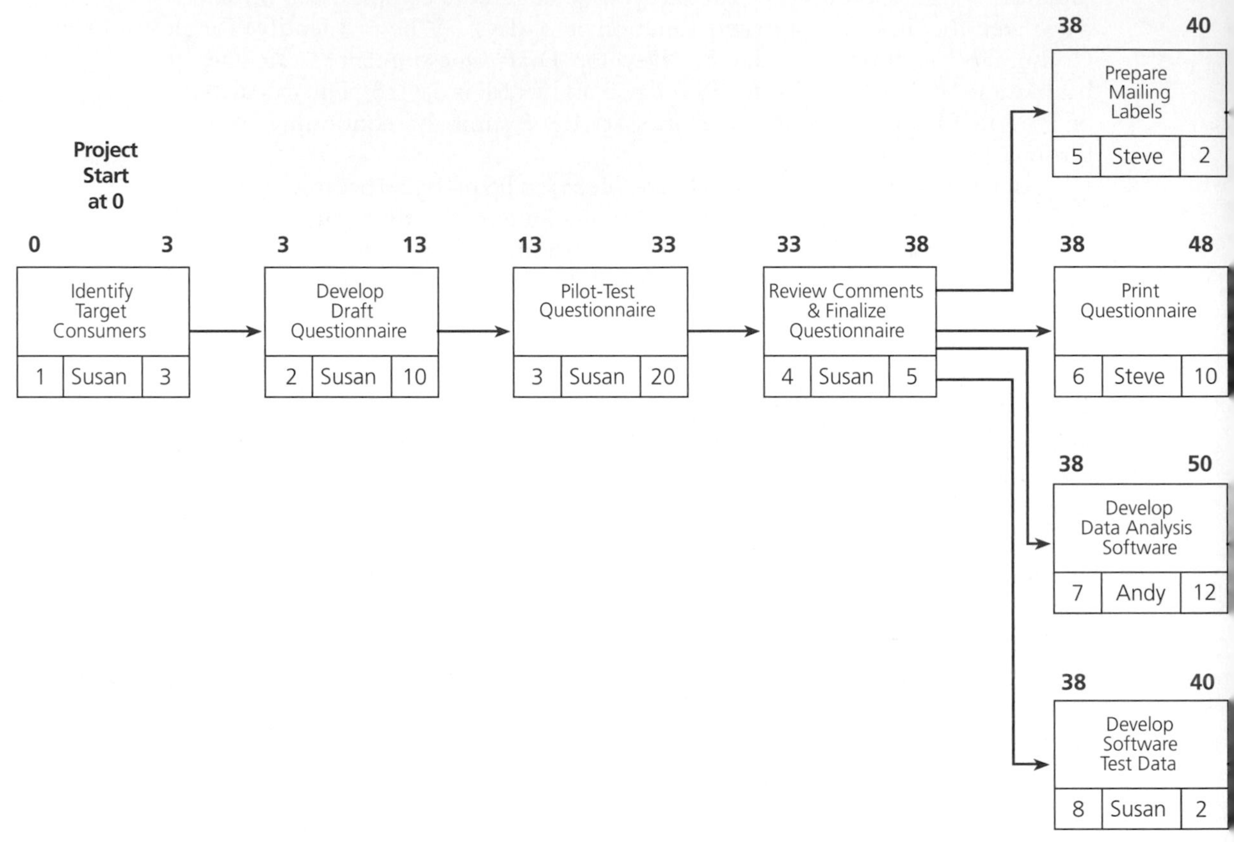

beginning of the project. There is one rule that must be followed in making these backward calculations.

Rule 2: The latest finish time for a particular activity must be the same as or earlier than the earliest of all the latest start times of all the activities emerging directly from that particular activity.

Reinforce Your Learning

7. What is the equation for calculating an activity's latest start time?

Reinforce Your Learning

8. The latest finish and latest start times are determined by calculating ____________ through the network diagram.

Figure 6.9 shows two activities emerging directly from "Print Posters & Brochures." This project is required to be completed by day 30. Therefore, "Distribute Posters" must be started by day 20, because it has a duration of 10 days, and "Mail Brochures" must be started by day 25, because it has a duration of 5 days. The earlier of these two LSs is day 20. Therefore, the latest that "Print Posters & Brochures" can finish is day 20, so that "Distribute Posters" can start by day 20. Even though "Mail Brochures" does not have to start until day 25, "Print Posters & Brochures" must finish by day 20, or else the whole project will be delayed. If "Print Posters & Brochures" does not finish until day 25, then "Distribute Brochures" will not be able to start until day 25. Because "Distribute Brochures" has an estimated duration of 10 days, it won't finish until day 35, which is 5 days beyond the project's required completion time.

Figures 6.10 and 6.11 show the backward calculations for the consumer market study project. The required completion time for the project is 130

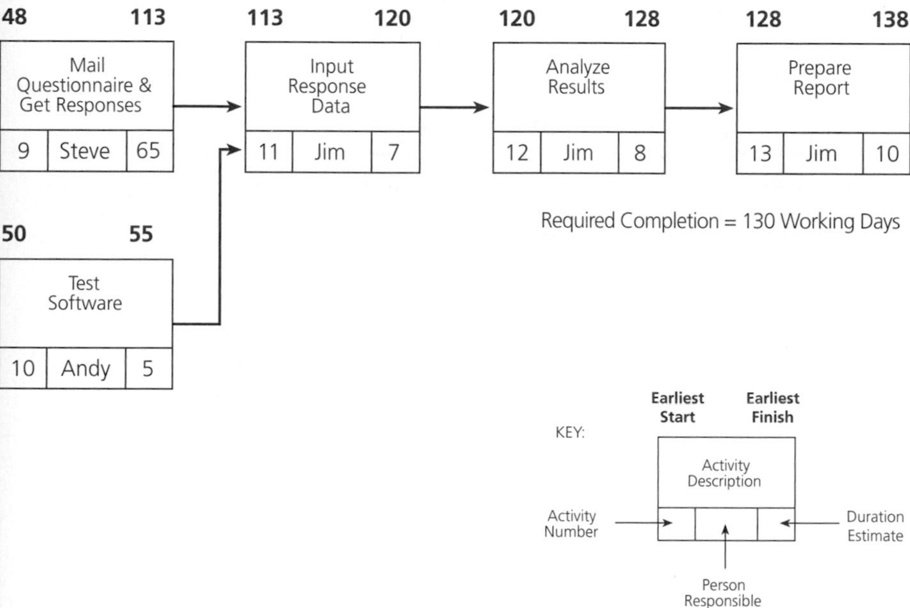

working days. Therefore, the latest that "Prepare Report," the last activity, can finish is day 130, and the latest that it can start is day 120, because its estimated duration is 10 days. In order for "Prepare Report" to start on day 120, the latest that "Analyze Results" can finish is day 120. If the LF for "Analyze Results" is day 120, then its LS is day 112, because its estimated duration is 8 days. The calculations of LF and LS for prior activities are done similarly, continuing backward through the network diagram.

Reinforce Your Learning

9. Refer to Figures 6.10 and 6.11. What are the latest finish and latest start times for "Input Response Data"?

Look at "Review Comments & Finalize Questionnaire." In order for the four activities emerging from this activity to start by their LS times (so that the project can finish by its required completion time of 130 days), "Review Comments & Finalize Questionnaire" must be finished by the earliest LS of all four activities, according to Rule 2. The earliest of the four LSs is day 30, the latest time by which "Print Questionnaire" must start. Therefore, the latest that "Review Comments & Finalize Questionnaire" can finish is day 30.

If you continue calculating the LF and the LS for each activity in the network diagram, you'll see that the very first activity, "Identify Target Consumers," has an LS of 8! This means that in order to complete the entire project by its required completion time of 130 days, the project must start 8 days earlier than it is estimated to start. Note that this difference of 8 days is equal to the difference we got when calculating forward through the network diagram to

Reinforce Your Learning

10. What determines a particular activity's latest finish time?

FIGURE 6.7 ***Network Diagram for Consumer Market Study Project, Showing Earliest Start and Finish Times (Activity-on-the-Arrow Format)***

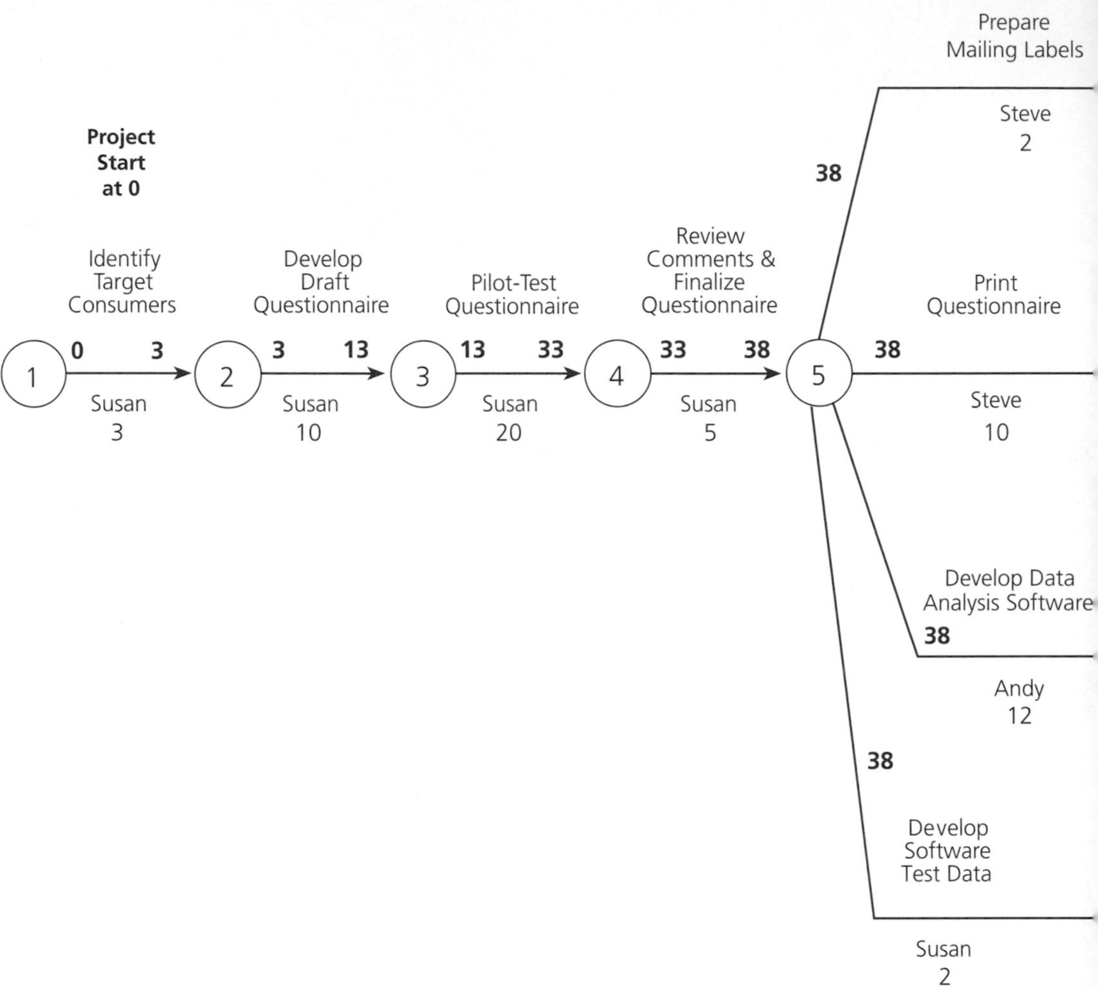

obtain the ES and EF times. In essence, what we have found is that this project may take 138 days to complete, even though its required completion time is 130 days.

Like the earliest start and earliest finish times, the latest start and latest finish times are usually not shown on the network diagram itself, but rather in a separate schedule table (see Figure 6.12).

Total Slack

In the consumer market study project, there is a difference of eight days between the calculated earliest finish time of the very last activity ("Prepare Report") and the project's required completion time. This difference is the **total slack (TS)**, sometimes called **float**. When the total slack is a negative number, as in this example, it indicates a lack of slack over the entire project.

If total slack is positive, it represents the maximum amount of time that the activities on a particular path can be delayed without jeopardizing completion of

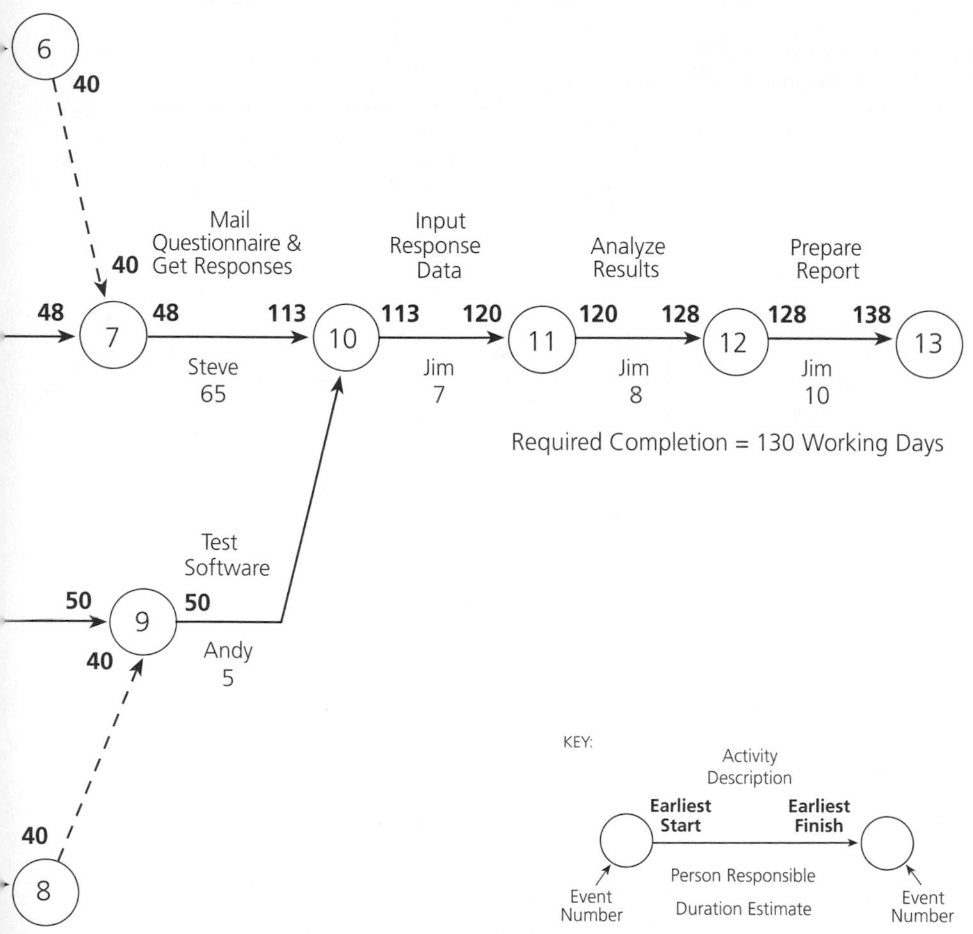

the project by its required completion time. On the other hand, if total slack is negative, it represents the amount of time that the activities on a particular path must be accelerated in order to complete the project by its required completion time. If total slack is zero, the activities on the path do not need to be accelerated but cannot be delayed.

The total slack for a particular path of activities is common to and shared among all the activities on that path. Consider the project diagrammed below.

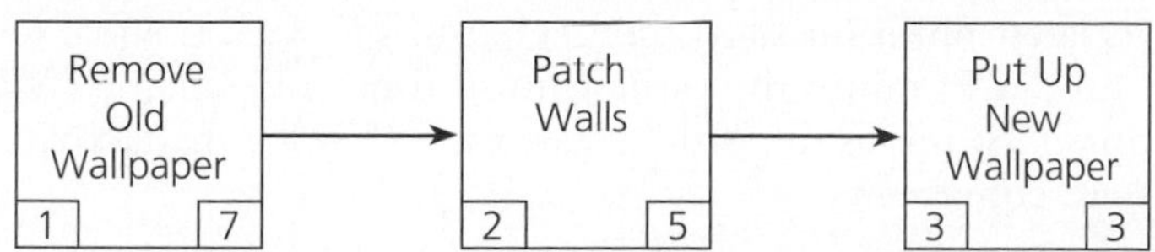

Reinforce Your Learning

11. When a project has a positive total slack, some activities can be ________ without jeopardizing completion of the project by its required completion time. When a project has negative total slack, some activities need to be ________ in order to complete the project by its required completion time.

FIGURE 6.8 ***Schedule for Consumer Market Study Project, Showing Earliest Start and Finish Times***

Consumer Market Study Project

	Activity	Respon.	Dur. Estim.	Earliest Start	Earliest Finish				
1	Identify Target Consumers	Susan	3	**0**	**3**				
2	Develop Draft Questionnaire	Susan	10	**3**	**13**				
3	Pilot-Test Questionnaire	Susan	20	**13**	**33**				
4	Review Comments & Finalize Questionnaire	Susan	5	**33**	**38**				
5	Prepare Mailing Labels	Steve	2	**38**	**40**				
6	Print Questionnaire	Steve	10	**38**	**48**				
7	Develop Data Analysis Software	Andy	12	**38**	**50**				
8	Develop Software Test Data	Susan	2	**38**	**40**				
9	Mail Questionnaire & Get Responses	Steve	65	**48**	**113**				
10	Test Software	Andy	5	**50**	**55**				
11	Input Response Data	Jim	7	**113**	**120**				
12	Analyze Results	Jim	8	**120**	**128**				
13	Prepare Report	Jim	10	**128**	**138**				

The earliest the project can finish is day 15 (the sum of the durations of the three activities, 7 + 5 + 3). However, the required completion time for the project is 20 days. The 3 activities on this path can therefore be delayed up to 5 days without jeopardizing completion of the project by the required time. This does *not* mean that each activity on the path can be delayed 5 days (because this would create a total delay of 15 days); rather, it means that all the activities that make up the path can have a total delay of 5 days among them. For example, if "Remove Old Wallpaper" actually takes 10 days (3 days longer than the estimated 7 days), then it will use up 3 of the 5 days of total slack, and only 2 days of total slack will remain.

Reinforce Your Learning

12. Total slack is the difference between the __________ times and the __________ times.

Total slack is calculated by subtracting the activity's earliest finish (or start) time from its latest finish (or start) time. That is, the slack is equal to either the latest finish time (LF) minus the earliest finish time (EF) for the activity or the latest start time (LS) minus the earliest start time (ES) for that activity. The two calculations are equivalent.

$$\text{Total Slack} = LF - EF \text{ or Total Slack} = LS - ES$$

FIGURE 6.9 *Latest Finish Times*

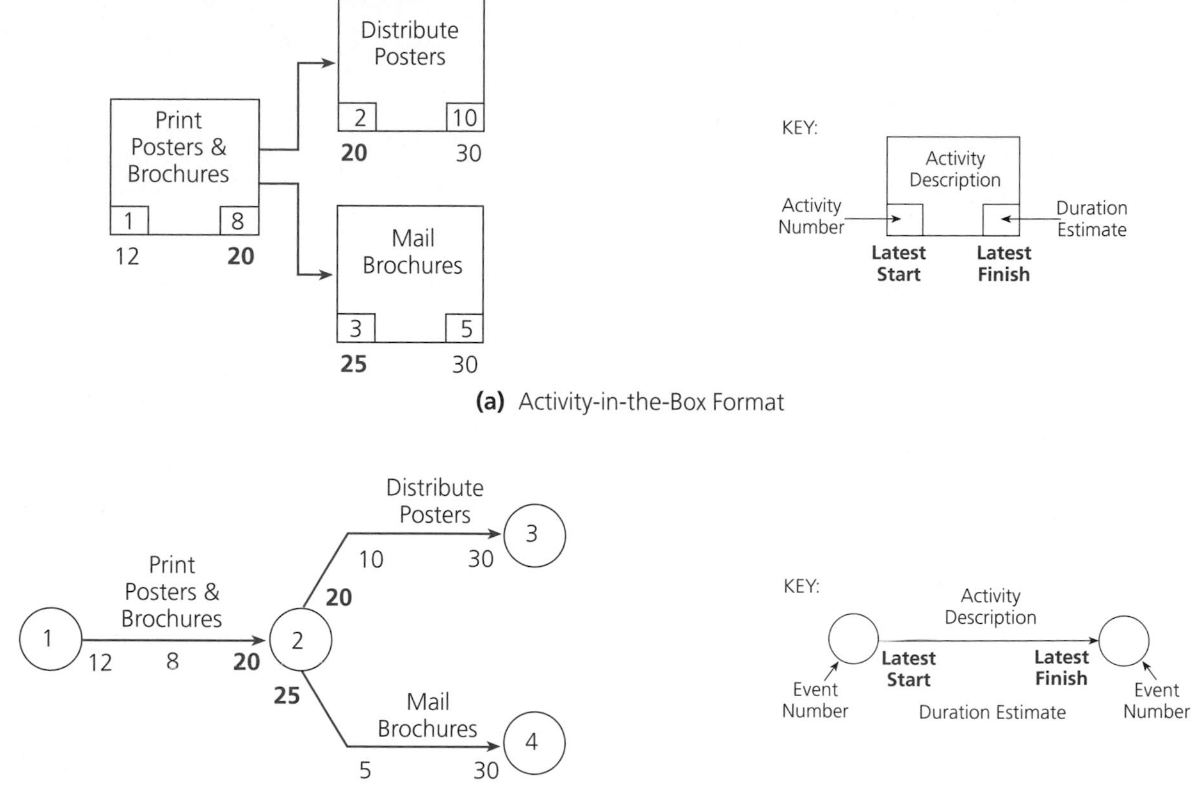

Critical Path

Not all networks are as simple as the one just used to illustrate total slack. In large network diagrams there may be many paths of activities from the project start to the project completion, just as there are many routes you can choose from to get from New York City to Los Angeles. If 20 friends were going to leave at the same time from New York City and each was going to drive a different route to Los Angeles, they couldn't get together for a party in Los Angeles until the last person had arrived—the one who took the longest (most time-consuming) route. Similarly, a project cannot be completed until the longest (most time-consuming) path of activities is finished. This longest path in the overall network diagram is called the **critical path**.

One way to determine which activities make up the critical path is to find which ones have the least slack. Subtract the earliest finish time from the latest finish time for each activity (or subtract the earliest start time from the latest start time—both calculations will result in the same value) and then look for all the activities that have the lowest value (either least positive or most negative). All the activities with this value are on the critical path of activities.

FIGURE 6.10 ***Network Diagram for Consumer Market Study Project, Showing Latest Start and Finish Times (Activity-in-the-Box Format)***

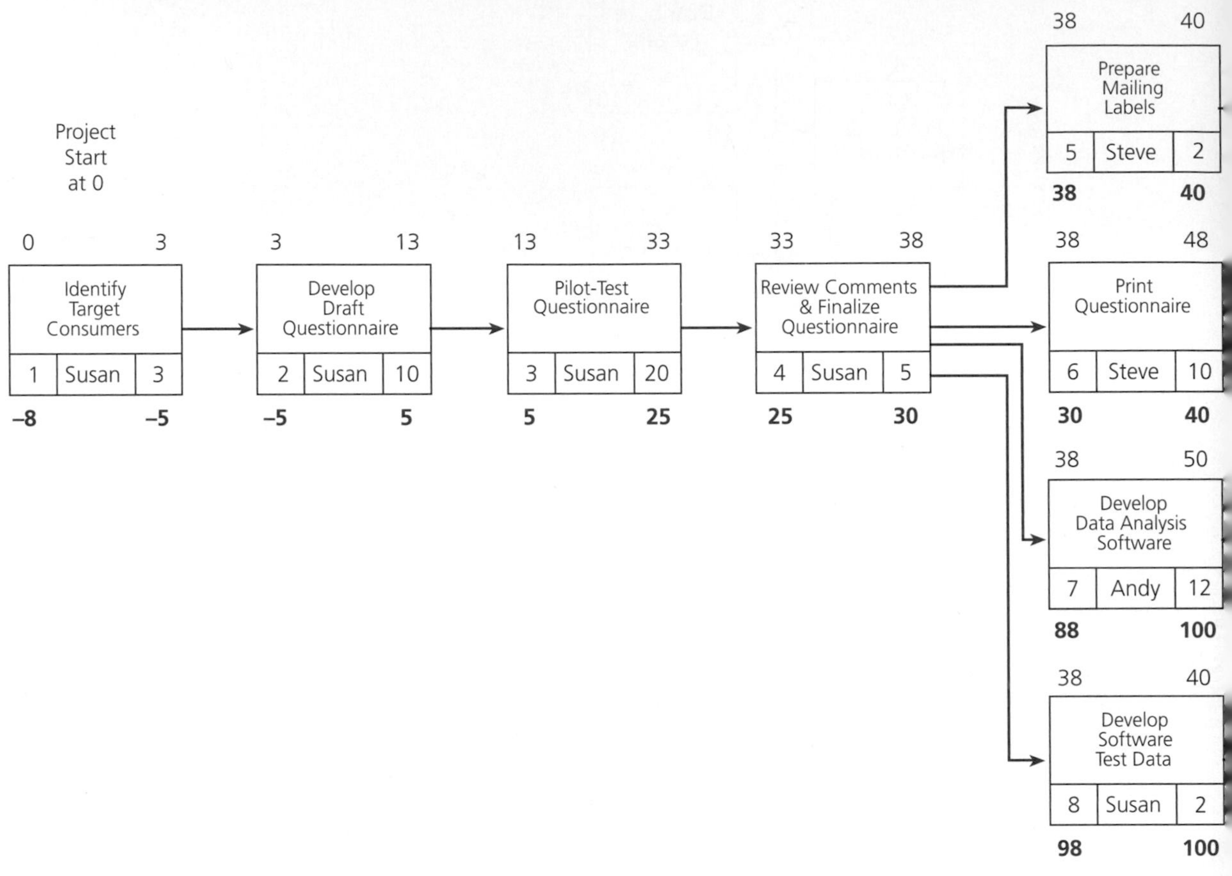

The values of total slack for the consumer market study project are shown in Figure 6.13. The lowest value is –8 days. The activities that have this same value of total slack make up the path 1–2–3–4–6–9–11–12–13. These nine activities comprise the critical, or most time consuming, path. The estimated durations of the activities on this path add up to 138 days (3 + 10 + 20 + 5 + 10 + 65 + 7 + 8 + 10). Among them, these activities need to be accelerated 8 days in order to complete the project by its required completion time of 130 days. Figures 6.14 and 6.15 highlight the activities that make up the critical path.

Reinforce Your Learning

13. The longest path of activities from the beginning to the end of a project is called the

________________ path.

To eliminate the –8 days of slack, the estimated durations of one or more activities on this critical path need to be reduced. Suppose we reduce the estimated duration of "Mail Questionnaire & Get Responses" from 65 days to 55 days, by reducing the time respondents are given to return the questionnaire. Because the estimated duration of an activity on the critical path is being reduced by 10 days, the total slack changes from –8 days to +2 days. The revised duration estimate of 55 days can be used to prepare a revised project schedule, as shown in Figure 6.16. This schedule shows that the critical path now has a total slack of +2 days, and the project is now estimated to finish in 128 days, which is 2 days earlier than the required completion time of 130 days.

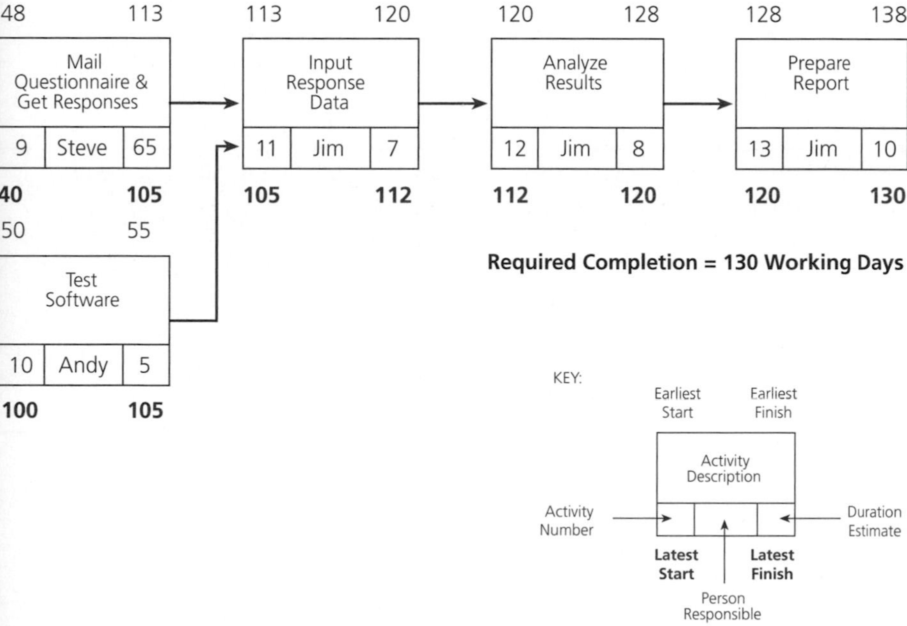

As stated earlier, a large network diagram can have many paths or routes from its beginning to its end. Some of the paths may have positive values of total slack; others may have negative values of total slack. Those paths with positive values of total slack are sometimes referred to as **noncritical paths**, whereas those paths with zero or negative values of total slack are referred to as *critical paths*. In this case the longest path is often referred to as the **most critical path**.

Free Slack

Another type of slack that is sometimes calculated is **free slack (FS)**. It's the amount of time a particular activity can be postponed without delaying the earliest start time of its immediately succeeding activities. It is the *relative difference* between the amounts of total slack for activities entering into the same activity. Free slack is calculated by finding the lowest of the values of total slack for all the activities entering into a particular activity and then subtracting it from the values of total slack for the other activities also entering into that same activity. Because free slack is the relative difference between values of total slack for activities entering into the same activity, it will exist only when two or more activities enter into the same activity. Also, because free slack is a relative difference between values of total slack, *it is always a positive value.*

FIGURE 6.11 ***Network Diagram for Consumer Market Study Project, Showing Latest Start and Finish Times (Activity-on-the-Arrow Format)***

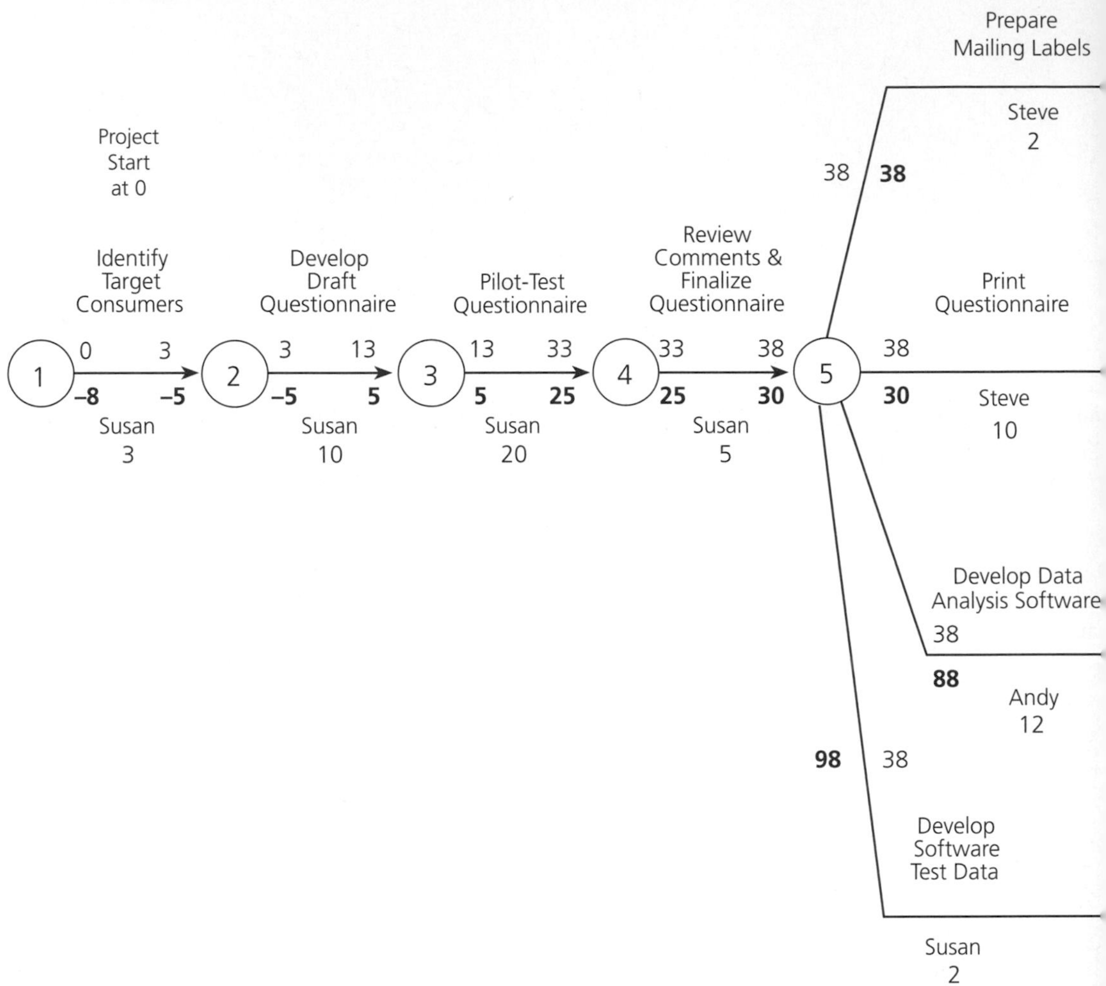

For an illustration of free slack, consider Figures 6.13 and 6.14. In the network diagram (Figure 6.14), there are three instances where a particular activity has more than one activity entering into it:

- Activity 9, "Mail Questionnaire & Get Responses," has activities 5 and 6 entering into it.
- Activity 10, "Test Software," has activities 7 and 8 entering into it.
- Activity 11, "Input Response Data," has activities 9 and 10 entering into it.

In the schedule (Figure 6.13), the values of total slack for activities 5 and 6 are 0 and –8 days, respectively. The lesser of these two values is –8 days for activity 6. The free slack for activity 5 is the relative difference between its total slack, 0, and –8. This relative difference is 8 days: 0 –(–8) = 8 days. This means that activity 5, "Prepare Mailing Labels," already has a free slack of 8 days and can slip by up to that amount without delaying the earliest start time of activity 9, "Mail Questionnaire & Get Responses."

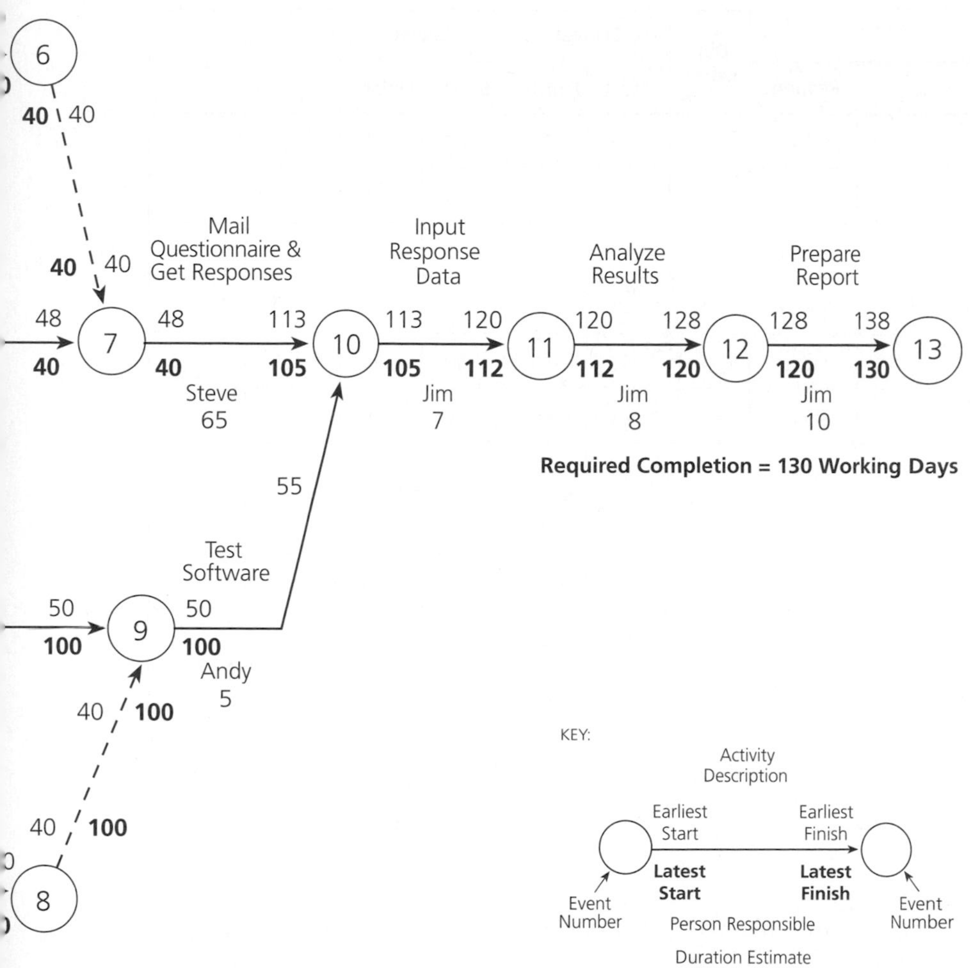

Similarly, the values of total slack for activities 7 and 8 are 50 and 60 days, respectively. The lesser of these two values is 50 days. Therefore, activity 8, "Develop Software Test Data," has a free slack of 10 days (60 – 50 = 10) and can slip by up to that amount without delaying the earliest start time of activity 10, "Test Software."

Reinforce Your Learning

14. Refer to Figures 6.13 and 6.14. Of the two activities entering into activity 11, "Input Response Data," which activity has free slack? What is its value?

SCHEDULING FOR INFORMATION SYSTEMS DEVELOPMENT

Chapter 5 defined an information system (IS) as a computer-based system that accepts data as input, processes the data, and produces information required by users. Scheduling the development of an information system is a challenging process. Unfortunately, such scheduling is often done in a haphazard manner, and thus a large percentage of IS projects are finished much later than originally promised or never finished at all. One of the most

FIGURE 6.12 *Schedule for Consumer Market Study Project, Showing Latest Start and Finish Times*

Consumer Market Study Project

	Activity	Respon.	Dur. Estim.	Earliest		Latest			
				Start	Finish	Start	Finish		
1	Identify Target Consumers	Susan	3	0	3	**–8**	**–5**		
2	Develop Draft Questionnaire	Susan	10	3	13	**–5**	**5**		
3	Pilot-Test Questionnaire	Susan	20	13	33	**5**	**25**		
4	Review Comments & Finalize Questionnaire	Susan	5	33	38	**25**	**30**		
5	Prepare Mailing Labels	Steve	2	38	40	**38**	**40**		
6	Print Questionnaire	Steve	10	38	48	**30**	**40**		
7	Develop Data Analysis Software	Andy	12	38	50	**88**	**100**		
8	Develop Software Test Data	Susan	2	38	40	**98**	**100**		
9	Mail Questionnaire & Get Responses	Steve	65	48	113	**40**	**105**		
10	Test Software	Andy	5	50	55	**100**	**105**		
11	Input Response Data	Jim	7	113	120	**105**	**112**		
12	Analyze Results	Jim	8	120	128	**112**	**120**		
13	Prepare Report	Jim	10	128	138	**120**	**130**		

important factors in effective scheduling is arriving at activity duration estimates that are as realistic as possible. This is not an easy task; however, it does become easier with experience.

Among the common problems that often push IS development projects beyond their required completion time are the following:

- failure to identify all user requirements
- failure to identify user requirements properly
- continuing growth of project scope
- underestimating learning curves for new software packages
- incompatible hardware
- logical design flaws
- poor selection of software
- failure to select the best design strategy
- data incompatibility issues
- failure to perform all phases of the SDLC

FIGURE 6.13 *Schedule for Consumer Market Study Project, Showing Total Slack Values*

Consumer Market Study Project

	Activity	Respon.	Dur. Estim.	Earliest		Latest		Total Slack	
				Start	Finish	Start	Finish		
1	Identify Target Consumers	Susan	3	0	3	–8	–5	–8	
2	Develop Draft Questionnaire	Susan	10	3	13	–5	5	–8	
3	Pilot-Test Questionnaire	Susan	20	13	33	5	25	–8	
4	Review Comments & Finalize Questionnaire	Susan	5	33	38	25	30	–8	
5	Prepare Mailing Labels	Steve	2	38	40	38	40	0	
6	Print Questionnaire	Steve	10	38	48	30	40	–8	
7	Develop Data Analysis Software	Andy	12	38	50	88	100	50	
8	Develop Software Test Data	Susan	2	38	40	98	100	60	
9	Mail Questionnaire & Get Responses	Steve	65	48	113	40	105	–8	
10	Test Software	Andy	5	50	55	100	105	50	
11	Input Response Data	Jim	7	113	120	105	112	–8	
12	Analyze Results	Jim	8	120	128	112	120	–8	
13	Prepare Report	Jim	10	128	138	120	130	–8	

An IS Example: Internet Applications Development for ABC Office Designs (Continued)

Recall from Chapter 5 that ABC Office Designs has a large number of sales representatives who sell office furniture to major corporations. Each sales representative is assigned to a specific state, and each state is part of one of four regions in the country. To enable management to monitor the number and amount of sales for each representative, for each state, and for each region, ABC has decided to build a web-based information system. In addition, the IS needs to be able to track prices, inventory, and the competition.

The IS Department within the corporation assigned Beth Smith to be the project manager of the web-based reporting system development project. Previously, Beth identified all of the major tasks that needed to be accomplished and developed the work breakdown structure, responsibility matrix, and network

FIGURE 6.14 ***Network Diagram for Consumer Market Study Project, Showing the Critical Path (Activity-in-the-Box Format)***

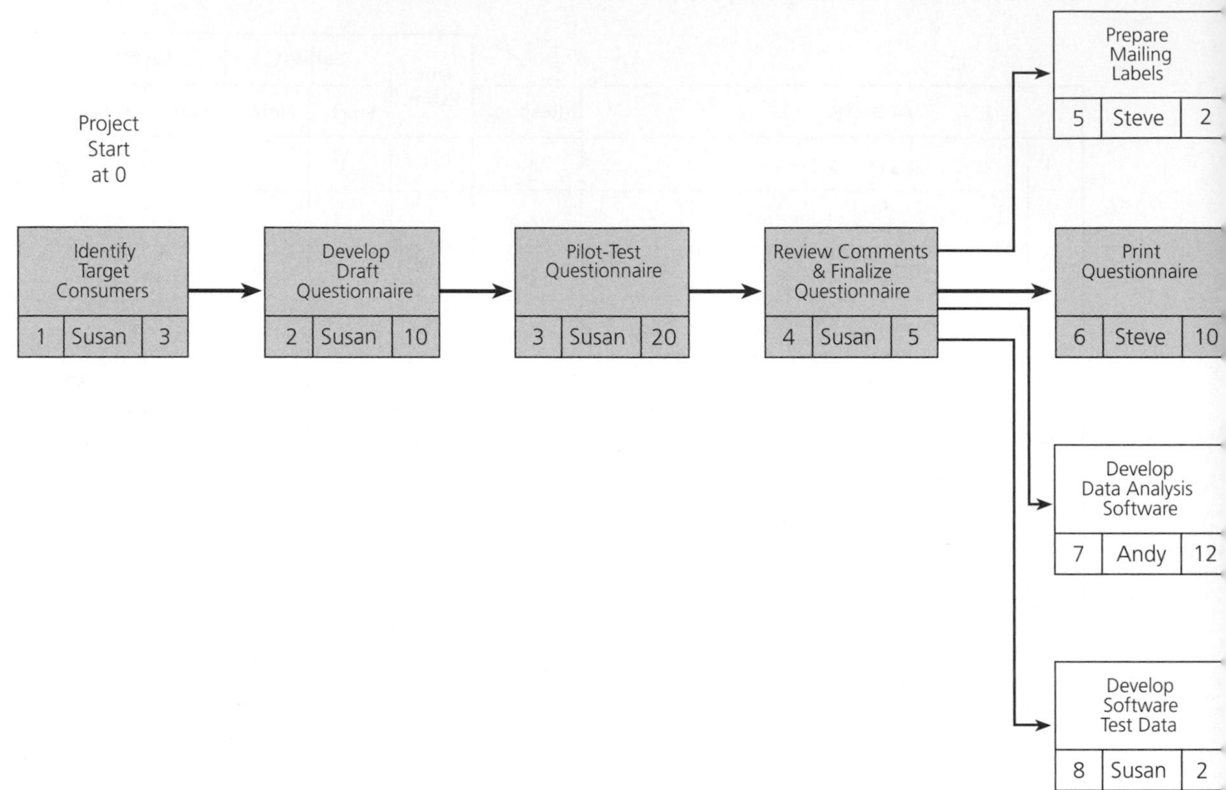

diagram. Her next step was to come up with activity duration estimates. After consulting extensively with the project team, she derived the estimates shown in Figure 6.17.

Recall from Chapter 5 that 50 days have been allotted for this project and the project needs to be started as soon as possible. Given each activity's duration estimate and the project's required start and finish times, Beth was ready to perform the calculations for the earliest start (ES) and earliest finish (EF) times for each activity. These values are shown above each activity in Figure 6.18.

Beth calculated the ES and EF times by going forward through the network. The first tasks, "Gather Data" and "Study Feasibility," have ES times of 0. Because "Gather Data" is expected to take 3 days, its EF is 0 + 3 = 3 days. Because "Study Feasibility" is expected to take 4 days, its EF is 0 + 4 = 4 days. Beth continued this process, moving forward through the network diagram until all activities had been assigned ES and EF times.

After the ES and EF times were calculated, Beth calculated the LS and LF times. The starting point here is the time by which the project must be completed—50 days. The LS and LF times are shown below each activity in Figure 6.19.

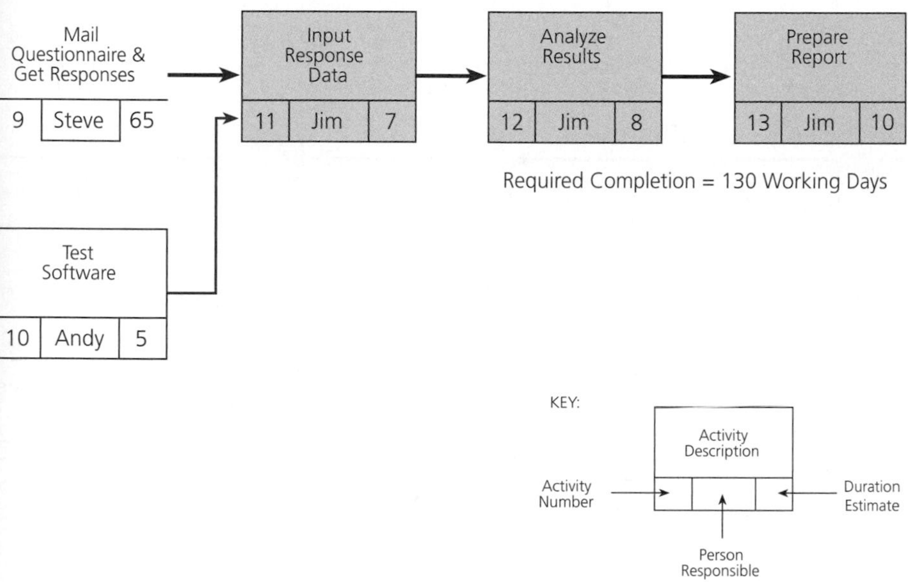

Beth calculated the LF and LS times by going backward through the network. The last task, "Prepare Implementation Report," has an LF time of 50—the time by which the project needs to be completed. Because "Prepare Implementation Report" is expected to take 1 day to perform, its LS is 50 – 1 = 49 days. This means that "Prepare Implementation Report" must be started by day 49 at the latest, or the project will not finish by its required completion time. Beth continued this process, moving backward through the network diagram until all activities had been assigned LF and LS times.

After the ES, EF, LS, and LF times were calculated, Beth calculated the total slack. These values are shown in Figure 6.20. Recall that the total slack is calculated by either subtracting ES from LS or subtracting EF from LF for each activity.

After she calculated the total slack for each activity, Beth had to identify the critical path. For the web-based reporting system development project, any activity with a slack of –9 is on the critical path. Figure 6.21 shows the critical path for this development project. At this point Beth and her team must either determine a way to reduce the development time by 9 days or request that the project completion date be extended from 50 to 59 days, or some compromise.

FIGURE 6.15 ***Network Diagram for Consumer Market Study Project, Showing the Critical Path (Activity-on-the-Arrow Format)***

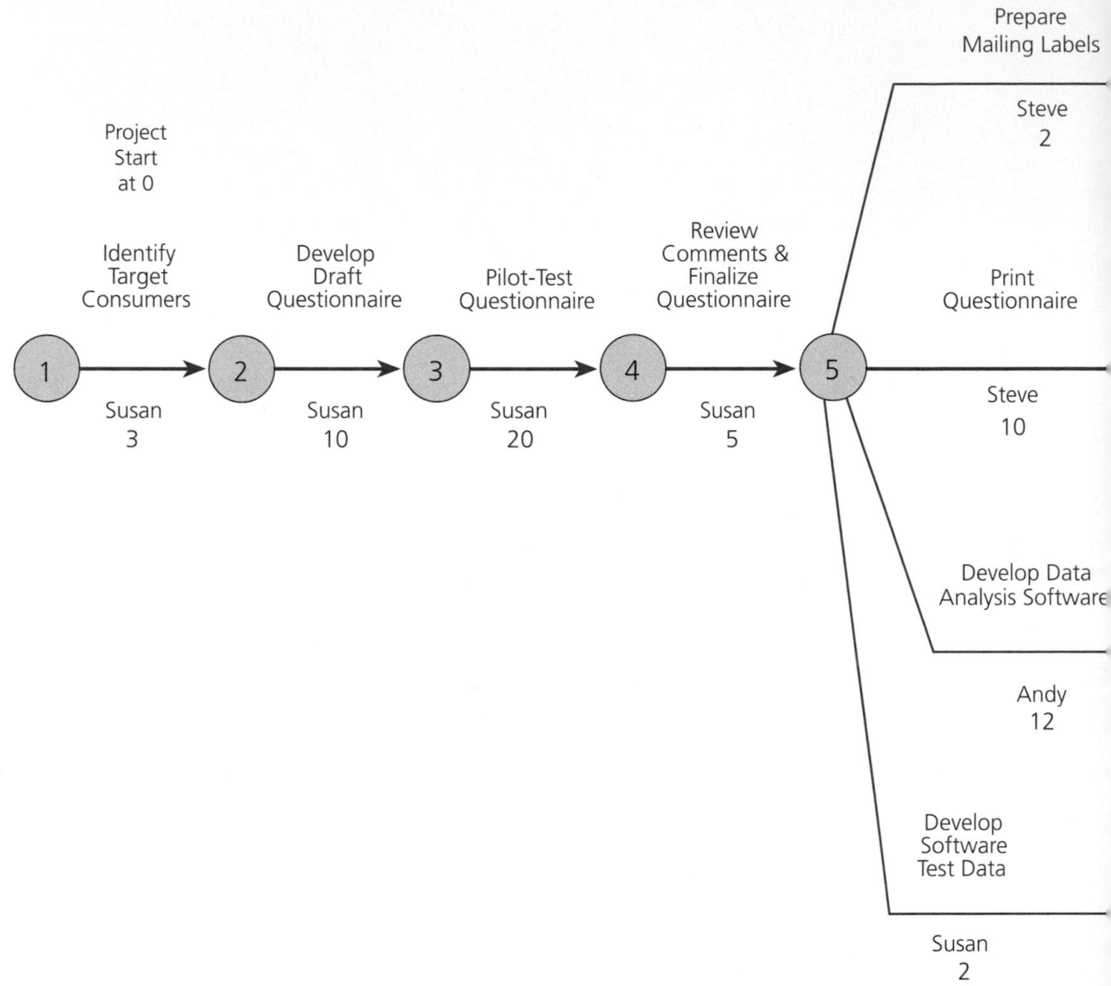

PROJECT MANAGEMENT SOFTWARE

Almost all project management software packages allow you to perform the scheduling functions identified in this chapter. Specifically, activity durations can be estimated in hours, days, weeks, months, or years, and with a click of the mouse, time scales can easily be converted from days to weeks, weeks to days, and so on. The duration estimates can easily be updated and revised. In addition, calendaring systems provide the project manager with the ability to handle weekends, company holidays, and vacation days.

Project start and finish times can be entered as specific calendar dates (for example, June 1, 2009 or December 31, 2010), or an overall number of days (or

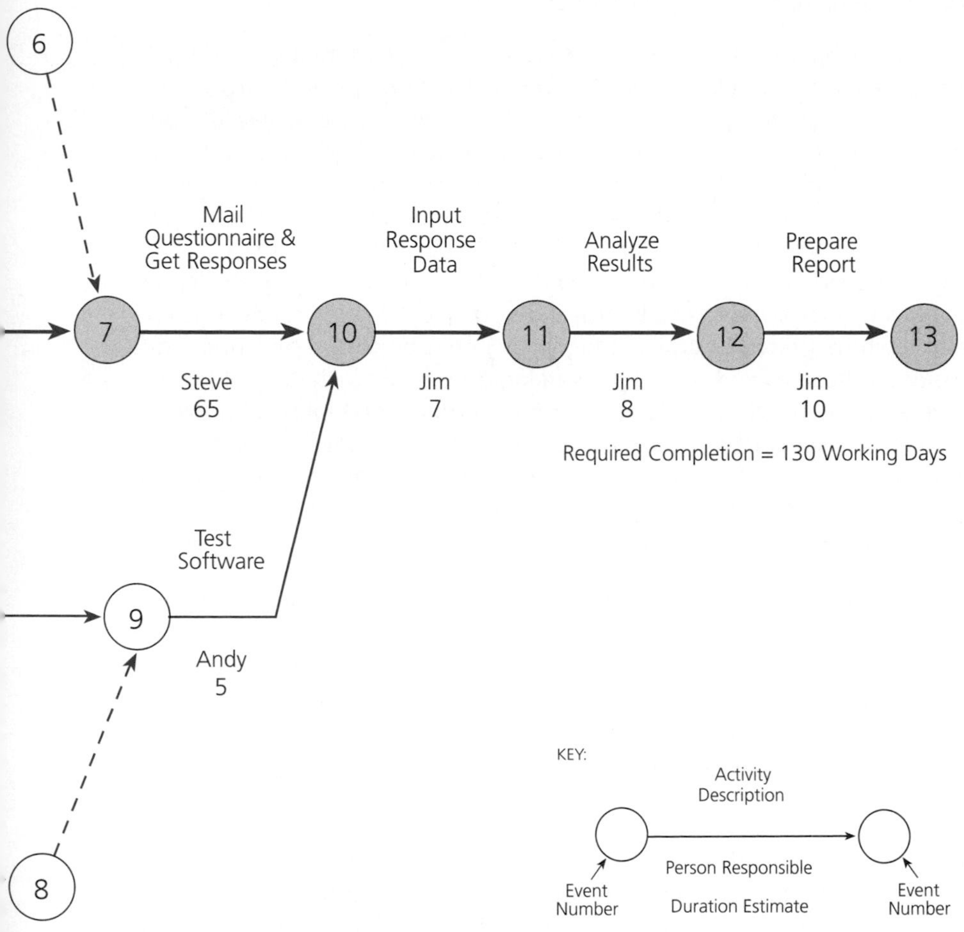

weeks or months), without specific calendar dates assigned, can be entered (for example, the project needs to finish by week 50). Given the required project completion date and the list of activities with their estimated durations, the software will calculate the date by which a project needs to start. Similarly, it will calculate the earliest project completion date, based on the actual start date and the list of activities with their estimated durations.

The software will also calculate ES, EF, LS, and LF times, total and free slack, and the critical path, all with a click of the mouse. It is important, however, for the project manager to understand what these terms are and what the calculations mean. See Appendix A at the end of the book for a thorough discussion of project management software.

Real World PROJECT MANAGEMENT

Fast-Track Innovation in Indiana

The major improvements necessary on a stretch of the combined I-65 and I-70 arteries posed numerous challenges to the Indiana Department of Transportation (INDOT). This area is located just south of downtown Indianapolis, where the bulk of the city's commute occurs. The project would involve 33 bridges and 35 lane miles of highway, and one side of the highway would need to be shut down, causing the project to easily stretch over two construction seasons. The project, however, was completed in just 55 days, truly earning its name, "Hyperfix."

INDOT developed an approach that would address each of the key challenges associated with the massive project. In order to decrease the duration of construction time, the whole stretch of affected highway would be closed and numerous contractors and subcontractors would be working on the job each day, 24 hours a day, 7 days a week. By closing down an entire portion of highway, however, 175,000 commuters would be displaced. So, the Hyperfix team arranged places for commuters to park, provided special shuttle buses, and planned routes for the shuttle buses to get commuters to their destinations. Finally, INDOT and contractors met with a variety of community stakeholders before the project was underway to discuss the options and get buy-in.

Public awareness for this project utilized media, public meetings, and numerous messaging strategies. This component was a critical element to the success of Hyperfix. The name "Hyperfix" itself became part of the local language, and provided advertising opportunities on billboards and radio shows.

The job was already planned on a fast track, yet managed to be completed in just 55 days. This was 30 days ahead of the extremely optimistic projections from engineers. Each day that was reduced from the 85-day construction time saved the public an estimated $1 million! The citizens of Indianapolis organized a huge block party and stock car rally to celebrate the completion of the project.

American Consulting, Inc., a local design and engineering firm, worked with INDOT from the beginning of the project to design a scope of work plan that would take into consideration stakeholder needs and apprehensions. This firm was instrumental in making Hyperfix a reality.

The old model of state DOTs was a formula known as "DAD," which stands for "Design, Announce, and Defend." American Consulting, Inc., helped to establish a new formula, "POP," which stands for "Priority on People." This approach enlisted the support of the community before the project ever began. The concept was so successful that the Indiana Chapter of the American Council on Engineering Companies presented American Consulting with its Grand Project Award.

Walsh Construction of Chicago was awarded the task of scheduling the very complicated project. Walsh staff implemented "hyper-management" to harness all of its resources and accomplish tasks simultaneously. "Most construction jobs are scheduled by the week—this one was scheduled by the hour," said Jeff Datzman, a Walsh Construction bridge superintendent. All of the subcontractors had to work together to make sure the entire sequence of activities wasn't completely thrown off target.

Commuters were still able to use all but one exit on either side of the closure and INDOT directed traffic onto the construction-free outer beltway. Downtown businesses were also encouraged to stagger work hours and use carpools. Project leaders made sure to include tourists and commuters as part of the team, despite expectations of widespread travel delays. Hetrick Communications, a local public relations firm, undertook a mass communication campaign to promote the commuter bus service "Hyperfix Park & Ride." The firm designed logos and graphics for road signage to accompany the project. They also designed a website that included detailed information about project progress. This website remains online and carries current traffic control updates.

The local media responded well to the public awareness campaign, running news and features about Hyperfix progress. Songs, parodies, talk radio segments, and discussions to "hyperfix" anything needing repairs allowed "Hyperfix" to become a community catchphrase. Excellent project management at all phases of this project resulted in successfully and quickly improving the highways, while minimizing any inconvenience to the drivers.

According to project manager, Dan Rogers, P.E., "With the combination of adequate planning, leveraging of resources, and a focused public information effort—a compressed schedule can be accomplished successfully!"

U.S. Department of Transportation, Federal Highway Administration, Highways for Life, Success Stories, www.fhwa.dot.gov/hfl, March 29, 2007.

Critical Success FACTORS

- The person who will be responsible for performing the activity should make the duration estimate for that activity. This generates commitment from the person.
- An activity's duration estimate must be based on the quantity of resources expected to used on the activity.
- Activity duration estimates should be aggressive yet realistic.
- Activities should not be longer in estimated duration than the time intervals at which the actual progress will be reviewed and compared to planned progress.

SUMMARY

After a plan is developed for a project, the next step is to develop a project schedule. The first step in this process is to estimate how long each activity will take, from the time it is started until the time it is finished. It's a good practice to have the person who will be responsible for an activity estimate its duration; however, with larger projects this is often not possible.

An activity's duration estimate must be based on the quantity of resources expected to be used on the activity. The estimate should be aggressive, yet realistic. A consistent time base, such as hours or days or weeks, should be used for all the activity duration estimates.

The earliest start and earliest finish (ES and EF) times and the latest start and latest finish (LS and LF) times can be calculated for each activity. The ES and EF

FIGURE 6.16 *Revised Schedule for Consumer Market Study Project*

Consumer Market Study Project

	Activity	Respon.	Dur. Estim.	Earliest		Latest		Total Slack	
				Start	Finish	Start	Finish		
1	Identify Target Consumers	Susan	3	0	3	2	5	2	
2	Develop Draft Questionnaire	Susan	10	3	13	5	15	2	
3	Pilot-Test Questionnaire	Susan	20	13	33	15	35	2	
4	Review Comments & Finalize Questionnaire	Susan	5	33	38	35	40	2	
5	Prepare Mailing Labels	Steve	2	38	40	48	50	10	
6	Print Questionnaire	Steve	10	38	48	40	50	2	
7	Develop Data Analysis Software	Andy	12	38	50	88	100	50	
8	Develop Software Test Data	Susan	2	38	40	98	100	60	
9	Mail Questionnaire & Get Responses	Steve	55	48	103	50	105	2	
10	Test Software	Andy	5	50	55	100	105	50	
11	Input Response Data	Jim	7	103	110	105	112	2	
12	Analyze Results	Jim	8	110	118	112	120	2	
13	Prepare Report	Jim	10	118	128	120	130	2	

times are calculated by working forward through the network. The earliest start time for an activity is calculated on the basis of the project's estimated start time and the duration estimates for preceding activities. The earliest finish time for an activity is calculated by adding the activity's duration estimate to the activity's earliest start time. The earliest start time for a particular activity must be the same as or later than the latest of all the earliest finish times of all the activities leading directly into that particular activity.

The LS and LF times are calculated by working backward through the network. The latest finish time for an activity is calculated on the basis of the project's required completion time and the duration estimates for succeeding activities. The latest start time is calculated by subtracting the activity's duration estimate from the activity's latest finish time. The latest finish time for a particular activity must be the same as or earlier than the earliest of all the latest start times of all the activities emerging directly from that particular activity.

The total slack for a particular path through the network is common to and shared among all activities on that path. If it's positive, it represents the maximum amount of time that the activities on a particular path can be delayed without jeopardizing completion of the project by the required time. If total slack is negative, it represents the amount of time that the activities on that path must be accelerated in order to complete the project by the required time. If it's

FIGURE 6.17 *List of Activities, Immediate Predecessors, and Duration Estimates*

Web-based Reporting System Project

Activity	Immediate Predecessors	Duration Estimate (days)
1. Gather Data	—	3
2. Study Feasibility	—	4
3. Prepare Problem Definition Report	1, 2	1
4. Interview Users	3	5
5. Study Existing System	3	8
6. Define User Requirements	4	5
7. Prepare System Analysis Report	5, 6	1
8. Input & Output	7	8
9. Processing & Database	7	10
10. Evaluation	8, 9	2
11. Prepare System Design Report	10	2
12. Software Development	11	15
13. Hardware Development	11	10
14. Network Development	11	6
15. Prepare System Development Report	12, 13, 14	2
16. Software Testing	15	6
17. Hardware Testing	15	4
18. Network Testing	15	4
19. Prepare Testing Report	16, 17, 18	1
20. Training	19	4
21. System Conversion	19	2
22. Prepare Implementation Report	20, 21	1

zero, the activities on that path do not need to be accelerated but cannot be delayed. The critical path is the longest (most time-consuming) path of activities in the network diagram and represents a series of activities that cannot be postponed without delaying the entire project.

Scheduling the development of an information system is a challenging process. Unfortunately, such scheduling is often done in a haphazard manner, and thus a large percentage of IS projects are finished much later than originally promised. One of the most important factors in effective scheduling is arriving at activity duration estimates that are as realistic as possible. The project manager should be aware of the common problems that often push IS development projects beyond their scheduled completion dates.

Project management software packages can help with the scheduling process.

QUESTIONS

1. Why does the scheduling function depend on the planning function? Which one must be done first? Why?
2. Describe what an activity duration estimate is. How is it determined? Can an activity have an estimated duration of 0? Why or why not?

FIGURE 6.18 ***Network Diagram for Web-Based Reporting System Project, Showing Earliest Start and Finish Times (Activity-in-the-Box Format)***

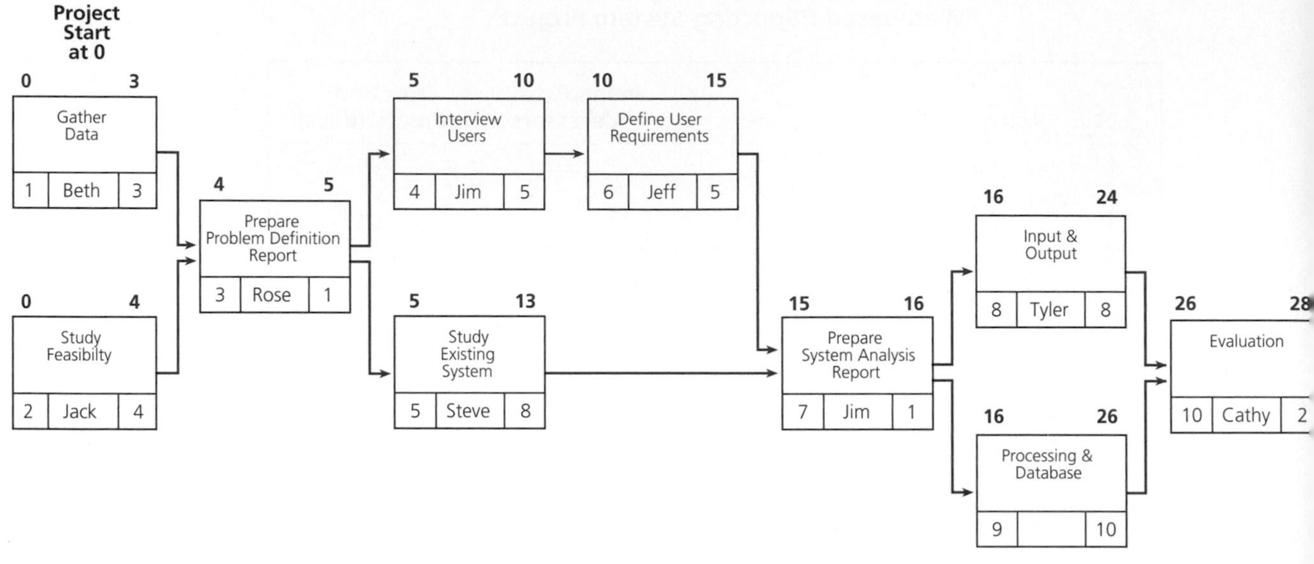

3. Why might a contractor prefer to state a project completion time in terms of number of days after the project starts rather than a specific date? Give some examples of instances when this would be appropriate.
4. Refer to Figures 6.6 and 6.7. Why is the earliest start time for “Review Comments & Finalize Questionnaire” day 33? Why is the earliest finish time day 38?
5. Refer to Figures 6.10 and 6.11. Why is the latest start time for “Mail Questionnaires & Get Responses” day 40? Why is the latest finish time day 105?
6. What is meant by the term *slack* as applied to a particular activity? What is the difference between positive slack and negative slack? How is it calculated?
7. What is meant by the term *total slack* as applied to a path? When is a path considered a critical path?
8. Why is it important to determine the critical path of a project? What happens if activities on this path are delayed? What happens if activities on this path are accelerated?

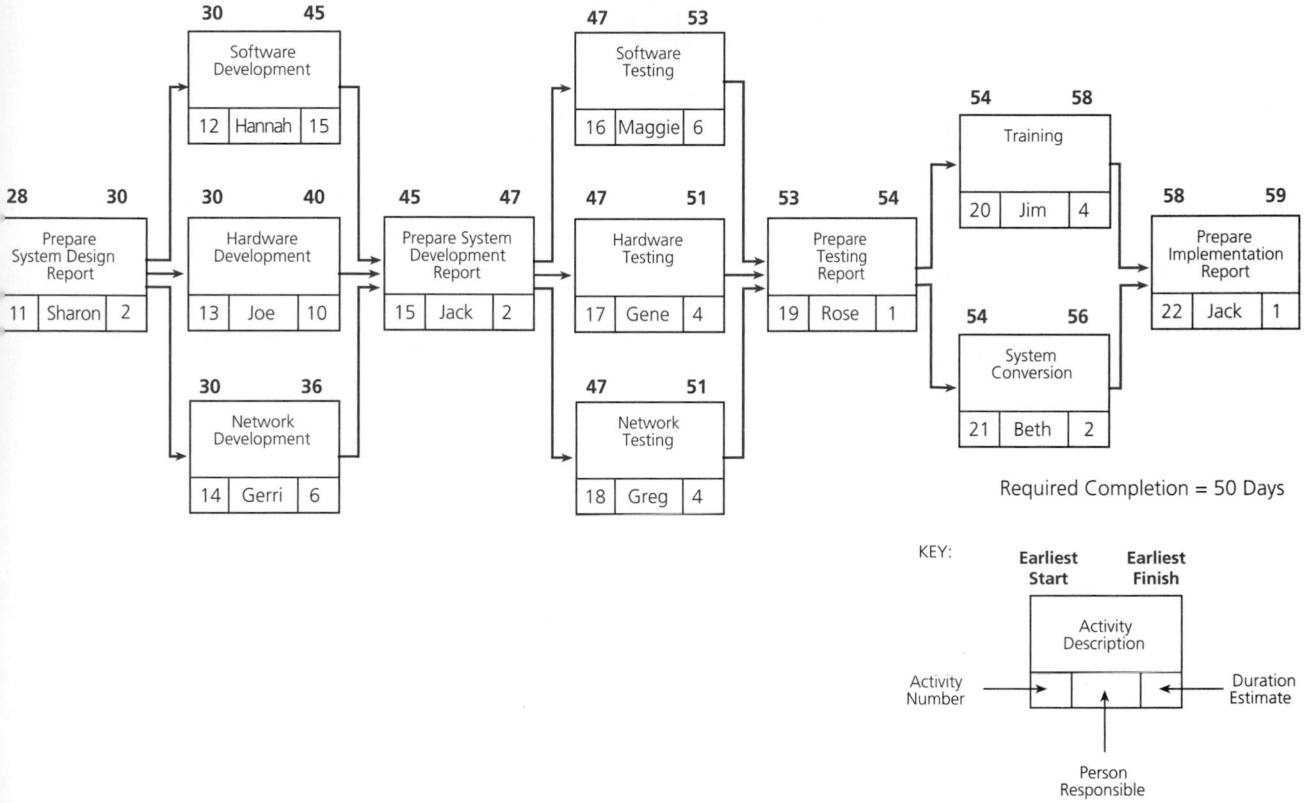

9. Why is the scheduling of IS projects so challenging? What are some of the common problems that push IS projects beyond their due dates?

10. Calculate the ES, EF, LS, and LF times and the slack for each activity in the figure below and identify the critical path for the project. Can the project be completed in 40 weeks?

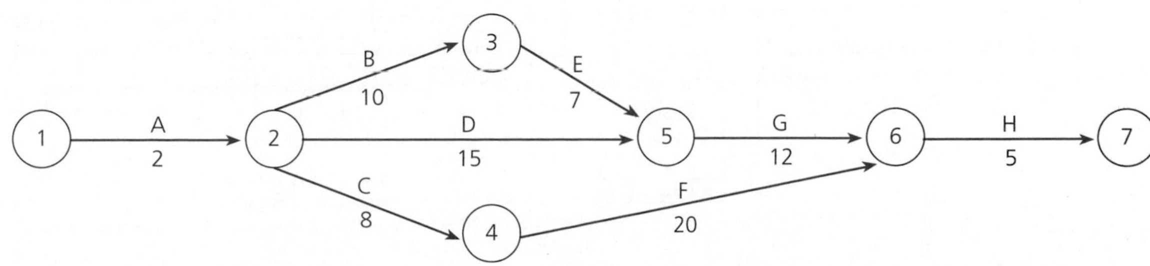

FIGURE 6.19 ***Network Diagram for Web-Based Reporting System Project, Showing Latest Start and Finish Times (Activity-in-the-Box Format)***

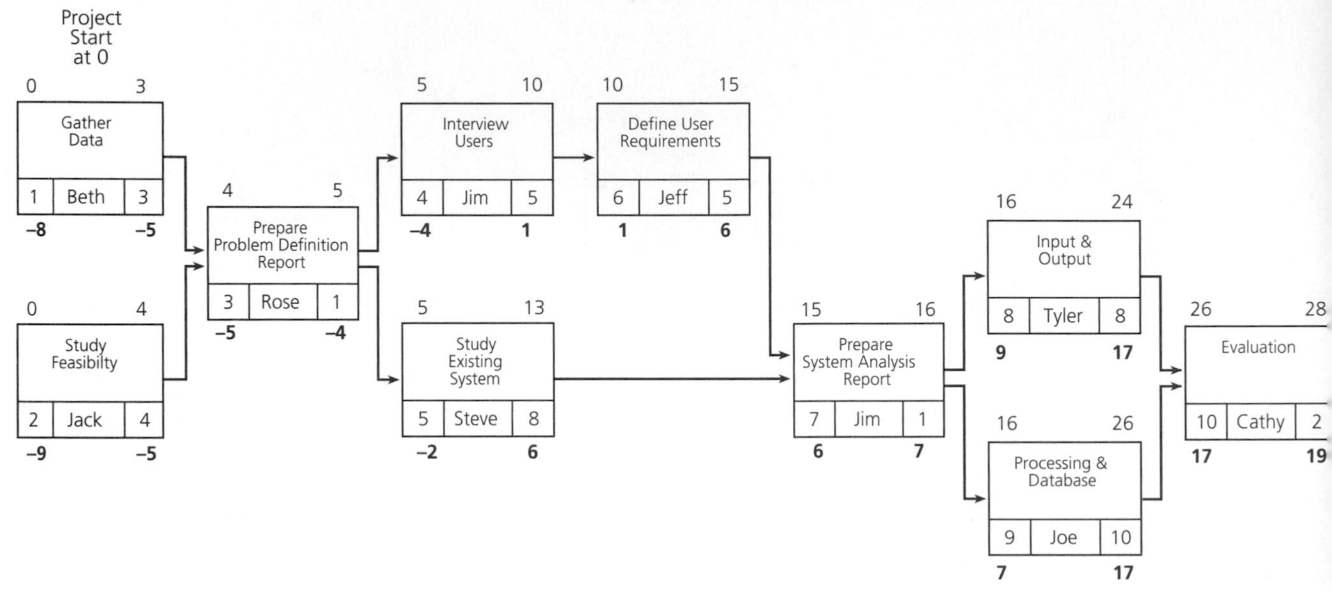

11. Calculate the ES, EF, LS, and LF times and the slack for each activity in the figure below and identify the critical path for the project. Can the project be completed in 30 weeks?

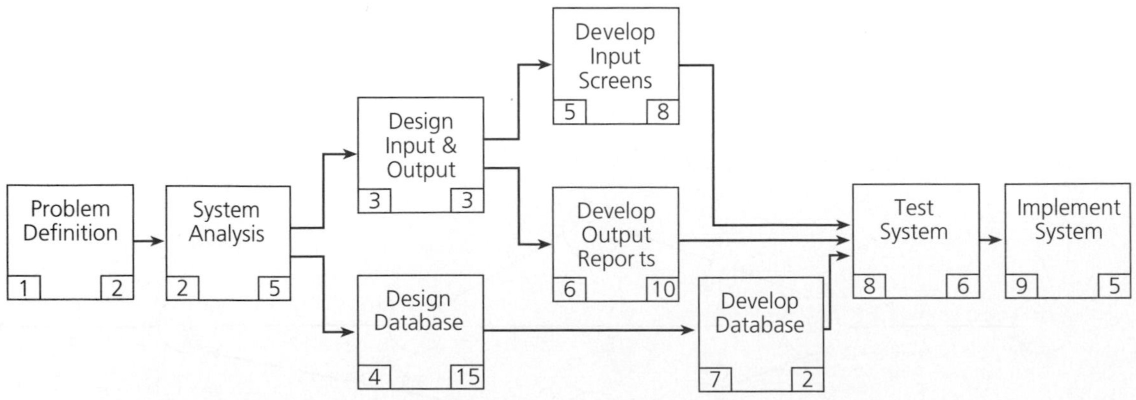

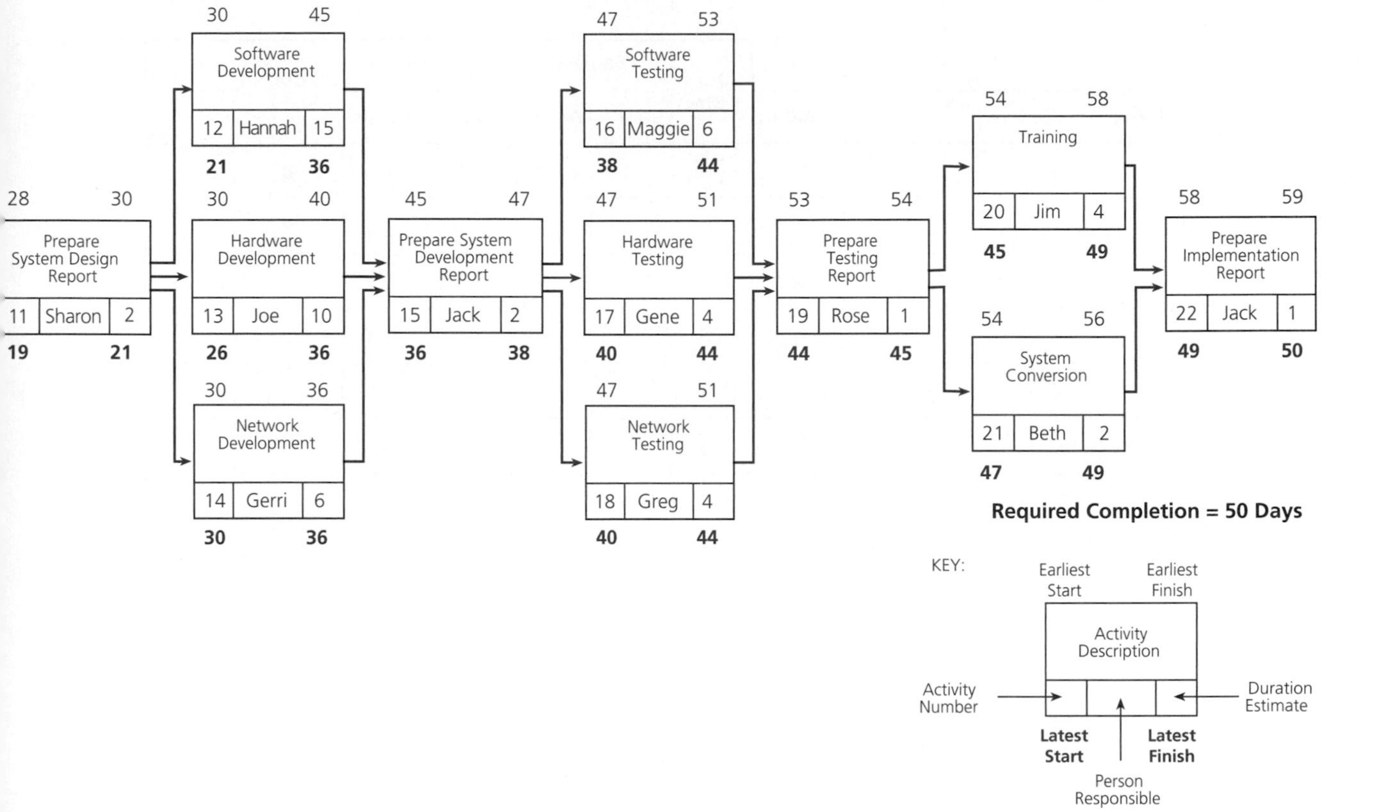

28 30
Prepare System Design Report
11 Sharon 2
19 21
30 45
Software Development
12 Hannah 15
21 36
30 40
Hardware Development
13 Joe 10
26 36
30 36
Network Development
14 Gerri 6
30 36
45 47
Prepare System Development Report
15 Jack 2
36 38
47 53
Software Testing
16 Maggie 6
38 44
47 51
Hardware Testing
17 Gene 4
40 44
47 51
Network Testing
18 Greg 4
40 44
53 54
Prepare Testing Report
19 Rose 1
44 45
54 58
Training
20 Jim 4
45 49
54 56
System Conversion
21 Beth 2
47 49
58 59
Prepare Implementation Report
22 Jack 1
49 50
Required Completion = 50 Days
KEY:
Earliest Start
Earliest Finish
Activity Description
Activity Number
Duration Estimate
Latest Start
Latest Finish
Person Responsible

12. Calculate the ES, EF, LS, and LF times and the slack for each activity in the figure below and identify the critical path for the project. Can the project be completed in 30 weeks?

1
2
3
4
5
6
7
8
A 3
B 5
C 18
D 7
E 10
F 5
G 8
H 2
I 9
J 5

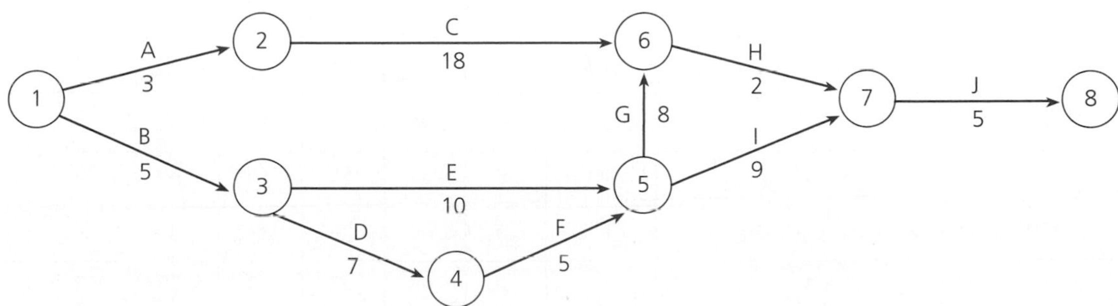

FIGURE 6.20 *Schedule for Web-Based Reporting System Project*

Web-based Reporting System Project

	Activity	Respon.	Dur. Estim.	Earliest		Latest		Total Slack	
				Start	Finish	Start	Finish		
1	Gather Data	Beth	3	0	3	–8	–5	–8	
2	Study Feasibility	Jack	4	0	4	–9	–5	–9	
3	Prepare Problem Definition Report	Rose	1	4	5	–5	–4	–9	
4	Interview Users	Jim	5	5	10	–4	1	–9	
5	Study Existing System	Steve	8	5	13	–2	6	–7	
6	Define User Requirements	Jeff	5	10	15	1	6	–9	
7	Prepare System Analysis Report	Jim	1	15	16	6	7	–9	
8	Input & Output	Tyler	8	16	24	9	17	–7	
9	Processing & Database	Joe	10	16	26	7	17	–9	
10	Evaluation	Cathy	2	26	28	17	19	–9	
11	Prepare System Design Report	Sharon	2	28	30	19	21	–9	
12	Software Development	Hannah	15	30	45	21	36	–9	
13	Hardware Development	Joe	10	30	40	26	36	–4	
14	Network Development	Gerri	6	30	36	30	36	0	
15	Prepare System Development Report	Jack	2	45	47	36	38	–9	
16	Software Testing	Maggie	6	47	53	38	44	–9	
17	Hardware Testing	Gene	4	47	51	40	44	–7	
18	Network Testing	Greg	4	47	51	40	44	–7	
19	Prepare Testing Report	Rose	1	53	54	44	45	–9	
20	Training	Jim	4	54	58	45	49	–9	
21	System Conversion	Beth	2	54	56	47	49	–7	
22	Prepare Implementation Report	Jack	1	58	59	49	50	–9	

INTERNET EXERCISES

For the website addresses of the organizations mentioned in these exercises, go to "Internet Exercises" at the book's companion website at **international.cengage.com**. It is suggested that you save this website in your "Favorites" for easy access in the future.

1. Search the web for project scheduling tools and describe at least three sites that you find.
2. For exercises 2 through 5, visit the website for the Software Program Managers Network (SPMN). Why was the SPMN established and what is their mission?
3. Click on the "16 Critical Software Practices" link. Briefly describe those 16 factors. Identify the factors that you think are relevant to all types of projects, not just software projects.
4. Click on the "Lessons Learned" section. Explore several of the links. Explore the links related to planning and scheduling and describe what you discover.
5. Click on their "Web Links" button. Explore and describe at least three of these links.

A Not-for-Profit Medical Research Center

CASE STUDY 1

This case study is a continuation of the one started in Chapter 5.

CASE QUESTIONS

1. Develop a duration estimate for each activity.
2. Using a project start time of 0 (May 15) and a required project completion time of 180 days (November 15), calculate the ES, EF, LS, and LF times and total slack for each activity. (*Note:* if your calculations result in a project schedule with negative total slack, don't make any revisions to any activity duration estimates or other changes to the network at this time. This will be done in Chapter 7.)
3. Determine the critical path and identify the activities that make up the critical path.
4. Develop a cost estimate for each activity and determine the total budget for the project.

GROUP ACTIVITY

Divide the course participants into the same groups of three or four as for the previous chapter's group activity and answer the questions listed above.

Note: This case study will continue in Chapters 7 through 9, so save the results of your work.

FIGURE 6.21 *Network Diagram for Web-Based Reporting System Project, Showing the Critical Path*

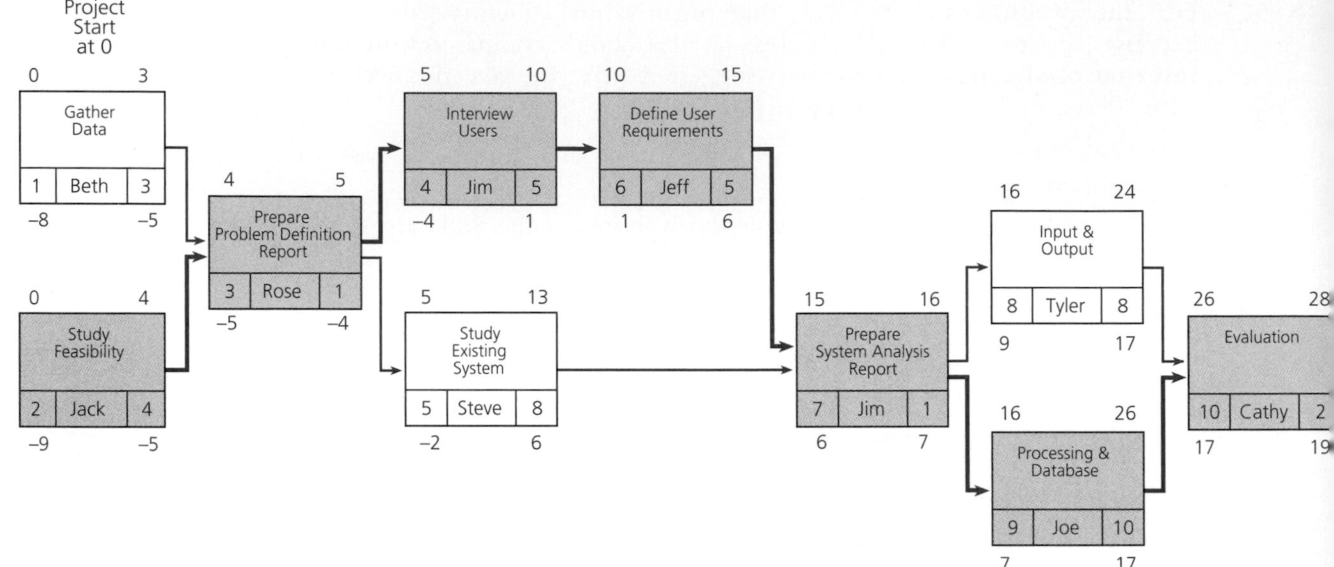

CASE STUDY 2

The Wedding

This case study is a continuation of the one started in Chapter 5.

CASE QUESTIONS

1. Develop a duration estimate for each activity.
2. Using a project start time of 0 (January 1) and a required project completion time of 180 days (June 30), calculate the ES, EF, LS, and LF times and total slack for each activity. (*Note:* If your calculations result in a project schedule with negative total slack, don't make any revisions to any activity duration estimates or other changes to the network at this time. This will be done in the Chapter 7.)
3. Determine the critical path and identify the activities that make up the critical path.
4. Develop a cost estimate for each activity and determine the total budget for the wedding.

GROUP ACTIVITY

Divide the course participants into the same groups of three or four as for the previous chapter's group activity and answer the questions listed above.

Note: This case study will continue in Chapters 7 through 9, so save the results of your work.

APPENDIX 1

Probability Considerations

Activity Duration Estimates

Recall that the duration estimate for each activity is the estimated total elapsed time from the time the activity is started until the time it is finished. With

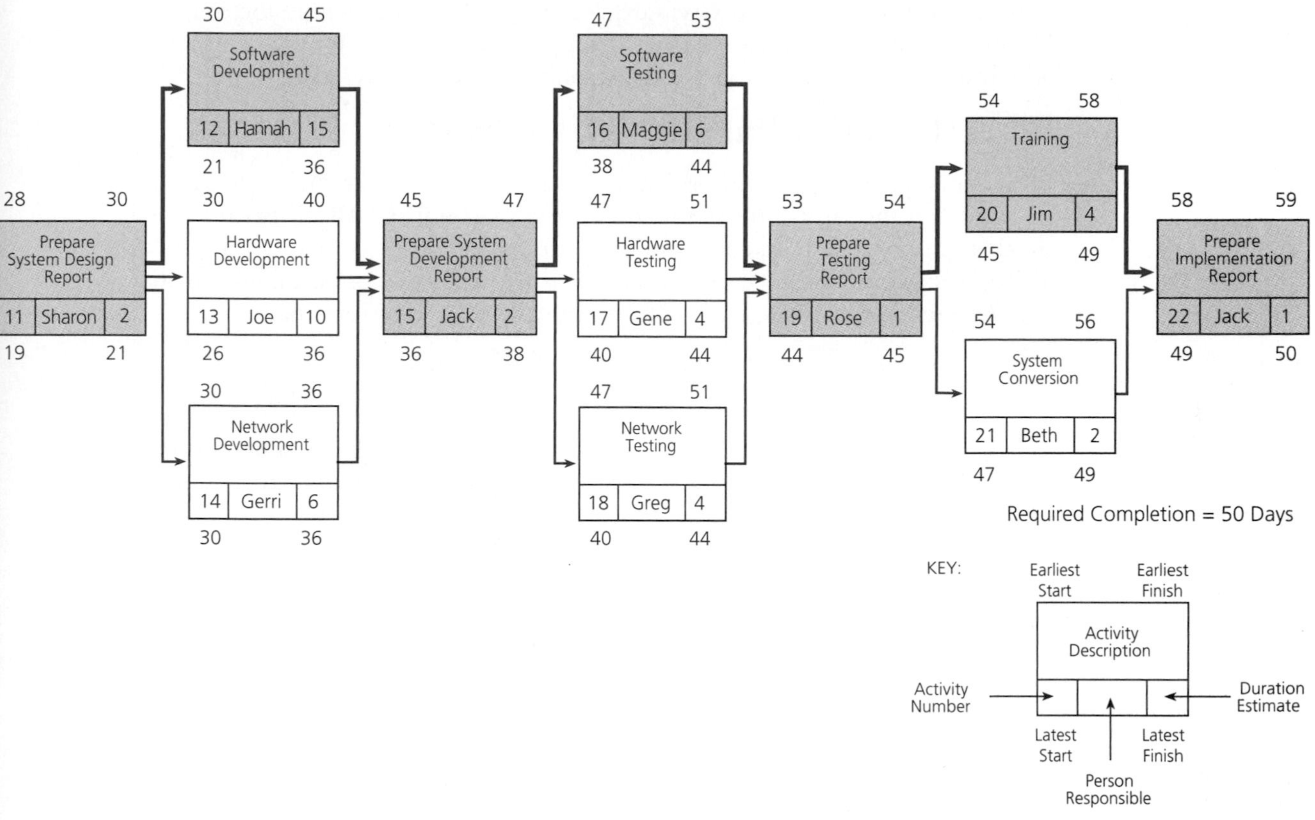

projects for which there is a high degree of uncertainty about the activity duration estimates, it is possible to use three estimates for each activity:

1. ***Optimistic time*** **(t_o)** is the time in which a particular activity can be completed if everything goes perfectly well and there are no complications. A rule of thumb is that there should be only one chance in 10 of completing the activity in less than the optimistic time estimate.
2. ***Most likely time*** **(t_m)** is the time in which a particular activity can most frequently be completed under normal conditions. If an activity has been repeated many times, the actual duration that occurs most frequently can be used as the most likely time estimate.
3. ***Pessimistic time*** **(t_p)** is the time in which a particular activity can be completed under adverse circumstances, such as in the presence of unusual or unforeseen complications. A rule of thumb is that there should be only one chance in ten of completing the activity in more than the pessimistic time estimate.

Establishing three time estimates makes it possible to take uncertainty into account when estimating how long an activity will take. The most likely time must be longer than or equal to the optimistic time, and the pessimistic time must be longer than or equal to the most likely time.

It is not required that three time estimates be made for each activity. If someone has wide experience or data on how long it took to perform very similar activities in completed projects, it may be preferable to make only one estimate for how long an activity is expected to take (as discussed in the chapter). However, using three time estimates (t_o, t_m, and t_p) can be helpful when there is a high degree of uncertainty as to how long an activity may take.

The Beta Probability Distribution

In network planning, when three time estimates are used for each activity, it is assumed that the three estimates follow a **beta probability distribution**. Based on this assumption, it's possible to calculate an expected (also called mean or average) duration, t_e, for each activity from the activity's three time estimates. The **expected duration** is calculated using the following formula:

$$t_e = \frac{t_o + 4(t_m) + t_p}{6}$$

Assume that the optimistic time for an activity is 1 week, the most likely time is 5 weeks, and the pessimistic time is 15 weeks. The beta probability distribution for this activity is shown in Figure 6.22. The expected duration for this activity is

$$t_e = \frac{1 + 4(5) + 15}{6} = 6 \text{ weeks}$$

Assume that the optimistic time for another activity is 10 weeks, the most likely time is 15 weeks, and the pessimistic time is 20 weeks. The beta probability distribution for this activity is shown in Figure 6.23. The expected duration for this activity is

$$t_e = \frac{10 + 4(15) + 20}{6} = 15 \text{ weeks}$$

Coincidentally, this happens to be the same as the most likely time estimate.

FIGURE 6.22 *Beta Probability Distribution*

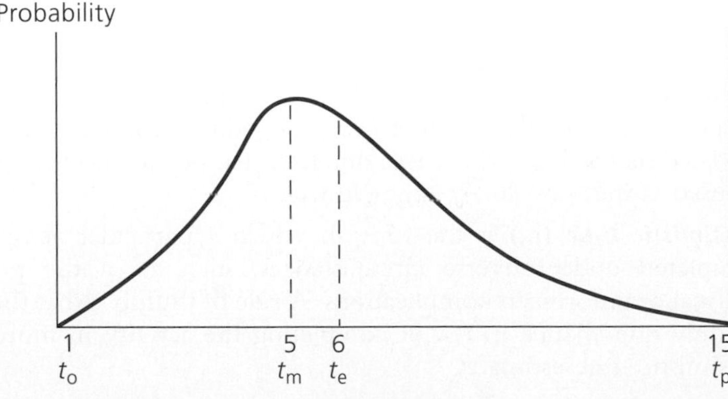

FIGURE 6.23 ***Beta Probability Distribution***

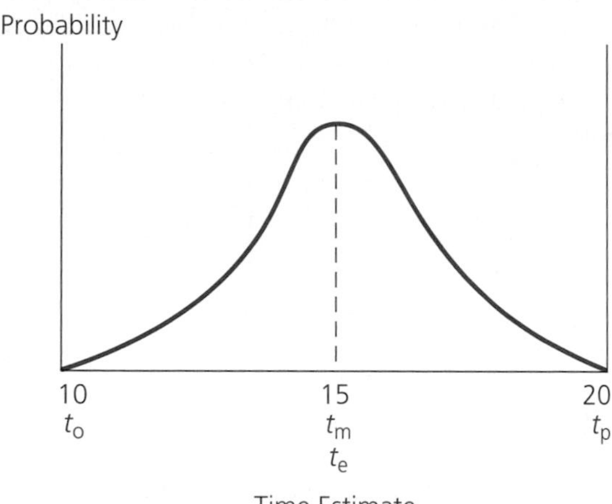

The peaks of the curves in Figures 6.22 and 6.23 represent the most likely times for their respective activities. The expected duration, t_e, divides the total area under the beta probability curve into two equal parts. In other words, 50 percent of the area under any beta probability curve will be to the left of t_e and 50 percent will be to the right. For example, Figure 6.22 shows that 50 percent of the area under the curve is to the left of 6 weeks and 50 percent of the area is to the right of 6 weeks. Thus, there is a 50–50 chance that an activity will actually take more or less time than its expected duration. Stated another way, there is a probability of 0.5 that an activity will take more time than t_e, and a probability of 0.5 that it will take less time then t_e. In Figure 6.22, there is a 50 percent chance that the activity will take longer than 6 weeks and a 50 percent chance that it will take less than 6 weeks.

It is assumed that, as a project progresses, some activities will take less time than their expected duration and some activities will take more time than their expected duration. It is further assumed that, by the time the entire project is completed, the total net difference between all *expected* durations and all *actual* durations will be minimal.

Reinforce Your Learning

15. Calculate the expected duration for an activity having the following time estimates: $t_o = 8$, $t_m = 12$, and $t_p = 22$.

Probability Fundamentals

Network planning in which three time estimates are used for each activity can be considered a *stochastic*, or *probabilistic, technique*, because it allows for uncertainty in activity duration by incorporating three estimates that are assumed to be distributed according to the beta probability distribution. Any technique that uses only one time estimate is considered a *deterministic technique*. Because it's assumed that the three time estimates for each activity follow a beta probability distribution, it is possible to calculate the probability, or likelihood, of actually completing the project before the required time. If only one time estimate is used for each activity, probability calculations cannot be made.

When three time estimates are used, all of the activities on the critical path of the network diagram can be added together to obtain a total probability distribution. The central limit theorem of probability theory states that this total probability distribution is not a beta probability distribution but a **normal probability distribution**, which is bell-shaped and symmetrical around its mean value. Furthermore, this total probability distribution has an expected duration that is equal to the sum of the expected durations of all of the activities that make up the total distribution. It also has a variance that is equal to the sum of the variances of all of the activities that make up the total distribution.

The **variance** for the beta probability distribution of an activity is found using the following formula:

$$\text{Variance} = \sigma^2 = \left[\frac{t_p - t_o}{6}\right]^2$$

Note that the variance of the normal distribution is the sum of the variances of the beta distribution.

Whereas the expected duration—which divides the area under a probability distribution into two equal parts—is a measure of the central tendency of a distribution, the variance is a measure of the dispersion, or spread, of a distribution from its expected value. The **standard deviation**, σ, is another measure of the dispersion of a distribution and *is equal to the square root of the variance.* The standard deviation gives a better visual representation of the spread of a distribution from its mean, or expected value, than does the variance. For a normal distribution (see Figure 6.24), the area within one standard deviation of the mean (to both sides) includes approximately 68 percent of the total area under the curve, the area within two standard deviations includes approximately 95 percent of the total area under the curve, and the area within three standard deviations includes approximately 99 percent of the total area under the curve.

Reinforce Your Learning

16. Compute the expected duration (t_e) and the variance (σ^2) for the following beta probability distribution.

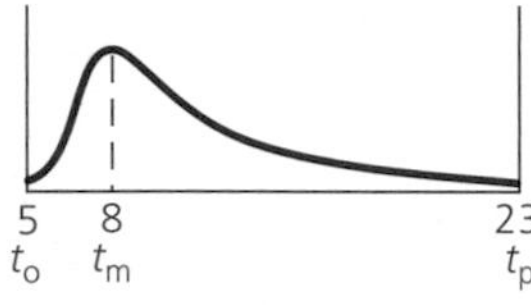

Reinforce Your Learning

17. What percentage of the area under this normal curve is shaded?

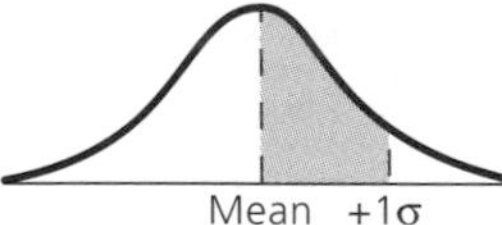

As noted above, the standard deviation is a measure of the dispersion of a distribution. Figure 6.25 shows two normal distributions. The distribution in (a) of Figure 6.25 is more widespread and thus has a larger standard deviation than that in (b). However, for both distributions 68 percent of the area under the curve is included within one standard deviation of the mean.

The total probability distribution of all the activities on the critical path of a network diagram is a normal distribution, with a mean equal to the sum of the individual activity expected durations and a variance equal to the sum of the individual activity variances. Consider the simple network in Figure 6.26. Assume that the project can start at time 0 and must be completed by day 42. The probability distributions for the activities in Figure 6.26 are shown in Figure 6.27.

FIGURE 6.24 *Normal Probability Distribution*

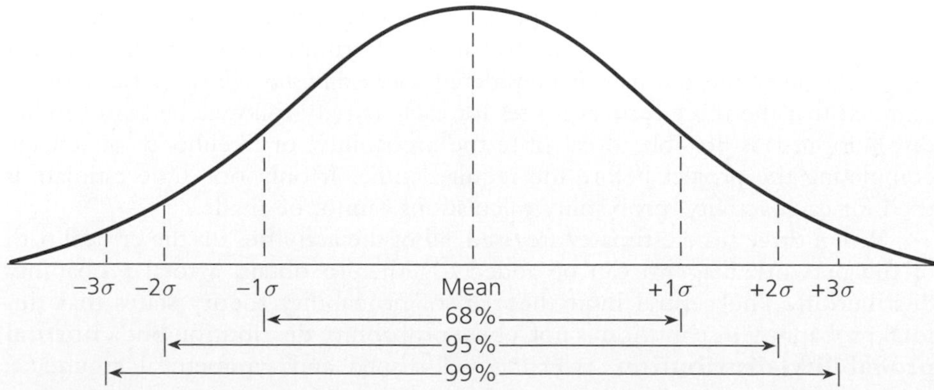

FIGURE 6.25 *Normal Probability Distributions*

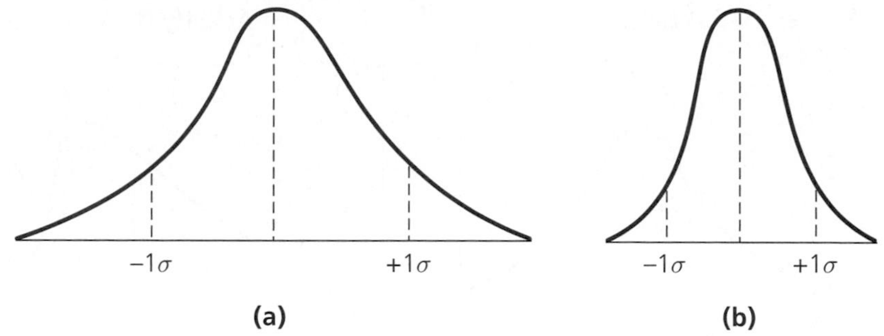

FIGURE 6.26 *Example Project*

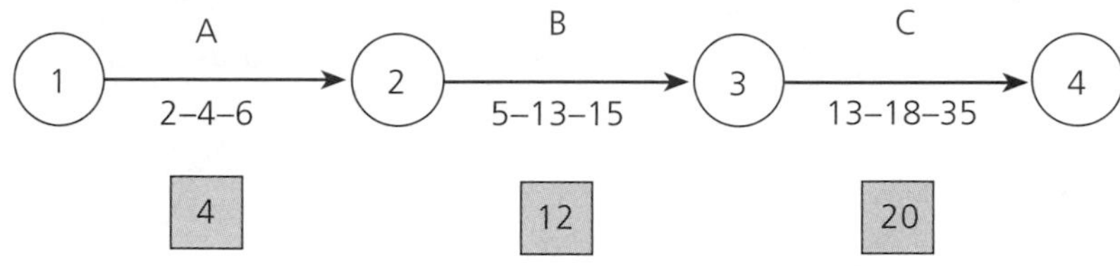

Required Completion = 42 Days

The expected duration for each activity is as follows.

$$\text{Activity A} \quad t_e = \frac{2 + 4(4) + 6}{6} = 4 \text{ days}$$

$$\text{Activity B} \quad t_e = \frac{5 + 4(13) + 15}{6} = 12 \text{ days}$$

$$\text{Activity C} \quad t_e = \frac{13 + 4(18) + 35}{6} = 20 \text{ days}$$

$$\text{Total} = 36 \text{ days}$$

If we sum the three distributions, we obtain a total mean, or total t_e:

Activity	t_o	t_m	t_p
A	2	4	6
B	5	13	15
C	13	18	35
Total	20	35	56

$$t_e = \frac{20 + 4(35) + 56}{6} = 36 \text{ days}$$

This result is the same as the sum of the three individual expected durations calculated previously: 4 + 12 + 20 = 36 days. The total probability distribution is shown in (d) of Figure 6.27. The total expected duration for

Reinforce Your Learning

18. If 95 percent of the area under the following normal curve is between the two labeled points, what is the standard deviation? What is the variance?

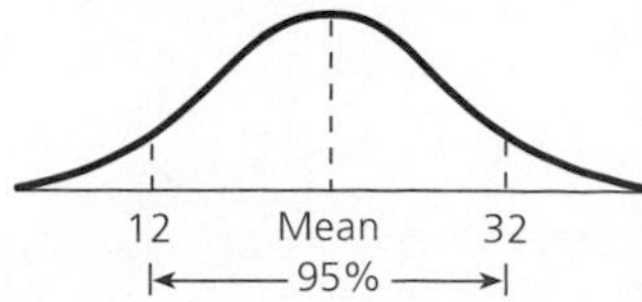

FIGURE 6.27 Probability Distributions

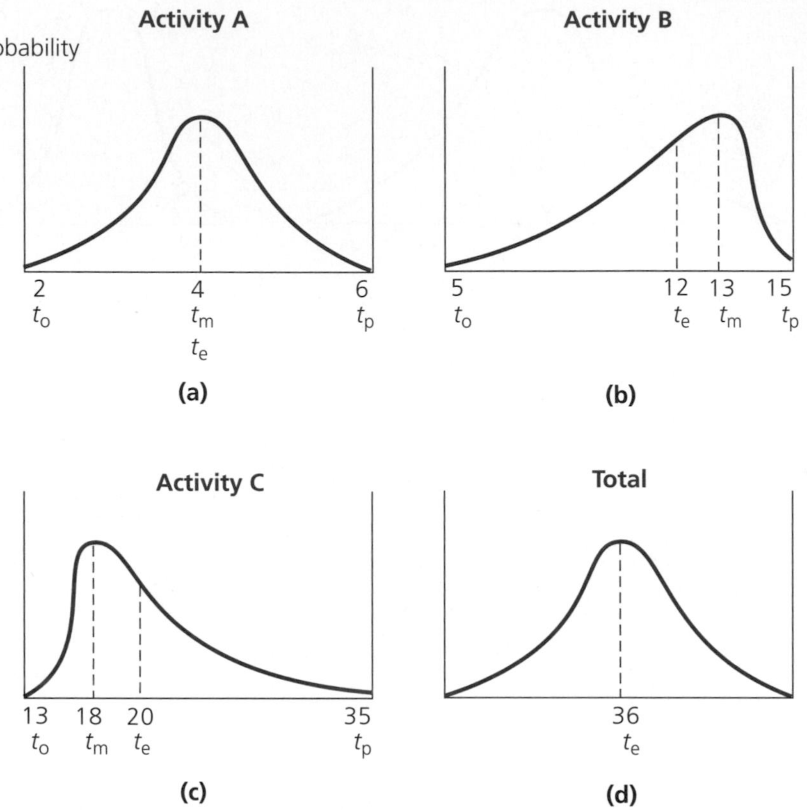

path 1–2–3–4 is 36 days. Thus, the project has an earliest expected completion time of day 36. As previously stated, the project has a required completion time of day 42.

The total distribution has a mean elapsed time equal to the sum of the three individual means, or expected durations. There is a probability of 0.5 that the project will be completed before day 36 and a probability of 0.5 that it will be completed after day 36.

For the simple example in Figure 6.26, the variances for the beta distributions of the three activities are as follows.

$$\text{Activity A} \quad \sigma^2 = \left(\frac{6-2}{6}\right)^2 = 0.444$$

$$\text{Activity B} \quad \sigma^2 = \left(\frac{15-5}{6}\right)^2 = 2.778$$

$$\text{Activity C} \quad \sigma^2 = \left(\frac{35-13}{6}\right)^2 = 13.444$$

$$\text{Total} = 16.666$$

The variance for the total distribution, which is a normal probability distribution, is the sum of the three individual variances, or 16.666. The standard deviation, σ, of the total distribution is

FIGURE 6.28 ***Normal Probability Distribution for Sample Project***

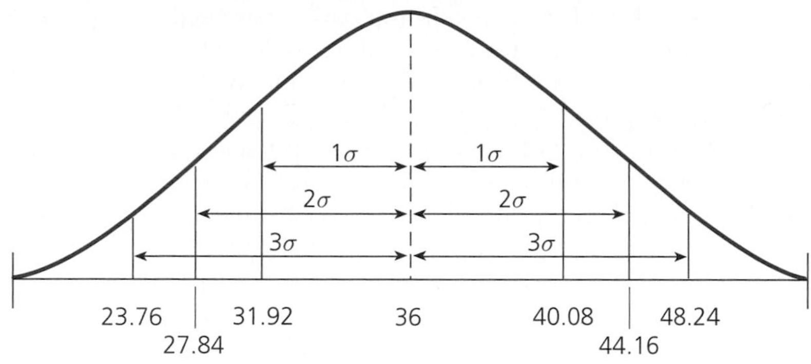

$$\text{Standard deviation} = \sigma = \sqrt{\sigma^2} = \sqrt{16.666} = 4.08 \text{ days}$$

Figure 6.28, like (d) of Figure 6.27, shows the total probability curve, with the addition of the standard deviations.

Figure 6.28 is a normal curve, so 68 percent of its total area is contained within $\pm 1\sigma$ (standard deviation) of t_e, or between 31.92 days and 40.08 days; 95 percent of its area is between 27.84 days and 44.16 days; and 99 percent of its area is between 23.76 days and 48.24 days. This probability distribution can be interpreted as follows:

- There is a 99 percent chance (0.99 probability) of completing the project in 23.76 to 48.24 days.
- There is a 95 percent chance (0.95 probability) of completing the project in 27.84 to 44.16 days.
- There is a 47.5 percent chance (0.475 probability) of completing the project in 27.84 to 36 days.
- There is a 47.5 percent chance (0.475 probability) of completing the project in 36 to 44.16 days.
- There is a 68 percent chance (0.68 probability) of completing the project in 31.92 to 40.08 days.
- There is a 34 percent chance (0.34 probability) of completing the project in 31.92 to 36 days.
- There is a 34 percent chance (0.34 probability) of completing the project in 36 to 40.08 days.
- There is a 13.5 percent chance (0.135 probability) of completing the project in 27.84 to 31.92 days.
- There is a 13.5 percent chance (0.135 probability) of completing the project in 40.08 to 44.16 days.
- There is a 0.5 percent chance (0.005 probability) of completing the project before 23.76 days.
- There is a 0.5 percent chance (0.005 probability) of completing the project after 48.24 days.

Thus, it can be stated that the ratio of the area under certain parts of the normal curve to the total area under the curve is related to the probability.

Calculating Probability

The earliest expected finish time for a project is determined by the critical path through the network diagram. It is equal to the scheduled start time of the project plus the sum of the expected durations of the activities on the critical path leading from project start to project completion. As stated previously, the probability of actually completing a project before its earliest expected finish time is 0.5, because half of the area under the normal distribution curve is to the left of this expected time; the probability of actually completing a project after its earliest expected finish time is also 0.5, because half of the area under the normal curve is to the right of this expected time. Knowing the required completion time for a project makes it possible to calculate the probability of actually completing the project before this time.

In order to find the probability of actually completing a project before its required completion time, the following formula is used:

$$Z = \frac{\text{LF} - \text{EF}}{\sigma_t}$$

The elements in this formula are as follows:

- LF is the required completion time (latest finish) for the project.
- EF is the earliest expected finish time for the project (mean of the normal distribution).
- σ_t is the standard deviation of the total distribution of the activities on the longest (most time-consuming) path leading to project completion.

In the above equation, Z measures the number of standard deviations between EF and LF on the normal probability curve. This Z value must be converted into a number that gives the proportion of the area under the normal curve that lies between EF and LF. Because the total area under a normal curve is equal to 1.0, the probability of finishing the project before its required completion time is equal to the proportion of the area under the curve that is to the left of LF.

The earliest expected finish time (EF) for the simple three-activity network in Figure 6.26 was calculated to be 36 days. Recall that the required completion time (LF) for the project is 42 days, or 6 days later than the EF. Figure 6.29 shows the normal curve for the project, with EF = 36 days and LF = 42 days.

The proportion of the area under the curve to the left of LF is equal to the probability of completing the project before 42 days. EF divides the area under

FIGURE 6.29 ***Normal Probability Distribution for Sample Project***

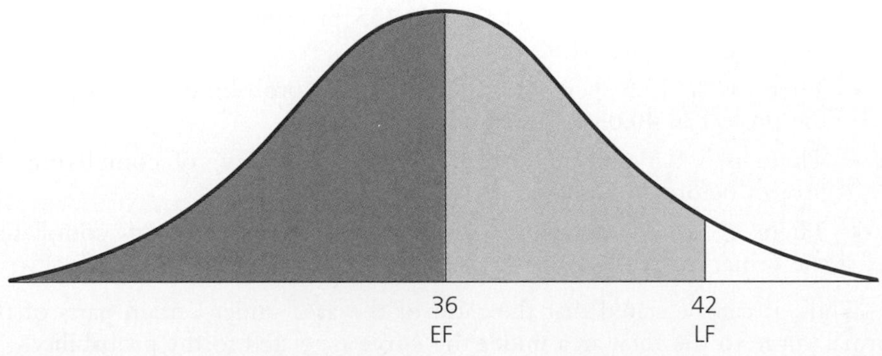

the curve into two equal parts, each containing half of the area, so we know that the proportion of the area to the left of EF is 0.5. We must now find the proportion of the area between EF and LF and add this to 0.5 to obtain the proportion of the total area to the left of LF. Using the previous equation to find the proportion of the area between EF and LF, we can calculate Z:

$$Z = \frac{\text{LF} - \text{EF}}{\sigma_t} = \frac{42 - 36}{4.08} = \frac{6}{4.08} = 1.47$$

The Z value of 1.47 indicates that there are 1.47 standard deviations (1 standard deviation 4.08 days) between EF and LF. However, the Z value does not directly give the proportion of the area under the curve between EF and LF. In order to find this area, we must convert the Z value to a number that gives the area directly, using a standard conversion table such as Table 6-1.

The first column and top row of the table are used to find the desired Z value with a significance of 0.01. To find the area for a Z value of 1.47, first go down the column on the far left to 1.4, then go across this row to the 0.07 column. The number there is 0.42922. This means that for a Z value of 1.47, the proportion of the area under a normal curve is 0.42922. This number tells us that the probability of actually completing the project between EF and LF, or in 36 to 42 days, is 0.42922; thus, there is a 42.922 percent chance. However, because we are interested in finding the probability of actually completing the project any time before 42 days, we must add the probability of finishing before 36 days. The probability of finishing the project any time before 42 days is equal to the probability of finishing before 36 days plus the probability of finishing between 36 days and 42 days:

$$0.50000 + 0.42922 = 0.92922$$

The probability of actually completing the project before its required completion time of 42 days is 0.92922; there is a 92.922 percent chance.

SUMMARY

If each activity in the network diagram for a project has three time estimates (optimistic, most likely, and pessimistic), it is possible to calculate the probability of actually completing the project before its required completion time using the methods discussed in this appendix. However, you should be careful in interpreting this probability, especially when there are several paths that are nearly as long as the critical path. If the standard deviations of these alternative paths are substantially different from that of the critical path, the probability of the project's actually being finished before its required completion time may be lower when these paths are used in the probability calculations than when the critical path is used. This discrepancy usually arises only when two or more paths that are equal or nearly equal in length lead to project completion.

QUESTIONS

1. True or false: In order to calculate the probability of finishing a project by its required completion time, it is necessary to have three time estimates for each activity and the required completion time for the project.
2. What are the expected duration, variance, and standard deviation for an activity whose three time estimates are $t_o = 2$, $t_m = 14$, and $t_p = 14$?

Table 6.1 *Table of Areas of the Normal Curve Between the Maximum Ordinate and Values of Z*

Z	0.00	0.01	0.02	0.03	0.04	0.05	0.06	0.07	0.08	0.09
0.0	.00000	.00399	.00798	.01197	.01595	.01994	.02392	.02790	.03188	.03586
0.1	.03983	.04380	.04776	.05172	.05567	.05962	.06356	.06749	.07142	.07535
0.2	.07926	.08317	.08706	.09095	.09483	.09871	.10257	.10642	.11026	.11409
0.3	.11791	.12172	.12552	.12930	.13307	.13683	.14058	.14431	.14803	.15173
0.4	.15542	.15910	.16276	.16640	.17003	.17364	.17724	.18082	.18439	.18793
0.5	.19146	.19497	.19847	.20194	.20540	.20884	.21226	.21566	.21904	.22240
0.6	.22575	.22907	.23237	.23565	.23891	.24215	.24537	.24857	.25175	.25490
0.7	.25804	.26115	.26424	.26730	.27035	.27337	.27637	.27935	.28230	.28524
0.8	.28814	.29103	.29389	.29673	.29955	.30234	.30511	.30785	.31057	.31327
0.9	.31594	.31859	.32121	.32381	.32639	.32894	.33147	.33398	.33646	.33891
1.0	.34134	.34375	.34614	.34850	.35083	.35314	.35543	.35769	.35993	.36214
1.1	.36433	.36650	.36864	.37076	.37286	.37493	.37698	.37900	.38100	.38298
1.2	.38493	.38686	.38877	.39065	.39251	.39435	.39617	.39796	.39973	.40147
1.3	.40320	.40490	.40658	.40824	.40988	.41149	.41309	.41466	.41621	.41774
1.4	.41924	.42073	.42220	.42364	.42507	.42647	.42786	.42922	.43056	.43189
1.5	.44319	.43448	.43574	.43699	.43822	.43943	.44062	.44179	.44295	.44408
1.6	.44520	.44630	.44738	.44845	.44950	.45053	.45154	.45254	.45352	.45449
1.7	.45543	.45637	.45728	.45818	.45907	.45994	.46080	.46164	.46246	.46327
1.8	.46407	.46485	.46562	.46638	.46712	.46784	.46856	.46926	.46995	.47062
1.9	.47128	.47193	.47257	.47320	.47381	.47441	.47500	.47558	.47615	.47670
2.0	.47725	.47778	.47831	.47882	.47932	.47982	.48030	.48077	.48124	.48169
2.1	.48214	.48257	.48300	.48341	.48382	.48422	.48461	.48500	.48537	.48574
2.2	.48610	.48645	.48679	.48713	.48745	.48778	.48809	.48840	.48870	.48899
2.3	.48928	.48956	.48983	.49010	.49036	.49061	.49086	.49111	.49134	.49158
2.4	.49180	.49202	.49224	.49245	.49266	.49286	.49305	.49324	.49343	.49361
2.5	.49377	.49396	.49413	.49430	.49446	.49461	.49477	.49492	.49506	.49520
2.6	.49534	.49547	.49560	.49573	.49585	.49598	.49609	.49621	.49632	.49643
2.7	.49653	.49664	.49674	.49683	.49693	.49702	.49711	.49720	.49728	.49736
2.8	.49744	.49752	.49760	.49767	.49774	.49781	.49788	.49795	.49801	.49807
2.9	.49813	.49819	.49825	.49831	.49836	.49841	.49846	.49851	.49856	.49861
3.0	.49865	.49869	.49874	.49878	.49882	.49886	.49889	.49893	.49897	.49900
3.1	.49903	.49906	.49910	.49913	.49916	.49918	.49921	.49924	.49926	.49929
3.2	.49931	.49934	.49936	.49938	.49940	.49942	.49944	.49946	.49948	.49950
3.3	.49952	.49953	.49955	.49957	.49958	.49960	.49961	.49962	.49964	.49965
3.4	.49966	.49968	.49969	.49970	.49971	.49972	.49973	.49974	.49975	.49976
3.5	.49977	.49978	.49978	.49979	.49980	.49981	.49981	.49982	.49983	.49983
3.6	.49984	.49985	.49985	.49986	.49986	.49987	.49987	.49988	.49988	.49989
3.7	.49989	.49990	.49990	.49990	.49991	.49991	.49992	.49992	.49992	.49992
3.8	.49993	.49993	.49993	.49994	.49994	.49994	.49994	.49995	.49995	.49995
3.9	.49995	.49995	.49996	.49996	.49996	.49996	.49996	.49996	.49997	.49997
4.0	.49997	.49997	.49997	.49997	.49997	.49997	.49998	.49998	.49998	.49998

3. Which of the following is *not* a measure of the dispersion, or spread, of a distribution: variance, mean, or standard deviation?
4. The earliest expected finish time for a project is 138 days, and its required completion time is 130 days. What is the probability of completing the project before its required time if σ_t (the standard deviation of the total distribution of the activities on the longest path) is 6?

Microsoft Project

APPENDIX 2

In this appendix we will discuss how Microsoft Project can be used to support the techniques discussed in this chapter based on the consumer market study example. To retrieve your project information, on the File menu, click Open and locate your consumer market study file. We are now ready to enter the estimated durations for each task as discussed in this chapter.

FIGURE 6A.1 *Add Duration Data and Show Critical Path*

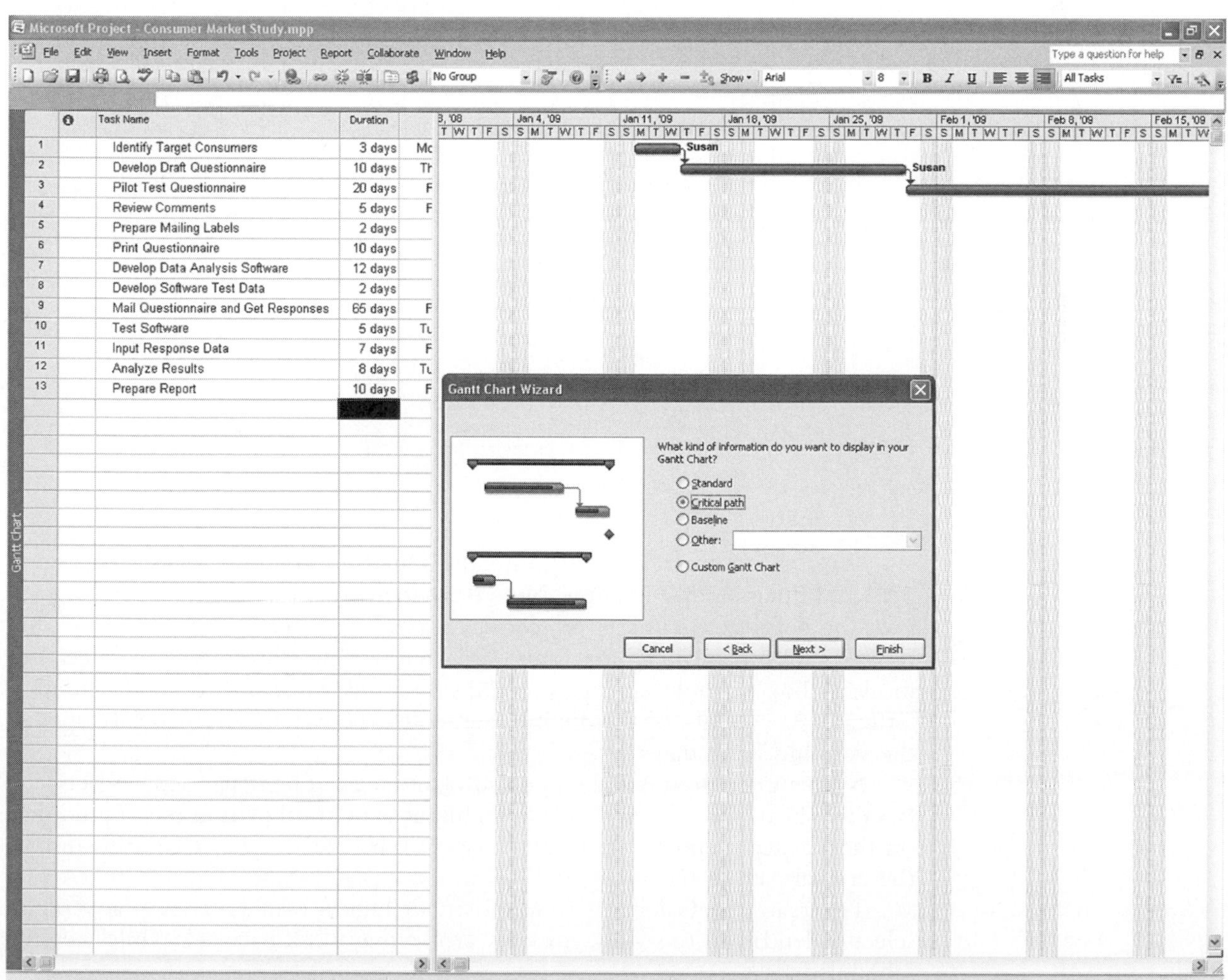

FIGURE 6A.2 *Calendar View*

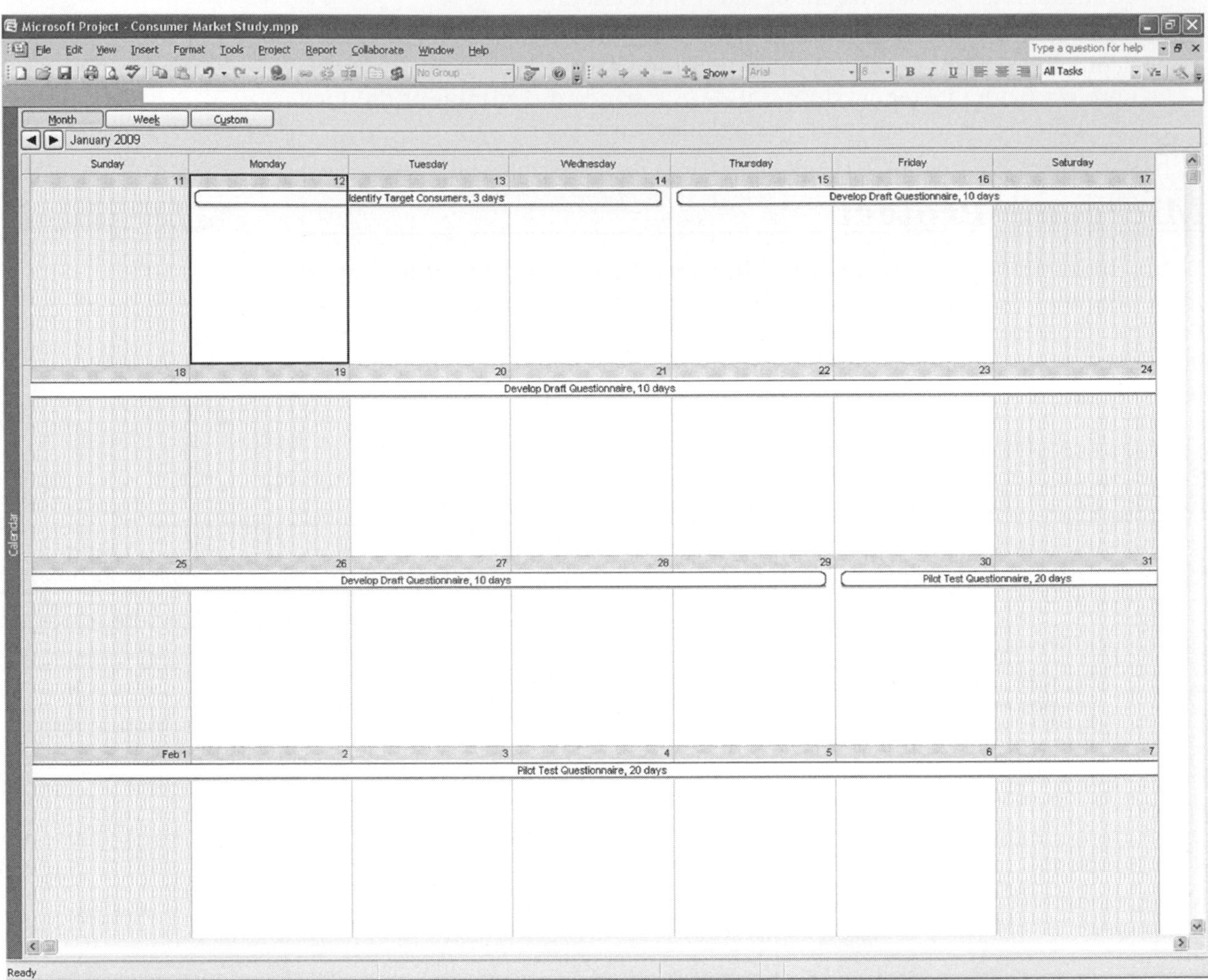

Enter duration data directly into the Duration column. Please see Figure 6A.1. for duration data to enter. Note that when you enter the duration for each task, the default time unit is "d" for days. You can enter "m" after the number to represent minutes; "h" for hours; "d" for days; "w" for weeks; or "mon" for months. For example, an entry of "2w" would equal a two-week duration estimate. As you modify the duration estimates, the system automatically updates the start and finish dates for each task.

Notice in Figure 6A.1 the updated Gantt chart. The dependencies between tasks are shown by arrows. You can highlight the critical path in red. To do this, on the Format menu, select Gantt Chart Wizard and use the wizard to display the critical path in red.

To create the Calendar View shown in Figure 6A.2, on the View menu select Calendar. In this view you can scroll along week by week while viewing scheduled tasks.

FIGURE 6A.3 ***More Views from the View menu***

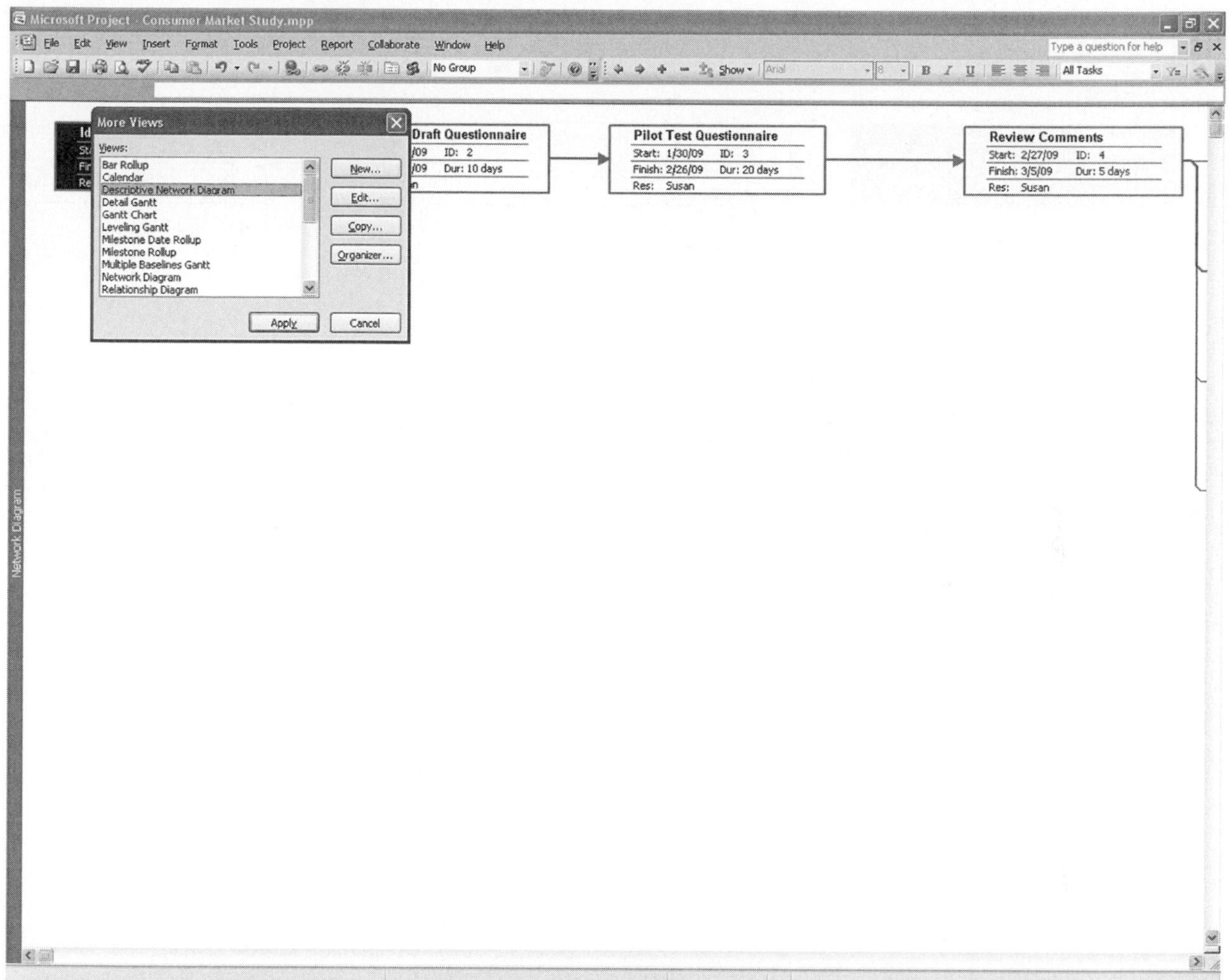

In the last chapter, you learned how to create two different PERT charts, one a simple Relationship Diagram, and the other, a standard Network Diagram. You can also produce a more detailed network diagram. On the View menu, select More Views, and choose Descriptive Network Diagram from the list, as shown in Figure 6A.3. The resulting screen would look as shown in Figure 6A.4.

Note that the critical path in the PERT diagram is also displayed in red.

Microsoft Project 2007 has already calculated the earliest and latest start and finish times for each task. To see these values, you need to view the Schedule Table from the Gantt Chart View. Start with the Gantt Chart View. On the View menu, click on Gantt Chart. Then, on the View menu, point to Table, and click on Schedule. You should see the table shown in Figure 6A.5.

You can request a report of all critical tasks in the Consumer Market Study project. On the Report menu, click on Reports. You should see the Reports window containing a menu of report types, as in Figure 6A.6. Choose Overview, click on Select, and choose Critical Tasks. You should see the Critical Tasks Report as in Figure 6A.7.

FIGURE 6A.4 *Descriptive Network Diagram*

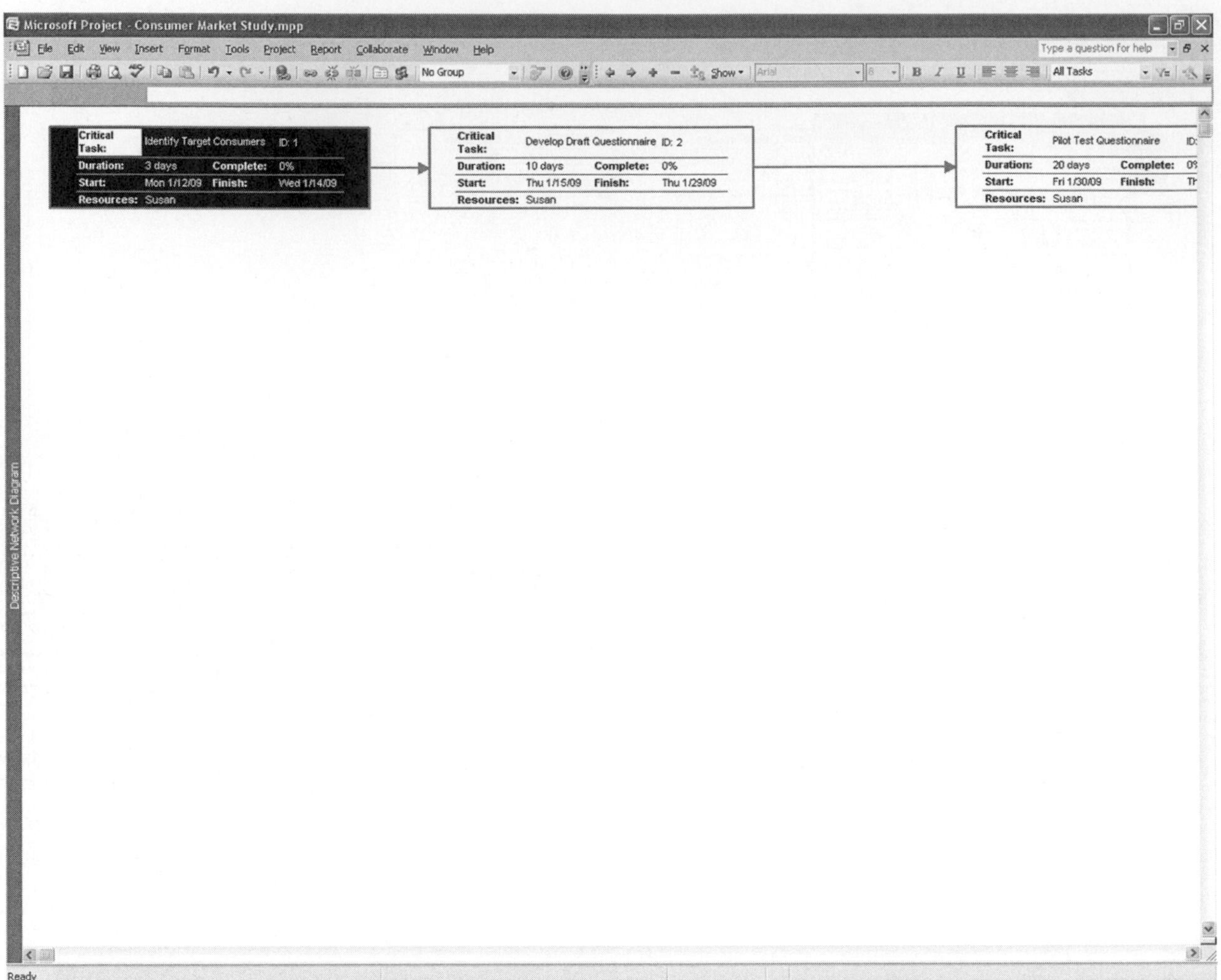

FIGURE 6A.5 *Gantt Chart View/ Schedule Table*

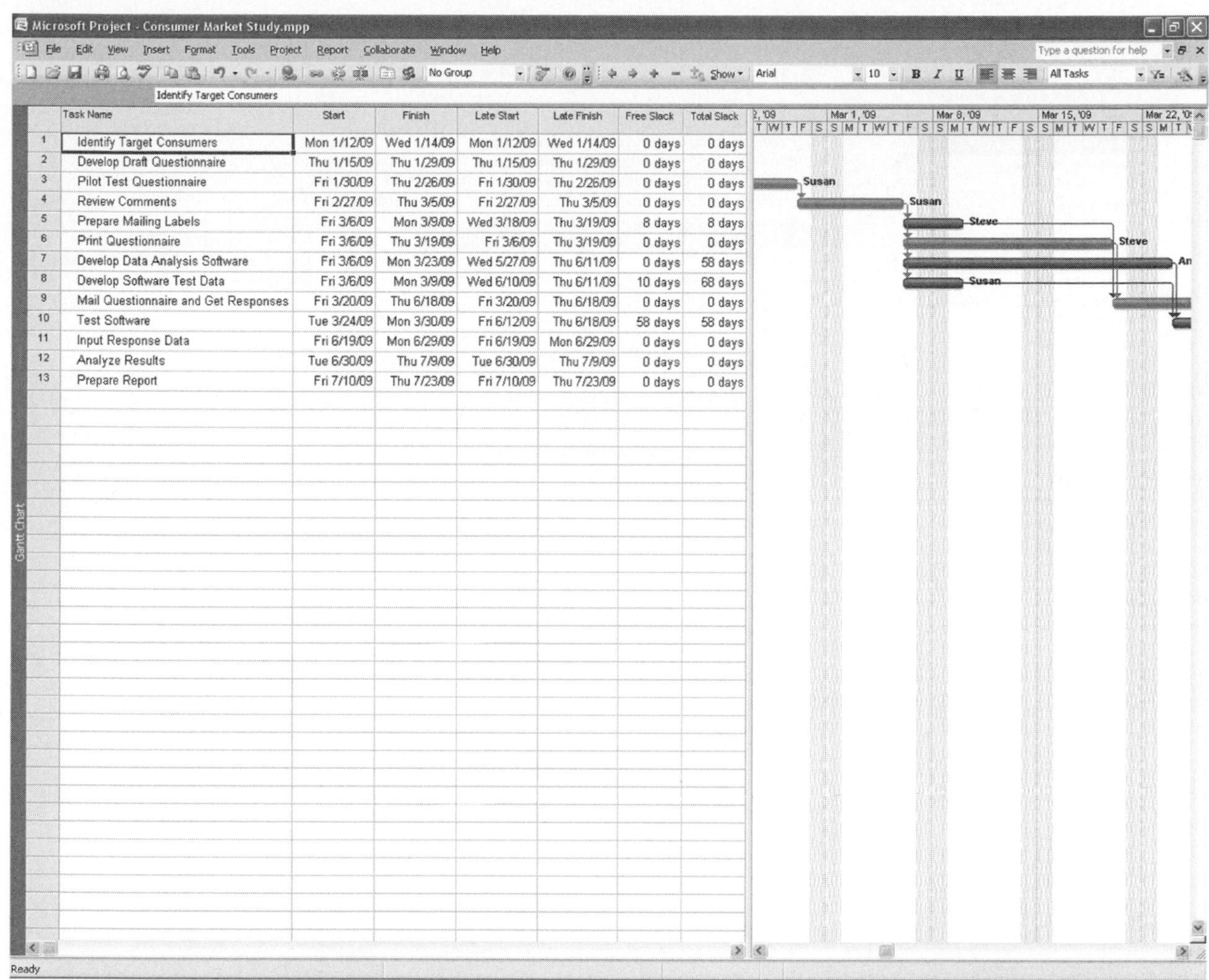

	Task Name	Start	Finish	Late Start	Late Finish	Free Slack	Total Slack
1	Identify Target Consumers	Mon 1/12/09	Wed 1/14/09	Mon 1/12/09	Wed 1/14/09	0 days	0 days
2	Develop Draft Questionnaire	Thu 1/15/09	Thu 1/29/09	Thu 1/15/09	Thu 1/29/09	0 days	0 days
3	Pilot Test Questionnaire	Fri 1/30/09	Thu 2/26/09	Fri 1/30/09	Thu 2/26/09	0 days	0 days
4	Review Comments	Fri 2/27/09	Thu 3/5/09	Fri 2/27/09	Thu 3/5/09	0 days	0 days
5	Prepare Mailing Labels	Fri 3/6/09	Mon 3/9/09	Wed 3/18/09	Thu 3/19/09	8 days	8 days
6	Print Questionnaire	Fri 3/6/09	Thu 3/19/09	Fri 3/6/09	Thu 3/19/09	0 days	0 days
7	Develop Data Analysis Software	Fri 3/6/09	Mon 3/23/09	Wed 5/27/09	Thu 6/11/09	0 days	58 days
8	Develop Software Test Data	Fri 3/6/09	Mon 3/9/09	Wed 6/10/09	Thu 6/11/09	10 days	68 days
9	Mail Questionnaire and Get Responses	Fri 3/20/09	Thu 6/18/09	Fri 3/20/09	Thu 6/18/09	0 days	0 days
10	Test Software	Tue 3/24/09	Mon 3/30/09	Fri 6/12/09	Thu 6/18/09	58 days	58 days
11	Input Response Data	Fri 6/19/09	Mon 6/29/09	Fri 6/19/09	Mon 6/29/09	0 days	0 days
12	Analyze Results	Tue 6/30/09	Thu 7/9/09	Tue 6/30/09	Thu 7/9/09	0 days	0 days
13	Prepare Report	Fri 7/10/09	Thu 7/23/09	Fri 7/10/09	Thu 7/23/09	0 days	0 days

FIGURE 6A.6 *Previewing a Report to Print*

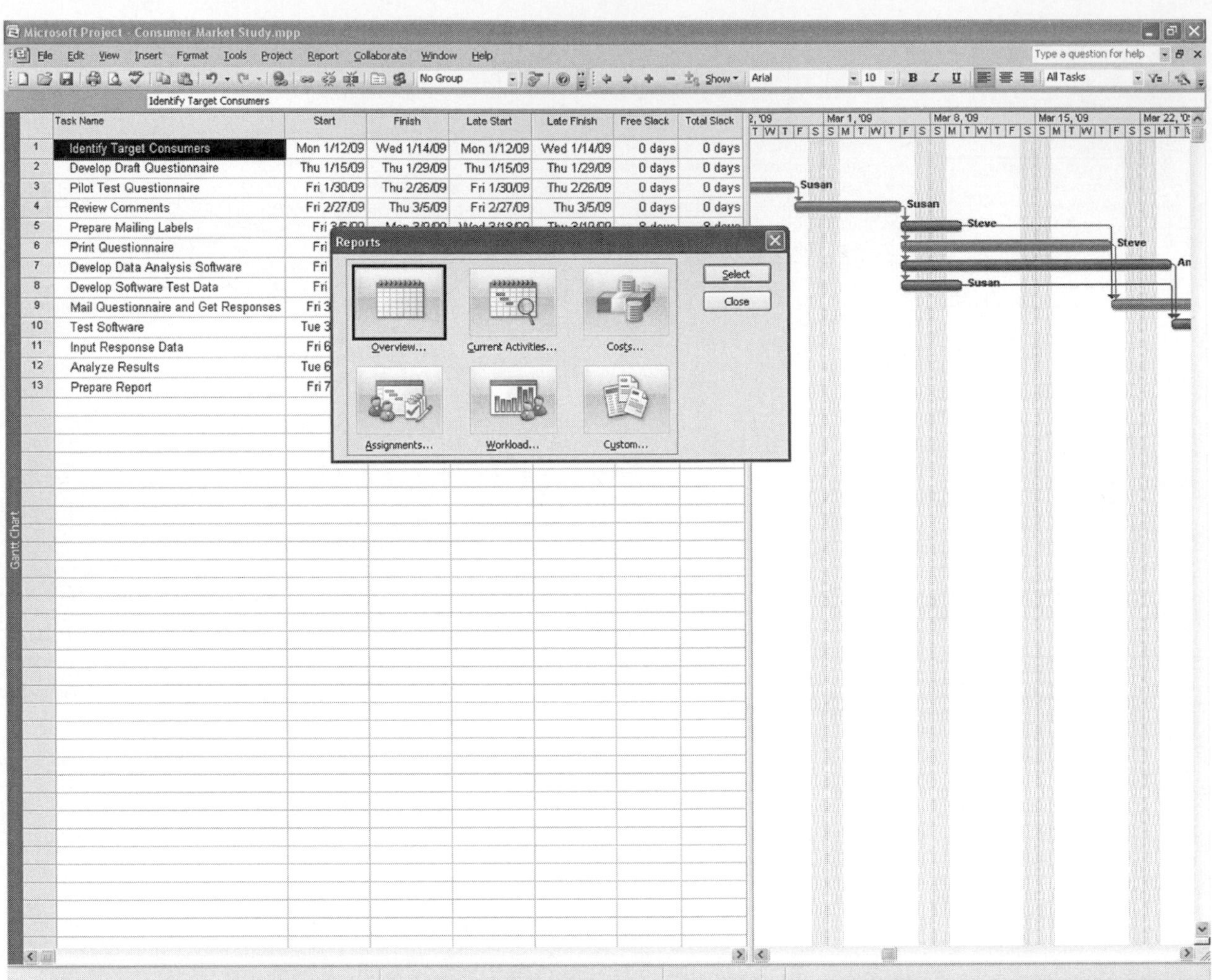

FIGURE 6A.7 *Critical Tasks Report*

Microsoft Project - Consumer Market Study.mpp

Page Setup... Print... Close Help

Critical Tasks as of Friday 1/02/09
Consumer Market Study.mpp

ID		Task Name			Duration	Start	Finish
1		Identify Target Consumers			3 days	Mon 1/12/09	Wed 1/14/09
	ID	*Successor Name*	*Type*	*Lag*			
	2	*Develop Draft Questionnaire*	*FS*	*0 days*			
2		Develop Draft Questionnaire			10 days	Thu 1/15/09	Thu 1/29/09
	ID	*Successor Name*	*Type*	*Lag*			
	3	*Pilot Test Questionnaire*	*FS*	*0 days*			
3		Pilot Test Questionnaire			20 days	Fri 1/30/09	Thu 2/26/09
	ID	*Successor Name*	*Type*	*Lag*			
	4	*Review Comments*	*FS*	*0 days*			
4		Review Comments			5 days	Fri 2/27/09	Thu 3/5/09
	ID	*Successor Name*	*Type*	*Lag*			
	5	*Prepare Mailing Labels*	*FS*	*0 days*			
	6	*Print Questionnaire*	*FS*	*0 days*			
	7	*Develop Data Analysis Software*	*FS*	*0 days*			
	8	*Develop Software Test Data*	*FS*	*0 days*			
6		Print Questionnaire			10 days	Fri 3/6/09	Thu 3/19/09
	ID	*Successor Name*	*Type*	*Lag*			
	9	*Mail Questionnaire and Get Responses*	*FS*	*0 days*			
9		Mail Questionnaire and Get Responses			65 days	Fri 3/20/09	Thu 6/18/09
	ID	*Successor Name*	*Type*	*Lag*			
	11	*Input Response Data*	*FS*	*0 days*			
11		Input Response Data			7 days	Fri 6/19/09	Mon 6/29/09
	ID	*Successor Name*	*Type*	*Lag*			
	12	*Analyze Results*	*FS*	*0 days*			
12		Analyze Results			8 days	Tue 6/30/09	Thu 7/9/09
	ID	*Successor Name*	*Type*	*Lag*			
	13	*Prepare Report*	*FS*	*0 days*			
13		Prepare Report			10 days	Fri 7/10/09	Thu 7/23/09

Page 1

Page: 1 of 2 Size: 1 row by 2 columns

© Chad Ehlers/Stock Connection/Jupiter Images

CHAPTER 7

Schedule Control

Real World PROJECT MANAGEMENT

A Fish Tale

Building an aquarium typically takes about seven years to complete. Bernie Marcus, co-founder of The Home Depot chain, decided he wanted to build one in half the time in Atlanta, Georgia. He wanted the aquarium to serve as a "thank you" for associates, customers, and stakeholders in the chain's home state. Heery International, Inc., a project management firm from Atlanta, created a clear and well-communicated vision to be used in conjunction with creative project planning. The Georgia Aquarium was completed for $290 million in less than three years and eight months. The project was declared a finalist in the Project Management Institute's (PMI) 2006 Project of the Year competition.

The aquarium houses more than 100,000 animals living in over eight million gallons of water. The aquarium has its own water treatment plant that has greater processing capabilities than the City of Atlanta Public Works Department. In most aquarium design projects, the building design dictates the types of animals that will eventually be living there. Mr. Marcus wanted to do the opposite: He first decided which animals he wanted and then built their habitats accordingly.

At first there was no project team. Mr. Marcus and Jeffrey Swanagan, executive director of the aquarium, were the only two working on the project. They visited 55 aquariums in 13 different countries. After they had gathered some information, they brought three more fish experts on board. The aquarium design was intended to be like a shopping mall as opposed to a large tank with spiraling walkways. The Georgia Aquarium was designed to have a main atrium, with five separate aquariums surrounding it. Each gallery would have its own story, mood, and music.

Mr. Marcus added Gary Goddard Entertainment to the team to help make the aquarium a place of entertainment. The entertainment firm worked with the "fish guys" to create an interactive virtual environment into the exhibits, with opportunities for viewing and touching tanks without compromising the dignity of the animals.

Heery International made sure that the team committed to work only on the aquarium project and on no others at the same time. The project was organized by program management, major designers, consultants, construction, design/build/operate, and purchase orders. Contracts were established with each company to ensure activities were in sync with one another. Mr. Marcus also decided to hold a portion of each company's profits depending on the completion of the aquarium. All fees for all companies were retained unless all projects were finished on time, which fostered a stronger collective project team.

All workers were encouraged to identify issues and suggest changes throughout the process. Senior personnel with decision-making authority were on-site at all times in order to make timely decisions. This helped to reduce change orders and save time. The team also tried to identify obstacles in advance and neutralize them before they became issues. The team established a partnership with the Atlanta Permits and Inspection group to join in the design and review process to eliminate any surprises.

It was critical for the marine life acquisitions to proceed on schedule to reduce any risk to the animals. Animals were arriving during construction, and the team turned over the aquarium tank by tank. Finally, the aquarium opened in November 2005, and as of early 2007 had already welcomed more than 3.6 million visitors.

Although Mr. Marcus explained, "We did it with planning, committed people, quick decision-making, and honestly, a lot of luck," it was effective project management that made the aquarium a wonderful success story!

Hildebrand, C., "A Fish Tale," *PM Network*, February 2007.

Chapters 5 and 6 established a baseline plan and a schedule, respectively, for the consumer market study project. Once a project actually starts, it's necessary to monitor the progress to ensure that everything is going according to schedule. This involves measuring actual progress and comparing it to the schedule. If at any time during the project it is determined that the project is behind schedule, corrective action must be taken to get back on schedule. If a project gets too far behind schedule, it may be very difficult to get back on track.

The key to effective project control is to measure actual progress and compare it to planned progress on a timely and regular basis and to take necessary corrective action immediately. A project manager must not simply hope that a problem will go away without corrective intervention—it won't. Based on actual progress and on consideration of other changes that may occur, it's possible to calculate an updated project schedule regularly and forecast whether the project will finish ahead of or behind its required completion time.

This chapter will cover the details of controlling a project and will focus mainly on the critical role of controlling the scheduling to ensure that the work gets done on time. By mastering the concepts discussed in this chapter, you should be well prepared to help control your projects. You will become familiar with

- performing the steps in the project control process
- determining the effects of actual schedule performance on the project schedule
- incorporating project changes into the schedule
- calculating an updated project schedule
- controlling the project schedule

PROJECT CONTROL PROCESS

The project control process involves regularly gathering data on project performance, comparing actual performance to planned performance, and taking corrective actions if actual performance is behind planned performance. This process must occur regularly throughout the project.

Figure 7.1 illustrates the steps in the project control process. It starts with establishing a baseline plan that shows how the project scope (tasks) will be accomplished on time (schedule) and within budget (resources, costs). Once this baseline plan is agreed upon by the customer and the contractor or project team, the project can start.

A regular **reporting period** should be established for comparing actual progress with planned progress. Reporting may be daily, weekly, biweekly, or

FIGURE 7.1 *Project Control Process*

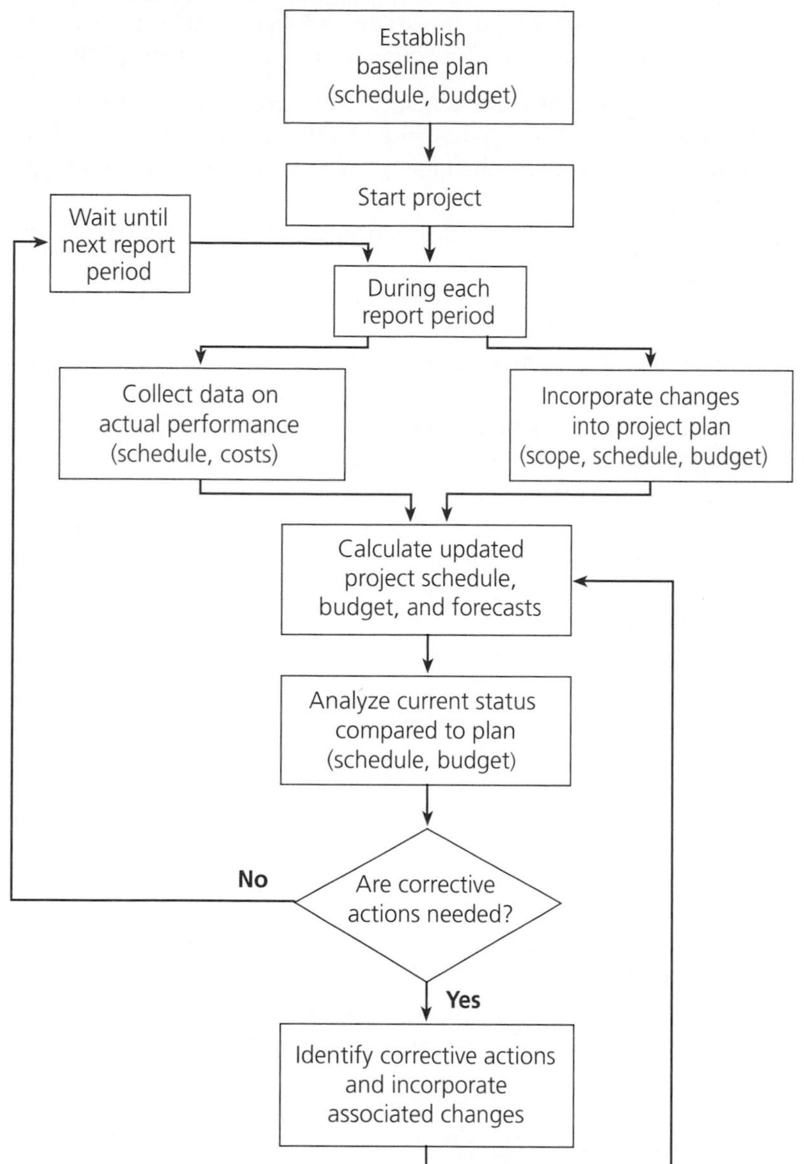

monthly, depending on the complexity or overall duration of the project. If a project is expected to have an overall duration of a month, the reporting period might be as short as a day. On the other hand, if a project is expected to run five years, the reporting period might be a month.

During each reporting period, two kinds of data or information need to be collected:

1. *Data on actual performance*. This includes
   - the actual time that activities were started and/or finished
   - the actual costs expended and committed

2. *Information on any changes to the project scope, schedule, or budget.* These changes could be initiated by the customer or the project team, or they could be the result of an unanticipated occurrence such as a natural disaster, a labor strike, or the resignation of a key project team member.

Reinforce Your Learning

1. What are the two kinds of data or information that need to be collected during each reporting period?

It should be noted that once changes are incorporated into the plan and agreed on by the customer, a new baseline plan has to be established. The scope, schedule, and budget of the new baseline plan may be different from those of the original baseline plan.

It is crucial that the data and information discussed above be collected in a timely manner and used to calculate an updated project schedule and budget. For example, if project reporting is done monthly, data and information should be obtained as late as possible in that monthly period so that when an updated schedule and budget are calculated, they are based on the latest possible information. In other words, a project manager should not gather data at the beginning of the month and then wait until the end of the month to use it to calculate an updated schedule and budget, because the data will be outdated and may cause incorrect decisions to be made about the project status and corrective actions.

Once an updated schedule and budget have been calculated, they need to be compared to the baseline schedule and budget and analyzed for variances to determine whether a project is ahead of or behind schedule and under or over budget. If the project status is okay, no corrective actions are needed; the status will be analyzed again for the next reporting period.

If it is determined that corrective actions are necessary, however, decisions must be made regarding how to revise the schedule or the budget. These decisions often involve a trade-off of time, cost, and scope. For example, reducing the duration of an activity may require either increasing costs to pay for more resources or reducing the scope of the task (and possibly not meeting the customer's technical requirements). Similarly, reducing project costs may require using materials of a lower quality than originally planned. Once a decision is made on which corrective actions to take, they must be incorporated into the schedule and budget. It is then necessary to calculate a revised schedule and budget to determine whether the planned corrective measures result in an acceptable schedule and budget. If not, further revisions will be needed.

Reinforce Your Learning

2. True or false: In general, it is better to have a shorter reporting period during a project.

Reinforce Your Learning

3. In addition to establishing a sound baseline plan, it is also necessary to proactively ______________ the project after it has started in order to assure that the project objective is achieved.

The project control process continues throughout the project. In general, the shorter the reporting period, the better the chances of identifying problems early and taking effective corrective actions. If a project gets too far out of control, it may be difficult to achieve the project objective without sacrificing the scope, budget, schedule, or quality. There may be situations in which it is wise to increase the frequency of reporting until the project is back on track. For example, if a five-year project with monthly reporting is endangered by a slipping schedule or an increasing budget overrun, it may be prudent to reduce the reporting period to one week in order to monitor the project and the impact of corrective actions more closely.

The project control process is an important and necessary part of project management. Just establishing a sound baseline plan is not sufficient, because even the best-laid plans don't always work out. *Project management is a proactive approach to controlling a project*, to ensure that the project objective is achieved even when things don't go according to plan.

EFFECTS OF ACTUAL SCHEDULE PERFORMANCE

Throughout a project, some activities will be completed on time, some will be finished ahead of schedule, and others will be finished later than scheduled. Actual progress—whether faster or slower than planned—will have an effect on the schedule of the remaining, uncompleted activities of the project. Specifically, the **actual finish times (AFs)** of completed activities will determine the earliest start and earliest finish times for the remaining activities in the network diagram, as well as the total slack.

Part (a) of Figure 7.2 is an AIB network diagram for a simple project. It shows that the earliest the project can finish is day 15 (the sum of the durations of the three activities, 7 + 5 + 3). Since the required completion time is day 20, the project has a total slack of +5 days.

Reinforce Your Learning

4. What three types of values will the actual finish times of completed activities affect?

Suppose that activity 1, "Remove Old Wallpaper," is *actually* finished on day 10, rather than on day 7 as planned, because it turns out to be more difficult than anticipated. (See part [b] of Figure 7.2.) This means that the earliest start and finish times for activities 2 and 3 will be 3 days later than on the original schedule. Because "Remove Old Wallpaper" is actually finished on day 10, the ES for "Patch Walls" will be day 10 and its EF will be day 15. Following through with the forward calculations, we find that "Put Up New Wallpaper" will have an ES of day 15 and an EF of day 18. Comparing this new EF of the last activity to the required completion time of day 20, we find a difference of 2 days. The total slack got worse—it changed in a negative direction, from +5 days to +2 days. This example illustrates how the actual finish times of activities have a ripple effect, altering the remaining activities' earliest start and finish times and the total slack.

It's helpful to indicate on the network diagram, in some manner, which activities have been completed. One method is to shade or crosshatch the activity box, as was done in part (b) of Figure 7.2.

FIGURE 7.2 *Effect of Actual Finish Times*

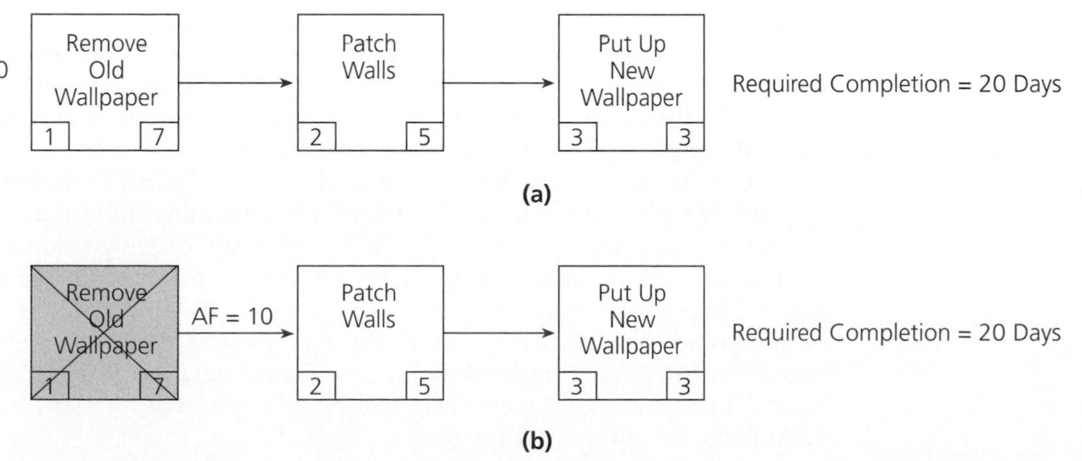

INCORPORATING PROJECT CHANGES INTO THE SCHEDULE

Throughout a project, changes may occur that have an impact on the schedule. As was noted earlier, these changes might be initiated by the customer or the project team, or they might be the result of an unanticipated occurrence.

Here are some examples of changes initiated by the customer:

- A home buyer tells the builder that the family room should be larger and the bedroom windows should be relocated.
- A customer tells the project team developing an information system that the system must have the capability to produce a previously unmentioned set of reports and graphics.

These types of changes represent revisions to the original project scope and will have an impact on the schedule and cost. The degree of impact, however, may depend on when the changes are requested. If they're requested early in the project, they may have less impact on cost and schedule than if they're requested later in the project. For example, changing the size of the family room and relocating the bedroom windows would be relatively easy if the house were still being designed and the drawings being prepared. If the changes were requested after the framing was put up and the windows were installed, however, the impact on costs and schedule would be far greater.

When the customer requests a change, the contractor or project team should estimate the impact on the project budget and schedule and then obtain customer approval before proceeding. If the customer approves the proposed revisions to the project schedule and budget, any additional tasks, revised duration estimates, and material and labor costs should be incorporated.

An example of a change initiated by a project team is the decision by a team planning a town fair to eliminate all amusement rides for adults because of space limitations and insurance costs. The project plan would then have to be revised to delete or modify all those activities involving adult rides. An example of a project manager-initiated change would be: a contractor, charged with developing an automated invoicing system for a customer, who suggests that, rather than incorporate custom-designed software, the system use standard available software in order to reduce costs and accelerate the schedule.

Some changes involve the addition of activities that were overlooked when the original plan was developed. For example, the project team may have forgotten to include activities associated with developing training materials and conducting training for a new information system. Or the customer or contractor may have failed to include the installation of gutters and downspouts in the work scope for the construction of a restaurant.

Other changes become necessary because of unanticipated occurrences, such as a snowstorm that slows down construction of a building, the failure of a new product to pass quality tests, or the untimely death or resignation of a key member of a project team. These events will have an impact on the schedule and/or budget and will require that the project plan be modified.

Still other changes can result from adding more detail to the network diagram as the project moves forward. No matter what level of detail is used in the initial network diagram, there will be some activities that can be broken down further as the project progresses.

Any type of change—whether initiated by the customer, the contractor, the project manager, a team member, or an unanticipated event—will require a modification to the plan in terms of scope, budget, and/or schedule. When such changes are agreed upon, a new baseline plan is established and used as the benchmark against which actual project performance will be compared.

Reinforce Your Learning

5. What three elements can project changes affect?

With respect to the project schedule, changes can result in the addition or deletion of activities, the resequencing of activities, the changing of activities' duration estimates, or a new required completion time for the project.

See Chapters 10 and 12 for further discussion of managing and controlling changes.

UPDATING THE PROJECT SCHEDULE

Network-based planning and scheduling allows project schedules to be dynamic. Because the network plan (diagram) and schedule (tabulation) are separate, they are much easier to update manually than a traditional Gantt chart. However, various project management software packages are available to assist with the automated generation of schedules, network diagrams, budgets, and even network-to-Gantt chart conversions.

Once data have been collected on the actual finish times of completed activities and the effects of any project changes, an updated project schedule can be calculated. These calculations are based on the methodology explained in Chapter 6:

- The earliest start and finish times for the remaining, uncompleted activities are calculated by working forward through the network, but they're based on the *actual finish times* of completed activities and the estimated durations of the uncompleted activities.
- The latest start and finish times for the uncompleted activities are calculated by working backward through the network.

As an illustration of the calculation of an updated schedule, let's consider the network diagram shown in Figure 7.3 for the consumer market study project. Assume the following:

1. Completed activities:
    a. Activity 1, "Identify Target Consumers," actually finished on day 2.
    b. Activity 2, "Develop Draft Questionnaire," actually finished on day 11.
    c. Activity 3, "Pilot-Test Questionnaire," actually finished on day 30.
2. Project changes:
    a. It was discovered that the database to be used to prepare the mailing labels was not up to date. A new database needs to be purchased before the mailing labels can be prepared. This new database was ordered on day 23. It will take 21 days to get it from the supplier.
    b. A preliminary review of comments from the pilot test of the questionnaire indicates that substantial revisions to the questionnaire are required. Therefore, the duration estimate for activity 4 needs to be increased from 5 days to 15 days.

FIGURE 7.3 *Network Diagram for Consumer Market Study Project, Incorporating Actual Progress and Changes*

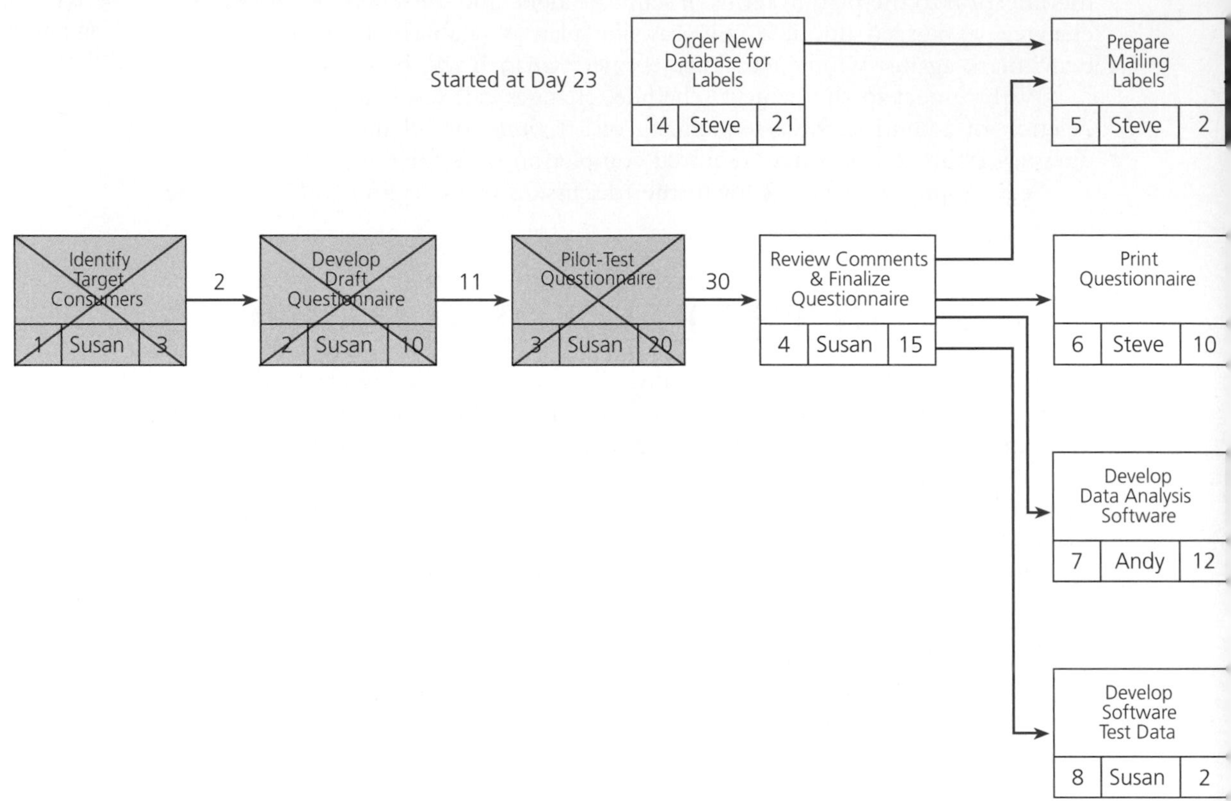

The network diagram in Figure 7.3 incorporates the above information. Figure 7.4 shows the updated schedule. Note that the total slack for the critical path is now –5 days, instead of the +2 days in the baseline schedule in Figure 6.16 in Chapter 6. The anticipated project completion time is now day 135, which is beyond the required completion time of 130 days.

APPROACHES TO SCHEDULE CONTROL

Schedule control involves four steps:

1. Analyzing the schedule to determine which areas may need corrective action
2. Deciding what specific corrective actions should be taken
3. Revising the plan to incorporate the chosen corrective actions
4. Recalculating the schedule to evaluate the effects of the planned corrective actions

If the planned corrective actions do not result in an acceptable schedule, these steps need to be repeated.

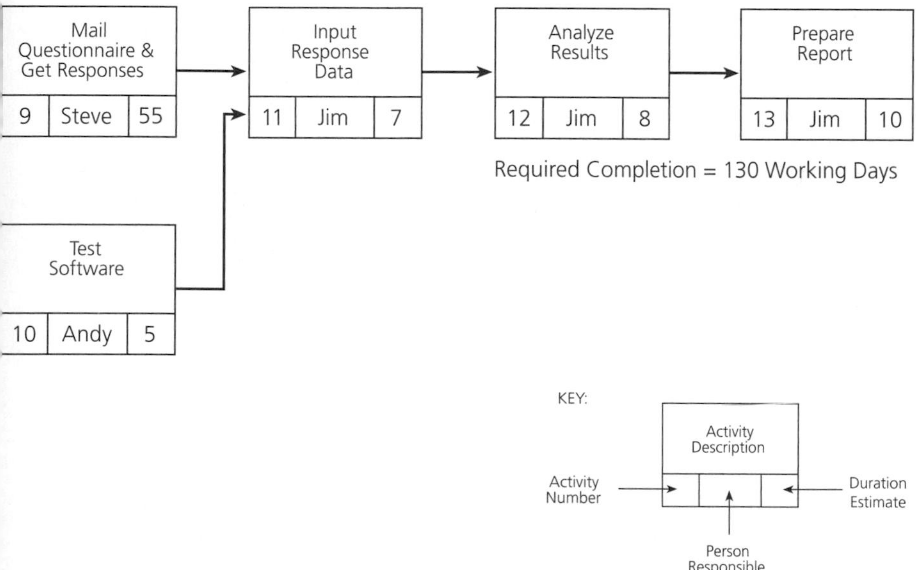

Throughout a project, each time a schedule is recalculated—whether it's after actual data or project changes are incorporated or after corrective actions are planned—it is necessary to analyze the newly calculated schedule to determine whether it needs further attention. The schedule analysis should include identifying the critical path and any paths of activities that have a negative slack, as well as those paths where slippages have occurred (the slack got worse) compared with the previously calculated schedule.

Reinforce Your Learning

6. In analyzing a project schedule, it is important to identify all the paths of activities that have a ____________ slack.

A concentrated effort to accelerate project progress must be applied to the paths with negative slack. The amount of slack should determine the priority with which these concentrated efforts are applied. For example, the path with the most negative slack should be given top priority.

Corrective actions that will eliminate the negative slack from the project schedule must be identified. These corrective actions must reduce the duration estimates for activities on the negative-slack paths. Remember, the slack for a path of activities is shared among all the activities on that path. Therefore, *a change in the estimated duration of any activity on that path will cause a corresponding change in the slack for that path.*

When analyzing a path of activities that has negative slack, you should focus on two kinds of activities:

1. *Activities that are near term (that is, in progress or to be started in the immediate future).* It's much wiser to take aggressive corrective action to reduce the

FIGURE 7.4 *Updated Schedule for Consumer Market Study Project*

Consumer Market Study Project

	Activity	Respon.	Dur. Estim.	Earliest		Latest		Total Slack	Actual Finish
				Start	Finish	Start	Finish		
1	Identify Target Consumers	Susan							2
2	Develop Draft Questionnaire	Susan							11
3	Pilot-Test Questionnaire	Susan							30
4	Review Comments & Finalize Questionnaire	Susan	15	30	45	25	40	–5	
5	Prepare Mailing Labels	Steve	2	45	47	48	50	3	
6	Print Questionnaire	Steve	10	45	55	40	50	–5	
7	Develop Data Analysis Software	Andy	12	45	57	88	100	43	
8	Develop Software Test Data	Susan	2	45	47	98	100	53	
9	Mail Questionnaire & Get Responses	Steve	55	55	110	50	105	–5	
10	Test Software	Andy	5	57	62	100	105	43	
11	Input Response Data	Jim	7	110	117	105	112	–5	
12	Analyze Results	Jim	8	117	125	112	120	–5	
13	Prepare Report	Jim	10	125	135	120	130	–5	
14	Order New Database for Labels	Steve	21	23	44	27	48	4	

durations of activities that will be done in the near term than to plan to reduce the durations of activities that are scheduled sometime in the future. If you postpone until the distant future taking corrective action that will reduce the durations of activities, you may find that the negative slack has deteriorated even further by that time. As the project progresses, there is always less time remaining in which corrective action can be taken.

Looking at Figure 7.4, we can see that it would be better to try to reduce the durations of the near-term activities on the critical path, such as "Review Comments & Finalize Questionnaire" or "Print Questionnaire," than to put off corrective action until the last activity, "Prepare Report."

Reinforce Your Learning

7. When analyzing a path of activities that has negative slack, what two kinds of activities should you look at carefully?

2. *Activities that have long duration estimates.* Taking corrective measures that will reduce a 20-day activity by 20 percent (that is, by four days) has a larger impact than totally eliminating a one-day activity. Usually, longer-duration activities present the opportunity for larger reductions.

Real World **PROJECT MANAGEMENT**

The Eaton Hotel Project

The Eaton Hotel project, the largest private historic rehabilitation project in Kansas history, was to be completed by December 22, 2000. Project manager Philip Wells set up a digital clock in a construction trailer outside the hotel that counted down the days, hours, minutes, and seconds until the deadline. Upon its completion, the hotel would rack up a total of 356 days, 230,000 worker-hours, and 750 truckloads of debris.

This construction project ranked as one of the largest in Wichita and required a great amount of attention to historical detail. Key Construction was selected to renovate the Eaton Hotel's historic, and badly deteriorated, building. The restoration of the hotel might not only restore its functionality, but also lead to new development in that stretch of downtown's East Douglas.

The Eaton block, where the hotel is located, was approved for the federal rehabilitation tax credit program by the National Park Service. This program allows investors in buildings on the block to claim tax credits equal to 20 percent of the total rehabilitation costs. To claim these credits, the project must be approved by the following entities: the state's historical preservation office and the state's historical society and park service. The project was to cost a total of $15.4 million, with construction costs of about $12 million, and had to be completed by December 31, 2000.

Key Construction crews had to knock down walls and tear down ceilings, while carefully maintaining stringent historic renovation requirements. Trim had to be maintained, while crumbling walls behind the trim needed to be replaced to meet today's construction standards. Original windows had to be refurbished rather than replaced. Numerous storey of the building had to be jacked up at one point so that structural improvements could be made.

Key Construction spent most of their time throughout the duration of the project on "ongoing value engineering," which consists of figuring out how the project would unfold and where the money would come from, as well as balancing changing bond rates, wage scales, and weather conditions. The company had never worked with so many funding mechanisms at once, with funds coming from numerous private and public sources.

To set the ground rules and ensure proper communication, city officials met with key people who would be involved in the project. An agreement was signed that they would work together as a team. This greatly attributed to the project's success. Another attributing factor was that Key Construction didn't request any unnecessary change order that would slow the work down and incidentally drive costs up.

One of Key's construction superintendents, Max Willhaus, was able to focus efforts where they were needed and keep the project rolling along on schedule. Christy Davis, a preservation specialist for the State Historic Preservation Office, explained how much of a challenge it was for the architect and contractor to meet the historic renovation standards, while still meeting the aggressive deadline.

The project ended as an overwhelming success. Key Construction met the deadline nine days early and stayed within the budget. The city's staff and community representatives from MetroPlains were extremely pleased with Key

Constructions' work on this project. City council member Joan Cole stated, "We had an extremely ambitious schedule, and frankly, I find it a miracle that we completed the project a little bit ahead of schedule!"

Keeping a project on schedule is one of the greatest challenges for a project manager and the project team. By sticking to the principles presented in this chapter you will definitely increase your likelihood of success!

Kratzer, D., "Key Construction had to Race the Clock to Finish the Eaton Hotel Project on Time," *Wichita Business Journal*, December 11, 2000.

Look again at Figure 7.4. There may be more opportunity to reduce the 55-day duration estimate for "Mail Questionnaire & Get Responses" by five days (9 percent) than to reduce the shorter duration estimates of other activities on the critical path.

There are various approaches to reducing the duration estimates of activities. One obvious way is to apply more resources to speed up an activity. This could be done by assigning more people to work on the activity or asking the people working on the activity to work more hours per day or more days per week. Additional appropriate resources might be transferred from concurrent activities that have positive slack. Sometimes, however, adding people to an activity may in fact result in the activity's taking longer, because the people already assigned to the activity are diverted from their work in order to help the new people get up to speed. Another approach is to assign a person with greater expertise or more experience to perform or help with the activity, so as to get it done in a shorter time than was possible with the less experienced people originally assigned to it.

Reducing the scope or requirements for an activity is another way to reduce its duration estimate. For example, it might be acceptable to put only one coat of paint on a room rather than two coats, as originally planned. In an extreme case, a decision might be made to totally eliminate some activities, deleting them and their durations from the schedule.

Increasing productivity through improved methods or technology is yet another approach to reducing activities' durations. For example, instead of having people keyboard data from a customer survey into a computer database, optical scanning equipment might be used.

Reinforce Your Learning

8. List four approaches to reducing the estimated durations of activities.

Once specific corrective actions to reduce the negative slack have been decided on, the duration estimates for the appropriate activities must be revised in the network plan. Then a revised schedule needs to be calculated to evaluate whether the planned corrective actions reduce the negative slack as anticipated.

In most cases, eliminating negative slack by reducing durations of activities will involve a trade-off in the form of an increase in costs or a reduction in scope. (For a more thorough discussion of this topic, see the appendix on time–cost trade-off at the end of this chapter.) If the project is way behind schedule (has substantial negative slack), a substantial increase in costs and/or reduction in work scope or quality may be required to get it back on schedule. This could jeopardize elements of the overall project objective: scope, budget, schedule, and/or quality. In some cases, the customer and the contractor or project team may have to acknowledge that one or more of these elements cannot be achieved. Thus, for example, the customer may have to extend the required completion time for the entire project, or there may be a dispute over who should absorb any increased cost to accelerate the schedule—the contractor or the customer.

Some contracts include a bonus provision, whereby the customer will pay the contractor a bonus if the project is completed ahead of schedule. Conversely, some contracts include a penalty provision, whereby the customer can reduce the final payment to the contractor if the project is not completed on time. Some of these penalties can be substantial. In either of these situations, effective schedule control is crucial.

The key to effective schedule control is to address any paths with negative or deteriorating slack values aggressively as soon as they are identified, rather than hoping that things will improve as the project goes on. Addressing schedule problems early will minimize the negative impact on cost and scope. If a project falls too far behind, getting back on schedule becomes more difficult, and it doesn't come free. It requires spending more money or reducing the scope or quality.

On projects that don't have negative slack, it's important not to let the slack deteriorate by accepting delays and slippages. If a project is ahead of schedule, a concentrated effort should be made to *keep* it ahead of schedule.

Project meetings are a good forum for addressing schedule control issues. See Chapter 12 for a discussion of project meetings and Chapter 11 for a discussion of problem solving.

SCHEDULE CONTROL FOR INFORMATION SYSTEMS DEVELOPMENT

Controlling the schedule for the development of an information system is a challenge. Numerous unexpected circumstances might arise that can push an IS development project well beyond its originally scheduled due date. However, just as with any other type of project, the key to effective project control is to measure actual progress and compare it to planned progress on a timely and regular basis and to take necessary corrective action immediately.

Like other forms of schedule control, schedule control for IS development projects is carried out according to the steps discussed earlier in this chapter. A project control process such as the one illustrated in Figure 7.1 should be used for comparing actual performance with the schedule. Once the customer and the project team agree on changes, these changes should be recorded and the schedule should be revised.

Among the changes that commonly become necessary during IS development projects are the following:

- *Changes to the interface*—such as added fields, different icons, different colors, different menu structures or buttons, or completely new screens.
- *Changes to reports*—such as added fields, different subtotals and totals, different sorts, different selection criteria, different order of fields, or completely new reports.
- *Changes to online queries*—such as different ad hoc capabilities, access to different fields or databases, different query structures, or additional queries.
- *Changes to database structures*—such as additional fields, different data field names, different data storage sizes, different relationships among the data, or completely new databases.

- *Changes to software processing routines*—such as different algorithms, different interfaces with other subroutines, different internal logic, or new procedures.
- *Changes to processing speeds*—such as higher throughput rates or response times.
- *Changes to storage capacities*—such as an increase in the maximum number of data records.
- *Changes to business processes*—such as changes in work or data flow, addition of new clients that must have access, or completely new processes that must be supported.
- *Changes to software resulting from hardware upgrades* or, conversely, *hardware upgrades resulting from the availability of more powerful software*.

An IS Example: Internet Applications Development for ABC Office Designs (Continued)

Recall from Chapters 5 and 6 that ABC Office Designs assigned Beth Smith to be the project manager of the web-based reporting system development project. Beth identified all of the major tasks that needed to be accomplished and developed the work breakdown structure, responsibility matrix, and network diagram. When she calculated the earliest and latest start and finish times for each activity, she discovered that the project would take 59 days to complete—9 days over the original 50 days that was requested. However, after extensive discussions with upper management in which she stressed the importance of developing the system right the first time and not having to rush through some critical phases of the SDLC, Beth convinced her superiors to extend the project completion time to 60 days.

Beth and her team proceeded with the project and completed activities 1 through 6:

Activity 1, "Gather Data," actually finished on day 4.

Activity 2, "Study Feasibility," actually finished on day 4.

Activity 3, "Prepare Problem Definition Report," actually finished on day 5.

Activity 4, "Interview Users," actually finished on day 10.

Activity 5, "Study Existing System," actually finished on day 15.

Activity 6, "Define User Requirements," actually finished on day 18.

They then discovered that, by using some reusable software for the database, they could reduce the estimated duration of activity 9, "Processing & Database," from 10 days to 8 days.

Figures 7.5 and 7.6 show the updated network diagram and project schedule, respectively, after these changes have been incorporated. Notice that because of the above occurrences, the critical path now has a total slack of 0.

Critical Success FACTORS

- Project management involves a proactive approach to controlling a project to ensure that the project objective is achieved even when things don't go according to plan.
- Once the project starts, it is important to monitor progress to ensure that everything is going according to plan.
- The key to effective project control is measuring actual progress and comparing it to planned progress on a timely basis and taking corrective action immediately, if necessary.
- The key to effective schedule control is to address any paths with negative or deteriorating slack values aggressively as soon as they are identified. A concentrated effort to accelerate project progress must be applied to these paths. The amount of negative slack should determine the priority for applying these concentrated efforts.
- When attempting to reduce the duration of a path of activities that has negative slack, focus on activities that are near term and on activities that have long duration estimates.
- Addressing schedule problems early will minimize the negative impact on cost and scope. If a project falls too far behind, getting it back on schedule becomes more difficult, and usually requires spending more money or reducing the scope or quality.
- If corrective actions are necessary, decisions must be made regarding a trade-off of time, cost, and scope.
- Use the time–cost trade-off methodology to reduce the project duration incrementally for the smallest associated increase in incremental cost.
- A regular reporting period should be established for comparing actual progress to planned progress.
- The shorter the reporting period, the better the chances of identifying problems early and taking corrective actions.
- During each reporting period, data on actual performance and information on changes to the project scope, schedule, and budget need to be collected in a timely manner and used to calculate an updated schedule and budget.

PROJECT MANAGEMENT SOFTWARE

Virtually all project management software packages allow you to perform the control functions identified in this chapter. Specifically, while an activity is in progress or once an activity has been completed, current information can be entered into the system and the software will automatically revise the project schedule. Likewise, if the estimated durations for any future activities change, these changes can be entered into the system and the software will automatically update the schedule. All network diagrams, tables, and reports produced by the software will be updated to reflect the most recent information. See Appendix A at the end of the book for a thorough discussion of project management software.

FIGURE 7.5 ***Network Diagram for Web-Based Reporting System Project, Incorporating Actual Progress and Changes***

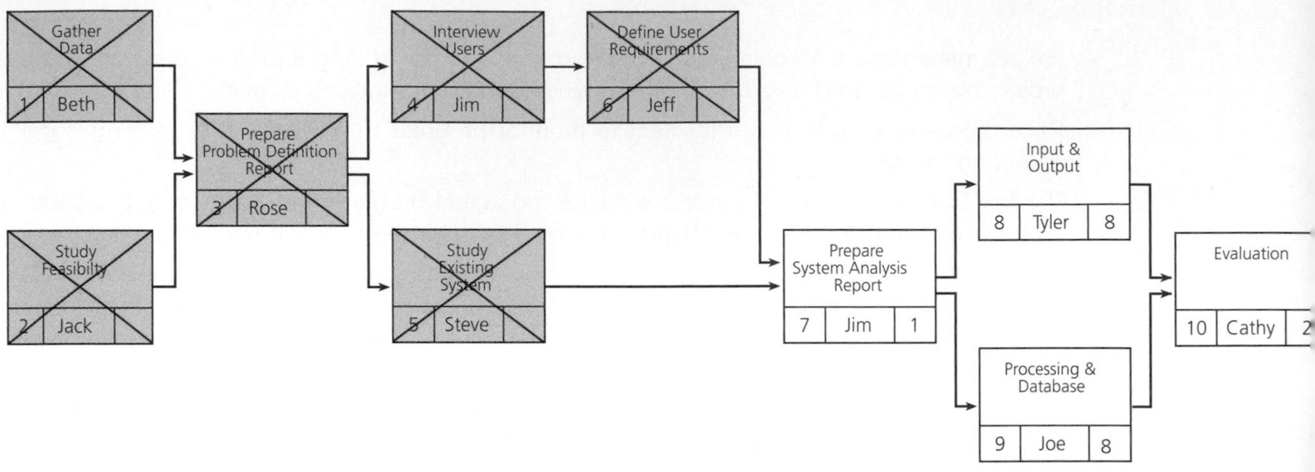

SUMMARY

Once a project actually starts, it's necessary to monitor the progress to ensure that everything is going according to schedule. This involves measuring actual progress and comparing it to the schedule. If at any time during the project it is determined that the project is behind schedule, corrective action must be taken to get back on schedule. The key to effective project control is to measure actual progress and compare it to planned progress on a timely and regular basis and to take necessary corrective action immediately. Based on actual progress and on consideration of other changes that may occur, it's possible to calculate an updated project schedule regularly and forecast whether the project will finish ahead of or behind its required completion time.

A regular reporting period should be established for comparing actual progress with planned progress. Reporting may be daily, weekly, biweekly, or monthly, depending on the complexity or overall duration of the project. During each reporting period, two kinds of data or information need to be collected: data on actual performance and information on any changes to the project scope, schedule, or budget.

The project control process continues throughout the project. In general, the shorter the reporting period, the better the chances of identifying problems

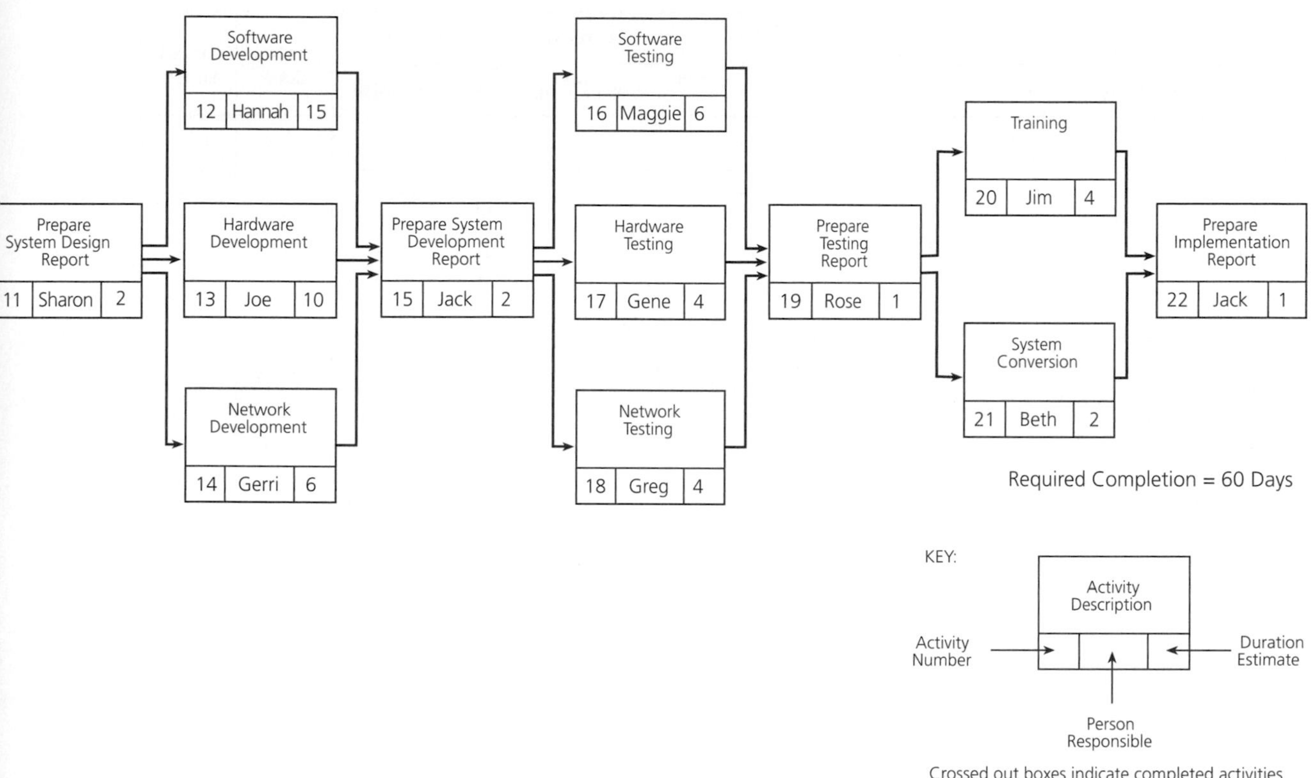

early and taking effective corrective actions. If a project gets too far out of control, it may be difficult to achieve the project objective without sacrificing the scope, budget, schedule, or quality.

Throughout a project, some activities will be completed on time, some will be finished ahead of schedule, and others will be finished later than scheduled. Actual progress—whether faster or slower than planned—will have an effect on the schedule of the remaining, uncompleted activities of the project. Specifically, the actual finish times (AFs) of completed activities will determine the earliest start and earliest finish times for the remaining activities in the network diagram, as well as the total slack.

Throughout a project, changes may occur that have an impact on the schedule. These changes might be initiated by the customer or the project team, or they might be the result of an unanticipated occurrence. Any type of change—whether initiated by the customer, the contractor, the project manager, a team member, or an unanticipated event—will require a modification to the plan in terms of scope, budget, and/or schedule. When such changes are agreed upon, a new baseline plan is established and used as the benchmark against which actual project performance will be compared.

Once data have been collected on the actual finish times of completed activities and the effects of any project changes, an updated project schedule

FIGURE 7.6 *Updated Schedule for Web-Based Reporting System Project*

Web-based Reporting System Project

	Activity	Respon.	Dur. Estim.	Earliest		Latest		Total Slack	Actual Finish
				Start	Finish	Start	Finish		
1	Gather Data	Beth							4
2	Study Feasibility	Jack							4
3	Prepare Problem Definition Report	Rose							5
4	Interview Users	Jim							10
5	Study Existing System	Steve							15
6	Define User Requirements	Jeff							18
7	Prepare System Analysis Report	Jim	1	18	19	18	19	0	
8	Input & Output	Tyler	8	19	27	19	27	0	
9	Processing & Database	Joe	8	19	27	19	27	0	
10	Evaluation	Cathy	2	27	29	27	29	0	
11	Prepare System Design Report	Sharon	2	29	31	29	31	0	
12	Software Development	Hannah	15	31	46	31	46	0	
13	Hardware Development	Joe	10	31	41	36	46	5	
14	Network Development	Gerri	6	31	37	40	46	9	
15	Prepare System Development Report	Jack	2	46	48	46	48	0	
16	Software Testing	Maggie	6	48	54	48	54	0	
17	Hardware Testing	Gene	4	48	52	50	54	2	
18	Network Testing	Greg	4	48	52	50	54	2	
19	Prepare Testing Report	Rose	1	54	55	54	55	0	
20	Training	Jim	4	55	59	55	59	0	
21	System Conversion	Beth	2	55	57	57	59	2	
22	Prepare Implementation Report	Jack	1	59	60	59	60	0	

can be calculated. These calculations are based on the methodology explained in Chapter 6.

Schedule control involves four steps: analyzing the schedule to determine which areas may need corrective action, deciding what specific corrective actions should be taken, revising the plan to incorporate the chosen corrective actions, and recalculating the schedule to evaluate the effects of the planned corrective actions. Corrective actions that will eliminate the negative slack from the project schedule must be identified. These corrective actions must reduce the duration estimates for activities on the negative-slack paths. When analyzing a path of activities that has negative slack, you should focus on two kinds of activities: activities that are near term and activities that have long duration estimates.

There are various approaches to reducing the duration estimates of activities. These include applying more resources to speed up an activity, assigning individuals with greater expertise or more experience to work on the activity, reducing the scope or requirements for the activity, and increasing productivity through improved methods or technology.

QUESTIONS

1. Explain why it is important to monitor the progress of a project continually.
2. Describe in your own words what is meant by *the project control process*. Give an example of its use.
3. Why should a project have a regular reporting period? Should all projects have the same reporting period? Why or why not? What types of data should be collected during each reporting period?
4. If a project schedule needs to be adjusted, what trade-offs might have to occur?
5. Who can initiate a change to a project schedule? Why would they do so? When would they do so? Give examples.
6. How are the network diagram and schedule updated after a project is initiated and changes have been requested?
7. Describe the four-step approach to schedule control. Give an example of its use.
8. When a schedule must be accelerated, which activities are likely candidates for adjustment? Why?
9. Why might the use of some slack by one activity affect other activities in a project?
10. Refer to question 10 at the end of Chapter 6. Assume that task A actually finished at 3 weeks, task B actually finished at 12 weeks, and task C actually finished at 13 weeks. Recalculate the expected project completion time. Which activities would you focus on in order to get the project back on schedule?
11. Refer to question 11 at the end of Chapter 6. Assume that "Systems Analysis" actually finished at 8 weeks, "Design Input & Output" actually finished at 15 weeks, and "Design Database" actually finished at 19 weeks. Recalculate the expected project completion time. Which

activities would you focus on in order to get the project back on schedule?

12. Refer to question 12 at the end of Chapter 6. Assume that task A actually finished at 5 weeks and task B actually finished at 5 weeks. Recalculate the expected project completion time. Which activities would you focus on in order to get the project back on schedule?

INTERNET EXERCISES

For the website addresses of the organizations mentioned in these exercises, go to "Internet Exercises" at the book's companion website at **international.cengage.com**. It is suggested that you save this website in your "Favorites" for easy access in the future.

1. Search the web for project schedule control and describe at least three sites that you find.
2. For exercises 2 through 5, visit the website for the organization 4PM. Explore the site. What kind of information does it provide?
3. Explore the topics in the "Articles and Videos" link. Watch a video that interests you. Provide a one-page summary.
4. Click on the "PMTalk Newsletter" link and subscribe to the free newsletter. In addition, under the "Articles and Videos" link read an article that interests you and provide a one-page summary.
5. Under the "Articles and Videos" link, explore the Project Management Blog. Describe what you find.

CASE STUDY 1

A Not-for-Profit Medical Research Center

This case study is a continuation of the case study from Chapters 5 and 6.

CASE QUESTIONS

1. If the schedule you calculated in Chapter 6 has negative slack, you need to revisit your plan and calculate a revised schedule to eliminate all negative slack. Also make any associated changes to the cost estimate for activities and calculate a revised total budget for the project.

   If the schedule you calculated in Chapter 6 did not have negative slack, proceed to item 2.
2. Assume it is August 15. Provide a list of activities that have been completed as of August 15, along with the actual finish (AFs) dates and actual costs expended for each of these completed activities.
3. Provide a scenario for problems that have come up that will cause a delay in at least two activities that are scheduled to be completed between September 15 and November 15.
4. Based on the actual finish times and the schedule delay problems identified in item 2, calculate a revised schedule, and then make the necessary revisions to the plan (including any duration and cost estimates) and schedule and continue to do so until all negative slack is eliminated.

GROUP ACTIVITY

Divide the course participants into the same groups of three or four as for the previous chapter's group activity and answer the questions listed above.

Note: This case study will continue in Chapters 8 and 9, so save the results of your work.

The Wedding

CASE STUDY 2

This case study is a continuation of the case study from Chapters 5 and 6.

CASE QUESTIONS

1. If the schedule you calculated in Chapter 6 has negative slack, you need to revise your plan and calculate a revised schedule to eliminate all negative slack. Also make any associated changes to the cost estimate for activities and calculate a revised total budget for the project.

   If the schedule you calculated in Chapter 6 did not have negative slack, proceed to item 2.
2. Assume it is March 31. Provide a list of activities that have been completed as of March 31, along with the actual finish (AFs) dates and actual costs expended for each of these completed activities.
3. Provide a scenario for problems that have come up that will cause a delay in at least two activities that are scheduled to be completed between May 1 and June 30.
4. Based on the actual finish times and the schedule delay problems identified in item 2, calculate a revised schedule, and then make the necessary revisions to the plan (including any duration and cost estimates) and schedule and continue to do so until all negative slack is eliminated.

GROUP ACTIVITY

Divide the course participants into the same groups of three or four as for the previous chapter's group activity and answer the questions listed above.

Note: This case study will continue in Chapters 8 and 9, so save the results of your work.

Time–Cost Trade-Off

APPENDIX 1

The time–cost trade-off methodology is used to reduce the project duration incrementally with the smallest associated increase in incremental cost. It is based on the following assumptions:

1. Each activity has two pairs of duration and cost estimates: normal and crash. The **normal time** is the estimated length of time required to perform the activity under normal conditions, according to the plan. The **normal cost** is the estimated cost to complete the activity in the normal time. The **crash time** is the shortest estimated length of time in which the activity can be completed. The **crash cost** is the estimated cost to complete the activity in the crash time. In Figure 7.7, each of the four activities has a pair of normal time and cost estimates and a pair of crash time and cost estimates. The estimated normal time to perform activity A is seven weeks, and its estimated normal cost is $50,000. The crash time

FIGURE 7.7 ***Network with Normal and Crash Times and Their Costs***

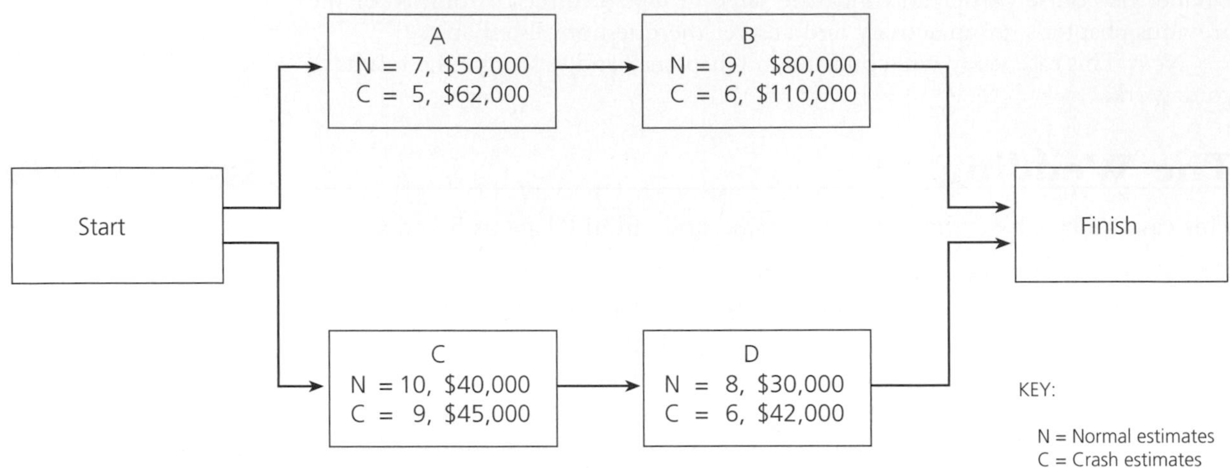

for this activity is five weeks, and the cost to complete the activity in this duration is $62,000.

Reinforce Your Learning

9. What are the normal and crash times and costs for activities B, C, and D in Figure 7.7?

	Normal Time	Normal Cost	Crash Time	Crash Cost
Activity B	___	___	___	___
Activity C	___	___	___	___
Activity D	___	___	___	___

2. An activity's duration can be incrementally accelerated from its normal time to its crash time by applying more resources—assigning more people, working overtime, using more equipment, and so on. Increased costs will be associated with expediting the activity.
3. An activity cannot be completed in less than its crash time, no matter how many additional resources are applied. For example, activity A cannot be completed in less than five weeks, no matter how many more resources are used or how much money is spent.
4. The resources necessary to reduce an activity's estimated duration from its normal time to its crash time will be available when needed.
5. Within the range between an activity's normal and crash points, the relationship between time and cost is linear. Each activity has its own *cost per time period* for accelerating the activity's duration from its normal time to its crash time. This acceleration cost per time period is calculated as follows:

$$\frac{\text{Crash Cost} - \text{Normal Cost}}{\text{Normal Time} - \text{Crash Time}}$$

Reinforce Your Learning

10. What are the cost-per-week rates to accelerate activities B, C, and D in Figure 7.7.

For example, in Figure 7.7, the cost per week to accelerate activity A from its normal time to its crash time is

$$\frac{\$62{,}000 - \$50{,}000}{7 \text{ weeks} - 5 \text{ weeks}} = \frac{\$12{,}000}{2 \text{ weeks}} = \$6{,}000 \text{ per week}$$

The network diagram in Figure 7.7 has 2 paths from start to finish: path A–B and path C–D. If we consider only the normal duration estimates, path A–B will take 16 weeks to complete, whereas path C–D will take 18 weeks to complete. Therefore, the earliest the project can be finished based on these time estimates is 18 weeks—the length of its critical path, made up of activities

C and D. The total project cost, based on the cost associated with performing each activity in its normal time, is

$$\$50{,}000 + \$80{,}000 + \$40{,}000 + \$30{,}000 + \$200{,}000$$

If all the activities were performed in their respective crash times, path A–B would take 11 weeks and path C–D would take 15 weeks. The earliest the project can be finished based on the crash time estimates is 15 weeks, which is 3 weeks earlier than if the activities were performed in their normal times.

Reinforce Your Learning

11. If all the activities in Figure 7.7 were performed in their crash times, what would be the total project cost?

It is usually not necessary or even constructive to crash all the activities. For example, in Figure 7.7, we want to crash only the appropriate activities by the amount necessary to accelerate project completion from 18 weeks to 15 weeks. Any additional crashing of activities will merely increase total project cost; it will not reduce the total project duration any further because that's determined by the length of the critical path. In other words, expediting activities not on the critical path will not reduce the project completion time but will increase total project cost.

The objective of the time–cost trade-off method is to determine the shortest project completion time based on crashing those activities that result in the smallest increase in total project cost. To accomplish this, it's necessary to shorten the total project duration, one time period at a time, crashing only those activities that are on the critical path(s) and have the lowest acceleration cost per time period. From Figure 7.7, we previously determined that, based on normal time and cost estimates, the earliest the project could be completed is 18 weeks (as determined by the critical path C–D), at a total project cost of $200,000. The cost per week of accelerating each of the activities is

Activity A	$6,000 per week
Activity B	$10,000 per week
Activity C	$5,000 per week
Activity D	$6,000 per week

To reduce the total project duration from 18 weeks to 17 weeks requires first identifying the critical path, which is C–D, and then determining which activity on the critical path can be accelerated at the lowest cost per week. Activity C costs $5,000 per week to accelerate, and activity D costs $6,000 per week to accelerate. Therefore, it's less expensive to expedite activity C. If activity C is crashed 1 week (from 10 weeks to 9 weeks), the total project duration is shortened from 18 weeks to 17 weeks, but the total project cost increases by $5,000, to $205,000.

To shorten the total project duration one more time period, from 17 weeks to 16 weeks, we must again identify the critical path. The durations of the 2 paths are 16 weeks for A–B and 17 weeks for C–D. Therefore, the critical path is still C–D, and it must be reduced again. Looking at path C–D, we see that although activity C has a lower acceleration cost per week than activity D, we cannot accelerate activity C any further because we reached its crash time of 9 weeks when the project was reduced from 18 weeks to 17 weeks. Therefore, the only choice is to accelerate activity D by 1 week, from 8 weeks to 7 weeks. This reduces the duration of critical path C–D to 16 weeks, but the total project cost increases by $6,000 (the cost per week for accelerating activity D), from $205,000 to $211,000.

Once again, let's reduce the project duration another week, from 16 weeks to 15 weeks. If we look at our 2 paths, we see that they are now of equal duration, 16 weeks, so we now have 2 critical paths. To reduce the total project

Table 7.1 *Time–Cost Trade-Off*

Project Duration (weeks)	Critical Path(s)	Total Project Cost
18	C–D	**$200,000**
17	C–D	$200,000 + $5,000 = **$205,000**
16	C–D	$205,000 + $6,000 = **$211,000**
15	C–D, A–B	$211,000 + $6,000 + $6,000 = **$223,000**

duration from 16 weeks to 15 weeks, it's necessary to accelerate each path by 1 week. In looking at path C–D, we see that the only activity with any remaining time to be crashed is activity D. It can be crashed 1 more week, from 7 weeks to 6 weeks, at an additional cost of $6,000. To accelerate path A–B by 1 week, we have a choice of crashing activity A or activity B. Activity A has a $6,000 cost per week to accelerate, compared with a $10,000 per week rate for activity B. Therefore, to reduce the total project duration from 16 weeks to 15 weeks, we need to crash activities D and A 1 week each. This increases the total project cost by $12,000 ($6,000 + $6,000), from $211,000 to $223,000.

Let's try again to shorten the total project duration by 1 week, from 15 weeks to 14 weeks. We again have 2 critical paths with the same duration, 15 weeks. Therefore, they must both be accelerated by 1 week. However, in looking at path C–D, we see that both activities are already at their crash time—9 weeks and 6 weeks, respectively—and therefore cannot be expedited any further. Accelerating path A–B would thus be of no value, because it would increase the total project cost but not reduce the total project duration. Our ability to reduce the total project duration is limited by the fact that path C–D cannot be reduced any further.

Table 7.1 displays the incremental acceleration in total project completion and the associated incremental increase in total project cost. It indicates that reducing the total project duration by 1 week would increase the total project cost by $5,000. To reduce it by 2 weeks would cost $11,000, and to reduce it by 3 weeks would cost $23,000.

If all 4 activities were crashed, the total cost of the project would be $259,000, but it would still not be completed any earlier than 15 weeks. Using the time–cost trade-off method, we were able to reduce the project duration from 18 weeks to 15 weeks at an additional cost of $23,000 by selectively crashing the critical activities with the lowest acceleration cost per time period. Crashing all the activities would have resulted in a waste of $36,000 because no reduction in total project duration beyond 15 weeks could be achieved.

SUMMARY

The time–cost trade-off methodology is used to reduce the project duration incrementally with the smallest associated increase in incremental cost. It is based on the assumptions that each activity has a normal and a crash duration and cost estimate, that an activity's duration can be incrementally accelerated by applying more resources, and that the relationship between time and cost is linear. Normal time is the estimated length of time required to perform the activity under normal conditions; normal cost is the estimated cost to complete the activity in the normal time. Crash time is the shortest estimated length of time in which the activity can be completed; crash cost is the estimated cost to complete the activity in the crash time.

QUESTIONS

1. What is the time–cost trade-off methodology, and when is it used?
2. Why do you need both normal and crash times and costs for this procedure?
3. Assume that an activity has a normal time of 20 weeks, a normal cost of $72,000, a crash time of 16 weeks, and a crash cost of $100,000. By how many weeks, at most, can this activity's duration be reduced? What is the cost per week to accelerate this activity?
4. Why isn't it appropriate to crash all of the activities in a project to achieve the shortest project schedule?

Microsoft Project

APPENDIX 2

In this appendix we will discuss how Microsoft Project can be used to support the techniques discussed in this chapter based on the Consumer Market Study example. As pointed out in Chapter 5, if you want to compare actual progress to planned progress you should save your project with a baseline plan before the project starts.

To save baseline project data, on the Tools menu, point to Tracking, and click on Save Baseline, as shown in Figure 7A.1. You can also use this tool to clear a baseline.

As discussed in Chapter 6, to update information about any task right-click on the task name to select Task Information from the menu. The General tab is selected by default. Here you can indicate the percentage of work completed for that task. You can also update other information such as time duration and required resources. Figure 7A.2 shows the input screen within the General tab. After the task information has been modified, the Gantt and PERT charts will automatically be updated.

To get information about current activities, on the Report menu click on Reports to open the Reports menu window. Choose Current Activities and click on Select. You should see the Current Activity Reports menu listing six different reports available, as shown in Figure 7A.3.

To obtain information on variances within your project, on the View menu, click on Gantt Chart. Next, you need to select the table that will display variance values. On the View menu, point to Table, and click on Variance. You should see the table that is shown in Figure 7A.4. This table shows the actual start and finish times compared to the baseline start and finish times for each activity, along with any variances. Note that at this point we are still assuming the project has not started yet, so all variances are zero. This might change as your project progresses.

Valuable tracking data can be displayed through the Tracking Table. While in the Gantt Chart view, on the View menu, point to Table, and click on Tracking. This table, as seen in Figure 7A.5, shows actual start and finish times, percent complete, actual duration, remaining duration, actual costs, and actual work time for each activity.

FIGURE 7A.1 ***Saving a Baseline***

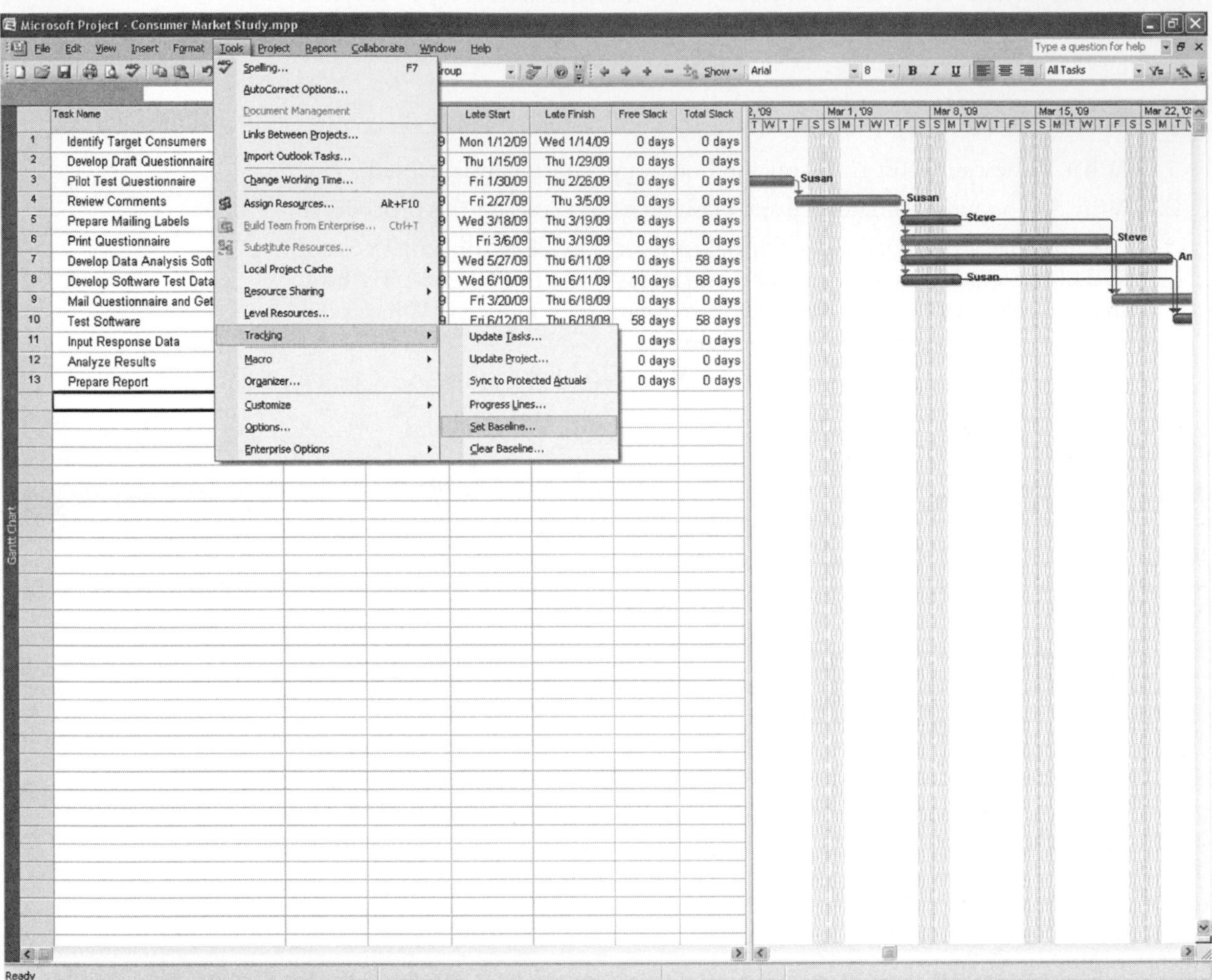

To get a visual representation of actual versus planned progress, on the View menu, click on More Views, and select Tracking Gantt. The Tracking Gantt chart, shown in Figure 7A.6, displays two bars for each task. The lower bar shows the baseline start and finish dates, and the upper bar shows the current start and finish dates, so that you can see the difference between your baseline plan and the current schedule.

FIGURE 7A.2 *Task Information*

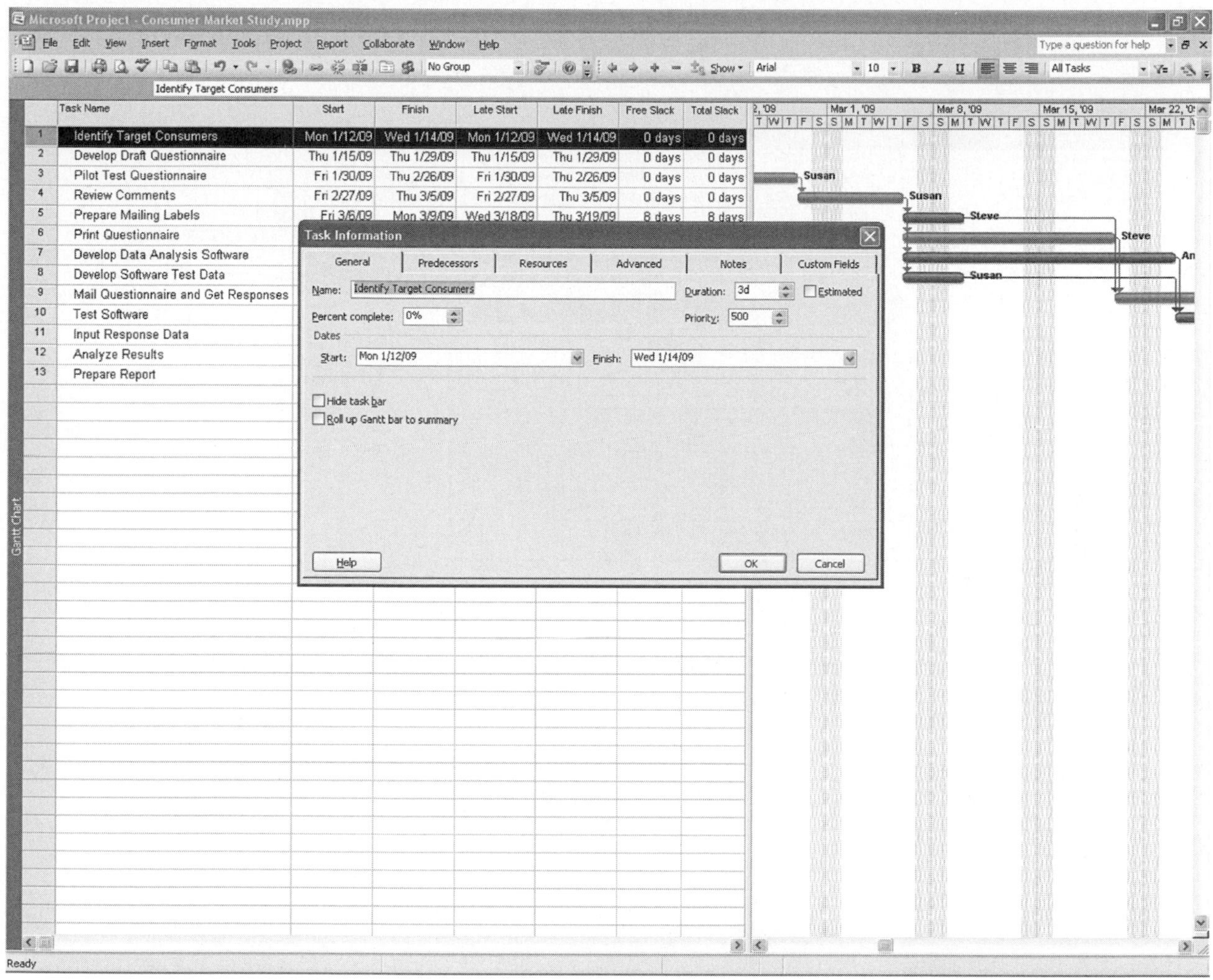

FIGURE 7A.3 *Current Activity Reports*

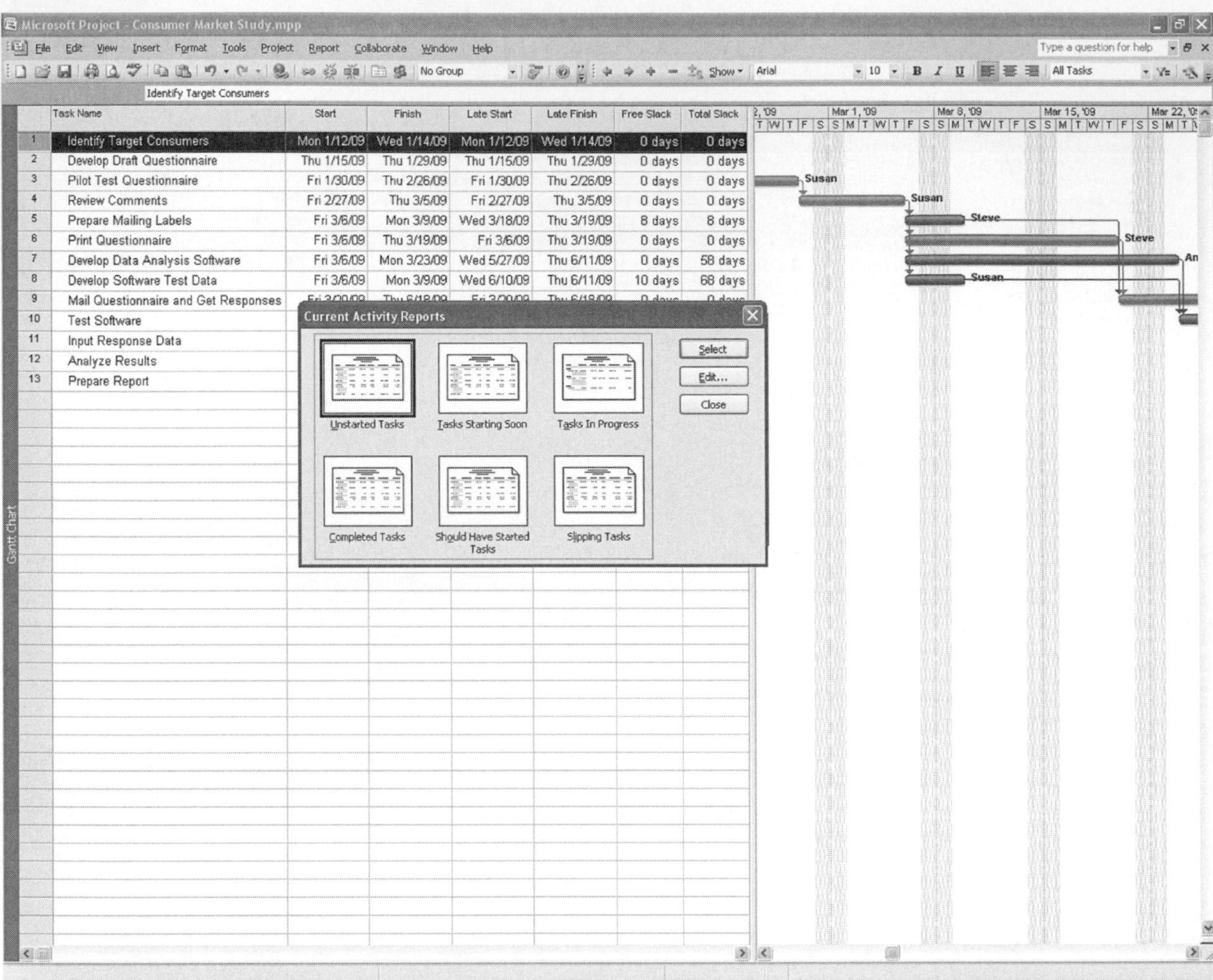

	Task Name	Start	Finish	Late Start	Late Finish	Free Slack	Total Slack
1	Identify Target Consumers	Mon 1/12/09	Wed 1/14/09	Mon 1/12/09	Wed 1/14/09	0 days	0 days
2	Develop Draft Questionnaire	Thu 1/15/09	Thu 1/29/09	Thu 1/15/09	Thu 1/29/09	0 days	0 days
3	Pilot Test Questionnaire	Fri 1/30/09	Thu 2/26/09	Fri 1/30/09	Thu 2/26/09	0 days	0 days
4	Review Comments	Fri 2/27/09	Thu 3/5/09	Fri 2/27/09	Thu 3/5/09	0 days	0 days
5	Prepare Mailing Labels	Fri 3/6/09	Mon 3/9/09	Wed 3/18/09	Thu 3/19/09	8 days	8 days
6	Print Questionnaire	Fri 3/6/09	Thu 3/19/09	Fri 3/6/09	Thu 3/19/09	0 days	0 days
7	Develop Data Analysis Software	Fri 3/6/09	Mon 3/23/09	Wed 5/27/09	Thu 6/11/09	0 days	58 days
8	Develop Software Test Data	Fri 3/6/09	Mon 3/9/09	Wed 6/10/09	Thu 6/11/09	10 days	68 days
9	Mail Questionnaire and Get Responses						
10	Test Software						
11	Input Response Data						
12	Analyze Results						
13	Prepare Report						

FIGURE 7A.4 *Variance Table*

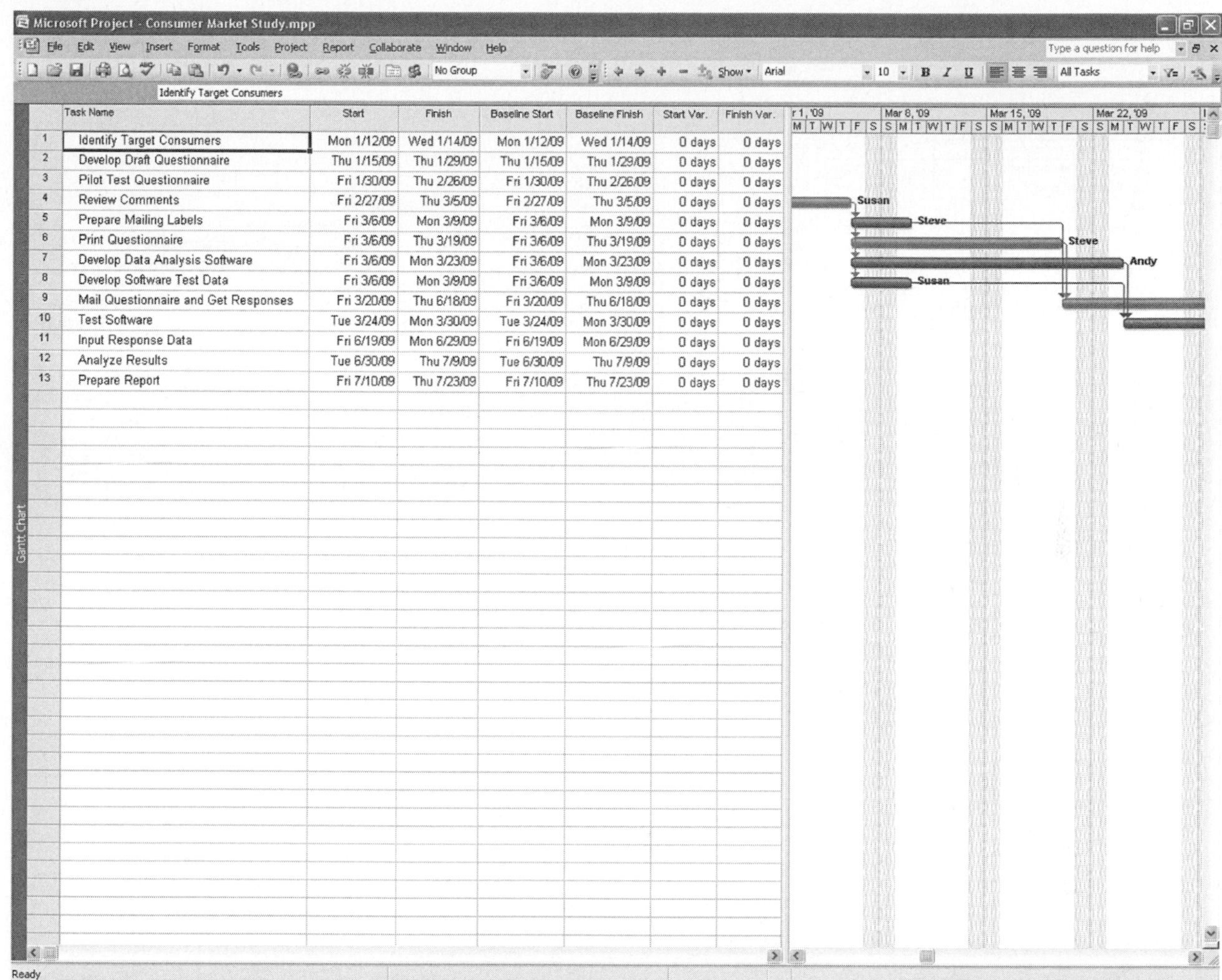

	Task Name	Start	Finish	Baseline Start	Baseline Finish	Start Var.	Finish Var.
1	Identify Target Consumers	Mon 1/12/09	Wed 1/14/09	Mon 1/12/09	Wed 1/14/09	0 days	0 days
2	Develop Draft Questionnaire	Thu 1/15/09	Thu 1/29/09	Thu 1/15/09	Thu 1/29/09	0 days	0 days
3	Pilot Test Questionnaire	Fri 1/30/09	Thu 2/26/09	Fri 1/30/09	Thu 2/26/09	0 days	0 days
4	Review Comments	Fri 2/27/09	Thu 3/5/09	Fri 2/27/09	Thu 3/5/09	0 days	0 days
5	Prepare Mailing Labels	Fri 3/6/09	Mon 3/9/09	Fri 3/6/09	Mon 3/9/09	0 days	0 days
6	Print Questionnaire	Fri 3/6/09	Thu 3/19/09	Fri 3/6/09	Thu 3/19/09	0 days	0 days
7	Develop Data Analysis Software	Fri 3/6/09	Mon 3/23/09	Fri 3/6/09	Mon 3/23/09	0 days	0 days
8	Develop Software Test Data	Fri 3/6/09	Mon 3/9/09	Fri 3/6/09	Mon 3/9/09	0 days	0 days
9	Mail Questionnaire and Get Responses	Fri 3/20/09	Thu 6/18/09	Fri 3/20/09	Thu 6/18/09	0 days	0 days
10	Test Software	Tue 3/24/09	Mon 3/30/09	Tue 3/24/09	Mon 3/30/09	0 days	0 days
11	Input Response Data	Fri 6/19/09	Mon 6/29/09	Fri 6/19/09	Mon 6/29/09	0 days	0 days
12	Analyze Results	Tue 6/30/09	Thu 7/9/09	Tue 6/30/09	Thu 7/9/09	0 days	0 days
13	Prepare Report	Fri 7/10/09	Thu 7/23/09	Fri 7/10/09	Thu 7/23/09	0 days	0 days

FIGURE 7A.5 *Tracking Table*

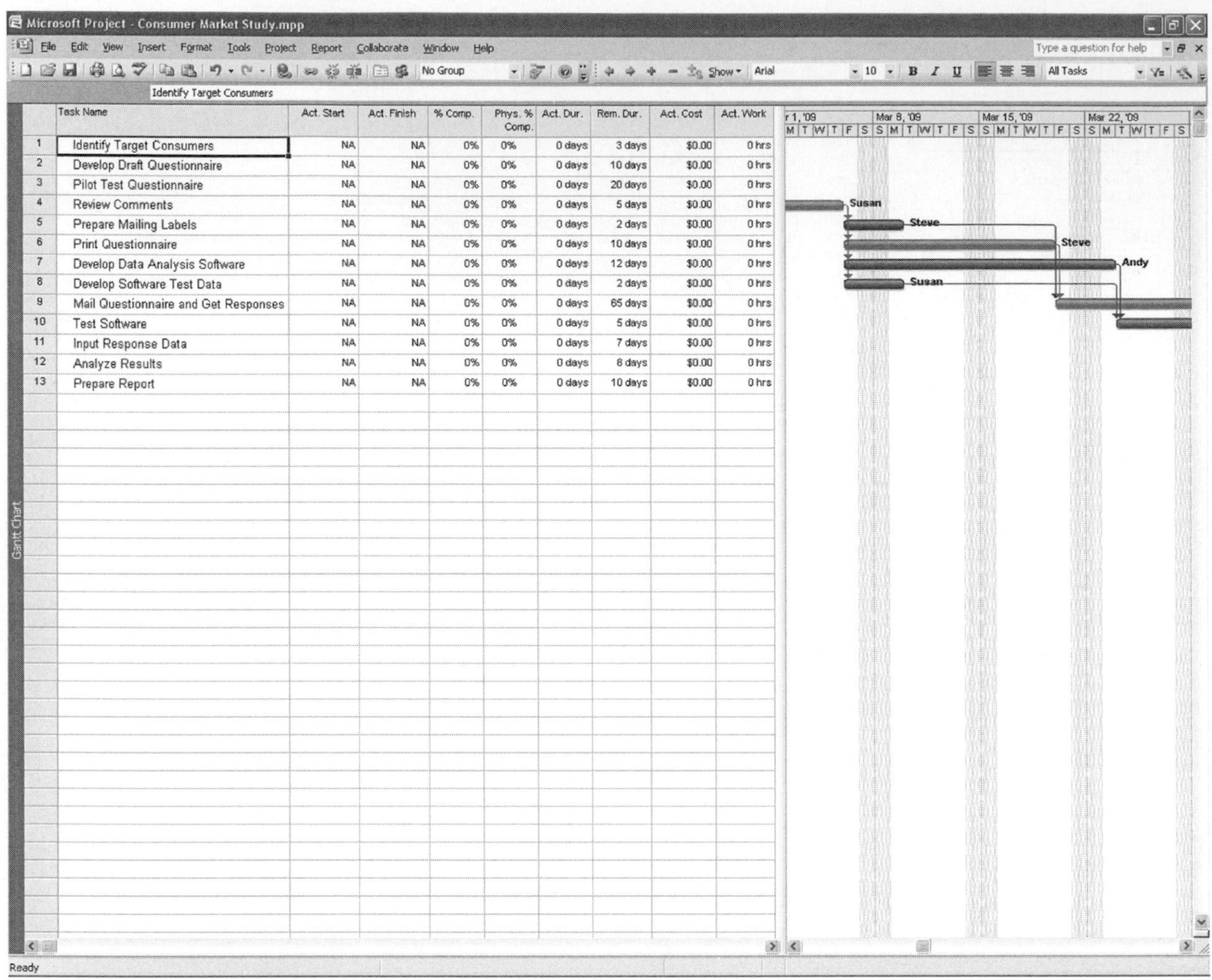

	Task Name	Act. Start	Act. Finish	% Comp.	Phys. % Comp.	Act. Dur.	Rem. Dur.	Act. Cost	Act. Work
1	Identify Target Consumers	NA	NA	0%	0%	0 days	3 days	$0.00	0 hrs
2	Develop Draft Questionnaire	NA	NA	0%	0%	0 days	10 days	$0.00	0 hrs
3	Pilot Test Questionnaire	NA	NA	0%	0%	0 days	20 days	$0.00	0 hrs
4	Review Comments	NA	NA	0%	0%	0 days	5 days	$0.00	0 hrs
5	Prepare Mailing Labels	NA	NA	0%	0%	0 days	2 days	$0.00	0 hrs
6	Print Questionnaire	NA	NA	0%	0%	0 days	10 days	$0.00	0 hrs
7	Develop Data Analysis Software	NA	NA	0%	0%	0 days	12 days	$0.00	0 hrs
8	Develop Software Test Data	NA	NA	0%	0%	0 days	2 days	$0.00	0 hrs
9	Mail Questionnaire and Get Responses	NA	NA	0%	0%	0 days	65 days	$0.00	0 hrs
10	Test Software	NA	NA	0%	0%	0 days	5 days	$0.00	0 hrs
11	Input Response Data	NA	NA	0%	0%	0 days	7 days	$0.00	0 hrs
12	Analyze Results	NA	NA	0%	0%	0 days	8 days	$0.00	0 hrs
13	Prepare Report	NA	NA	0%	0%	0 days	10 days	$0.00	0 hrs

FIGURE 7A.6 *Tracking Gantt*

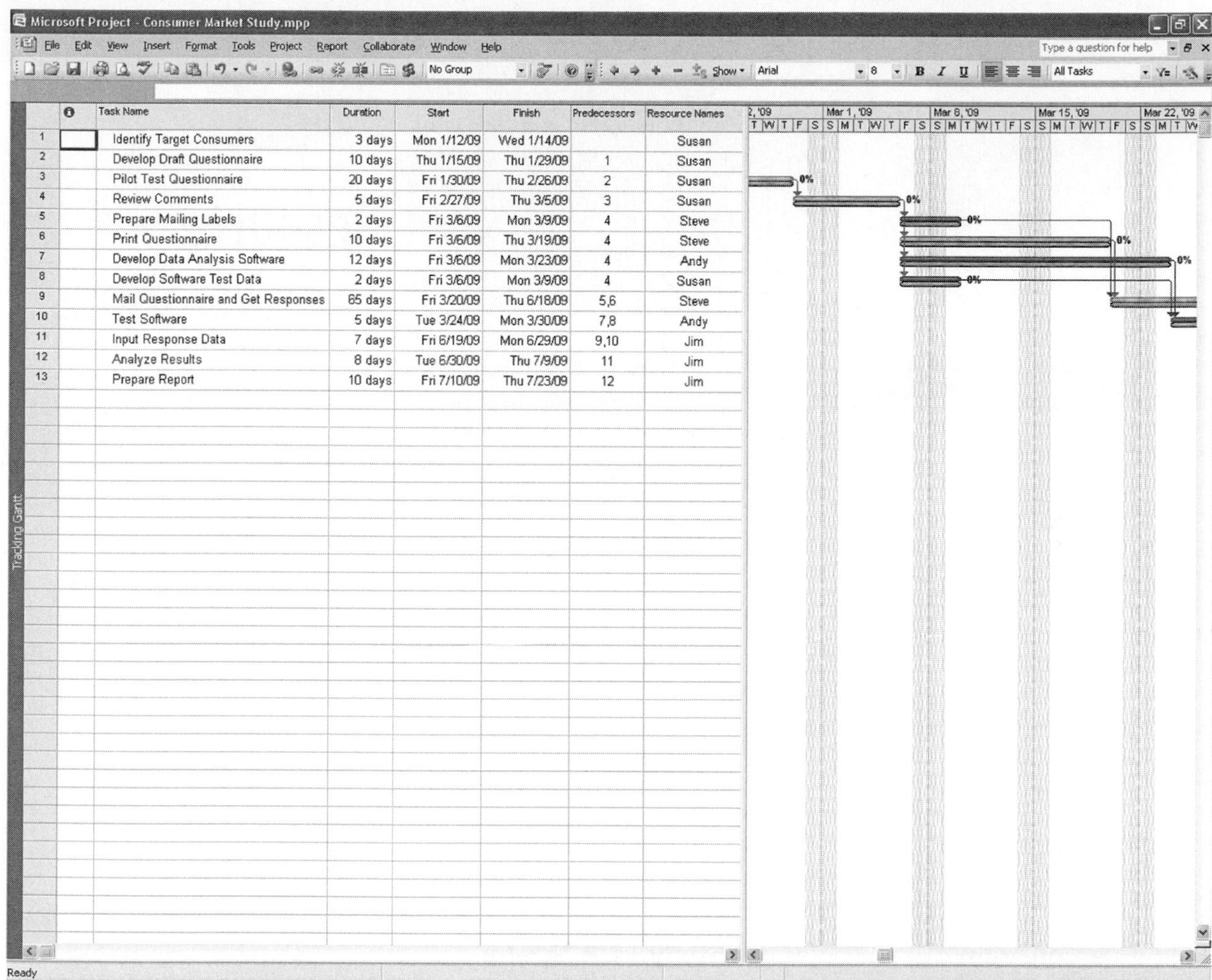

Microsoft Project - Consumer Market Study.mpp

	Task Name	Duration	Start	Finish	Predecessors	Resource Names
1	Identify Target Consumers	3 days	Mon 1/12/09	Wed 1/14/09		Susan
2	Develop Draft Questionnaire	10 days	Thu 1/15/09	Thu 1/29/09	1	Susan
3	Pilot Test Questionnaire	20 days	Fri 1/30/09	Thu 2/26/09	2	Susan
4	Review Comments	5 days	Fri 2/27/09	Thu 3/5/09	3	Susan
5	Prepare Mailing Labels	2 days	Fri 3/6/09	Mon 3/9/09	4	Steve
6	Print Questionnaire	10 days	Fri 3/6/09	Thu 3/19/09	4	Steve
7	Develop Data Analysis Software	12 days	Fri 3/6/09	Mon 3/23/09	4	Andy
8	Develop Software Test Data	2 days	Fri 3/6/09	Mon 3/9/09	4	Susan
9	Mail Questionnaire and Get Responses	65 days	Fri 3/20/09	Thu 6/18/09	5,6	Steve
10	Test Software	5 days	Tue 3/24/09	Mon 3/30/09	7,8	Andy
11	Input Response Data	7 days	Fri 6/19/09	Mon 6/29/09	9,10	Jim
12	Analyze Results	8 days	Tue 6/30/09	Thu 7/9/09	11	Jim
13	Prepare Report	10 days	Fri 7/10/09	Thu 7/23/09	12	Jim

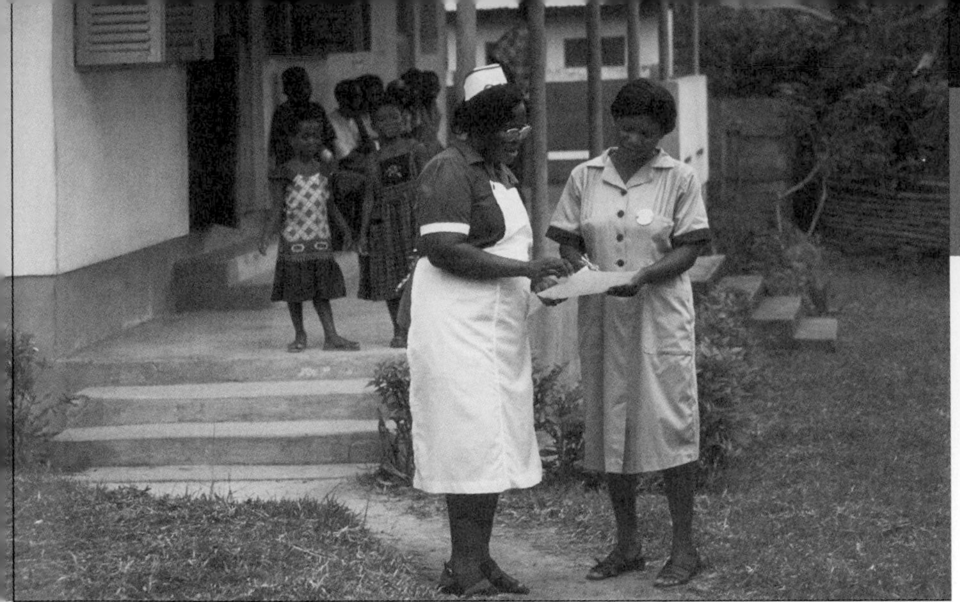

© GS International/Greenshoots Communication/Alamy Ltd.

CHAPTER

8

Resource Considerations

Real World PROJECT MANAGEMENT

Resource-Constrained Health Services Planning in Ghana

The Ghana Community-based Health Planning and Services (CHPS) initiative was designed to translate innovations from an experimental study of the Navrongo Health Research Centre (NHRC). The experiment centered around the implementation of a national program for improving accessibility, efficiency, and overall quality of health and family planning services. In response to the CHPS initiative, the Navrongo project experiment became the paradigm for health care development in Ghana. Despite the existence of "health for all" policies for two decades, as of 1990 it was estimated that more than 70 percent of all Ghanaians resided more than eight kilometers from the nearest providers. Additionally, rural infant mortality rates were 50 percent higher than urban infant mortality rates.

As a direct response to the need for health care reform, a phased research project was initiated to aid in changing the system from having a clinical facility–focused approach to a community-based approach. The aim of this experimental project was to serve as a tool for guiding reform by identifying underused cultural and organization resources, mobilizing these resources, and guiding health care reform in the direction of evidence-based practice.

The initiative involved extending the evidence-based knowledge necessary for organization change to the community level in a sector-wide approach to effectively transition from facility-based health care to integrated community-based health care. The CHPS initiative was composed of three components: (1) research to provide evidence for guiding the overall process, (2) providing policies, resources, and mechanisms for communicating the overall process and priorities necessary for organizational change, and (3) informal mechanisms utilized to foster innovation and change between and within districts.

Research in the CHPS processes proceeded in many distinct stages and each had a role in developing policy. The first phase was the Navrongo pilot project to determine the proper elements of a community health care program. Focus groups were held with men and women, community leaders, and health care workers to assess perceptions of service needs. The pilot services were designed and implemented to transform operational strategies to meet the needs expressed in the focus group sessions.

Results of this pilot project were used to plan the operational design of the Navrongo Community Health and Family Planning Project. This project was a factorial experiment that would test the impact of two general sets of existing underused resources for primary health care.

The Navrongo project design addressed the fact that traditional social institutions playing a power role in village life organization were being completely overlooked by the health care system. The Navrongo experiment was able to bring together health care and traditional leaders. This enabled health professionals to recruit, train, and deploy community-accountable volunteers, and enabled traditional leaders to support all community health operations. The hypothesis of the Navrongo experiment was based upon mobilizing the traditional leadership system, communication, and governance to develop health care service accessibility and accountability and reduce mortality and fertility.

In the early 1990s, community health nurses were required to complete 18 months of training; they were then assigned to subdistrict health centers throughout Ghana to provide treatment for malaria, childhood immunization, and family planning and health education services. The nursing coverage was plagued by logistical problems, resource shortages, and lapses in supervision. The nurses were also confined to their subdistrict centers. The Navrongo project experiment attempted to end social isolation of the nurses by retraining, renaming, and recertifying them as "community health officers" to serve as resident health care providers.

By 1997, evidence had shown that the Navrongo project experiment was having a measurable impact. If a single nurse had access to a motorbike and relocated to a village health center, she or he could perform better than an entire subdistrict health center. She or he could increase the volume of heath service encounters in a service area, while improving immunization and coverage of family planning. Consequently, fertility and mortality began to decline. In 1998, the Ghana Health Service held a conference for national managers to discuss the implications of the Navrongo project experiment. They declared it the national model for community-based health care, and proceeded with national policy and action for implementation.

Nyonator, F., Awoonor-Williams, J., Phillips, J., Jones, T. and Miller, R., "The Ghana Community-based Health Planning and Services Initiative: Fostering Evidence-based Organizational Change and Development in a Resource-Constrained Setting," Population Council, Policy Research Division, No. 180, 2003.

In previous chapters, we established schedules based on the time element. We assumed that the resources required to perform the individual activities would be available when they were needed. These resources can include people, equipment, machines, tools, facilities, and space. Among the people there may be many different types, such as painters, designers, cooks, computer programmers, and assembly workers.

The consideration of resources adds another dimension to planning and scheduling. In many projects, the amounts of the various types of resources available to perform the project activities are limited. Several activities may require the same resources at the same time, and there may not be sufficient resources available to satisfy all the demands. In a sense, these activities are *competing* for the use of the same resources. If sufficient resources are not available, some activities may have to be rescheduled for a later time when resources *are* available for them. Therefore, resources can constrain the project schedule. They can also be an obstacle to completing the project within budget if it is determined that additional resources are needed to complete the project on time.

This chapter covers several approaches to incorporating resource considerations into the project plan and schedule. You will become familiar with

- taking resource constraints into account when developing a network diagram
- determining the planned resource utilization for a project
- leveling the use of resources within the required time frame of the project
- determining the shortest project schedule with the limited resources available

RESOURCE-CONSTRAINED PLANNING

One way to consider resources is to take them into account when drawing the logical relationships among activities in the network diagram. At a minimum, network diagrams illustrate the *technical constraints* among activities. Activities are

FIGURE 8.1 *Technically Constrained Activity Sequence*

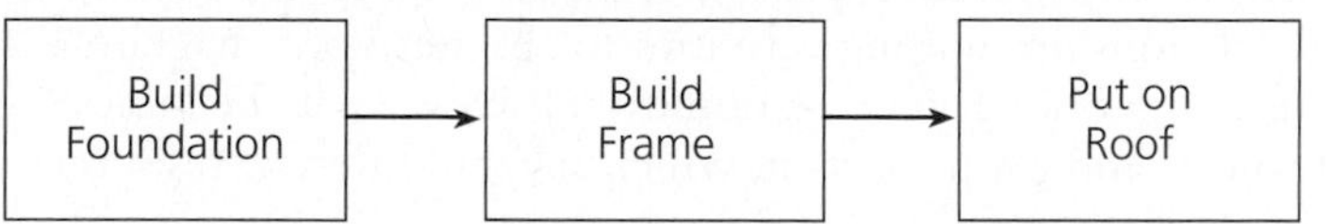

FIGURE 8.2 *Resource-Constrained Planning*

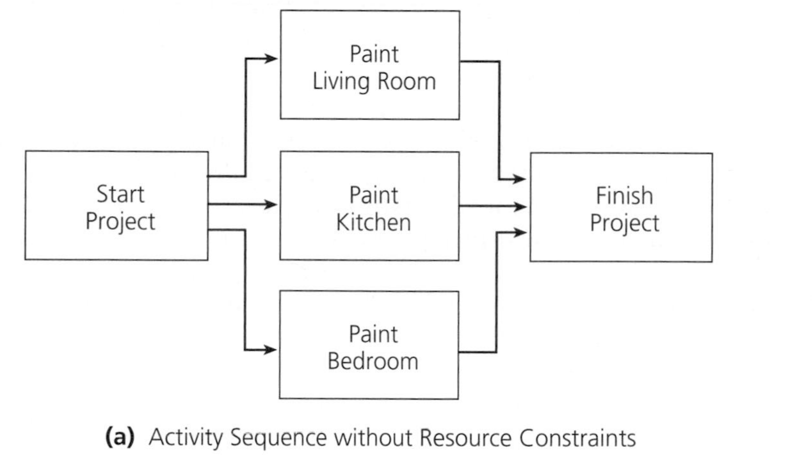

(a) Activity Sequence without Resource Constraints

(b) Activity Sequence Based on Resource Constraints

drawn in a serial relationship because, from a technical standpoint, they must be performed in that sequence. For example, Figure 8.1 shows that the three house-building activities—build foundation, build frame, and put on roof—must be done in series. Technically, these activities must be performed in this sequence. The roof cannot be put on before the frame is built!

In addition to showing the technical constraints among activities, the network logic can also take into account *resource constraints*. The sequence of activities can be drawn to reflect the availability of a limited number of resources. Part (a) of Figure 8.2 shows that, technically, three activities—paint living room, paint kitchen, and paint bedroom—could be performed concurrently; that is, there is no technical reason why the start of any one of these activities should depend on the completion of any other one. Suppose, however, that there is only one person available to do all the painting; this limitation introduces a resource constraint on the painting activities. That is, although technically all three activities could be done concurrently, they will have to be performed in series because only one painter is available to do all three. To incorporate this resource constraint, the diagram will have to be drawn as shown in part (b) of Figure 8.2. The exact sequence of these three activities—which particular room gets painted first, second, and third—is another decision that must be made when the network diagram is drawn.

Reinforce Your Learning

1. At a minimum, network diagrams illustrate the ________ constraints among activities. However, when limited resources are available, the network diagram can be drawn to also reflect ________ constraints.

This example illustrates how resource limitations can be considered when a network plan is drawn. This approach of incorporating resource constraints into the logical relationships among activities in the network diagram is feasible for small projects involving few resources. However, it becomes complicated for large projects and for projects in which several different resources are needed for some of the activities.

PLANNED RESOURCE UTILIZATION

If resources are to be considered in planning, it's necessary to indicate the amounts and types of resources needed to perform each activity. Figure 8.3 is a network diagram for a painting project; each activity box shows the estimated activity duration (in days), as well as the number of painters needed to accomplish the activity within its estimated duration.

Using the information in Figure 8.3, we can prepare a resource utilization chart as shown in Figure 8.4, which indicates how many painters are needed each day based on the earliest start and finish times for each activity. The resource utilization chart shows that four painters are needed on days 1 through 4, three painters are needed on days 5 and 6, two painters are needed on days 7 through 10, and only one painter is needed on days 11 and 12. A total of 32 painter-days are needed. The resource profile for painters is illustrated in Figure 8.5. It shows an uneven utilization of painters. A peak of four painters is needed during one portion of the project, and a low of only one painter is needed during another portion of the project.

Resources such as painters cannot usually be hired on a day-to-day basis to meet fluctuating requirements. If the same number of painters must be employed throughout the project, it will be necessary to pay some painters to work overtime during periods of peak demand and to pay some painters to remain idle during periods of low demand. Thus, it's preferable to have a more uniform, or level, application of resources.

FIGURE 8.3 ***Painting Project Showing Needed Resources***

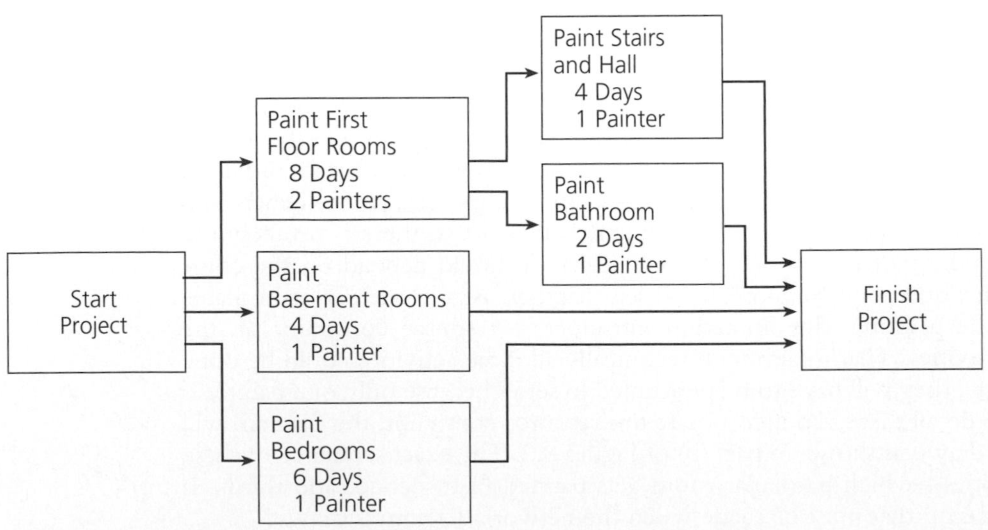

FIGURE 8.4 *Planned Resource Utilization*

Activity	Painter Days
First Floor Rooms (2 Painters)	16
Stairs & Hall (1 Painter)	4
Bathroom (1 Painter)	2
Basement Rooms (1 Painter)	4
Bedrooms (1 Painter)	6

Day	1	2	3	4	5	6	7	8	9	10	11	12	
Painters	4	4	4	4	3	3	2	2	2	2	1	1	32

FIGURE 8.5 *Resource Profile for Painters*

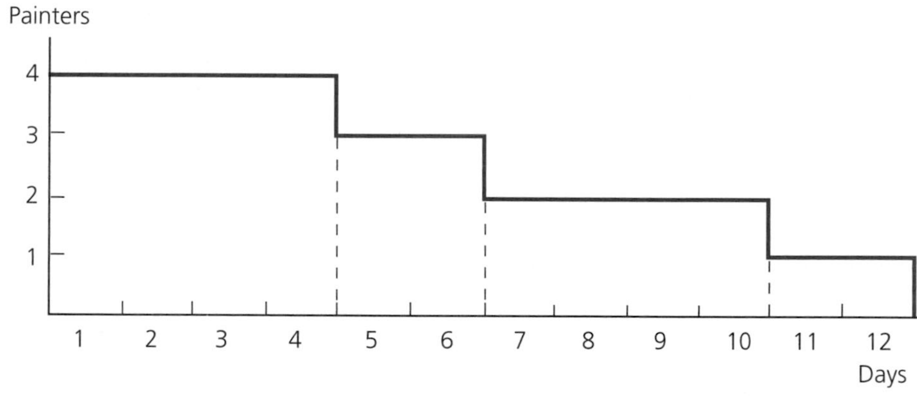

It should be noted that the resource utilization charts shown in Figures 8.4 and 8.5 are based on each activity's earliest start time. Such resource utilization charts are said to be based on an **as-soon-as-possible (ASAP) schedule**. Resource utilization charts based on each activity's latest start time are said to be based on an **as-late-as-possible (ALAP) schedule**.

RESOURCE LEVELING

Resource leveling, or **smoothing**, is a method for developing a schedule that attempts to minimize the fluctuations in requirements for resources. This method levels the resources so that they are applied as uniformly as possible without extending the project schedule beyond the required completion time. It's a trial-and-error method in which the start of noncritical activities (those with positive slack values) are delayed beyond their earliest start times (but not beyond their latest start times) in order to maintain a uniform level of required resources. Activities can be delayed only to the point where all their positive slack is used up, as any further delays would cause the project to extend beyond the project due date. Resource leveling attempts to establish a schedule in which resource use is made as level as possible without extending the project beyond the required completion time.

Reinforce Your Learning

2. Resource leveling attempts to establish a schedule in which resource use is made as level as possible without extending the project beyond the ________ ________ time.

Let us look at the painting project in Figures 8.3, 8.4, and 8.5 to determine whether resource utilization can be leveled. Figures 8.3 and 8.4 show that the critical path for the project is made up of two activities and is 12 days long (8 days to paint the first-floor rooms plus 4 days to paint the stairs and hall). Therefore, these two activities cannot be delayed without extending the project completion time beyond 12 days. Looking at Figure 8.4, however, we can see that "Bathroom" could be delayed up to 2 days, "Basement Rooms" could be delayed up to 8 days, and "Bedrooms" could be delayed up to 6 days—all without extending the project completion time beyond 12 days. Looking at Figure 8.4, we can see that two alternative actions could be taken to level the daily resource requirements for painters:

> *Alternative 1.* Delay the activity with the most positive slack—"Basement Rooms" (+8 days slack)—by six days so that it will start after "Bedrooms" is finished. Rather than have two separate painters paint the basement rooms and bedrooms concurrently, the resource-leveled schedule will use the same painter to first paint the bedrooms and then paint the basement rooms.
>
> *Alternative 2.* Delay "Bedrooms" so that it will start on day 4, after "Basement Rooms" is completed. This alternative will use the same painter to first paint the basement rooms and then paint the bedrooms (the reverse of alternative 1, achieving the same result).

Figures 8.6 and 8.7 illustrate the resource profile for the resource-leveled schedule if we choose alternative 1. Comparing Figure 8.6 with Figure 8.4, we

FIGURE 8.6 *Resource-Leveled Utilization*

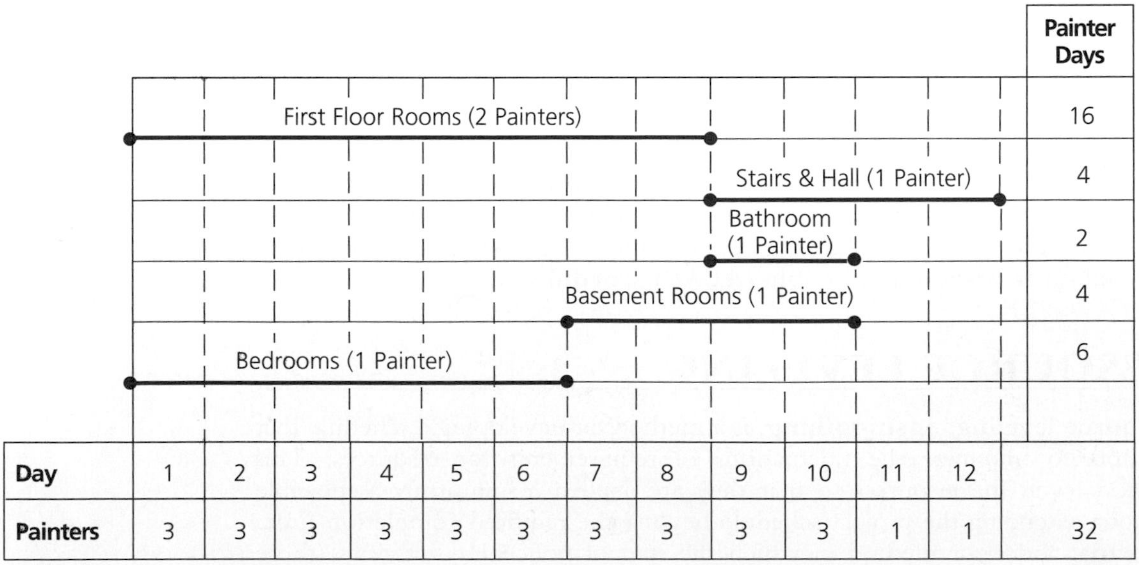

Activity	Painter Days
First Floor Rooms (2 Painters)	16
Stairs & Hall (1 Painter)	4
Bathroom (1 Painter)	2
Basement Rooms (1 Painter)	4
Bedrooms (1 Painter)	6

Day	1	2	3	4	5	6	7	8	9	10	11	12	
Painters	3	3	3	3	3	3	3	3	3	3	1	1	32

FIGURE 8.7 ***Resource-Leveled Profile for Painters***

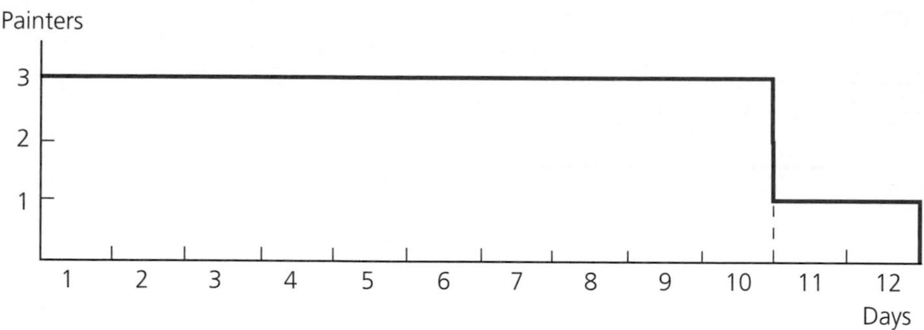

see that the earliest start time for "Basement Rooms" has been delayed from time 0 to day 6, and its earliest finish time is now day 10 rather than day 4. Figure 8.7 shows a more uniform utilization of painters than Figure 8.5, except for days 11 and 12, which remain the same. In both cases 32 painter-days are required, but in the resource-leveled schedule they're utilized with less fluctuation.

For a large project with many different resources, resource leveling can get very complicated. Various project management software packages are available that will assist in generating a resource-leveled schedule and resource utilization charts and profiles.

RESOURCE-LIMITED SCHEDULING

Resource-limited scheduling is a method for developing the shortest schedule when the number or amount of available resources is fixed. This method is appropriate when the resources available for the project are limited and these resource limits cannot be exceeded. This method will extend the project completion time if necessary in order to keep within the resource limits. It is an iterative method in which resources are allocated to activities based on the least slack. When several activities need the same limited resource at the same time, the activities with the least slack have first priority. If resources are left over, the activities with the second least slack have the next priority, and so forth. If other activities need the resource but the resource has been totally allocated to higher-priority activities, the lower-priority activities get delayed; as their slack becomes worse, they eventually move up the priority ladder. This delaying of activities can extend the project completion time.

Figure 8.8 illustrates what would happen if only a limited number of painters—two—were available to do the painting project. When we push down on the level of resources because no more than two painters can be used, we push out the project completion time. If only two painters are available at any time, the project completion time has to be extended from day 12 to at least day 16, in order to get the 32 painter-days required.

Let us apply resource-limited scheduling to the painting project shown in Figure 8.3. Figure 8.9, which is the same as Figure 8.4, is our original resource utilization; it shows a project completion time of 12 days. Let us now assume, however, that we're limited to only two painters.

Reinforce Your Learning

3. Resource-limited scheduling develops ______ the schedule when the number or amount of available resources is fixed. This method will ______ the project completion time if necessary in order to keep within the limits.

FIGURE 8.8 ***Effect of Limited Resource Availability***

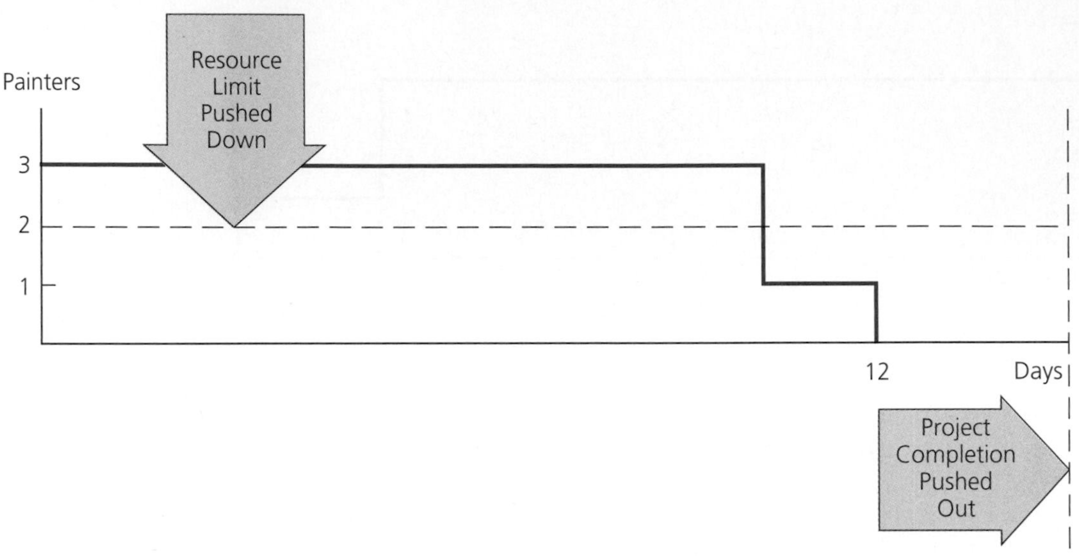

FIGURE 8.9 ***Original Resource Utilization***

Activity	Slack
First Floor Rooms (2 Painters)	0
Stairs & Hall (1 Painter)	0
Bathroom (1 Painter)	+2
Basement Rooms (1 Painter)	+8
Bedrooms (1 Painter)	+6

Day	1	2	3	4	5	6	7	8	9	10	11	12
Painters	4	4	4	4	3	3	2	2	2	2	1	1

Figure 8.9 shows that, as the project starts, three activities require a total of four painters ("First-Floor Rooms," "Basement Rooms," and "Bedrooms"). Only two painters are available, though, so they will be allocated to the activities based on a priority determined by slack.

"First-Floor Rooms" has a slack of 0, whereas "Basement Rooms" has a slack of +8 days and "Bedrooms" has a slack of +6 days. Therefore, the two painters will be allocated to the first-floor rooms and will continue to be assigned to that activity until it is finished. (In this example, it's assumed that, once an

FIGURE 8.10 ***First Resource Allocation***

First Floor Rooms (2 Painters)
Stairs & Hall (1 Painter)
Bathroom (1 Painter)
Basement Rooms (1 Painter)
Bedrooms (1 Painter)

Activity	Slack
First Floor Rooms (2 Painters)	0
Stairs & Hall (1 Painter)	0
Bathroom (1 Painter)	2
Basement Rooms (1 Painter)	0
Bedrooms (1 Painter)	–2

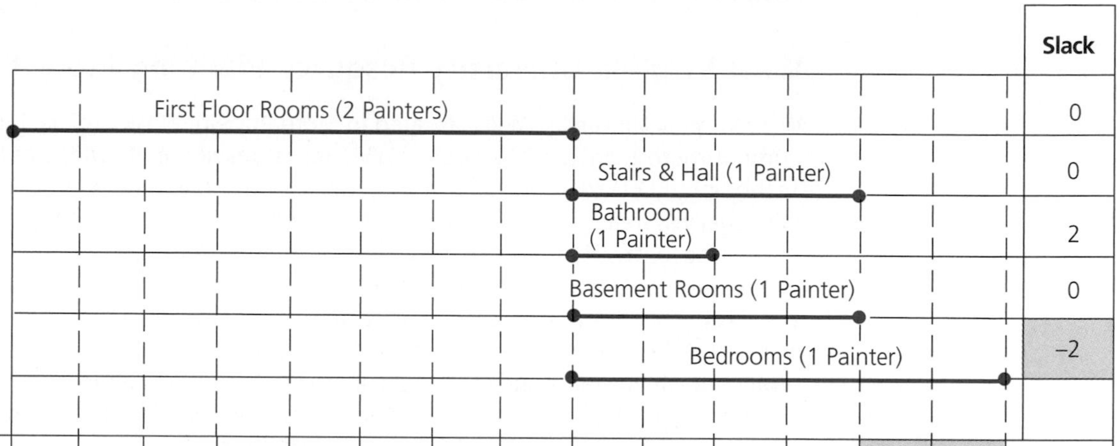

Day	1	2	3	4	5	6	7	8	9	10	11	12	13	14
Painters	2	2	2	2	2	2	2	2	4	4	3	3	1	1

activity starts, it continues until it's finished and cannot be stopped and restarted.) Because all the available resources are assigned to "First-Floor Rooms" from time 0 through day 8, the other two activities ("Basement Rooms" and "Bedrooms") will have their starts delayed until after day 8. This first resource allocation is shown in Figure 8.10.

The result of this first iteration of allocating the painters is extension of project completion from day 12 to day 14 because of the delay of "Bedrooms." Additionally, there is still a problem on days 9 through 12 because the resource requirements exceed the limit of two painters. So it's now necessary to do a second allocation of painters on day 9. "Bedrooms" has the least slack, with –2 days; its earliest expected finish time is now day 14, and the required project completion time is 12 days. "Bedrooms" requires one painter, so one of the two available painters is allocated to it. One painter is still to be allocated. Two activities, "Stairs and Hall" and "Basement Rooms," have the same next lowest value of slack (0). One way to choose between these two is to determine which has been critical for a longer time. Looking back, we see that "Stairs and Hall" was more critical (0 slack) than "Basement Rooms" (+8 days slack) in Figure 8.9. Therefore, the remaining painter should be allocated to "Stairs and Hall." "Bedrooms" will start after day 8 and will continue through day 14. "Stairs and Hall" will also start after day 8 and will continue through day 12. The next time a painter will become available is after "Stairs and Hall" is finished on day 12. Therefore, the remaining two activities, "Basement Rooms" and "Bathrooms," will have their starts delayed until after day 12. This second resource allocation is shown in Figure 8.11.

The result of this second iteration of allocating the painters is another extension of project completion, this time from day 14 to day 16, because of the delay of "Basement Rooms." There is still a problem on days 13 and 14 because the resource requirements exceed the limit of two painters. So it's now necessary to do a third allocation of painters on day 13, when one painter becomes available after finishing "Stairs and Hall." (Remember that the second

Real World PROJECT MANAGEMENT

West Virginia University Resource Planning Project

West Virginia University (WVU), located in Morgantown, West Virginia, has a student body of more than 32,000 students. WVU relies heavily on its Office of Information Technology (OIT) to implement new systems, perform technology upgrades, maintain legacy systems, build communication networks, and deliver new online services.

In the past, OIT's staff of about 130 full-time employees were divided into individual teams that created proposals for submission to a central committee for approval. This approach resulted in a few problems, including the inability to estimate and manage resource needs for IT projects. It also made evaluation of project portfolio status and costs difficult across the organization. In addition, there was no way to determine whether approved projects could be handled in actuality by the number of people available to work on them.

The Academic and Administration Information Management System (AAIMS) committee was assembled to consider project proposals that were created manually from disparate tools and formats. Even to present the proposals, substantial effort was required to gather the necessary information from the workstations of project managers because of their lack of consistency. This ineffective system resulted in over-tasked teams and missed deadlines. The problems became evident to the state government, who mandated an update to OIT's course management system.

WVU had three major objectives in mind when they initiated a project to tackle the problems with OIT: (1) to achieve better resource planning and utilization, (2) to have easy access to project portfolio status, and (3) to accurately determine costs of IT projects.

OIT considered several solutions, and decided to implement IBM's Rational Portfolio Manager for its strengths in project staffing and resource management, reusable templates, and what-if analysis capabilities. The Rational Portfolio Manager is also designed to establish better planning and execution of resource allocations.

During the implementation, OIT focused on defining resources and setting up the system to do critical analysis on resource demands versus resource supply. The Rational Portfolio Manager also helped put a new project approval process in place. Assistant directors of OIT and members of the AAIMS committee were given portfolio manager status within the Rational Portfolio Manager. The initial implementation also included project managers and OIT staffers (database administrators, developers, and testers). With this process in place, the AAIMS committee can now make better-informed decisions based upon estimated resource requirements and resource availability.

Once a project is approved, it is published so team members can see the project description and tasks. The project manager can also make minor schedule adjustments or add detail to the project plan through the Rational Portfolio Manager. OIT staff can also report their individual efforts on each project task.

Additionally, WVU needed a way to track the amount of time OIT staffers devoted to maintenance on existing systems. This time was tracked for each group of employees and became useful in determining maintenance costs for its various systems. Although it was barely ever done in the past, accounting for the amount of time spent by WVU staff is, as expected, one of the largest components of a total project's estimated cost.

OIT is now going to reuse project plans by creating templates for future use. Templates can be valuable resources in terms of developing accurate cost and resource estimates for future projects. Since Rational Project Manager has been so successful in OIT, WVU is planning to implement it in other departments within the university in order to better manage resources and projects.

Its implementation has resulted in significant improvements to a number of IT processes as noted above. In addition, information for proposals is now organized and readily accessible to the project management office and other decision makers, and project and portfolio management has now become a part of doing business at WVU. Continued improvements in project management and resource utilization are expected.

"West Virginia University Sees Improved IT Governance with Resource Planning and Cost Accounting," http://www-360.ibm.com/software/success, February 14, 2007.

painter is still working on "Bedrooms.") Two activities, "Bathrooms" and "Basement Rooms," need a painter on day 13. "Basement Rooms" has less slack (–4 days) than the other activity, so the available painter will be allocated to it. "Basement Rooms" will start after day 12 and will continue through day 16. The next time a painter will become available is after "Bedrooms" is finished on day 14. Therefore, "Bathroom" will have its start delayed until after day 14. This third resource allocation is shown in Figure 8.12.

As a result of this third iteration of allocating the painters, the project completion time is still four days beyond the required project completion time, but all the activities have been scheduled to start and finish so as to stay within the limit of two painters. No further iterations are needed.

In order to accelerate the schedule to complete the project by day 12, it would be necessary to implement one or more of the approaches to schedule control mentioned in Chapter 7, such as adding more painters, working overtime, reducing the scope of work or the requirements for some of the activities, or increasing productivity.

FIGURE 8.11 ***Second Resource Allocation***

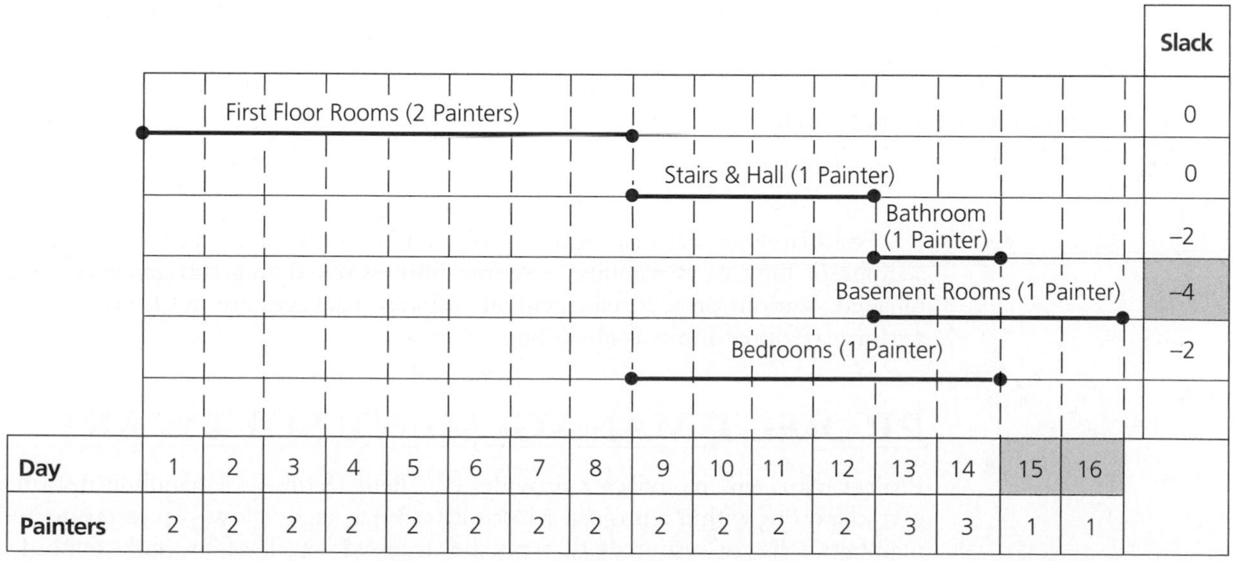

Activity	Slack
First Floor Rooms (2 Painters)	0
Stairs & Hall (1 Painter)	0
Bathroom (1 Painter)	–2
Basement Rooms (1 Painter)	–4
Bedrooms (1 Painter)	–2

Day	1	2	3	4	5	6	7	8	9	10	11	12	13	14	15	16
Painters	2	2	2	2	2	2	2	2	2	2	2	2	3	3	1	1

FIGURE 8.12 *Third Resource Allocation*

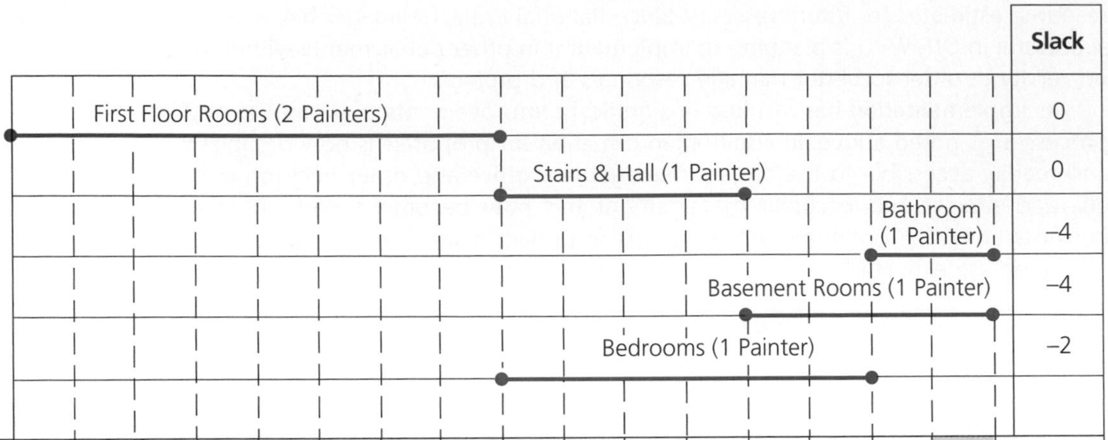

Activity	Slack
First Floor Rooms (2 Painters)	0
Stairs & Hall (1 Painter)	0
Bathroom (1 Painter)	−4
Basement Rooms (1 Painter)	−4
Bedrooms (1 Painter)	−2

Day	1	2	3	4	5	6	7	8	9	10	11	12	13	14	15	16
Painters	2	2	2	2	2	2	2	2	2	2	2	2	2	2	2	2

Critical Success FACTORS

- Resources can constrain the project schedule because the amounts of various types of resources available to perform the project activities may be limited.
- If resources are to be considered in planning, it is necessary to estimate the amounts and types of resources needed to perform each activity.
- If sufficient resources are not available, some activities may have to be rescheduled for a later time when resources become available to perform the activities.
- Resource leveling or smoothing is a method for developing a schedule that attempts to minimize the fluctuations in requirements for resources. It levels the resources so that they are applied as uniformly as possible without extending the project schedule beyond the required completion time.
- Resource-limited scheduling is a method for developing the shortest schedule when the number or amount of resources is fixed. It will extend the project completion time if necessary in order to keep within the resource limits.

For a large project that requires many different resources, each of which has a different limit of availability, resource-limited scheduling can get very complicated. Various project management software packages are available that will perform resource-limited scheduling.

PROJECT MANAGEMENT SOFTWARE

Project management software provides excellent features for handling resource considerations within a project. Most software packages allow you to create and maintain a list of resources that can be accessed by all of the tasks within a project. The list typically allows you to store the resource name, maximum number of units available, standard and overtime rates, and costs. In addition, because the expenses for resources can be accrued at different times throughout a project, most software systems allow you to create charges for a resource at the beginning of its use, at fixed intervals, or at the end of the project. Each resource can also be assigned a calendar of availability.

The software will typically inform the user if any resources have time conflicts or if any resources are overallocated within a project or among concurrent projects. Tables and graphs of resource usage are often available.

To resolve any conflicts or to level, or smooth, the resources, the software typically provides two options. The first is to correct the situation manually. With this option, the user modifies the task information and requirements or the resource list and then sees whether the situation has been resolved. The second option is to allow the software to perform this process automatically. If the automatic process is selected, the software typically asks the user whether the deadline can be extended if that's the only way to resolve the conflict or smooth the resources.

As with the other features of project management software that have been discussed, all of this can be done with simple point-and-click commands. See Appendix A for a thorough discussion of project management software.

SUMMARY

Resources can include people, equipment, machines, tools, facilities, and space. Among the people may be many different types, such as painters, designers, cooks, computer programmers, and assembly workers.

The consideration of resources adds another dimension (beyond the element of time) to planning and scheduling. In many projects, the amounts of the various types of resources available to perform the project activities are limited. Several activities may require the same resources at the same time, and there may not be sufficient resources available to satisfy all the demands. If sufficient resources are not available, some activities may have to be rescheduled for a later time when resources *are* available for them.

One way to consider resources is to take them into account when drawing the logical relationships among activities in the network diagram. In addition to showing the technical constraints among activities, the network logic can also take into account resource constraints. The sequence of activities can be drawn to reflect the limited availability of a number of resources. If resources are to be considered in planning, it's necessary to indicate the amounts and types of resources needed to perform each activity. For this reason, a resource profile is often developed.

Resource leveling, or smoothing, is a method for developing a schedule that attempts to minimize the fluctuations in requirements for resources. This method levels the resources so that they are applied as uniformly as possible without extending the project schedule beyond the required completion time. Resource leveling attempts to establish a schedule in which resource use is made as level as possible without extending the project beyond the required completion time. In resource leveling, the required project completion time is fixed, and the resources are varied in an attempt to eliminate fluctuation.

FIGURE 8.13 ***Fixed Variable Elements for Resource Leveling and Resource-Limited Scheduling***

	Fixed	Variable
Resource Leveling	Project Required Completion Time	Resources
Resources-Limited Scheduling	Resources	Project Required Completion Time

Resource-limited scheduling is a method for developing the shortest schedule when the number or amount of available resources is fixed. This method is appropriate when the resources available for the project are limited and these resource limits cannot be exceeded. This method will extend the project completion time if necessary in order to keep within the resource limits. It is an iterative method in which resources are allocated to activities based on the least slack. The steps are repeated until all resource constraints have been satisfied. In resource-limited scheduling, the resources are fixed, and the project completion time is varied (extended) in order not to exceed the resource limits.

Figure 8.13 shows the differences between resource leveling and resource-limited scheduling.

For a large project that requires many different resources, each of which has a different limit of availability, resource-limited scheduling can get very complicated. Various project management software packages are available that will assist with this process.

QUESTIONS

1. Give at least 10 examples of resources.
2. Think about a project that you are currently working on or have worked on. List all of the resources used in this project.
3. Discuss why resources need to be considered when developing a schedule.
4. Describe how resources can be considered when drawing a network diagram.
5. What are technical constraints? Give some examples.
6. What are resource constraints? Give some examples.
7. Describe what is meant by *resource leveling* or *smoothing*. Why is it used? When is it used?
8. Does resource leveling keep a project on schedule? If so, how?
9. Describe what is meant by *resource-limited scheduling*. Why is it used? When is it used?
10. Does resource-limited scheduling keep a project on schedule? If so, how?
11. Using the following figure, perform resource leveling. Assume that each task can be performed independently of the other tasks.

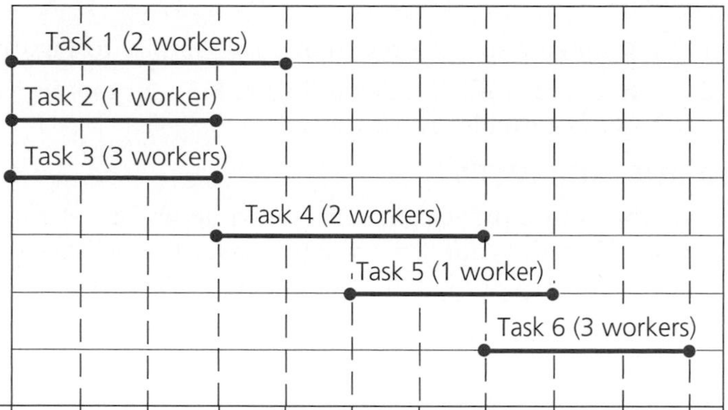

Task 1 (2 workers)
Task 2 (1 worker)
Task 3 (3 workers)
Task 4 (2 workers)
Task 5 (1 worker)
Task 6 (3 workers)

Day	1	2	3	4	5	6	7	8	9	10
Workers	6	6	6	4	2	3	3	4	3	3

12. Using the figure in question 11, perform resource-limited scheduling. Assume that you have only three workers available at any given time. What is the new completion date for the project?

INTERNET EXERCISES

For the website addresses of the organizations mentioned in these exercises, go to "Internet Exercises" at the book's companion website at **international.cengage.com**. It is suggested that you save this website in your "Favorites" for easy access in the future.

1. Search the web for resource leveling or resource limited scheduling and describe what you find.
2. Find and describe how at least one project management software package handles the resource considerations discussed in this chapter.
3. For exercises 3 through 5, visit the website of the Association for Project Management. Click on the "About Us" link and describe the mission of the organization.
4. Click on the "Resources" link. Explore the resources offered on this website and summarize one that interests you.
5. Explore either the "Latest News" or "Upcoming Events" links. Describe what you find.

A Not-for-Profit Medical Research Center

CASE STUDY 1

This case study is a continuation of the case study from Chapters 5, 6, and 7.

CASE QUESTIONS

Using the revised schedule you calculated in response to item 1 in Chapter 7 to eliminate all the negative slack (or if you did not have any negative slack to eliminate, then use the schedule you calculated in item 2 of

Chapter 6), and the responsibility matrix you developed in Chapter 5, now develop:

1. a planned resource utilization chart (similar to Figure 8.4); and
2. a resource profile (similar to Figure 8.5), for *each* resource, based on an as-soon-as-possible (ASAP) schedule.

GROUP ACTIVITY

Divide the course participants into the same groups of three or four as for the previous chapter's group activity and answer the questions listed above.

Note: This case study will continue in Chapter 9, so save the results of your work.

CASE STUDY 2

The Wedding

This case study is a continuation of the one from Chapters 5, 6, and 7.

CASE QUESTIONS

Using the revised schedule you calculated in response to item 1 in Chapter 7 to eliminate all the negative slack (or if you did not have any negative slack to eliminate, then use the schedule you calculated in item 2 of Chapter 6), and the responsibility matrix you developed in Chapter 5, now develop:

1. a planned resource utilization chart (similar to Figure 8.4); and
2. a resource profile (similar to Figure 8.5), for *each* resource, based on an as-soon-as-possible (ASAP) schedule.

GROUP ACTIVITY

Divide the course participants into the same groups of three or four as for the previous chapter's group activity and answer the questions listed above.

Note: This case study will continue in Chapter 9, so save the results of your work.

APPENDIX

Microsoft Project

In this appendix we will discuss how Microsoft Project can be used to support the techniques discussed in this chapter based on the Consumer Market Study example.

Figure 8A.1 shows a resource sheet for the consumer market study. To obtain the resource sheet, on the View menu click on Resource Sheet. As you learned in Chapter 5, this table allows you to enter information such as standard and overtime pay rates and specific work calendars for each of your resources. Note that for each worker in the Consumer Market Study pay rates have been entered. Resources other than human resources can also be entered into this table.

Additional information can be entered about each resource by double-clicking on a resource name in the Resource Name column. You will see the Resource Information window with 4 tabs: General, Costs, Notes, and Custom Fields, as shown in Figure 8A.2.

FIGURE 8A.1 *Resource Sheet*

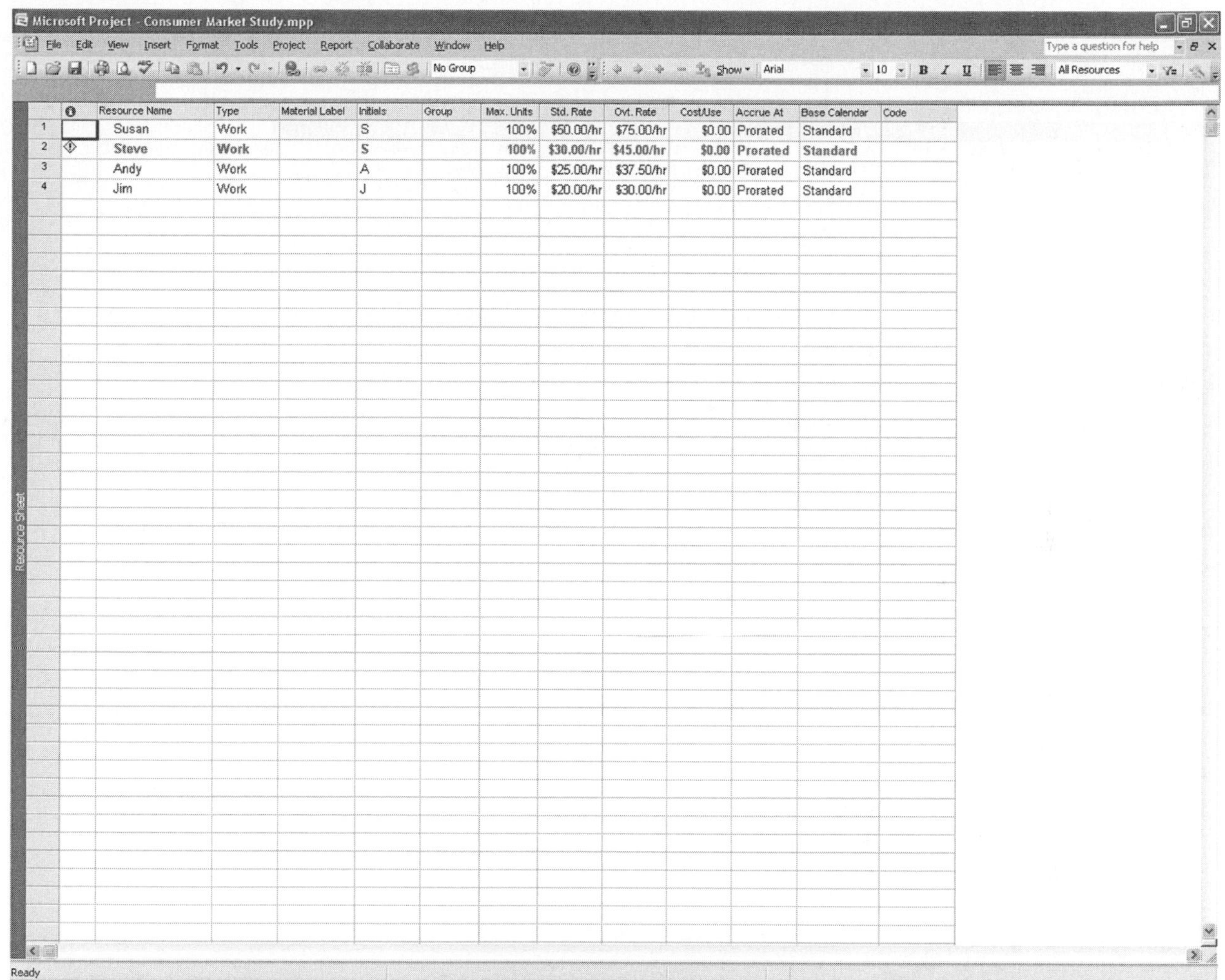

	Resource Name	Type	Material Label	Initials	Group	Max. Units	Std. Rate	Ovt. Rate	Cost/Use	Accrue At	Base Calendar	Code
1	Susan	Work		S		100%	$50.00/hr	$75.00/hr	$0.00	Prorated	Standard	
2	Steve	Work		S		100%	$30.00/hr	$45.00/hr	$0.00	Prorated	Standard	
3	Andy	Work		A		100%	$25.00/hr	$37.50/hr	$0.00	Prorated	Standard	
4	Jim	Work		J		100%	$20.00/hr	$30.00/hr	$0.00	Prorated	Standard	

To view various reports related to your resources, on the Report menu click on Reports, select Assignments, and click on Select. You will see four different types of assignment reports (Figure 8A.3).

From the Assignment Reports menu, select Overallocated Resources, and click on Select.

This report (Figure 8A.4.) provides information about any resources that are overallocated. In this example, note that Steve is assigned to Prepare Mailing Labels on Friday 3/6/09 and on Mon 3/9/09, for eight hours each day. He is also assigned to Print Questionnaire on the same days, eight hours each day. In other words, this report indicates that Steve is assigned to work 16 hours per day on both Friday (March 6) and Monday (March 9).

The Resource Usage report in Figure 8A.5 shows resource and task assignments on a weekly schedule. To produce this report, on the Report menu, click on Reports to open the Reports menu window. From the menu, click on Workload, and then click on Select. You should see a menu of 2 different types of Workload Reports: Task Usage and Resource Usage. Select Resource Usage, and then click on Select.

FIGURE 8A.2 *Resource Notes*

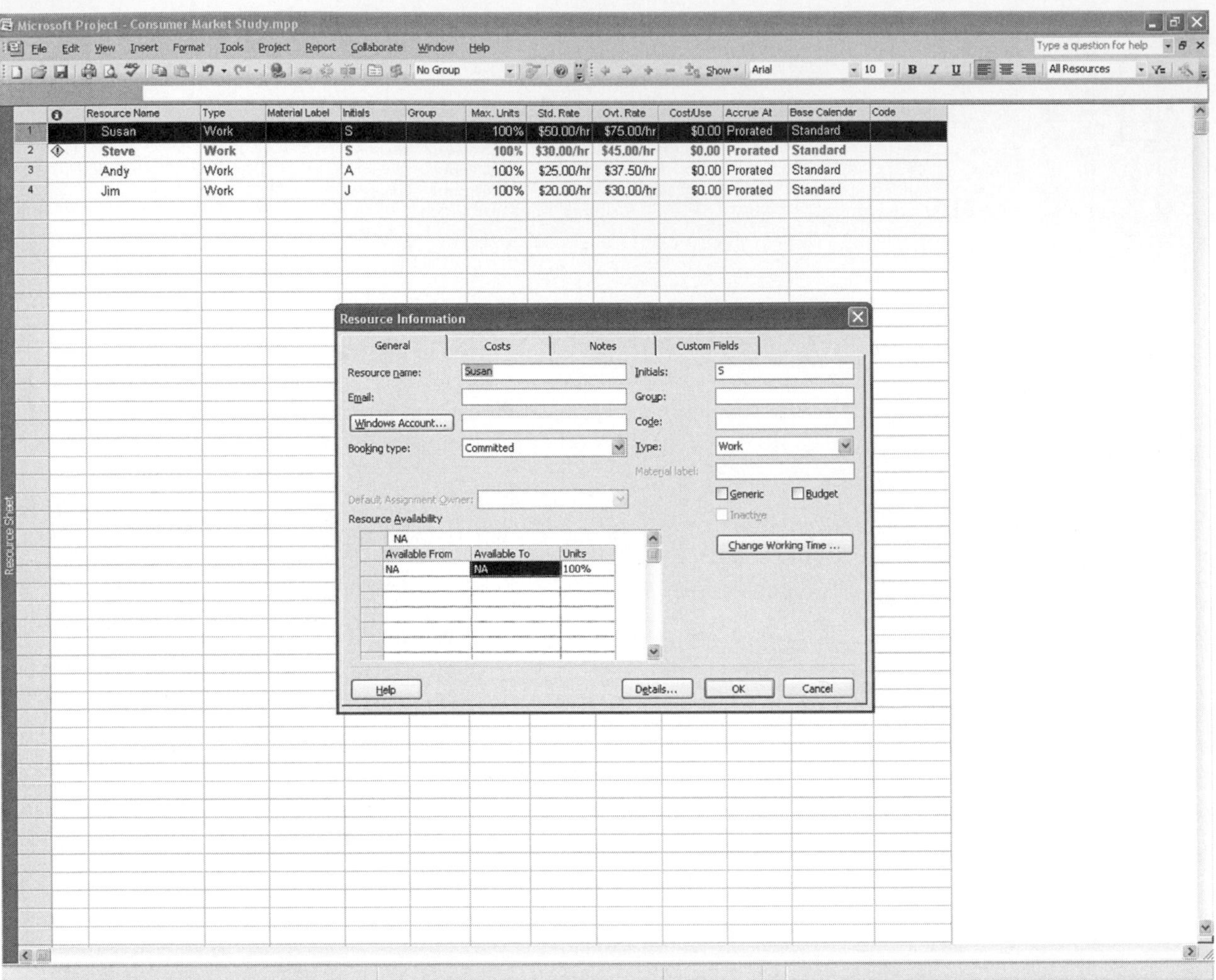

To perform Microsoft's version of resource leveling, on the Tools menu, click on Level Resources to open the Resource Leveling tool window (Figure 8A.6). In Microsoft Project, the resource-leveling tool basically just looks at overallocated resources and typically resolves those overallocations by extending the project deadline. When this leveling is done, Microsoft Project does not change resource assignments, and it does not change task information; it only delays tasks that have resources that are overallocated. The leveling can be performed by clicking on the Level Now button. Leveling can be removed by clicking on the Clear Leveling button.

To get a breakdown of all resources on your project along with the total hours of work, total costs, and peak utilization rates, on the View menu, click on Resource Sheet. Then on the View menu, point to Table, and then click on Summary (Figure 8A.7).

FIGURE 8A.3 *Assignment Reports*

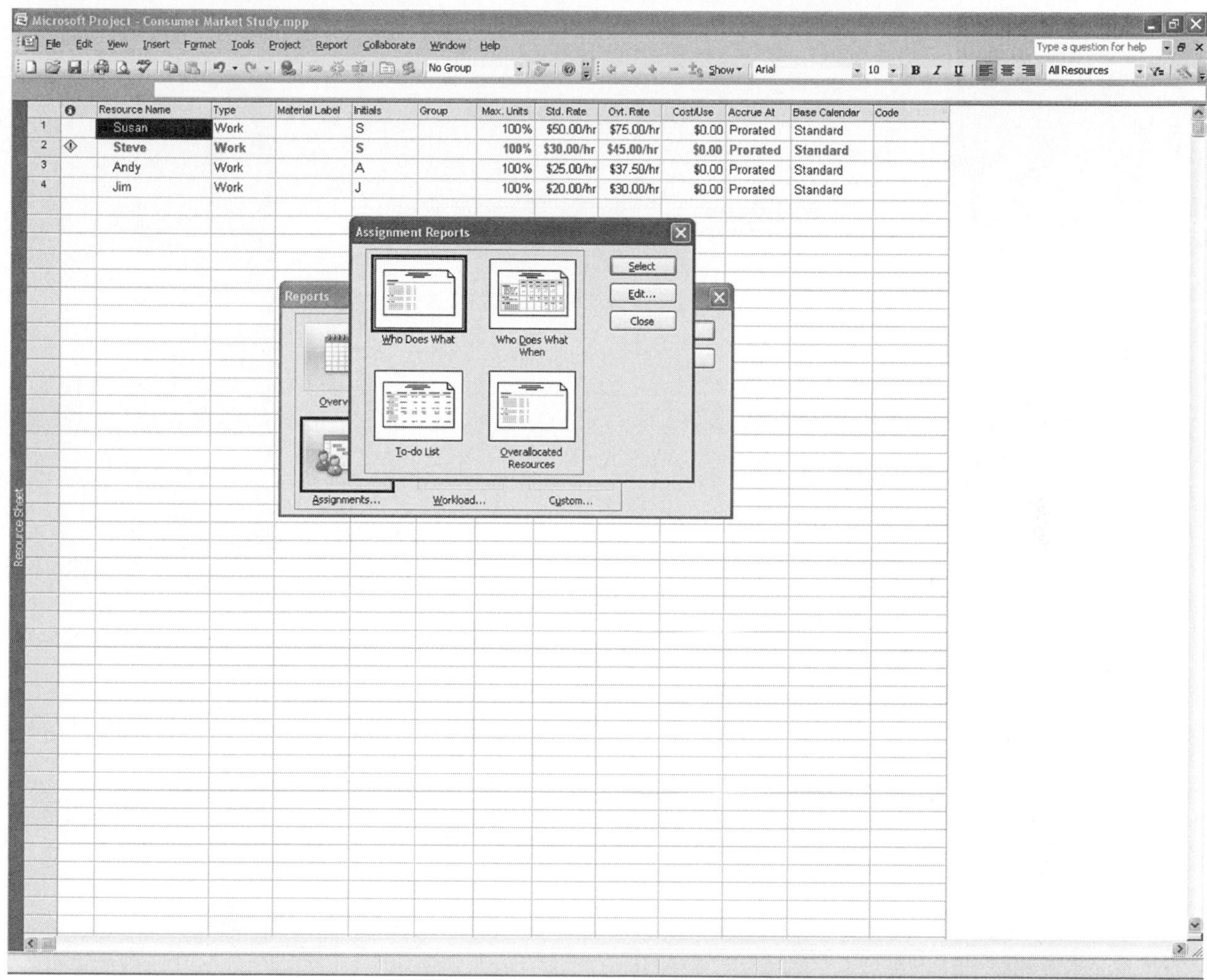

FIGURE 8A.4 *Overallocated Resources Report*

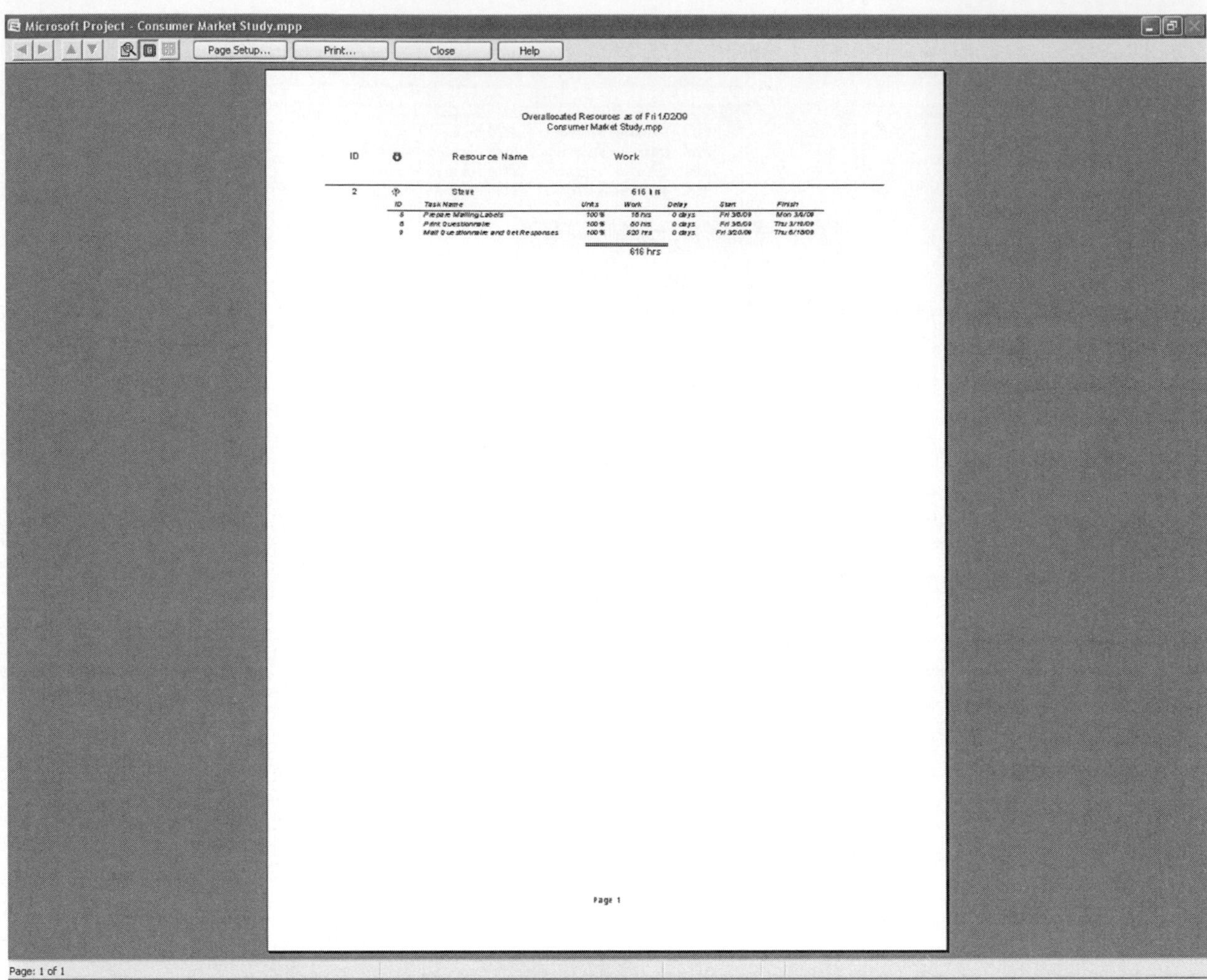

Overallocated Resources as of Fri 1/02/09
Consumer Market Study.mpp

ID	Resource Name	Work
2	Steve	616 hrs

ID	Task Name	Units	Work	Delay	Start	Finish
5	Prepare Mailing Labels	100%	16 hrs	0 days	Fri 3/6/09	Mon 3/9/09
6	Print Questionnaire	100%	80 hrs	0 days	Fri 3/6/09	Thu 3/19/09
9	Mail Questionnaire and Get Responses	100%	520 hrs	0 days	Fri 3/20/09	Thu 6/18/09
			616 hrs			

FIGURE 8A.5 *Resource Usage Report*

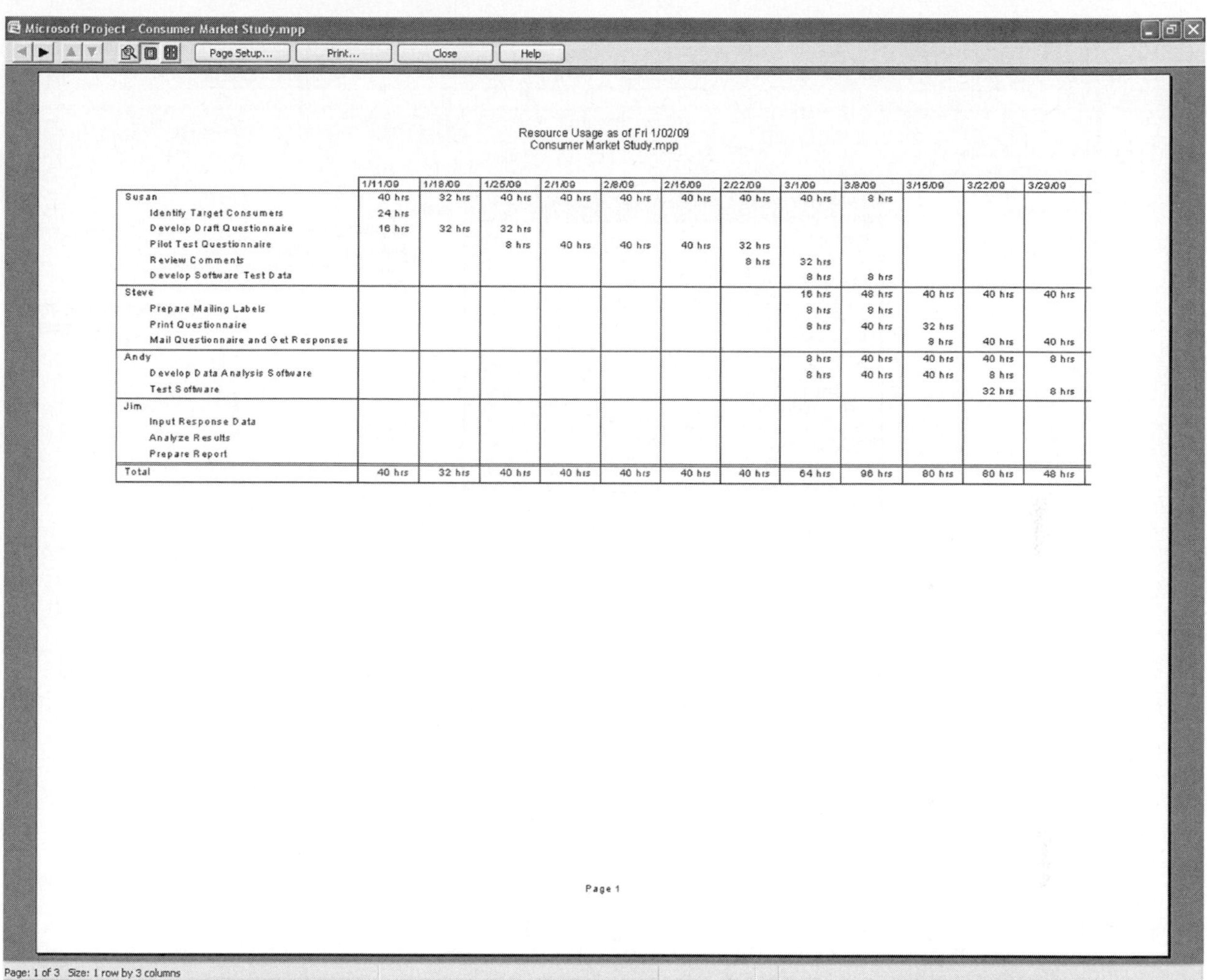

Resource Usage as of Fri 1/02/09
Consumer Market Study.mpp

	1/11/09	1/18/09	1/25/09	2/1/09	2/8/09	2/15/09	2/22/09	3/1/09	3/8/09	3/15/09	3/22/09	3/29/09
Susan	40 hrs	32 hrs	40 hrs	40 hrs	40 hrs	40 hrs	40 hrs	40 hrs	8 hrs			
Identify Target Consumers	24 hrs											
Develop Draft Questionnaire	16 hrs	32 hrs	32 hrs									
Pilot Test Questionnaire			8 hrs	40 hrs	40 hrs	40 hrs	32 hrs					
Review Comments							8 hrs	32 hrs				
Develop Software Test Data								8 hrs	8 hrs			
Steve								16 hrs	48 hrs	40 hrs	40 hrs	40 hrs
Prepare Mailing Labels								8 hrs	8 hrs			
Print Questionnaire								8 hrs	40 hrs	32 hrs		
Mail Questionnaire and Get Responses										8 hrs	40 hrs	40 hrs
Andy								8 hrs	40 hrs	40 hrs	40 hrs	8 hrs
Develop Data Analysis Software								8 hrs	40 hrs	40 hrs	8 hrs	
Test Software											32 hrs	8 hrs
Jim												
Input Response Data												
Analyze Results												
Prepare Report												
Total	40 hrs	32 hrs	40 hrs	40 hrs	40 hrs	40 hrs	40 hrs	64 hrs	96 hrs	80 hrs	80 hrs	48 hrs

FIGURE 8A.6 *Resource Leveling*

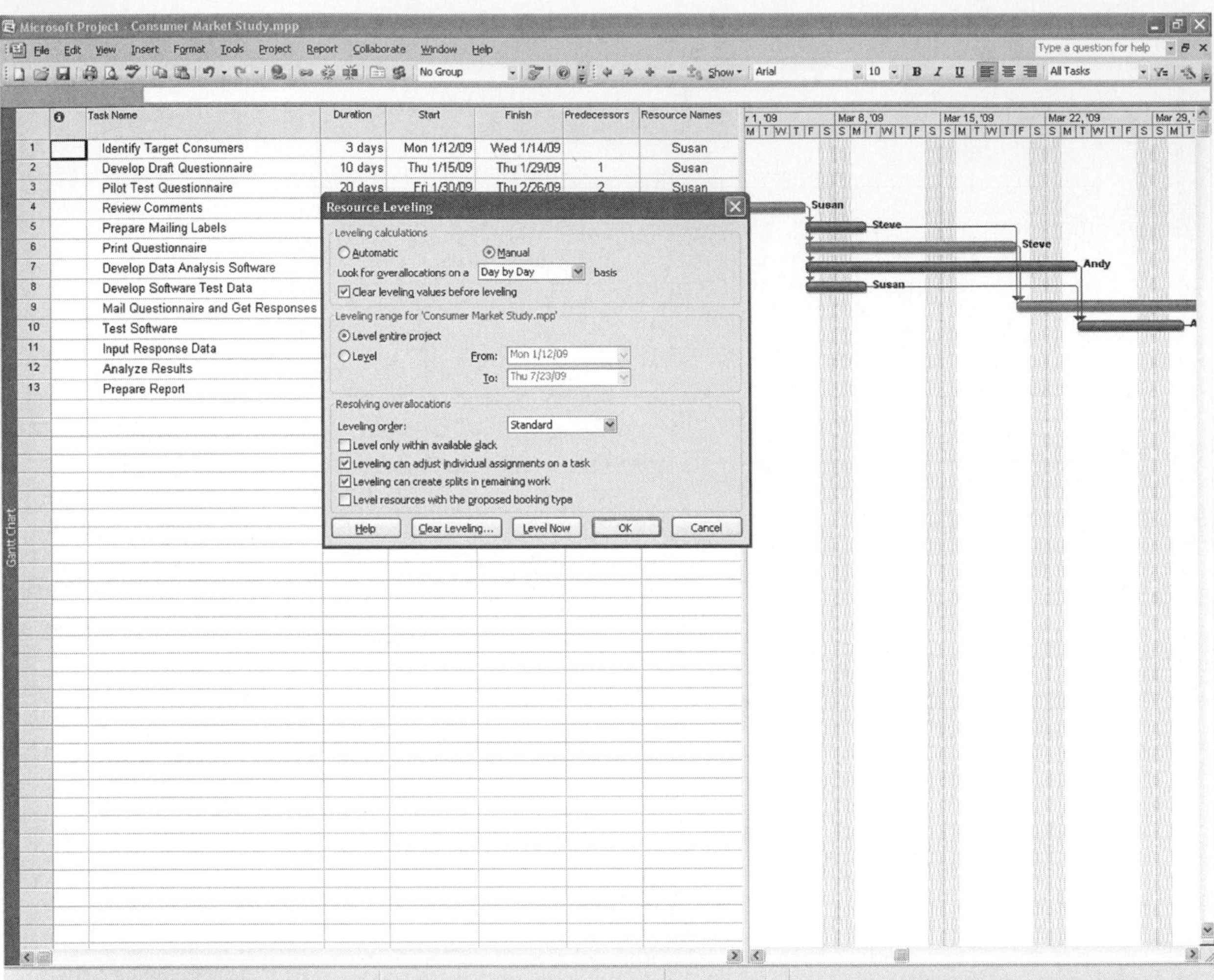

FIGURE 8A.7 *Resource Summary Table*

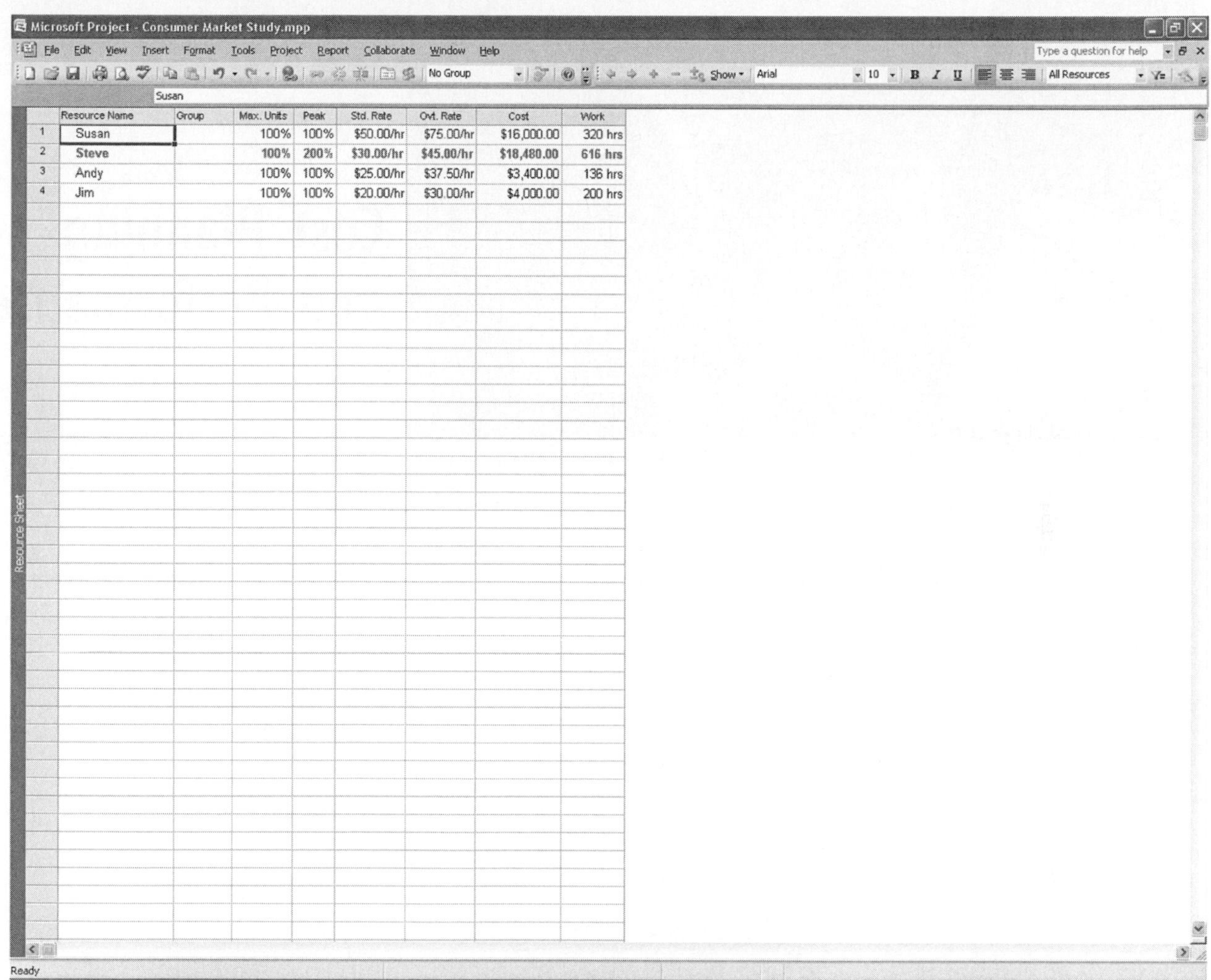

	Resource Name	Group	Max. Units	Peak	Std. Rate	Ovt. Rate	Cost	Work
1	Susan		100%	100%	$50.00/hr	$75.00/hr	$16,000.00	320 hrs
2	**Steve**		**100%**	**200%**	**$30.00/hr**	**$45.00/hr**	**$18,480.00**	**616 hrs**
3	Andy		100%	100%	$25.00/hr	$37.50/hr	$3,400.00	136 hrs
4	Jim		100%	100%	$20.00/hr	$30.00/hr	$4,000.00	200 hrs

© Kevin Lamarque/Reuters/Landov

CHAPTER 9

Cost Planning and Performance

Real World PROJECT MANAGEMENT

Feds Miscalculate Costs

According to the *Ocean County Observer*, by July 2005, the Department of Defense (DOD) knew that the data used to calculate costs of closing Fort Monmouth were incorrect and would lead to underestimating the project's cost by hundreds of millions of dollars. Fort Monmouth officials had written a 32-page memo warning the DOD about the inaccurate data submitted, and in several instances warned that the data would inevitably lead to erroneous calculations. However, the day before the decision was made to close the fort, the then Under Secretary of Defense guaranteed the panel's chairman in writing that there was "no evidence" to support any claims that the closing cost estimates were wrong.

DOD spokespeople refused to disclose information about who made the decision to disregard the accurate data despite repeated written requests from the news organization Gannett New Jersey, which publishes the *Ocean County Observer*. Under these pretenses, the Base Realignment and Closure (BRAC) commission voted in August 2005 to close the fort and move it to Aberdeen Proving Ground for a cost of about $780 million. The correct estimate to close the fort, however, could be closer to $1.5 billion, utilizing what was believed to be more accurate data.

Two years later, the DOD was forced to admit the miscalculation when its Fiscal Year 2008 budget estimated the total cost at about $1.5 billion for closing the fort. A one-time closing cost of $822 million was estimated using the faulty information. The DOD relayed this figure to Congress, which the BRAC commission later cut to $780 million when the fort's closure was approved. A Gannett New Jersey review revealed that a warning about the incorrect information was sent to the DOD on July 8, 2005, by Fort Monmouth officials.

The faulty data included a number of miscalculations about closing costs and projected savings. For example:

- The DOD projected that the move of the U.S. Military Academy Preparatory School to West Point, NY, would cost about $29 million; however, this cost was believed to be nearly $180 million below the actual cost.
- The cost of moving $650 million worth of specialized equipment to Aberdeen was also seriously underestimated.
- The amount of laboratory space needed at Aberdeen was grossly underestimated as 300,000 square feet, when in actuality, it would need to be at least 800,000 square feet.
- The DOD estimated that about 80 percent of the Fort's employees would need to relocate to Aberdeen. Fort officials, however, estimated that no more than 20 percent of employees would need to relocate.
- In addition, questions about whether or not electronic sensor "test-beds" could be re-established at Aberdeen were also raised, along with the cost of doing so.

Two of the nine BRAC commissioners on the panel had concerns and questions drafted to ask DOD officials regarding discrepancies in data, such as those listed above. The hearing's transcript did not reflect that those questions were asked. The Fort Monmouth memo was designed to help the DOD respond to 22 questions posed by the BRAC commission; however, DOD officials used only some of this information in their official response letter to the commission although documents reviewed by the press revealed that corrected financial data were also included in the Fort's memo. The DOD did not include this information in its response letter.

In the 2005 memo, the following information was included: corrected numbers for the cost of operating the base, the correct amount of square footage needed for construction at Aberdeen, costs for training personnel, and rationale for the closure of the Fort, with the closure estimated at $1.5 billion, nearly double the original number. DOD officials responded, however, that the implementation would begin yielding annual savings of $150M in FY 2012 due to reduced infrastructure overhead.

Bowman, B. and Brown, K., "Feds Ignored Ft. Monmouth Warnings on Data: Memo Advised Cost Estimates were Wrong," *Ocean County Observer*, July 15, 2007.

In addition to establishing a baseline schedule for a project, it's also necessary to develop a baseline budget. Project costs are estimated when a proposal is prepared for the project. Once a decision is made to go forward with the proposed project, it's necessary to prepare a budget, or plan, for how and when funds will be spent over the duration of the project. Once the project starts, it's important to monitor actual costs and work performance to ensure that everything is within budget. At regular intervals during the project, the following cost related parameters should be monitored:

- cumulative actual amount spent since the start of the project
- cumulative earned value of the work performed since the start of the project
- cumulative budgeted amount planned to be spent, based on the project schedule, from the start of the project

Comparisons must be made among these three parameters to evaluate whether the project is being accomplished within budget and whether the value of the work performed is in line with the actual amount expended.

If at any time during the project it is determined that the project is overrunning the budget or the value of the work performed isn't keeping up with the actual amount expended, corrective action must be taken. Once project costs get out of control, it will be very difficult to complete the project within budget. As you will see in this chapter, the key to effective cost control is to analyze cost performance on a timely and regular basis. Early identification of cost variances allows corrective action to be taken before the situation gets worse. In this chapter, you will learn how to regularly forecast, based on the actual amount spent and the value of the work performed, whether the entire project will be completed within budget. You will become familiar with

- items to be considered when estimating project cost
- preparation of a baseline budget, or plan, for how and when funds will be spent over the duration of the project

- cumulating actual costs
- determining the earned value of the work performed
- analyzing cost performance
- forecasting project cost at completion
- controlling project costs
- managing cash flow

PROJECT COST ESTIMATES

Cost planning starts with the proposal for the project. It is during the development of the proposal by the contractor or project team that project costs are estimated. In some cases, the proposal will indicate only the total bottom-line cost for the proposed project. In other cases, the customer may request a detailed breakdown of various costs. The cost section of a proposal may consist of tabulations of the contractor's estimated costs for such elements as the following:

1. *Labor.* This portion gives the estimated costs for the various classifications of people who are expected to work on the project, such as painters, designers, and computer programmers. It might include the estimated hours and hourly rate for each person or classification.
2. *Materials.* This portion gives the cost of materials the contractor or project team needs to purchase for the project, such as paint, lumber, wallpaper, shrubbery, carpeting, paper, art supplies, food, computers, or software packages.
3. *Subcontractors and consultants.* When contractors or project teams do not have the expertise or resources to do certain project tasks, they may outsource some of the work to subcontractors or consultants to perform those tasks. Examples of such tasks include designing a brochure, developing a training manual, developing software, or catering a reception.
4. *Equipment and facilities rental.* Sometimes the contractor may need special equipment, tools, or facilities solely for the project. The equipment may be too expensive to purchase if it's going to be used on only one or a few projects. In such cases, the contractor may decide to rent the equipment for as long as it is needed on the project.
5. *Travel.* If travel (other than local travel) is required during the project, the costs for travel (such as airfare), hotel rooms, and meals need to be included.
6. *Contingencies.* In addition to the above items, the contractor or project team may include an amount for contingencies to cover unexpected situations that may come up during the project. For example, items may have been overlooked when the project cost estimates were prepared, tasks may have to be redone because they did not work the first time, or the costs of labor (wages, salaries) or materials may escalate during a multiyear project.

It is good practice to have the person who will be responsible for the costs associated with the work make the cost estimates. This generates a commitment from the responsible person and prevents any bias that might result from having

Reinforce Your Learning

1. List the items for which costs should be estimated.

one person make all the cost estimates for the entire project. In large projects involving several hundred people, it is not practical to have every person provide cost estimates. In such cases, each organization or subcontractor involved may designate an experienced individual to make the cost estimates for which that organization or subcontractor will be responsible. If a contractor or organization has performed similar projects in the past and has kept records of the actual costs for various items, these historical data can be used as guides in estimating costs for the current project.

Cost estimates should be aggressive yet realistic. They should not be so heavily "padded" that they include contingency funds for every conceivable thing that might come up or go wrong. If cost estimates are overly conservative, the total estimated cost for the project is likely to be more than the customer is willing to pay—and higher than that of competing contractors. On the other hand, if cost estimates are overly optimistic and some unexpected expenditures arise, the contractor is likely to either lose money (on a fixed-price contract) or have to suffer the embarrassment of going back to the customer to request additional funds to cover cost overruns.

PROJECT BUDGETING

The project budgeting process involves two steps. First, the project cost estimate is allocated to the various work packages in the project work breakdown structure (see Chapter 5). Second, the budget for each work package is distributed over the duration of the work package so that it's possible to determine how much of its budget should have been spent at any point in time.

Allocating the Total Budgeted Cost

Allocating total project costs for the various elements—such as labor, materials, and subcontractors—to the appropriate work packages in the work breakdown structure will establish a **total budgeted cost (TBC)** for each work package. There are two approaches to establishing the TBC for each work package. One is a top-down approach, in which total project costs (for labor, materials, and so forth) are reviewed in relation to the work scope for each work package, and a proportion of the total project cost is allocated to each work package. The other is a bottom-up approach, which is based on an estimate of the costs for the detailed activities associated with each work package. The project cost is usually estimated when the proposal for the project is prepared, but detailed plans are not usually prepared at this time. At the start of the project, however, detailed activities are defined and a network plan is developed. Once detailed activities have been defined, time, resource, and cost estimates can be made for each activity. The TBC for each work package will be the sum of the costs of all the activities that make up that work package.

Reinforce Your Learning

2. The first step in the project budgeting process is to allocate the total project costs to each

____

in the work breakdown structure, thereby establishing a

____

____

for each work package.

Figure 9.1 illustrates the allocation of costs to individual work packages in the work breakdown structure for a $600,000 project. The amount allocated to each work package represents the TBC for completing all the activities associated with the work package. Whether the top-down or the bottom-up approach is used to establish the total budgeted cost for each work package, *when the budgets for all the work packages are summed, they cannot exceed the total project budgeted cost.*

FIGURE 9.1 *Work Breakdown Structure with Allocated Budgets*

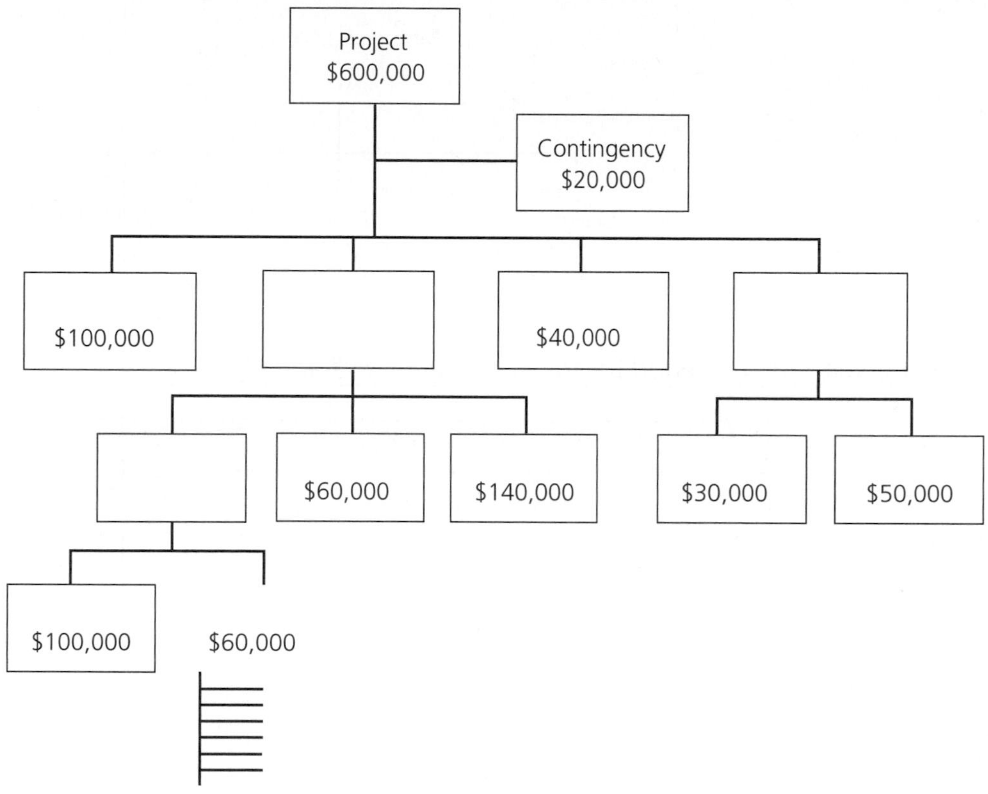

FIGURE 9.2 *Network Diagram for the Packaging Machine Project*

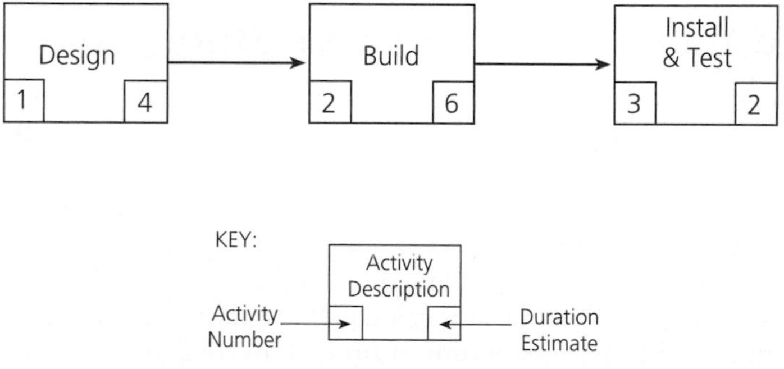

Figure 9.2 is a network diagram for a project to make a specialized automated packaging machine and install it at the customer's factory. The machine will insert the customer's product into boxes rolling by at high speed on a conveyor. *This project will be used as an example throughout the remainder of this chapter, so it has been kept simple.* The project consists of three activities, and the network diagram shows the duration (in weeks) for each activity. Figure 9.3 shows the work breakdown structure with the total budgeted cost for each work package.

FIGURE 9.3 *Work Breakdown Structure for the Packaging Machine Project*

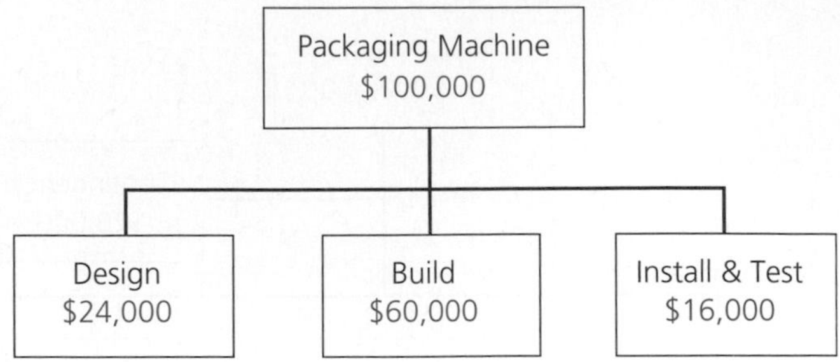

FIGURE 9.4 *Budgeted Cost by Period for the Packaging Machine Project*

		Week											
	TBC	1	2	3	4	5	6	7	8	9	10	11	12
Design	24	4	4	8	8								
Build	60					8	8	12	12	10	10		
Install & Test	16											8	8
Total	100	4	4	8	8	8	8	12	12	10	10	8	8
Cumulative		**4**	**8**	**16**	**24**	**32**	**40**	**52**	**64**	**74**	**84**	**92**	**100**

Amounts are in thousands of dollars.

Developing the Cumulative Budgeted Cost

Once a total budgeted cost has been established for each work package, the second step in the project budgeting process is to distribute each TBC over the duration of its work package. A cost is determined for each period, based on when the activities that make up the work package are scheduled to be performed. When the TBC for each work package is spread out by time period, it can be determined how much of the budget should have been spent at any point in time. This amount is calculated by adding up the budgeted costs for each time period up to that point in time. This total amount, known as the **cumulative budgeted cost (CBC)**, is the amount that was budgeted to accomplish the work that was scheduled to be performed up to that point in time. The CBC is the *baseline* that will be used in analyzing the cost performance of the project.

Reinforce Your Learning

3. Once a total budgeted cost has been established for each work package, the second step in the project budgeting process is to

__________ each TBC over the

__________ of its work package.

For the packaging machine project, Figure 9.4 shows how the TBC for each work package is spread over the time periods, based on the estimated durations shown in Figure 9.2. Also shown is the period-by-period budgeted cost for the entire project, as well as its cumulative budgeted cost (CBC). Figure 9.4 indicates that $32,000 was budgeted to accomplish the work that was scheduled to be performed through week 5. The periods over which budgeted costs are

FIGURE 9.5 ***Cumulative Budgeted Cost Curve for the Packaging Machine Project***

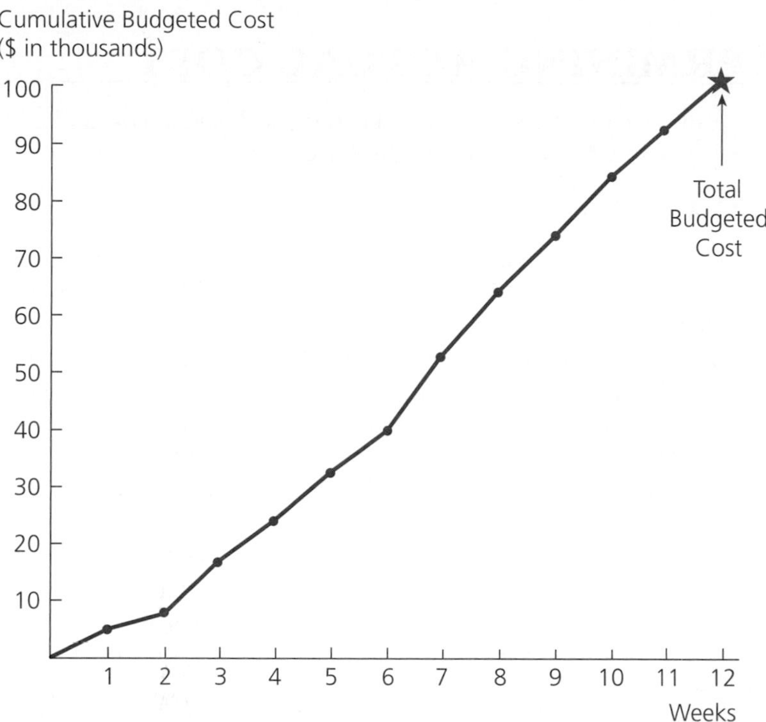

spread usually are determined by the earliest start and finish times for the activities in the baseline project schedule (adjusted to take into account resource leveling or resource-limited scheduling).

With the CBC values, it's possible to draw a cumulative budgeted cost curve to illustrate budgeted expenditures over the duration of the project. Figure 9.5 shows the cumulative budgeted cost curve for the packaging machine project. Although the table in Figure 9.4 and the cost curve in Figure 9.5 display cumulative budgeted cost for the total project, a similar cumulative table and curve can be made for each work package, if desired.

The CBC for the entire project or each work package provides a baseline against which actual cost and work performance can be compared at any time during the project. It would be misleading to merely compare actual amounts expended to the total budgeted cost for the project or work package, as cost performance will always look good as long as actual costs are below the TBC. In the packaging machine example, we would think that the project cost was under control as long as the total actual cost was below $100,000. But what happens when one day the total actual cost exceeds the $100,000 TBC, and the project isn't finished? It's too late to control the project so as to complete it within budget—the project budget has been exceeded and work remains to be done, so more costs have to be incurred to complete the project!

To avoid such nightmares, it's important to use the cumulative budgeted cost, rather than the total budgeted cost, as the standard against which actual cost is compared. This way, if actual cost begins to exceed the CBC, corrective action can be taken before it's too late.

Reinforce Your Learning

4. The ______________ ______________ ______________ is the amount that was budgeted to accomplish the ______________ that was scheduled to be performed up to that point in time.

For large projects involving many work packages or activities, project management software is available that will assist with project budgeting.

DETERMINING ACTUAL COST

Once the project starts, it's necessary to keep track of actual cost and committed cost so that they can be compared to the CBC.

Actual Cost

To keep track of **actual cost** on a project, it's necessary to set up a system to collect, on a regular and timely basis, data on funds actually expended. Such a system might include procedures and forms for gathering data. An accounting structure should be established based on the work breakdown structure numbering system so that each item of actual cost can be charged to the appropriate work package. Each work package's actual cost can then be totaled and compared to its CBC.

Weekly timesheets are often used to collect actual labor costs. Individuals working on the project indicate the numbers of the work packages on which they worked and the number of hours they spent on each work package. These hours are then multiplied by the hourly cost rate for each individual to determine the actual dollar cost. In companies using a matrix organization structure, individuals may be assigned to several projects concurrently. In such cases, the individual has to indicate the proper project number as well as the work package number on the timesheet to ensure that the actual labor costs are charged to the appropriate project. When invoices are received for materials or services that were purchased for use on the project, they, too, have to be charged to the proper work package number.

Committed Cost

In many projects, large dollar amounts are expended for materials or services (subcontractors, consultants) that are used over a period longer than one cost reporting period. These **committed costs** need to be treated in a special way so that the system periodically assigns a portion of their total cost to actual cost, rather than waiting until the materials or services are finished to charge to the total actual costs.

Committed costs are also known as *commitments* or *encumbered costs*. Costs are committed when an item (material, subcontractor) is ordered, usually by means of a purchase order, even though actual payment may take place at some later time—when the material or service has been completed, delivered, and invoiced. When a purchase order is issued to a supplier or subcontractor for an item, the funds for that purchase order are committed and are no longer available to be spent on other project activities. The committed amount must be considered as encumbered, or set aside, because funds will be needed to pay the supplier or subcontractor at some time in the future, when the material or service is delivered and an invoice is received. For example, if you hire a contractor to paint your home for $5,000, you have committed $5,000, even though you may not actually pay the contractor until the work is finished.

To permit a realistic comparison of actual cost to cumulative budgeted cost, portions of the committed amount should be assigned to actual cost while the work is being performed. In some cases, the supplier or subcontractor may require progress payments, rather than waiting until all the work is finished before being paid. In such situations, when an invoice is received from the supplier or subcontractor for a partial or progress payment, the amount of that invoice should be charged to the actual cost for the proper work package. Suppose a project to develop a computerized inventory control system includes a subcontract with a consultant to develop six different software modules for $12,000. As each module is completed and delivered, the consultant submits an invoice for $2,000. When the invoice is received, the $2,000 should be considered an actual cost.

Now let's consider a different scenario, in which the subcontractor or supplier does not issue invoices for partial or progress payments, but rather waits until all the work is finished and delivered and then submits an invoice for the total amount. Even in such a case, a portion of the total committed amount should be periodically assigned as an actual cost, because work is actually being performed. For example, suppose a project to remodel an office building includes a subcontract with a heating contractor to install new heating units in each office throughout the building over four months for $80,000. Even though the subcontractor will submit only one invoice for $80,000 when all the work has been completed, $20,000 should be assigned to actual cost each month, because work is actually being performed.

Comparing Actual Cost to Budgeted Cost

As data are collected on actual cost, including portions of any committed cost, they need to be totaled by work packages so that they can be compared to the cumulative budgeted cost. For the packaging machine project, Figure 9.6 shows actual cost by time period for each work package through week 8. Also shown is the period-by-period actual cost for the entire project, as well as the **cumulative actual cost (CAC)**.

Figure 9.6 indicates that at the end of week 8, $68,000 has actually been expended on this project. The CBC in Figure 9.4 reveals that only $64,000 was budgeted to have been spent by the end of week 8. There is a variance of $4,000-the project is overrunning its budget.

FIGURE 9.6 *Actual Cost by Period for the Packaging Machine Project*

	Week								Total Expended
	1	2	3	4	5	6	7	8	
Design	2	5	9	5	1				22
Build				2	8	10	14	12	46
Install & Test									0
Total	2	5	9	7	9	10	14	12	**68**
Cumulative	**2**	**7**	**16**	**23**	**32**	**42**	**56**	**68**	**68**

Amounts are in thousands of dollars.

FIGURE 9.7 ***Cumulative Budgeted and Actual Cost for the Packaging Machine Project***

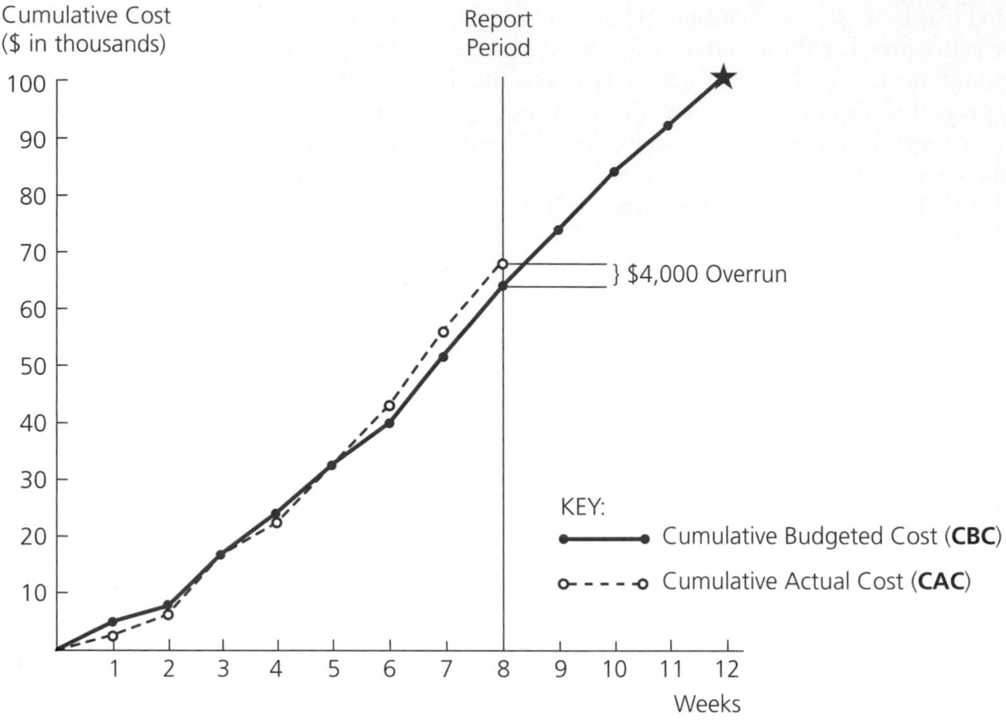

Reinforce Your Learning

5. Look at Figures 9.4 and 9.6. How much did the "Design" work package and the "Build" work package each contribute to the $4,000 cost overrun at the end of week 8?

	Amount	Overrun or Underrun?
Design	______	______
Build	______	______

With the CAC values, it's possible to draw a cumulative actual cost curve. Drawing this curve on the same axes as the cumulative budgeted cost curve, as shown in Figure 9.7, provides a good visual comparison.

Although the table in Figure 9.6 and the cost curves in Figure 9.7 display data for the total project, similar cumulative tables and curves can be made for each work package, if desired. Generating individual curves will help pinpoint the particular work packages that are contributing to the overrun.

DETERMINING THE VALUE OF WORK PERFORMED

Consider a project that involves painting 10 similar rooms over 10 days (1 room per day) for a total budgeted cost of $2,000. The budget is $200 per room. At of the end of day 5, you determine that $1,000 has actually been spent. When you compare expenditures to the cumulative budgeted cost of $1,000 for five days, it looks as if actual costs are tracking the budget. But that's only part of the story.

What if, at the end of day 5, only 3 rooms have been painted? That wouldn't be very good, because half of the budget has been spent on only 3 of the 10 rooms that need to be painted. On the other hand, what if, at the end of day 5, 6 rooms have been painted? That would be excellent, because only half of the budget has been spent and 6 of the 10 rooms have been painted. This example introduces the concept of *earned value* of the work performed. The fact that half the budget was actually expended doesn't necessarily mean that half the work was performed. If the work performed isn't keeping up with the actual cost, there's trouble, even if the actual cost is in line with the CBC.

Earned value (EV), the value of the work actually performed, is a key parameter that must be determined throughout the project. Comparing the cumulative actual cost to the cumulative budgeted cost tells only part of the story and can lead to wrong conclusions about the status of the project.

Just as it's important to track actual cost for a project, it's also necessary to set up a companion system to collect data on a regular and timely basis regarding the earned value of the work performed on each work package. Determining the earned value involves collecting data on the **percent complete** for each work package and then converting this percentage to a dollar amount by multiplying the TBC of the work package by the percent complete.

The percent complete data usually are obtained each period from the individual responsible for the work package. In many cases, the estimate is subjective. It's extremely important that the person who comes up with the percent complete estimate make an honest assessment of the work performed relative to the entire work scope for the work package. There often seems to be an inclination to be overly optimistic and make a high percent complete estimate too soon. For example, suppose the team leader of a work package with a 20-week duration reports, at the end of week 10, that the work is 90 percent complete. If this report is unrealistic, it will create a false sense of security that work performance is outpacing actual cost. An unrealistic report will lead the project manager to conclude that project performance is better than it actually is and keep her or him from taking any corrective action. As the percent complete begins to stretch out while the actual cost continues to pile up, it will appear that project performance is deteriorating over the final weeks. By week 20, the percent complete may be only 96 percent and the actual cost may have exceeded the cumulative budgeted cost. If corrective action had been taken earlier, problems could have been prevented. One way to prevent premature inflated percent complete estimates is to keep the work packages or activities small in terms of scope and duration. It's important that the person estimating the percent complete not only assess how much work has been performed but also consider what work remains to be done.

Once the percent complete data have been gathered, the earned value can be calculated. This is done by multiplying the total budgeted cost for the work package by its percent complete. For example, in the project involving painting 10 rooms for \$2,000, if three rooms were completed, it's safe to say that 30 percent of the work has been performed. The earned value is

$$0.30 \times \$2{,}000 = \$600$$

Let's now return to the example of the packaging machine project. At the end of week 8, the "Build" work package is the only one in progress, and it's estimated to be 50 percent complete. The "Design" work package had previously been finished, so it's 100 percent complete; and the "Install & Test" work package hasn't yet started, so it's 0 percent complete. Figure 9.8 shows the cumulative percent complete estimates reported during each of the first 8 weeks for each work package. Figure 9.9 shows the associated **cumulative earned value (CEV)** for each work package, calculated by multiplying each percent complete by the TBC for the work package. Figure 9.9 indicates that, at the end of week 8, the earned value of the work performed on this project is \$54,000.

Reinforce Your Learning

6. Cumulative earned value is calculated by first determining the

____

for each work package and then multiplying it by the

____

for the work package.

FIGURE 9.8 ***Cumulative Percent Complete by Period for the Packaging Machine Project***

	Week							
	1	2	3	4	5	6	7	8
Design	10	25	80	90	100	100	100	100
Build	0	0	0	5	15	25	40	50
Install & Test	0	0	0	0	0	0	0	0

Amounts are cumulative percentages complete.

FIGURE 9.9 ***Cumulative Earned Value by Period for the Packaging Machine Project***

		Week							
	TBC	1	2	3	4	5	6	7	8
Design	24	2.4	6	19.2	21.6	24	24	24	24
Build	60				3	9	15	24	30
Install & Test	16								
Cumulative	100	**2.4**	**6**	**19.2**	**24.6**	**33**	**39**	**48**	**54**

Amounts are in thousands of dollars.

With the CEV values, it's possible to draw a cumulative earned value curve. Drawing this curve on the same axes as the cumulative budgeted cost and cumulative actual cost curves, as shown in Figure 9.10, provides an excellent visual comparison. Although the cost curves in Figure 9.10 illustrate the CBC, CAC, and CEV for the entire project, similar curves can be made for each work package, if desired. Generating individual curves will help identify how much each work package is affecting project cost performance.

COST PERFORMANCE ANALYSIS

The following four cost-related measures are used to analyze project cost performance:

- TBC (total budgeted cost)
- CBC (cumulative budgeted cost)
- CAC (cumulative actual cost)
- CEV (cumulative earned value)

FIGURE 9.10 ***Cumulative Budgeted, Actual, and Earned Value for the Packaging Machine Project***

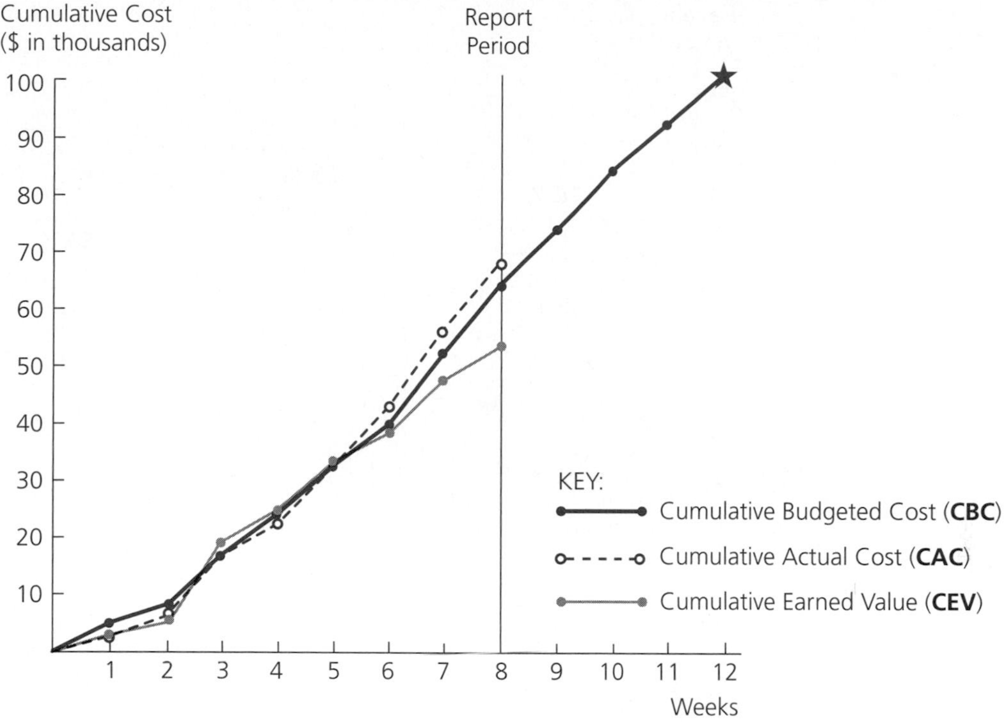

They are used to determine whether the project is being performed within budget and whether the value of the work performed is in line with the actual cost.

In analyzing Figures 9.4, 9.6, and 9.9 for the packaging machine project at the end of week 8, we see that

- $64,000 was budgeted through the end of week 8 to perform all the work scheduled to be performed during the first 8 weeks
- $68,000 was actually expended by the end of week 8
- $54,000 was the earned value of work actually performed by the end of week 8

Reinforce Your Learning

7. List the four cost-related measures used to analyze project cost performance.

A quick analysis indicates that the actual cost is exceeding the budgeted cost. Aggravating the situation further is the fact that the value of the work performed isn't keeping up with the actual cost.

It is a good idea to plot CBC, CAC, and CEV curves on the same axes, as shown in Figure 9.10, at the end of each report period. This will reveal any trends toward improving or deteriorating cost performance.

Another way to approach the situation is to analyze progress in terms of percentages of the total budgeted cost of $100,000 for the project. Using the format in Figure 9.11, we could say that, at the end of week 8,

- 64 percent of the total budget for the project was to have been spent to perform all the work scheduled to be performed during the first 8 weeks
- 68 percent of the total budget was actually expended by the end of week 8
- 54 percent of the total project work was actually performed by the end of week 8

FIGURE 9.11 *Packaging Machine Project Status as of Week 8*

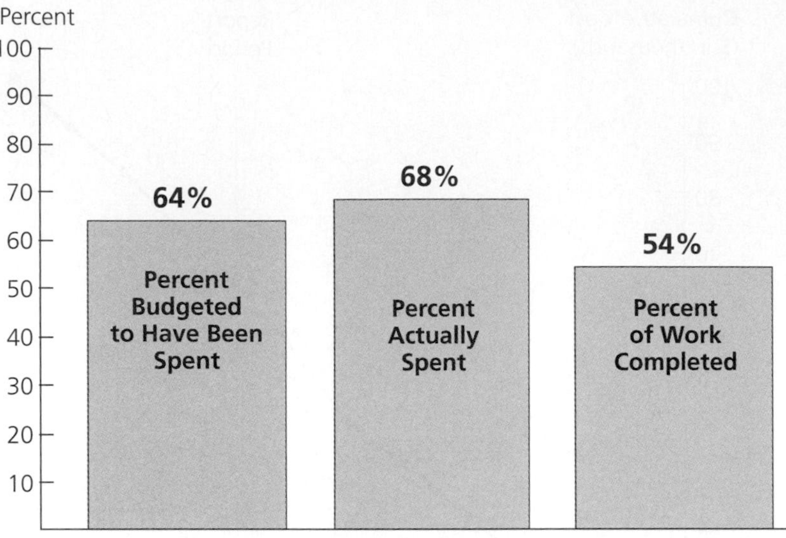

In addition to plotting the CBC, CAC, and CEV curves on the same axes, it may be useful to tabulate or draw curves for the percentages. This, too, will indicate any trends toward improving or deteriorating cost performance.

Cost Performance Index

Another indicator of cost performance is the **cost performance index (CPI)**, which is a measure of the cost efficiency with which the project is being performed. The formula for determining the CPI is

$$\text{Cost performance index} = \frac{\text{Cumulative earned value}}{\text{Cumulative actual cost}}$$

$$\text{CPI} = \frac{\text{CEV}}{\text{CAC}}$$

Reinforce Your Learning

8. What is the cost performance index for the "Design" work package in the packaging machine project at the end of week 5?

In the packaging machine project, the CPI as of week 8 is given by

$$\text{CPI} = \frac{\$54{,}000}{\$68{,}000} = 0.79$$

This ratio indicates that for every $1.00 actually expended, only $0.79 of earned value was received. Trends in the CPI should be watched carefully. When the CPI goes below 1.0 or gradually gets smaller, corrective action should be taken.

Cost Variance

Another indicator of cost performance is **cost variance (CV)**, which is the difference between the cumulative earned value of the work performed and the cumulative actual cost. The formula for determining the cost variance is

$$\text{CV} = \text{CEV} - \text{CAC}$$

Real World **PROJECT MANAGEMENT**

A $4 Million Landscape Project

Despite the fact that the total cost of fixing the massive landslide problem next to Rancho Santa Fe Road in Carlsbad, California, had risen from $1 million to almost $4 million, city officials remained optimistic and believed they had now made positive strides toward fixing the problem. Deputy City Engineer Skip Hammann explained that conditions resulting from the Agua Dulce landslide site had been stabilized and that progress toward recovery had been made.

The landslide has been a challenge for officials and private contractors for quite some time as it threatened two homes and a major commuter route. At the Agua Dulce landslide site, when work had begun on building a retaining wall the project was estimated to cost less than $1 million. However, once work had begun the City realized they underestimated the scope and complexity of the project and began adding additional costs. They believe they have finalized their project costs after adding in another $1.95 million on top of other costs already included, bringing the new total to almost $3.9 million.

Contractors have tried several times to build walls that could hold the soil. However, the landslides kept twisting the metal rods that would have supported the retaining walls. In another attempt at recovery, the City drilled holes in the hillside and pumped water out to reduce the water that made the hill soggy. The hillside eventually dried out slowly, and the work on the retaining wall concluded a few months later, leaving city officials feeling like they found a viable solution.

Russell Kurtz, owner of one of the mudslide-damaged homes, believed the City finally stopped the soil from moving. He had been living temporarily in a rental home for sometime. The backyard of his house was basically non-existent as a result of all of the work being done on the hillside—all of the trees, flowers, and grass had been stripped away. In addition, his pool also needed to be resurfaced because of debris from the construction work on the retaining walls. However, despite these inconveniences, he remained optimistic that the City and contractors have the landslide situation under control.

Meanwhile across town, another project has been started on another landslide site, the Marbella landslide. After extended legal battles, the La Costa de Marbella Homeowners Association decided that they would work with the City to revise their landslide agreement. Attorney Patrick Catalano represented the homeowners' association and accused the City of not working quickly enough to restore the Marbella site.

Officials of the city fired back and accused Catalano of delaying the job in order to incur more costs upon the City. The new and revised agreement stated details of exactly what type of work needed to be done. It also stated that repairs would cost no more than $1.2 million. Catalano pushed for the revisions in order to safeguard the assets of the residents, while the City's attorney, Brad Bartlett, stated that the revisions didn't change the work the city originally planned to do. According to the City, the next step was to meet with contractors to determine when repair work could begin.

City officials are hoping they won't face the same kind of project cost overruns that happened on the Agua Dulce landslide!

Henry, B., "City to Spend $4 Million on Landslide Project," *North County Times*, August 30, 2007.

Like the CPI, this indicator shows the gap between the value of the work performed and the actual cost, but the CV is expressed in terms of dollars.

Reinforce Your Learning

9. What is the cost variance for the "Build" work package in the packaging machine project at the end of week 8?

In the packaging machine project, the cost variance as of week 8 is given by

$$CV = \$54{,}000 - \$68{,}000 = -\$14{,}000$$

This calculation indicates that the value of the work performed through week 8 is $14,000 less than the amount actually expended. It's another indication that the work performed is not keeping pace with the actual cost.

For analyzing cost performance, it's important that the data collected all be as current as possible and all be based on the same reporting period. For example, if the costs are collected as of the 30th of each month, then the percent complete estimates for the work packages should be based on work performed through the 30th of the month.

COST FORECASTING

Based on analysis of *actual* cost performance throughout the project, it's possible to forecast what the total costs will be at the completion of the project or work package. There are three different methods for determining the **forecasted cost at completion (FCAC)**.

The first method assumes that the work to be performed on the remaining portion of the project or work package will be done at the same rate of efficiency as the work performed so far. The formula for calculating the FCAC using this first method is

$$\text{Forecasted cost at completion} = \frac{\text{Total budgeted cost}}{\text{Cost performance index}}$$

$$\text{FCAC} = \frac{\text{TBC}}{\text{CPI}}$$

For the packaging machine project, the forecasted cost at completion is given by

$$\text{FCAC} = \frac{\$100{,}000}{0.79} = \$126{,}582$$

Reinforce Your Learning

10. Using the first forecasting method described, calculate the forecasted cost at completion for the "Build" work package in the packaging machine project.

As of week 8, the project has a cost efficiency, or CPI, of 0.79, and if the remainder of the project continues to be performed at this same efficiency rate, then the entire project will actually cost $126,582. If this forecast is correct, there will be an overrun of $26,582 beyond the total budgeted cost for the project of $100,000.

A second method for determining the forecasted cost at completion assumes that, regardless of the efficiency rate the project or work package has experienced in the past, the work to be performed on the remaining portion of the project or work package will be done according to budget. The formula for calculating the FCAC using this method is

$$\begin{matrix}\text{Forecasted}\\\text{cost at}\\\text{completion}\end{matrix} = \begin{matrix}\text{Cumlative}\\\text{actual}\\\text{cost}\end{matrix} + \left(\begin{matrix}\text{Total}\\\text{budgeted}\\\text{cost}\end{matrix} - \begin{matrix}\text{Cumulative}\\\text{earned}\\\text{value}\end{matrix}\right)$$

$$\text{FCAC} = \text{CAC} + (\text{TBC} - \text{CEV})$$

For the packaging machine project, the forecasted cost at completion is given by

$$\begin{aligned} \text{FCAC} &= \$68{,}000 + (\$100{,}000 - \$54{,}000) \\ &= \$68{,}000 + \$46{,}000 \\ &= \$114{,}000 \end{aligned}$$

As of week 8, the cumulative actual cost was $68,000, but the cumulative earned value of the work performed was only $54,000. Therefore, work with an earned value of $46,000 needs to be performed to complete the project. This method assumes that the remaining work will be performed at an efficiency rate of 1.0, even though the project has been experiencing an efficiency rate of 0.79 as of the end of week 8. This method results in a forecasted cost at completion of $114,000, a forecasted overrun of $14,000 beyond the total budgeted cost for the project.

A third method for determining the forecasted cost at completion is to re-estimate the costs for all the remaining work to be performed and then add this reestimate to the cumulative actual cost. The formula for determining the FCAC using this third method is

$$\text{FCAC} = \text{CAC} + \text{Re-estimate of remaining work to be performed}$$

This approach can be time-consuming, but it may be necessary if the project experiences persistent deviations from the plan or if there are extensive changes.

Reinforce Your Learning

11. Using the second forecasting method described, calculate the forecasted cost at completion for the "Build" work package in the packaging machine project.

As part of the regular cost performance analysis, the FCAC for the project should be calculated, using the first or second method described above. The forecasted overrun or underrun can then be determined. When cost is forecasted to the completion of the project or work package, a small variance in a given reporting period can expand to a much greater overrun, signaling the need for corrective action.

COST CONTROL

The key to effective cost control is to analyze cost performance on a regular and timely basis. It's crucial that cost variances and inefficiencies be identified early so that corrective action can be taken before the situation gets worse. Once project costs get out of control, it may be very difficult to complete the project within budget.

Cost control involves the following:

1. Analyzing cost performance to determine which work packages may require corrective action
2. Deciding what specific corrective action should be taken
3. Revising the project plan, including time and cost estimates, to incorporate the planned corrective action

The cost performance analysis should include identifying those work packages that have a negative cost variance or a cost performance index of less than 1.0. Also, those work packages for which the CV or CPI has deteriorated since the prior reporting period should be identified. A concentrated effort must be applied to the work packages with negative variances, to reduce cost or improve the efficiency of the work performed. The amount of CV should determine the priority for applying these concentrated efforts; that is, the work package with the largest negative CV should be given top priority.

When evaluating work packages that have a negative cost variance, you should focus on taking corrective actions to reduce the costs of two types of activities:

Reinforce Your Learning

12. In analyzing cost performance, it's important to identify all of the work packages that have a ______________ cost variance or a cost performance index of less than ______________.

1. *Activities that will be performed in the near term.* Don't plan to reduce the costs of activities that are scheduled sometime in the distant future. You'll get more timely feedback on the effects of corrective actions if they are done in the near term. If you put off corrective actions until some point in the distant future, the negative cost variance may deteriorate even further before the corrective actions are ever implemented. As the project progresses, less and less time remains in which corrective actions can be taken.
2. *Activities that have a large cost estimate.* Taking corrective measures that reduce the cost of a $20,000 activity by 10 percent will have a larger impact than eliminating a $300 activity. Usually, the larger the estimated cost for an activity, the greater the opportunity for a large cost reduction.

Reinforce Your Learning

13. When evaluating work packages that have a negative cost variance, you should focus on taking corrective actions to reduce the costs of activities that will be performed in the ______________ term and those that have a ______________ cost estimate.

There are various ways to reduce the costs of activities. One way is to substitute less expensive materials that meet the required specifications. Maybe another supplier can be found who can supply the same material but at a lower cost. Another approach is to assign a person with greater expertise or more experience to perform or help with the activity to get it done more efficiently.

Reducing the scope or requirements for the work package or specific activities is another way to reduce costs. For example, a contractor might decide to put only one coat of paint on a room rather than two coats, as originally planned. Increasing productivity through improved methods or technology is yet another approach to reducing costs. For example, by renting automatic paint spraying equipment, a contractor may substantially lower the cost and time of painting a room below what it would be for painters working with rollers and brushes.

In many cases, there will be a trade-off—reducing cost variances will involve a reduction in project scope or a delay in the project schedule. If the negative cost variance is very large, a substantial reduction in the work scope or quality may be required to get the project back within budget. The scope, budget, schedule, or quality of the overall project could be in jeopardy. In some cases, the customer and contractor or project team may have to acknowledge that one or more of these elements cannot be achieved. This could result in the customer's providing additional funds to cover the forecasted overrun, or it could result in a contract dispute over who caused the cost overrun and who should pay for it—the customer or the contractor.

The key to effective cost control is aggressively addressing negative cost variances and cost inefficiencies as soon as they are identified, rather than hoping that things will get better as the project goes on. Cost problems that are addressed early will have less impact on scope and schedule. Once costs get out of control, getting back within budget is likely to require reducing the project scope or extending the project schedule.

Even when projects have only positive cost variances, it's important not to let the cost variances deteriorate. If a project's cost performance is positive, a concentrated effort should be made to keep it that way. Once a project gets in trouble with cost performance, it becomes difficult to get it back on track.

MANAGING CASH FLOW

It is important to manage the cash flow on a project. Managing cash flow involves making sure that sufficient payments are received from the customer in time so that you have enough money to cover the costs of performing the project—employee payroll, charges for materials, invoices from subcontractors, and travel expenses, for example.

The key to managing cash flow is to ensure that cash comes in faster than it goes out. If sufficient cash isn't available to meet expenses, money must be borrowed. Borrowing increases project cost because any money borrowed must be paid back to the lender, along with a charge for borrowing the money—the interest.

Reinforce Your Learning

14. The key to managing cash flow is to ensure that cash ________________ faster than it ________________.

The flow of cash coming in from the customer can be controlled by the terms of payment in the contract. From the contractor's point of view, it's desirable to receive payments from the customer early in the project rather than later. The contractor might try to negotiate payment terms that require the customer to do one or more of the following:

- Provide a down payment at the start of the project. This requirement is reasonable when the contractor needs to purchase a significant amount of materials and supplies during the early stages of the project.
- Make equal monthly payments based on the expected duration of the project. Cash outflow usually is smaller in the early stages of a project. If more cash is coming in than is going out during the early part of the project, the contractor may be able to invest some of the excess cash and earn interest. The saved funds can then be withdrawn to meet the greater cash outflow requirements later in the project.
- Provide frequent payments, such as weekly or monthly payments rather than quarterly payments.

The worst scenario from the contractor's point of view is to have the customer make only one payment at the end of the project. In this situation, the contractor will need to borrow money to have cash available to meet expenses throughout the project.

The contractor's outflow of cash can also be controlled by the terms of payment, in this case in contracts with suppliers. The contractor wants to delay payments (cash outflow) as long as possible. For example, a contractor who has ordered $100,000 worth of material would want to wait until it has all been delivered before paying the supplier. If the supplier's invoice states that it must be paid within 30 days, the contractor would probably hold off until about the 27th day before making the payment.

Reinforce Your Learning

15. If sufficient funds are not available to meet expenses, a contractor may need to ________________ money. This adds to the cost of the project, because the contractor then has to pay ________________ also.

PROJECT MANAGEMENT SOFTWARE

Project management software makes it fairly easy to handle the cost considerations of a project. All costs associated with each resource in a project can be stored, and the software will calculate the budget for each work package and for the entire project. It will calculate the actual costs as the project proceeds and will forecast the final costs as well. Because various resources have different rate structures and charge their rates at various points in the project, project management software usually allows the user to define different rate structures for each

Critical Success FACTORS

- Cost planning starts with the proposal for the project, at which time project costs are estimated.
- The person who will be responsible for the costs associated with the work should make the cost estimates. This will generate commitment from the person.
- Cost estimates should be aggressive yet realistic.
- Once the project starts, it is important to monitor actual costs and work performance to ensure that everything is within budget.
- A system should be set up to collect, on a regular and timely basis, data on costs actually expended and committed, and the earned value (percent complete) of the work performed, so they can be compared to the cumulative budgeted cost (CBC).
- If at any time during the project it is determined that the project is overrunning the budget, or the value of the work performed isn't keeping up with the actual amount of costs expended, corrective action must be taken immediately.
- It is important to use the cumulative budgeted cost (CBC), rather than the total budgeted cost (TBC), as the standard against which cumulative actual cost (CAC) is compared. It would be misleading to compare the actual costs expended to the total budgeted cost, because cost performance will always look good as long as actual costs are below the TBC.
- To permit a realistic comparison of cumulative actual cost to cumulative budgeted cost, portions of the committed costs should be assigned to actual costs while the associated work is in progress.
- The earned value of the work actually performed is a key parameter that must be determined and reported throughout the project.
- For each reporting period, the percent complete data should be obtained from the person responsible for the work. It is important that the person make an honest assessment of the work performed relative to the entire work scope.
- One way to prevent inflated percent complete estimates is to keep the work packages or activities small in terms of scope and duration. It is important that the person estimating the percent complete assess not only how much work has been performed, but also what work remains to be done.
- The key to effective cost control is to analyze cost performance on a timely and regular basis. Early identification of cost variances (CV) allows corrective actions to be taken before the situation gets worse.
- For analyzing cost performance, it is important that all the data collected be as current as possible and be based on the same reporting period.
- Trends in the cost performance index (CPI) should be monitored carefully. If the CPI goes below 1.0, or gradually gets smaller, corrective action should be taken.
- As part of the regular cost performance analysis, the forecasted cost at completion (FCAC) should be calculated.
- The key to effective cost control is to address work packages or activities with negative cost variances and cost inefficiencies aggressively as soon as they are identified. A concentrated effort must be applied to these areas. The amount of negative cost variance should determine the priority for applying these concentrated efforts.
- When attempting to reduce negative cost variances, focus on activities that will be performed in the near term and on activities that have a large cost estimate.

- Addressing cost problems early will have less impact on scope and schedule. Once costs get out of control, getting back within budget becomes more difficult and is likely to require reducing the project scope or extending the project schedule.
- The key to managing cash flow is to ensure that cash comes in faster than it goes out.
- It is desirable to receive payments (cash inflow) from the customer as early as possible, and to delay making payments (cash outflow) to suppliers or subcontractors as long as possible.

resource and when charges for those resources will actually be accrued. At any time during a project, cost estimates, allocated total budgeted cost, cumulative budgeted cost, actual cost, earned value, committed costs, a cost performance index, cost variance, and a cost forecast can be calculated for each task, each work package, or the entire project, with a click of the mouse. Cost tables and graphs are often available to help analyze cost performance. See Appendix A for a thorough discussion of project management software.

SUMMARY

Project costs are estimated when a proposal is prepared for the project. Once a decision is made to go forward with the proposed project, it's necessary to prepare a budget, or plan, for how and when funds will be spent over the duration of the project. Once the project starts, it's important to monitor actual costs and work performance to ensure that everything is within budget. Several parameters should be monitored at regular intervals during the project: cumulative actual amount spent since the start of the project, cumulative earned value of the work performed since the start of the project, and cumulative budgeted amount planned to be spent, based on the project schedule, from the start of the project.

Cost planning starts with the proposal for the project. The cost section of a proposal may consist of tabulations of the contractor's estimated costs for such elements as labor, materials, subcontractors and consultants, equipment and facilities rental, and travel. In addition, the proposal might also include an amount for contingencies, to cover unplanned expenses.

The project budgeting process involves two steps. First, the project cost estimate is allocated to the various work packages in the project work breakdown structure. Second, the budget for each work package is distributed over the duration of the work package so that it's possible to determine how much of its budget should have been spent at any point in time.

Allocating total project costs for the various elements, such as labor, materials, and subcontractors, to the appropriate work packages in the work breakdown structure will establish a total budgeted cost (TBC) for each work package. Once a total budgeted cost has been established for each work package, the second step in the project budgeting process is to distribute each TBC over the duration of its work package in order to determine how much of the budget should have been spent at any point in time. This amount is calculated by adding up the budgeted costs for each time period up to that point in time. This total amount, known as the cumulative budgeted cost (CBC), will be used in analyzing the cost performance of the project. The CBC for the entire project or each work package provides a baseline against which actual cost and work performance can be compared at any time during the project.

Once the project starts, it's necessary to keep track of actual cost and committed cost so that they can be compared to the CBC. In addition, it is also necessary to monitor the earned value of the work that has been performed. Determining the earned value involves collecting data on the percent complete for each work package and then converting this percentage to a dollar amount by multiplying the TBC of the work package by the percent complete. This figure can then be compared to the cumulative budgeted cost and the cumulative actual cost.

After this has been done, the project cost performance can be analyzed by looking at the total budgeted cost, the cumulative budgeted cost, the cumulative actual cost, and the cumulative earned value. They are used to determine whether the project is being performed within budget and whether the value of the work performed is in line with the actual cost.

Another indicator of cost performance is the cost performance index (CPI), which is a measure of the cost efficiency with which the project is being performed. The CPI is calculated by dividing the cumulative earned value by the cumulative actual cost. Another indicator of cost performance is cost variance (CV), which is the difference between the cumulative earned value of the work performed and the cumulative actual cost.

Based on analysis of actual cost performance throughout the project, it's possible to forecast what the total costs will be at the completion of the project or work package. There are three different methods for determining the forecasted cost at completion (FCAC). The first method assumes that the work to be performed on the remaining portion of the project or work package will be done at the same rate of efficiency as the work performed so far. The second method assumes that, regardless of the efficiency rate the project or work package has experienced in the past, the work to be performed on the remaining portion of the project or work package will be done according to budget. The third method for determining the forecasted cost at completion is to reestimate the costs for all the remaining work to be performed and then add this reestimate to the cumulative actual cost.

The key to effective cost control is to analyze cost performance on a regular and timely basis. It's crucial that cost variances and inefficiencies be identified early so that corrective action can be taken before the situation gets worse. Cost control involves analyzing cost performance to determine which work packages may require corrective action, deciding what specific corrective action should be taken, and revising the project plan (including time and cost estimates) to incorporate the planned corrective action.

It is important to manage the cash flow on a project. Managing cash flow involves making sure that sufficient payments are received from the customer in time so that you have enough money to cover the costs of performing the project (employee payroll, charges for materials, invoices from subcontractors, and travel expenses, for example). The key to managing cash flow is to ensure that cash comes in faster than it goes out.

QUESTIONS

1. Describe why it is necessary to develop a baseline budget for a project.
2. A proposal for a project often includes a cost section. List and describe the items that should be included in this section.
3. What does the term *contingencies* mean? Should contingency costs be included in a project proposal? Explain your answer.

4. What is the problem with making cost estimates too conservative or too aggressive?
5. Describe the project budgeting process.
6. Define the following: TBC, CBC, CAC, CEV, CPI, CV, and FCAC. How is each calculated?
7. Why is it necessary to track actual and committed costs once a project starts?
8. Why is it necessary to calculate the earned value of work performed? How is this done?
9. How is a cost performance index calculated? What does it mean when it's below 1.0? What does it mean when it's above 1.0?
10. How is cost variance calculated? What does it mean when it's negative? What does it mean when it's positive? When evaluating a work package with a negative cost variance, on what two types of activities should you focus? Why?
11. What is the key to managing cash flow? How can this goal be accomplished?
12. a. Refer to the table below. What is the cumulative budgeted cost at the end of week 6?

		Week									
	TBC	1	2	3	4	5	6	7	8	9	10
Task 1	30	10	15	5							
Task 2	70		10	10	10	20	10	10			
Task 3	40					5	5	25	5		
Task 4	30								5	5	20
Total	170	10	25	15	10	25	15	35	10	5	20
Cumulative											

Amounts are in thousands of dollars.

b. Below is a table of actual costs. What is the cumulative actual cost at the end of week 6? Determine whether there is a cost overrun or underrun. What is causing it?

	Week					
	1	2	3	4	5	6
Task 1	10	16	8			
Task 2		10	10	12	24	12
Task 3					5	5
Task 4						
Total	10	26	18	12	29	17
Cumulative						

Amounts are in thousands of dollars.

c. Below is a table of the cumulative percentages of work completed by the end of week 6. What is the cumulative earned value of the project at the end of week 6? Is it good?

	Week					
	1	2	3	4	5	6
Task 1	30	80	100			
Task 2		10	25	35	55	65
Task 3					10	20
Task 4						

Amounts are cumulative percentages complete.

d. What is the CPI at the end of week 6? What is the CV?
e. Calculate the FCAC using the first two methods described in the chapter.

In addition, describe a third FCAC method you could use.

INTERNET EXERCISES

For the website addresses of the organizations mentioned in these exercises, go to "Internet Exercises" at the book's companion website at **international.cengage.com**. It is suggested that you save this website in your "Favorites" for easy access in the future.

1. Search the web for cost analysis tools. Provide a description of what you find. If possible, download a demo copy of a software package that provides some cost analysis tools.
2. Search the web for cost forecasting and discuss how it is similar to and/or different from the methods described in the chapter.
3. For exercises 3 through 5, visit the website of PMFORUM. Click on the "PM World Today" link and sign up for a free subscription. Read a recent article and provide a one-page summary.
4. Click on the "PM Library" link, then on "PM Case Studies" and review at least one case study. Was the project a success? Why or why not? What did the project manager do right and wrong?
5. Search the website for "Cost Planning". Describe what you find and how it relates to this chapter.

CASE STUDY 1

A Not-for-Profit Medical Research Center

This case study is a continuation of the one from Chapters 5, 6, 7, and 8.

CASE QUESTIONS

1. From item 2 in Chapter 7, you have the actual costs for each completed activity. Now determine actual costs expended through August 15

(including any portion of committed costs) for each activity that is scheduled to be in progress as of August 15. Make an estimate of the percent complete of the work performed for each of those same activities that are in progress as of August 15.

2. Using the plan, schedule, and activity cost estimates from item 1 in Chapter 7, prepare a budgeted cost by period table (similar to Figure 9.4) and graph a cumulative budgeted cost (CBC) curve (similar to Figure 9.5) for the project.
3. Using the actual cost data (through August 15) from item 1 above, prepare an actual cost by period table (similar to Figure 9.6) and add a cumulative actual cost (CAC) curve to the CBC graph prepared in item 2 above (similar to Figure 9.7).
4. Using the percent complete data (through August 15) from item 1 above, prepare a cumulative earned value by period table (similar to Figure 9.9) and add a cumulative earned value (CEV) curve to the CBC and CAC graph (similar to Figure 9.10).
5. As of August 15, calculate for the total project, the:
   - cost performance index (CPI)
   - cost variance (CV)
   - forecasted cost at completion (FCAC)
6. If the FCAC in item 5 exceeds the total budgeted cost (TBC) for the project, what suggestions could your team make to reduce the costs of any in-progress activities or those activities not yet started, to get the FCAC within the TBC for the project?

GROUP ACTIVITY

Divide the course participants into the same groups of three or four as for the previous chapter's group activity and answer the questions listed above.

Nice work on completing this case study! If you developed the network, schedules, tables, and graphs manually using pencil and paper, it was probably tedious, prone to errors, frustrating, and time-consuming. Project management software, such as Microsoft Project, can automate these tasks, and allow you to use your time more effectively to analyze the project schedule and cost performance and manage the project successfully.

The Wedding

CASE STUDY 2

This case study is a continuation of the one from Chapters 5, 6, 7, and 8.

CASE QUESTIONS

1. From item 2 in Chapter 7, you have the actual costs for each completed activity. Now determine actual costs expended through March 31 (including any portion of committed costs) for each activity that is scheduled to be in progress as of March 31.

   Make an estimate of the percent complete of the work performed for each of those same activities that are in progress as of March 31.
2. Using the plan, schedule, and activity cost estimates from item 1 in Chapter 7, prepare a budgeted cost by period table (similar to Figure 9.4) and graph a

Real World PROJECT MANAGEMENT

The Cleanup Act!

Can you imagine running a project that came in 12 years early and $7.8 billion (yes, billion) below estimates? It would be pretty hard to imagine or to believe, wouldn't it? Well, that is exactly what Fluor Corporation, based in Dallas, Texas, did during one of the largest environmental cleanup projects in the history of the United States.

The Fernald Feed Materials Production Center, located northwest of Cincinnati, Ohio, had produced uranium metal products for the U.S. Military throughout the Cold War. Residents of this area were not happy to have such a facility located in their backyards. This feeling of ill will was compounded by the fact that all of the activity during the 37 years of production in the Center was top secret and left the residents angry over the perceived risks they felt to their community.

In 1989, it was determined that the facility was no longer needed and it was closed. Within a few years, the Department of Energy (DOE) hired Fluor Corporation to begin the cleanup of the site. The project was massive and very dangerous due to the nature of the materials located on the site. The site contained:

Four hundred acres of contaminated soil

Thirty-one million pounds of nuclear products

More than 1,000,000 tons of radioactive waste

Nearly 200,000 gallons of liquid mixed waste

Two silos with nearly 9,000 cubic yards of radium-filled sludge

One silo of 5,100 cubic yards of cold metal oxides

Additional waste pits, containers, and low-level wastes

Given the lack of trust from the community, the inherent risks, and the politics of the situation, the project seemed like one doomed for failure. Extensive television, radio, and newspaper coverage brought lots of attention from the community and from politicians. Rex Norton, director of contracts and acquisitions for the project, stated, "When I first came here I thought there was no way we'd be able to clean this up!"

The original estimates to clean up the site were projected at 30 years and $12 billion! However, Fluor was ready for the challenge. They demonstrated incredible leadership and dedication, as well as an amazing ability to work together with all interested stakeholders. Con Murphy, president and site manager at the Fluor Fernald closure project, noted that there was an overwhelming sense of camaraderie and everybody was in the same boat rowing in the same direction.

In 1996, Fluor presented the first closure plan, which greatly accelerated the cleanup. They negotiated a contract that put the majority of the risks on themselves. The bottom line was that they needed to clean up the site as specified by the EPA and that the DOE would pay X dollars if the work was done by that date. However, if they finished earlier than that date, they would get additional profits of $8.1 million per month or approximately $256,000 per day! Likewise, if they finished the project behind schedule, they would pay a significant price for missing the deadline.

The project was broken down into subprojects, with an integrated plan of more than 17,000 activities. An aggressive schedule was built and interdependencies among activities were clearly defined and all the proper project controls were put into place. A project war room was created and an on-site project location clearly displayed the latest cost and schedule information so that anyone, including the client, could review it. The company held regular public meetings and created a citizens' advisory board.

In 2006, the last pieces of contaminated wastes were shipped off-site and the site was certified as meeting all the regulatory mandated cleanup levels. In 2007, a public ceremony was held to introduce the new Fernald Preserve, a 1050-acre nature reserve and park open to the public. The final results—the project completed 12 years and $7.8 billion below the initial estimates—earned it the Project Management Institute's 2007 Project of the Year award!

Hildebrand, C., "The Clean Up Act," *PM Network*, January 2008.

It is the people—not the procedures and techniques (covered in other chapters)—that are critical to accomplishing the project objective. Procedures and techniques are merely tools that help people do their jobs. For example, an artist needs to have paint, canvas, and brushes to paint a portrait, but it is the skills and knowledge of the artist that allow a portrait to be created with these tools. So, too, in project management: the skills and knowledge of the people involved are vital for producing the result. This chapter focuses on one very important person: the project manager. You will become familiar with

- the responsibilities of the project manager
- the skills needed to successfully manage projects and techniques for developing those skills
- approaches to effective delegation
- ways the project manager can manage and control changes to the project

RESPONSIBILITIES OF THE PROJECT MANAGER

It is the responsibility of the project manager to make sure that the customer is satisfied that the work scope is completed in a quality manner, within budget, and on time. The project manager has primary responsibility for providing leadership in planning, organizing, and controlling the work effort to accomplish the project objective. In other words, *the* ***project manager*** *provides the leadership to the project team to accomplish the project objective.* If the project team were an athletic team, the project manager would be the coach; if it were an orchestra, the project manager would be the conductor. The project manager coordinates the activities of the various team members to ensure that they perform the right tasks at the proper time, as a cohesive group.

Planning

First, the project manager clearly defines the project objective and reaches agreement with the customer on this objective. The manager then communicates this objective to the project team in such a manner as to create a vision of what will constitute successful accomplishment of the objective. The project manager spearheads development of a plan to achieve the project objective. By involving the project team in developing this plan, the project manager ensures a more comprehensive plan than he or she could develop alone. Furthermore, such participation gains the commitment of the team to achieve the plan. The project manager reviews the plan with the customer to gain endorsement and then sets up a project management information system—either manual or computerized—for comparing actual progress to planned progress. It's important that this system be explained to the project team so that the team can use it properly to manage the project.

Reinforce Your Learning

1. What two benefits does the project manager realize by involving the team in developing the plan?

Organizing

Organizing involves securing the appropriate resources to perform the work. First, the project manager must decide which tasks should be done in house and which tasks should be done by subcontractors or consultants. For tasks that will be carried out in house, the project manager gains a commitment from the specific people who will work on the project. For tasks that will be performed by subcontractors, the project manager clearly defines the work scope and deliverables and negotiates a contract with each subcontractor. The project manager also assigns responsibility and delegates authority to specific individuals or subcontractors for the various tasks, with the understanding that they will be accountable for the accomplishment of their tasks within the assigned budget and schedule. For large projects involving many individuals, the project manager may designate leaders for specific groups of tasks. Finally, and most important, the task of organizing involves creating an environment in which the individuals are highly motivated to work together as a project team.

Reinforce Your Learning

2. The project manager secures the

____

____

to perform the work and then assigns

____

and delegates

____

to specific individuals for the various tasks.

Controlling

To control the project, the project manager implements a project management information system designed to track actual progress and compare it with planned progress. Such a system helps the manager distinguish between busy-ness and accomplishments. Project team members monitor the progress of their assigned tasks and regularly provide data on progress, schedule, and costs. These data are supplemented by regular project review meetings. If actual progress falls behind planned progress or unexpected events occur, the project manager takes immediate action. He or she obtains input and advice from team members regarding appropriate corrective action and how to replan those parts of the project. It's important that problems, and even potential problems, be identified early and action taken. The project manager cannot take a "let's wait and see how things work out" approach—things never work out on their own. He or she must intervene and be proactive, resolving problems before they become worse.

The project manager plays the leadership role in planning, organizing, and controlling the project but does not try to do it alone. She or he involves the project team in these functions to gain their commitment to successful completion of the project.

Reinforce Your Learning

3. The project manager implements a project management information system to serve what two functions?

SKILLS OF THE PROJECT MANAGER

The project manager is a key ingredient in the success of a project. In addition to providing leadership in planning, organizing, and controlling the project, the manager should possess a set of skills that will both inspire the project team to

Reinforce Your Learning

4. The project manager has primary responsibility for providing leadership for what three management functions?

succeed and win the confidence of the customer. Effective project managers have strong leadership ability, the ability to develop people, excellent communication skills, good interpersonal skills, the ability to handle stress, problem-solving skills, and time management skills.

Leadership Ability

Leadership is getting things done through others; the project manager achieves results through the project team. Project leadership involves inspiring the people assigned to the project to work as a team to implement the plan and achieve the project objective successfully. The project manager needs to create for the team a vision of the result and benefits of the project. For example, the project manager may describe a new layout for a plant that will be the result of a project and articulate the benefits of this project, such as the elimination of bottlenecks, increased throughput, and reduced inventory. When project team members can envision the results, they will be more motivated to work as a team to complete the project successfully.

Reinforce Your Learning

5. Project leadership involves ________ the people assigned to the project to work as a team to implement the ________ and achieve the ________ ________ successfully.

Effective project management requires a participative and consultive leadership style, in which the project manager provides guidance and coaching to the project team. This style is preferred over a hierarchical, autocratic, and directive management approach. Leadership requires that the project manager provide *direction*, not *directions*. The project manager establishes the parameters and guidelines for what needs to be done, and the project team members determine how to get it done. The effective manager does not tell people how to do their jobs.

Project leadership requires involvement and empowerment of the project team. Individuals want to have ownership and control of their own work. They want to show that they can accomplish goals and meet challenges. The project manager should involve individuals in decisions affecting them and should empower them to make decisions within their assigned areas of responsibility. Creating a project culture that empowers the project team means not only assigning responsibility for tasks to team members but also delegating the authority to make decisions regarding the accomplishment of those tasks. Team members will embrace the responsibility for planning their work, deciding how to accomplish their tasks, controlling the progress of their work, and solving problems that may impede progress. They will accept accountability for performing their work scope within budget and on schedule.

Reinforce Your Learning

6. Project leadership requires ________ and ________ of the project team.

In empowering individuals to make decisions affecting their work, the project manager should establish clear guidelines and, if appropriate, any limits. For example, team members may be authorized to implement their own remedy for solving a problem as long as the decision doesn't result in overrunning the budget or schedule; otherwise, consultation with a team leader or the project manager may be required. Likewise, when a decision by an individual or group of individuals within the team could have a negative impact on the work, budget, or schedule of other team members, consultation with the project manager would be required. For example, suppose one team member wants to hold up ordering certain materials until she confirms particular test results, but doing so will cause the work of other team members to fall behind schedule. In this instance, the project manager might want to involve all appropriate team members in a problem-solving meeting.

The capable project manager understands what motivates team members and creates a supportive environment in which individuals work as part of a high-performing team and are energized to excel. A project manager can create such an environment by encouraging participation and involvement by all members of the project team. Techniques include facilitating project meetings so as to draw all individuals into the discussions, soliciting an individual's ideas when meeting separately with that person, and having various team members participate in presentations to the customer or the company's upper management. The project manager shows that he or she values the contributions of each team member by seeking advice and suggestions. By example, the project manager encourages team members to seek advice from one another. In addition to allowing each member to tap into the knowledge and expertise of other team members, this approach creates a sense of support and mutual respect within the team for the unique expertise each person brings to the team.

Reinforce Your Learning

7. The capable project manager understands what ______________ team members and creates a ______________ environment in which individuals work as part of a high-performing team.

The project manager must be careful not to create situations that cause individuals to become discouraged. When expectations are unclear, discouragement is likely to result. Consider the following example. On Monday, the project manager tells Gayle to get a specific task done as soon as possible. Then, on Friday, he asks her whether the task is done yet. When Gayle says she won't have it done until next Friday, he looks annoyed and says, "I really needed it done by today!" If he had a specific deadline, he should have communicated it to Gayle at the start.

Another way of discouraging a project team is to subject members to unnecessary procedures, such as the weekly preparation of written status reports that basically duplicate what is verbalized at the weekly project meetings. Unproductive team meetings can also decrease motivation.

The underutilization of individuals creates another problematic situation. Assigning people to work that is well below their level of competence and not challenging will decrease their motivation. Even more detrimental is "over-managing" people by telling them how to do their work. Such an approach will cause individuals to think that the project manager doesn't trust them; it will create a feeling of "If you're going to tell me how to do my job, why don't you just do it yourself!" So, effective project managers not only do things that establish a supportive environment but also are careful not to do things that can have the opposite effect.

The project manager can foster motivation through recognition of the project team as a whole and of individual members. This is done throughout the project, not just at the end of the project. People want to feel that they are contributing to the project and need to be recognized. Recognition can take many forms—it need not be monetary. It can come in the form of verbal encouragement, praise, a sign of appreciation, or rewards. Such positive reinforcement helps stimulate desired behavior; behavior that is recognized or rewarded is repeated. A project team might be recognized for completing a major task under budget and ahead of schedule or for identifying an innovative way to accelerate the project schedule. Such recognition will encourage the team to try to repeat such feats in the future.

One way the project manager provides recognition is by exhibiting a genuine interest in the work of each person on the project team. This can be accomplished by focusing full and undivided attention on individuals when they are explaining their work and then asking them questions about the work. A brief concluding comment such as "thank you," "good job," or "sounds great" will show the person that her or his contributions are recognized and appreciated. Other forms of recognition include a congratulatory or "thanks for the nice

Reinforce Your Learning

8. People want to feel that they are making a ______________ to the project and need to be ______________.

job" memo; or some publicity, such as an article or photograph in the company newsletter, a presentation of a certificate or plaque, or assigning the person a more responsible position on the project team.

Recognition should be carried out as soon as possible after the action that is being recognized. If too much time elapses between the good deed and the recognition, there will be little impact on future performance. In fact, the individual may feel that the project manager is not interested in the contribution that he or she made. When possible, recognition activities should involve other people in addition to the person being recognized. Individuals appreciate being acknowledged in front of their peers. The project manager, for example, might make a positive comment about the team or specific individuals during a project meeting or in front of the customer or the company's upper management. The project manager should try to make the recognition event fun, perhaps by presenting the person with some type of novelty award or taking the person to lunch. The effective project manager never monopolizes the spotlight or tries to take credit for the work of others.

Reinforce Your Learning

9. A project manager sets the tone for the project team by establishing an environment of

______________,

high

______________,

and

______________.

The project manager sets the tone for the project team by establishing an environment of trust, high expectations, and enjoyment. To foster an atmosphere of trust, the project manager lives up to his or her word and follows through on his or her commitments. By doing so, the project manager sets an example, demonstrating that follow-through is expected of everyone on the project team. If the project manager fails to follow up on any suggestions, questions, or concerns, he or she will lose credibility. In cases where things can't or don't work out as intended or expected, the project manager needs to provide an explanation so that his or her credibility is not damaged.

Capable project managers have high expectations of themselves and of each person on the project team. They believe that people tend to live up to what is expected of them. If the project manager shows confidence in the team members and has high expectations for their performance, team members will usually rise to the occasion and deliver. Project managers tend to be optimistic that, at times, even apparently insurmountable obstacles to accomplishing the project can be overcome. If the project manager doesn't balance her or his high expectations and optimism with reality, however, the project team can become frustrated. Examples of unrealistic expectations include committing to an overly ambitious schedule for completing a complicated task or expecting a newly developed sophisticated software product to work right the first time without any glitches. A project manager who is perceived as foolhardy or reckless will not win the confidence of the project team or the customer.

Reinforce Your Learning

10. People working on projects look for

____

and

______________;

they don't want to work in

______________.

Projects should be fun. Project managers should enjoy their work and encourage the same positive attitude on the part of the project team members. Most people working on projects look for affiliation and socialization; they don't want to work in isolation. The project team needs to go through socialization before it can function effectively as a high-performing team. The project manager can facilitate this socialization process by creating a sense of camaraderie among team members. One technique is to initiate periodic social gatherings—lunches, picnics, or pizza parties—for the project team. Another technique is to try to situate all the project team members in one office location, if feasible. Having an open office environment, rather than having everyone behind a closed door, will further foster socialization by making it easier for people to interact. Finally, the project manager should look for opportunities to celebrate successes, especially early in the project. As early milestones are achieved, the project manager might bring donuts to a team meeting or order boxed lunches for everyone at the conclusion of a staff meeting. Such activities create a forum for socialization, informal chatter, and team building, and they make the job enjoyable. Who said work shouldn't be fun!

Leadership requires that the project manager be highly motivated and set a positive example for the project team—in other words, practice what she or he preaches. If a project manager expects people to stay late to finish up work to keep the project on schedule, she has to be there too; she can't leave early. Everything the project manager does and says sets an example for the team in terms of expected behavior. A project manager must maintain a positive attitude—no negative comments, no whining, no bad-mouthing or blaming, and no derogatory remarks—and make it clear that such behavior is not acceptable while working on the team. Effective project managers have a "can do" attitude—a desire to achieve and overcome obstacles. They thrive on challenges and getting things done. They focus on ways to get the job done rather than on reasons why it can't be done. A good project manager is not deterred by barriers or excuses. She or he has self-confidence and exhibits confidence in the project team members.

Reinforce Your Learning

11. Leadership requires that the project manager be highly ________________ and set a ________________ ________________ for the project team.

It is said . . .

> There are those who make things happen
> those who let things happen, and
> those who wonder what happened.

The project manager leads by making things happen!

Ability to Develop People

The effective project manager has a commitment to the training and development of people working on the project. He or she uses the project as an opportunity to add value to each person's experience base so that all members of the project team are more knowledgeable and competent at the end of the project than when they started it. The project manager should establish an environment where people can learn from the tasks they perform and the situations they experience or observe, and he or she must communicate to the team the importance of continuous self-development activities. One way of encouraging such activities is to talk about the importance of self-development at project team meetings. Another way is to meet with project team members individually at the start of their project assignments and encourage them to take advantage of their assignments to expand their knowledge and skills. A good project manager believes that all individuals are valuable to the organization and that they can make greater contributions through continuous learning. He or she stresses the value of self-improvement by encouraging individuals to take the initiative—for example, to ask for new or challenging assignments or to participate in seminars. A project presents many opportunities for people to expand their technical knowledge as well as further develop skills in communication, problem solving, leadership, negotiating, and time management.

Reinforce Your Learning

12. A good project manager believes that all individuals are ________________ to the organization and that they can make greater contributions through ________________ ________________.

Reinforce Your Learning

13. Rather than create a fear of ________________, the project manager acknowledges that mistakes are part of the ________________ and ________________ experience.

A capable project manager provides opportunities for learning and development by encouraging individuals to assume the initiative, take risks, and make decisions. Rather than create a fear of failure, the manager acknowledges that mistakes are part of the learning and growth experience. The project manager can try to provide "stretch" assignments that require individual team members to extend their knowledge and accomplish more than they may think they can. For instance, a design task that involves the use of optics technology for sensors may be assigned to an engineer who has only limited familiarity with optics technology. This will require the engineer to learn more about optics, making her more valuable to the organization on future projects.

Another thing the project manager can do is identify situations in which less experienced people can learn from more experienced people. For example, a person who has been compiling test data may be assigned to work with an analyst so that he can learn how to analyze and interpret the data. In such situations, the project manager should tell the experienced people that part of their job on the project is to mentor, coach, and teach the less experienced people.

A final way in which the project manager can develop people is by having them attend formal training sessions. For example, if an individual on the project team has no experience in making stand-up presentations or has poor presentation skills, the project manager might have him attend a seminar on how to make effective presentations. The individual might then be given opportunities to apply what he has learned by making presentations at team meetings. The project manager might even provide coaching to help him improve to the point where he can make an effective presentation to the customer.

Reinforce Your Learning

14. A good project manager values and expects continuous ____________.

During discussions with individual team members, the project manager should ask, "What have you learned from working on the project?" Each response will help the manager determine what further development activities or learning opportunities are needed. Asking such questions also sends the message that the project manager values and expects continuous self-improvement.

Communication Skills

Project managers must be good communicators. They need to communicate *regularly* with the project team, as well as with any subcontractors, the customer, and their own company's upper management. Effective and frequent communication is crucial for keeping the project moving, identifying potential problems, soliciting suggestions to improve project performance, keeping abreast of customer satisfaction, and avoiding surprises. A high level of communication is especially important early in the project to build a good working relationship with the project team and to establish clear expectations with the customer.

Reinforce Your Learning

15. List five reasons why it is important for the project manager to have frequent communication.

Reinforce Your Learning

16. A high level of communication is especially important early in the project to help build a good ____________ ____________ with the project team and to establish clear ____________ with the customer.

Effective project managers communicate and share information in a variety of ways. They have meetings and informal conversations with the project team, the customer, and the company's upper management. They also provide written reports to the customer and upper management. All these tasks require that the project manager have good oral and written communication skills. We learn more by listening than by talking. Therefore, good project managers spend more time listening than talking. They don't dominate a conversation. They listen to the expectations and needs expressed by the customer and the ideas and concerns expressed by the project team. To initiate dialogue on important issues, they start discussions and conversations; to stimulate dialogue, they ask questions and solicit comments and ideas. For example, when a project manager introduces a topic at a team meeting, she might ask for others' reactions or ideas, rather than just giving her views on the topic and then moving to the next agenda item. Every project manager should get out of her or his office on a regular basis and drop in on individual team members—for instance, to follow up on a comment

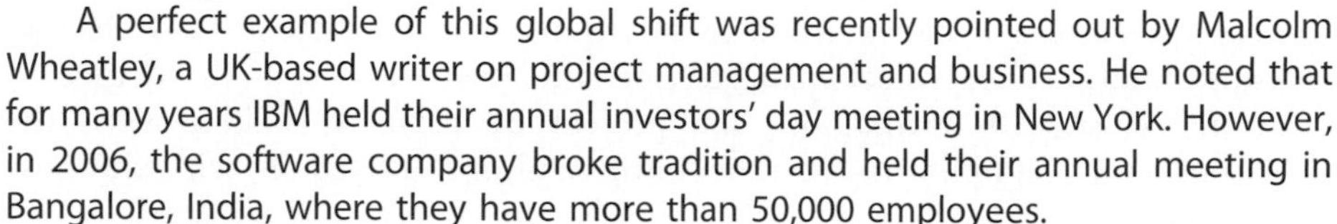

Real World PROJECT MANAGEMENT

The Borderless Leader

According to David Eaton, co-founder and president of Aperian Global, a consulting and training firm with offices in Copenhagen, Denmark; Tokyo, Japan; California, USA; and Massachusetts, USA, globalization has resulted in increased connectivity, integration, and interdependence in the cultural, ecological, economic, political, social, and technological spheres of countries around the world. Because of this, cross-cultural skills are of the utmost importance to global project leaders who must learn to be sensitive to the wide range of cultures with which they interact. It is now commonplace for project managers to have team members scattered around the globe.

A perfect example of this global shift was recently pointed out by Malcolm Wheatley, a UK-based writer on project management and business. He noted that for many years IBM held their annual investors' day meeting in New York. However, in 2006, the software company broke tradition and held their annual meeting in Bangalore, India, where they have more than 50,000 employees.

Today's leaders of global projects must recognize when and where cultural differences exist and they must be sensitive to these differences. An effective leader will capitalize on and build on these differences. Fons Trompenaars, a Belgian researcher, noted that cultures can be characterized by various dimensions such as uncertainty avoidance; the level of individualism compared with the level of collectivism; and the level of hierarchy in decision making. According to Trompenaars, certain cultures place a greater value on human relationships whereas others place a greater value on following rules. Likewise, some cultures allow a certain level of ambiguity in decision making, whereas others require very clear, well-defined structures and a specific level of detail before discussions can proceed. With proper understanding of these differences, project leaders can adjust their policies and the work environment to fit the cultural expectations.

Another factor pointed out by Rudolf Melik, chief executive of Tenrox, a California-based project management firm, is that leaders should never underestimate the importance of face-to-face time. In certain cultures, walking through the hallways while checking e-mail on a handheld phone or PDA is quite acceptable and routine; however, in other cultures this is viewed as a serious insult and as completely disrespectful because in those cultures people expect more eye contact and personal acknowledgment. Similarly, certain cultures expect a consensual management style, while others are comfortable with a highly individualistic approach. Leading a project effectively means understanding which style is appropriate based on the circumstances.

According to global project manager, Carla Catalano, PMP, a lot of the cross-cultural challenges can be overcome if project managers and project teams show respect, listen to others, and show an interest in the culture they are dealing with. She suggests that project managers should never hesitate to ask for clarification and that they should repeat their understanding of what has been said when an agreement is being made.

Daniel Hepp, director of professional services at BlueCat Networks, a Canada-based manufacturing firm, is absolutely right when he insists that we should celebrate cultural differences. He states, "People from different cultural perspectives bring with them a different way of looking at issues, and it's the diversity of ideas and viewpoints that should be captured and leveraged."

Having a multicultural workforce is the future and it can drive an organization to new heights by bringing insights that otherwise would never be considered. These different and often fresh perspectives can allow project teams to be more innovative when tackling problems and opportunities. Project leaders who acknowledge this and capitalize on cross-cultural differences will be better positioned to deliver successful projects in the new "flat" world.

Wheatley, M., "Globalization: The Borderless Leader," *PMI Leadership in Project Management*, Vol. 4, 2008. pp. 8–15.

or idea that the person expressed at a team meeting but that was not pursued at the meeting.

Reinforce Your Learning

17. What are three ways in which a project manager communicates?

The project manager establishes ongoing communication with the customer to keep the customer informed and to determine whether there are any changes in expectations. The project manager needs to keep abreast of the degree of customer satisfaction throughout the project by regularly talking with the customer—for example, maybe scheduling a phone discussion with the customer every Friday afternoon.

Reinforce Your Learning

18. Good project managers spend more time

____

than

__________________.

Communication by project managers needs to be timely, honest, and unambiguous. Effective communication establishes credibility and builds trust. It also prevents rumors from starting. Suppose a team member is temporarily assigned to another project where her expertise is needed to help solve a critical problem. When the project team discovers that one of the members is no longer working on the project, rumors may start that she was let go for overrunning her budget or that she quit because she was unhappy. The project manager needs to call a team meeting to inform the members that she was temporarily reassigned and will return to the project in a couple of weeks.

Reinforce Your Learning

19. Give three reasons the project manager should establish ongoing communication with the customer.

It's important for the project manager to provide timely feedback to the team and customer. Both the good news and the bad news should be shared promptly. For the project team to be effective, members need to have up-to-date information—especially customer feedback that may necessitate changes to the project work scope, budget, or schedule.

Reinforce Your Learning

20. Why does communication by project managers need to be timely, honest, and unambiguous?

The project manager should create an atmosphere that fosters timely and open communication without any fear of reprisal, and he or she must accept differing viewpoints. For example, an individual who is having difficulty completing a task should feel that he can bring the problem to the attention of the project manager without being penalized.

Project communication is discussed further in Chapter 12.

Interpersonal Skills

Interpersonal skills are essential for a project manager. Such skills depend on good oral and written communication skills, as discussed in the previous section. The project manager needs to establish clear expectations of members of the project team so that everyone knows the importance of his or her role in achieving the project objective. The project manager can do so by involving the team in developing a project plan that shows which people are assigned to which tasks and how those tasks fit together. Much like the coach of an athletic team, the project manager should emphasize that everyone's contribution is valuable to executing the plan successfully.

It's important that the project manager develop a relationship with each person on the project team. This may sound like a time-consuming activity, but it isn't necessarily so. It requires making the time to have an informal conversation with each person on the project team and with each key individual in the customer's organization. These conversations, initiated by the project manager, can take place during work or outside the office. They can occur over lunch, while traveling with the person on a business trip, or while sitting next to the individual at a Little League game. Such situations provide an opportunity for the project manager to get to know the various people on the project team—what motivates them, how they think things are going, what concerns they have, and how they feel about things. For example, suppose Carlos mentions that he enjoys doing demonstrations but would like to further develop his formal presentation skills. With such knowledge, the project manager can ask Carlos to provide a demonstration at the next customer review meeting of the graphics software he has developed. Or, the project manager might ask Carlos to give a presentation at the next internal project review meeting, which Carlos may find a less stressful forum for practicing his presentation skills. Carlos's self-improvement goal might not have been uncovered in any situation other than an informal conversation initiated by the project manager.

Reinforce Your Learning

21. The project manager should have an informal ________________ with each person on the project team and with each key individual in the ________________ organization.

The project manager should try to learn about the personal interests of each individual without being intrusive. The project manager might mention his or her own hobbies or family and see whether the team member picks up on the topic. The project manager should look for areas of common interest with each individual, such as tennis, cooking, college sports, children, or hometown.

In informal conversations, the project manager should use open-ended questions and do a lot of listening. It's amazing how much information you can get in response to a simple question like "How are things going?" Show genuine interest in what an individual says, however; if you seem disinterested, the person will not pursue the conversation. Thus, it is important to provide feedback and encouraging comments, such as "That's interesting" or "Tell me more about that."

Reinforce Your Learning

22. The project manager should use ________________ questions and do a lot of ________________.

Good interpersonal skills enable a project manager to empathize with individuals when special circumstances arise—whether a team member is discouraged because of technical problems in developing software or is distracted by the stress of a spouse's recuperation from an automobile accident. Of course, the project manager must be genuine in offering encouragement and support.

When he or she encounters a member of the project team, whether in the hallway or at the supermarket, the project manager should capitalize on the opportunity. Rather than make do with a mere "Hi" or "Good afternoon," she or he should stop and try to engage the team member in a conversation, even if brief. It can be on any topic, from "Are you ready for our meeting with the customer next week?" to "Did your daughter's soccer team win yesterday?" An effective project manager develops and maintains these interpersonal relationships throughout the duration of the project.

A project manager needs good interpersonal skills to try to influence the thinking and actions of others. Throughout the project, the project manager will have to persuade and negotiate with the customer, the project team, and the company's upper management. For example, the manager of a construction project might need to try to persuade the customer to forgo a change in the project scope that would require an increase in costs. Or the manager of a project to present a talent show for the benefit of a local charity might have to use her interpersonal skills to persuade a local celebrity to work on the project. These situations cannot be handled in a heavy-handed manner; good interpersonal skills are required to bring about the desired outcome.

A project manager also needs good interpersonal skills to deal with disagreement or divisiveness among team members. Such situations can require delicate handling on the project manager's part in order to mediate a resolution in which no one loses face and the project work is not affected. The subject of conflict resolution is discussed further in Chapter 11.

Ability to Handle Stress

Project managers need to be able to handle the stress that can arise from work situations. Stress is likely to be high when a project is in jeopardy of not meeting its objective because of a cost overrun, a schedule delay, or technical problems with the equipment or system; when changes in scope are requested by the customer; or when conflict arises within the project team regarding the most appropriate solution to a problem. Project activity can get both tense and intense at times. The project manager cannot panic; she or he has to remain unruffled. The effective project manager is able to cope with constantly changing conditions. Even with the best-laid plans, projects are subject to unforeseen events that can cause immediate turmoil. The project manager needs to remain composed and make sure that panic and frustration do not beset the project team, the customer, or the company's upper management.

In certain situations, the project manager needs to act as a buffer between the project team and either the customer or upper management. If the customer or upper management is not satisfied with the progress of the project, the project manager has to take the blame and make sure that the project team doesn't become discouraged. She or he needs to communicate any discontent to the project team in a manner that will inspire the team to meet the challenge. Similarly, there may be times when the project team has complaints about the customer's requirements or unwillingness to make changes. Here, too, the project manager needs to act as the buffer, absorbing the complaints and redirecting them into challenges for the project team to overcome.

The project manager needs to have a good sense of humor. Used appropriately, humor can help a project manager handle the stress and break the tension. Since the project manager sets an example for the project team and demonstrates what is acceptable behavior on the project, any humor must be in good taste. A manager should not tell inappropriate jokes or have improper items hanging on the office wall, and he or she must make it known to the project team right from the beginning that such behavior is unacceptable and will not be tolerated.

Reinforce Your Learning

23. The project manager needs to have a good sense of

____

and needs to stay

____

fit.

The project manager can improve her or his ability to handle stress by keeping physically fit through regular exercise and good nutrition. The project manager also can organize stress relief activities for the project team, such as a softball game, golf outing, or hiking trip.

Problem-Solving Skills

A project manager needs to be a good problem solver. Although it's easier to identify problems than to solve them, good problem solving starts with the early identification of a problem or potential problem. Early identification of a problem will allow more time to develop a well-thought-out solution. In addition, if a problem is identified early, it may be less costly to solve and may have less impact on other parts of the project. Good problem identification requires a timely and accurate data-driven information system; open and timely communication among the project team, the subcontractors, and the customer; and some "gut feelings" based on experience.

The project manager should encourage project team members to identify problems early and solve them on their own. The project team needs to be self-directed in solving problems and not wait for or depend on the project manager to get them started.

When a problem is potentially critical and likely to jeopardize accomplishment of the project objective, team members need to communicate this information to the project manager early so that he or she can lead the problem-solving effort. Once such a problem has been identified, the project manager may need to seek additional data and ask clarifying questions to really understand the problem and its magnitude. Team members should be asked whether they have any suggestions for how the problem might be solved. Working with the appropriate members of the project team, the project manager should then use analytical skills to evaluate the information and develop the optimal solution. It's important that the project manager possess the ability to see the "big picture" and how potential solutions might affect other parts of the project, including relationships with the customer or upper management. After the optimal solution has been developed, the project manager delegates implementation of the solution to the appropriate individuals on the project team.

Reinforce Your Learning

24. In solving problems, the project manager needs to be able to see the

____

____

and how potential solutions might affect other parts of the project.

Problem solving is discussed further in Chapter 11.

Time Management Skills

Good project managers manage their time well. Projects require a lot of energy because they involve many concurrent activities and unexpected events. To make optimal use of the time available, project managers need to have self-discipline, be able to prioritize, and show a willingness to delegate.

Time management is discussed thoroughly in Chapter 11.

Reinforce Your Learning

25. What skills do effective project managers have?

DEVELOPING THE SKILLS NEEDED TO BE A PROJECT MANAGER

People are not born with the skills effective project managers need; rather, they develop these skills. There are various ways to develop the skills necessary to be an effective project manager.

1. *Gain experience.* Work on as many projects as you can. Each project presents a learning opportunity. It's helpful if the projects aren't all the same. For example, if you're a civil engineer with a large architectural firm and you just worked on a project to design a high school, you might then look for an opportunity to be assigned to another type of project, such as designing a museum or a church. Also, look for different assignments on each project. On one project you might develop software, whereas on another project you might ask to be a group leader or to have an opportunity to interact more with the customer. The purpose of varying projects and assignments is to expose yourself to as many project managers, customers, and other experienced project people as

possible. Each experience presents an opportunity to learn from other people.

You can ask someone to be your *mentor* while you work on a project. This should be someone who you think has the skills that you're trying to develop. You should also observe how the other project participants employ their skills. See what they do—right and wrong. For example, suppose you want to develop your presentation skills. When people make presentations on the project, observe what they do right (such as showing enthusiasm or engaging the audience) and what they do wrong (such as blocking the visual aids so that not everyone can see them or telling an inappropriate joke at the start of the presentation). Making mental notes of such things will help you when you have to make a presentation. It is less painful to learn from others' mistakes than from your own.

2. *Seek out feedback from others*. If you want to improve your problem-solving skills, for example, ask a mentor whether she has observed anything you could do better in problem-solving situations. If she tells you that you have a tendency to jump to conclusions prematurely, you can work on taking more time to find out all the facts or listen to others' viewpoints.
3. *Conduct a self-evaluation, and learn from your mistakes*. If you completed a project task but overran the budget or were behind schedule, for example, ask yourself what happened, what you could have done differently, and what you will do differently the next time. Maybe you need to work on time management—focusing on the most important activities first.
4. *Interview project managers who have skills that you want to develop in yourself*. If you want to develop leadership skills, for example, seek out project managers who you think are effective leaders. Ask them how they developed their skills and what suggestions they have. Offer to buy them lunch, if that's the only time you can meet them. It could be a worthwhile investment.
5. *Participate in training programs*. There are plenty of seminars, workshops, videotapes, DVDs, and audiotapes, and self-study materials on all of the skills discussed in the previous section. There are even courses and seminars on the topic of project management. When participating in seminars, look for opportunities to learn from three sources: the instructor, the materials, and the other participants.
6. *Join organizations*. For example, membership in the Project Management Institute will provide opportunities for you to participate in meetings and conferences with other people involved in project management. Joining Toastmasters will give you a chance to develop effective presentation skills. See Appendix B for a list of project management organizations.
7. *Read*. Subscribe to journals, or look up articles related to the skills you want to develop. There are plenty of articles on improving your skills. Ask other people if they know of any good books or articles on a specific topic; their endorsement may save you time searching for good materials.
8. *Volunteer*. The workplace is not the only place where you can develop skills. Opportunities may not be available at work to develop certain skills. Consider getting involved with a volunteer organization, in which you not only can contribute to the community or a specific cause but also can try your hand at developing leadership skills.

Learning and development are lifetime activities—there's no finish line. Your employer can support and encourage you and provide the resources (time and money). The organization has to budget funds for training and staff development activities. You, however, have the primary responsibility for developing your skills. You have to take the initiative and have the desire. You have to make it happen.

Reinforce Your Learning

26. a. Identify one skill you want to develop.
    b. Identify three things you can do to develop that skill.
    c. Select one of the three things listed above and pick a date by which you will have done it.

DELEGATION

Delegation involves empowering the project team to achieve the project objective and empowering each team member to accomplish the expected results for his or her area of responsibility. It's the act of allowing individuals to carry out assigned tasks successfully. Delegation implies more than just assigning tasks to specific members of the project team. It includes giving team members the responsibility to accomplish job objectives and the authority to make decisions and take actions to achieve the expected results, as well as accountability for accomplishing those results.

Members of the project team are given specific results to achieve in terms of the work scope, tangible results or products to be delivered, the available budget, and the allowable time frame or schedule for their assigned areas of responsibility. They plan their own methods for accomplishing the desired results, and they exercise control over the resources they need to do the work.

Reinforce Your Learning

27. Delegation involves ____________ the project team to achieve the ____________ ____________ and each team member to accomplish the ____________ ____________ for his or her area of responsibility.

Delegation is a must for an effective project manager. It is part of the project manager's responsibility for organizing the project. Delegation is *not* "passing the buck." The project manager is still ultimately responsible for achieving the project results. The project manager who understands and practices delegation ensures effective performance by the project team and creates the conditions necessary for cooperation and teamwork.

Effective delegation requires effective communication skills. The project team members need to realize that the job of implementing the project has been delegated to them. The project manager has the responsibility for providing a clear understanding of what is expected in terms of specific results. It's not sufficient for the project manager to say, "Rashid, you work on the mechanical design" or "Rosemary, you handle the publicity." Rather, she or he needs to define what specifically constitutes each task and the desired result of the task. This includes its work scope, tangible results or products to be delivered, expected quality, budget, and schedule. These elements should be defined and agreed upon by the project manager and project team members before any work begins. However, the project manager *should not tell the individuals how to do the task.* That should be left up to the individuals so that they can be creative. If people are told how to do tasks, they will not be as committed to achieving the desired result and will feel that the project manager lacks confidence in their capabilities.

If team members are to accomplish their tasks successfully, they need to be given the necessary resources and authority to exercise control over those resources. Resources can include people, money, and facilities. Team members should be able to call on other team members' expertise, purchase materials, and have access to facilities as needed. Team members should be given the authority to make decisions regarding the use of resources as long as they stay within the constraints of the budget and schedule.

Reinforce Your Learning

28. Project managers should not tell individuals ____________ to do the assigned tasks.

Delegation involves selecting the project team members who are best qualified to perform each task and then empowering them to do it. The project manager needs to know the capabilities, capacity, and limitations of each member of the project team when making assignments. The project manager can't delegate to a particular individual a set of tasks that requires more person-days than the individual has available. For example, one person, working alone, can't be expected to paint six rooms in a week when it is estimated that it takes two days to paint each room. Similarly, the project manager can't expect individuals to perform tasks for which they do not have the appropriate expertise. For example, an individual without the appropriate knowledge of chemistry or analysis techniques cannot be expected to perform a chemical analysis. Delegation, however, does provide an opportunity to give challenging, or "stretch," assignments to individuals in order to develop and extend their expertise and skills. Therefore, when the project manager is delegating, he or she considers not only the person's current capabilities, but also the person's potential. Stretch assignments energize people to take on the challenge and show that they can meet the project manager's expectations.

Reinforce Your Learning

29. When assigning individuals to specific tasks, the project manager needs to take into consideration the person's __________, __________, and __________.

When a project manager empowers team members to make decisions associated with performing their work, he or she gives them freedom to take action to accomplish the work without interference. Yet, the project manager should realize that in performing the work and making decisions, people may make errors and failure may occur. If the project manager is critical of mistakes, he or she will train people to seek him or her out to review and approve every little thing they do. Such fear of failure will paralyze the project team. Effective delegation requires that the project manager have confidence in each member of the project team.

Reinforce Your Learning

30. Effective delegation requires that the project manager have __________ in each member of the project team.

When the project team is carrying out its tasks, the project manager should let team members do their jobs; however, he or she should be available to coach and advise individuals when needed. An effective project manager is careful not to disempower individuals by giving them directives, by telling them how to do things, or by making decisions for them. Rather, he or she shows confidence in their capabilities and encourages them.

Delegation requires that individuals be accountable for achieving the expected results of their tasks. To support team members in controlling their work efforts, the project manager needs to establish a project management information and control system. This system should keep the project manager and the team informed and support decision making. The system may include a computerized information reporting system and the requirement that regular meetings be held with the project team or individual team members to check on progress. Such a system should focus on measuring and evaluating progress toward the expected result of each task, not merely on monitoring busy-ness. The project manager is interested in knowing whether the work scope for each task is progressing according to plan and whether it will be completed within the available budget and on the required schedule. He or she cannot accept a report that "the team worked until 10:00 P.M. all week" as an indication that the work is on track. The project manager makes it known that delegation requires team members to be accountable for achieving the expected results, not just to keep busy. Empowered individuals accept this accountability. When monitoring progress, the project manager should offer encouragement to team members. He

Reinforce Your Learning

31. Delegation requires that individuals be __________ for achieving the expected results.

or she should show genuine interest in their work and offer recognition and appreciation of their progress.

Following are some common barriers to effective delegation and what can be done to overcome them.

- The project manager has a personal interest in the task or thinks she can do it better or faster herself. In this case, she must force herself to let go and have confidence in other individuals. She needs to understand that other people may not do things exactly the way she would.
- The project manager lacks confidence in the capability of others to do the work. In this case, he should be sure that he knows the capabilities, potential, and limitations of each member of the project team so that he can select the most appropriate person for each task.
- The project manager is afraid that he will lose control of the work and not know what is going on. In this case, he should set up a system for regularly monitoring and evaluating progress toward the expected results.
- Team members fear criticism for mistakes or lack self-confidence. In this case, the project manager has to show confidence in each individual, offer regular encouragement, and understand that mistakes are opportunities for learning rather than occasions for criticism.

Figure 10.1 shows various degrees of delegation. The sixth degree supports full empowerment of the project team. In most cases, the project manager

FIGURE 10.1 *Degrees of Delegation*

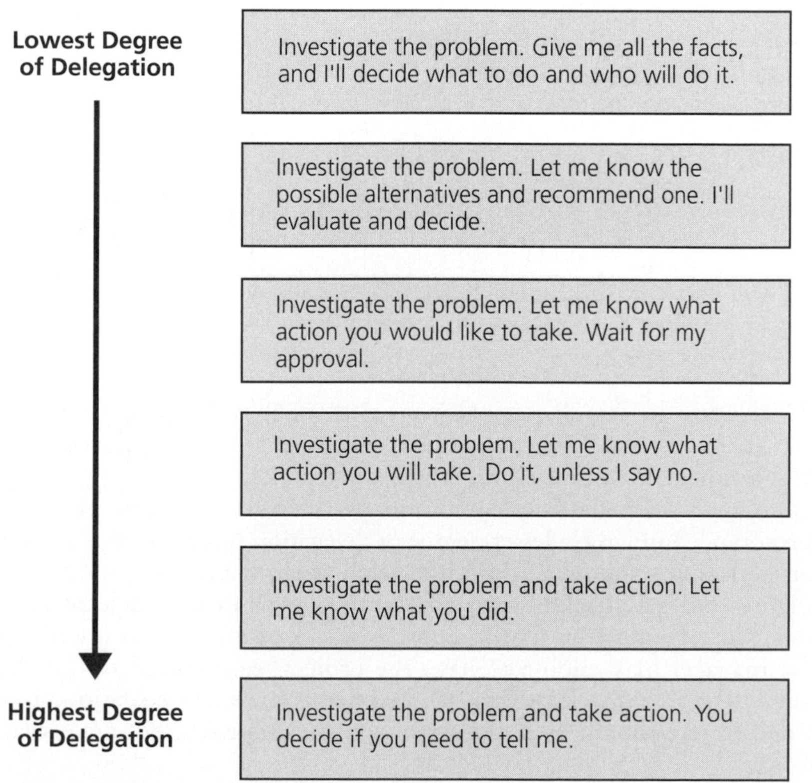

FIGURE 10.2 ***Delegation Checklist***

How Effective Are You at Delegating?

	Not at All		Somewhat		Very Much
1. Does your team have a clear understanding of the results expected?	1	2	3	4	5
2. Does your team have all the resources needed to accomplish what was delegated?	1	2	3	4	5
3. Do you focus on the results you expect from team members, rather than on the details of how they do their work?	1	2	3	4	5
4. Do you have a system to follow up and monitor progress?	1	2	3	4	5
5. Do team members understand how and when they are to let you know how they are progressing and when to seek your advice?	1	2	3	4	5
6. Does your team understand how progress will be measured and evaluated?	1	2	3	4	5
7. Can your team speak freely to you about problems, without fear of criticism?	1	2	3	4	5
8. Do team members feel they have the freedom to perform their work without your over-managing them?	1	2	3	4	5
9. Do team members feel they can perform their work without fear of making a mistake?	1	2	3	4	5
10. Do you encourage team members to make decisions within the level of authority you delegated to them?	1	2	3	4	5
11. Do you provide coaching as needed?	1	2	3	4	5
12. Do you encourage and are you supportive of your team's suggestions?	1	2	3	4	5

should delegate to this degree. However, there may be some situations that require delegating to a lesser degree. For example, a lesser degree of delegation might be advisable if there was a critical problem in meeting the project objective, such as a potentially significant cost overrun or continuing test failures of a prototype. Similarly, a lesser degree of delegation might be appropriate if the person performing the work was in a stretch assignment.

Figure 10.2 is a checklist for rating your effectiveness at delegation. It can be used by the project manager as a self-assessment instrument, or the project manager may choose to have the project team complete the checklist in order to get feedback on his or her effectiveness at delegation. In either case, the project manager should then focus on improving in areas that were rated low.

MANAGING CHANGE

The one thing that you can be sure will happen during a project is change. Despite the best-laid plans, changes will still occur. Changes may be

- initiated by the customer,
- initiated by the project team,
- caused by unanticipated occurrences during the performance of the project, or
- required by the users of the project results.

An important aspect of the project manager's job is to manage and control changes to minimize any negative impact on the successful accomplishment of the project objective. Some changes are trivial, but others may significantly affect the project work scope, budget, or schedule. Deciding to change the color of a room before it is painted is a trivial change. Deciding that you want a two-story house after the contractor has already put up the framing for a single-story house is a major change, which would certainly increase the cost and probably delay the completion date.

The impact a change has on accomplishing the project objective may be affected by when during the project the change is identified. Generally, *the later in the project that changes are identified, the greater their effect on accomplishing the project objective*. The aspects most likely to be affected are the project budget and the completion date. This is particularly true when work that has already been completed needs to be "undone" to accommodate the required change. For example, it would be very expensive to change the plumbing or wiring in a new office building after the walls and ceilings are completed because some of them would need to be torn out first. Then new ones would have to be installed. However, if such a change was made much earlier in the project—for instance, while the building is still being designed—accommodation would be easier and less costly. The drawings could be changed so that the plumbing and wiring could be installed correctly the first time.

At the start of the project, procedures need to be established regarding how changes will be documented and authorized. These procedures must cover communication between the project manager and the customer and between the project manager and the project team. If changes are agreed upon orally rather than in writing and there is no indication of the impact the changes will have on the work scope, cost, or schedule, project costs can be greater than expected and schedules can run later than expected. Let's say, for example, that Mrs. Smith calls her contractor and tells him to add a fireplace to the house he is building for her. Based on her oral authorization, the contractor installs the fireplace and chimney. Then, when he informs Mrs. Smith of the additional costs, she is shocked.

"You should have told me before you went ahead and did the work," she says.

"But you told me to go ahead and do it. It sounded like your mind was made up," he says.

"Well, I'm not going to pay this much; it's outrageous!" Mrs. Smith responds. And the hassle continues.

Reinforce Your Learning

32. Changes may be initiated by the

____

or by the

____

____

or may be caused by

____

____

during the performance of the project.

Reinforce Your Learning

33. The project manager's job is to

____

and

____

changes in order to

____

any negative impact on the successful accomplishment of the project objective.

Reinforce Your Learning

34. At the start of the project, the project manager needs to establish ______________ regarding how changes will be ______________ and ______________.

Whenever a customer requests changes, the project manager should have the appropriate project team members estimate the effects on the project cost and schedule. The project manager should then present these estimates to the customer and request the customer's approval before proceeding. If the customer agrees to the changes, the project schedule and budget should be revised to incorporate the additional tasks and costs. Sometimes customers try to squeeze in changes for free by making them sound trivial or by circumventing the project manager and dealing with one of the individuals on the project team. The project manager needs to be sure that team members won't casually agree to changes that may require additional person-hours. Otherwise, if the customer does not agree to pay for the changes, the contractor will have to absorb the costs for the additional person-hours and risk overrunning costs for a particular task or the entire project.

Sometimes changes are initiated by the project manager or project team. For example, suppose a member of the project team comes up with a new design approach that uses a different type of computer system than the customer originally wanted that will substantially reduce the project cost. In this case, the project manager would present a proposal for the change to the customer and get the customer's approval before making the change. The customer would probably give approval if the change reduced costs without any degradation to system performance. On the other hand, if the project manager asked the customer to extend the project completion date or to provide additional funding because the project team had run into difficulties that had caused schedule slippage or cost overruns, the customer might not agree. The contractor might have to absorb the cost overrun or spend additional money to add more resources temporarily to get the project back on schedule.

The project manager needs to make it clear to the project team that team members should not make any changes to their work that will increase costs beyond budgeted amounts, delay the schedule, or produce results that do not meet the customer's expectations. For example, on a technical project a software engineer may think that he will please the customer by making slight enhancements to the software beyond what is required. However, he will not please the project manager if he overruns the budget for the software development task because of all the time he spends making a bunch of "slight enhancements" that are nice but aren't necessary!

Some changes become necessary as a result of unanticipated occurrences, such as an early snowstorm that slows down the construction of a building, failure of a new product to pass tests, or the untimely death or resignation of a key member of the project team. These occurrences will have an impact on the project schedule or cost and will require that the project plan be modified. In some cases, unanticipated events can cause the project to be terminated. For example, if early test results in a research project to develop an advanced ceramic material are not promising, the company may decide to terminate the project rather than spend more money with diminishing chances of success.

Perhaps the most difficult type of change to manage is that required of the users of the project results. In some situations, the project manager is responsible not only for managing the project to develop a new or improved

Critical Success FACTORS

- Successful project managers accept responsibility for making sure the customer is satisfied and the work scope is completed in a quality manner, within budget, and on time.
- The project manager needs to be proactive in planning, communicating, and providing leadership to the project team to accomplish the project objective.
- The project manager needs to inspire the project team to succeed and to win the confidence of the customer.
- By involving the project team in developing the project plan, the project manager ensures a more comprehensive plan and gains the commitment of the team to achieve the plan.
- Successful project managers are proactive in addressing problems. They don't take a "let's wait and see how things work out" approach.
- The project manager needs to have a project management information system that distinguishes accomplishments from busy-ness.
- Effective project managers have strong leadership ability, the ability to develop people, excellent communication skills, good interpersonal skills, the ability to handle stress, problem-solving skills, and time management skills.
- Successful project management requires a participative and consultative leadership style in which the project manager provides guidance and coaching to the project team. The effective project manager does not tell people how to do their jobs.
- Project managers show they value the contributions of team members when they seek advice and suggestions from team members.
- Project managers can foster motivation through recognition. People want to feel they are making a contribution and need to be recognized. Positive reinforcement helps stimulate desired behavior; behavior that is recognized or rewarded gets repeated.
- The effective project manager doesn't monopolize, seek the spotlight, or try to take credit for the work of others.
- Capable project managers are optimistic and have high, yet realistic, expectations of themselves and each person on the project team.
- Projects should be fun. Project managers should enjoy their work and encourage the same positive attitude on the part of the project team members. The project manager should set a positive example for the team in terms of expected behavior.
- A good project manager provides opportunities for learning and development by encouraging team members to take the initiative, take risks, and make decisions. Rather than create a fear of failure, the project manager realizes that mistakes are part of the learning and growth experience.
- Good project managers spend more time listening than talking. They listen to the needs expressed by the customer and the ideas and concerns expressed by the project team.
- Communication by project managers needs to be timely, honest, and unambiguous.
- The project manager should create an atmosphere that fosters timely and open communication without fear of reprisal, and must be understanding of differing viewpoints.
- When unforeseen events cause turmoil on a project, effective project managers remain composed and do not panic.

- To make effective use of their time, project managers need to have self-discipline, be able to prioritize, and be willing to delegate.
- At the start of a project, the project manager needs to establish procedures for how changes will be documented and authorized.

system but also for implementing the resultant system among its users, who will have to change the way they perform their work. For example, in a project to design, develop, and implement a new computerized ordering, billing, and collection system to replace the current manual systems, the project manager might be responsible not only for managing the project to design and develop the new system, but also for getting the users to accept the change from the old manual system to the new computerized system.

There are some things a project manager can do to facilitate implementation of such a change. Open communication and a climate of trust are prerequisites for introducing change, reducing resistance to change, and gaining commitment to the change. It is important to gain the users' support for and commitment to the new system, not merely their agreement that they need a better system. The project manager needs to share information about the change with the users. Such communication has to be carried out promptly, fully, honestly, and regularly. This means that the project manager must initiate discussions with the users before the new system is even designed, not wait until it is ready to be implemented. Discussing the system early will help squelch the rumor mill. The project manager needs to tell the users why the change is being made and how it will affect and benefit them. They need to believe that the change will benefit them; otherwise, they will resent it that the change will benefit them; otherwise, they will resent it rather than support it.

Discussions or meetings provide a good opportunity for people to express their concerns, fears, and anxieties. Anxiety and fear of the unknown can induce stress in people and build up resistance to change. During meetings to discuss the impending change, the project manager should not get into debates or be defensive. He or she should empathize with people's concerns and fears, not discount or trivialize them. If possible, the project manager should have users participate up front in the decision to change from, say, manual methods to a computerized system. Then he or she needs to involve them in planning and designing the system; after all, they are the people who will be using it. The users also need to be involved in planning how to implement the new system—how to make the changeover from the manual system to the computerized one. The project manager can provide support and rewards to help ensure successful implementation of the new system. A reward to the users might be that they receive computer skills training that will make them more knowledgeable and valuable. Finally, the project manager needs to be patient; only when the new system becomes fully utilized will the expected benefits be achieved.

Changes are going to occur on projects. The project manager has to manage and control the changes so that the project doesn't get out of control.

SUMMARY

It is the responsibility of the project manager to make sure that the customer is satisfied that the work scope is completed in a quality manner, within budget, and on time. The project manager has primary responsibility for providing leadership in planning, organizing, and controlling the work effort to accomplish the project objective. In terms of planning, the project manager has to clearly define the project objective and reach agreement with the customer on this objective. In terms of organizing, the project manager must secure the appropriate resources to perform the work. In terms of controlling, the project manager needs to track actual progress and compare it with planned progress.

The project manager is a key ingredient in the success of a project and needs to possess a set of skills that will help the project team succeed. The project manager should be a good leader who inspires the people assigned to the project to work as a team to implement the plan and achieve the project objective successfully; be committed to the training and development of the people working on the project; be an effective communicator who interacts regularly with the project team, as well as with any subcontractors, the customer, and her or his own company's upper management; and have good interpersonal skills. It is important that the project manager develop a relationship with each person on the project team and effectively use his or her interpersonal skills to try to influence the thinking and actions of others.

An effective project manager can handle stress and has a good sense of humor. In addition, he or she is a good problem solver. Although it's easier to identify problems than to solve them, good problem solving starts with the early identification of a problem or potential problem. Good project managers also manage their time well.

These essential skills can be developed through experience, by seeking out feedback from others, by conducting a self-evaluation and learning from your own mistakes, by interviewing effective project managers, by participating in training programs, by joining organizations, through reading, and through involvement with volunteer organizations in which these skills can be tested.

Project managers need to be good delegators. Delegation involves empowering the project team to achieve the project objective and empowering each team member to accomplish the expected results for her or his area of responsibility. It's the act of allowing individuals to carry out assigned tasks successfully.

One other important component of the project manager's job is managing and controlling changes to minimize any negative impact on the successful accomplishment of the project objective. To do this successfully, the project manager, at the beginning of the project, should establish procedures regarding how changes will be documented and authorized.

QUESTIONS

1. Describe what the project manager should do to perform the planning function. Give some specific examples.
2. Describe what the project manager should do to perform the organizing function. Give some specific examples.

3. Describe what the project manager should do to perform the controlling function. Give some specific examples.
4. What are some essential skills for an effective project manager? How can these skills be developed?
5. Describe why a project manager needs good oral and written communication skills.
6. What is meant by the term *interpersonal skills*? Give some examples of interpersonal skills, and explain why they are important.
7. What are some things a project manager can do to help create an environment in which a project team will feel motivated?
8. What is meant by the term *delegation*? Why is delegation essential for project management? Give some examples.
9. What are some barriers to effective delegation?
10. Why is it important to manage change during a project? How is change initiated? Give some specific examples.
11. Describe some ways a project manager can make a project more fun and team members more committed.
12. Think of a project that you have worked on. Describe what made the project manager for that project effective or ineffective. How could the project manager have done a better job?

INTERNET EXERCISES

For the website addresses of the organizations mentioned in these exercises, go to "Internet Exercises" at the book's companion website at **international.cengage.com**. It is suggested that you save this website in your "Favorites" for easy access in the future.

1. Jerry Madden, who recently retired from the Flight Projects Directorate at NASA's Goddard Space Flight Center, compiled an excellent list of more than 100 lessons learned for NASA project managers. These lessons cover a wide range of areas, including communication, decision making, ethics, and failures. The list can be found by searching for "100 Lessons Learned for Project Managers." Review the list and write down your favorite five items.
2. In the NASA website you found in exercise 1, click on the "Stories" link. Read and summarize one of the stories. What did the project manager do right or wrong in this story?
3. Search the web for "Effective Project Leadership." Based on your search, briefly describe some of the suggestions you found.
4. Search the web for "Effective Delegation." Describe what you find. How does it relate to the topics presented in this chapter?
5. Visit the home page of the Project Management Institute. Check out the "Career Development" link and then the "Career Headquarters" link. Describe at least three of the project management jobs that are posted.

Codeword

CASE STUDY 1

Codeword is a medium-size firm that designs and manufactures electronic systems for the mass transit industry. It competes with other firms to win contracts to provide such systems. When Codeword receives a contract, it creates a project to complete the work. Most projects range from $10 million to $50 million in cost and from one to three years in duration. Codeword can have 6 to 12 projects going on at any one time, in various stages of completion—some just starting and others finishing.

Codeword has a handful of project managers who report to the general manager; other people report to their functional manager. For example, the electronics engineers all report to the manager of electrical engineering, who reports to the general manager. The functional manager assigns particular individuals to work on various projects. Some people work full-time on a project, whereas others split their time among two or three projects. Although individuals are assigned to work for a project manager on a specific project, administratively they still report to their functional manager.

Jack Kowalski has been with the company for about 12 years, since graduating from college with a B.S. in electronic engineering. He has worked his way up to senior electronics engineer and reports to the manager of electrical engineering. He has worked on many projects and is well respected within the company. Jack has been asking for an opportunity to be a project manager. When Codeword is awarded a $15 million contract to design and manufacture an advanced electronics system for a new aircraft, the general manager promotes Jack to project manager and asks him to run this project.

Jack works with the functional managers to get the best people available assigned to the project. Most of the people are buddies who have worked with Jack on previous projects. However, with Jack's position as senior electronics engineer vacant, the manager of electrical engineering has no one with the appropriate level of expertise to assign to Jack's project. So the manager hires a new person, Alfreda Bryson. Lured away from a competitor, she has a Ph.D. in electronic engineering and eight years experience. She was able to command a high salary—more than Jack is making. She is assigned to Jack's project full-time as the senior electronics engineer.

Jack takes a special interest in Alfreda's work and asks to meet with her to discuss her design approaches. Yet most of these meetings turn into monologues, with Jack suggesting how Alfreda should do the design and paying little attention to what she says.

Finally, Alfreda asks Jack why he is spending so much more time reviewing her work than that of the other engineers on the project. He responds, "I don't have to check theirs. I know how they work. I've worked with them on other projects. You're the new kid on the block, and I want to be sure you understand the way we do things here, which may be different than at your previous employer."

On another occasion, Alfreda shows Jack what she thinks is a creative design approach that will result in a lower-cost system. Jack tells her, "I don't even have a Ph.D. and I can see that that won't work. Don't be so esoteric; just stick to basic sound engineering."

During a business trip with Dennis Freeman, another engineer assigned to the project who has known Jack for six years, Alfreda says that she is frustrated with the way Jack treats her. "Jack is acting more like the electronics engineer for the project than the project manager," she tells Dennis. "Besides, I have forgotten more about designing electronics than Jack ever knew! He really isn't up to date on electronic design methodologies." She also tells Dennis that she's planning to discuss the matter with the manager of electrical engineering and that she'd never have taken the job with Codeword if she'd known it was going to be like this.

CASE QUESTIONS

1. Do you think Jack is ready to serve as a project manager? Why or why not? How could Jack have prepared for his new role?
2. What is the major problem with the way Jack interacts with Alfreda?
3. Why do you think Alfreda hasn't had an open discussion with Jack about the way he's treating her? If Alfreda approaches Jack directly, how do you think he will respond?
4. How do you think the manager of electrical engineering will respond to this situation? What should the manager do?

GROUP ACTIVITY

Course participants should split into groups of four or five students to discuss the following questions:

- What should be done to remedy the situation?
- What could have been done to prevent the situation?

Each group must then choose a spokesperson to present its conclusions to the entire class.

CASE STUDY 2

A Growing E-Business Company

Ivana is the owner of ICS, Inc., an information systems consulting firm of 20 employees. They mostly design and implement information technology projects for small and medium-size businesses in the metropolitan area. Although ISC has a sufficient level of business, the environment is becoming more competitive as more entrepreneurs are starting their own information technology consulting businesses. Ivana does all the marketing for ICS and is the primary contact between ICS and its customers.

ICS just received a contract from a Fortune 100 company to design and implement an e-business system for one of their distribution centers. ICS beat out several competitors, including some larger national consulting firms, to win this contract. This was due in part to ICS bidding a bare bones low price, and Ivana promising the customer that ICS would complete the project in six months, even though the customer specified that the project had to be completed in nine months or less. She knows that if ICS successfully completes this project and shows that they can beat the customer's expected schedule, it could lead to a larger contract to implement similar systems in the client's other distribution centers throughout the country.

As soon as Ivana heard that ICS won the contract, she called eight of her employees together whom she wanted to work on the project. "Some of you may not be aware of it, but I submitted a proposal to a very large client, our largest ever, to implement an e-business system for one of their distribution centers. This is a really important project for me because if we are successful, there will be other future projects with this customer, and ICS can become a major consulting firm—my dream come true. I must tell you, this is a fixed-price contract, and I cut our price as low as I could to increase our chances of winning the contract. I also promised them that we could complete the project in six months, even though they would have been satisfied with nine months. So I want to be very clear with all of you, this project is very important to me and ICS, so I expect each of you to put in whatever time is necessary to get it done on time. You'll have to figure out how to get your other work done in the meantime. And, I want to emphasize, *mistakes will not be tolerated*. There is too much at stake. I need to leave for a business lunch now. But here are copies of the proposal I submitted. Look it over, and then get together and get to it."

As they left the conference room, Patrick, a systems designer, said, "Let's all read the proposal and get together about 9 o'clock tomorrow morning to figure out who needs to do what."

Ivana overheard Patrick's comment, and she piped in, "Tomorrow! Maybe you didn't hear me say how important this project is. I suggest you read the proposal now, and get together this afternoon or evening."

Ester, a programmer spoke up, "I have an appointment with my obstetrician this afternoon for my six-month checkup."

Ivana snapped, "Well, you'll just have to reschedule it. The baby's not due for three more months anyway. What's the big deal? My mother delivered five children with a midwife, no doctor, and we all survived."

After Ivana left, Ester, with tears in her eyes, told the others, "What a witch. If I didn't need the health insurance benefits, I'd quit today."

The group got together later that afternoon. Patrick took the lead in facilitating the discussions, only because he was the longest term employee. Harvey, the other systems designer in the group, and one of the newer and younger people in the group, asked, "Patrick, are you like going to be like the leader on this project?"

"That's not the way things really work around here. We all know who the real project manager is, don't we?" responded Patrick. And most of the group answered in unison "Ivana!" and laughed.

As the group discussed the proposal, many questions came up. And there was a difference of opinion between Patrick and Harvey regarding the system design approach. Patrick's approach was less risky, but might be more time-consuming; Harvey's approach was more risky, but would take less time if it worked. Patrick said, "Let me try to meet with Ivana in the morning and get some answers, if that's possible."

"Maybe we should all meet with her," said Harvey.

"Ivana's not a big fan of long meetings with a lot of people. She thinks they're a waste of everyone's time," answered Patrick.

Patrick met with Ivana the next morning. "Well, does everybody have everything figured out?" asked Ivana.

"Actually, we stayed late last night discussing the proposal, and we have some questions. The proposal seemed ambiguous in some . . . "

Ivana interrupted, "Ambiguous! The customer didn't think it was ambiguous. I don't think it's ambiguous. So now you tell me why you think it's ambiguous."

"Well, for example, Harvey and I have come up with two different design schemes; one more risky but might take less time, the other less risky but could take longer," stated Patrick.

"One meeting and you guys are arguing with each other like little children," Ivana jumped in. "Didn't you ever hear of teamwork? Here is what I want—less risky and less time. No should's, could's, or might's. You two are just going to have to figure it out and not waste any time. Do I have to make all the decisions around here? What else, I don't have all day? And I'm glad to hear that everyone was willing to work late last night because that's the kind of commitment it's going to take to get this project done on time. You know, I pay top salaries, and I expect people to do whatever it takes to get the job done. And if anybody can't handle it, they can go find a job somewhere else. They'll see that the grass isn't always greener on the other side of the fence."

As Patrick turned and left Ivana's office, she said, "By the way, as a reward for winning the contract, I'm treating myself to a two-week vacation in Europe. And tell the others that when I get back, I hope to find the project is well on its way; and no fighting."

Later in the day, as Ivana was walking down the hallway, she saw Ester and said, "I assume you were able to reschedule your doctor appointment."

Ester replied, "Yes, but not for two more weeks. It's going to be tough trying to keep up with the work during these last three months."

"Tough?" responded Ivana. "Let me tell you what tough is. I helped raise my four younger brothers and sisters after my mother died giving birth to my youngest sister. Then I worked my way through college going at night for almost 10 years while raising four children of my own. So the next time you think you have it tough, just think about how tough some other people have had it. I hope you can get most of your part of the work done on the project before your baby arrives. I'm counting on you."

At about 6 o'clock, Harvey stopped by Ivana's office. "Gotta minute?" asked Harvey.

"Only a minute," responded Ivana. "I'm meeting a friend for dinner, so make it quick."

"There is a computer conference in Las Vegas next month," Harvey said, "and I was wondering if I could have your approval to go? There are a lot of new things I could learn that may help us on this project."

"You've got to be kidding!" answered Ivana. "You want me to pay to send you to some conference to party while we have a deadline to make on this project? And everybody else is going to be back here working their butts off? Where is your sense of priorities? Don't you feel any responsibility to the rest of the project team? I swear, I am the only one around here who thinks about teamwork! Maybe when the project is over, you can find some conference that's closer and cheaper. I've got to go. By the way, tell whoever leaves last tonight to make sure the coffee pot is turned off. It was left on last night." As Ivana walked briskly by Harvey, she murmured, "Sometimes I feel like I have to be everybody's mommy around here."

CASE QUESTIONS

1. Considering Ivana's management style, how should the group of employees assigned to the project proceed?
2. How should the project members interact with Ivana throughout the project?

3. Why do you think Ivana behaves the way she does?
4. Should the project members approach Ivana about her management style? If so, how?

GROUP ACTIVITY

Select five course participants to perform a skit of this case in front of the class. One person will be the narrator describing the scene and the transitions between scenes. The other four participants will play the roles of Ivana, Patrick, Ester, and Harvey and read their lines.

At the conclusion of the skit, have the entire class discuss their responses to the case questions.

© AP Images

CHAPTER 11

The Project Team

Real World PROJECT MANAGEMENT

Teamwork Creates a Miracle on Ice

Sports Illustrated stated that Team USA's gold medal run in the 1980 Winter Olympic Games might just be the single most indelible moment in all of U.S. sports history. Herb Brooks, NCAA coach and student of international hockey, coached the legendary team. He played for the U.S. hockey team in two previous Olympics. In the 1970s, he served as head coach at the University of Minnesota, where he led the team to three NCAA titles.

After numerous defeats in the 1970s, the USSR re-emerged as the pinnacle of the hockey world going into the 1980 Winter Games held at Lake Placid. The Soviet team had many returning veterans and exciting young players, which led to a 1979 World Championship win.

Brooks held tryouts for the 1980 U.S. Hockey Team and selected a roster from over a hundred prospects. The team spent four months playing exhibition games across Europe and North America. Many of these players went on to lengthy NHL careers. Despite Brooks' emphasis on speed, conditioning, and discipline, his team wasn't considered a match for the Europeans in terms of skill. Rivalries were present among the players because they hailed from rival colleges and regions. Brooks worked tirelessly to unite the players as a team. He challenged them not only physically, but verbally as well. He was constantly making the players question whether they were good enough or tough enough.

Before the Olympics, Brooks made a series of positional changes to the team. He thought that a bronze medal was within the team's reach. They were considered competitive, but underdogs, from the beginning. In a pre-Olympic exhibition game, the Soviets beat the American team 10-3. Brooks blamed his conservative game plan. However, once the games began, the United States tied Sweden, and beat Czechoslovakia, Norway, Romania, and Germany. The Soviets remained undefeated in their group. The USSR and the USA teams were set to meet in the first medal round.

The Soviets came out strong in the game, outshooting the Americans. However, thanks to the goalie, the U.S. team remained in the game, down 2-1 near the end of the first period. Mark Johnson, for the U.S. team, crashed between the Soviet defensemen to score at the buzzer. The officials decided that the goal was confirmed, and the teams were tied to end the period. During the second period, the Soviet team came out even more dominant. The Americans only had two shots on goal and the second period ended with the Soviets leading 3-2.

In the final period, Brooks' strategy of focusing on speed came to the forefront. The American team tied the score once again on a power play. Then, a defensive mistake resulted in Mike Eruzione making a 25-foot wrist shot, giving the American team the 4-3 lead with ten minutes remaining in the game. The Russian coach left his veteran players in the game despite their tired legs. The American team took advantage of that and rolled in four lines in quick shifts. At this point, the Soviets started to panic for the first time in the game.

As the Soviets made a last-ditch effort, broadcaster Al Michaels made the most famous comment in all of American sport, "Eleven seconds. You got ten seconds, the countdown going on right now. Five seconds left in the game! So you believe in miracles? Yes!"

The crowd erupted, as the Soviets offered their congratulations, even smiling at the U.S. team and left the arena quietly. Still to this day the win is called a "Miracle on Ice." However, at that point two games remained in the tournament. If the American team lost to Finland, and the Soviets defeated the Swedish team, based on points the USSR would be gold medalists.

With the support of millions of new American hockey fans watching, the USA team began the final game of the 1980 Winter Games. Finland built a lead of 2-1 after two periods of play. Brooks warned his players that if they lost, that loss would haunt them for the rest of their lives.

The team responded with three goals, securing the gold medal. The U.S. team gathered on the medal podium sealing American hockey's most defining moment. The inspiring story of this team was captured in a motion picture made by Disney in 2004, titled "Miracle."

Fitzpatrick, J., "Miracle on Ice: American Hockey's Defining Moment," http://proicehockey.about.com, copyright 2007 About.com, Inc., a part of The New York Times Company.

Reinforce Your Learning

1. A project team is a group of individuals working __________ to achieve the project __________.

A ***project team*** is a group of individuals working interdependently to achieve the project objective. ***Teamwork*** is the cooperative effort by members of a team to achieve that common goal. The effectiveness—or lack thereof—of the project team can make the difference between project success and project failure. Although plans and project management techniques are necessary, it is the people—the project manager and the project team—that are the key to project success; project success requires an effective project team. This chapter covers the development and maintenance of an effective project team. You will become familiar with

Reinforce Your Learning

2. Teamwork is the __________ effort by members of a team to achieve a __________ goal.

- the development and growth of teams
- characteristics of effective project teams and barriers to effectiveness
- team building
- valuing team diversity
- ethical behavior
- sources of conflict during the project and approaches to handling conflict
- problem solving
- effective time management

PROJECT TEAM DEVELOPMENT AND EFFECTIVENESS

A personal relationship between two people takes time to develop. Initially, you may be curious about each other, but apprehensive about letting your guard down and opening yourself up to the other person. As you get to know each other a little more, you may begin to notice differences in your attitudes and values, and disagreements may arise. You may be anxious about whether the relationship will or should continue. As you work through your differences, you may get to know each other better and become friends. Finally, you may develop a close relationship that helps you to be open with each other, accept each other's differences, and enjoy participating together in activities that are of mutual interest.

Likewise, teams evolve through various stages of development. In many projects, people who have never worked together are assigned to the same project team. This group of individuals must develop into an effective team to achieve the project objective successfully.

Stages of Team Development and Growth

B. W. Tuckman has defined four stages of team development: forming, storming, norming, and performing (see Figure 11.1).

FORMING

Forming is the initial stage of the team development process. It involves the transition from individual to team member. Similar to the early "courting" phase of a relationship, it is when individuals on the team begin to get acquainted. During this stage, team members generally have positive expectations and are eager to get started on the work to be accomplished. The group begins to establish an identity and attempts to define and plan the tasks that need to be done. In this phase, however, little actual work is accomplished because of the high level of anxiety that individuals have about the work itself and about their relationships with each other. Team members are unsure of their own roles and the roles of the other members of the project team. In the forming stage, the team needs direction. Members depend on the project manager to provide direction and structure.

Feelings characteristic of this stage include excitement, anticipation, suspicion, anxiety, and hesitancy. Individuals do a lot of questioning in the forming stage: What is our purpose? Who are the other team members? What are they

Reinforce Your Learning

3. During the forming stage, ______________ actual work is accomplished because of the ______________ level of anxiety that individuals have.

Reinforce Your Learning

4. In the forming stage, individuals do a lot of ______________.

FIGURE 11.1 *Stages of Team Development*

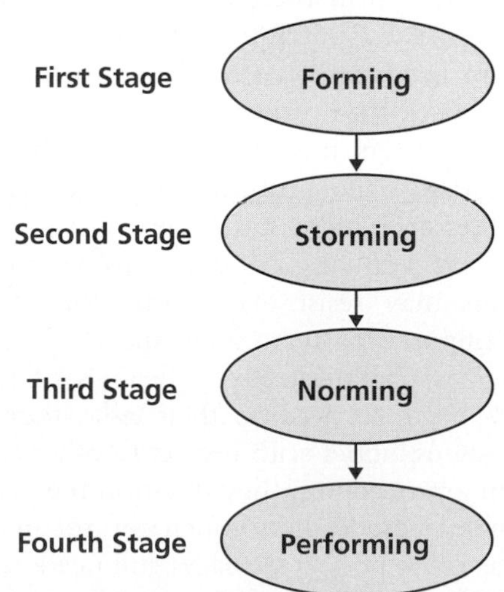

like? Individuals are anxious about whether they will fit in with the other members and be accepted. They may be hesitant to participate because they are unsure how other members will react. Members wonder whether their input will be valued and whether their role in the project aligns with their personal and professional interests.

Reinforce Your Learning

5. During the forming stage, the project manager must provide

________________ and

________________ for the project team.

During the forming stage, the project manager needs to provide direction and structure. In giving orientation to the project team, the project manager must clearly communicate the project objective and create a vision of the successful result of the project and the benefits it will provide. Project constraints regarding the work scope, quality levels, budget, and schedule must be stated. The project manager also needs to discuss the makeup of the project team: the reasons team members were selected, their complementary skills and expertise, and each person's role in helping to accomplish the project objective. Establishing structure is another task the project manager must perform in this phase. This includes defining initial processes and procedures for team operation and addressing such items as communication channels, approvals, and paperwork. These processes and procedures may be improved by the team as it develops through its later stages. To relieve some of the anxiety, the project manager should discuss his or her management style and expectations regarding the work and behavior of the people on the project team. It's also important to get the team working on some initial tasks. Here is where the project manager gets the team to participate in developing the project plans.

STORMING

The second stage of team development is known as *storming*. Like the teenage years, it's usually tough on everyone, but you have to go through it. You can't get around it or avoid it.

The project objective is clearer in this stage. Members start to apply their skills to work on their assigned tasks, and work begins to progress slowly. Reality sets in, though, and it may not match individuals' initial expectations. For example, tasks may be more extensive or difficult than anticipated, or cost or schedule constraints may be tighter than expected. As team members begin to perform their tasks, they feel increasing dissatisfaction with dependence on the direction or authority of the project manager. For example, they may have negative reactions to the project manager and to the operating processes and procedures that were established in the forming stage. Team members now begin to test the limits and flexibility of the project manager and the ground rules. During the storming stage, conflict emerges and tension increases. There is a need for agreement on methods for handling and resolving conflict. Motivation and morale are low in this stage. Members may resist team formation—they want to express their individuality as opposed to team allegiance.

Reinforce Your Learning

6. During the storming stage,

________________ emerges and

________________ increases.

The storming stage is characterized by feelings of frustration, anger, and hostility. As individuals begin to perform their tasks, they have more questions about their roles and responsibilities with respect to other team members. As they begin to follow operating procedures, they question the viability and necessity of such procedures. Members wonder how much control and authority they have.

Reinforce Your Learning

7. During the storming stage, team members wonder how much

________________ and

________________ they have.

In the storming stage, the project manager still needs to be directive, but less directive than in the forming stage. She or he needs to provide clarification and better definition of individual responsibilities and of interfacing activities among team members. It is necessary to begin involving the team in problem-solving activities and to start sharing decision making so as to empower the team. The project manager should acknowledge and tolerate any dissatisfaction expressed by team members—not become defensive or take it personally. This is the time for the project manager to provide an understanding and supportive environment. It's important to give members an opportunity to express their concerns. The project manager has to provide guidance and foster conflict resolution—not try to suppress any dissatisfaction, hoping that it will go away by itself. If dissatisfaction is not addressed, it will build up and could result in dysfunctional behavior later, putting the successful completion of the project at risk.

Reinforce Your Learning

8. During the storming stage, the project manager needs to provide ____________ and foster ____________ ____________.

NORMING

After struggling through the storming stage, the project team moves into the *norming* stage of development. Relationships among team members and between the team and the project manager have become settled. Interpersonal conflicts have been resolved for the most part. In general, the level of conflict is lower than it was in the storming stage. Dissatisfaction, too, is reduced, as individuals' expectations align with the reality of the situation—the work to be done, the resources available, the constraints, and the other individuals involved. The project team has accepted its operating environment. Project procedures are improved and streamlined. Control and decision making are transferred from the project manager to the project team. Cohesion begins to develop. There is a sense of team. Individuals feel accepted as part of the team, and they accept others as part of the team. There is an appreciation of each member's contribution to achieving the project objective.

Trust begins to develop in this stage, as team members start to confide in one another. There is a greater sharing of information, ideas, and feelings; cooperation increases. Team members give and ask for feedback and feel that they can freely and constructively express their emotions and criticisms. A feeling of camaraderie emerges as the team goes through a socialization process. Personal friendships may develop that reach beyond the work environment.

During the norming stage, the project manager minimizes directiveness and takes on a more supportive role. Work performance accelerates and productivity increases. The project manager should recognize the project team for the progress being made.

Reinforce Your Learning

9. In the norming stage, ____________ and ____________ are reduced, ____________ begins to develop, and there is a sense of ____________.

Reinforce Your Learning

10. During the norming stage, ____________ begins to develop. There is a greater sharing of ____________, ____________, and ____________; ____________ increases.

Reinforce Your Learning

11. In the norming stage, ____________ ____________ accelerates and ____________ increases.

PERFORMING

The fourth and final stage of team development and growth is the *performing* stage. In this stage, the team is highly committed and eager to achieve the project objective. The level of work performance is high. The team feels a sense of unity and pride in its accomplishments. Confidence is high. Communication is open, frank, and timely. During this stage, members work individually or in temporary subteams, as needed. There is a great degree of interdependency—members frequently collaborate and willingly help each other with work beyond their own assigned tasks. The team feels fully empowered. As problems are identified, appropriate team members form subteams to solve the problems and decide how the solution should be implemented. There is a feeling of satisfaction as progress is made and recognized. Individual members realize that they are experiencing professional growth as a result of working on the project.

Reinforce Your Learning

12. During the performing stage, there is a great degree of ____________—members frequently ____________ and willingly ____________ each other with work beyond their own assigned tasks.

FIGURE 11.2 *Level of Functioning at Various Stages of Team Development*

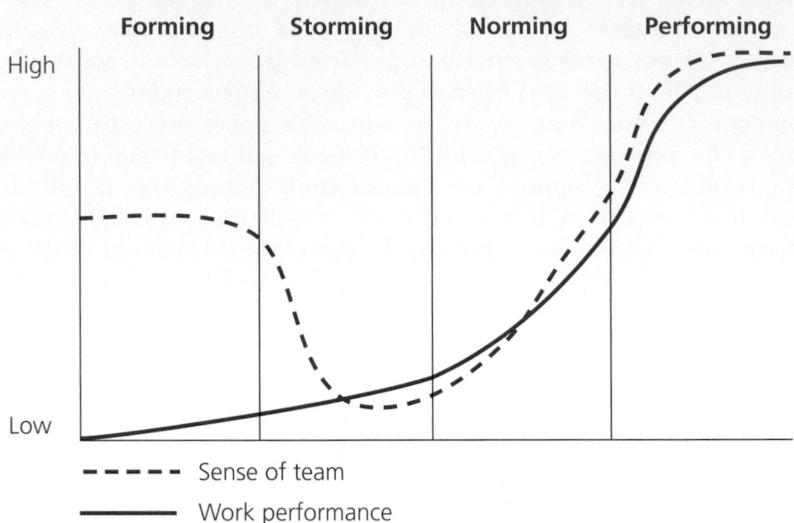

Reinforce Your Learning

13. During the performing stage, the project manager fully ________________ responsibility and authority, thereby empowering the project team.

During the performing stage, the project manager fully delegates responsibility and authority, thereby empowering the project team. He or she focuses on helping the team execute the project plan and giving recognition to team members for their progress and accomplishments. At this stage, the project manager concentrates on project performance with respect to the budget, schedule, scope, and plan. The project manager's role is to facilitate and support the development and implementation of corrective actions if actual progress falls behind planned progress. It is also at this stage that the project manager acts as a mentor, supporting the professional growth and development of the people working on the project.

Reinforce Your Learning

14. What are the four stages of team development and growth?

Figure 11.2 graphically illustrates the levels of work performance and sense of team during the four stages of team development and growth. The amount of time and effort it takes a team to move through each of the stages depends on several factors, including the number of people on the team, whether team members have worked together before, the complexity of the project, and the teamwork skills of the members.

The Effective Project Team

A project team is more than a group of individuals assigned to work on one project. A project team is a group of interdependent individuals working cooperatively to achieve the project objective. Helping these individuals develop and grow into a cohesive, effective team takes effort on the part of the project manager and each member of the project team. As was noted at the beginning of the chapter, the effectiveness—or lack thereof—of the project team can make the difference between project success and project failure. Although plans and project management techniques are necessary, it is the people— the project manager and project team—that are the key to project success; project success requires an effective project team.

Characteristics associated with effective project teams include

- a clear understanding of the project objective
- clear expectations of each person's role and responsibilities
- a results orientation
- a high degree of cooperation and collaboration
- a high level of trust

Reinforce Your Learning

15. An effective project team has a clear understanding of the

____

and clear expectations of each person's

____

and

______________.

A CLEAR UNDERSTANDING OF THE PROJECT OBJECTIVE

The scope, level of quality, budget, and schedule must be well defined for a project team to be effective. If the project objective is to be achieved, each team member must have the same vision of the project result and the benefits it will provide.

CLEAR EXPECTATIONS OF EACH PERSON'S ROLE AND RESPONSIBILITIES

Members of an effective team know how their work must fit together, because they participated in developing the project plans. Team members appreciate each other's expertise, skills, and contributions to achieving the project objective. Each person accepts responsibility for carrying out her or his part of the project.

A RESULTS ORIENTATION

Each person on an effective project team has a strong commitment to achieving the project objective. By setting a good example, the project manager sets the tone for the energy level. Team members are enthusiastic and willing to spend the time and energy necessary to succeed. For example, individuals are willing to work extra hours or weekends or skip lunches when necessary in order to keep the project on track.

Reinforce Your Learning

16. Effective project teams have a

____

orientation; each person has a strong commitment to achieving the

____

______________.

There is a high degree of

____

and

______________.

A HIGH DEGREE OF COOPERATION AND COLLABORATION

Open, frank, and timely communication is the norm on an effective project team. Members readily share information, ideas, and feelings. They are not shy about asking other members for help. Team members act as resources for each other, beyond just doing their assigned tasks. They want to see other members succeed in their tasks and are willing to help and support them if they are stuck or faltering. They give and accept feedback and constructive criticism. Because of this cooperation, the team is creative in problem solving and timely in decision making.

A HIGH LEVEL OF TRUST

Members of an effective team understand interdependency and accept that everyone on the team is important to project success. Each member can count on the other members to do what they say they will do—and at the expected level of quality. There is a shared sense of trust. Team members care for and about one another. Because differences are accepted, members feel free to be themselves. Differences of opinion are encouraged, freely expressed, and respected. Individuals are able to raise issues that may result in disagreement or conflict without concern about retribution. Effective project teams resolve conflict through constructive and timely feedback and positive confrontation of the issues. Disagreement is not suppressed; rather, it is seen as normal and as an opportunity for growth and learning.

Reinforce Your Learning

17. Effective project teams have a high level of

______________.

They are able to resolve conflict through constructive and timely

____

and positive

____

of the issues.

Figure 11.3 is a checklist for rating the effectiveness of a project team. It is recommended that team members complete this assessment instrument periodically during the project. After the scores of all team members have been summarized, the team, including the project manager, should discuss how to improve in any areas that were rated low.

FIGURE 11.3 ***Team Effectiveness Checklist***

How Effective Is Your Project Team?

	Not at All		Somewhat		Very Much
1. Does your team have a clear understanding of its goal?	1	2	3	4	5
2. Are the project scope, level of quality, budget, and schedule well defined?	1	2	3	4	5
3. Does everyone have clear expectations of his or her own role and responsibilities?	1	2	3	4	5
4. Does everyone have clear expectations of other members' roles and responsibilities?	1	2	3	4	5
5. Does everyone know the expertise and skills that each person brings to the team?	1	2	3	4	5
6. Is your team results oriented?	1	2	3	4	5
7. Does everyone have a strong commitment to achieving the project objective?	1	2	3	4	5
8. Does your team have a high level of enthusiasm and energy?	1	2	3	4	5
9. Does your team have a high degree of cooperation and collaboration?	1	2	3	4	5
10. Are open, frank, and timely communications the norm?	1	2	3	4	5
11. Do members readily share information, ideas, and feelings?	1	2	3	4	5
12. Do members feel free to ask other members for help?	1	2	3	4	5
13. Do members willingly help one another?	1	2	3	4	5
14. Do team members give feedback and constructive criticism?	1	2	3	4	5
15. Do team members accept feedback and constructive criticism?	1	2	3	4	5
16. Is there a high level of trust among the project team members?	1	2	3	4	5
17. Do members follow through on what they say they will do?	1	2	3	4	5
18. Is there an openness to differing viewpoints?	1	2	3	4	5
19. Do team members accept one another and their differences?	1	2	3	4	5
20. Does your team constructively resolve conflicts?	1	2	3	4	5

Barriers to Team Effectiveness

Although every project team has the potential to be highly effective, there are often barriers that impede a team's achievement of the level of effectiveness of which it is capable. Following are barriers that can hinder project team effectiveness and some suggestions for overcoming them.

UNCLEAR GOALS

The project manager needs to articulate the project objective, as well as the project scope, level of quality, budget, and schedule. He or she needs to create a vision of the project result and the benefits it will provide. This information needs to be communicated at the very first project meeting. At this meeting, the project manager needs to ask team members if they understand this information and answer any questions they may have. The information should then be provided in written form, along with any clarification given during the initial project meeting, to each individual on the project team.

Periodically, the project manager needs to discuss the project objective at project status review meetings. At these meetings, he or she should always ask whether anyone has any questions about what must be accomplished. Telling the team what the project objective is only once, at the beginning of the project, is not sufficient. The project manager must say it, write it, distribute it, and repeat it frequently.

Reinforce Your Learning

18. The project manager needs to articulate the project ____________ frequently. At periodic meetings, he or she should always ask whether anyone has any ____________ about what must be accomplished.

UNCLEAR DEFINITION OF ROLES AND RESPONSIBILITIES

Individuals may feel that their roles and responsibilities are ambiguous or that there is overlap in the responsibilities of some individuals. At the beginning of the project, the project manager should meet individually with each member of the project team, to explain why she or he was selected for the project, describe her or his expected role and responsibilities, and detail how they relate to the other team members' roles and responsibilities. Project team members need to feel free to ask the project manager to clarify any areas of ambiguity or overlap whenever they become apparent. As the project team develops the project plan, each member's tasks should be identified using a tool such as a work breakdown structure, a responsibility matrix, a Gantt chart, or a network diagram (all of these were discussed in Part 2 of the text). Copies of these documents should be given to everyone so that each team member can see not only her or his own assigned tasks but also other members' tasks and how they all fit together.

Reinforce Your Learning

19. The project manager should meet individually with each team member, to tell the member why he or she was ____________ for the project and describe her or his expected ____________ and ____________.

LACK OF PROJECT STRUCTURE

Individuals may feel that everyone is working in a different direction or that there are no established procedures for team operation. This, too, is a reason for the project manager to have the team participate in developing the project plan.

A tool such as a network diagram (discussed in Part 2) shows how everyone's work fits together to accomplish the project objective. At the beginning of the project, the project manager should establish preliminary operating procedures that address such issues as communication channels, approvals, and documentation requirements. Each procedure, as well as the rationale for establishing it, needs to be explained to the team at a project meeting. The procedures should also be provided in written form to all team members. If some team members do not follow the procedures or circumvent them, the project manager needs to reinforce the importance of everyone consistently following established procedures. However, the project manager needs to be open to suggestions for eliminating or streamlining procedures when they no longer contribute to the effective and efficient performance of the project.

Reinforce Your Learning

20. The project manager needs to establish preliminary operating ________ at the beginning of the project, but be open to suggestions for ________ or ________ them when they no longer ________ to the effective and efficient performance of the project.

LACK OF COMMITMENT

Team members may not appear to be committed to their project work or the project objective. To counter such indifference, the project manager needs to explain to each individual the importance of his or her role on the team and how he or she can contribute to the success of the project. The project manager also needs to ask team members what their personal and professional interests are and look for ways that the project assignment might help satisfy these interests. She or he should try to determine what motivates each individual and then create a project environment where these motivators are available. The project manager also needs to recognize the accomplishments of each person and support and encourage his or her progress.

Reinforce Your Learning

21. The project manager should try to determine what ________ each individual and then create a project ________ where these motivators are available.

POOR COMMUNICATION

Poor communication occurs when team members lack knowledge about what is happening on the project and individuals don't share information. It's important for the project manager to have regular project status review meetings with a published agenda. Various project team members should be asked to give a briefing on the status of their work. Participation and questions should be encouraged. All project documents, such as plans, budgets, schedules, and reports, should be kept up to date and distributed in a timely manner to the entire project team. The project manager should encourage team members to get together to share information, collaborate, and solve problems as needed, rather than wait for official project meetings. Also, physically locating all members of the project team in the same office area can enhance project communications.

Reinforce Your Learning

22. It's important for the project manager to have regular project ________ ________ meetings with a published agenda. ________ and questions should be encouraged during such meetings.

POOR LEADERSHIP

To keep the project team from feeling that the project manager is not providing effective leadership for the team, the project manager has to be willing to solicit feedback from the project team periodically by asking questions like "How am I doing?" or "How can I improve my leadership?" However, she or he must first establish a project environment in which individuals feel free to provide feedback without fear of retribution. The project manager should state at an early project meeting that feedback will be requested periodically and that others' suggestions for improving her or his leadership skills are welcome. For example, a project manager might say that she is interested in improving her leadership skills so as to enhance her own contribution to the success of the project. Of course, she then must be willing to follow up on appropriate suggestions, whether they involve additional training, changing her behavior, or modifying project procedures.

Reinforce Your Learning

23. A project manager should periodically solicit others' suggestions for improving her or his ________ skills.

TURNOVER OF PROJECT TEAM MEMBERS

When team composition changes often—that is, when new people are continually being assigned to a project and others are leaving—the flow of individuals may be too dynamic for the team to jell. A project team made up of a small number of individuals with long-term assignments will be more efficient than a project team composed of a large number of individuals with short-term assignments. The project manager should select for the project team people who are sufficiently versatile in expertise and skills that they can contribute to many areas of the project and thus be assigned to a project for a long period of time. Although the project manager should not try to run the project with a multitude of individuals with narrow expertise who will be assigned to the project for only short intervals, in some cases it may be appropriate for individuals with specific expertise to be assigned to the project for only one task or for a limited time.

Reinforce Your Learning

24. A project team made up of a ______________ number of individuals with ______________ -term assignments will be more efficient than a project team composed of a ______________ number of individuals with ______________ -term assignments.

DYSFUNCTIONAL BEHAVIOR

Sometimes an individual exhibits behavior that is disruptive to the development of an effective team—hostility, excessive clowning around, or making disparaging personal remarks, for example. The project manager needs to meet with this individual, point out the disruptive behavior, and explain that it is unacceptable because of the impact it's having on the rest of the project team. The individual might be offered coaching, a training seminar, or counseling, if appropriate. The project manager must make it clear, however, that if the dysfunctional behavior continues, the person will be released from the project team. Of course, the project manager needs to be prepared to follow through, if necessary.

Being an Effective Team Member

Being a member of a project team should be an enriching and satisfying growth experience for each individual. However, growth will not just happen by itself. It requires a sense of responsibility, hard work, open-mindedness, and a desire for further self-development. Although the project manager is ultimately responsible for the success of a project, each member of the project team shares in that responsibility. Each member of the project team needs to help create and foster a positive and effective project environment.

Reinforce Your Learning

25. What are some barriers to team effectiveness?

Effective team members plan, control, and feel accountable for their individual work efforts. They have high expectations of themselves and strive to accomplish their assignments under budget and ahead of schedule. They manage their time well. They make things happen, they don't just let them happen. Effective team members don't simply work on a task until they are told to stop—they're self-directed and follow through on assignments and action items. They take pride in doing quality work instead of expecting other team members to finish, clean up, or redo any of their shabby or incomplete work. Each team member can count on all the other team members to perform their respective tasks in a quality and timely manner so as not to delay or impede the work of other team members.

Reinforce Your Learning

26. Effective team members plan, control, and feel ______________ for their individual work efforts. They have high ______________ of themselves.

Effective team members participate and communicate. They don't sit back and wait to be asked; they speak up and participate in meetings. They take the initiative, communicating with other team members and the project manager in a clear, timely, and unambiguous manner. They provide constructive feedback to each other. In particular, effective team members feel responsible for identifying problems—or potential problems—as early as possible, without pointing the finger or blaming other individuals, the customer, or the project manager for causing the problems. Effective team members are not only problem identifiers but also problem solvers. When a problem has been identified, they suggest alternative solutions and are ready and willing to collaborate with other team members to solve the problem, even if it is outside of their assigned area of responsibility. Effective team members do not have a "that's not my problem" or "that's not my job" attitude; rather, they are willing to pitch in to help the team achieve the project objective.

Reinforce Your Learning

27. Effective team members ______________ and ______________. They are not only problem identifiers, but also ______________ ______________.

Real World PROJECT MANAGEMENT

Honesty in Project Management

According to Richard Fox, Associate Director at Project Management Institute's Information Systems Specific Interest Group (ISSIG) and editor of the *ISSIG Review*, honesty is a topic that is very often overlooked when people write about, or talk about, project management. And, he is absolutely right! However, the proper application of honesty can allow project managers to be more effective, ease the stress of their jobs, and help them gain the trust of their clients, which can lead to additional projects.

Fox defines honesty very simply as "telling the truth." This applies to all project management activities including time and cost estimates; resource assignments; evaluation of risks; and communications to clients, community groups, management, project sponsors, team members, users, and vendors. The concept of honesty must apply to all team members as well.

Honesty must start right at the beginning of the project when the objective, costs, schedules, risk, etc., are being defined. Projects of all types fail because (1) there is not enough time, money, and/or other resource available and (2) there are often unclear expectations and unrealistic deadlines. Building an honest plan at the beginning of the project can make a project much easier to manage.

Fox suggests that all project managers should ask themselves whether they have ever:

1. Fudged an estimate to increase their likelihood of success?
2. Deliberately over/under-estimated a completion date?
3. Deliberately over/under-estimated the cost or time needed for a change request?
4. Reported actual days or hours worked that weren't exactly right?
5. Reported that a task was complete when it really wasn't?

Additional questions might include:

1. Have you ever over/under-estimated the risks of a project to your client?
2. Have you ever withheld pertinent information when communicating information about your project?
3. Have you ever realized the budget or schedule was slipping and not taken immediate action to communicate the situation and/or not taken immediate corrective actions to get the project back on track?

The list could go on and on.

Honesty should be an integral part of all project phases from project definition to project planning to project implementation to project control to project completion/termination. During project definition, the project manager should avoid setting the expectations too high and she should clearly communicate all goals and objectives to the stakeholders. During project planning, the project manager must do her best to identify all required tasks, properly estimate the duration and costs for each activity, and assign resources without a hidden agenda. In addition, she must honestly identify each risk and the probability of the risk occurring, and honestly assess the impact of each risk. Deliberately over- or underestimating a risk can doom a project to failure.

In the course of the project, the project manager must do her best to collect accurate figures on percentages of work complete and actual costs. She must also do her best to be honest when projecting the impact of the true cost/time needed to handle a change request. And finally, the project manager must be fair and honest when communicating with clients, team members, and numerous people within and outside of the organization. A project manager with a reputation as an honest person, whose words and actions can be trusted, will have a better chance of success on current and future projects.

Fox presents the following "Magic Elements" for honesty in project management: 1) a true understanding and agreement among the team, users, and management, 2) a fair and accurate project plan, and 3) constant and open communications. Being honest in all aspects of project management will increase your effectiveness, build trust with all stakeholders, and result in obtaining additional projects in the future!

Fox, R., "Honesty in Project Management," *ISSIG Review*, Vol. XI, Issue 2, 2007.

Effective team members help to create a positive, constructive project environment in which there is no room for divisiveness. They're sensitive to the diverse composition of the project team and show respect for all members of the team. They respect others' viewpoints. They don't let pride, stubbornness, or arrogance get in the way of collaboration, cooperation, and compromise. Effective team members put the success of the project above personal gain.

It has been said that there is no I in TEAM—there are no individual winners or losers. When a project is successful, everybody wins!

Reinforce Your Learning

28. Think about projects in which you have been involved. What are some characteristics of individual team members that made them effective contributors?

Team Building

Legendary baseball manager Casey Stengel once said, "It's easy to get the players. Gettin' 'em to play together, that's the hard part." **Team building**—developing a group of individuals to accomplish the project objective—is an ongoing process. It is the responsibility of both the project manager and the project team. Team building helps to create an atmosphere of openness and trust. Members feel a sense of unity and a strong commitment to accomplishing the project objective. Chapter 10 discussed various things that the project manager can do to foster and support team building. Here we will discuss a few things that the project team can do to help the team-building process.

Reinforce Your Learning

29. Team building is the responsibility of both the ______________ ______________ and the ______________ ______________.

Socializing among team members supports team building. The better team members get to know one another, the more team building is enhanced. To ensure that individual members communicate with one another frequently, situations need to be created that foster socializing among team members. Team members can initiate some of these situations.

Reinforce Your Learning

30. ______________ among team members supports ______________ ______________. Individual members need to ______________ with one another frequently.

The team can request that team members be physically located in one office area for the duration of the project. When team members are located near one another, there is a greater chance that they will go to each other's offices or work areas to talk. Also, they will pass each other more frequently in common areas such as hallways and have a chance to stop and talk. Discussions should not always be work related. It's important that team members get to know one another on a personal basis, without being intrusive. A certain number of personal friendships will develop during the project. Having the entire project team located in one area prevents that "us versus them" feeling that can arise when parts of the team are located in different parts of a building or plant. Such a situation can result in a project team that is really a set of several subgroups rather than a true team.

The project team can initiate social events to celebrate project events, such as reaching a critical milestone—a system's passing a test or a successful design review meeting with the customer—or events can be scheduled periodically just for stress relief. An after-work pizza party, a team luncheon, an informal lunch in the conference room, a weekend family picnic, and a trip to see a sports event or theater production are examples of events the team can organize to foster socializing and team building. It's important that such activities include everyone on the team. Although some individuals may not be able to participate, everyone should at least be invited and encouraged to participate. Team members should use these events to get to know as many other team members (and their families, if they participate) as possible. A good rule of thumb is to always try to sit next to someone you don't know too well and strike up a conversation—ask questions, listen to what the other person says, look for areas of common interest. It is important for individuals to avoid forming cliques composed of several people who always hang together at every event. Engaging in social events not only helps to develop a sense of camaraderie but also makes it easier for team members to engage in open and frank communication while working on the project.

In addition to organizing social activities, the team can periodically call team meetings, as opposed to project meetings. The purpose of team meetings is to discuss openly such questions as the following: How are we working as a team? What barriers are impeding teamwork (such as procedures, resources, priorities, or communications)? What can we do to overcome these barriers? What can we do to improve teamwork? If the project manager participates in team meetings, he or she should be treated as an equal—team members should not look to the manager for the answers, and he or she should not pull rank and override the consensus of the team. It's a team meeting, not a project meeting. Only team-related issues, not project items, should be discussed.

Team members should foster team building in whatever ways they can. They should not expect the project manager alone to be responsible for team building.

Valuing Team Diversity

Globalization, changes in demographics and the need for individuals with unique skills are causing changes in the make-up or diversity of project teams. *Diversity* is differences among people. Diversity is about acknowledging, understanding, and valuing differences and creating a work environment that recognizes, respects, and harnesses differences among team members for the benefits of accomplishing a shared goal, such as the project objective. However, differences can create barriers to team performance. Miscommunication and misunderstanding may be more likely to happen between people who are different. If the differences within the project team are not valued as a strength, they can lead to low morale, diminished trust, reduced productivity, greater tension, and suspicion and become a serious impediment to team performance. Team members should feel valued and have a sense of belonging. Diversity of the team brings unique ideas and perspectives to projects. Each team member has unique experiences, skills, and values they bring to the team. Such differences can lead to more creative, faster, and higher-quality problem solving and decision making.

Reinforce Your Learning

31. Diversity of the team brings ________ ideas and ________ to projects.

Chances are that most project teams are diverse in more ways than you think. The following are some dimensions of diversity:

- *Age* or generational. Many teams have a mix of members of various age groups—younger, older, and in-between. Three or four generations can be represented on a team. Each generation has different experiences that shaped their values and perspectives and thus responds to different motivational factors. Older team members may value security, a strong work ethic, adherence to rules, and prefer face-to-face meetings, whereas younger members may value work/life balance and informality, dislike close supervision, and prefer electronic connections with others.
- *Appearance.* Team members are different in weight, height, facial features, hairstyle, dress, jewelry, body piercing, and tattoos. These characteristics can become a barrier to team effectiveness if some team members make assumptions about other members' competence or performance based on their appearance.
- *Ethnicity* or ancestry. Driven by globalization, projects have team members located around the globe as well as project work packages that may be outsourced to subcontractors on several continents. Moreover, decedents of immigrants are accessing higher education and attaining skilled positions. Therefore more project teams include people in or from different countries or with various national ancestries. Team members may have not only different levels of language proficiency, but different customs and norms as well. Behaviors, and words or phrases that are not considered offensive in one culture may be considered offensive in another culture. Team members may have different concepts of time (punctuality), communication styles (greetings, eye contact, hand gestures, personal space), protocol (formality, hierarchical) as well as on the role of women or elders. Team members need to exhibit patience when another person is struggling with the language or pronunciations.
- *Gender.* Project teams increasingly include a higher proportion of women as more women enter and stay in the workforce, particularly in positions that require specific high demand skills, such as in information and technology positions. Men and women may behave and communicate differently due to differences in their socialization process. Different communication styles can lead to misinterpretation and misunderstanding.
- *Health.* Teams are diverse with respect to the health or wellness of their members. This includes physical and mental abilities as well as behavioral disorders. Some of these differences are visible, such as prostheses or a cane, while other health matters are less visible (heart condition, anxiety disorder). Team members need to accommodate each other with respect to health matters and not "label" people or discount their capabilities and contributions.
- *Job Status.* Many project teams include members of different levels of experience and skills, as well as different levels of seniority and job titles. Team members should not make assumptions about the potential contribution of another member based on their job title or position. Excluding team members from meetings or problem-solving discussions because they may be considered in a lower level position or do not have the specific expertise can be a missed opportunity for some new or creative ideas.

- *Marital and Parental Status*. With respect to conditions such as people getting married at a later age, divorced, married several times, widowed, and so on, and with blended families, both spouses working, single parents, and childless couples or partners, the composition of project teams is more diverse. Team members should not make assumptions about the availability or effectiveness of other members based on their marital or parental status, such as assuming that a single person would have more time to work on a challenging assignment. Members need to accommodate the unique needs of team members, such as finishing a meeting on time so a member can pick up their child from child care by a certain time.
- *Race*. With globalization, migration between countries, and racial minorities accessing higher education and attaining skilled positions, project teams increasingly have a mix of people of traditionally under-represented races. Team members should avoid stereotyping others in the team from different races. Individuals from various races can bring different and enriching perspectives to project team discussions and processes.
- *Religious Affiliation*. Just as globalization affects the make-up of project teams with respect to ethnic and racial diversity, it also impacts teams with respect to religious diversity. There are variety of religions worldwide, including Buddhism, Christianity, Hinduism, Islam, and Judaism. Each religion has particular practices such as daily prayer times, observance of holy days, dietary restrictions, avoiding touching the opposite gender, etc. Individuals may have great devotion to their religious beliefs and practices. Team members need to respect other members' religious practices and accommodate them in accomplishing the project schedule.
- Other aspects of diversity among the project team can include sexual orientation, political affiliation, personal habits, such as smoking, and personal interests, such as hunting, traveling, etc. Like the other dimensions of diversity mentioned above, these elements need to be respected, even if there may be personal disagreement, such as regarding political affiliation, in order to create an environment of trust and support that is necessary for successful team performance.

Reinforce Your Learning

32. What are some dimensions of diversity?

Stereotyping is categorizing individuals into a group and then conferring on them the characteristics that we believe apply universally to all members of that group. Project team members should not stereotype or make assumptions about a team member's behavior or performance based on their diversity. Don't attribute a team member's performance to their difference or to a particular diversity characteristic (gender, age, race, etc.); for example, "That activity was very tedious and required attention to detail. Kim did a good job on it because Asians and women are good at those kinds of tasks." Similarly, don't blame team members for something that went wrong and relate it to their diversity (e.g. physical disability, language skills); for example, "His task didn't get done on time because he couldn't keep up with the rest of the team due to his heart condition" or, "We had to do everything over because her directions were not clear because of her poor language skills."

Team members should not exclude or have lower expectations of certain diverse groups, as seen by, for example, assigning them less challenging tasks or assuming that a female team member can't handle additional responsibilities because of her family obligations. Differences do not imply inferiority or superiority. Don't discount a team member's comments or their contribution just because of their diverse characteristics; for example, not asking the opinion of a younger team member or a clerical worker or craftsperson.

Do not identify or refer to team members by drawing attention to their diversity; for example, "He's the one in the wheelchair" (or "the good-looking one," or "the fat guy," or "the short woman," etc.). Nor should team members make derogatory or insensitive remarks or engage in behavior that demeans the dignity of others; such as making fun of the spelling or pronunciation of a person's name (rather than asking them for the correct pronunciation), what they wear (turban, earring, etc.), or a religious practice such as saying a prayer before they eat their meal.

It is inappropriate for team members to tell jokes, ridicule, or make fun of a diversity characteristic of a team member or a particular group. Such behavior often reinforces stereotypes. Innuendoes are also made by what is said or written (e-mailed), the words used ("those people," "them"), how it is said (disdainful tone), or body language used (smirk, raised eye brows, shaking head). Even if unintentional, a person may use a phrase or term that confuses or embarrasses another team member. Although one team member may think a comment is funny, another person may consider it offensive or hurtful. Also, there is a chance that a person may be offended because they have an acquaintance such as a spouse, child, or parent who may be in the group that is the brunt of the joke; for example, people with a physical disability.

Inappropriate behavior regarding diversity includes closed-mindedness, stereotyping, labeling, exclusion, ridiculing, insulting, harassment, intimidation, and discrimination. An individual who is offended or a victim of such behavior may not react or speak up. They may develop resentment for certain team members, which could affect team cohesion, morale, and performance. If a team member feels something that was said or done is offensive, they should address it with the offender and perhaps take the opportunity to educate the person about why it was offensive. Any diversity issues or conflicts should be addressed immediately so they can be resolved before they fester and "explode" at a later time. If a team member exhibits unacceptable behavior regarding the various aspects of diversity, or sees such behavior among the team, the concern needs to be discussed with the project manager or the organization's management about how the issues should be addressed—on an individual basis, with the group of individuals involved, or with the entire team. If diversity-related issues are not addressed, it can have serious impacts on the project team and work environment, such as frequent conflicts, a hostile climate, strained communication, and poor performance, as well as affect specific team members due to increased anxiety, nervousness, and stress. It could also lead to a formal complaint by an individual or group and could possibly result in lawsuits against the project contractor and/or specific team members. It could also lead to disciplinary action against individual team members, including dismissal from the team or termination of employment.

Reinforce Your Learning

33. Team members should not ______________ or make ______________ about a team member's behavior or ______________ based on their ______________.

What can a project organization do to create and sustain a supportive and positive climate for diversity? There are things that can be done by the project organization, project manager, and individual team members in this regard.

Two actions the project organization can take are to develop a written policy regarding diversity and to provide training about diversity in the workplace. The goals of the policy might be to create a work environment where (1) all team members flourish; (2) differences are respected and valued; (3) the right of all team members to participate and contribute is respected; (4) each team member is valued and respected for their unique contributions; and (5) there will be zero tolerance for breach of respect or intolerant behavior.

Reinforce Your Learning

34. Two actions an organization can take to support a positive climate for diversity are to have a written ____________ regarding diversity and provide ____________ about diversity in the workplace.

Barriers to valuing diversity include lack of awareness and lack of understanding. Therefore, a training session on diversity should raise awareness, create understanding, and help diminish misunderstanding and conflict. Providing a training session on diversity to the project team at the beginning of the project to inform them of the organization's policy, and incorporating case studies and role plays, is a helpful approach. Mandating such training sends a message that the project organization places high importance on valuing diversity. One outcome of the training might be that team members become comfortable asking questions about differences and preferred interactions in the workplace. An example of how additional informal training can take place throughout the project might be to have team lunches where team members of different nationalities bring ethnic food to share and explain some of their customs.

Reinforce Your Learning

35. Barriers to valuing diversity include lack of ____________ and lack of ____________.

The project manager must promote and foster a respectful and supportive work environment that removes barriers to valuing diversity, values differences, and encourages participation by all team members. She must establish and clearly communicate expectations and exemplify that expected behavior. The project manager should discuss the importance of respecting and valuing diversity at a project team meeting at the beginning of the project and periodically throughout the project, as well as discuss those expectations with new members as part of their orientation when they join the team.

Team members can also do things to support valuing diversity and the contributions of all team members. Individual team members can make a personal commitment to understand and value diversity and respect the differences of other team members. Don't make assumptions about other team members' value or potential contributions. Be aware of and acknowledge your own stereotypes of diverse groups. Learn from team members who are different than you and demonstrate respect by striving to learn from differences among team members. Look for occasions for "learning opportunities." Make an effort to enhance your awareness and understanding of the various dimensions of diversity through participation in training, reading, social activities, informal discussions, etc. For example, take the time to get to know other team members outside of the work environment in a more relaxed social setting. Be open-minded, exhibit professional behavior, act in a civilized manner, and have a considerate regard for others.

Diversity is about acknowledging, understanding and valuing differences, and creating a work environment that recognizes, respects, and harnesses differences for the benefits of accomplishing a shared goal. It should be seen and valued by the project team as a strength that can enrich communication, foster better relationships, create an enjoyable workplace, and enhance team performance. Diversity of the team brings unique ideas and perspectives to projects. Each team member has unique experiences, skills and values they contribute to the team. Such differences can lead to more creative, faster, and higher quality problem solving and decision making. Team members need to interact with each other differently based on each person's unique differences. Having a common goal such as the project objective can bring a diverse group together.

Key points to remember regarding valuing team diversity:

- Don't make assumptions or judgments about team members' value-added contributions just because of their diversity characteristics.
- Think before you speak. Once something is said, you can't take it back; and you may lose the respect of other team members.

Reinforce Your Learning

36. What are some reasons why the project team should value diversity as a strength?

ETHICAL BEHAVIOR

Bill stopped by Pat's office and said, "Hey Pat, what'd ya say we skip out this afternoon and go golfing. The boss isn't around. If anybody asks, we can just say we're going to the construction site to check on some stuff. We've been working hard so we deserve it, so we shouldn't have to charge it to our vacation time. We're a lot more productive than some of the other people around here anyway. I told the boss the task we're working on would take us 10 days, and we should easily finish in about 6 days, just like I figured we would anyway. So hey, we've got some time coming to us."

Is Bill's behavior ethical? What should Pat do? If you were the owner of a small business and some of your employees did this and you found out about it, what would you do?

There are situations when, rather than doing the right thing, individuals rationalize their actions—" It's not hurting anyone," "Everybody does it." Some people will try to get others to go along with them, or be party to the action, to validate that it must be okay if another person also agrees to do it.

Not only is ethical behavior necessary within a project organization, but it is crucial in project business relationships with the customer, suppliers, and subcontractors. Customers and suppliers want to do business with a contractor or project organization they can trust. This is especially important in what information the project manager or team members communicate to the customer. Withholding or falsifying information is unacceptable, especially in situations where potential safety consequences are concerned. There certainly may be gray areas of reporting. For example, when do you tell a customer of a potential problem—immediately when the problem is identified, after you have attempted to resolve the problem, or once you've developed an action plan to resolve the problem? Will the customer overreact too soon? It is important to communicate honestly about such situations in a timely manner that is objective and neither unnecessarily alarming nor misleading.

Reinforce Your Learning

37. Customers and suppliers want to do business with a project contractor they can ______________.

Throughout a project there are situations that can provide an opportunity for unethical behavior or misconduct. Some examples are:

- Intentionally submitting a low bid on a proposal with the intention that you will make up the price by charging the customer for high-priced changes after you get the contract.
- Purchasing materials from suppliers who give you "kickbacks" or gifts for doing business with them, rather than using fair, open competition practices.
- Dishonesty in time card reporting of hours worked, resulting in over-charges to the customer.
- Padding or falsifying travel expense reports.
- Plagiarizing the work of others and taking credit for it.
- Knowingly using marginal or unsafe materials or designs.
- Taking project supplies or using project equipment for personal use.
- Putting pressure on the project team to charge more or less hours than they actually worked to mislead management or the customer that the project expenditures are within budget.
- Knowingly approving test results that are inaccurate.
- Paying off inspectors to approve work that otherwise may not have passed inspection.

There are many circumstances during a project that are debatable regarding misbehavior. For example, if a project schedule slips, is it because the contractor or a project team member intentionally provided unrealistic time estimates originally, or was he or she genuinely optimistic that the work could get done in the estimated duration? It really points to "intention" or doing something knowingly—was the intent to knowingly mislead? Intentional distortion, deception, or misrepresentation is outright unethical.

What can a project organization do to promote ethical behavior and reduce the chances of any misconduct?

Certainly the project manager must set the tone and expectations and must exemplify ethical behavior. If the project team sees the project manager taking actions or making decisions that are ethically questionable, they will think that it is okay for them to do the same thing. The project manager must be committed to always doing what is right and fair and communicate the same expectations to the project team.

Two actions a project organization can take to help prevent any wrongdoing are to have a written policy on ethical behavior and to provide training about ethics in the workplace. A policy on ethical behavior should include topics on expectations, process for reporting misconduct, and consequences of engaging in unethical practices. The project manager should discuss the importance of ethical behavior at a project team meeting at the beginning of the project, and mention it regularly at meetings throughout the project. Ethical actions, such as a project team member raising an issue about an unsafe design, should be encouraged, acknowledged and appreciated. Misconduct or conflict of interest activities must be addressed and appropriate disciplinary action taken to show that such behavior is unacceptable and will not be tolerated.

Providing a training session on ethical behavior to inform the project team of the organization's policy, and incorporating case studies or role-plays, is a helpful approach. Employees who participate in ethics training are less likely to engage in wrongdoing. Mandating such training sends a message that the project organization places high value on ethical behavior. Also when new members are brought onto the project team, the project manager should discuss the importance of, and expectations for, ethical behavior as part of an orientation meeting.

Reinforce Your Learning

38. Two actions an organization can take to help prevent any wrongdoing are to have a

____

______________________ on ethical behavior and to provide

______________________ about ethics in the workplace.

Project team members need to be informed that if they are not sure of or hesitant about a possible ethical or conflict of interest situation, they should bring it to the attention of the project manager before taking action. The project organization should also establish a nonthreatening process for individuals to report any actions by others that they consider unethical or misconduct. For example, this process might include a procedure for individuals to report such matters anonymously, or to be able to report them to or discuss them with an independent party, such as the Human Resources manager. If a case of wrongdoing is reported—for example, someone alleges that a person on the project team is falsifying their travel expense reports—the organization must thoroughly investigate such allegations for facts versus hearsay before any disciplinary action is taken.

Ethical behavior is everyone's responsibility, not just the project manager's. Every member of the project team must feel accountable for his or her actions. Personal integrity is the foundation for workplace ethics. Individuals who have a mind-set of trying to "get away (from being caught) with things" will erode that foundation. Other members of the project team need to put peer pressure on such individuals to help modify such behavior by communicating that they do not agree with, condone, accept, or want to be party to such behavior.

Key principles to guide ethical behavior on projects are:

- Treat others the way you would like to be treated.
- Don't do anything that you wouldn't want your family, friends, neighbors, or coworkers to read about in the newspaper or hear on the news.

Reinforce Your Learning

39. ______________________

______________________ is the foundation for workplace ethics.

CONFLICT ON PROJECTS

Conflict on projects is inevitable. You might think that conflict is bad and should be avoided. Differences of opinion are natural, however, and must be expected. It would be a mistake to try to suppress conflict, as it can be beneficial. It provides an opportunity to gain new information, consider alternatives, develop better solutions to problems, enhance team building, and learn. As part of the team-building process, the project manager and project team need to openly acknowledge that disagreement is bound to occur during the performance of the project and reach a consensus on how it should be handled. Such a discussion needs to take place at the beginning of the project, not when the first situation occurs or after there has been an emotional outburst.

The following sections discuss the sources of conflict on a project and approaches to handling these conflicts.

Sources of Conflict

During a project, conflict can emerge from a variety of situations. It can involve members of the project team, the project manager, and even the customer. Here are seven sources of potential conflict on projects.

WORK SCOPE

Conflict can arise from differences of opinion on how the work should be done, how much work should be done, or at what level of quality the work should be done. Take the following cases:

- In a project to develop an order-tracking system, one team member thinks that bar coding technology should be used, whereas another individual thinks that keypad data entry stations should be used. This is a conflict over the technical approach to the job.
- In a town festival project, one team member thinks that mailing an advertisement about the festival to each household in the town is sufficient, whereas another thinks that the mailing should be sent to all residents in the county and advertisements should be placed in newspapers. This is a conflict over how much work should be included.
- As part of a project to build a home, a contractor has put one coat of paint on each room in the house. Upon inspection, however, the customer is not satisfied that one coat is sufficient and demands that the contractor put on a second coat at no additional cost. This is a conflict over the level of quality of the work.

RESOURCE ASSIGNMENTS

Conflict can arise over the particular individuals assigned to work on certain tasks or over the quantity of resources assigned to certain tasks. In the project to develop an order-tracking system, the person assigned the task of developing the application software might want to be assigned to work on the database because it would give her an opportunity to expand her knowledge and skills. In the town festival project, the team members charged with painting the booths might think that they need more volunteers assigned to help them in order to finish the work in time.

SCHEDULE

Conflict can result from differences of opinion about the sequence in which the work should be done or about how long the work should take. When, during the planning stage at the beginning of the project, a team member estimates that her tasks will take six weeks to complete, the project manager may respond, "That's too long. We'll never get the project done on time. You have to do it in four weeks."

COST

Conflict often arises over how much the work should cost. For example, suppose a market research company provided a customer with an estimated cost for conducting a nationwide survey and then, when the project was about 75 percent complete, told the customer that the project would probably cost 20 percent more than originally estimated. Or suppose more people were assigned to a late project to bring it back on schedule, but now expenditures are way above budget. Who should pay for the cost overruns?

PRIORITIES

Conflict is likely to result when people are assigned to work on several different projects concurrently or when various people need to use a limited resource at the same time. For example, suppose an individual has been assigned to work part of her time on a project team within her company to streamline some of the company's procedures. However, she has a sudden increase in her regular workload, and her failure to spend the anticipated amount of time on her project assignments is holding up the project. Which has priority—her project assignment or her regular work? Or suppose a company has one powerful computer capable of doing complicated scientific data analysis. Several project teams need access to the computer during the same time period in order to maintain their respective schedules. The team that can't use the computer will be behind schedule. Which project team has priority?

ORGANIZATIONAL ISSUES

A variety of organizational issues can cause conflict, particularly during the storming stage of team development (discussed earlier in the chapter). There may be disagreement over the need for certain procedures established by the project manager with respect to paperwork or approvals. Conflict can result from poor or ambiguous project communication, lack of information sharing, or failure to make timely decisions. For example, conflict is likely to arise if the project manager insists that all communications flow through him or her. Another case may be that there are not enough project status review meetings. When one is held, information is unveiled that would have been helpful to others if it had been known several weeks earlier. As a result, some team members may have to redo some of their work. Finally, there could be conflict between some or all of the project team members and the project manager because of his or her leadership style.

PERSONAL DIFFERENCES

Conflict can emerge among members of the project team because of prejudices or differences in individuals' values and attitudes. In the case of a project that is behind schedule, if one team member is working evening hours to try to get the work back on schedule, she may resent the fact that another member always leaves at the normal time to have dinner with his wife before she leaves for her evening job.

There may be times during the project when there are no conflicts. On the other hand, there will be times when there are many conflicts from various sources that need to be handled. Conflict is inevitable on projects, but it can be beneficial if handled properly.

Reinforce Your Learning

40. What are common sources of conflict on projects?

Handling Conflict

41. Handled properly, conflict can be ______________.

Conflict is not just for the project manager to resolve; conflict between team members should be handled by the individuals involved. Dealt with properly, conflict can be beneficial. It causes problems to surface and be addressed. It stimulates discussion and requires individuals to clarify their views. Conflict can force individuals to search for new approaches; it can foster creativity and enhance the problem-solving process. If it is handled properly, conflict helps team building. However, if it is not handled properly, conflict can have a negative impact on the project team. It can destroy communication—people stop talking and sharing information. It can diminish team members' willingness to listen to and respect others' viewpoints. It can break down team unity and reduce the level of trust and openness.

Researchers Blake and Mouton and Kilmann and Thomas have identified five approaches that people use to handle conflict.

AVOIDING OR WITHDRAWING

In the avoiding or withdrawing approach, individuals in conflict retreat from the situation to avoid an actual or potential disagreement. For example, if one person disagrees with a second person, the second individual may simply remain silent. This approach can cause the conflict to fester and then escalate at a later time.

COMPETING OR FORCING

In the competing or forcing approach, conflict is viewed as a win-lose situation. The value placed on winning the conflict is higher than the value placed on the relationship between the individuals, and the individual who is in a position to do so handles the conflict by exerting power over the other individual. For example, in a conflict between the project manager and a member of the project team regarding which technical approach to use for designing a system, the project manager may simply pull rank and say, "Do it my way." This approach to handling conflict can result in resentment and deterioration of the work climate.

ACCOMMODATING OR SMOOTHING

The accommodating or smoothing approach emphasizes the search for areas of agreement within the conflict and minimizes the value of addressing differences. Topics that may cause hurt feelings are not discussed. In this approach, the value placed on the relationship between the individuals is greater than the value placed on resolution of the issue. Although this approach may make a conflict situation livable, it does not resolve the issue.

COMPROMISING

In the compromising approach, team members search for an intermediate position. They focus on splitting the difference. They search for a solution that will bring some degree of satisfaction to each individual. The solution, however, may not be the optimal one. Take the case where members of the project team are establishing duration estimates for various project tasks. One member says, "I think it'll take 15 days." Another says, "No way; it shouldn't take that long. Maybe 5 or 6 days." So they quickly split the difference and agree on 10 days, which may not be the best estimate.

COLLABORATING, CONFRONTING, OR PROBLEM SOLVING

In the collaborating, confronting, or problem-solving approach, team members confront the issue directly. They look for a win-win outcome. They place high value on both the outcome and the relationship between the individuals. Each person must approach the conflict with a constructive attitude and a willingness to work in good faith with the others to resolve the issue. There is an open exchange of information about the conflict as each sees it. Differences are explored and worked through to reach the best overall solution. Each individual is willing to abandon or redefine his or her position as new information is exchanged, in order to arrive at the optimal solution. For this approach to work, it is necessary to have a healthy project environment (see the earlier discussion of effective project teams) in which relationships are open and nonhostile and people don't fear retribution if they're honest with each other.

Differences can escalate into emotional arguments. When individuals try to resolve a conflict, they cannot let themselves be drawn into an emotional state. They need to be able to manage, but not suppress, their emotions. They need to take the time to understand the other person's point of view. The following section provides a helpful approach to collaborative problem solving.

Unnecessary conflict can be avoided or minimized through early involvement of the project team in planning; clear articulation of each member's role and responsibilities; open, frank, and timely communication; clear operating procedures; and sincere team-building efforts by the project manager and project team.

Reinforce Your Learning

42. What are five approaches to handling conflict?

PROBLEM SOLVING

It is unusual for a team to complete a project without encountering some problems. Normally, various kinds of problems arise along the way, some more serious than others. For example, the project can fall a few weeks behind schedule, jeopardizing completion by the customer's required date. Or the project may be in budget trouble— maybe 50 percent of the money has been spent, but only 40 percent of the work has been accomplished. Some problems are of a technical nature—a new optical sensor system is not providing the required data accuracy, or a new piece of high-speed assembly equipment continues to jam up and ruin expensive components. How effectively the project team solves problems may make the difference between project success and project failure. Therefore, a disciplined, creative, and effective approach to problem solving is needed. Here is a nine-step approach to problem solving, followed by a discussion of brainstorming—a technique helpful in several steps of the problem-solving approach.

A Nine-Step Approach to Problem Solving

1. *Develop a problem statement.* It's important to start with a written statement of the problem, which gives definition and boundaries to the problem. The problem statement provides a vehicle for the members of the problem-solving team to agree about the exact nature of the problem they are trying to solve. The problem statement should include a quantitative measure of the extent of the problem.

- An example of a poor problem statement is "We are behind schedule." An example of a better problem statement is "We are two weeks behind schedule. It looks as if we will miss our customer's due date, which is four weeks from now, by two weeks unless we do something. If we don't make the customer's due date, she will be entitled to a 10 percent price reduction according to the contract."
- Another example of a poor problem statement is "The sensor system doesn't work." A better statement is "The sensor system is giving erroneous data when it measures the rounded corners of parts."

The more specific or quantitative the problem statement, the better, because any measures can be used as criteria later on to evaluate whether the problem has indeed been solved.

2. *Identify potential causes of the problem.* There can be many reasons why a problem has occurred or is occurring. This is especially true of technical problems. Take a project involving the development of a multiple-user computer system, in which data are not being passed from the central computer to all the user work stations. The cause could be a hardware or software problem, or it could be a problem with the central computer or with some of the work stations. A technique often used to identify potential causes of a problem is *brainstorming*. This technique will be discussed later in this chapter.
3. *Gather data and verify the most likely causes.* In the early stages of the problem-solving process, the team is often reacting to symptoms rather than dealing with what might be causing the problem. This is particularly likely to happen when the problem is described in terms of symptoms. Suppose a person goes to a doctor and says he has been getting headaches. The doctor realizes that there could be many causes, such as stress, a tumor, a change in diet, or a problem in the environment. So the doctor will attempt to gather additional data about some of the most likely causes by asking questions and possibly having the patient undergo some tests. The doctor will then use this information to narrow down the list of possible causes of the problem. It's important for the team to get beyond the symptoms and gather the facts before moving on to the next step: identifying possible solutions. Otherwise, much time may be wasted developing solutions to symptoms rather than to the cause of the problem. Gathering data, whether it be through asking questions, interviewing people, running tests, reading reports, or analyzing data, takes time. However, it must be done to focus the team's work in the rest of the problem-solving process.
4. *Identify possible solutions.* This is the fun and creative step in the problem-solving process. It's also a critical step in the process. Team members need to be careful not to jump to the first solution suggested or even the most obvious solution. They will be disappointed later on when that first or obvious solution doesn't work and it's back to the drawing board. For example, when a project is two weeks behind schedule, the obvious solution may be to just ask the customer if it's okay for the project to be delivered two weeks late. However, that solution could backfire. If the

project manager approaches the customer and asks if it's okay for the project to be delivered late, the customer may react negatively, threaten not to do business with his company ever again, and call his boss to complain about the project's being late. The brainstorming technique, discussed later, is very useful in this step to help identify several possible solutions.

5. *Evaluate the alternative solutions.* Once various potential solutions have been identified in step 4, it is necessary to evaluate them. There may be many good, yet different, solutions to the problem. Each viable solution should be evaluated. The question then becomes, "Evaluated against what?" Criteria have to be established. So in this step, the problem-solving team has to first establish the criteria against which alternative solutions will be evaluated. Once the criteria have been established, the team may want to use an evaluation scorecard similar to the one in Figure 3.3. Each criterion can be weighted differently, depending on how important it is. For example, the cost of implementing the solution may be weighted more heavily than the estimated time it will take to implement. Like step 3, this step may take some time if you need to gather data to evaluate the alternative solutions intelligently. For example, it may take time to pull together information on the costs of parts or materials needed for some of the solutions, especially if you need to get price estimates from other vendors or suppliers. Each person on the problem-solving team should complete an evaluation scorecard for each of the possible solutions. These scorecards will be used in the next step.
6. *Determine the best solution.* In this step, the evaluation scorecards completed in step 5 by each member of the problem-solving team are used to help determine the best solution. They become a basis for discussion among the team members. The scorecards are not used as the sole mechanism for determining the best solution; they are used as input to the decision-making process. Here is where it becomes important to have a well-rounded team in terms of relevant expertise. The decision as to which is the best solution is based on the knowledge and expertise of the members of the problem-solving team, in conjunction with the evaluation scorecards.
7. *Revise the project plan.* Once the best solution has been selected, it's necessary to prepare a plan for implementing that solution. Specific tasks need to be identified, along with their estimated costs and durations. The persons and resources needed for each task must also be identified. The project team members who will be responsible for implementing the solution should develop this planning information. It must then be incorporated into the overall project plan to determine what impact the solution will have, if any, on other parts of the project. Of specific interest is whether the selected solution will cause other problems. For example, the best solution to the technical problem with the sensor system may be to order a new part from a vendor, but if it takes two months for the vendor to make and ship the part, this solution may cause the whole project to fall behind schedule and jeopardize meeting the required project completion date. If this risk wasn't taken into account in step 5, the problem-

solving team may have to revisit the solution to determine whether it is still the best solution.

8. *Implement the solution.* Once a plan has been developed for implementing the best solution, the appropriate team members should go ahead and perform their respective tasks.
9. *Determine whether the problem has been solved.* Once the solution has been implemented, it's important to determine whether the problem has indeed been solved. Here is where the team goes back to the problem statement in step 1 and compares the results of implementing the solution to the measure of the problem defined in the problem statement. The team has to ask itself, "Did the selected solution accomplish what we hoped it would? Is the problem solved?" The solution may have only partially solved the problem, or perhaps it didn't solve the problem at all. For example, maybe after the new part ordered for the sensor system was installed, the system still gave erroneous data. If the problem has not been solved, the problem-solving team needs to go back to steps 2 and 3 to see what else could be causing the problem.

Reinforce Your Learning

43. What are the nine steps involved in problem solving?

Depending on the magnitude and complexity of the problem, the above nine-step problem-solving process can take a few hours or several months. The problem-solving team should include those individuals most familiar with the problem as well as individuals with specific expertise that may be required. Sometimes the individual with the necessary expertise may be an outsider to the project team, such as a consultant who can provide a fresh perspective.

Brainstorming

Brainstorming is a technique used in problem solving in which all members of a group contribute spontaneous ideas. Before team members select a solution to a problem, they should make sure that they have explored as broad a range of options and ideas as possible. Brainstorming is a way to generate a lot of ideas and have fun doing it. Brainstorming generates excitement, creativity, better solutions, and greater commitment. It is particularly useful in two of the steps in the nine-step approach to problem solving: step 2, identify potential causes of the problem, and step 4, identify possible solutions.

In brainstorming, the *quantity* of ideas generated is more important than the *quality* of the ideas. The objective is for the group to produce as many ideas as possible, including novel and unorthodox ones.

The team sits around a table, with a facilitator at a flip chart or chalkboard to record ideas. To start the process, one member states an idea. For example, during a brainstorming session for a project that is two weeks behind schedule, the first member might say, "Work overtime." It would then be the next member's turn to state an idea, such as "Bring in some temporary help." And so forth. The process continues around the table, with each person stating only one idea at a time. Anyone who can't think of an idea when it's his or her turn can simply say, "Pass." Some people will come up with ideas that *build* on ideas previously mentioned by others. *Building* involves combining several ideas into one idea or improving on another's idea. As the ideas are given, the facilitator writes them on the flip chart or chalk board. This round-robin process continues until no one can come up with any more ideas or the time limit is up.

Two important rules must be followed for brainstorming to work: *no discussion and no judgmental comments.* As soon as a participant has stated his or her idea, it's the next person's turn. Individuals should simply state an idea—not discuss, justify, or try to sell it. Other participants are not allowed to make any comments at all, supportive or judgmental, and no one may ask questions of the person who stated the idea. Obviously such "killer" comments as "That will never work," "That's a stupid idea," or "The boss won't go for that" are not allowed, but participants also must be cautioned not to use body language—raised eyebrows, a cough, a smirk, or a sigh—to send judgmental messages.

Brainstorming can be an effective and fun way of helping a problem-solving team come up with the best possible solution.

Reinforce Your Learning

44. In brainstorming, the ____________ of ideas generated is more important than the ____________ of the ideas.

TIME MANAGEMENT

People involved in projects are usually very busy working on their assigned tasks, communicating, preparing documents, attending meetings, and traveling. Therefore, good time management is essential for a high-performance project team. Following are some suggestions to help you effectively manage your time:

1. *At the end of each week, identify several (two to five) goals that you want to accomplish the following week.* List the goals in priority order, with the most important (not the most urgent) first. Take into consideration the time you will have available; look at your schedule for the week to see whether you have meetings or other commitments. Don't attempt to create a multiple-page, exhaustive list of all the things you would like to do. Keep this list of goals within sight so you will look at it frequently.
2. *At the end of each day, make a to-do list for the next day.* The items on the daily to-do list must support the achievement of the goals you set for the week. List items in priority order, again with the most important (not necessarily the easiest or the most urgent) first. Before you prepare the to-do list, look at your schedule for the day to see how much time you have available to devote to accomplishing the items on your list. You may have meetings or appointments that will reduce the amount of time available. You should also allow some flextime in your day's schedule to accommodate unexpected things that may come up. Don't make an exhaustive list of everything you'd like to accomplish when there's no time to get it all done—that just causes frustration.

   List only what you can realistically accomplish. Don't get in the habit of feeling that whatever isn't accomplished can just be rolled over to the next day. You will find more items rolled over than accomplished!

   It's important to write out the to-do list, not just keep it in your head. Writing it out builds commitment to doing it.
3. *Read the daily to-do list first thing in the morning, and keep it in sight all day.* Set everything else aside, and start working on the first item. Focus and

Critical Success FACTORS

- Project success requires an effective project team. Although plans and project management techniques are necessary, it is the people—the project manager and project team—that are the key to project success.
- Putting a group of people together to work on a project does not create a team. Helping these individuals develop and grow into a cohesive, effective team takes effort on the part of the project manager and each member of the project team.
- Characteristics of effective project teams include a clear understanding of the project objective, clear expectations of each person's roles and responsibilities, a results orientation, a high degree of cooperation and collaboration, and a high level of trust.
- Each member of the project team needs to help create and foster a positive project environment.
- Effective team members have high expectations of themselves. They plan, control, and feel accountable for their individual work efforts.
- Members of effective teams have open, frank, and timely communication. They readily share information, ideas, and feelings. They provide constructive feedback to each other.
- Effective team members go beyond just doing their assigned tasks; they act as a resource for each other.
- Diversity of the team brings unique ideas and perspectives to projects.
- Individual team members make a personal commitment to understand and value diversity and respect the differences of other team members.
- Diversity is valued as a strength that will enrich communication, foster better relationships, create an enjoyable workplace, and enhance team performance.
- Ethical behavior is crucial in project business relationships with the customer, suppliers, and subcontractors.
- The project manager and the project team need to acknowledge openly that disagreement is bound to occur during the performance of the project and reach consensus on how it should be handled.
- Effective project teams resolve conflict through constructive and timely feedback and positive confrontation of the issues. Disagreement is not suppressed; rather, it is seen as normal and as an opportunity for growth.
- Handled properly, conflict can be beneficial. It causes problems to surface and be addressed. It stimulates discussion and requires individuals to clarify their views. It can foster creativity and enhance problem solving.
- Conflict is not just for the project manager to handle and resolve; conflict between team members should be handled by the individuals involved.
- Each person must approach the conflict with a constructive attitude and a willingness to work in good faith with others to resolve the issues.
- To effectively manage their time, team members should establish weekly goals and make a daily to-do list each day.

self-discipline are extremely important. Don't divert your attention to less important items that may be less challenging, such as reading nonessential e-mail or filing. As you complete an item, cross it off the list; this will provide a sense of accomplishment. Then start right in on the next item. Again, don't let yourself get sidetracked into working on less important items in between completing the items on your list.

4. *Control interruptions.* Don't let phone calls, e-mail messages, or walk-in visitors divert you from working on the items on your to-do list. You may want to set aside a block of time each day to return and make phone calls and e-mail rather than letting them interrupt your work throughout the day. There may be times when you want to close your door so that people will know not to interrupt you. When you are working on a particular item on your to-do list, clear away other paperwork to eliminate the temptation to reach over and start working on something else.
5. *Learn to say no.* Don't let yourself get drawn into activities that will consume your time but not contribute to accomplishing your goals. You might have to turn down invitations to participate in meetings or trips, serve on committees, or review documents. You may have to cut short hallway conversations. Learn to say no, or you'll overcommit yourself and end up a very busy person without accomplishing your goals.
6. *Make effective use of waiting time.* For example, always carry reading material with you in case you get stuck in an airport, a traffic jam, or a dentist's office.
7. *Try to handle most paperwork and e-mail only once.* Go through your incoming mail or e-mail at the end of the day so that it won't divert you from working on your day's to-do list. There may be something in your mail that will lead you to add an item to the to-do list you prepare for the next day. When going through your mail, take action on each document while you are holding or reading it:

- If it's junk mail, throw it out or delete it without reading it.
  - If you can throw it out or delete it after you read it, do so; file it only if you can't get it somewhere else if you need it.
  - If a response is required, either hand-write a response on the document and return it to the originator or type a brief e-mail reply.
  - If the document will require an extended period of time to read, either incorporate time to read it on one of your future to-do lists (if the item could make an important contribution to your weekly goals) or put it in your briefcase so that you can read it when you're stuck waiting somewhere (see item 6 above).

8. *Reward yourself at the end of the week if you accomplished all your goals.* Make sure you're honest with yourself. Reward yourself for accomplishing all your goals, not for working hard and being busy but not accomplishing your goals. In your mind, the reward must be an incentive and payoff tied directly to accomplishing your goals. If you don't accomplish your weekly goals, you should not reward yourself. Otherwise, the reward will be meaningless and will not constitute an incentive to accomplish the goals.

Reinforce Your Learning

45. What are some things you can do to manage your time effectively?

SUMMARY

A team is a group of individuals working interdependently to achieve a common goal. Teamwork is the cooperative effort by members of a team to achieve that common goal. The effectiveness—or lack thereof—of the project team can make the difference between project success and project failure.

Project teams evolve through various stages of development. Forming, the initial stage of the team development process, involves the transition from individual to team member. During this stage, individuals on the team begin to get acquainted. During the storming stage, conflict emerges and tension increases. Motivation and morale are low. Members may even resist team formation. However, after struggling through the storming stage, the team moves into the norming stage of development. Relationships among team members and between the team and the project manager have become settled, and interpersonal conflicts have been resolved for the most part. The fourth and final stage of team development and growth is the performing stage. In this stage, the team is highly committed and eager to achieve the project objective. The members feel a sense of unity.

Characteristics often associated with effective project teams include a clear understanding of the project objective, clear expectations of each person's role and responsibilities, a results orientation, a high degree of cooperation and collaboration, and a high level of trust. Barriers to team effectiveness include unclear goals, unclear definition of roles and responsibilities, lack of project structure, lack of commitment, poor communication, poor leadership, turnover of project team members, and dysfunctional behavior.

Team building—developing a group of individuals to accomplish the project objective—is an ongoing process. It is the responsibility of both the project manager and the project team. Socializing among team members supports team building. To facilitate socializing, team members can request that they be physically located in one office area for the duration of the project and they can participate in social events.

Diversity is about acknowledging, understanding, and valuing differences, and creating a work environment that recognizes, respects, and harnesses differences among team members for the benefits of accomplishing a shared goal, such as the project objective. Diversity of the team brings unique ideas and perspectives to projects. Each team member has unique experiences, skills, and values they bring to the team. Such differences can lead to more creative, faster, and higher-quality problem solving and decision making. Some dimensions of diversity include age or generational, appearance, ethnicity or ancestry, gender, health, job status, marital and parental status, race and religious affiliation. Project team members should not stereotype or make assumptions about a team member's behavior or performance based on their diversity. Barriers to valuing diversity include lack of awareness and lack of understanding. Two actions a project organization can take to create and sustain a supportive and positive climate for diversity are to develop a written policy regarding diversity and to provide training about diversity in the workplace. Individual team members can make a personal commitment to understand and value diversity and respect the differences of other team members. Diversity should be seen and valued by the project team as a strength that can enrich communication, foster better relationships, create an enjoyable workplace, and enhance team performance.

Ethical behavior is necessary within a project organization and is crucial in project business relationships with the customer, suppliers and subcontractors. Customers and suppliers want to do business with a contractor or project organization that they can trust. Intentional distortion, deception or misrepresentation is outright unethical. Two actions a project organization can take to help prevent any wrongdoing is to have a written policy on ethical behavior and to provide training about ethics in the workplace. A policy on ethical behavior should include topics on expectations, process for reporting misconduct, and consequences of engaging in unethical practices. Misconduct or conflict of interest activities must be addressed and appropriate disciplinary action taken to show that such behavior is unacceptable and will not be tolerated. Every member of the project team must feel accountable for his or her actions. Personal integrity is the foundation for workplace ethics.

Conflict on projects is inevitable. During a project, conflict can emerge from a variety of situations. It can involve members of the project team, the project manager, and even the customer. Sources of potential conflict on projects include differences of opinion on how the work should be done, how much work should be done, at what level of quality the work should be done, who should be assigned to work on which tasks, the sequence in which the work should be done, how long the work should take, and how much the work should cost. Conflict can also arise because of prejudices or differences in individuals' values and attitudes.

Conflict is not just for the project manager to resolve; conflict among team members should be handled by the individuals involved. Dealt with properly, conflict can be beneficial because it causes problems to surface and be addressed.

It is unusual for a team to complete a project without encountering some problems along the way. A good nine-step problem-solving approach is to develop a problem statement, identify potential causes of the problem, gather data and verify the most likely causes, identify possible solutions, evaluate the alternative solutions, determine the best solution, revise the project plan, implement the solution, and determine whether the problem has been solved. Brainstorming is a technique used in problem solving in which all members of a group contribute spontaneous ideas. In brainstorming, the quantity of ideas generated is more important than the quality of the ideas.

Good time management is essential for a high-performance project team. To manage their time effectively, team members should identify weekly goals, make a to-do list for each day, focus on accomplishing the daily to-do list, control interruptions, learn to say no to activities that don't move them closer to their goals, make effective use of waiting time, handle paperwork and e-mail only once, and reward themselves for accomplishing their goals.

QUESTIONS

1. Discuss the stages of team development. Address the process, problems, and level of productivity of each.
2. What are some characteristics associated with effective project teams? Can the same be said for an effective couple, orchestra, or professional sports team? Why or why not?

3. What are some common barriers to team effectiveness? Think of a team project that you have worked on. Discuss any barriers to success.
4. Why is it said that there is no I in TEAM? Do you agree or disagree? How can you be an effective team member?
5. Describe three activities that facilitate the process of team building. Must the project manager initiate all of these?
6. Describe some of the dimensions of diversity. List some ways you can capitalize on diversity in order to achieve your project objective.
7. What role does the project manager have related to ethical behavior on the team? What steps can be taken to help ensure a high level of ethical behavior? Describe a situation in which you were confronted with an ethical decision and the outcome of your decision.
8. Discuss some types of conflict that might arise during a project. Describe two situations in which you have experienced these types of conflict.
9. Describe the methods for handling conflict on a project. How was the conflict handled in the two situations you described in your answer to question 8?
10. The manager at a local bank noticed that after a new information system was installed at the bank, some of the customer transactions were not getting posted. The manager knew that this problem could lead to serious financial difficulties as well as unhappy customers. Describe how she could apply the nine-step problem-solving process described in the chapter to solve the problem.
11. With a friend, conduct a brainstorming session and list as many uses of a pen or pencil as you can.
12. How can people more effectively manage their time? Which of these suggestions do you currently practice? For the next week, attempt to manage your time better. Heed all the advice given in the book. At the end of the week, write a summary of your experience.

INTERNET EXERCISES

For the website addresses of the organizations mentioned in these exercises, go to "Internet Exercises" at the book's companion website at **international.cengage.com**. It is suggested that you save this website in your "Favorites" for easy access in the future.

1. Search the web for ideas on effective project teams. Summarize what you find and compare it to what was presented in this chapter.
2. Search the web for ideas on sources of conflict and strategies for conflict resolution. Summarize what you found and compare it to what was presented in this chapter.
3. Search the web for ideas on time management. Print out the ideas listed on at least one site and discuss what you believe are the five most effective strategies for managing your time.
4. Search the web for a case study in project team building. Was the project manager successful in building his or her team? Why or why not? Describe at least one ethical dilemma that the project manager or team might have faced on the project.

5. Visit the home page for the Project Management Institute. Search the website for "PMI Code of Ethics." Print and summarize the PMI Code of Ethics and Professional Conduct.

Team Problems

CASE STUDY 1

Colin and Raouf had been having one of their typical sidebar conversations during the meeting when an obviously irritated Henri looked at Colin. "In my 20 years of experience, I've never seen such a shabby hardware design. A first-year college student could do better," said Henri, raising his voice at Colin. "No wonder we're a month behind schedule. Now we're going to have to spend more time and money on redesign. If you were in over your head, Colin, you should have asked someone for help. I'll review the situation with Jack when he gets back on Friday. That's it—the meeting is over. We need to spend more time working than chitchatting at meetings." Everyone else on the project team was somewhat stunned by Henri's tirade, but it wasn't the first time. They all felt badly for Colin, but others had experienced the wrath of Henri in the past.

Henri is the hardware systems team leader, and Colin is a hardware system designer assigned to Henri's team. Jack, the project manager, was out of town several days for a meeting with the customer, and asked Henri to run the weekly project meeting in his absence.

After the meeting, Colin went to Raouf's office. Raouf is an application software designer. Colin and Raouf have developed a friendship during the past year. They discovered that they both graduated from the same university, but a couple years apart. They are among the younger members of the project team, along with Fatima, the software system team leader. "I'm gonna get that jerk if it's the last thing I do," Colin told Raouf.

"Take it easy Colin. You're right; he's a jerk. Everybody knows he doesn't know what he's doing, and he is in over his head. We all have his number," responded Raouf. "But notice that Henri never behaves like that in front of Jack. Only when Jack isn't around or in meetings when Jack isn't there," continued Raouf.

"Well, I'm gonna see Jack first thing on Friday when he gets back and tell him about Henri. Nobody needs to take that kind of crap in front of everybody," Colin said.

"Maybe you should talk to Henri first, Colin," suggested Raouf.

"Yea right!" chuckled Colin.

"What do you think Jack will do?" asked Raouf.

"Fire him, I hope," answered Colin.

"I doubt it," Raouf said, "Jack seems to always cut him a break, like he feels sorry for him or something."

"Maybe Jack should be concerned about all the good apples, and get rid of the one bad apple!" replied Colin.

Jack was back in the office Friday morning. He was just taking off his jacket when Colin appeared. "Jack, at one of the project meetings you said you had an open door policy, so I'm here to talk to you about a problem with Henri," Colin said. Jack began unpacking his briefcase and had a lot of things to catch up on after being out the whole week. He saw Colin was upset so he said, "Sure,

Colin, I have about 10 minutes before I need to meet with our contracts department to go over some amendments to the contract."

Colin blurted out, "This won't take long. I just want to say that while you were out, Henri accused me of being a lousy designer in front of the whole project team. He blamed me for the project being a month behind schedule. He always does this kind of stuff. Why do you let him get away with it? Nobody likes him. Can't you get rid of him or assigned to some other project?"

Jack was taken aback. He responded, "Colin, you really seem upset. Let's get together on Monday when I have more time, and you can have the weekend to cool off."

"There's nothing more to talk about. That's all there is to it. You can ask anybody if you don't believe me," replied Colin as he left Jack's office.

Jack asked Rosemary, his administrative assistant, who had been intently eavesdropping on the conversation from outside of Jack's office, to schedule a meeting with Henri for later that afternoon. At that meeting, Jack told Henri about Colin's comments. Jack knew Henri has been under stress because his son has recently been arrested for selling drugs. Henri told Jack, "It sounds to me like Colin overreacted and blew things way out of proportion. At the meeting I told Colin that there were some shortcomings in his design and suggested he get together with some folks and take another look at it. You know how these young people are; they have got to learn to be responsible for their actions."

"What about the project being behind schedule? That's news to me," asked Jack.

Henri replied, "Well, I didn't mean it was Colin's fault. To be honest with you, Fatima and her group of software whiz kids aren't the hardest workers. I mean I always see them clowning around and yakking with each other and bothering my hardware team. No wonder the project is behind schedule. Anyway, don't worry about Colin. He's young and will have to learn to develop a thick skin. I'll talk to him. I'll tell him to stop hanging around with those software people so he doesn't develop any bad habits."

That same Friday afternoon, Colin went around asking most of the younger members of the project team to meet for a few drinks at a Happy Hour after work. They were most of the software people, and Rosemary, Jack's administrative assistant. She is attracted to Colin, and has been hoping he'd ask her out. She told Colin that she overheard Henri tell Jack that Fatima and the software group was causing delays in the project because they spend too much time fooling around rather than working. Later in the evening, Colin went over to talk with Fatima and Raouf who had been sitting together. Colin told them, "I have firsthand information that Henri told Jack that the project is way behind schedule because of your software team. I suggest you go and talk with Jack. Henri is poisoning this project. If Jack believes him, we'll all be fired before this project is over. Hey, I had the guts to go to Jack. Now you got to do it too. We got to stand together against Henri. Jack has got to be told that Henri is a big bag of wind and is disrupting the whole project team and causing dissension, and that's why the project is behind schedule. Simply put, the project will never be successful as long as Henri is working on it. And that is going to affect all of our careers—being associated with a failed project. Jack won't have any choice when he sees it's all of us against Henri."

CASE QUESTIONS

1. What are some things Colin could have done in or after the meeting when Henri verbally attacked him?
2. Is there anything more Raouf could have done during or after his meeting with Colin to prevent the situation from escalating?
3. Could Jack have handled his meeting with Colin in a better way? Was there anything Jack could have done after his meeting with Colin and before he met with Henri? What are some things Jack could have done in his meeting with Henri?
4. What should Fatima do?

GROUP ACTIVITY

Divide the class into four groups and assign one of the case questions to each group to discuss and develop responses. Each group must identify a spokesperson to present its responses to the entire class.

New Team Member

CASE STUDY 2

Straight Arrow Systems Corp., located in Los Angeles, develops and builds custom systems. Its major customer is the military market. One of its current projects is to develop a personnel identification and tracking system, referred to as the PITS.

Bob Slug is the team leader for the hardware development work package. There has been a higher than normal turnover of people on Bob's team. Today, Bob is just finishing up a brief orientation meeting with his newest team member, Brad. It is Brad's first day at Straight Arrow Systems. Brad recently graduated from a large university in southern California. Brad's father is in the military; and prior to college, Brad lived in various countries where his father was stationed.

"Before I introduce you to the rest of the team at the weekly project team meeting this afternoon, I want to briefly give you some background on each of the people so you know what you're in for," Bob told Brad as he rolled his eyes. He continued, "They certainly are a different group of characters. Sometimes I wonder how we get anything done. You'll probably eventually hear that we've had some turnover on the team, but I think it was for the best. There were people who just didn't fit in, if you know what I mean."

"First, there's the Asian lady; Yoko something or other. I can't pronounce it so I just call her 'Yoyo,'" Bob says with a chuckle. He continues, "Those people are good at detailed tasks so I pretty much assign her to double-check the work of some of the other people. By the way, whenever she brings in lunch, it smells up the whole place, as you can imagine. Who knows what kinds of food they eat.

Then there's Autumn. Cute! She looks like she's still in high school. She's always got one of those iPods plugged into her ears. So it's hard to take her seriously. When she talks, she uses all these 'techie' terms. These young people just don't know how to communicate; all they do is sit in front of their computer all day. And she is always asking me how she is doing. I mean, like I'm not her mommy. Anyway, I kind of got my arm-twisted into hiring her because management said I didn't have enough females on my team. Then they wonder why I have turnover. Next thing you know she'll be pregnant and leave too."

"And I have Jared, the kid with the tattoo. Need I say anything more?" said Bob as he shook his head. "If he doesn't respect his own body, how can I expect him to respect my authority? He probably gave his parents a hard time too.

Tyrell is the black guy obviously. He doesn't say much; probably doesn't feel like he fits in since he's the only black on the team, and you know how they like to always hang out with each other. I expect he'll probably leave so I don't give him any long-term tasks.

Jay is the guy with the turban. Does he really have to wear that? I mean come on, this is America; when in Rome, do as the Romans do!

There is Tanya. She's got a couple of small kids. I'm not sure if she's married. Anyway, I can't count on her because she's always out because her kids are sick; and she can't work late because she has to pick up the kids from the babysitter. A mother with young kids should be staying home with them, like my wife.

And you'll see that Jose is always on the phone talking in Spanish so nobody else knows what he's saying. Obviously he's not pulling his weight, and I think the rest of the team resents him. By the way, he has five kids; and before you ask, yes he is Catholic." Bob said with a laugh. He went on, "He's another one I got pressured to hire.

And there is Brenda 'the blimp.' You won't miss her," Bob said with a big grin. "When we have meetings with the customer, I obviously make sure Brenda has other things to do. I don't want them to get any bad images of the team. On the other hand, I try to make sure Autumn comes to those meetings; she's a real 'looker' if you get my drift," Bob said as he winked.

"Stan is the guy who looks like he's a hundred years old. He should have retired a long time ago. He's too old to have any good ideas; I never even bother asking him. He's just hanging on to collect a bigger pension and everyone knows it.

Fred is the guy in the wheelchair. He's okay, but takes forever to get things done and keep up. I have to make sure I don't give him any tasks that are too challenging or he'll slowdown the rest of the team.

Finally, there is Sandy. Nobody likes her. She has a hard time building relationships with the rest of the team; seems like she doesn't trust anybody. No wonder she's divorced. Somebody told me she has a kid on drugs. I guess that's no surprise; she's not the greatest role model. She also never seems to hang around any of the guys on the team; what does that tell you?" Bob said, raising his eyebrows.

"How does management expect me to drive this bus, when I have so many flat tires?

Thank goodness I have Bill on the team. I have known him for a long time. We went to the State University together, and both of our families go to the same Methodist church. We also both served in the military together; so he's a real task master that I know I can always count on."

Bob goes on, "I want you to know Brad that I'm not prejudiced or anything like that. I'm just a straight shooter and call things as I see them. Some of the people may not like that, but at least they know where I stand. These people are who they are. I don't know where they all come from; I certainly don't see them in my neighborhood or at my church on Sundays. They just don't have the work ethic they should have, like Bill and me. They just have some strange values. Most of them will never get ahead if they don't change their attitudes. I got to do my best to get the job done with who I got. But it's difficult to get anything done, let alone having to always worry about who might get offended by what you say and then they might go whining to management or threaten to sue you. It's not like the good old days, when everybody was the same. Frankly, I don't think some of them like working with each other because they can't see past their differences. Some of them even think I'm the one who is different; can you believe that?"

"So you can see that with the team I am stuck with, that it is a real challenge to complete our hardware development tasks on time. Some days I REALLY think this project is the "PITS!" If I had more people like Bill on the team, things would be a lot simpler.

Brad, it looks like Bill, you, and I are going to have to carry the team. We are the only ones who are different. I hope I can count on you to pick up the slack and help get the hardware development back on schedule. And Brad, don't go telling anybody what I told you about these people because if word got back to them it would probably get them all stirred up and they'd go running off to complain to management; and I'd lose my trust in you."

CASE QUESTIONS

1. What behaviors is Bob demonstrating with respect to valuing team diversity? What are some alternative choices for what Brad can do next? What should he do?
2. What should any of the team members do?
3. What could be done to improve the climate for diversity in this case?
4. What do you think Bob's direct supervisor would do if she was aware of Bob's actions?

GROUP ACTIVITY

Divide the course participants into teams of three or four to discuss this case and develop responses to the case questions. Have each team select a spokesperson to present its responses to the entire class.

© Hill Street Studios/Blend Images/Jupiter Images

CHAPTER 12

Project Communication and Documentation

Personal Communication
- Oral Communication
- Written Communication

Effective Listening

Meetings
- Types of Project Meetings
- Effective Meetings

Presentations
- Preparing for the Presentation
- Delivering the Presentation

Reports
- Types of Project Reports
- Preparing Useful Reports

Project Documentation and Controlling Changes

Collaborative Communication Tools

Summary

Questions

Internet Exercises

Case Study #1 Office Communications
- Case Questions
- Group Activity

Case Study #2 International Communications
- Case Questions
- Group Activity

Real World PROJECT MANAGEMENT

Major Projects in Brazil

When Arthur Costa Neto, project manager for Sociedade Potiguar de Empreendimentos Ltd., was developing a golf course and tourist destination resort in Natal, Brazil, he quickly realized that communication complications could easily arise between team members from different countries or cultures. Twelve of his team members were from Brazil and eight were from Spain. It quickly became evident that the two groups had very different ways of communicating. Mr. Costa Neto noted that the Brazilian team members normally maintained continuous communication among team members of the project, while the Spanish team members provided reports only when they had new information to share. The differences in communication styles became an issue.

Costa Neto decided that he and his project team needed to schedule regular weekly conference calls to keep both the Brazilian and Spanish team members on track with the project's progress. In doing so, he was able to accommodate the different approaches to communication of each team member and build a sense of trust. Projects with team members from different countries and cultures can be expensive and can be viewed as a higher risk with little margin for error in communications. Therefore, it is the responsibility of the project manager to communicate in a way that crosses cultural boundaries.

In another instance, Mr. Costa Neto was managing a project for WBS Gerenciamento e Empreedimentos Ltd., who had been hired to provide project management services for Companhia Petroquimica do Sul (COPESUL). In this project, he noted that cultural differences can cause problems with communications even when team members are from the same country. In this project, his team was asked to customize a project management software application and then train the employees on that application.

In this project, all his team members came from Brazil, which should have made things easy, right? Well, not necessarily. His team came from both the northern and southern parts of Brazil and there were clear differences in their communication styles. Costa Neto noted that the team members from the South were much more direct and open, and would more freely express themselves than their colleagues from the North. This mismatch in styles led Costa Neto to develop a project plan to minimize potential conflicts in communication. To keep everyone moving in the same direction, he implemented a well-defined, disciplined communication plan that required team members to assemble weekly performance and progress reports so other team members could be properly informed as the project moved forward.

The reports were divided into four sections: (1) actions that were performed during the past week, (2) problems that occurred and any corrective actions that were taken, (3) tasks that were required during the following week, and (4) any assistance that was needed during the following week. With team members communicating on a regular basis, and in a standard format, the team members from the North and the South gained a better understanding of their colleagues from the other side of the country and the project progressed very well.

According to Karen Kroll, writer on business and technology, it is also important for project managers to determine the method and frequency of communication that will be used during the span of their projects. Most often face-to-face communications are best, but e-mail is popular with geographically dispersed, cross-cultural teams because team members can thoroughly read the messages and respond at their convenience in their time zone. If additional communication is required, phone and videoconferencing can be used in these cases. It is just important to keep in mind that when these channels are used time differences may result in some team members talking outside of their normal working hours, and issues such as these should be taken into account by project managers in order to make communication as effective as possible.

This chapter will introduce you to some very important communication strategies and, by properly implementing those ideas, just like Mr. Costa Neto, you will bring your projects in on time and within budget!

Kroll, K., "What Did You Say?" *PM Network*, November, 2006.

This chapter discusses an element vital to the effective performance of a project: communication. Communication takes place between the project team and the customer, among the project team members, and between the project team and its upper management. Communication may involve two people or a group of people. It can be oral or written. It can be face to face or involve some medium, such as phone, voice mail, e-mail, letters, memos, videoconferencing, or groupware. It can be formal, such as a report or a presentation at a meeting, or informal, such as a hallway conversation or an e-mail message. This chapter covers many communication formats. You will become familiar with

- suggestions for enhancing personal communications, such as face-to-face discussions and written communications
- effective listening
- various types of project meetings and suggestions for effective meetings
- formal project presentations and suggestions for effective presentations
- project reports and suggestions for preparing useful reports
- project documentation and keeping track of changes
- collaborative communication tools.

PERSONAL COMMUNICATION

Effective and frequent personal communication is crucial to keep the project moving, identify potential problems, solicit suggestions for improving project performance, keep abreast of whether the customer is satisfied, and avoid surprises. Personal communication can occur through words or nonverbal behavior, such as body language. It can be face to face or use some medium, including telephone, voice mail, e-mail, letters, memos, videoconferencing, or groupware. Personal communication can be oral or written.

Oral Communication

Personal oral communication can be face to face or via telephone. It can be by means of voice mail or videoconferencing. Information can be communicated in a more accurate and timely manner through oral communication. Such communication provides a forum for discussion, clarification, understanding, and immediate feedback. Face-to-face communication also provides an opportunity to observe the body language that accompanies the communication. Even phone conversations allow the listener to hear the tone, inflection, and emotion of the voice. Body language and tone are important elements that enrich oral communication. Face-to-face situations provide an even greater opportunity for enriched communication than phone conversations do.

Reinforce Your Learning

1. Identify two types of personal oral communication.

Body language can be used not only by the person talking, but also by the listener, as a way of providing feedback to the person talking. Positive body language can include direct eye contact, a smile, hand gestures, leaning forward, and nodding in acknowledgment or agreement. Negative body language can be a frown, crossed arms, slouching, fidgeting, gazing or looking away, doodling, or yawning. In personal communications people need to be sensitive to body language reflective of the cultural diversity of the participants, whether they're other team members or the customer. When communicating with individuals from other cultures or countries, you need to be aware of their customs regarding greetings, gestures, eye contact, and protocol. For example, hand gestures, proximity to the person with whom you are communicating, and touching have different meanings in different cultures.

Reinforce Your Learning

2. Body language can be used not only by the person talking, but also by the ____________________, as a way of providing ____________________ to the person talking.

When communicating orally, a person must be careful not to use remarks, words, or phrases that can be construed to be sexist, racist, prejudicial, or offensive. Comments do not have to be made directly to a particular person to be offensive. Remarks made in a group setting can be distasteful to some individuals in the group. They may find certain statements hurtful to themselves or to an acquaintance. Comments about ethnic customs, surnames, dialects, religious practices, physical characteristics or appearance, or mannerisms can be offensive, even if the offense is unintentional or the comment is said in jest.

A high degree of face-to-face communication is especially important early in a project to foster team building, develop good working relationships, and establish mutual expectations. Locating the project team in a common area facilitates communication. It's much easier to walk over to someone's office to ask something than to call the person on the phone and maybe wait several days for your call to be returned. However, voice mail allows individuals to communicate orally in a timely manner when face-to-face communication is not possible. It is not always feasible to locate the project team in a common area, especially if the team includes members or subcontractors from different geographic locations. In such cases, videoconferencing can be helpful, if available.

Reinforce Your Learning

3. In personal communication, people need to be sensitive to body language reflective of the ____________________ ____________________ of the participants.

Project team members need to be proactive in initiating timely communication with other team members and the project manager to get and give information, rather than waiting for an upcoming project team meeting that could be several weeks away. The project manager, in particular, should get out of the office on a regular basis and drop in on individual team members. She or he should take the initiative to visit the customer or the firm's upper management for face-to-face communication, rather than waiting to be summoned to a meeting. If a visit to the customer requires distant travel, the manager should initiate regular phone discussions between visits.

Reinforce Your Learning

4. Project team members need to be ____________________ in initiating timely communication to ____________________ and ____________________ information.

Oral communication should be straightforward and unambiguous. Sometimes attempting to be overly tactful, especially in communicating a problem or concern, can mislead and result in unclear expectations. You should check for understanding of what you wanted to communicate by asking for feedback. If you're not sure whether a point you made was understood by the other person,

Reinforce Your Learning

5. Identify two methods you can use to generate feedback during oral communication.

ask the other person to state his or her understanding of what you said. Similarly, if you aren't clear on a point the other person was trying to communicate, paraphrase what you think the other person said to ensure mutual understanding.

Finally, the timing of oral communication is important. For example, you shouldn't barge into a colleague's office and interrupt him if he is in the middle of doing something important. Rather, in such a situation, ask him when would be a good time to get together. You should indicate about how long you need to talk with him and what you want to discuss. He will then know whether to expect a 10-minute discussion on a trivial subject or a one-hour discussion on a critical subject. Similarly, when making a phone call to another person, you should state at the start what topics you want to discuss and how long it might take, then ask if now is a good time or if you should call back at a more convenient time.

Written Communication

Personal written communication is generally carried out through internal memos to the project team and external letters to the customer or others outside the firm, such as subcontractors. Written correspondence is normally transmitted through e-mail or can be sent as hardcopy. Formal project documents such as contracts and amendments, which require signatures, are usually sent in hardcopy.

Reinforce Your Learning

6. What are two forms of personal written communication?

E-mail is a way to communicate efficiently with a group of people when it's impractical to have a meeting or when the information needs to be disseminated in a timely manner. Written communication should be used only when necessary and not just to generate paperwork. Project participants are usually very busy and do not have time to read trivial or irrelevant memos containing information that could have been communicated orally at the next project meeting.

A memo or letter may be appropriate as a follow-up to a face-to-face conversation or a phone call, confirming decisions or actions rather than relying on a person's memory. When a memo is used to confirm oral communication, other people who were not involved in the oral communication but who may need to know the information should also be provided copies. Also, such written communication can be important if a member of the project team leaves the project—the replacement person will have a record of communications regarding previous actions and decisions.

Written communication should be used mostly to inform, confirm, and request—for example, to remind the project team that the customer will be visiting on a certain date or to ask team members to provide written input for a quarterly project progress report to the client.

Memos and letters should be clear and concise and should not include lengthy dissertations or voluminous extraneous attachments. Project participants are busy with their assigned work tasks and will perceive being flooded with paperwork or e-mail as more of a hindrance than a help.

EFFECTIVE LISTENING

Reinforce Your Learning

7. Failure to ____________ can cause a ____________ in communication between people.

"I know that you believe that you understand what you thought you heard me say. But what you don't realize is that what you thought you heard is not what I meant."

The heart of communication is not words, but understanding—not only to be understood, but also to understand. Half of making communication effective is listening. Failure to listen can cause a breakdown in communication.

Here are some common barriers to effective listening:

- *Pretending to listen.* You listen and think faster than the average person talks. This may lead to drifting, boredom, or thinking about what you want to say in response.
- *Distractions.* If you try to do something else, such as answer the phone or read, while someone is talking to you, you won't be able to focus on the person talking. It's also easy to get distracted by people walking by or what's happening outside the window.
- *Bias and closed-mindedness.* Hearing what supports your views and turning off the things with which you disagree is known as selective listening. Bias in listening can also be attributed to feelings about the speaker's dress, looks, tone of voice, or mannerisms.
- *Impatience.* If you are anxious for the person talking to get to the point or waiting for a chance to interrupt and speak, you may tune out what the speaker is saying.
- *Jumping to conclusions.* If you begin to draw conclusions about what is being said before the person talking has finished, you may not hear the whole story or all the facts.

Listening is more than just letting the other person talk. It must be an active, not a passive, process. Active listening increases understanding and reduces conflict. Here are some suggestions for improving listening skills:

Reinforce Your Learning

8. List some common barriers to effective listening.

- *Focus on the person talking.* Looking at the person who is speaking helps you concentrate and to pay attention to the speaker's body language.
- *Engage in active listening.* Provide verbal and nonverbal feedback to the person talking. This can include body language, such as nodding in acknowledgment of something the person said, smiling, or simply leaning forward attentively. It can be a verbal comment that doesn't require a response from the speaker, such as, "That's interesting," "I see," or "Uh huh." It can be paraphrasing what the speaker said, as in "What you're saying is . . ." or "What you mean is . . ." Such paraphrasing will give the speaker an opportunity to clear up any misunderstandings.
- *Ask questions.* When you need clarification or more information about something the person said, ask a probing question such as "Could you tell me more about that?"
- *Don't interrupt.* When a person is talking, listen to the whole thought or wait for an appropriate pause before breaking in with a question or comment. Don't interrupt and change the subject before the person talking has completed the message.

Good listening skills are important if project team members are to be effective in communicating with one another and with the customer.

Reinforce Your Learning

9. What are some things you can do to improve your listening skills?

MEETINGS

A meeting can be a vehicle for fostering team building and reinforcing team members' expectations, roles, and commitment to the project objective. This section covers various types of meetings that may take place during a project and provides suggestions for ensuring that meetings are effective.

Real World PROJECT MANAGEMENT

Silence can be Deadly

The Concours Group and VitalSmarts LC recently conducted a major study entitled "Silence Fails: The Five Crucial Conversations for Flawless Execution." The study was aimed at determining the major causes of project failure. The study was conducted worldwide and included more than 1000 executives and project management professionals, more than 2200 projects, and 40 different companies. The projects they analyzed ranged from $10,000 efforts to projects valued at more than $1 billion.

The five crucial conversations identified by the study as the most prevalent, and most costly, barriers to project success are:

1. Fact-Free Planning—when a project plan is created with unrealistic deadlines and resource constraints.
2. AWOL Sponsors—when a project sponsor doesn't provide the political clout, time, or energy to see a project through to completion.
3. Skirting—when people work around the priorities.
4. Project Chicken—when project managers and/or team members don't speak up when there is a problem.
5. Team Failures—when team members perpetuate dysfunction when they are unwilling or unable to support the project.

In order to overcome these problems, The Concours Group and VitalSmarts study recommends that senior leaders should develop a business case for change; measure behaviors; invest in skills; and hold senior management accountable. The study's website provides a nice assessment and checklist to help project managers address the five issues noted in the study.

Robert Scott, Vice President at Proctor & Gamble, participated in the study. He notes that the study showed that there is a set of project communication problems that are extremely common and plague far more projects than most senior leaders tend to realize. He notes that it is estimated that 90 percent of all project managers come across one or more of the five critical communication problems throughout the course of a project.

One of the major findings of the study was that projects tend to be derailed when people do not have conversations about problems they see along the way. When crucial conversations do not occur, the problems in the projects tend to fester, work deteriorates, politics prevail, and failure becomes likely.

The study also demonstrated that when project team members discuss core problems effectively, projects tend to stay on course. This finding was significant for Proctor & Gamble, where a significant number of their projects are considered to be high-stake projects run in a global environment. Proctor & Gamble's view, which was consistent with the results of the study, indicated that the single most important factor affecting project success or failure was communication.

P&G has now established project guidelines that require teams to clarify expectations with leadership, with other team members, and their partner companies and employees. It was also determined that when these expectations were changed, met, or not met, it would be communicated to all of those involved.

At P&G, people are placed on appropriate projects, backed by rewards tied to requirements, and encouraged to have discussions of any issues in a timely manner. Information, whether it is good or bad, is shared immediately. These strategies have helped to promote trust on the project teams and have produced results that were considered to be beyond expectations.

Mr. Scott believes the best predictor of project success is a constant and open line of communication. Senior managers at Proctor & Gamble are now encouraged to conduct early assessments to identify potential problems as early as possible and are also educated on how to create an organizational culture that encourages communication with project managers and team members. And, the bottom line is—it is working!

Scott, R., "For IT Projects, Silence can be Deadly," *Computerworld*, February 5, 2007.

Types of Project Meetings

The three most common types of project meetings are

- Status review meetings.
- Problem-solving meetings.
- Technical design review meetings.

It's not unusual for a contract between a customer and a project contractor to outline requirements for periodic status review meetings and specific technical review meetings.

STATUS REVIEW MEETINGS

A project status review meeting is usually led or called by the project manager; it generally involves all or some of the project team, and may also include the customer and/or the project team's upper management. The primary purposes of such a meeting are to inform, to identify problems, and to identify action items. Project status meetings should be held on a regularly scheduled basis so that problems and potential problems can be identified early and surprises that could jeopardize accomplishing the project objective can be prevented. For example, project status review meetings might be held weekly with the project team and less frequently with the customer—perhaps monthly or quarterly, depending on the overall duration of the project and the contractual requirements.

A sample agenda for a project status review meeting is shown in Figure 12.1. Here are some of the subjects that might be discussed under each of the agenda items:

Reinforce Your Learning

10. What are the primary purposes of a status review meeting?

- *Accomplishments since the last meeting.* Key project milestones that were reached should be identified, and actions on items from previous meetings should be reviewed.
- *Cost, schedule, and work scope—status.* Performance should be compared to the baseline plan. It's important that status be based on up-to-date information regarding completed tasks and actual expenditures.
- *Cost, schedule, and work scope—trends.* Any positive or negative trends in project performance should be identified. Even if a project is ahead of schedule, the fact that the schedule has been slipping over the past several weeks might indicate that corrective action should be initiated now, before the project falls behind schedule.

FIGURE 12.1 ***Project Status Review Meeting Agenda***

Project Status Review
Team Meeting

Agenda

8:00 AM	Accomplishments since last meeting	
	• Hardware	Steve
	• Software	Alex
	• Documentation	Wendy
8:30	Cost, schedule, and work scope	Jack
	• Status	
	• Trends	
	• Forecasts	
	• Variances	
8.50	Risk assessment update	Teresa
9.00	Corrective actions, if necessary	As appropriate
9:15	Opportunities for improvement	All
9:30	Open discussion	All
9:50	Action item assignments	Jack
10:00	Adjourn	

- *Cost, schedule, and work scope—forecasts.* Based on current status, trends, and the project tasks yet to be completed, the forecasted project completion date and forecasted cost at completion should be reviewed and compared to the project objective and the baseline plan.
- *Cost, schedule, and work scope—variances.* Any differences between actual progress and planned progress with respect to cost and schedule for project work packages and tasks should be identified. These variances can be positive (for example, being ahead of schedule) or they can be negative (such as overrunning the budget given the amount of work that has been accomplished). Negative variances will help pinpoint both current problems and potential problems. Particular attention should be given to those parts of the project that have had negative variances that are continuing to get worse.
- *Risk assessment update.* Particular attention should be given to reviewing the trigger points for each risk to determine if any risk response plans are on the verge of having to be implemented.
- *Corrective actions.* In some instances, corrective actions to address problems and potential problems might take place right at the status review meeting—for example, receiving customer or management approval to proceed with the purchase of certain materials or authorization of overtime to get the project back on schedule. In other cases, separate problem-solving meetings may be required so that appropriate members of the project team can develop corrective actions.

- *Opportunities for improvement.* These should also be identified, along with problem areas and associated corrective actions. For example, a member of the project team might point out that the technical specifications could be met by using an alternative material or piece of equipment, which is substantially less expensive than the one the team originally planned to use. Or a team member might suggest that substantial time could be saved by replicating and slightly modifying existing computer software rather than developing completely new software.
- *Action item assignment.* Specific action items should be identified and assigned to specific team members. For each action item, the person responsible and the estimated completion date should be noted. The completion date should be estimated by the person responsible for the action item. When people verbalize their commitment to a date at a meeting in front of other people, they will usually strive to meet that date.

It should be noted that listening to the information provided at a status review meeting is one way, but not the only way, for a project manager to get a true understanding of the project status. He or she needs to validate what was said at the status review meeting through personal communication with individual members of the project team. The project manager should also ask to see any tangible products, or deliverables, such as drawings, prototypes, or reports. This will both validate that the item is really complete (and not just almost or essentially complete) and show that the project manager is genuinely interested in the individual's work and acknowledges its importance to the successful achievement of the project objective.

PROBLEM-SOLVING MEETINGS

When a problem or potential problem is identified by an individual project team member, that person should promptly call a problem solving meeting with other appropriate individuals, not wait for a future status review meeting. Identifying and resolving problems as early as possible is critical to project success.

The project manager and the project team need to establish guidelines at the beginning of the project regarding who should initiate problem-solving meetings and when, as well as the level of authorization required to implement corrective actions.

Problem-solving meetings should follow a good problem-solving approach, such as the following:

1. Develop a problem statement.
2. Identify potential causes of the problem.
3. Gather data and verify the most likely causes.
4. Identify possible solutions.
5. Evaluate the alternative solutions.
6. Determine the best solution.
7. Revise the project plan.
8. Implement the solution.
9. Determine whether the problem has been solved.

This nine-step problem-solving approach was discussed in greater detail in Chapter 11.

Reinforce Your Learning

11. True or false: when members of the project team identify problems or potential problems, they should wait until the next scheduled status review meeting to bring them up for discussion.

TECHNICAL DESIGN REVIEW MEETINGS

Projects that involve a design phase, such as an information system project or development of a new marketing brochure, may require one or more technical design review meetings to ensure that the customer agrees with or approves of the design approach developed by the project contractor.

Take the example of a company that hires a consultant to design, develop, and implement an information system to track customer orders from order entry through receipt of payment. The company may require that the consultant review the system design with appropriate company representatives before the next phase of the project—detailed development of the system and purchase of hardware and software—is approved. At a later stage in the project, the company may want certain employees to review and approve the computer interface and output formats developed by the consultant to ensure that they meet the needs and expectations of the people who will be using the system.

Reinforce Your Learning

12. On technical projects there are often two design review meetings: a ____________ design review meeting and a ____________ design review meeting.

In many technical projects there are two design review meetings:

1. *A preliminary design review meeting* when the contractor has completed the initial conceptual specifications, drawings, or flowcharts. The purpose of this preliminary design review meeting is to get the customer's agreement that the design approach meets the technical requirements and to gain approval from the customer before the contractor orders materials that have a long delivery time (so as not to delay the project schedule).
2. *A final design review meeting* when the contractor has completed the detailed specifications, drawings, screen and report formats, and the like. The purpose of this final design review meeting is to gain approval from the customer before the contractor starts building, assembling, and producing the project deliverables.

Effective Meetings

Before, during, and after a meeting, the person organizing or leading the meeting can take various steps to ensure that the meeting is effective.

BEFORE THE MEETING

- *Determine whether a meeting is really necessary* or whether another mechanism, such as a conference call, is more appropriate.
- *Determine the purpose of the meeting*. For instance, is it to share information, plan, collect input or ideas, make a decision, persuade or sell, solve a problem, or evaluate status?
- *Determine who needs to participate in the meeting*, given its purpose. The number of participants should be the minimum number needed to achieve the purpose of the meeting. Project team members are usually busy on their work tasks and do not want to participate in meetings to which they have nothing to contribute or from which they have nothing to gain. Individuals who are invited to attend the meeting should know why they are being asked to participate.
- *Distribute an agenda well in advance of the meeting* to those invited. The agenda should include:

Purpose of the meeting.

Topics to be covered. (Items should be listed from most important to least important. If time runs out, the most important items will have been covered.)

Time allocated for each topic and who will cover the topic, make the presentation, or lead the discussion.

Figure 12.2 is a sample agenda for a project review meeting with a customer. Accompanying the agenda should be any documents or data the participants need to review *prior* to the meeting. Sufficient time should be given between distribution of the announcement and the date of the meeting to allow participants to prepare for the meeting adequately. Some participants may need to collect and analyze data or prepare presentation or handout materials.

- *Prepare visual aids or handouts.* Graphics, charts, tables, diagrams, pictures, and physical models are effective visual aids. Often these materials focus the discussion and prevent a lot of rambling and misunderstanding. A picture is worth a thousand words!
- *Make meeting room arrangements.* The room should be large enough that people aren't cramped and uncomfortable. Seats should be arranged so that all participants can see each other; this will foster participation. The appropriate visual aids and accessories (projector, screen, computer, flip charts) should be in the room and be tested before the meeting starts. If any presenters are going to use PowerPoint slides, it is time-saving to

FIGURE 12.2 ***Customer Project Review Meeting Agenda***

Project Review
Meeting with Customer

Agenda

8:00 AM	Opening comments	Jeff
8:15	Technical review	
	• System design	Joe
	• Training	Cathy
	• Installation plans	Jim
10:00	Break	
10:15	Project status	Jeff
	• Schedule	
	• Cost	
11:00	Proposed changes	Joe
11:45	Decisions and action items	Jeff
12:00	Open discussion (box lunches)	
1:00	Adjourn	

have the files loaded on the computer before the meeting starts. Refreshments should be ordered if the meeting is going to be long. For example, box lunches may be served in order to allow meeting discussions to continue over a working lunch.

Reinforce Your Learning

13. To ensure that a meeting is effective, what are some steps that the person organizing or leading the meeting should take before the meeting?

In some cases, a conference room may be designated the "project room," where all project meetings are held or where project team members can meet for problem-solving discussions. Sometimes such project rooms have project plans, schedules, status charts, and system diagrams posted on the walls for easy reference by all project team members.

DURING THE MEETING

- *Start the meeting on time.* If the meeting leader waits for a few latecomers, people will get in the habit of showing up late, because they know the meeting won't start on time anyway. If the meeting starts on time, people will get in the habit of arriving on time rather than suffer the embarrassment of entering a meeting already in progress.
- *Designate a note-taker.* Someone should be assigned (preferably before the meeting) to take notes. The notes should be concise, and they should cover decisions and action items, assignments, and estimated completion dates. Detailed meeting minutes can be a burden both to take and to read later and therefore should be avoided.
- *Review the purpose of the meeting and the agenda.* Be concise, and don't give a lengthy discourse.
- *Facilitate—don't dominate—the meeting.* The project manager should not lead all the discussions, but should get other participants to lead the discussions on their assigned topics.

  A good facilitator will:

  Keep the meeting moving and within the scheduled time frame.

  Encourage participation, especially from individuals who appear hesitant to participate.

  Limit discussion by participants who have a tendency to talk too much, repeat themselves, or stray from the topic at hand.

  Control interruptions and side conversations.

  Clarify points that are made.

  Summarize discussions and make transitions to the next topics on the agenda.

  It's helpful to discuss meeting guidelines at a project team meeting at the beginning of the project so that everyone understands what behavior is expected during project meetings. An example of a code of conduct for team meetings is shown in Figure 12.3.

Reinforce Your Learning

14. True or false: It's always a good idea to wait for everyone to arrive before starting a meeting, even if it's beyond the scheduled start time.

- *Summarize the meeting results* at the end of the meeting, and make sure all participants have a clear understanding of all decisions and action items. The meeting leader should verbalize these items to help avoid any misunderstandings.
- *Do not overrun the scheduled meeting time.* Participants may have other commitments or subsequent meetings. If all agenda items are not covered,

FIGURE 12.3 *Team Meeting Code of Conduct*

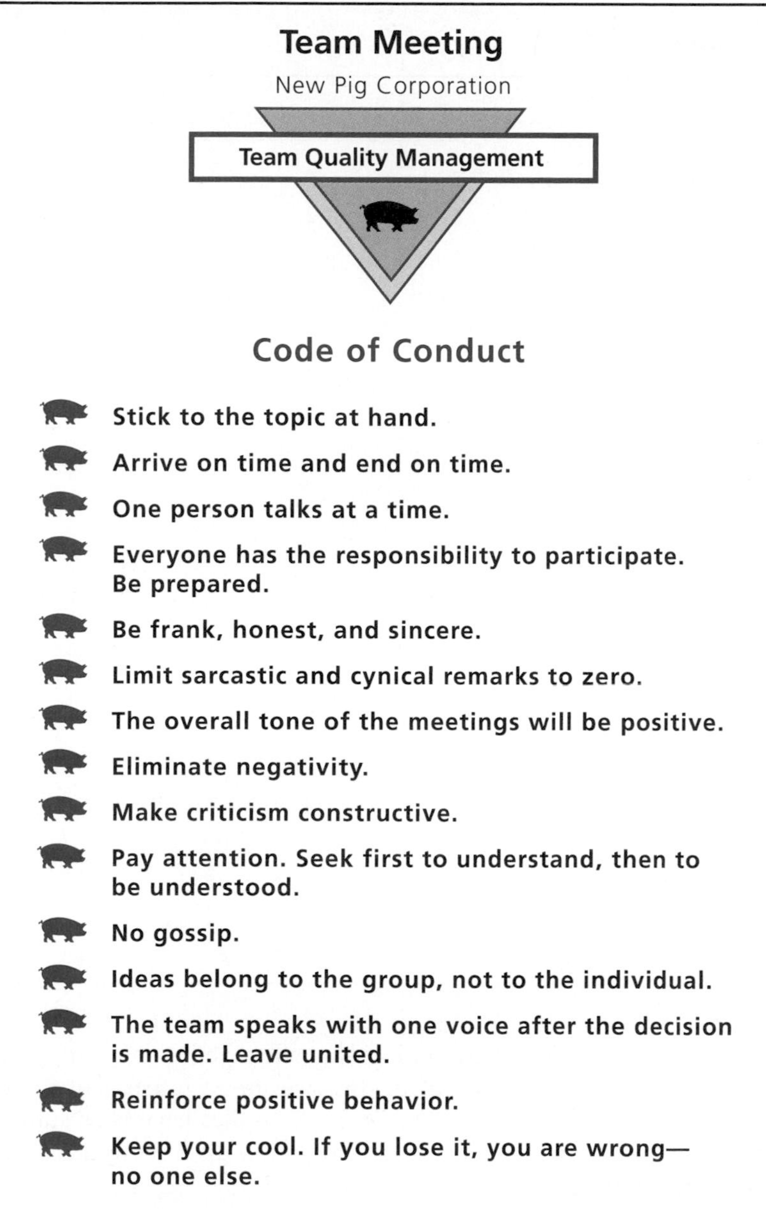

it's better to schedule another meeting for the people involved with those items. These should be the lower-priority items anyway, because the agenda topics should have been arranged in order of most to least important.

- *Evaluate the meeting process.* Occasionally, at the end of a meeting, the participants should openly discuss what took place and determine whether any changes should be made to improve the effectiveness of future meetings.

FIGURE 12.4 *Meeting Effectiveness Checklist*

How Effective Are Your Meetings?

	Not at All		Somewhat		Very Much
1. Is the agenda sent in time to allow preparation?	1	2	3	4	5
2. Is the agenda properly sequenced?	1	2	3	4	5
3. Is sufficient time allocated for each item?	1	2	3	4	5
4. Is the room set up appropriately?	1	2	3	4	5
5. Do appropriate participants attend?	1	2	3	4	5
6. Do meetings start on time?	1	2	3	4	5
7. Do attendees know why they were invited?	1	2	3	4	5
8. Are meeting objectives understood?	1	2	3	4	5
9. Are objectives for each agenda item clear?	1	2	3	4	5
10. Are meetings kept on track and not allowed to digress?	1	2	3	4	5
11. Is there balanced participation of all attendees?	1	2	3	4	5
12. Do attendees listen to each other?	1	2	3	4	5
13. Does the leader maintain control?	1	2	3	4	5
14. Do meetings have a positive, productive tone?	1	2	3	4	5
15. Do meetings finish on time?	1	2	3	4	5
16. Are decisions and action items documented and the documents distributed?	1	2	3	4	5
17. Are meetings a valuable use of time?	1	2	3	4	5

Figure 12.4 is a checklist for rating the effectiveness of a meeting. The project team members might complete this assessment instrument periodically during the project. After the scores of all team members have been summarized, the team, including the project manager, should discuss how to improve in the areas that were rated low.

AFTER THE MEETING

Publish the meeting results within 24 hours after the meeting. The summary document should be concise and kept to one page if possible.

It should confirm decisions that were made and list the action items, including who is responsible, the estimated completion date, and expected deliverables. It may also list who attended and who was absent. The meeting results should be distributed to all individuals who were invited, whether or not they actually attended the meeting. The meeting notes should not include a detailed narrative of the meeting discussions. Figure 12.5 is a sample action item list from a meeting.

Effective meetings, like successful projects, require good planning and good performance.

FIGURE 12.5 *Action Item List*

Action Items
from March 1 Project Status Review Meeting

Action	Who	By When
1. Revise system requirements document	Tyler	March 10
2. Schedule review meeting with customer	Jim	March 11
3. Change purchase order for computers from 15 to 20	Maggie	March 19
4. Evaluate feasibility of bar coding and optical character recognition for data entry	Hannah	March 19

PRESENTATIONS

Often the project manager or members of the project team are called on to give a formal presentation. The audience may be representatives of the customer's organization, the project organization's upper management, the project team itself, or the public, such as at a conference. The audience may be one person (the customer) or several hundred attendees at a national conference. The presentation may last 10 minutes or an hour or more. The subject could be an overview of the project; the current status of the project; a serious problem that is jeopardizing successful achievement of the project objective, such as a forecasted schedule delay or cost overrun; or an attempt to persuade the customer to expand or redirect the project work scope.

In such situations, you, the speaker, are in the spotlight. Following are some suggestions that may help you prepare and deliver your presentation.

Preparing for the Presentation

- *Determine the purpose of the presentation.* Is it to inform or to persuade? What do you want to accomplish? For example, do you want the audience to understand the project, or do you want the customer to agree to suggested changes in the project work scope?
- *Know the audience.* What is their level of knowledge or familiarity with the subject? What is their rank—are they senior managers and key decision makers, or are they your peers?
- *Make an outline of the presentation.* Only after you have made an outline should you write out the presentation. Read it over and over and over, but don't try to memorize it.
- *Use simple language that the audience will understand.* Don't use jargon, acronyms, or sophisticated or technical vocabulary that the audience may not understand. Don't try to impress the audience with your word power!

Don't make remarks that can be construed to be sexist, racist, prejudicial, offensive, sarcastic, or profane.

- *Prepare notes or a final outline that you will use or refer to during your presentation.* Yes, it is all right to use notes.
- *Practice, practice, practice—more than you think you should.* You may want to do a trial run in front of your peers. Ask for their feedback; solicit suggestions on how you might improve the presentation.
- *Prepare visual aids and test them.* Make sure the visual aids are readable from the most distant seat in the room where the presentation will be given. If it will be given in a large auditorium, make sure the visual aids are very large. Visual aids such as graphs, diagrams, and tables should be simple and not too busy—there shouldn't be a lot of text and diagrams shouldn't be too detailed. There should be one idea per chart or slide. Multicolor graphics are more appealing than plain black and white, but choose colors carefully—you can overwhelm your audience with too many colors or color combinations that are difficult to read.
- *Make copies of handout materials.* If audience members don't have to take a lot of notes, they will be able to give their full attention to the presentation.
- *Request the audiovisual equipment well in advance.* Whether it's a computer, projector, microphone, lectern, or pointer, you don't want to find at the last minute that it's not available.
- *Go into the meeting room when it's empty or not in use and get a feel for the surroundings.* Stand in the place where the presentation will be made (in the front of the room, at the lectern, or on the stage). Test the projector and microphone.

Reinforce Your Learning

15. What are some important things to do in preparing a presentation?

Delivering the Presentation

- *Expect a bit of nervousness; all speakers experience it.* Just remember that you know more about what you are talking about than most of the audience members do.
- *Know the first two or three sentences of your presentation.* The opening lines are crucial; have them down pat. They must be delivered in a confident and relaxed manner. This is where credibility is established with the audience. You can't afford to fumble over the opening lines or say something that may alienate the audience.
- *Use the 3-T approach in your presentation:*

  First, tell them what you are going to tell them (your outline).

  Then, tell them (the body of your presentation).

  Finally, tell them what you told them (your summary).
- *Talk to the audience, not at it.* Maintain as much eye contact with the audience as possible, and refer to your notes as little as possible (you'll be glad you practiced plenty of times beforehand).
- *Speak clearly and confidently.* Don't speak too quickly or too slowly. Speak in short, understandable sentences—not long, complex, rambling sentences.

Pause appropriately after a key point or before moving on to a new item. Use appropriate inflection in your voice to help make a point. Do not present your speech in a monotone.

- *Use appropriate animation to help make a point.* Use hand movements, facial expressions, and body language. Don't stand frozen to one spot; move around, if appropriate. In a large auditorium, it's better to have a portable microphone than to be locked to a lectern with a fixed microphone. If you do walk around, whether in a small meeting room or an auditorium, always face the audience when you speak; never speak with your back to the audience. For example, do not face the projector screen and read your visual aid to the audience. Elaborate on the single idea illustrated by each visual aid and give examples, if appropriate.
- *Do not stand in front of your visual aids.* Don't stand in a position where you block any of the audience's view of the projector screen, flip chart, or whatever.
- *Build interest in your presentation.* Develop your "story" with logic and reason. Gradually increase the tempo of your presentation.
- *Keep to the key points in your outline.* Don't digress or wander off the topic or your outline. You will waste time and confuse the audience.
- *When making key points, explain to the audience why they are important.*
- *Sum up your points on a particular item before moving on to the next item on your outline.*
- *Know your closing lines.* The closing is as important as the opening. Tie the closing to the purpose of the presentation. Finish with conviction and confidence.
- *Allow time for interaction with the audience, if appropriate.* Ask if there are any questions. You should state at the beginning of your presentation whether there will be time for questions at the end of the presentation or whether the audience can interrupt with questions during the presentation. The latter option can be risky if you have a fixed time slot or an agenda to complete. However, if it's a presentation to a customer conducted in a small meeting room, responding to questions on the fly may be more appropriate than expecting the customer to hold all questions until the end of the presentation. In fact, part of your presentation strategy may be to draw the customer into a discussion to expose his or her opinions.
- *When responding to questions, be sincere, candid, and confident.* If you don't know the answer or can't divulge the answer, say so; that's a legitimate answer. Don't be defensive in responding.

16. What are some important things to keep in mind when delivering a presentation?

REPORTS

Written reports are just as important as oral reports in communicating information about a project. The required types, content, format, frequency, and distribution of reports that the project organization must prepare may be specified by the customer in the contract.

Some reports may be distributed to a large audience. It's important to know who will be receiving copies of reports. The audience could be very diverse and could include people who are very knowledgeable about the project, as well as individuals who know only what they read in the periodic reports they receive. Recipients of the reports may have different levels of technical sophistication, and some may not understand certain technical language or jargon.

It is important to keep in mind that *reports must be written to address what is of interest to the readers, not what is of interest to the person writing the report.*

The following sections discuss two common types of project reports and offer suggestions for ensuring that reports are useful.

Reinforce Your Learning

17. Project reports should be written to address what is of interest to the ________________, not what is of interest to the person ________________ the report.

Types of Project Reports

The two most common types of project reports are

- Progress reports.
- Final report.

PROGRESS REPORTS

It is important to keep in mind that a progress report is not an activity report. *Do not confuse activity or busy-ness with progress and accomplishment.* The customer, in particular, is interested in project accomplishments—what progress has been made toward achieving the project objective—rather than what activities the project team was busy on.

Reinforce Your Learning

18. The primary purpose of progress reports is to report on project ________________ rather than what ________________ the project team was busy on.

Reports on project progress can be prepared by project team members for the project manager or their functional manager (in a matrix organization), by the project manager for the customer, or by the project manager for the project company's upper management.

Progress reports usually cover a specified period, called the **reporting period**. This period could be a week, a month, a quarter, or whatever best fits the project. Most progress reports cover only what happened during the reporting period rather than cumulative progress since the beginning of the project.

A sample outline for a project progress report is shown in Figure 12.6. Items that might be included in a project progress report include the following:

- *Accomplishments since the previous report.* This section should identify key project milestones that were reached. It could also include a report on achievement (or lack of achievement) of specific goals set for the reporting period.
- *Current status of project performance.* Data on cost, schedule, and work scope are compared to the baseline plan.
- *Progress toward resolution of previously identified problems.* If no progress has been made on items brought up in previous progress reports, an explanation should be provided.
- *Problems or potential problems since prior report.* Problems can include (1) technical problems such as prototypes that do not work or test results that are not what they were expected to be; (2) schedule problems such as delays encountered because some tasks took longer than expected, materials were delivered late, or bad weather caused construction delays; and (3) cost problems such as cost overruns because materials cost more than originally estimated or more person-hours were expended on tasks than had been planned.

FIGURE 12.6 ***Project Progress Report Outline***

Progress Project Report
for the period July 1 to September 30

Table of Contents

1. Accomplishments since prior report
2. Current status of project performance
   - 2.1 Cost
   - 2.2 Schedule
   - 2.3 Work scope
3. Progress toward resolution of previously identified problems
4. Problems or potential problems since prior report
5. Planned corrective actions
6. Milestones expected to be reached during next report period

- *Planned corrective actions.* This section should specify the corrective actions to be taken during the next reporting period to resolve each of the identified problems. It should include a statement explaining whether the project objective will be jeopardized, with respect to scope, quality, cost, or schedule, by any of these corrective actions.
- *Milestones expected to be reached during next reporting period.* These goals should be in accordance with the latest agreed-upon project plan.

None of the information in the progress report should be a surprise to the readers. For example, any identified problems should already have been discussed orally prior to the preparation of the written progress report.

FINAL REPORT

The project final report is usually a summary of the project. It is not an accumulation of the progress reports, nor is it a blow-by-blow story of what happened throughout the project. The final report might include the following:

- *Customer's original need.*
- *Original project objective.*
- *Customer's original requirements.*
- *Actual versus anticipated benefits* to the customer as a result of the project.
- *Degree to which the original project objective was met.* If it was not met, an explanation should be included.
- *Brief description of the project.*
- *Future considerations.* This section could include actions the customer might want to consider in the future to enhance or expand the project results. For example, if the project was constructing an office building,

future considerations might be to add a parking deck, a fitness center, or a day care center adjacent to the building. If the project was organizing an arts festival, future considerations might be to change the time of year or to take action to improve the pedestrian traffic flow.

- *A list of all deliverables* (equipment, materials, software, documents such as drawings and reports, and so on) provided to the customer.
- Test data from the final-acceptance testing of a system or piece of equipment, on the basis of which the customer accepted the project results.

Reinforce Your Learning

19. True or false: A project final report is an accumulation of the progress reports prepared during the project.

Preparing Useful Reports

Taking into consideration the following guidelines when you are preparing project reports will help ensure their usefulness and value to the recipients:

- *Make your reports concise.* Don't try to impress the recipients with volume. The volume of a report does not equate with project progress or accomplishment. If reports are kept brief, there is a better chance that they will be read. Furthermore, report preparation can be a time-consuming activity; the project manager should therefore try to minimize the time needed by the project team to develop input to the project reports.
- *Write as you would speak.* Use short, understandable sentences rather than compound, complex, paragraph-length sentences. Long paragraphs will tempt the reader to skip down the page and miss important points. Use simple language that the various recipients will understand. Don't use jargon or acronyms that some readers may not understand. Read the report aloud for content and style. Is it easily readable and understandable, or does it sound stilted and confusing?
- *Put the most important points first*—in the report and in each paragraph. Some readers have a tendency to read the first sentence and then skim over the rest of the paragraph.
- *Use graphics where possible*—such as charts, diagrams, tables, or pictures. Remember, a picture is worth a thousand words. Don't make the graphics too busy. Have one concept or point per graphic. It's better to have several clean graphics than a single cluttered one.
- *Pay as much attention to the format of the report as to the content.* The report should be open, inviting, and organized in a manner that is understandable to the readers. It should not be cluttered or in a small-sized type font that is difficult to read. It should not contain unclear copies of materials or graphics or forms that have been reduced to an illegible size.

Reinforce Your Learning

20. What are some important guidelines to keep in mind when preparing a report?

Written reports, like oral communication, leave an impression—positive or negative—with the audience. Care and thought should be given to preparing reports, and report preparation should be looked upon as an opportunity to make a positive impression, rather than as a burdensome, time-consuming activity. It may be worthwhile to ask periodically for feedback from the recipients of the reports regarding the usefulness of the reports in meeting their needs and interests and to solicit any suggestions they might have for enhancing the reports.

PROJECT DOCUMENTATION AND CONTROLLING CHANGES

In addition to project reports, many other documents may be created by either the contractor's project team or the customer during the project. Some examples are a map of tent locations at a campground for a scout camping trip, assembly instructions for booths for a town festival, drawings for a house addition, and a printout of a computer program for controlling the movements of a robot. Project documents can be text, drawings, forms, lists, manuals, photographs, videos, or software. They can be on large paper (for example, an engineering drawing or blueprints) or on a CD or DVD (for example, a document or simulation).

Revisions to project documents can result from changes initiated by the customer or by the project team. Some changes are trivial; others are major, affecting the project work scope, cost, and schedule. An example of a minor change is updating the drawings and assembly instructions for festival booths because a benefactor donated canopies for all the booths. An example of a major change is a change in the location, size, and type of some of the windows requested by the customer upon seeing the house being built. In this case, it's important that the contractor stop work on those particular windows and inform the customer of any additional costs or schedule delays that might be caused by the requested changes. These changes should be documented in writing for the customer, and the customer should approve the changes before work proceeds and any new materials are ordered.

Throughout a project, various project documents will be revised to incorporate changes. It is important for the project team to know which is the latest version of a document, so that they can perform their work correctly based on the most current information and documentation. For example, the buyer wouldn't want the builder to use outdated drawings if the architect had just made revisions that changed the locations of interior walls.

Reinforce Your Learning

21. Revisions to project documents can result from changes initiated by the

____

or by the

____

____________________.

It's good practice to put on each page of each type of document (1) the date of the latest revision, (2) a sequential revision number, and (3) the initials of the person who made the changes. For example, a notation in the lower right corner of a floor plan for an office arrangement may indicate

Rev.4, 12/29/07, ES

This means that the latest version of the floor plan is revision number 4, which was made on December 29, 2007, by Elisabeth Smith (ES).

Just as important as keeping up to date with revision numbers and dates on documents is timely distribution of updated documents to appropriate people on the project. When changes are made to documents, the updated documents should immediately be given to any project team members whose work will be affected by the changes. Also, when revised documents are distributed, they should be accompanied by a cover memo explaining the changes that were made to the previous document. This will be helpful to people receiving the document—they won't need to go back and compare the new document to the old one and try to find the changes. If only a few changes are made to a document, distribution of the particular pages that were changed may be all that is required. When changes are extensive, it may make sense to distribute the entire revised document rather than all the revised pages.

Early in the project, agreement should be reached between the contractor and the customer, as well as between the project manager and the project team, regarding the way changes will be documented and authorized. If changes are consented to orally rather than in writing and there is no indication given of the impact the changes will have on the work scope, cost, or schedule, there are bound to be problems down the road.

Reinforce Your Learning

22. Early in the project, agreement should be reached regarding the way changes will be ______ and ______.

Project team members should be careful about casually agreeing to changes without knowing whether they will necessitate additional person-hours. If the customer does not agree to pay for extra person-hours, the contractor must absorb the costs and risk overrunning costs for a particular task or the project. See Chapter 10 for a further discussion of managing change.

COLLABORATIVE COMMUNICATION TOOLS

Meetings create a forum and opportunity for team collaboration. However, face-to-face meetings are not always feasible, timely, or practical, especially when many team members are involved and because of constraints such as travel. Project teams may be geographically dispersed, with team members located in various buildings in an office complex, or in different offices in various cities within a state, across the country, or on several continents. Also with telecommuting, some team members may have arrangements in which they work from their domiciles.

There are various collaborative communication tools, such as teleconferencing, groupware, content management systems, extranets, and collaborative project workspaces on the web that allow all or some of the members of the project team, including subcontractors and the customer, to communicate with each other. Use of such communication tools can be important when team members are in different geographic locations, making it inconvenient or impractical for them to physically come together in a common location for a face-to-face meeting. These tools facilitate the sharing of project information and can enhance the communication, collaboration, teamwork, productivity, and performance of the project team. Collaborative communication tools range from e-mail, which relies on writing and reading; to audio-based tools such as conference calls; to videoconferencing, which is based on both audio and video. For project communications that are not face to face, e-mail is the most frequently used method for transmitting and distributing project information. . Information can be distributed quickly and efficiently to the project team or various subgroups through an assortment of distribution lists.

Reinforce Your Learning

23. Teleconferencing includes tools such as ______ calls and ______.

Teleconferencing allows the live exchange of information among members of the project team. It includes tools such as conference calls and videoconferencing. It can help facilitate the sharing of information in a more interactive way than perhaps e-mail. Teleconferencing eliminates travel costs and allows team members to be more productive by not having to travel to meetings. Conference calls allow people at different locations to interact using voice/audio, while videoconferencing enriches the interaction by using both audio and video. Videoconferencing can involve multiple locations where several team members gather in rooms equipped with cameras and displays. Web videoconferencing, where each participant is connected using their own personal computer and webcam, is another tool used to conduct live meetings over the Internet. This technique may be particularly helpful to team members who are telecommuting and may not be able to travel to a common location where the videoconferencing equipment is set up. Web or desktop videoconferencing may allow participants to also share data, documents, or video, such as a spreadsheet, PowerPoint slides, or a web cast, for other participants to view from their personal computer during the session. Similar to preparing for a face-to-face meeting, it is good practice to prepare and distribute an agenda to participants before the session, and provide copies of materials (project documents, presentation slides, etc.) that will be referenced during the session. When scheduling a teleconference, you need to be sensitive to differences in the time zones of the participants.

Groupware is another collaborative tool. It is software that helps people involved in a common task. Groupware can support team idea generation, brainstorming, problem solving, and decision making. An example of such groupware is a group decision support system, which is software that facilitates group decision making. It is particularly useful for idea generation and brainstorming. Session participants provide their own input simultaneously. The system allows participants to contribute anonymously when appropriate. It also allows the group to categorize, rank, or vote on various statements or entries. Reports, including graphics, of the results can be produced automatically.

Document management systems are another collaboration tool that can provide a central repository for project information and capture the efforts of team members into a managed content environment. A content management system is used to manage the content of a website, documents, or files. Such a system can be used by a group of contributors to share, develop, add to, and edit documents, such as a project report, technical specification, or an instruction manual. Such systems can also provide document management information, such as who accessed which documents and when, and what changes they may have made. Some systems may also incorporate automatic routing of documents for approvals, including e-mail notification, for example.

A computer server may be dedicated to a specific project, or there can be reserved space on a server as a place to share project documents and files, such as requirements documents, proposals, specifications, contracts, drawings, forms, plans, schedules, budgets, a common project calendar, meeting agenda and action items, project reports, presentation materials, etc. An extranet is a "private" network that uses the Internet to securely share a repository of project information among the project team, subcontractors, and customer. It can be a restricted part of a website where registered users need to log in to access project information and documents. Project workspaces on the web, such as those that can be created with Microsoft Office Project Professional 2007, allow for complete web access to all project information across multiple projects and provide numerous reporting and communication tools.

Cell phones, to some extent, have features that provide team members with greater access and flexibility while using various interactive telecommunication technologies and collaboration tools such as e-mail, Internet access, document management, etc.

Critical Success FACTORS

- Effective and frequent personal communication is crucial to successful project management.
- A high degree of face-to-face communication is important early in the project to foster team building, develop good working relationships, and establish mutual expectations.
- Body language and customs reflective of cultural diversity must be considered in communications.
- Be careful not to use remarks, words, or phrases that can be construed to be sexist, racist, prejudicial, or offensive.
- The heart of communication is understanding—not only to be understood, but to understand. Half of making communication effective is listening. Failure to listen can cause a breakdown in communication.
- Communication should be straightforward, unambiguous, free of technical jargon, and not offensive.
- Achieving customer satisfaction requires ongoing communication with the customer to keep the customer informed and to determine whether expectations have changed. Regularly ask the customer about the level of satisfaction with the progress of the project.
- Keep the customer and project team informed of the project status and potential problems in a timely manner.
- Project status meetings should be held on a regular basis. Discuss meeting guidelines at a project team meeting at the beginning of the project so everyone understands what behavior is expected during project meetings.
- Do not confuse busy-ness and activity with accomplishment when communicating project progress.
- Reports must be written to address what is of interest to the readers, not what is of interest to the person writing the report.
- Make reports concise. Pay as much attention to format, organization, appearance, and readability, as to the content.
- Early in the project, agreement should be reached regarding how changes will be authorized and documented.
- When documents are updated, they should immediately be distributed to all team members whose work will be affected.

SUMMARY

Project communication takes various forms, including personal communication, meetings, presentations, reports, and project documentation. Communication can be face to face or use some medium, including telephones, voice mail, e-mail, videoconferencing, or groupware. It can be formal or informal. Personal communication can be either oral or written. Oral communication can be face to face or via telephone. Information can be communicated in a more accurate and timely manner through oral communication. Such communication provides a forum for discussion, clarification, understanding, and immediate feedback.

Body language and tone are important elements in oral communication. Body language and customs reflective of cultural diversity must be considered in communications. Oral communication should be straightforward, unambiguous, free of technical jargon, and not offensive. Asking for or providing feedback enhances understanding.

Personal written communication is generally carried out through internal memos or external letters. Such means can be used to communicate effectively with a large group of people, but should not be used for trivial matters. Written communications should be clear and concise and should be used mostly to inform, confirm, and request.

Listening is an important part of making communication effective. Failure to listen can cause a breakdown in communication. Common barriers to effective listening include pretending to listen, distractions, bias and closed-mindedness, impatience, and jumping to conclusions. Listening skills can be improved by focusing on the person talking, engaging in active listening, asking questions, and not interrupting.

Project meetings are another forum for project communication. The three most common types of project meetings are status review, problem-solving, and technical design review meetings. The purposes of a status review meeting are to inform, identify problems, and establish action items. Items often covered include accomplishments since the previous meeting; cost, schedule, and work scope—status, trends, forecasts, and variances; risk assessment update; corrective actions; opportunities for improvement; and action item assignment. Problem-solving meetings are called when problems or potential problems arise. They should be used to develop a problem statement, identify potential causes, gather data, identify and evaluate possible solutions, determine the best solution, revise the plan, implement the solution, and evaluate it. Technical design review meetings are for projects that include a design phase. They often include a preliminary design review meeting, in which the customer reviews the initial conceptual design, and a final design review meeting, in which the customer reviews completed, detailed design documents. These meetings are a mechanism for gaining customer approval before proceeding with the remainder of the project effort.

Before any meeting, the purpose of the meeting and the people who need to participate should be determined, an agenda should be drawn up and distributed, materials should be prepared, and room arrangements should be made. The actual meeting should start on time, notes should be taken, and the agenda should be reviewed. The meeting leader should facilitate, not dominate, the meeting. After the meeting, decision and action items should be published and distributed.

Project managers and team members are often called on to give formal presentations. In preparing for the presentation, it's important to determine the purpose of the presentation, find out about the target audience, make an outline, develop notes and visual aids, make copies of handout materials, and practice. You should start by telling the audience what you are going to tell them, then tell it to them, then summarize the presentation by telling them what you told them. The presentation should be clear, simple, and interesting, and should conclude within the allotted time.

Written reports are often required during a project. The two most common types of project reports are progress reports and final reports. Progress reports often cover accomplishments since the prior report, the current project status, any potential problems that have been identified and corrective actions that are planned, and goals that should be accomplished during the next reporting period. Final reports provide a summary of the project and often include items such as the customer's original need, the original project objective and requirements, benefits resulting from the project, a description of the project, and a list of deliverables produced. All reports should be clear and concise and written as you would speak. They should be written to address what is of interest to the readers, not the writer.

Throughout a project, many types of documents may be created, such as manuals or drawings. They may need to be revised as a result of changes made by the customer or the project team. Early in the project, agreement should be reached regarding how changes will be documented and authorized.

Collaborative communication tools allow all or some of the members of the project team, including subcontractors and the customer to communicate with each other. This can be important when team members are in different geographic locations from where it is not convenient or practical for them to physically come together in a common location for a face-to-face meeting. These tools facilitate the sharing of project information and can enhance the communication, collaboration, teamwork, productivity, and performance of the project team. They can also support and advance team idea generation, brainstorming, problem solving, decision making, and document development and management.

QUESTIONS

1. Discuss why oral and written communication are important to project success, and describe several ways of enhancing such communication.
2. Why are listening skills important in effective communication? How can you improve your listening skills?
3. For the next few days, observe the body language of the people with whom you communicate. Describe some of the positive and negative things they do.
4. Discuss why it's important to be sensitive to the diverse composition of a project team, especially with regard to communication.
5. What is the purpose of status review meetings? When should they be conducted? What should be covered at such meetings?
6. Why are problem-solving meetings conducted? Who should call such meetings? Describe the approach that should be followed.
7. What is the purpose of technical design review meetings? What are the two different types of technical design reviews? Who participates? What should be covered in each type of meeting?
8. What should be done before a meeting to properly prepare for the meeting? What should be done during a meeting to ensure that the meeting will be effective?
9. If you were asked to advise someone on how to prepare for and deliver an important presentation, what would you say? For each step listed, state why it is important.
10. Why are progress reports an integral part of project communications? What should they include? How are they different from a final report?

11. Why is it important to control the changes made to project documents? How can you achieve effective control?
12. Describe what is meant by the term *collaborative communication tools* and provide a list of some of these tools. How can these tools help improve project communications?

INTERNET EXERCISES

For the website addresses of the organizations mentioned in these exercises, go to "Internet Exercises" at the book's companion website at **international.cengage.com**. It is suggested that you save this website in your "Favorites" for easy access in the future.

1. Search the web for "Effective Project Communications." Summarize at least one website and compare it to what was presented in this chapter. What new insights did you gain from this website?
2. Search the web for "Effective Listening Skills." Identify several helpful techniques that were not presented in this chapter.
3. Search the web for "Effective Meeting Strategies." Identify several helpful techniques that were not presented in this chapter. In addition, identify at least one tool that allows you to run electronic or online meetings. Describe the features of this tool.
4. Search the web for "Project Reports." Print out and describe at least one website that discusses methods for writing effective project reports or provide a one-page review of a software package that helps you write project reports.
5. To improve communications, many projects today have their own website. Search the web for at least one web-based collaborative communications software tool. Describe what this tool does. Do you think this product can be used to improve project communications?

Office Communications

CASE STUDY 1

Cathy Buford is the design leader on a project team for a large, complex technical project for a very demanding customer. Joe Jackson is an engineer assigned to her design team.

It's about 9:30 A.M. when Joe walks into Cathy's office. Her head is down and she's hard at work.

"Hey, Cathy," says Joe, "going to the Little League game tonight? Ya know, I volunteered to coach this year."

"Oh. Hi, Joe. I'm really busy," Cathy tells him.

Joe then proceeds to sit down in Cathy's office. "I hear your kid is a pretty good ball player."

Cathy shuffles some papers and tries to focus on her work. "Huh? I guess so. I am so swamped."

"Yeah, me too," Joe says. "I had to take a break to get away from it for a while."

"Since you're here," Cathy says, "I've been thinking that maybe you should evaluate using bar coding or optical character recognition technology for data entry. It might ..."

Joe interrupts. "Look at those dark clouds forming outside. I hope the game isn't rained out tonight."

Cathy continues, "Some of the advantages of these technologies are . . ." She goes on for a few minutes. "So what do you think?"

"Huh? No, they won't work," is Joe's response. "Trust me. Besides, the customer is a low-tech kind of guy, and it would increase the project costs."

"But if we can show the customer that it could save him money and reduce input errors," Cathy persists, "he probably would pay the extra needed to implement the technologies."

"Save him money!" Joe exclaims. "How? By laying off people? We already have too much downsizing in this country. And the government and politicians aren't doing anything about it. It doesn't matter who you vote for. They're all the same."

"By the way, I still need your input for the progress report," Cathy reminds him. "I need to e-mail it to the customer tomorrow. As you know, I'll need about 8 to 10 pages. We need a thick report to show the customer how busy we've been."

"What? Nobody told me," says Joe.

"I sent the design team an e-mail a couple of weeks ago saying I needed everyone's input by last Friday. You could probably use the material you've prepared for the project status review meeting tomorrow afternoon," Cathy responds.

"I have to make a presentation at the meeting tomorrow? That's news to me," Joe tells her.

"It was on the agenda distributed last week," says Cathy.

"I don't have time to keep up with all the e-mails in my Inbox," Joe snorts. "Well, I'll just have to wing it. I'll use some of the slides from my pitch six months ago. Nobody will know the difference. Those meetings are a waste of time anyway. Nobody cares about them. Everybody thinks they are just a waste of two hours each week."

"Anyway, can you e-mail me your input for the progress report by the end of the day?" asks Cathy.

"I have to leave early for the game."

"What game?"

"Aren't you listening to anything I say? The Little League game."

"Maybe you should start working on it now," Cathy suggests.

"I just have to talk to Jim first about the game tonight." says Joe. "Then I'll write up a couple of paragraphs. Can't you just take notes at the meeting tomorrow when I give my pitch? That should give you what you need for the report."

"It can't wait until then. The report has to be e-mailed tomorrow, and I'll be working on it late into the night."

"So, you won't be at the game?"

"Just e-mail me your input."

"I'm not being paid to be a typist," Joe declares. "I can write it much faster. You can get somebody to type it. You'll probably want to edit it anyway. The last report to the customer looked completely different from the input I provided. It looked like you completely rewrote it."

Cathy looks back down at her desk and attempts to continue her work.

CASE QUESTIONS

1. What are some of the communication problems?
2. What should Cathy do? What do you think Joe will do?
3. How could Cathy and Joe have handled this situation better?
4. What could have been done to prevent the communication problem between Cathy and Joe?

GROUP ACTIVITY

Have two participants in the class act out this scenario. Immediately afterward, have a class discussion that addresses the four questions above.

International Communications

CASE STUDY 2

"Samuel, this is Angelique calling again. It is Wednesday at 9 o'clock. I need to talk to you. I haven't heard from you in a while, and I need an update on the project. There are also some changes to the equipment placement in the building that I want to discuss with you. I tried to e-mail you several times over the past couple weeks, but I get a message back that my e-mails are undeliverable. Are you having a problem with your e-mail? Please call me today. I have to give a report to our board of directors on Monday, and I need to know the status of the project."

Angelique hung up the phone after leaving the voice message. She was not happy. She had been trying to get in touch with Samuel for several weeks. She thought to herself, "That's it! If he doesn't call back today, I'm calling his boss first thing in the morning."

Angelique was the newly appointed plant manager for ElectroTech Corporation's new manufacturing facility that Thomson Industries was designing and building for ElectroTech in Ireland. She was currently located at ElectroTech's headquarters in Boston, but would be relocating to Ireland as soon as the construction started.

Samuel was the project manager for Thomson Industries, the prime contractor for the design and construction of the new factory. His office was in Dallas. Although he had managed several projects in the past, they were smaller and were in the Dallas region. He got to know most of the subcontractors from working with them on various projects. The ElectroTech project was by far the largest and most complex project ever assigned to him. For example, on this project, two of the major subcontractors who would be supplying equipment for the factory were located in Germany and Japan.

At the start of the project, Samuel called a brief team meeting and confidently told them, "Boston and Ireland are no different than Dallas. And as far as the German and Japanese subcontractors are concerned, my approach will be straightforward. Build the equipment according to our specifications and deliver it on time, or they don't get paid. It's as simple as that. No excuses, no negotiations. The ElectroTech contract has a bonus clause in it for early completion, and I intend to make it. So we got to play hardball with all our subcontractors; we can't let any of their delays screw up our chances for the bonus. And another thing—we need to be very tough on entertaining any changes from the customer. That will give them a reason for delays and an excuse for not paying the bonus."

"We got some pretty good senior people assigned to this project so we should be able to start fast. Everyone should pretty much know what needs to be done, so we shouldn't have to spend a lot of time in meetings discussing and figuring things out. We can focus all our time on doing the job rather than talking about it. Don't bog me down with paperwork or e-mails. I'll have enough to do tracking our budgets and schedules, keeping on top of our subcontractors, keeping ElectroTech from making a bunch of changes, and keeping our own management off our backs."

When Samuel came back to his office after lunch, Penny, his administrative assistant, said, "I checked your voice messages, and Angelique left another one. She said she needs to talk to you—something about changes. She also said something about your e-mail not working."

Samuel responded, "Changes, I knew it! That's exactly why I don't want to talk to her. Just like a woman, changing her mind already about something or another. Thank god men don't do that or we'd never get anything done. And as for my e-mails, I had Larry do something to my computer so whoever sends me an e-mail will get a message back that it's undeliverable. After a while they'll get the message that I'm not interested in getting copies of everybody's e-mails full of trivia and details."

Penny told Samuel, "You really should check your e-mails; some could be very important."

Samuel snapped back, "I've managed plenty of successful projects—all without e-mail. More work and less talk—that's the key to project success."

Penny said, "Maybe I can ask Larry to have your e-mails forwarded to me, so at least I can screen them."

"Go ahead if you want to," replied Samuel. "You're just going to make a whole lot of work for yourself. If something is really important, people will figure out how to get in touch with me. How do you think we managed before we had e-mail? Besides, with you screening my voice mail, I can control my time and decide who I need to talk to and when, and not get snagged with people calling me and telling me why they can't do something; because they always figure a way to get it done anyway. They just got to get in the habit of solving problems when they come up, and not running to the boss and whining about it."

Samuel didn't return Angelique's voice message. The next morning she called Michael Jetson, vice president of projects for Thomson Industries and Samuel's boss. She blasted him about Samuel not returning her phone calls and e-mails. She threatened to put a hold on all future payments of Thomson's invoices if Samuel didn't get back to her.

Michael walked to Samuel's office. Samuel was reviewing the project cost reports. "Samuel, I got a call from Angelique at ElectoTech. She was pretty upset. She said you haven't returned her calls, and she needs to talk with you."

Samuel responded, "That's absolutely right. And you know why I'm not getting back to her? Because she wants to make a whole bunch of changes and that will delay this project big time and screw up our chances for that early completion bonus."

"I told her you'd call her back, Samuel, so please get back to her today. This is an important project for us; and I don't want an unhappy customer," said Michael.

"Michael, you know how women are. They get emotional over things. I'll get back to her and calm her down. It would have been nice if she would have told me that she was going to call you rather than just going around my back, but that's a woman for you!" replied Samuel.

After Michael left Samuel's office, Penny brought in a fax from the Japanese subcontractor. It stated, "We have reviewed the recently revised equipment specifications that you sent us. We found that they were changed without our knowledge. Some of the performance requirements have changed significantly, and we regret that they cannot be met unless we do substantial engineering redesign. We would like to meet with you to discuss the additional costs required for such additional design efforts to meet your revised specifications."

Samuel said, "That's a joke. We're not paying them an extra dime. They got plenty of money in the subcontract to do any more design that is needed. I'm not about to negotiate with them for more money. They better realize that in America we don't do business that way, or at least I don't. Penny, draft a letter to them for my signature telling them that we do not see a basis to provide additional funds. They knew the initial specifications were marked Preliminary and should have anticipated that further engineering design would be required once things got firmed up. Make the letter short and firm. I don't want to leave any opening for getting into any of those you-got-to-save-face negotiations."

"Two more things Penny," said Samuel. "Schedule a project meeting tomorrow with whoever is around. I got to get an update on some of this stuff that's going on. I need to find out if anyone has been talking with the Japanese or Angelique without me knowing about it. I tell you, if I find out that's been going on, some folks are going to have some sore butts after the meeting. Don't people know it's their job to keep me informed? And a second item. Call Angelique and see if she can fly to Dallas on Friday for a meeting. I don't have time to go there; I got a tennis match with an old buddy Friday night. Besides she's the one who needs to talk to me, so let her come here. Maybe that will cool her down. Also make reservations for us at that new restaurant near the mall. After I sweet-talk her over a couple drinks at lunch, I'll suggest she go to the mall to shop before she heads back to Boston. Shopping—that's what women need to get rid of their stress, right Penny?"

CASE QUESTIONS

1. What are the communication errors Samuel made?
2. What should Angelique do when she gets the phone call from Penny asking her to come to Dallas to meet with Samuel?
3. Is there anything more Michael could have said or done in his conversation with Samuel about Angelique's phone call? Should Penny do anything about Samuel's communication style and insensitive comments?
4. What would be the elements of a good communication plan for managing a multinational project such as this?

GROUP ACTIVITY

Divide the course participants into groups of three or four to develop responses to the case questions. Each group should identify a spokesperson to present its responses to the entire class.

© Image Source Black/Jupiter Images

CHAPTER 13

Types of Project Organizations

Real World PROJECT MANAGEMENT

The Customer is Always Right

NCR Financial Solutions Group Ltd., based in Dundee, Scotland, develops software, hardware, and electronics for the leading share of the world's automated teller machines. Several years ago, Andrew Christie, PMP, director of the program management office at NCR Financial Solutions Group, realized that things weren't running very smoothly. He noted that they were missing internal customer commitments, and projects were taking too long to get from the development phase to the market. Many project management processes were not being followed and a great deal of time was spent putting out fires.

In 2001, Christie and four other project managers decided to establish a program management office (PMO). They began a six-month process in order to develop a strategy for the office geared to drive project improvement. Christie hired an outside firm to conduct assessments and interviews of the company's project managers. Interviews were also conducted with key internal customers to determine what they valued in a program management office.

Christie and his team decided that the mission of the program management office should be focused on customer management. So they identified three levels of internal customer base: executive management, middle management, and project management. Four types of customers were identified across those levels: executives, engineering managers, product managers, and project managers.

Once the customers were identified, plans formed around determining the needs of those customers. Christie's team formulated a plan detailing times and ways of communication with its customers. One communication used was an annual two-page satisfaction survey. This feedback was used to justify the work that the program management office would do the following year. For example, two years ago customers called for an improved project management software system. The group replaced their old in-house system with a new customized off-the-shelf system, which is now in the implementation stage.

The program management office's website communicates to the customers what they are doing, including the office's plan and the status of its activities. The website also provides best practice and project management process information and references.

In 2002, the program management office launched a competency assessment for its project managers. A five-point scale in 34 areas was used by functional managers to rate project managers. The project managers also used the scale to rate themselves. These assessments provided an accurate picture with respect to training and mentoring needs. For example, one project manager had low scores in risk management. He was then enrolled in two half-day training sessions and one-on-one follow-up sessions as needed.

The program management office also developed an internal certification program with the objective to complement PMI's Project Management Professional (PMP) certification to demonstrate the application of best practices. Employees had to demonstrate the application of all 34 competencies, achieve certain training levels, and give a 30-minute presentation to senior management. To date, six project managers have satisfied these criteria and have achieved internal certification.

Mr. Christie and his colleagues used an evidence- and assessment-driven approach, which included analyzing a set of case studies to determine exactly how things were being done. The result was a set of objective feedback on what did and didn't work. Mr. Christie explained, "A major aspect is being in continual assessment of both customers' needs and the maturing project management environment to ensure that activities can be aligned appropriately."

The program management office is now averaging far better success rates on its projects than in the past. About a 30 percent to 40 percent reduction in cycle time was noted over a five-year period. The majority of projects are now hitting their schedules as opposed to a minority of projects just five-years ago!

Jedd, M., "The Customer Is Always Right," *PM Network*, December, 2006.

Although there are various ways in which people can be organized to work on projects, the most common types of organization structures are functional, project, and matrix. The examples here relate to industrial companies; however, the concepts are applicable to other sectors, such as service businesses and not-for-profit organizations (for example, educational institutions and hospitals). You will become familiar with

- the characteristics of the three types of organization structures
- the advantages and disadvantages of each.

FUNCTIONAL-TYPE ORGANIZATION

Figure 13.1 represents a **functional organization structure** for an industrial business that sells standard electronics products. Functional organization structures are typically used in businesses that primarily sell and produce standard products and seldom conduct external projects. For example, a company that manufactures and sells video recorders and players may have a functional organization structure. In the functional organization structure, groups consist of individuals who perform the same function, such as engineering or manufacturing, or have the same expertise or skills, such as electronics engineering or testing. Each functional group, or component, concentrates on performing its own activities in support of the company's business mission. The focus is on the technical excellence and cost competitiveness of the company's products, as well as the importance of the contribution of each functional component's expertise to the company's products.

Reinforce Your Learning

1. The functional organization emphasizes the importance of the contribution of each functional component's ________________ to the company's products.

A company with a functional structure may periodically undertake projects, but these are typically in-house projects rather than projects for external customers. Projects in a functional-type organization might involve developing new products, designing a company information system, redesigning the office floor plan, or updating the company policy and procedures manual. For such projects, a *multifunctional project team or task force* is formed, with members selected by company management from the appropriate subfunctions in marketing, engineering, manufacturing, and procurement. Team members may be assigned to the project either full-time or part-time, for a part of the project or for the entire project duration. In most cases, however, individuals continue to perform their regular functional jobs while they serve part-time on the project task force. One of the team members—or possibly one of the functional vice presidents—is designated as the project leader or manager.

In a functional-type organization, the project manager does not have complete authority over the project team, because administratively the members still work for their respective functional managers. Because they view their contribution to the project in terms of their technical expertise, their allegiance remains to their functional managers. If there is conflict among the team members, it usually works its way through the organization hierarchy to be resolved, slowing down the project effort. On the other hand, if the company president does give the project manager the authority to make decisions when there is disagreement among team members, decisions might reflect the interests of the project manager's own functional component rather than the best interests of the overall project. For example, take the situation in which there is disagreement about the design of a new product and the project manager, who is from the engineering function, makes a decision that reduces the engineering design cost of the product but increases the manufacturing cost. In reporting project progress to the company president, the project manager then makes some biased comments regarding the viewpoints of team members from other functional components, such as, "If manufacturing were more willing to consider other production methods, they could make the product for a lower cost. Engineering has already reduced its design costs." Such a situation could require the company president to get drawn into handling the conflict.

Reinforce Your Learning

2. True or false: In a functional organization, individuals continue to perform their regular functional jobs while they serve part-time on a project task force.

The functional organization structure can be appropriate for internal company projects. However, because projects are not a part of the normal routine, it's necessary to establish a clear understanding of the role and responsibilities of each person assigned to the project task force. If the project manager does not have full authority for project decisions, then she or he must rely on leadership and persuasion skills to build consensus, handle conflict, and unify the task force members to accomplish the project objective. The project manager also needs to take the time to update the other functional managers in the company regularly on the status of the project and thank them for the support of their people assigned to the task force.

There may be situations in which a task force is assigned to work on a project that is strictly within a particular functional component. For example, the manager of technical documentation may form a task force of editors and documentation specialists to develop common standards for all technical documents. In such a case, the particular functional manager has full authority over the project, and conflict can be handled more quickly than when it arises within a multifunctional project team.

Reinforce Your Learning

3. A company with a functional structure may periodically form project task forces to work on ______________ projects, but will seldom perform projects involving ______________ customers.

Companies with functional organization structures seldom perform projects involving external customers, as such organizations do not have project managers designated to manage customer-funded projects. Rather, functional-type organizations concentrate on producing their products and selling them to various customers.

FIGURE 13.1 *Functional Organization Structure*

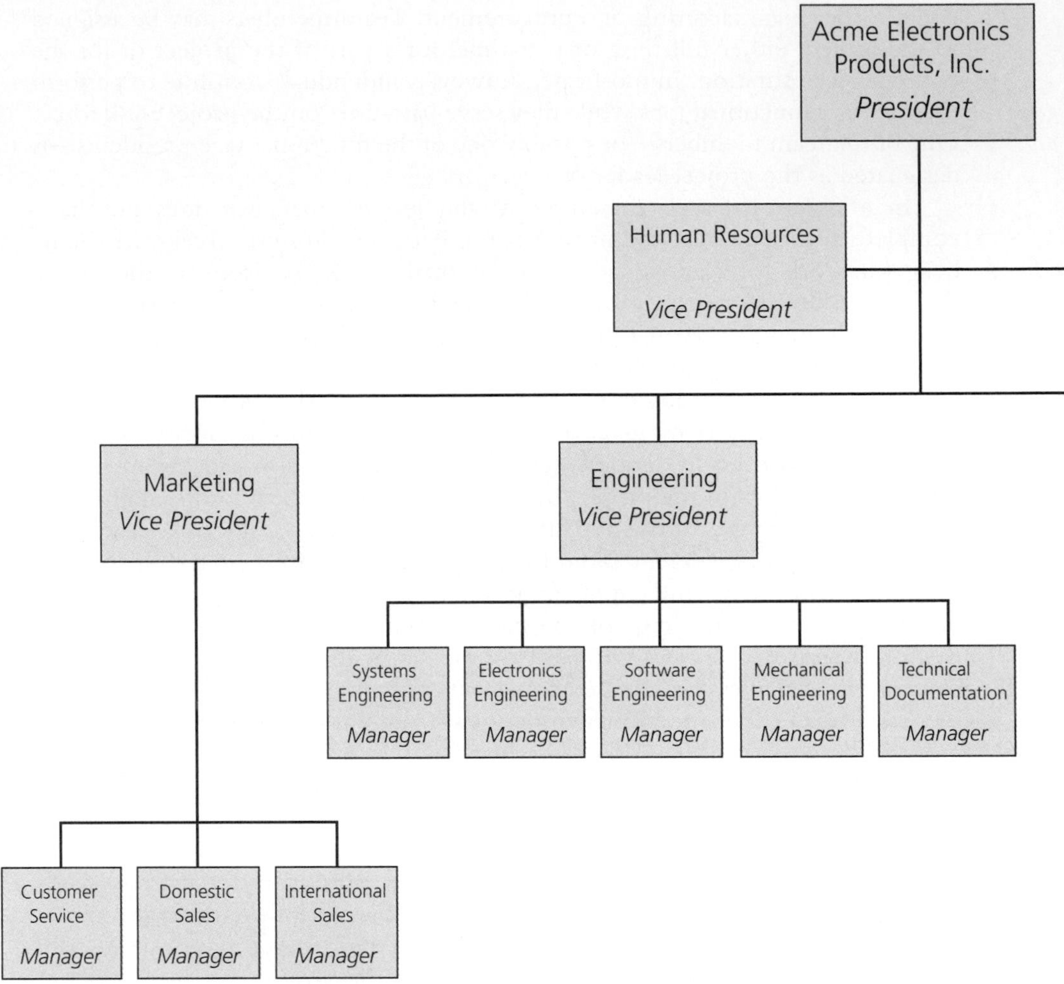

PROJECT-TYPE ORGANIZATION

Figure 13.2 illustrates a **project organization structure** for a business that sells rapid transit projects to cities and counties. An average customer order will be for a multimillion-dollar project that will require several years for engineering, manufacturing, and installation. This company is in the projects business; it does not produce standard products. It's working on multiple projects at any one time, at various stages of completion. As projects wind down and are completed, the company hopes to get contracts for new projects. People are hired to work on a specific project; they may be reassigned from a project just completed if they have the appropriate expertise. Each project team is dedicated to only one project. When their project is completed, unless team members are assigned to another project they might be laid off.

In the project-type organization, each project is operated like a minicompany. All the resources needed to accomplish each project are assigned full-time to work on that project. A full-time project manager has complete project and

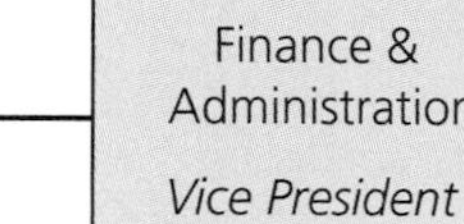

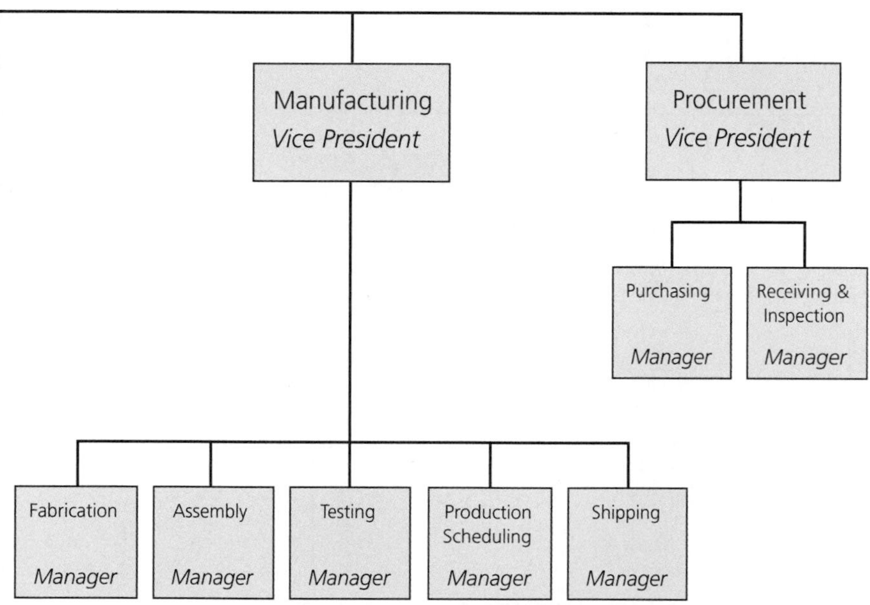

administrative authority over the project team. (In the functional-type organization, the project manager may have project authority, but the functional manager retains administrative and technical authority over his or her people who are assigned to the team.) The project-type organization is well positioned to be highly responsive to the project objective and customer needs because each project team is strictly dedicated to only one project.

A project-type organization can be cost-inefficient both for individual projects and for the company. Each project must pay the salaries of its dedicated project team, even during parts of the project when they are not busy. For example, if a delay in one part of the project leaves some resources with no work to do for several weeks, project funds must cover these costs. If the amount of unapplied time becomes excessive, the project can become unprofitable and drain the profits from other projects. From a company-wide viewpoint, a project-type organization can be cost-inefficient because of the duplication of resources or tasks on several concurrent projects. Because resources are not shared, they may not be diverted to a similar concurrent project even when

Reinforce Your Learning

4. In a project-type organization, all resources are assigned ________________-time to work on a particular project. The project manager has complete ________________ and ________________ authority over the project team.

Reinforce Your Learning

5. A project-type organization can be cost-________________.

FIGURE 13.2 ***Project Organization Structure***

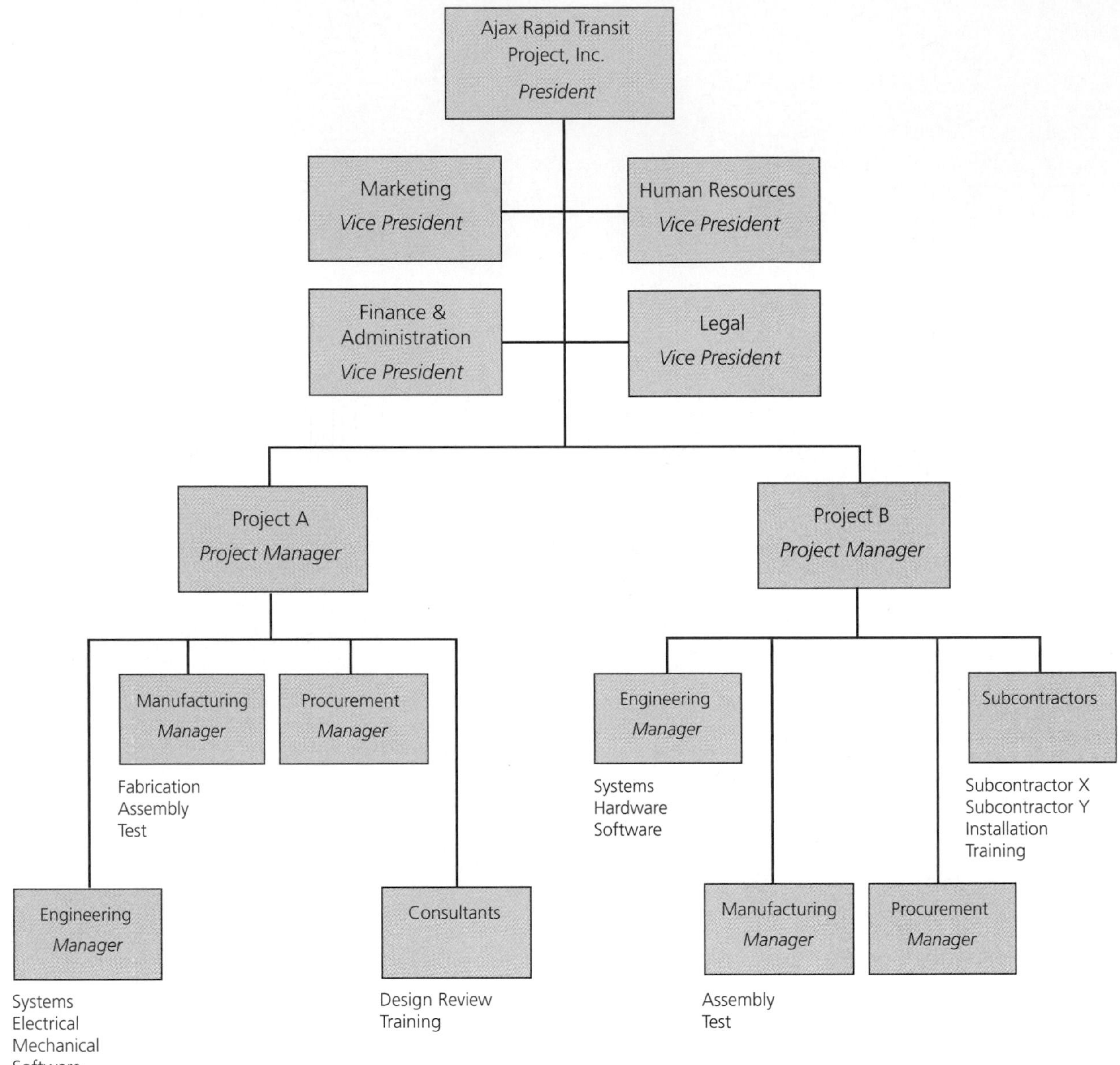

they are not busy on or being used for the project to which they are dedicated. Also, there is little opportunity for members of different project teams to share knowledge or technical expertise, since each project team tends to be isolated and focused strictly on its own project. However, there may be some company-wide support functions that serve all the projects. Figure 13.2 shows, for example, that the human resources function serves all projects, because it wouldn't make sense for each project to hire its own human resources staff. And, by having a common human resources functional component, the company is likely to have consistent human resources policies and employee benefits.

In a project-type organization, detailed and accurate planning and an effective control system are required to assure optimum utilization of the project resources in successfully completing the project within budget.

Project organization structures are found primarily in companies that are involved in very large projects. Such projects can be of high (multimillion) dollar value and long (several years) duration. Project organization structures are prevalent in the construction and aerospace industries. They are also used in the nonbusiness environment, such as for a volunteer-managed fund-raising campaign, town centennial celebration, class reunion, or variety show.

Reinforce Your Learning

6. Project organization structures are found primarily in companies that are involved in very ________ projects.

MATRIX-TYPE ORGANIZATION

Figure 13.3 shows a **matrix organization structure** for a business that sells custom computer-based automation systems. Each customer order is for a unique system. Some systems sell for as little as $50,000 and take four to six months to design and produce, whereas others cost several million dollars and take up to three years to complete. Like Ajax Rapid Transit Project, Inc. in Figure 13.2, Specialized Computer Systems, Inc. is in the projects business; however, its business involves a greater number of smaller-sized projects. It's working on multiple projects at any one time, and these projects vary in size and complexity. Projects are continually being completed and started.

The matrix-type organization is kind of a hybrid—a mix of both the functional and project organization structures. It provides the project and customer focus of the project structure, but it retains the functional expertise of the functional structure. The project and functional components of the matrix structure each have their responsibilities in contributing jointly to the success of each project and the company. The project manager is responsible for the project results, whereas the functional managers are responsible for providing the resources needed to achieve the results.

Reinforce Your Learning

7. The matrix organization structure provides the project and customer focus of the ________ structure, but it retains the functional expertise of the ________ structure.

The matrix-type organization provides for effective utilization of company resources. The functional components (systems engineering, testing, and so forth), home of the technical staff, provide a pool of expertise to support ongoing projects.

Project managers come under the projects component of the organization. When the company receives an order for a new system, the vice president of projects assigns a project manager to the project. A small project may be assigned to a project manager who is already managing several other small projects. A large project may be assigned a full-time project manager.

Reinforce Your Learning

8. In a matrix organization, the ________ components provide a pool of ________ to support ongoing projects.

The project manager then meets with the appropriate functional managers to negotiate the assignment of various individuals from the functional components to work on the project. These individuals are assigned to the project for the length of time they are needed. Some individuals may be assigned to the project full-time, whereas others may be assigned only part-time. Some people may be assigned to a project for its entire duration; others may work on only one part of the project or even off and on throughout the project, depending on when their expertise is needed and how many of their hours the project budget can support. In a matrix-type organization, it's not unusual for an individual from a functional component to be assigned part-time to several concurrent projects. Figure 13.3 shows, for example, that Jack, Cathy, Rose, Chris, and Alex are all working part-time on two projects. Some projects do not require certain types of expertise. For example, projects A and C do not require any mechanical engineering activity, and project A does not include any training.

FIGURE 13.3 *Matrix Organization Structure*

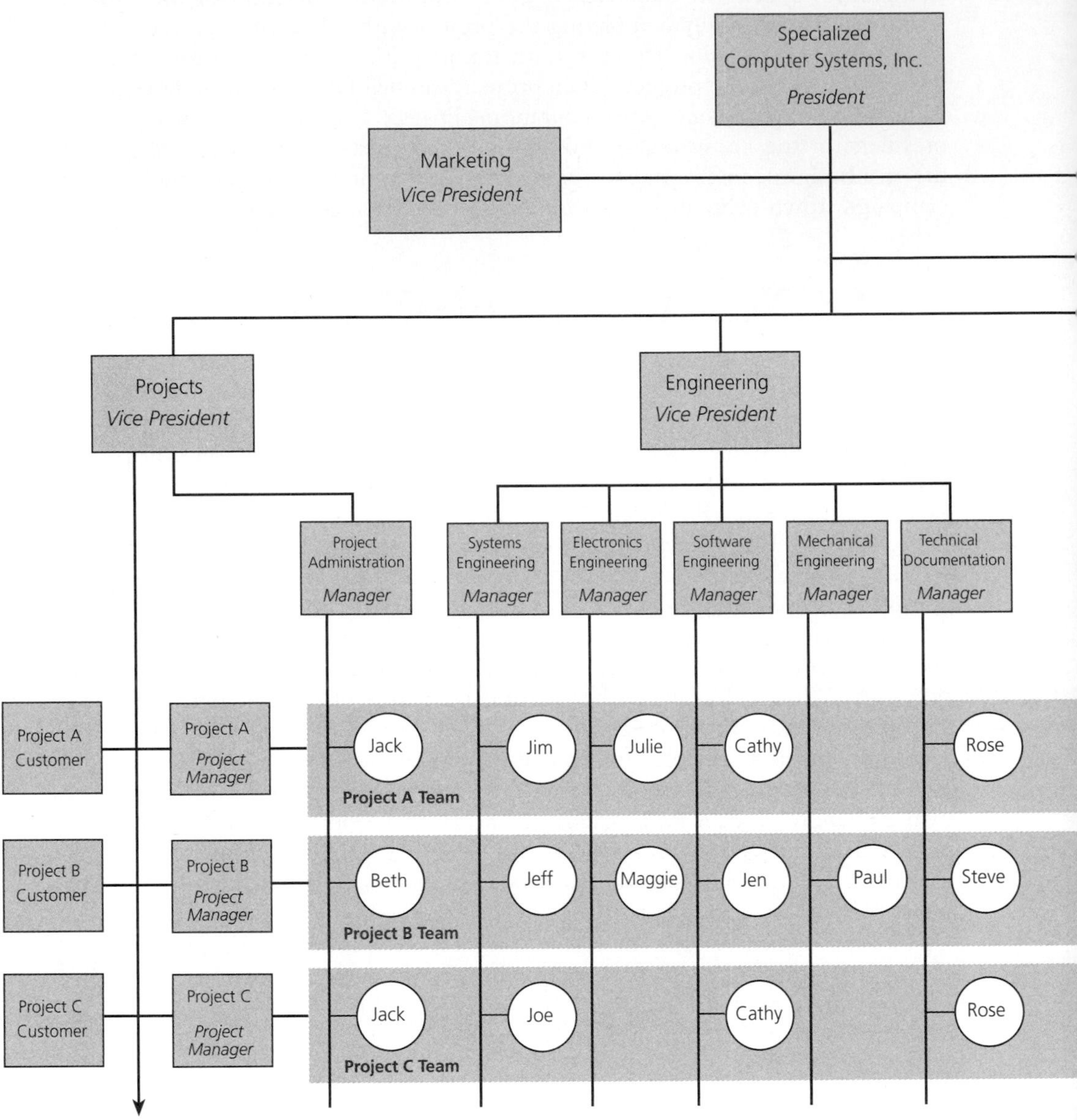

Reinforce Your Learning

9. The matrix organization structure results in effective utilization of ____________ and minimizes overall ____________ because it allows for the ____________ of individuals' time among several ____________.

Thus, sharing of individuals' time among several projects results in effective utilization of resources and minimizes overall costs for each project and for the entire company.

As projects or particular assignments are completed, available individuals are assigned to new projects. The objective is to maximize the number of functional person-hours applied to work on projects (within the constraints of individual project budgets) and minimize the unapplied time (because the salary costs for unapplied time have to be absorbed by the company, reducing overall company profitability). Of course, unapplied time must be provided for vacations, holidays, illness, training activities, and work on proposals for new projects.

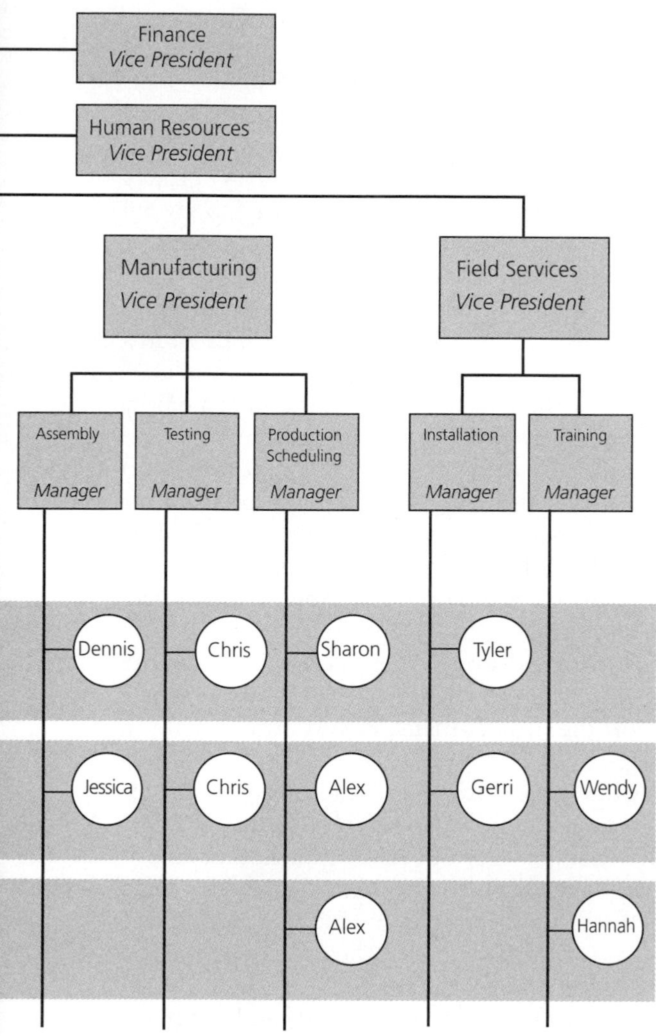

It is important to note that if the total amount of unapplied time of the functional staff is high, the company may be unprofitable even though each project is completed within its budgeted hours. This will happen if the company is not working on enough projects to utilize the people in some of the functional components. The company always needs to have new projects coming in as other projects are completed, in order to maintain a high applied-time rate for the functional staff. If the amount of unapplied time is excessive, individuals may have to be laid off. The company needs to be continually on the lookout for opportunities to develop projects for new or past customers or to develop proposals in response to requests for proposal, as discussed in Chapter 3.

The matrix-type organization provides opportunities for people in the functional components to pursue career development through assignment to various types of projects. As they broaden their experience, individuals become more valuable for future assignments and enhance their eligibility for higher-level positions within the company. As each individual in a particular functional component develops a broad base of experience, the functional manager gains greater flexibility to assign individuals to different kinds of projects.

Reinforce Your Learning

10. In a matrix-type organization, each member of a

____

____

has a dual reporting relationship—to the temporary

____

manager and to a permanent

____

manager.

All of the individuals assigned to a given project comprise the project team, under the leadership of a project manager who integrates and unifies their efforts. Individuals assigned to several small projects will be members of several different project teams. Each member of a project team has a dual reporting relationship; in a sense, each member has two managers—a (temporary) project manager and a (permanent) functional manager. For a person assigned to several concurrent projects, changing work priorities can cause conflict and anxiety.

It's critical to specify to whom the team member reports and for what responsibilities or tasks. Therefore, it's important that the project management responsibilities and the functional management responsibilities be delineated in a matrix-type organization.

In the matrix organization structure, the *project manager* is the intermediary between the company and the customer. The project manager defines what has to be done (work scope), by when (schedule), and for how much money (budget) to meet the project objective and satisfy the customer. She or he is responsible for leading the development of the project plan, establishing the project schedule and budget, and allocating specific tasks and budgets to the various functional components of the company organization. Throughout the project, the project manager is responsible both for controlling the performance of the work within the project schedule and budget and for reporting project performance to the customer and to the company's upper management. A project administrator may be assigned to each project to support the project manager and project team in planning, controlling, and reporting.

Reinforce Your Learning

11. In a matrix organization, the project manager defines

____

has to be done, by

____________________,

and for how much

____

to meet the project

____

and satisfy the customer.

Each functional manager in a matrix organization structure is responsible for how the assigned work tasks will be accomplished and who (which specific people) will do each task. The functional manager of each organization component provides technical guidance and leadership to the individuals assigned to projects. He or she is also responsible for ensuring that all tasks assigned to that functional component are completed in accordance with the project's technical requirements, within the assigned budget, and on schedule.

Reinforce Your Learning

12. In a matrix organization, each functional manager is responsible for

____

the work will be accomplished and

____

will do each task.

In a multiple-project environment, each functional manager can have many individuals assigned to parts of many concurrent projects, particularly if projects are too small to require full-time people or if projects need certain expertise for only brief periods. The functional manager must continually monitor the assignments of the individuals within her or his functional component and make any needed reallocations in response to changing conditions on various projects, such as schedule delays or customer changes. For example, if a project is delayed because the customer is taking longer than anticipated to review and approve engineering drawings or because the shipment of a piece of equipment from a vendor is taking longer than estimated, individuals assigned to the project should be temporarily reassigned to other projects, if possible. In a situation in which a project is behind schedule and in jeopardy of not being completed by the customer's required due date, the functional manager might temporarily assign people from projects that are not in jeopardy.

The matrix-type organization provides a checks-and-balances environment. The fact that potential problems can be identified through both its project and its functional structure reduces the likelihood that problems will be suppressed beyond the point where they can be corrected without jeopardizing the success of the project. The matrix organization structure allows for fast response upon problem identification because it has both a horizontal (project) and a vertical (functional) path for the flow of information.

The vice president of projects, to whom the project managers report, plays an important role in the matrix structure (see Figure 13.3). This individual can resolve priority conflicts between two or more projects within the organization. For example, if two projects are competing to use a particular resource (a technical specialist, maybe, or a piece of test equipment) the vice president of projects can decide the priority in terms of least overall risk to the company and customer relationships (especially if the company has other current or proposed projects for a given customer). Through the project administration function, the vice president of projects can establish consistent procedures for managing projects, such as planning and budgeting, data gathering, using information systems, and project reporting.

Reinforce Your Learning

13. The matrix organization structure allows for fast response upon problem identification because it has both a ____________ and a ____________ path for the flow of ____________.

ADVANTAGES AND DISADVANTAGES

The previous sections discussed the characteristics of the functional-, project-, and matrix-type organizations. Table 13.1 lists some of the more significant advantages and disadvantages that are particular to each of the three organization structures.

Reinforce Your Learning

14. List three common types of structures that can be used to organize people to work on projects.

Functional Organization Structure

By bringing specialists from the same discipline together in one organizational unit, a functional-type organization reduces duplication and overlap of activities. It provides the benefits associated with specialization: an environment in

Table 13.1 *Advantages and Disadvantages of Organization Structures*

	Advantages	Disadvantages
Functional Structure	• No duplication of activities • Functional excellence	• Insularity • Slow response time • Lack of customer focus
Project Structure	• Control over resources • Responsiveness to customers	• Cost-inefficiency • Low level of knowledge transfer among projects
Matrix Structure	• Efficient utilization of resources • Functional expertise available to all projects • Increased learning and knowledge transfer • Improved communication • Customer focus	• Dual reporting relationships • Need for balance of power

which individuals can share and keep up with the knowledge and skills of their particular discipline. For example, all individuals in a computer engineering unit can share software and discuss approaches to developing computer systems.

Functional-type organizations can be insular, though, with each functional component concerned about only its own performance. Teamwork with other functions is not emphasized, and there is little cross-fertilization of ideas among functions. Project focus is not emphasized either, and decisions may be parochial rather than in the best interests of the overall project. The hierarchical structure causes communication, problem resolution, and decision making to be slow.

Reinforce Your Learning

15. What are some advantages and disadvantages of the functional organization structure?

Take the case in which there is a problem with product failures. Engineering thinks it's because manufacturing is not producing the product properly. Manufacturing claims it's because engineering didn't design it properly or because there were errors in the engineering drawings provided to manufacturing. Such a problem could work its way up and down through the chain of command, and its resolution may rest with the company president. The functional-type organization lacks customer focus. There is a stronger allegiance to the function than to the project or the customer.

Project Organization Structure

In a project-type organization, all the individuals on the project team work for the project manager. Therefore, she or he has full control over the resources, including authority over how the work gets done and by whom. There is no conflict with other projects over priorities or resources, because all the resources for a project are totally dedicated to that project. The project organization is highly responsive to the customer. For example, if the customer makes changes to the project work scope, the project manager has the authority to reassign resources to accommodate the changes immediately.

The project organization structure can be cost-inefficient because of underutilization of resources. With individuals assigned full-time to the project, there may be times when things are slow and team members are not working at a high level of productivity. When things are slow, individuals have a tendency to stretch out their work to fill up the time available. If there's nothing else to work on, a one-week task can stretch out to two or three weeks, causing project costs to increase. Also, if some people do not have any tasks to do for temporary periods, their unapplied time is still a cost to the company and erodes the company's profitability. Another factor increasing cost-inefficiency is the potential for duplication of activities on several concurrent projects. For example, if project teams ordered their materials and supplies jointly instead of independently, they could probably get better prices from vendors.

Reinforce Your Learning

16. What are some advantages and disadvantages of the project organization structure?

In the project organization structure, there is a low level of knowledge transfer among projects. Individuals are dedicated to working on one project. They do not have a functional "home" to be a source of shared functional expertise and knowledge. Also, at the end of a project, people may be laid off if there is not a new project to which they can be assigned. In such cases, what they learned on the project is lost to the company. In a project-type organization, team members experience high anxiety about reassignment as their project nears completion, especially because they don't have a functional home to which they can return.

Real World PROJECT MANAGEMENT

What's Your Organizational Quotient?

According to Jennifer Reingold and Jia Lynn Yang, in almost every company there is an organization chart, and then there's the way things really get done. A number of companies are now bringing those hidden power structures out into the light. These informal structures tend to be just as important as the company's formal power structure. A recent study conducted by Katzenbach Partners explains why it is critical to understand the collaborations, relationships, and networks of the informal organization.

As part of the study, a recent survey was conducted, where one-third of the 390 respondents admitted to ignoring their company's rules when they felt they could do daily work more effectively their own way. Additionally, respondents were three times more likely to describe their job environment as positive when managers worked closely with informal employee networks.

Katzenbach refers to the ability to balance both formal and informal power structures as "organizational quotient" or "OQ." Social analysis is one of the most effective ways for project managers to figure out how the hidden workplace can work for them. In a social analysis, a graphic is used to show relationships between employees, bosses, and units. Some companies are now using this information to encourage awareness of informal organization, without trying to control it. These informal power structures are valuable and can be used to remedy classic business issues.

One challenge facing many companies is finding a way to energize a sluggish working environment. Michael Sabia, Bell Canada's new CEO, decided that he needed to do away with its monopolist mentality in order to function effectively. He initially tried traditional business strategies, like cutting costs, but that wasn't enough. Sabia worked with Katzenbach to conduct surveys, performance reviews, and collect recommendations from executives to locate 14 low- and mid-level employees who were committed, passionate, and competitive—all of the traits Bell sought. They found that these 14 individuals shared the ability to get people to work with them to solve problems and established trusting relationships. The initial group recommended 40 more associates. Bell Canada named these employees "Pride Builders" and asked them to help lead a cultural transformation with much less of a hierarchy.

The group grew to 150 people, who worked on solving problems identified during the company "gripe-sessions." The Pride Builders have changed into a more formal organization, consisting of 2500 people. The company realized that the impact of "pride behaviors" has directly resulted in significant and measurable increases in employee and customer satisfaction.

Another challenge many companies face is grooming future leadership. Lehman Brothers is an investment bank that is notorious for being an extremely competitive company. Lately, they have been placing emphasis upon their OQ in order to try to retain their top talent. They recently used social network analysis to identify the company's 300 vice presidents who were considered top performers and sent them to a leadership workshop. The group was given a survey, which resulted in a graphic representation of connections between the executives. Lehman executives used this information to try to build a better social network and encourage informal ties between employees.

Informal social networks can be used effectively to solve numerous business problems. However, companies need to resist the urge to try to micromanage these relationships. They must also be sure not to completely rely on this power structure to solve company problems that rely on concrete structures. It is recommended that executives and project managers try to create loose parameters around informal organizations that operate independently. It is critical for companies to locate the right people to place in project management positions—people who can cross over from the formal to the informal social networks and use both to contribute to the overall success of the company's projects.

Reingold, J. and Yang, J., "What's Your OQ?" *Fortune*, July 23, 2007.

Matrix Organization Structure

The matrix organization structure tries to capitalize on the advantages of both the functional and project structures while overcoming their disadvantages. The matrix structure allows efficient utilization of resources by having individuals from various functions assigned to work part-time, if necessary, on specific projects or by having them assigned for only a limited duration to certain projects. Furthermore, it's not unusual for individuals in a specific function to be working on two or more projects concurrently. Because they have a functional home, individuals can be moved among projects as necessary to accommodate any project changes. For example, if one project is delayed, the functional manager can deploy some of its team members to other projects rather than have their unapplied time increase costs to the company.

The matrix structure provides a core of functional expertise that is available to all projects, and thus this expertise is better utilized. Individuals in a functional component have a common discipline and can collaborate with and learn from one another. This functional component provides a home for individuals at the end of a project while they are waiting to be assigned to other projects. Their knowledge stays with the company, ready to be used on future projects. As people work on more and various projects, they experience greater learning and growth, and their knowledge and skills are transferred from project to project.

The matrix structure also facilitates improved communication, allowing for more timely problem identification and conflict resolution.

Project team members have two channels through which to send up a warning about a potential problem—the project manager and the functional manager. These dual communication paths increase the chances that problems will be identified rather than suppressed.

Finally, the matrix organization is customer-focused. The project manager is the designated focal point for communication with the customer, and the functional units are set up to support projects.

Members of a project team in a matrix organization structure have a dual reporting relationship: temporarily they report to a project manager, while administratively they still report to their functional manager. If an individual is assigned to work on several projects, she or he can have several managers. This can cause anxiety and conflict over work priorities. These individuals have a permanent allegiance to their functional home, which is strained by their required allegiance to the project team. A company that uses a matrix

Critical Success FACTORS

- In a matrix-type organization, it is important to delineate the project management responsibilities and the functional management responsibilities.
- When implementing a matrix organization structure, operating guidelines should be established to assure proper balance of power between project managers and functional managers.

organization structure must establish operating guidelines to assure a proper balance of power between project managers and functional managers. Conflicts will arise between project managers and functional managers regarding priorities, the assignment of specific individuals to projects, technical approaches to the work, and changes to projects. If there is an imbalance of power, such conflicts may not be resolved in a manner that will be in the best interests of either the customer or the company.

Reinforce Your Learning

17. What are some advantages and disadvantages of the matrix organization structure?

SUMMARY

The three most common structures used to organize people to work on projects are functional, project, and matrix. These structures are applicable to a large majority of businesses and not-for-profit organizations.

The functional organization structure is typically used in businesses that primarily sell and produce standard products and seldom conduct external projects. The focus is on the technical excellence and cost competitiveness of the company's products, as well as the importance of each functional component's contribution of expertise to the company's products. For projects, a multifunctional project team or task force is formed, with members selected from the appropriate subfunctions. In this structure, the project manager does not have complete authority over the project team, because administratively the members still work for their respective functional managers. If there is conflict among the team members, it usually works its way through the organization hierarchy to be resolved. A company with a functional organization structure may periodically form project task forces to work on internal projects, but will seldom perform projects involving external customers.

The project organization structure is used by companies that are working on multiple projects at any one time and do not produce standard products. People are hired to work on a specific project, and each project team is dedicated to only one project. When the project is completed, team members may be assigned to another project if they have the appropriate expertise. A full-time project manager has complete project and administrative authority over the project team. A project-type organization is well positioned to be highly responsive to the project objective and customer needs because each project team is strictly dedicated to only one project. From a company-wide viewpoint, a project-type organization can be cost-inefficient because of the duplication of resources or tasks on several concurrent projects. Also, there is little opportunity for members of different project teams to share knowledge or technical expertise. Project organization structures are found primarily in companies that are involved in very large projects with high dollar values and long durations.

The matrix-type organization is kind of a hybrid—a mix of both the functional and project organization structures. It's appropriate for companies that are working on multiple projects at any one time and projects that vary in size and complexity. It provides the project and customer focus of the project structure while retaining the functional expertise of the functional structure. The project and functional components of the matrix structure each have their responsibilities in contributing jointly to the success of each project and the company. In addition, the matrix-type organization provides for effective utilization of company resources. The sharing of individuals' time among several projects results in effective utilization of resources and minimizes overall costs for each project and for the entire company. All of the individuals assigned to a given project comprise the project team, under the leadership of a project manager who integrates and unifies their efforts.

In the matrix structure, the project manager is the intermediary between the company and the customer. The project manager defines what has to be done, by when, and for how much money to meet the project objective and satisfy the customer. The project manager is responsible for leading the development of the project plan, establishing the project schedule and budget, and allocating specific tasks and budgets to various functional components of the company organization. Each functional manager is responsible for how the assigned work tasks will be accomplished and who will do each task.

The advantages of a functional organization structure are no duplication of activities and functional excellence. Disadvantages include insularity, slow response time, and lack of customer focus. The project organization structure has control over resources and responsiveness to customers as advantages. Cost-inefficiency and low level of knowledge transfer among projects are its disadvantages. The advantages of a matrix organization structure include efficient utilization of resources, functional expertise available to all projects, increased learning and knowledge transfer, improved communication, and customer focus. Its disadvantages are the dual reporting relationships and the need for a balance of power.

QUESTIONS

1. Describe what a functional-type organization is. Make sure you discuss the advantages and disadvantages of this structure.
2. Describe what a project-type organization is. Make sure you discuss the advantages and disadvantages of this structure.
3. Describe what a matrix-type organization is. Make sure you discuss the advantages and disadvantages of this structure.
4. Which type of organization structure is often used by companies that produce standard products? Why?
5. Discuss some of the problems that might be encountered when a functional-type organization develops new products.
6. Why is a project-type organization considered to be like a mini-company?

7. Why is a project-type organization sometimes considered to be expensive?
8. Which organization structure is considered to be a hybrid? How so?
9. How does a matrix-type organization provide for career development?
10. What are the responsibilities of the project manager in a matrix-type organization?
11. What are the responsibilities of the functional manager in a matrix-type organization?
12. What are the responsibilities of the vice president of projects in a matrix-type organization?

INTERNET EXERCISES

For the website addresses of the organizations mentioned in these exercises, go to "Internet Exercises" at the book's companion website at **international.cengage.com**. It is suggested that you save this website in your "Favorites" for easy access in the future.

1. Search the web for "Functional Organization Structures." Summarize at least one website and compare it to what was presented in this chapter. What new insights did you gain from this website?
2. Search the web for "Project-Based Organization Structures." Summarize at least onc website and compare it to what was presented in this chapter. What new insights did you gain from this website?
3. Search the web for "Matrix Organization Structures." Summarize at least one website and compare it to what was presented in this chapter. What new insights did you gain from this website?
4. Search the web for "Project Management Successes and Failures." Write a one-page review of a story or case study that you found and include your thoughts as to how the project organization might have effected the outcome.
5. Visit the website of the Project Management Institute**.** Click on the "Training and Events " link and then on the "Calendar" link. Search through the calendar for upcoming events. Find one related to the different types of project organizations. Where is the event taking place and what topics are being discussed?

Multi Projects

CASE STUDY 1

Multi Projects, Inc. is a well-established consulting firm with 400 employees. It has many projects going on at the same time for various clients. It has a good reputation, and nearly 30 percent of its business is from previous clients. It targets growing companies for future business and has been successful in this area, too. Because of the growth, things have been quite hectic, with employees trying to keep up with the work, keep old clients satisfied, and bend over backward to accommodate new clients. Multi Projects has been hiring new employees—in fact, it has grown from 300 to 400 employees over the past 2 years.

Multi Projects has a matrix organization structure. As new projects come in, a project manager is assigned. One project manager may be assigned to several projects at one time, depending on the sizes of the projects. Projects range in value from $20,000 to $1 million and can be from one month to two years in duration. Most projects are about six months in duration and worth about $60,000 to $80,000. The firm performs a range of consulting services, including market research, manufacturing system design, and executive recruiting. Its clients are medium to large corporations and include banks, manufacturers, and government agencies.

Multi Projects just got a call from Growin Corporation, which wants to go forward with a project that Multi Projects proposed nearly six months ago. Partners at Multi Projects are surprised by the good news. They had thought the project was dead. They're also very interested in carrying out a first project for Growin Corporation because it's a rapidly growing company. Multi Projects sees an opportunity to do several projects with Growin Corporation in the future.

Jeff Armstrong has been assigned as project manager for the Growin Corporation project. He has been with Multi Projects for about a year and has been anxious to get a challenging project to manage. He worked on the proposal for the Growin project.

Tyler Bonilla is a senior systems engineer. He has been with Multi Projects eight years. He has an excellent reputation, and previous clients with whom he has worked usually request that he be assigned to their projects. He enjoys his work even though he's extremely busy. He is currently working full-time on a project for Goodold Company, a previous client. Goodold said that one of the reasons it does business with Multi Projects, rather than with another consulting firm, is the great work Tyler does on their projects.

Jennifer Fernandez is the manager of systems engineering. She has been with Multi Projects about 15 years. Tyler reports to Jennifer, but because of his heavy workload and associated travel he doesn't get to see Jennifer very often, other than at her monthly staff meetings.

Julie Capriolo is the project manager for the Goodold Company project. She has been with Multi Projects about two years. Tyler is assigned to her project full-time. The project has a tight schedule, and everyone is putting in extra hours. Julie feels a lot of pressure, but she has a good project team—she relies heavily on Tyler. She had heard from a friend who used to work with Jeff that Jeff is very ambitious and will do whatever it takes to make himself look good. This hadn't been of concern to Julie because she and Jeff have separate projects and don't run into each other very often.

The day Jeff is assigned to be project manager on the Growin Corporation project, he runs into Tyler in the hallway. "We got the Growin project," he tells Tyler.

"Great," responds Tyler.

Jeff continues, "You know, one of the big reasons they gave the project to us rather than another consulting firm is because we promised you'd be the lead systems engineer on the project, Tyler. They were impressed with you when we met with them to present our proposal. When do you think you can start work on the project?"

"Unfortunately, I can't. I'm tied up on the Goodold project, and things are really hectic. I'll be on that project for another four months," says Tyler.

"No way!" exclaims Jeff. "This Growin project is too important to me—I mean, to us. I'll take care of it."

"You'd better talk to Jennifer," Tyler tells him.

Jeff stops by Jennifer's office. She's busy, but he interrupts her. "I gotta have Tyler Bonilla on my Growin project. He wants to work on it, but he said I should talk to you."

"That's impossible," says Jennifer. "He's assigned to Julie Capriolo's Goodold project for the next four months."

"Julie? Who's she? Never mind. I'll find her and work it out. You probably have somebody else you can assign to her project," replies Jeff as he quickly bolts out of her office in search of Julie.

"That's my decision, not yours or Julie's!" shouts Jennifer. But by that time Jeff is gone and doesn't hear what she says.

Julie is meeting with her project team in the conference room. Jeff knocks on the door and opens it. "Is there a Julie in here?" he asks.

"I'm Julie," she responds.

"I need to talk to you ASAP. It's important. Oh, by the way, sorry for interrupting." Looking toward Tyler, who's in the meeting, Jeff says, "Hey, Tyler, catch you later, buddy, after I talk with Julie." Jeff then shuts the door and goes back to his office. Julie is noticeably disturbed at the interruption.

After her meeting, Julie calls Jeff. "This is Julie. What did you want to talk to me about that was so urgent?"

"About reassigning Tyler to my project. He's interested, and I've already talked to Jennifer about it," answers Jeff.

"That's impossible," declares Julie. "He's critical to the Goodold project."

"Sorry," says Jeff, "but if the Growin project is successful, we'll get more business from them than we ever got from the Goodold Company."

"It's already after 6 o'clock and I have to be out of town for a week, but I'll discuss this with Jennifer as soon as I get back," snaps Julie.

"Yeah, sure, whatever," responds Jeff.

The next day Jeff calls a meeting with Jennifer and Tyler. He starts by telling them, "I called this meeting to figure how soon Tyler can begin working on the Growin project and how you [looking toward Jennifer] can get somebody to take his place on what's-her-name's project."

"I think Julie should be here for this discussion," says Jennifer.

"She couldn't make it. Apparently she's out of town for a week, and we need to get going on the Growin project." Jeff tells her. "We need to prepare for a meeting with them next week. Besides, Tyler is the one we're talking about, and he'd rather work on the Growin project. Right, Tyler?"

"Ah, well, now that you've asked, I am getting tired of working on the Goodold projects," replies Tyler. I'm not learning anything new. I mean, it's okay, but I'd like a change."

Jennifer is astonished. "You never mentioned that to me, Tyler."

Jeff breaks in, "Well, I guess it's settled. Jennifer, you assign somebody else to the Goodold project who'll feel a little more challenged and tell Julie when she gets back. In the meantime, me and my buddy Tyler have got a lot of work to do to look good for our meeting with the Growin people next week."

CASE QUESTIONS

1. Why is Jeff so anxious to get started on the Growin project?
2. What is wrong with Jeff's approach to handling this situation?
3. What should Jennifer do to resolve this situation?
4. What advantages and disadvantages of the matrix-type organization are apparent from this story?

GROUP ACTIVITY

Have an open discussion among course participants regarding the following questions:

- What should Jennifer do next?
- What should Tyler do?
- What could have been done to prevent this situation?
- How could each of the four individuals have handled the situation better?

CASE STUDY 2

Organize for Product Development

Stevens Corporation is a multidivision manufacturing company with diversified products serving the aerospace, automotive, and medical markets. Its Medical Instruments Division is located in the Midwest and has a plant with over 1,000 employees. It sells various medical instruments, such as analyzers, monitoring equipment, and testing instruments to hospitals and medical laboratories. It is a market leader, and its business has been steady. It has a very good reputation and commands a premium price for its products. However, the business is not growing as fast as the rest of Stevens' divisions or as fast as the board of directors thinks it should. They feel that the division's management has become complacent. There are several new competitors entering the market with products that have more features and lower prices. Last year the chief executive officer told Kareem, the Medical Instruments Division general manager, that he had to start developing new and enhanced products in order not to lose market share to the emerging competitors.

Kareem has worked his entire 20-year career in the division and is an electronics engineer who worked on many of the current products. He thinks they are still quality products and that his Marketing Department needs to do a better job of convincing the customers that Stevens' products are still the best value compared to unproven competitors' products. He also believes his Manufacturing Department can reduce costs through tougher negotiations with suppliers and by making process improvements.

He believes that Stevens' reputation will eventually knock the new competitors' products out of the market. Therefore, he is hesitant to allocate any more resources into any product development efforts than are necessary to pacify the CEO and board of directors. He wants to maintain the division's profit margin, which is used to determine his year-end bonus.

Kareem's approach was to establish four product development teams. Each team was assigned a different product that was being threatened by competitor products, with the goal of developing enhancements that would match or beat the competing products. He simply assigned each of his four department managers to head the four product development teams. He thought this would create some friendly rivalry. The four department managers are:

1. Tanya—Manager, Marketing
2. Khalid—Manager, Electronic Engineering
3. Lee—Manager, Computer Systems Engineering
4. Tony—Manager, Manufacturing.

Kareem has been getting more frequent questions from the CEO about the status of the product developments. Kareem knows that progress has been slow, and that he really hasn't put a priority on it because he believes Stevens will simply outlast its competitors, who he thinks are losing money on their lower-priced products.

Kareem had his annual performance review sessions with his department managers last week and asked them about the product development projects. Here is what each of them told him:

Tanya, manager of marketing, said that none of the managers, including Kareem, are giving priority to the product development projects because they are too busy with their regular work. She said the product development efforts should be market-driven, not engineering-driven. The other product development teams led by Khalid and Lee are not interested in any input from the Marketing Department; they just want to develop highly sophisticated, over-engineered products that will be too complicated for customers to use. She also said that Tony is only interested in how to make any new products cheaper, not necessarily better, because he thinks that a lower manufacturing cost per unit is the ultimate goal. Tanya suggested to Kareem that he approve a new position of product development manager, who should report directly to her and would have full responsibility for all product development projects.

She told Kareem that several key people from each of the other departments should be permanently reassigned to the product development manager to work solely on product development projects. She told Kareem the other three department managers seem to side with each other against her because she is a woman and has only been with the division a short time. She accused them of being a bunch of "good old boys" who have never gone outside the plant to talk with customers in the 20 plus years they have all been there. She told Kareem that if he doesn't approve hiring a product development manager who would report to her, then she would seriously have to reconsider her interest in staying at Stevens Corporation. She has an excellent reputation in the industry; many other companies would welcome her. Kareem knows that it took him a while to fill the marketing manager position, and he had to pay a higher salary than he wanted to get her to come to Stevens.

Khalid, manager of electronic engineering, told Kareem that the product development projects are not progressing because the Computer Systems Engineering Department is always fighting among themselves about whether product features should be done with hardware or software. He said that Lee has already announced that he intends to retire at the end of the year. Khalid told Kareem that when Lee retires, he should not be replaced; rather, the Computer Systems Engineering Department should be merged into Khalid's department. He said he would then have better control over the product development projects which should be led by engineering anyway because all product enhancements require engineering and design expertise. He saw no need for Marketing or Manufacturing to be involved. He said Marketing's job should be to sell the products Engineering develops, and it's Manufacturing's job to make the products the way Engineering designs them. He also said that by not replacing Lee, Kareem can make up some of the money to pay for the "overpriced" marketing manager.

Lee, manager of computer systems engineering, told Kareem that he evaluated the competitors' products and the big difference is that their products are software based whereas Stevens' products are electronics based, as they have been for years. Lee reminded Kareem that it was years ago that both of them engineered those electronic products. But today it's a different environment, with new technologies and approaches, and Stevens has to redesign its products to be software based. He suggested that when he retires at the end of the year, that Kareem should appoint Nicole as the new manager of the Computer Systems Engineering Department. Lee said she is young, bright, knows software design better than anyone in his department, and could do a great job in leading the product development projects. She has a master's degree in computer engineering and an MBA. She is interested in having Stevens' products meet customers' needs. She frequently has discussions with Tanya about marketing and customers and competitors. Lee told Kareem that if Nicole is not promoted that she will probably leave Stevens and go to another company, maybe even one of the competitors, where her talents might be better utilized.

Tony, manager of manufacturing, told Kareem that he (Kareem) needs to get more involved in the product development projects and "start knocking some heads together." He said Marketing and Khalid and Lee are trying to make too many changes to the products and that will just increase the price or reduce profit margins. He said they have no concern for costs or any manufacturing process changes that would have to be made. Tony suggested that Kareem start having regular product development status meetings to find out what is "really" going on and see all the "politics." He said all the department managers only cared about their own department looking good, and they weren't willing to share information or cooperate with the other teams. As a result, all the product development teams were suffering, and it was getting worse each day. He told Kareem that what started out as a friendly rivalry among the teams has turned into outright nasty competition. He again warned Kareem to do something before the CEO has all their jobs or even recommends selling the division to a competitor, if it begins to drag down the corporation's overall profitability.

Finally, the CEO calls Kareem to a meeting and tells him that the latest marketing report shows the Medical Instruments Division has lost market share for the second consecutive quarter and wants to know why Kareem doesn't have any new product enhancements out in the market yet. Kareem admitted that he hasn't been on top of the product development efforts and hasn't given them the priority that he should. He thought the competitors would fold. Kareem discussed his approach to establishing the product development teams and the feedback he just got from his department managers. The CEO was not happy and told Kareem that he was relying too much on doing things the same old ways and that he'd better look for new ideas and approaches or his position will be in jeopardy.

The CEO told Kareem that the situation is critical and the board of directors is losing their patience. When the board hired her last year, they expected her to move Stevens from a good national company to a great global one, and that all the other divisions are moving in that direction while the Medical Instruments Division is staying flat in spite of an increasing global market for their products. She told Kareem that she is going to bring in a management consultant to evaluate what is going on in his division and make recommendations to her about how to get the product development effort organized and on an accelerated track.

CASE QUESTIONS

You are the management consultant hired by the CEO.

1. How would you initiate your assignment with Kareem and the department managers?
2. Develop a list of questions you would ask.

3. Assuming the department managers tell you the same things they told Kareem, what recommendations would you make to the CEO, including any changes to the organization structure, to improve the management of product development projects?
4. What guidelines would you recommend for how the departments or new functions should work together on product development projects?

GROUP ACTIVITY

Divide the course participants into groups of three or four members to develop responses to the case questions. Each group should choose a spokesperson to present its responses to the entire class.

Appendix A

Project Management Software

Numerous project management software systems are available that allow the user to plan, track, and manage their projects. In recent years, the software has become very easy to use and often can be customized to fit the needs of the users. The software provides a powerful suite of web-based tools to support many of the topics covered in this text. This appendix provides

- a discussion of the common features available in most project management software systems
- criteria for selecting a project management software system
- a discussion of some advantages of using project management software
- a discussion of some disadvantages of using project management software
- a discussion of vendors offering project management software

PROJECT MANAGEMENT SOFTWARE FEATURES

The following list of features offered by most of today's project management software, although by no means complete, gives a general overview of the types of features available. It should be noted, however, that different project management software systems provide different features, and some of the features listed are not found in every project management package. In addition, some products do a much better job than others at providing software support for some of these features.

1. **Budgeting & Cost Management**

   One of the most important features that project management software provides is the ability to effectively plan and manage the costs of projects. Features often include:

   - *Billing and billing methods*

     As discussed in the text, projects can be charged to customers in a variety of ways. Most software allows selection of fixed price, time and materials, milestone completion, and/or percent-to-completion billing methods. In addition, automated billing procedures can be defined.

   - *Cost-to-completion tracking*

     This feature permits the user to track the progress of each task and automatically calculate the expected remaining cost to complete each task and the expected cost to complete the entire project.

- *Earned value management*

  As described in Chapter 9 it is important for the project manager to understand the value of work actually performed. Tools to support earned-value calculations and management are common in project management software systems.

- *Multiple currency*

  With the global business environment of today, many projects have components that span several countries. Some project management software systems can handle the tracking and reporting of currency from multiple countries.

- *Payroll integration*

  Many of the project management software systems comply with the direct integration of project data with the most common payroll systems that are available.

- *Percent-to-complete tracking*

  It is extremely important for the project manager to track each task as a project is being worked on. Percent-to-complete tracking lets the user to report their progress, on a percentage basis, as a means to help keep a project within its budget.

- *Project accounting and cost control*

  The ability to track projected vs. actual expenses, labor and non-labor costs, earned value, and to forecast revenue and profitability are just a few features of project accounting software. Numerous tools exist for helping the project manager track and control costs.

- *Project cost estimating*

  As discussed in Chapters 3 and 9 of the text, it is very important for the project manager and the project team to properly estimate the costs of individual tasks and the cost of the entire project. Project management software helps to do this and also provides features for capturing and using historical data to help better estimate future projects.

- *Time and expense reporting*

  All project management software provides features for tracking time and expenses. Timesheet functions provide the ability to designate billable and non-billable time, and various work schedules and holidays. Expense reporting features help you to create customized expense reports, define expense categories, and track receipts and paid items.

2. Communications

In the past few years the communication features of project management software systems have come a long way. Most systems provide a suite of tools such as those noted below.

- *Automatic e-mail notifications*

  These features can be used to automatically inform a team member when he or she has a task that is due in a few days. They can also be used to inform a team member if he or she has a task that is past due. Due to the interdependencies of many tasks, this feature can also automatically inform others who might be affected by a task that is behind schedule.

- *Collaboration management*

  Because the project management systems are now web-based, they have the capability to provide access to project data from virtually any computer in the world that has Internet connectivity. Therefore, each project team member and the client can have their own log-in access and receive real-time information about the project.

- *Customer collaboration*

  Customer collaboration features allow for project managers to receive client's input and approval electronically. It also permits the client to view real-time progress reports on the project.

- *Discussion forums*

  In order to facilitate an open exchange of ideas, newer versions of project management software often include web-based discussion forums that allow the project team and the customer to have an open, electronic dialogue about any aspect of the project. Users can see previous comments and create a string of ideas and suggestions.

- *E-mail integration*

  The ability to send virtually all project information, from the system, directly to a team member or customer's e-mail account is a nice feature of modern software. E-mails can also be sent at predefined times and in predefined formats; for example, providing a daily morning update on the budget to the client.

- *File attachments*

  The ability to attach multiple files and multiple file formats to project information is now a common feature of project management software systems.

- *International characters*

  With the globalization of projects, many project management software systems allow the selection from multiple international character sets when planning, tracking, or communicating information about your project.

- *Message center*

  This feature allows for a virtual location to be set up for the posting of critical information about a project. For example, if a shipment of materials was delayed, a message could be posted to the message center informing all team members and the client.

- *Mobile access*

  With the convergence of the latest technologies, many of the project management software systems now allow for mobile access to project information from cell phones and PDAs, thereby allowing the users to access data virtually anytime and anywhere.

- *Multiple languages*

  In addition to working in English, many systems now allow users to work in several languages such as Chinese, French, Spanish, and many other languages.

- *Online meetings*

  Several systems provide features that support online meetings, web conferencing, webinars, screen sharing, and live collaboration tools. This can save time and reduce travel expenses for geographically dispersed users.

3. **Documentation Management**

   One of the most important features of project management software systems is the ability to document a project from beginning to end. The following is a list of some features that are available to help.

   - *Approval process and routing*

     To streamline the workflow, process documents can be routed electronically via pre-defined paths and can include sections so that approvals can be noted before items are processed.

   - *Change order management*

     This feature makes possible the tracking of billable and non-billable change orders, and to estimate and track their effect on project budgets and schedules. Change orders can often be billed and tracked via numerous methods.

   - *Contract management and automation*

     Several software systems have contract templates and allow implementation of some business rules and billing rates for specific projects. Many of the common contract provisions, such as those discussed in Chapter 3, are provided in the templates.

   - *Meeting management and action items*

     As discussed above, many of the newer project management software systems provide an environment for online meetings. However, from a documentation standpoint, the software allows the project team to track relevant discussion, decisions, and action items.

   - *Project charter information*

     The project charter feature captures critical information about a project. For example, who is the project sponsor, what is the project supposed to accomplish, why is the project being done, what are the major assumptions and/or risks.

   - *Requirements management*

     This feature supports the documentation and tracking of the major deliverables for the project.

   - *Time-off requests*

     This feature tracks personal and vacation time of project members, and automates requests for time off and the approval or rejection of that request as well. Workload reports can be automatically updated in order to properly manage the human resources.

4. **Integration and Customization**

   Most project management software systems allow for the customization of the user interface and the reports to suit the particular needs of a project. In addition, they provide linkages with many other popular software systems.

- *Customizable user interfaces*

  Users often have the ability to change the look and feel of the user interface. They can change colors, fonts, and backgrounds, as well as customize input screens and project reports.

- *Importing/exporting*

  Many project management software systems allow the user to bring in information from other applications, such as word processing, spreadsheet, and database applications. The process of bringing information into the project management software is called *importing*. Similarly, it's often possible to send information from the project management software to those applications. The process of sending out information is called *exporting*.

- *Multimedia integration*

  Many project management software systems allow for the full range of graphics, animation, voice, and video to be incorporated into the project. This can be very useful, for example, to use a video or animation to show the customer the latest design of a bridge or a building.

5. Online Tutorials

During the past few years the online help tools for project management software systems have come a long way. The systems now often include very detailed demos, online help, in-depth tutorials, and even full video presentations.

6. Project Planning

All project management software systems allow the user to define the activities and resources that are needed to perform a project. The list below provides an overview of some of the important project planning features.

- *Gantt & PERT charts*

  One of the important features of project management software is the ability to generate easily and quickly a variety of charts, including Gantt charts, PERT charts, and other network diagrams, based on current data. Once the baseline plan has been created, any modifications to the plan can easily be entered into the system, and the charts will automatically reflect those changes. Project management software lets tasks in Gantt charts to be linked together so that the precedence activities can be shown. Typically, the user can jump back and forth between Gantt chart and network diagram displays with a single command.

- *Project time estimating*

  During the planning phase, all activities can be defined along with their appropriate time estimates. Based on the interdependencies, and other factors such as vacation time and holidays, the software will calculate an overall project time estimate.

- *Scheduling*

  Project management software systems provide extensive support for scheduling. Most systems will build Gantt charts and network diagrams based on the task and resource lists and all of their associated information. Any changes to those lists will automatically be reflected in the schedules. In addition, users can schedule recurring tasks, set priorities for scheduled tasks, perform reverse scheduling (from the end date backward to the beginning), define work shifts, schedule elapsed time, schedule tasks to start as late as possible or as soon as possible, and specify a must-start-by or must-finish-by date or a no-earlier-than or no-later-than date.

- *Task management and interdependencies*

  Just as the software lets a resource list to be maintained, it also permits an activity or task list to be maintained. For each task, the user can provide a title, a start date, a finish date, comments, and estimated durations (including optimistic, most likely, and pessimistic estimates in various time scales) and can specify any precedent relationships with other tasks, as well as the person(s) responsible. Typically, project management software allows several thousand tasks to be associated with a project.

- *What-if analysis*

  One very helpful feature of project management software is the ability to perform what-if analysis. This feature lets the user explore the effects of various scenarios. At some point in a project, the user might ask the system, "What if __________ were delayed by a week?" The effects of the delay on the entire project would automatically be calculated, and the results would be presented. Almost any variable (people, pay rates, costs) in a project can be tested to see the effects of certain occurrences. This type of analysis enables the manager to better control any risks associated with the project.

- *Work breakdown structure*

  In addition to the features mentioned above, most systems allow you to create a work breakdown structure (WBS) similar to the one presented in Chapter 5. Work breakdown structures are very useful tools to aid in the planning process.

7. Project Portfolio Management

Many project managers today are running multiple projects and tracking significant issues related to those projects. The list below provides some features that can help.

- *Issue management*

  The issue management feature helps team members or the customer to electronically note any issues that they have with a project. The issues can cover a wide range of topics and can be tracked and responded to electronically.

- *Knowledge management*

  There are often certain business rules and/or historical data and/or experiences that can help provide insights and guidance into successfully completing your projects. A few of the newer project management software systems have functions that allow you to build in some of this knowledge and expertise.

- *Multiple project management*

  Experienced project managers often oversee several projects simultaneously, and team members are assigned to more than one project simultaneously, with their time divided between the projects. Most project management software systems provide support for these situations. They often can store multiple projects in separate files, with connecting links between the files, store multiple projects in the same file, handle several hundred or even several thousand projects at the same time, and create Gantt charts and network diagrams for multiple projects.

8. **Project Tracking and Control**

   Tracking progress, actual costs, and actual resource use is a fundamental component of project management. Project management software systems allow the user to define a baseline plan and compare actual progress and costs with those in the baseline plan. Most systems can track tasks in progress, completed tasks, associated costs, time expended, start and finish dates, actual dollars committed or spent, and resources used, as well as remaining durations, resources, and expenses.

   - *Critical path analysis*

     The software will calculate the critical path for the project and often display it in red. In addition, for any activities not on the critical path, the software will calculate the slack.

   - *Milestone tracking*

     Milestones should be defined for each project and the software will support tracking progress toward those milestones. Any milestone that has been successfully completed can be displayed on a variety of reports and team members can be informed electronically.

   - *Subcontractor tracking*

     This feature allows tracking subcontractors who are assigned to projects. Time on task, fee, and numerous other items can be tracked.

   - *Task priorities*

     When tracking the progress of a project, the level of priorities can often change. This feature permits setting and redefining the priority of any given task based on a particular situation. Tasks priorities are often defined as low, normal, high, or urgent but they can also be defined on a numerical scale such as 1–10.

   - *Task reminders*

     As noted above under point 2 "Communications," automatic e-mail notifications can be sent. These can take many forms. One popular form is to remind the person responsible that a task is scheduled to start, scheduled to finish, or that certain levels of progress should have been achieved.

9. **Report Generation**

   Most of today's project management software systems have extensive reporting capabilities. Among the reports they can generate are (a) reports on the project as a whole; (b) reports on the major milestones; (c) reports that provide a variety of information with respect to a date range—such as tasks that have been completed within that range, tasks that are in progress, and tasks that will start within that range; (d) financial reports that show a full range of information, including budgets for all tasks as well as the entire project, tasks and resources that are over budget, cumulative budgeted costs, actual costs, and committed costs; (e) earned value analysis and management reports; (f) resource allocation reports for each resource or group of resources involved in a project; and (g) baseline-to-actual variance reports

- *Customizable reporting*

  Almost all of the systems allow the user to customize reports, selecting the data wanted along with the report format (i.e. font, color, etc.)

- *Dashboard indicators*

  Dashboard indicators provide a visual report that the project manager can customize in order to get a quick snapshot of information that is most important to him or her. For example, their dashboard can provide a visual summary of what tasks are done, which are due, and which are overdue. Likewise, it could present a visual summary of which tasks are under- or over-budget.

- *Filtering*

  Filtering enables the user to select only certain data that meet some specified criteria. For example, if the user wants information on just the tasks that require a certain resource, a simple request tells the software to ignore tasks that don't use that resource and display only tasks that do use that resource.

- *Real-time reporting*

  All of the reports generated via project management software can provide real-time, up-to-date information, assuming the project database has been properly updated.

- *Sorting*

  Sorting lets the user view information in a desired order, such as pay rates from highest to lowest, resource names in alphabetical order, or task names in alphabetical order. Most programs allow multiple levels of sorting (for example, by last name and then by first name).

10. Resource Management

Project management software can maintain a resource list consisting of resource names, the maximum amount of time resources are available, standard and overtime rates for resources, accrual methods, and textual descriptions of the resources. Constraints can be assigned to each resource, such as the number of hours or times that it is available.

The system will highlight and help correct overallocation and perform resource leveling and resource smoothing.

- *Assignment tracking*

  Users can also assign resources to a task, a percentage of a task, set priority levels for resource assignments, assign more than one resource to the same task, and keep memos or notes on each resource.

- *Calendars*

  All resources can have their own individualized calendar, stating when they are and are not available.

- *Resource allocation and planning*

  The system will track any resource assignments that are made and make sure they are not overallocated. Many systems can also perform some version of resource leveling and/or resource smoothing as discussed in Chapter 8.

- *Resource utilization*

  Resource utilization charts can be created to provide an overview of the utilization rates for each resource. This can be very helpful as project managers try to make the best use of available resources.

- *Skills tracking*

  This feature allows the assignment of resources by skill level. Resource profiles can include skill levels, certifications, experience levels, and training and educational levels.

11. **Risk Management**

    Project risks are uncertain events or circumstances that could have an impact on a project. The degree to which project management software systems support risk management varies greatly. Several tools allow the user to define possible risks, determine the probability that they will occur, and predict the impact on the schedule and budget if they occur. These risks can be directly associated with individual tasks within a project or to the project as a whole.

12. **Sales and Business Development**

    Several of the newer project management software systems include a feature related to business development. Some of the features include:

    - *Automated lead generation*

      This feature automatically takes information directly from web-based lead forms and informs the sales team so they can follow up. Should a project be created, that information can then be imported into the project database.

    - *Client management*

      Some systems provide an integrated view of sales and client information. Project managers, with approved access, can see any relevant notes, history, contacts, and on-going communications with the client and/or potential client.

    - *Sales dashboard*

      A sales dashboard provides a visual summary of pertinent sales information. This information might include sales pipeline information, sales metrics, sales quotas and expectation, geographical territory displays, and numerous actual vs. projected reports.

13. **Security & Access Controls**

    A relatively new, but critically important, feature in project management software systems is security and access rights features. Some systems provide password access to the project management program itself, password access to individual project files, and password access to specific data within a project file (such as pay rates). Different views can be given to the project manager, team members, and the client.

CRITERIA FOR SELECTING PROJECT MANAGEMENT SOFTWARE

Following is a list of factors to consider before purchasing a project management software system. Depending on your individual needs, and the needs of your organization, certain factors may be more or less important to you than they are to other people.

1. *Capacity.* Here the main concern is whether the system can handle the number of tasks you expect to perform, the number of resources you think you will need, and the number of projects you expect to be managing simultaneously. For most organizations the software capacity is not an issue.
2. *Documentation and on-line help facilities.* The quality of documentation and on-line help facilities varies greatly among project management software systems. Consideration should be given to the readability of the online user's manual, the logical presentation of ideas in the user's manual, the level of detail of the on-line help, the number and quality of examples provided, and the level of the discussion of advanced features.
3. *Ease of use.* This is often an important factor in the selection of any type of software package. Consideration should be given to the "look" and "feel" of the system, the menu structures, available short-cut keys, color displays, the amount of information in each display, the ease with which data can be entered, the ease with which existing data can be modified, the ease with which reports can be generated, the quality of the reports that are produced, the consistency among screens, and the amount of learning required to become proficient with the system.
4. *Features available.* Here consideration must be given to whether the system provides the features that are required for your organization. For example, does the package include work breakdown structures and both Gantt charts and network diagrams? How good are the resource-leveling and smoothing algorithms? Can the system sort and filter information, monitor the budget, produce customized calendars, and help with tracking and control? Does it have the capability to check for and help resolve over allocation of resources?
5. *Installation requirements.* The considerations here are the hardware and software required to run the project management software: the memory required, the amount of hard disk space required, the processing speed and power required, the type of graphics display needed, and operating system requirements.
6. *Integration with other systems.* More and more in today's digital world there is a convergence of numerous electronic systems. If you are working in an environment where pertinent data are stored in various places, such as databases and spreadsheets, then special attention should be given to the integration capabilities of the project management software. Some systems allow very basic integration with a few popular software systems, whereas others provide sophisticated integration with distributed databases and even object-oriented databases. In addition, the ability of the project management software to export information to word processing, spreadsheets, human resources systems, and payroll systems may affect your decision.

7. *Internet features.* Although all modern project management software systems allow project information to be posted and shared directly through the Internet, there is great variance in the web-based tools they contain. For example, the online support for the communications features mentioned in the previous section should be evaluated.
8. *Reporting capabilities.* Project management systems vary in the number and types of reports they can provide. Some support just the basic planning, scheduling, and cost reports, whereas others have extensive facilities for providing reports on individual tasks, resources, actual costs, committed costs, progress, and so on.

   In addition, some systems are easier to customize than others. Reporting capabilities should be given a fairly high priority, because the ability to produce extensive and powerful reports is a feature that most users rate very highly.
9. *Security.* Some project management software systems provide greater levels of security than others. If security is important, then special attention should be given to the methods of restricting access to the project management software system itself, to each project file, and to the data within each file.
10. *Vendor support.* Special attention should be given to whether the vendor or dealer provides technical support, the price of that support, and the reputation of the vendor.

ADVANTAGES OF USING PROJECT MANAGEMENT SOFTWARE

There are numerous advantages of using project management software. Some of these are as follows:

1. *Ability to handle complexity.* It's obvious that software can handle certain aspects (especially numeric aspects) of large-scale projects more easily than a person can manually. For projects that have just a few activities and span a short period of time, a manual approach may be feasible. But for projects that involve thousands of activities and thousands of resources and span a few years' time, project management software provides indispensable assistance with the level of complexity.
2. *Accuracy.* A major benefit of using project management software is that accuracy is greatly improved. For large projects, manually drawing network diagrams, calculating start and finish times, and monitoring resource usage are very difficult. Project management software systems have accurate algorithms for calculating project information and contain numerous built-in routines that check for user errors.
3. *Affordability.* Excellent PC-based project management software can be purchased for under $200.
4. *Ease of use.* Over the past few years, project management software systems have become extremely easy to use. They can often be mastered with only a minimal amount of training.

5. *Maintainability and modifiability.* With manual systems it's often difficult to maintain and modify project information. With project management software, any change in the data will automatically be reflected in all the project documents, such as the diagrams, the cost tables, and the resource allocation charts.
6. *Record keeping.* A major benefit of project management software is its ability to keep excellent records. For instance, data can be kept on individual team members' schedules, each task, costs, and resources used. These data can be used to produce high-quality reports and can be helpful in planning future projects.
7. *Speed.* Once input data have been collected and entered, almost every imaginable calculation can be done very rapidly by the software. Manually creating or revising plans, schedules, and budgets can take hours, days, or weeks.
8. *What-if analysis.* One further feature of project management software that's a great benefit is the ability to perform what-if analysis. What-if analysis, as discussed earlier, allows the user to see the effects of various scenarios on a project. These different scenarios can be run on the software, and their effects can be evaluated. This helps the project manager to prepare and plan for certain contingencies and to assess consequences.

CONCERNS ABOUT USING PROJECT MANAGEMENT SOFTWARE

Although there are numerous benefits to using project management software, there are also a few concerns to be considered and pitfalls to be avoided, if possible.

1. *Becoming distracted by the software.* For some project managers, project management software can be distracting. A manager can spend too much time playing with, and focusing on, the software, with all of its reports and features, and forget about the most important part of a project: the people.
2. *False sense of security.* The software can sometimes lull project managers into a false sense of security. First, project managers might believe that, because they have powerful software, they can manage and accomplish more than is actually feasible. Second, managers might think that, although a project is slipping, the software will be able to figure out a way to get it back on track. Third, if the software is not used properly, it might report that the project is doing fine, when in reality it's not. Just because the software says everything is all right doesn't necessarily make it so.
3. *Information overload.* Project management software systems provide a great number of features and a huge amount of information. At times the sheer quantity can be overwhelming. Only needed features of the software should be used. Project managers have to resist the temptation to use features that produce more reports or more data without contributing to the successful completion of the project.
4. *Learning curve.* It does take a certain amount of time to become proficient in the use of project management software systems. The amount of time

required varies, depending on the individual's background. For those not currently using computers and business software, there can be a significant learning curve. However, the amount of training typically required to master the software has been decreasing over the past few years as the systems have become easier and easier to use.

5. *Overreliance on software.* Because project management software has become so easy to use and because it provides so many appealing features, project managers have started relying heavily on it. Individuals with little or no knowledge of the fundamentals of project management sometimes use the software without really understanding what they're doing. If the basic concepts of project management have not been mastered, the software won't make much of a difference. Stated simply, the software is just a tool to help you do your job more effectively and efficiently—the software itself cannot manage a project. You must manage the project, relying mainly on your skills and the skills of your team.

PROJECT MANAGEMENT SOFTWARE VENDORS

Numerous project management software systems are available that provide support for the project management process. Almost all of the vendors provide on-line demos of their products or free trial software that can be downloaded.

A simple Internet search for "project management software" or "project management software directory" will provide links for hundreds of vendors and consultants. Several of the websites provide a list of the top-selling project management software systems, as well as a review of their features. Other sites actually compare popular systems and report which features they provide and a give a summary of the strengths and weaknesses of each.

SUMMARY

This appendix discusses several features that are typically found in project management software systems. Among the most common are budgeting and cost management; communications; documentation management; integration and customization; portfolio management; online tutorials; project planning; project tracking and control; report generation; resource management; risk management; sales and business development; and security and access controls.

Criteria are given for selecting a project management software system, including capacity, documentation and on-line help facilities, ease of use, features available, integration with other systems, installation requirements, reporting capabilities, Internet features, security, and vendor support.

Finally, a list is provided of advantages of and concerns about using project management software. The benefits include accuracy, affordability, ease of use, ability to handle complexity, maintainability and modifiability, record keeping, speed, and what-if analysis. Concerns include becoming distracted by the software, a false sense of security, information overload, the learning curve, and overreliance on software.

QUESTIONS

1. Discuss at least 10 common features of project management software systems. In your opinion, which of these are the most important?
2. Discuss how the Internet can facilitate project communications.
3. Discuss the criteria that should be considered when purchasing project management software. If you had to rank these in order of importance, how would you rank them?
4. What are some of the advantages of using project management software?
5. What are some of the concerns about using project management software? Do the advantages outweigh the concerns? Explain your answer.

INTERNET EXERCISES

1. Perform a search for "project management software." Provide a summary of three different software systems.
2. Perform a search for "project management software directory." Provide a list of the top-selling project management software systems.
3. Search the Internet for a website that compares two popular project management software systems. Provide a printout of the review.
4. Download a free trial version of a project management software system. What software did you choose? What features does it contain?

Appendix B

Project Management Organizations Around the Globe

For the updated website addresses of the organizations in this appendix, go to the book's student companion website at **international.cengage.com**. Click on ***Effective Project Management, 4th edition*** and navigate to Appendix B. It is suggested that you save the book's companion website in your "Favorites" for easy access in the future.

Agile Project Leadership Network
American Society for the Advancement of Project Management
Asociacion Espanola de Direccion Integrada de Proyecto (Spain)
Asociacion Espanola de Ingenieria de Proyectos (Spain)
Asociacion Espanola de Project Management
Associacao Portuguesa de Gestao de Projectos (Portugal)
Association for Project Management
Association for Project Management Hong Kong
Association Francophone de Management de Projet (France)
Association of Danish Project Management
Associazione Nazionale di Impiantistica Industriale (Italy)
Australian Institute of Project Management
Azerbaijan Project Management Association
Brazilian Association for Project Management
Bulgarian Project Management Association
Croatian Association for Project Management
Deutsche Gesellschaft fur Projektmanagement e. V. (Germany)
Emirates Project Management Association
Institute of Project Management of Ireland
International Association for Project and Program Management
International Construction Project Management Association
International Project Management Association
Iran Project Management Association
Kazakhstan Project Management Association
Kenya Institute of Project Management
Latvian National Project Management Association

Major Projects Association (United Kingdom)
Network of Project Managers in Greece
NewGrange Center for Project Management
Norwegian Association of Project Management
PMFORUM
Project Management Associates (India)
Project Management Association Czech Republic
Project Management Association Finland
Project Management Association for Professionals, Pakistan
Project Management Association of Canada
Project Management Association of Hungary
Project Management Association of Iceland
Project Management Association of Japan
Project Management Association of Poland (Stowarzyszenie Project Management Polska)
Project Management Association of Slovakia
Project Management Association Turkey
Projekt Management Austria
Project Management Benchmarking Network
Project Management Institute
Project Management Instituut Nederland
Project Management Research Committee, China
Project Management Romania
Project Management South Africa
Project Manager Union (China)
Russian Project Management Association
Slovenian Project Management Association
Societe de Management de Projet (France)
Swedish Project Management Association
Swiss Project Management Association
Taiwan Project Management Association
Ukrainian Project Management Association

Appendix C

Project Management Websites

For the updated website addresses of the organizations in this appendix, go to the book's student companion website at **international.cengage.com**. Click on ***Effective Project Management, 4th edition*** and navigate to Appendix C. It is suggested that you save the book's companion website in your "Favorites" for easy access in the future.

Department of Defense (DOD) Software Program Managers Network

International Project Management Association (IPMA)

MIT Information Systems Project Management Resources and Exploration

New Grange Center for Project Management

One Hundred Rules for NASA Project Managers

Project Management Boulevard

Project Management Center

Project Management Forum

Project Management Insight

Project Management Institute

Project Management Knowledge Base

Project Management Website

Project Manager

Project Manager's Home Page

Project Net

Project Smart

Research on Temporary Organizations and Project Management

Internet Guide to Project Management Research Sites

Appendix D

Abbreviations

AF	Actual finish time
AIB	Activity in the box
ALAP	As late as possible
AOA	Activity on the arrow
ASAP	As soon as possible
CAC	Cumulative actual cost
CBC	Cumulative budgeted cost
CEV	Cumulative earned value
CPI	Cost performance index
CPM	Critical path method
CV	Cost variance
EF	Earliest finish time
ES	Earliest start time
EV	Earned value
FCAC	Forecasted cost at completion
FS	Free slack
LF	Latest finish time
LS	Latest start time
MIS	Management information system
PERT	Program evaluation and review technique
RFP	Request for proposal
SDLC	Systems development life cycle
SOW	Statement of work
TBC	Total budgeted cost
TS	Total slack
WBS	Work breakdown structure

References

Chapter One

Andersen, E.S., Birchall, D., Jessen, S.A., & Money, A.H. (2006). Exploring project success. *Baltic Journal of Management*, 1(2), 127.

Baker, B. (2006). Project management in a flat world. *Contract Management*, 46(10), 66–68.

Besner, C. & Hobbs, B. (2006). The perceived value and potential contribution of project management practices to project success. *Project Management Journal*, 37(3), 37–49.

Cicmil, S. (2006). Understanding project management practice through interpretative and critical research perspectives. *Project Management Journal*, 37(2), 27–38.

Crawford, L. (2006). Developing organizational project management capability; Theory and practice. *Project Management Journal*, 37(3), 74–87.

Crawford, L. & Pollack, J. (2007). How generic are project management knowledge and practice. *Project Management Journal*, 38(1), 87–97.

Hegazy, T. (2006). Simplified project management for construction practitioners. *Cost Engineering*, 48(11), 20–29.

Holmes, A. Maine's medical mistake. *CIO Magazine*, April 15, 2006.

Hyväri, I. (2006). Success of projects in different organizational conditions. *Project Management Journal*, 37(4), 31–42.

Milosevic, D.Z. & Srivannaboon, S. (2006). A theoretical framework for aligning project management with business strategy. *Project Management Journal*, 37(3), 98–111.

Reich, B.H. (2007). Managing knowledge and learning in IT projects: A conceptual framework and guidelines for practice. *Project Management Journal*, 38(2), 5–18.

Shenhar, A.J. & Dvir, D. (2007). Project Management Research- the challenge and opportunity. *Project Management Journal*, 38(2), 93–100.

Songini, M. Irish agency halts work on two SAP application projects. *Computerworld*, October 17, 2005.

Sutterfield, J.S., Friday-Stroud, S.S., & Shivers-Blackwell, S.L. (2006). A case study of project and stakeholder management failures: Lessons learned. *Project Management Journal*, 37(5), 26–36.

Chapter Two

Anonymous. (2007). Managing the innovation portfolio: Doing the right projects. *Strategic Direction*, 23(3), 35–37.

Boivie, C. Red light, green light. *CIO Magazine*, June 15, 2006.

Buchanan, J. (2007). Ranking projects for an electricity utility using ELECTRE III. *International Transactions in Operational Research*, 14(4), 309–323.

Cadenillas, A., Cvitanic, J., & Zapatero, F. (2007). Optimal risk-sharing with effort and project choice. *Journal of Economic Theory*, 133(1), 403–440.

De Paola, M. & Calabria, U. (2006). Organizational design, project selection and incentives. *Journal of Institutional and Theoretical Economics*, 162(3), 424–449.

Kendrick, J.D. & Saaty, D. (2007). Use analytic hierarchy process for project selection. *ASQ Six Sigma Forum Magazine*, 6(4), 22–31.

Magni, C.A. (2007). Project selection and equivalent CAPM-based intervention criteria. *Applied Financial Economics Letters*, 3(1/3), 165–168.

Mavrotas, G., Diakoulaki, D., & Kourentzis, A. (2008). Selection among ranked projects under segmentation, policy and logical constraints. *European Journal of Operational Research*, 187(1), 177–192.

Omitaomu, O.A. (2007). Fuzzy present value analysis model for evaluating information system projects. *Engineering Economist*, 52(2), 157–178.

Soutar, S. (2005). Get better ROI from your RFP. *Association Management*, 13(3).

Sun Microsystems. Sun helps polish telecom maintain market leadership with messaging migration solution, www.sun.com/software/customers, July 23, 2007.

Tripathy, B.B. & Biswal, M.P. (2007). A zero-one goal programming approach for project selection. *Journal of Information & Optimization Sciences*, 28(4), 619.

Viaene, S., Fagan, S., & Almeida, S. (2005). Belgacome: IT project selection 2005. *Communications of the Association for Information Systems*, 19, 11.

Wei, C., Liang, G.-S., & Wang, M.-J.J. (2007). A comprehensive supply chain management project selection framework under fuzzy environment. *International Journal of Project Management*, 25(6), 627–636.

Chapter Three

Boon, T. (2007). Preparing cost-effective contracts by meeting fringe benefit responsibilities. *Contract Management*, 47(7), 58–61.

Burleson, R.C. & Wilson, L. (2007). Incentive contracts. *Contract Management*, 47(9), 18–23.

Cogan, J.P. (2005). Contracting practices evolve for new global LNG trade. *Oil & Gas Journal*, 14–18.

DuPont, M.J. & Hennessey, W.M. (2002). Contract formation and the impact of contingent payment provisions. *Business Credit*, 104(3), 65–68.

Frey, R.S. (2001). Knowledge management, proposal development and small business. *The Journal of Management Development*, 20(1), 38.

Garrett, G.A. (2007). Bid/no bid decision-making: Tools + techniques. *Contract Management*, 47(4), 20–27.

Keating, M. (2006). To boost bid response rates, purchasing pros get the word out. *Government Procurement*, 14(4), 12–16.

Kiehl, S. New ballgame: The BDC entertains ideas for a sports and concert facility to replace 1st Mariner Arena. *Sun Paper*, November 14, 2007.

Kiehl, S. Group wants Arena site near M&T. *Sun Paper*, November 18, 2007.

Larkin, H. (2007). How to do an RFP for an EHR. *Medical Economics*, 84(2), 45–49.

Lieberman, R.D. (2007). 10 Big mistakes in government contract bidding. *Contract Management*, 47(1), 30–39.

Lin, C.T. & Chen, Y.T. (2004). Bid/no bid decisions-making- a fuzzy linguistic approach. *International Journal of Project Management*, 22(7), 585.

Marshall, R.A. (2005). The case for earned value management with fixed-price contracts. *Contract Management*, 45(10), 30–34.

Overby, S. Enterprise application suites fading out. *CIO Magazine*, February 15, 2003.

Rendon, P.-M. (2007). RFP Madness!. *Marketing*, 112(2), 16–18.

Chapter Four

Day, G.S. (2007). Is it real? Can we win? Is it worth doing?: Managing risk and reward in an innovation portfolio. *Harvard Business Review*, 85(12), 110.

Flyvbjerg, B. (2006). From Nobel prize to project management: Getting risks right. *Project Management Journal*, 37(3), 5–16.

Gwynne, P. (2007). Predicting project performance. *Research Technology Management*, 50 (4), 5–8.

Hines, M. IBM pitches risk management strategy. *InfoWorld*, May 15, 2007.

Kaliprasad, M. (2006). Proactive risk management. *Cost Engineering*, 48(12), 26–37.

Kayis, B., Zhou, M., Savci, S., & Khoo, Y.B. (2007). IRMAS- development of a risk management tool for collaborative multi-site, multi-partner new product development projects. *Journal of Manufacturing Technology Management*, 18(4), 387.

Lehman, B. (2007). Project risk management. *Mortgage Banking*, 67(5), 99–101.

Palomo, J., Insua, D.R., & Ruggeri, F. (2007). Modeling external risks in project management. *Risk Analysis*, 27(4), 961.

Patterson, D. (2006). Managing project cost risk. *AACE International Transactions*, IT51–IT58.

Regev, S., Shtub, A., & Ben-Haim, Y. (2006). Managing project risks as knowledge gaps. *Project Management Journal*, 37(5), 17–26.

Strischek, D. (2006). Putting a name to construction risk: Where and what. *The RMA Journal*, 89(3), 54–57.

Tesch, D., Kloppenborg, T.J., & Frolick, M.N. (2007). IT project risk factors: The project management professionals perspective. *The Journal of Computer Information Systems*, 47(4), 61–70.

Waggener, S. UC Berkeley's data center success story. *IST Publication UC Berkeley*, http://istpub.berkeley.edu. October 1, 2004.

Zwikael, O. & Sadeh, A. (2007). Planning effort as an effective risk management tool. *Journal of Operations Management*, 25(4), 755.

Chapter Five

Charmicheal, D.G. (2006). Project planning and control. *Net Library*, xi, 328.

Cotton, G. (2007). Planning a contract and setting parameters. *Occupational Health*, 59(10), 24–26.

Donaldson, S.E. & Siegel, S.G. (2007). Enriching you project planning: Tying risk assessment to resource estimation. *IT Professional Magazine*, 9(5), 20.

Dvir, D., Ben-Gurion, U., & Lechler, T. (2004). Plans are nothing, changing plans is everything: The impact of changes on project success. *Research Policy*, 33(1), 1–15.

Hans, E.W., Herroelen, W., & Wullink, G. (2007). A hierarchical approach to multi-project planning under uncertainty. *Omega*, 35(5), 563–577.

Hormozi, A.M. & Dube, L.F. (1999). Establishing project control: Scheduling, cost, and quality. *S.A.M. Advanced Management Journal*, 64(4), 32–39.

Kerzner, H. (2001). Strategic planning for project management using a project management maturity model. *Net Library*, xiv, 255.

Kohlin, G. & Goteborg, U. (2001). Contingent valuation in project planning and evaluation: The case of social forestry in Orissa, India. *Environment and Development Economics*, 6(2), 237–258.

Mentrup, L. Broad appeal. *PM Network*, December 2006.

Mitchell, V.L. & Nault, B.R. (2007). Cooperative planning, uncertainty, and managerial control in concurrent design. *Management Science*, 53(3), 375–400.

Schultz, S. Hopkins project delayed, over budget. *Baltimore Business Journal*, December 24, 2007.

Westland, J. (2006). The project management life cycle: A complete step-by-step methodology for initiating, planning, executing and closing a project successfully. *Net Library*, xviii, 237.

Winn, M.T. (2007). The benefits of work breakdown structures. *Contract Management*, 47(5), 16–22.

Zwikael, O. & Globerson, S. (2006). Benchmarking of project planning and success in selected industries. *Benchmarking*, 13(6), 688.

Chapter Six

Dodin, B. & Elimam, A.A. (2008). Integration of equipment planning and project scheduling. *European Journal of Operational Research*, 184(3), 962.

Herroelen, W. & Leus, R. (2005). Project scheduling under uncertainty: Survey and research potentials. *European Journal of Operational Research*, 165(2/1), 289–306.

Kent, S. Game plan. *PM Network*, August 2007.

Khodakarami, V., Fenton, N., & Neil, N. (2007). Project scheduling: Improved approach to incorporate uncertainty using Bayesain networks. *Project Management Journal*, 38(2), 39–50.

Liess, O. & Michelon, P. (2008). A constraint programming approach for the resource-constrained project scheduling problem. *Annals of Operations Research*, 157(1), 25–37.

Ruwanpura, J.Y., Ahmed, T.N., Kaba, K., & Mulvany, G.P. (2006). Project planning and scheduling and its impact to project outcome: A study of EPC projects in Canada. *AACE International Transactions*, 201–210.

Sappe, R. (2007). A schedule success: Hartsfield-Jackson Atlanta airport's runway delivered 11 days early and $102 million under budget. *Cost Engineering*, 49(4), 21–24.

U.S. Department of Transportation. Federal Highway Administration, Highways for Life, Success Stories, www.fhwa.dot.gov/hfl. March 29, 2007.

Van de Vonder, S., Demeulemeester, E., & Herroelen, W. (2007). A classification of predictive-reactive project scheduling procedures. *Journal of Scheduling*, 10(3), 195–208.

Van de Vonder, S., Ballestín, F., Demeulemeester, E., & Herroelen, W. (2007). Heuristic procedures for reactive project scheduling. *Computers & Industrial Engineering*, 52(1), 11.

Yamashita, D.S., Armentano, V.A., Laguna, M. (2007). Robust optimization models for project scheduling with resource availability cost. *Journal of Scheduling*, 10(1), 67–77.

Yang, J.-B. (2007). How the critical chain scheduling method is working for construction. *Cost Engineering*, 49(4), 25–33.

Zack, J.G. (2007). The roles and value of schedulers. *Cost Engineering*, 49(4), 3–6.

Zbigniew, A. & Zaremba, B.B. (2006). Project-driven planning and scheduling support for virtual manufacturing. *Journal of Intelligent Manufacturing*, 17(6), 641.

Chapter Seven

Al-Fawzan, M.A. & Haouari, M. (2005). A bi-objective model for robust resource-constrained project scheduling. *International Journal of Production Economics*, 96(2), 175–187.

Charoenngam, C. & Kazi, A.S. (1997). Cost/schedule information system: A human-centered approach. *Cost Engineering*, 39(9), 29–36.

Cummings, J.N. & Kiesler, S. (2007). Coordination costs and project outcomes in multi-university collaborations. *Research Policy*, 36(10), 1620–1634.

Davey, K. R. (2004). Cost and schedule control for engineering contracts. *Cost Engineering*, 46(9), 16–23.

Farris, J.S. & Wilkerson, R. (2001). Cost/schedule control on disaster recovery projects. *Cost Engineering*, 43(1), 24–29.

Henry, R.M., McCray, G.E., Purvis, R.L., & Roberts, T.L. (2007). Exploiting organizational knowledge in developing IS project cost and schedule estimates: An empirical study. *Information & Management*, 44(6), 598–612.

Hildebrand, C. A fish tale. *PM Network*, February 2007.

Knoke, J.R. & de la Garza, J. (2003). Practical cost/schedule modeling for CIP management. *AACE International Transactions*, PM61.

Kratzer, D. Key construction had to race the clock to finish the Eaton hotel project on time. *Wichita Business Journal*, December 11, 2000.

Longworth, S.R. (2002). Evolving project control practices. *AACA International Transactions*, 04.1.

Mika, M., Waligora, G., & Weglarz, J. (2008). Tabu search for multi-mode resource-constrained project scheduling with schedule-dependent setup times. *European Journal of Operational Research*, 187(3), 1238–1250.

Ranjbar, M., De Reyck, B., & Kianfar, F. (2007). A hybrid scatter search for the discrete time/resource trade-off problem in project scheduling. *European Journal of Operational Research*, In press, Available online November 5, 2007.

Ranjbar, M. (2007). Solving the resource-constrained project scheduling problem using filter-and-fan approach. *Applied Mathematics and Computation*, In press, Available December 2007.

Youngsoo, J. (2004). Flexible work breakdown structure for integrated cost and schedule control. *Journal of Construction, Engineering & Management*, 130(5), 616–625.

Chapter Eight

Al-jibouri, S. (2002). Effects of resource management regimes on project schedule. *International Journal of Project Management*, 20(4), 271–277.

Engwall, M. & Jerbrant, A. (2003). The resource allocation syndrome: The prime challenge of multi-project management? *International Journal of Project Management*, 21(6), 403–409.

Laslo, Z. & Goldberg, A. (2007). Resource allocation under uncertainty in a multi-project matrix environment: Is organizational conflict inevitable? *International Journal of Project Management*, In Press, Available online November 26, 2007.

Li, H., Chen, Z., Wong, C.T.C., & Love, P.E.D. (2002). A quantitative approach to construction pollution control based on resource leveling. *Construction Innovation*, 2(2), 71.

Lova, A., Maroto, C., & Tormos, P. (2000). A multicriteria heuristic method to improve resource allocation in multiproject scheduling. *European Journal of Operational Research*, 127(2), 408.

Neumann, K. & Zimmermann, J. (1999). Resource leveling for projects with schedule-dependent time windows. *European Journal of Operational Research*, 117(3), 591–596.

Neumann, K. & Zimmermann, J. (2000). Procedures for resource leveling and net present value problems in project scheduling with general temporal and resource constraints. *European Journal of Operational Research*, 127(2), 425.

Nosbisch, M.R. & Winter, R.M. (2006). Managing resource leveling. *Cost Engineering*, 48(7), 24–35.

Nyonator, F., Awoonor-Williams, J., Phillips, J., Jones, T., & Miller, R. (2003). The Ghana Community-based Health Planning and Services Initiative: Fostering Evidence-based Organizational Change and Development in a Resource-Constrained Setting. Population Council, Policy Research Division, No. 180.

Stevens, P. & Dietschw, E. (2008). Resource curse: An analysis of causes, experiences and possible ways forward. *Energy Policy*, 36(1), 56.

Vandersluis, C. (1995). Making sense of resource management. *Computing Canada*, 21(24), 28.

Vanhoucke, M. & Debels, D. (2008). The impact of various activity assumptions on the lead time and resource utilization of resource-constrained projects. *Computers & Industrial Engineering*, 54(1), 140.

"West Virginia University Sees Improved IT Governance with Resource Planning and Cost Accounting," http://www-360.ibm.com/software/success. February 14, 2007.

Younis, M.A. & Saad, B. (1996). Optimal resource leveling of multi-resource projects. *Computers & Industrial Engineering*, 31(1,2), 1–5.

Chapter Nine

Al-Jibouri, S.H. (2003). Monitoring systems and their effectiveness for project cost control in construction. *International Journal of Project Management*, 21(2), 145.

Bent, J.A. (2006). Are today's project cost professionals a bunch of bean counters? *Cost Engineering*, 48(10), 23–28.

Berends, T. C. & Dhillon, J. S. (2004). An analysis of contract cost phasing on engineering and construction projects. *The Engineering Economist*, 49(4), 327–338.

Bowman, B. & Brown, K. Feds ignored Ft. Monmouth warnings on data: Memo advised cost estimates were wrong. *Ocean County Observer*, July 15, 2007.

Bredehoeft, P.R. (2005). Controlling non-construction costs. *AACE International Transactions*, ES81–ES88.

Cullen, S. (2004). Essentials of cost management. *AACE International Transactions*, CS11–CS18.

Fleming, Q. & Koppelman, J. (2003). What's your project's real price tag?, *Harvard Business Review*, 81(9), 20.

Hamilton, A.C. (2004). Cost management. *AACE International Transactions*, CS121-133.

Henry, B. City to spend $4 million on landslide project. *North County Times*, August 30, 2007.

Kohl, B. & Wulke, R.J. (2004). Supplementing accounting systems for project costs management. *AACE International Transactions*, IT31-37.

Moon, S.W., Kim, J.S., & Kwon, K.N. (2007). Effectiveness of OLAP-based cost data management in construction cost estimate. *Automation in Construction*, 16(3), 336–344.

Stukel, J. (2003). Cost-conscious construction. *Commercial Investment Real Estate*, 22(5), 36.

Tichacek, R.L. (2005). Effective cost management-back to basics. *AACE International Transactions*, CS111– 118.

Verzuh, E. (2004). Project status reporting using earned value analysis. *CHIPS*, 22(2), 31.

Chapter Ten

Baca, C.M. (2007). Project manager! Who? Me?. *Machine Design*, 79(20), 64–68.

Barber, E. & Warn, J. (2005). Leadership in project management: From firefighter to firelighter. *Management Decision*, 43(7/8), 1032–1040.

Blomquist, T. & Müller, R. (2006). Practices, roles, and responsibilities of middle managers in program and portfolio management. *Project Management Journal*, 37(1), 52–67.

Dvir, D., Sadeh, A., & Malach-Pines, A. (2006). Projects and project managers: The relationship between project manager's personality, project types, and project success. *Project Management Journal*, 37(5), 36–49.

Eskerod, P. & Skriver, H.J. (2007). Organizational culture restraining in-house knowledge transfer between project managers- a case study. *Project Management Journal*, 38(1), 110–123.

Gehring, D.R. (2007). Applying traits theory of leadership to project management. *Project Management Journal*, 38(1), 44–55.

Grosse, D. (2007). Leadership in R&D projects. *Creativity and Innovation Management*, 16(4), 447.

Hildebrand, C. The clean up act. *PM Network*, January 2008.

Krishna, R.V. (2006). Project management goal setting: Questions to consider. *Contract Management*, 46(8), 60–62.

Neuhauser, C. (2007). Project manager leadership behavior and frequency of use by female project managers. *Project Management Journal*, 38(1), 21–32.

Peterson, J. (2007). Winning contract managers borrow plays from project management playbook. *Contract Management*, 47(4), 50–56.

Richmond, A. & Skitmore, M. (2006). Stress and coping: A study of project managers in a large ICT organization. *Project Management Journal*, 37(5), 5–17.

Van Ingen, S. (2007). Leadership of project teams. *Chemical Engineering*, 114(1), 55–59.

Wheatley, M. (2008). Globalization: The borderless leader. *PMI Leadership in Project Management*, 4, 8–15.

Chapter Eleven

Akgun, A.E., Byrne, J.C., Lynn, G.S., & Keskin, H. (2007). Team stressors, management support, and project and process outcomes in new product development projects. *Technovation*, 27(10), 628.

Blake, R.R. & Mouton, J.S. *The Managerial Grid*, Gulf, 1964.

Bourgeon, L. (2007). Staffing approach and conditions for collective learning in project teams: The case of new product development projects. *International Journal of Project Management*, 25(4), 413.

Brenner, D.A. (2007). Achieving a successful project by motivating the project team. *Cost Engineering*, 49(5), 16–21.

Chiocchio, F. (2007). Project team performance: A study of electronic task and coordination communication. *Project Management Journal*, 38(1), 97–110.

Fitzpatrick, J. Miracle on ice: American hockey's defining moment, http://proicehockey.about.com, copyright 2007 About.com, Inc., a part of The New York Times Company.

Fox, R. (2007). Honesty in project management. *ISSIG Review*, XI(2).

Gardenswartz, L. & Rowe, A. (1994). *Diverse Teams at Work: Capitalizing on the Power of Diversity*. Irwin Publishing.

Garris, L.B. (2007). Building the perfect project team. *Buildings*, 101(4), 34–39.

Sackmann, S. A. & Friesl, M. (2007). Exploring cultural impacts on knowledge sharing behavior in project teams—results from a simulation study. *Journal of Knowledge Management*, 11(6), 142.

Thomas, K. & Kilmann, R. (1974). *Thomas-Kilmann Conflict Mode*. Xicom.

Tuckman, B. W. (1965). Developmental sequence in small groups. *Psychological Bulletin*,63, 384–399.

Uday-Riley, M. (2006). Eight critical steps to improve workplace performance with cross-cultural teams. *Performance Improvement*, 45(6), 28–34.

Van Ingen, S. (2007). Leadership of project teams. *Chemical Engineering*, 114(1), 55–59.

Chapter Twelve

Anonymous. (2004). Listening may not be as easy as you think. *Dispute Resolution Journal*, 59(2), 88.

Delisle, C.L. & Olson, D. (2004). Would the real project management language please stand up? *International Journal of Project Management*, 22(4), 327–337.

Dyer, S. (2006). The root causes of poor communication. *Agency Sales*, 36(12), 52–55.

Gillard, S. & Johansen, J. (2004). Project management communication: A systems approach. *Journal of Information Science*, 30(1), 23.

Gillard, S. (2005). Managing IT projects: Communication pitfalls and bridges. *Journal of Information Science*, 31(1), 37

Koskinen, K.U. (2004). Knowledge management to improve project communication and implementation. *Project Management Journal*, 35(2), 13–20.

Kraus, W.E. (2006). The "cool hand Luke" theory of project communication. *International Transactions*, PM91–PM95.

Kroll, K. What did you say? *PM Network*, November, 2006.

LaBrosse, M. (2005). 5 ways to improve engineering communications. *Control Engineering*, 52(9), 81.

Müller, R. (2003). Determinants for external communications of IT project managers. *International Journal of Project Management*, 21(5), 345–354.

Müller, R. & Turner, J.R. (2005). The impact of principal–agent relationship and contract type on communication between project owner and manager. *International Journal of Project Management*, 23(5), 398–403.

Reed, B. (2002). Actually making things happen. *Information Executive*, 6(2), 10.

Scott, R. For IT projects, silence can be deadly. *Computerworld*, February 5, 2007.

Tucker, J. (2007). Communicating change. *Mortgage Banking*, 67(8), 1115–116.

Chapter Thirteen

Aubry, M., Hobbs, B., & Thuillier, D. (2008). Organizational project management: An historical approach to the study of PMOs. *International Journal of Project Management*, 26(1), 38–43.

Hobday, M. (2000). The project-based organisation: An ideal form for managing complex products and systems? *Research Policy*, 29(7/8), 871–893.

Jedd, M. The customer is always right. *PM Network*, December, 2006.

Johansson, S. (2007). Separation of integration? A dilemma when organizing development projects. *International Journal of Project Management*, 25(5), 457–464.

Kaleba, R. (2006). Strategic planning getting from here to there. *Healthcare Financial Management*, 60(11), 74–78.

Kathuria, R., Joshi, M.P., & Porth, S.J. (2007). Organizational alignment and performance: Past present and future. *Management Decision*, 45(3), 503.

Lester, A. (2007). Organization structures. *Project Management Planning and Control*, 5, 32–34.

Lindkvist, L. (2008). Project organization: Exploring its adaptation properties. *International Journal of Project Management*, 26(1), 13–20.

Manning, S. (2008). Embedding projects in multiple contexts—a structuration perspective. *International Journal of Project Management*, 26(1), 30–37.

Reingold, J. & Yang, J. What's your OQ? *Fortune*, July 23, 2007.

Turner, J.R. & Simister, S.J. (2001). Project contract management and a theory of organization. *International Journal of Project Management*, 19(8), 457–464.

Turner, J.R. & Müller, R. (2003). On the nature of the project as a temporary organization. *International Journal of Project Management*, 21(1), 1–8.

van Donk, D.P. & Molloy, E. (2007). From organizing as projects to projects as organizations. *International Journal of Project Management*, In Press, Corrected Proof, Available online June 27, 2007.

von Bernuth C. & Bathelt, H. (2007). The organizational paradox in advertising and the reconfiguration of project cooperation. *Geoforum*, 38(3), 545–557.

Appendix A

Anonymous. (2007). Focus on software. *EC&M Electrical Construction & Maintenance*, 106(3), 57.

Anonymous. (2007). Project management software. *Stores Magazine*, 89, 134.

Bednarz, A. & Dubie, D. (2006). Project mgmt. software can limit IT woes. *Network World*, 23(45), 1–31.

Feldman, W. (2007). Software selection considerations. *Landscape Management*, 46(10), 56–60.

Fischbach, A.F. (2003). Effectively Managing Projects Remotely. *EC&M Electrical Construction & Maintenance*, 102(11), C4–C11.

Jepson, K. (2005). How 1 CU is using a project management solution. *Credit Union Journal*, 9(28), 11.

King, N. (2002). Handle projects with the web's help. *PC Magazine*, 21(18), 28–32.

Liberatore, M. & Pollack-Johnson, B. (2003). Factors influencing the usage and selection of project management software. *IEEE Transactions on Engineering Management*, 50(2), 164–175.

McMorrow, E. (2004). Project management software-deployed for the basics. *Architecture*, 93(8), 69–70.

Mohamed, A. (2006). On time, on budget. Police get it cracked. *Computer Weekly*, 1.

Setzer, S. & Bonafair, M. (2004). Project management software comes of age. *EC&M Electrical Construction & Maintenance*, 103(4), C16–C22.

Smith, J. (2002). Is project management software right for you? *Plant Engineering*, 56(6), 36–39.

Reinforce Your Learning Answers

Chapter One

1. What are some attributes of a project?
   - A well-defined objective
   - Interdependent tasks
   - Use of various resources
   - A specific time frame
   - A unique or one-time endeavor
   - A customer
   - Degree of uncertainty
2. Identify five projects in which you have been involved during your lifetime.

   Answers will vary.
3. What are four factors that constrain the achievement of a project objective?
   - Scope
   - Cost
   - Schedule
   - Customer satisfaction
4. Match the phases of the project life cycle, in the column on the left, with the descriptions, in the column on the right:

C	First phase	A. Developing the proposed solution
A	Second phase	B. Implementing the proposed
B	Third phase	C. Identifying the need or problem
D	Fourth phase	D. Terminating the project

5. The project *objective* must be agreed upon by the *customer* and the individual or organization who will *perform* the project.
6. The front-end effort of managing a project involves establishing a *baseline plan*.
7. Implementing the baseline plan for a project involves *performing* the work according to the plan and *controlling* the work so that the project scope is achieved within the *budget* and *schedule* to the customer's *satisfaction*.
8. *Cultural awareness* and sensitivity are not only important, but *imperative* for successful *global* project management.

Chapter Two

1. The initial phase of the project life cycle is *needs identification*. It starts with the recognition of a need or opportunity and ends with the issuance of a *request for proposal*.

2. Project selection involves *evaluating* various needs or opportunities, and then *deciding* which of these should move forward as a *project*.
3. Benefits and consequences can be both *quantitative* and tangible or qualitative and *intangible*.
4. What are the four steps in the project selection process?
   - Develop a set of evaluation criteria.
   - List assumptions for each opportunity.
   - Gather data and information for each opportunity.
   - Evaluate each opportunity against the criteria.
5. What is the purpose of a request for proposal?

   An RFP states, comprehensively and in detail, what is required, from the customer's point of view, to address the identified need.
6. What are some elements that may be included in a request for proposal?
   - Statement of work
   - Customer requirements
   - Deliverables
   - Customer-supplied items
   - Approvals required
   - Type of contract
   - Payment terms
   - Required schedule
   - Instructions for the format and content of contractor proposals
   - Due date
   - Proposal evaluation criteria
   - Funds available
7. Care should be taken not to provide *information* to only some of the *contractors* that is not provided to all interested contractors because it would give some of them an *unfair competitive advantage*.

Chapter Three

1. *Relationships* establish the foundation for successful funding and contract *opportunities*.
2. Relationship building requires being *proactive* and *engaged*.
3. Establishing and building *trust* is key to developing *effective* and successful *relationships*.
4. Building effective and successful relationships takes *time* and *work*.
5. Contractors need to *develop relationships* with potential customers *before* customers prepare an RFP.
6. What is the outcome of a successful pre-RFP/proposal marketing effort?

   The outcome is eventually winning a contract from the customer to perform the project.

7. What are some factors that a contractor should consider when deciding whether to respond to an RFP?
   - Competition
   - Risk
   - Consistency with business mission
   - Opportunity to extend and enhance capabilities
   - Reputation with the customer
   - Availability of customer funds
   - Availability of resources to prepare a quality proposal
   - Availability of resources to perform the project
8. Contractors need to be *realistic* about their ability to prepare proposals and about the *probability* of winning the contract.
9. The proposal process is a *competitive* process. A proposal is a *selling* document.
10. In a proposal, the contractor must highlight the *unique* factors that *differentiate* it from *competitors'* proposals.
11. A proposal should address three topics or contain three sections. What are they?
    - Technical section
    - Management section
    - Cost section
12. What is the objective of the technical section of a proposal? The objective is to convince the customer that the contractor understands the need or problem and can provide the least risky and most beneficial solution.
13. What is the objective of the management section of a proposal? The objective is to convince the customer that the contractor can do the proposed work and achieve the intended results.
14. What is the objective of the cost section of a proposal? The objective is to convince the customer that the contractor's price for the proposed project is realistic and reasonable.
15. What elements might each of the three sections of a proposal contain?

    Technical section
    - Understanding of the problem
    - Proposed approach or solution
    - Benefits to the customer

    Management section
    - Description of work tasks
    - Deliverables
    - Project schedule
    - Project organization
    - Related experience
    - Equipment and facilities

Cost section

- Labor
- Materials
- Subcontractors and consultants
- Equipment and facilities rental
- Travel
- Documentation
- Overhead or indirect costs
- Escalation
- Contingency or management reserve
- Fee or profit

16. What are some items a contractor needs to consider when determining a price for a proposed project?
    - Reliability of the cost estimates
    - Risk
    - Value of the project to the contractor
    - Customer's budget
    - Competition
17. Contractors must continue to be *proactive* even after the proposal is submitted.
18. A contractor bidding on a fixed-price contract must develop *accurate* and *complete* cost estimates and include sufficient *contingency* costs.
19. Write the word *low* or *high* in each box, depending on the degree of risk for the customer and contractor associated with each type of contract.

	Customer	Contractor
Fixed price	Low	High
Cost reimbursement	High	Low

20. A measure used to determine the success of proposal efforts is known as the *win ratio*.

Chapter Four

1. What are the two parts of the project phase of the life cycle? The two parts are planning and then implementing the plan to accomplish the project objective.
2. The first part of the project phase of the life cycle involves establishing a *baseline plan*.
3. Planning determines: *what* needs to be done; *who* will do it; how *long* it will take; and how much it will *cost*.
4. Risk management involves *identifying, assessing* and *responding* to project risks to minimize the *likelihood* and *impact* of the *consequences* of adverse events on the achievement of the project *objective*.

5. Risk response planning involves developing an *action plan* to reduce the impact or likelihood of each risk, establishing a *trigger point* for when to implement the actions, and assigning *responsibility* to individuals for implementing each response plan.
6. A *contingency plan* is a pre-defined set of actions that would be implemented if the risk event occurs.
7. What are the two kinds of data or information that need to be collected during each reporting period?
   - Data on actual performance
   - Information on any changes to the project scope, schedule, or budget
8. In addition to establishing a baseline plan, it is also necessary to *control* the project proactively to ensure that the project *objective* is achieved and the customer is *satisfied.*
9. What is the purpose of properly terminating a project?

   The purpose is to learn from the experience in order to improve performance on future projects.
10. What are the two types of internal post-project evaluation meetings the project manager should have?
    - An individual meeting with each team member
    - A group meeting with the entire project team
11. List three reasons for having a post-project evaluation meeting with the customer.
    - To determine whether the project provided the customer with the anticipated benefits
    - To assess the level of customer satisfaction
    - To obtain feedback
12. For a contractor, what are two potential consequences of having a project terminated early by a dissatisfied customer?
    - The contractor may suffer a financial loss.
    - The contractor's reputation will be tarnished.

Chapter Five

1. For a project, the objective is usually defined in terms of *scope, schedule,* and *cost.*
2. State the project objective for a project you are currently working on (or have recently worked on).

   Answers will vary.
3. What is a work breakdown structure?

   A work breakdown structure is a hierarchical tree of end items that will be accomplished or produced by the project team during the project.
4. The lowest-level work item for any given branch of the work breakdown structure is called a *work package.*
5. A responsibility matrix shows which individual is responsible for accomplishing each *work item* in the work breakdown structure.

6. Identify two formats for drawing a network diagram.
   - Activity in the box
   - Activity on the arrow
7. Activities are linked in a *precedential* order to show which activities must be *finished* before others can be *started.*
8. In the activity-on-the-arrow format for drawing a network diagram, activities are linked together by circles called *events.*
9. Dummy activities are used only when the *activity-on-the-arrow* format is used for drawing a network diagram. Dummy activities are shown using a *dashed arrow.*
10. Refer to Figure 5.8.
    a. When "Prepare Mailing Labels" and "Print Questionnaire" are finished, what activity can be started?

       "Mail Questionnaire & Get Responses"
    b. In order to start "Input Response Data," which activities must have been finished immediately beforehand?

       "Mail Questionnaire & Get Responses" and "Test Software"
11. Refer to Figure 5.9.
    a. In order to start "Test Software," which activities must have been completed immediately beforehand?

       "Develop Data Analysis Software" and "Develop Software Test Data"
    b. True or false: Once "Print Questionnaire" is finished, "Mail Questionnaire & Get Responses" can start immediately. False; "Prepare Mailing Labels" must also be finished in order for "Mail Questionnaire" to start.

Chapter Six

1. True or false: The duration estimate for an activity should include the time required to perform the work plus any associated waiting time.

   True
2. The overall window of time in which a project must be completed is defined by its *estimated start* time and *required completion* time.
3. What is the equation for calculating an activity's earliest finish time?

$$\text{EF} = \text{ES} + \text{Duration Estimate}$$

4. The earliest start and earliest finish times for activities are determined by calculating *forward* through the network diagram.
5. Refer to Figures 6.6 and 6.7. What are the earliest start and earliest finish times for "Pilot-Test Questionnaire"?

$$\text{ES} = \text{Day } 13, \text{EF} = \text{Day } 33$$

6. What determines a particular activity's earliest start time? It is determined by the latest of all the earliest finish times of all the activities leading directly into that particular activity.

7. What is the equation for calculating an activity's latest start time?

$$\text{LS} = \text{LF} - \text{Duration Estimate}$$

8. The latest finish and latest start times are determined by calculating *backward* through the network diagram.
9. Refer to Figures 6. 10 and 6. 11. What are the latest finish and latest start times for "Input Response Data"?

$$\text{LF} = \text{Day } 112, \text{LS} = \text{Day } 105$$

10. What determines a particular activity's finish time? It is determined by the earliest of all the latest start times of all the activities emerging directly from that particular activity.
11. When a project has a positive total slack, some activities can be *delayed* without jeopardizing completion of the project by its required completion time. When a project has negative total slack, some activities need to be *accelerated* in order to complete the project by its required completion time.
12. Total slack is the difference between the *latest* times and the *earliest* times.
13. The longest path of activities from the beginning to the end of a project is called the *critical* path.
14. Refer to Figures 6.13 and 6.14. Of the two activities entering into activity 11, "Input Response Data," which activity has free slack? What is its value?

$$\text{Activity } 10, \text{"Test Software"}; 50 - (-8) = 58 \text{ days}$$

15. Calculate the expected duration for an activity having the following time estimates: to $t_o = 8$, $t_m = 12$, and $t_p = 22$.

$$t_e = \frac{8 + 4(12) + 22}{6} = 13$$

16. Compute the expected duration (t_e) and the variance (σ^2) for the following beta probability distribution.

$$t_e = \frac{5 + 4(8) + 23}{6} = 10$$

$$\sigma^2 = \left(\frac{23 - 5}{6}\right)2 = 9$$

17. What percentage of the area under this normal curve is shaded?

    34 percent
18. If 95 percent of the area under the following normal curve is between the two labeled points, what is the standard deviation? What is the variance?

    Since there are a total of four standard deviations (+2 and –2) between 12 and 32, $4\sigma = 32 - 12 = 20$, and thus $1\sigma = 5$. Variance $= \sigma^2 = (5)^2 = 25$.

Chapter Seven

1. What are the two kinds of data or information that need to be collected during each reporting period?
   - Data on actual performance
   - Information on any changes to the project scope, schedule, or budget
2. True or false: In general, it is better to have a shorter reporting period during a project.

   True
3. In addition to establishing a sound baseline plan, it is also necessary to proactively *control* the project after it has started in order to assure that the project objective is achieved.
4. What three types of values will the actual finish times of completed activities affect?

   The actual finish times will affect the earliest start times and the earliest finish times of the remaining activities and the total slack.
5. What three elements can project changes affect?

   Project changes can affect the scope, the budget, and the schedule of the project.
6. In analyzing a project schedule, it is important to identify all the paths of activities that have a *negative* slack.
7. When analyzing a path of activities that has negative slack, what two kinds of activities should you look at carefully?
   - Activities that are in progress or to be started in the immediate future
   - Activities that have long duration estimates
8. List four approaches to reducing the estimated durations of activities.
   - Apply more resources.
   - Assign a person with greater expertise or more experience.
   - Reduce the scope or requirements.
   - Increase productivity through improved methods or technology.
9. What are the normal and crash times and costs for activities B, C, and D in Figure 7.7?

	Normal Time	Normal Cost	Crash Time	Crash Cost
Activity B	9 weeks	$80,000	6 weeks	$110,000
Activity C	10 weeks	$40,000	9 weeks	$45,000
Activity D	8 weeks	$30,000	6 weeks	$42,000

10. What are the cost-per-week rates to accelerate activities B, C, and D in Figure 7.7?

    B, $10,000 per week; C, $5,000 per week; D, $6,000 per week
11. If all the activities in Figure 7.7 were performed in their crash times, what would be the total project cost?

    $259,000

Chapter Eight

1. At a minimum, network diagrams illustrate the *technical* constraints among activities. However, when limited resources are available, the network diagram can also be drawn to reflect *resource* constraints.
2. Resource leveling attempts to establish a schedule in which resource use is made as level as possible without extending the project beyond the *required completion* time.
3. Resource-limited scheduling develops the *shortest* schedule when the number or amount of available resources is fixed. This method will *extend* the project completion time if necessary in order to keep within the limits.

Chapter Nine

1. List the items for which costs should be estimated.
   - Labor
   - Materials
   - Subcontractors and consultants
   - Equipment and facilities rental
   - Travel
2. The first step in the project budgeting process is to allocate the total project costs to each *work package* in the work breakdown structure, thereby establishing a *total budgeted cost* for each work package.
3. Once a total budgeted cost has been established for each work package, the second step in the project budgeting process is to *distribute* each TBC over the *duration* of its work package.
4. The *cumulative budgeted cost* is the amount that was budgeted to accomplish the *work* that was scheduled to be performed up to that point in time.
5. Look at Figures 9.4 and 9.6. How much did the "Design" work package and the "Build" work package each contribute to the $4,000 cost overrun at the end of week 8?

	Amount	Overrun or Underrun?
Design	$2,000	underrun
Build	$6,000	overrun

6. Cumulative earned value is calculated by first determining the *percent complete* for each work package and then multiplying it by the *total budgeted cost* for the work package.
7. List the four cost-related measures used to analyze project cost performance.
   - TBC (total budgeted cost)
   - CBC (cumulative budgeted cost)
   - CAC (cumulative actual cost)
   - CEV (cumulative earned value)

8. What is the cost performance index for the "Design" work package in the packaging machine project at the end of week 5?

$$\text{CPI} = \frac{\$24{,}000}{\$22{,}000} = 1.091$$

9. What is the cost variance for the "Build" work package in the packaging machine project at the end of week 8?

$$\text{CV} = \$30{,}000 - \$46{,}000 = -\$16{,}000$$

10. Using the first forecasting method described, calculate the forecasted cost at completion for the "Build" work package in the packaging machine project.

$$\text{FCAC} = \frac{\$60{,}000}{0.65} = \$92{,}300 \left(\textit{Note}\text{: CPI} = \frac{\$30{,}000}{\$46{,}000} = 0.65 \right)$$

11. Using the second forecasting method described, calculate the forecasted cost at completion for the "Build" work package in the packaging machine project.

$$\text{FCAC} = \$46{,}000 + (\$60{,}000 - \$30{,}000) = \$76{,}000$$

12. In analyzing cost performance, it's important to identify all of the work packages that have a *negative* cost variance or a cost performance index of less than 1. 0.
13. When evaluating work packages that have a negative cost variance, you should focus on taking corrective actions to reduce the costs of activities that will be performed in the *near* term and those that have a *large* cost estimate.
14. The key to managing cash flow is to ensure that cash *comes in* faster than it *goes out*.
15. If sufficient funds are not available to meet expenses, a contractor may need to *borrow* money. This adds to the cost of the project, because the contractor then has to pay *interest* also.

Chapter Ten

1. What two benefits does the project manager realize by involving the team in developing the plan?

   The project manager ensures a more comprehensive plan and gains the commitment of the team to achieve the plan.

2. The project manager secures the *appropriate resources* to perform the work and then assigns *responsibility* and delegates *authority* to specific individuals for the various tasks.
3. The project manager implements a project management information system to serve what two functions?

   The two functions are to track actual progress and compare it with planned progress.

4. The project manager has primary responsibility for providing leadership for what three management functions?
   - Planning
   - Organizing
   - Controlling
5. Project leadership involves *inspiring* the people assigned to the project to work as a team to implement the *plan* and achieve the *project objective* successfully.
6. Project leadership requires *involvement* and *empowerment* of the project team.
7. The capable project manager understands what *motivates* team members and creates a *supportive* environment in which individuals work as part of a high-performing team.
8. People want to feel that they are making a *contribution* to the project and need to be *recognized.*
9. A project manager sets the tone for the project team by establishing an environment of *trust,* high *expectations,* and *enjoyment.*
10. People working on projects look for *affiliation* and *socialization;* they don't want to work in *isolation.*
11. Leadership requires that the project manager be highly *motivated* and set a *positive example* for the project team.
12. A good project manager believes that all individuals are *valuable* to the organization and that they can make greater contributions through *continuous learning.*
13. Rather than create a fear of *failure,* the project manager acknowledges that mistakes are part of the *learning* and *growth* experience.
14. A good project manager values and expects continuous *self-improvement.*
15. List five reasons it is important for the project manager to have frequent communication.
    - To keep the project moving
    - To identify potential problems
    - To solicit suggestions for improving project performance
    - To keep abreast of customer satisfaction
    - To avoid surprises
16. A high level of communication is especially important early in the project to help build a good *working relationship* with the project team and to establish clear *expectations* with the customer.
17. What are three ways in which a project manager communicates?
    - Meetings
    - Informal conversations
    - Written reports
18. Good project managers spend more time *listening* than *talking.*
19. Give three reasons the project manager should establish ongoing communication with the customer.
    - To keep the customer informed
    - To determine whether there are any changes in expectations
    - To keep abreast of the degree of customer satisfaction

20. Why does communication by project managers need to be timely, honest, and unambiguous?

    Such communication establishes credibility, builds trust, and prevents rumors.
21. The project manager should have an informal *conversation* with each person on the project team and with each key individual in the *customer* organization.
22. The project manager should use *open-ended* questions and do a lot of *listening*.
23. The project manager needs to have a good sense of *humor* and needs to stay *physically* fit.
24. In solving problems, the project manager needs to be able to see the *big picture* and how potential solutions might affect other parts of the project.
25. What skills do effective project managers have?
    - Leadership ability
    - Ability to develop people
    - Communication skills
    - Interpersonal skills
    - Ability to handle stress
    - Problem-solving skills
    - Time management skills
26. a. Identify one skill you want to develop.
    b. Identify three things you can do to develop that skill.
    c. Select one of the three things listed above and pick a date by which you will have it done.

    Answers will vary.
27. Delegation involves *empowering* the project team to achieve the *project objective* and each team member to accomplish the *expected results* for his or her area of responsibility.
28. Project managers should not tell individuals *how* to do the assigned tasks.
29. When assigning individuals to specific tasks, the project manager needs to take into consideration the person's *capabilities, potential,* and *workload.*
30. Effective delegation requires that the project manager have *confidence* in each member of the project team.
31. Delegation requires that individuals be *accountable* for achieving the expected results.
32. Changes may be initiated by the *customer* or by the *project team* or may be caused by *unanticipated occurrences* during the performance of the project.
33. The project manager's job is to *manage* and *control* changes in order to *minimize* any negative impact on the successful accomplishment of the project objective.
34. At the start of the project, the project manager needs to establish *procedures* regarding how changes will be *documented* and *authorized*.

Chapter Eleven

1. A project team is a group of individuals working *interdependently* to achieve the project *obejective.*
2. Teamwork is the *cooperative* effort by members of a team to achieve a *common* goal.
3. During the forming stage, *little* actual work is accomplished because of the *high* level of anxiety individuals have.
4. In the forming stage, individuals do a lot of *questioning.*
5. During the forming stage, the project manager must provide *direction* and *structure* for the project team.
6. During the storming stage, *conflict* emerges and *tension* increases.
7. During the storming stage, team members wonder how much *control* and *authority* they have.
8. During the storming stage, the project manager needs to provide *guidance* and foster *conflict resolution.*
9. In the norming stage, *conflict* and *dissatisfaction* are reduced, *cohesion* begins to develop, and there is a sense of *team.*
10. During the norming stage, *trust* begins to develop. There is a greater sharing of *information, ideas,* and *feelings; cooperation* increases.
11. In the norming stage, *work performance* accelerates and *productivity* increases.
12. During the performing stage, there is a great degree of *interdependency*—members frequently *collaborate* and willingly *help* each other with work beyond their own assigned tasks.
13. During the performing stage, the project manager fully *delegates* responsibility and authority, thereby empowering the project team.
14. What are the four stages of team development and growth?
    - Forming
    - Storming
    - Norming
    - Performing
15. An effective project team has a clear understanding of the project *objective* and clear expectations of each person's *role* and *responsibilities.*
16. Effective project teams have a *results* orientation; each person has a strong commitment to achieving the *project objective.* There is a high degree of *cooperation* and *collaboration.*
17. Effective project teams have a high level of *trust.* They are able to resolve conflict through constructive and timely *feedback* and positive *confrontation* of the issues.
18. The project manager needs to articulate the project *objective* frequently. At periodic meetings, he or she should always ask whether anyone has any *questions* about what must be accomplished.
19. The project manager should meet individually with each team member, to tell the member why she or he was *selected* for the project and describe her or his expected *role* and *responsibilities.*

20. The project manager needs to establish preliminary operating *procedures* at the beginning of the project, but be open to suggestions for *eliminating* or *streamlining* them when they no longer *contribute* to the effective and efficient performance of the project.
21. The project manager should try to determine what *motivates* each individual and then create a project *environment* where these motivators are available.
22. It's important for the project manager to have regular project *status review* meetings with a published agenda. *Participation* and questions should be encouraged during such meetings.
23. A project manager should periodically solicit others' suggestions for improving her or his *leadership* skills.
24. A project team made up of a *small* number of individuals with *long*-term assignments will be more efficient than a project team composed of a *large* number of individuals with *short*-term assignments.
25. What are some barriers to team effectiveness?
    - Unclear goals
    - Unclear definition of roles and responsibilities
    - Lack of project structure
    - Lack of commitment
    - Poor communication
    - Poor leadership
    - Turnover of project team members
    - Dysfunctional behavior
26. Effective team members plan, control, and feel *accountable* for their individual work efforts. They have high *expectations* of themselves.
27. Effective team members *participate* and *communicate*. They are not only problem identifiers, but also *problem solvers*.
28. Think about projects in which you have been involved. What are some characteristics of individual team members that made them effective contributors?

    Answers will vary.
29. Team building is the responsibility of both the *project manager* and the *project team*.
30. *Socializing* among team members supports *team building*. Individual members need to *communicate* with one another frequently.
31. Diversity of the team brings *unique* ideas and *perspectives* to projects.
32. What are some dimensions of diversity?
    - *Age or generational*
    - *Appearance*
    - *Ethnicity or ancestry*
    - *Gender*
    - *Health*
    - *Job status*

- *Marital and parental status*
- *Race*
- *Religious affiliation*

33. Team members should not *stereotype* or make *assumptions* about a team member's behavior or *performance* based on their *diversity*.
34. Two actions an organization can take to support a positive climate for diversity are to have a written *policy* regarding diversity and provide *training* about diversity in the workplace.
35. Barriers to valuing diversity include lack of *awareness* and lack of *understanding*.
36. What are some reasons why the project team should value diversity as a strength?
    - *Enrich communication*
    - *Foster better relationships*
    - *Create an enjoyable workplace*
    - *Enhance team performance*
37. Customers and suppliers want to do business with a project contractor they can *trust*.
38. Two actions an organization can take to help prevent any wrongdoing are to have a *written policy* on ethical behavior and to provide *training* about ethics in the workplace.
39. *Personal integrity* is the foundation for workplace ethics.
40. What are common sources of conflict on projects?
    - Work scope
    - Resource assignments
    - Schedule
    - Cost
    - Priorities
    - Organizational issues
    - Personal differences
41. Handled properly, conflict can be *beneficial*.
42. What are five approaches to handling conflict?
    - Avoiding or withdrawing
    - Competing or forcing
    - Accommodating or smoothing
    - Compromising
    - Collaborating, confronting, or problem solving
43. What are the nine steps involved in problem solving?
    - Develop a problem statement.
    - Identify potential causes of the problem.
    - Gather data and verify the most likely causes.
    - Identify possible solutions.
    - Evaluate the alternative solutions.

- Determine the best solution.
- Revise the project plan.
- Implement the solution.
- Determine whether the problem has been solved.

44. In brainstorming, the *quantity* of ideas generated is more important than the *quality* of the ideas.
45. What are some things you can do to effectively manage your time?
    - Identify weekly goals.
    - Make a to-do list each day.
    - Focus on accomplishing your daily to-do list.
    - Control interruptions.
    - Learn to say "no."
    - Make effective use of waiting time.
    - Handle paperwork only once.
    - Reward yourself.

Chapter Twelve

1. Identify two types of personal oral communication.
   - Face-to-face communication
   - Telephone conversations
2. Body language can be used not only by the person talking, but also by the *listener,* as a way of providing *feedback* to the person talking.
3. In personal communication, people need to be sensitive to body language reflective of the *cultural diversity* of the participants.
4. Project team members need to be *proactive* in initiating timely communication to *get* and *give* information.
5. Identify two methods you can use to generate feedback during oral communication.
   - Ask the other person to state her or his understanding of what you said.
   - Paraphrase what you think the other person said.
6. What are two forms of personal written communication?
   - Internal memos
   - External letters
7. Failure to *listen* can cause a *breakdown* in communication between people.
8. List some common barriers to effective listening.
   - Pretending to listen
   - Distractions
   - Bias and closed-mindedness
   - Impatience
   - Jumping to conclusions

9. What are some things you can do to improve your listening skills?
   - Focus on the person talking.
   - Engage in active listening.
   - Ask questions.
   - Don't interrupt.
10. What are the primary purposes of a status review meeting?
    - Inform
    - Identify problems
    - Identify action items
11. True or false: When members of the project team identify problems or potential problems, they should wait until the next scheduled status review meeting to bring them up for discussion.

    False; they should immediately initiate a problem-solving meeting with the appropriate team members.
12. On technical projects there are often two design review meetings: a *preliminary* design review meeting and a *final* design review meeting.
13. To ensure that a meeting is effective, what are some steps that the person organizing or leading the meeting should take before the meeting?
    - Determine whether a meeting is really necessary.
    - Determine the purpose of the meeting.
    - Determine who needs to participate.
    - Distribute an agenda.
    - Prepare visual aids or handouts.
    - Make meeting room arrangements.
14. True or false: It's always a good idea to wait for everyone to arrive before starting a meeting, even if it's beyond the scheduled start time. False; if the meeting leader waits for latecomers, people will get in the habit of showing up late because they know the meeting won't start on time anyway.
15. What are some important things to do in preparing a presentation?
    - Determine the purpose of the presentation.
    - Know the audience.
    - Make an outline.
    - Use simple language.
    - Prepare notes.
    - Practice.
    - Prepare visual aids.
    - Make copies of handout materials.
    - Request audiovisual equipment.
    - Go into the meeting room and get a "feel" for the surroundings.

16. What are some important things to keep in mind when delivering a presentation?
    - Expect a bit of nervousness.
    - Know your opening lines.
    - Use the 3-T approach.
    - Talk to the audience, not at it.
    - Speak clearly and confidently.
    - Use appropriate animation.
    - Do not stand in front of your visual aids.
    - Build interest by developing your story.
    - Don't digress.
    - State why key points are important to the audience.
    - Sum up each point before moving on.
    - Know your closing lines.
    - Allow time for questions from the audience.
    - Be sincere, candid, and confident in responding to questions.
17. Project reports should be written to address what is of interest to the *readers,* not what is of interest to the person *writing* the report.
18. The primary purpose of progress reports is to report on project *accomplishments* rather than what *activities* the project team was busy on.
19. True or false: A project final report is an accumulation of the progress reports prepared during the project.

    False; it's a summary of the project.
20. What are some important guidelines to keep in mind when preparing a report?
    - Make it concise.
    - Write as you would speak.
    - Put the most important points first.
    - Use graphics.
    - Make the format inviting and easy to read.
21. Revisions to project documents can result from changes initiated by the *customer* or by the *project team.*
22. Early in the project, agreement should be reached regarding the way changes will be *documented* and *authorized.*
23. Teleconferencing includes tools such as *conference* calls and *videoconferencing.*

Chapter Thirteen

1. The functional organization emphasizes the importance of the contribution of each functional component's *expertise* to the company's products.
2. True or false: In a functional organization, individuals continue to perform their regular functional jobs while they serve part-time on a project task force.

   True

3. A company with a functional structure may periodically form project task forces to work on *internal* projects, but will seldom perform projects involving *external* customers.
4. In a project-type organization, all resources are assigned *full*-time to work on a particular project. The project manager has complete *project* and *administrative* authority over the project team.
5. A project-type organization can be cost-*inefficient*.
6. Project-type organization structures are found primarily in companies that are involved in very *large* projects.
7. The matrix organization structure provides the project and customer focus of the *project* structure, but it retains the functional expertise of the *functional* structure.
8. In a matrix organization, the *functional* components provide a pool of *expertise* to support ongoing projects.
9. The matrix organization structure results in effective utilization of *resources* and minimizes overall *costs* because it allows for the *sharing* of individuals' time among several *projects*.
10. In a matrix-type organization, each member of a *project team* has a dual reporting relationship to the temporary *project* manager and to a permanent *functional* manager.
11. In a matrix organization, the project manager defines *what* has to be done, by *when,* and for how much *money* to meet the project *objective* and satisfy the customer.
12. In a matrix organization, each functional manager is responsible for *how* the work will be accomplished and *who* will do each task.
13. The matrix organization structure allows for fast response upon problem identification because it has both a *horizontal* and a *vertical* path for the flow of *information*.
14. List three common types of structures that can be used to organize people to work on projects.
    - Functional
    - Project
    - Matrix
15. What are some advantages and disadvantages of the functional organization structure?

    Advantages:
    - No duplication of activities
    - Functional excellence

    Disadvantages:
    - Insularity
    - Slow response time
    - Lack of customer focus

16. What are some advantages and disadvantages of the project organization structure?

    Advantages:

    - Control over resources
    - Responsiveness to customers

    Disadvantages:

    - Cost-inefficiency
    - Low level of knowledge transfer among projects

17. What are some advantages and disadvantages of the matrix organization structure?

    Advantages:

    - Efficient utilization of resources
    - Functional expertise available to all projects
    - Increased learning and knowledge transfer
    - Responsiveness
    - Customer focus

    Disadvantages:

    - Dual reporting relationships
    - Need for balance of power

Glossary

A

Activity A defined piece of work that consumes time; task.

Activity in the box (AIB) A form of network diagramming in which activities are represented by boxes.

Activity on the arrow (AOA) A form of network diagramming in which activities are represented by arrows.

Actual cost The amount that has actually been expended.

Actual finish time (AF) The time at which a particular activity is actually completed.

As-late-as-possible (ALAP) schedule A schedule based on the latest start time of each activity in the project.

As-soon-as-possible (ASAP) schedule A schedule based on the earliest start time of each activity in the project.

B

Bar chart *See* Gantt chart.

Baseline plan The original plan, or roadmap, laying out the way in which the project scope will be accomplished on time and within budget.

Best and final offer (BAFO) A final price for a project, submitted by a contractor at the request of a customer who is considering proposals from several contractors for the same project.

Beta probability distribution A distribution that is frequently used to calculate the expected duration and variance for an activity based on the activity's optimistic, most likely, and pessimistic time estimates.

Bid/no-bid decision An evaluation by a contractor of whether to go ahead with the preparation of a proposal in response to a customer's request for proposal.

C

Committed cost The funds that are unavailable to be spent elsewhere because they will be needed at some later time to pay for an item, such as material, that has been ordered; commitment; encumbered cost.

Contingency An amount a contractor may include in a proposal to cover unexpected costs that may arise during a project; management reserve.

Contingency plan A pre-defined set of actions that would be implemented if the risk event occurs.

Contract An agreement between a contractor, who agrees to provide a product or service (deliverables), and a customer, who agrees to pay the contractor a certain amount of money in return.

Cost The amount the customer has agreed to pay for acceptable project deliverables.

Cost estimate Estimate of total cost of an activity, work package or project based on the types and quantities of resources required.

Cost performance index (CPI) A measure of the cost efficiency with which the project is being performed; the cumulative earned value divided by the cumulative actual cost.

Cost-reimbursement contract A contract in which a customer agrees to pay a contractor for all actual costs incurred during a project, plus some agreed-upon profit.

Cost variance (CV) An indicator of cost performance; the cumulative earned value minus the cumulative actual cost.

Crash cost The estimated cost of completing an activity in the shortest possible time (the crash time).

Crash time The shortest estimated length of time in which an activity can be completed.

Critical path In a network diagram, any path of activities with zero or negative total slack. *See also* Most critical path.

Critical path method (CPM) A network planning technique.

Cumulative actual cost (CAC) The amount that has actually been expended to accomplish all the work performed up to a specific point in time.

Cumulative budgeted cost (CBC) The amount budgeted to accomplish all the work scheduled to be performed up to a specific point in time.

Cumulative earned value (CEV) The value of the work actually performed up to a specific point in time; total budgeted cost multiplied by the percentage of the work estimated to be complete.

Customer The entity that provides the funds necessary to accomplish a project. A customer may be a person, an organization, or a group of people or organizations.

Customer requirements Specifications for a project and/or attributes of a deliverable specified by a customer in a request for proposal. Requirements may include size, quantity, color, speed, and other physical or operational parameters that a contractor's proposed solution must satisfy.

D

Deliverables The tangible items or products that the customer expects the contractor to provide during performance of the project.

Due date The date, specified in a request for proposal, by which a customer expects potential contractors to submit proposals.

Dummy activity A special type of activity, used in the activity-on-the-arrow form of network diagramming, that consumes no time. A dummy activity is represented by a dashed arrow.

Duration estimate The estimated total time an activity will take from start to finish, including associated waiting time; time estimate.

E

Earliest finish time (EF) The earliest time by which a particular activity can be completed; the activity's earliest start time plus the activity's estimated duration.

Earliest start time (ES) The earliest time at which a particular activity can begin; the project's estimated start time plus the estimated duration of preceding activities.

Earned value (EV) The value of the work actually performed.

Estimated start time The time or date when a project is expected to begin.

Evaluation criteria The standards, specified in a request for proposal, that a customer will use to evaluate proposals from competing contractors.

Events Interconnecting points that link activities in the activity-on-the-arrow form of network diagramming. An event is represented by a circle.

Exception A variation from a customer's specified requirements, stated by a contractor in a proposal.

Expected duration (t_e) Also called the mean or average duration. The expected duration for an activity, calculated from the activity's optimistic, most likely, and pessimistic time estimates, as follows:

$$t_e = \frac{t_o + 4(t_m) + t_p}{6}$$

F

Fixed-price contract A contract in which a customer and a contractor agree on a price that will not change no matter how much the project actually costs the contractor.

Float *See* Total slack.

Forecasted cost at completion (FCAC) The projected total cost of all the work required to complete a project.

Free slack (FS) The amount of time that a particular activity can be delayed without delaying the earliest start time of its immediately succeeding activities; the relative difference between the amounts of total slack for activities entering into that same activity. It's always a positive value.

Functional organization structure An organizational structure in which groups are made up of individuals who perform the same function, such as engineering or manufacturing, or have the same expertise or skills, such as electronics engineering or testing.

G

Gantt chart A planning and scheduling tool that displays project activities along a time scale; bar chart.

Graphical evaluation and review technique (GERT) A type of network planning technique.

I

Indirect costs *See* Overhead.

Information system (IS) A computer-based system that accepts data as input, processes the data, and produces information for users.

L

Laddering A method of showing the logical precedential relationship of a set of activities that is repeated several times consecutively.

Latest finish time (LF) The latest time by which a particular activity must be completed in order for the entire project to be finished by its required completion time.

Latest start time (LS) The latest time by which a particular activity must be started in order for the entire project to be finished by its required completion time; the activity's latest finish time minus the activity's estimated duration.

M

Management reserve *See* Contingency.

Matrix organization structure A hybrid of the functional and project organizational structures, in which resources from appropriate functional components of a company are temporarily assigned to particular projects.

Most critical path In a network diagram, the most time-consuming (longest) path of activities; the path of activities that has the lowest value—either least positive or most negative—for total slack.

Most likely time estimate (t_m) The time in which an activity can most frequently be completed under normal conditions.

N

Network diagram A graphic display of the activities to be performed to achieve the overall project work scope, showing their sequence and interdependencies.

Noncritical path In a network diagram, any path of activities with positive total slack.

Normal cost The estimated cost of completing an activity under normal conditions, according to the plan.

Normal probability distribution A bellshaped distribution of values that is symmetrical around its mean value.

Normal time The estimated length of time required to perform an activity under normal conditions, according to the plan.

O

Objective The expected result or product of a project, usually defined in terms of scope, schedule, and cost.

Optimistic time estimate (t_o) The time in which an activity can be completed if everything goes perfectly well and there are no complications.

Overhead A percentage of the direct costs of a particular project, added to a contractor's proposal to cover costs of doing business, such as insurance, depreciation, general management, and human resources; indirect costs.

P

Percent complete An estimate in percentage form, of the proportion of the work involved in a particular work package that has been completed.

Pessimistic time estimate (t_p) The time in which an activity can be completed under adverse conditions, such as in the presence of unusual or unforeseen complications.

Planning The systematic arrangement of tasks to accomplish an objective; determining what needs to be done, who will do it, how long it will take, and how much it will cost.

Precedence diagramming method (PDM) A type of network planning technique.

Precedential relationship The order in which activities must be finished before other activities can start.

Predecessor event The event at the beginning of an activity (tail of the arrow) in the activity-on-the-arrow form of network diagramming; start event.

Program evaluation and review techniques (PERT) A network planning technique.

Project An endeavor to accomplish a specific objective through a unique set of interrelated tasks and the effective utilization of resources.

Project control Regularly gathering data on actual project performance, comparing actual performance to planned performance, and taking corrective measures if actual performance is behind planned performance.

Project control process *See* Project control.

Project life cycle The four phases through which a project moves: identification of a need, problem, or opportunity; development of a proposed solution; implementation of the proposed solution; and termination of the project.

Project manager The individual who provides leadership to the project team to accomplish the project objective.

Project organization structure An organization structure in which each project has its own project manager and project team and all the resources needed to accomplish an individual project are assigned full-time to that project.

Project scope All the work that must be done to accomplish the project's objective to the customer's satisfaction; scope of the project; work scope; scope of work.

Project selection Evaluating various needs or opportunities and then deciding which of these should move forward as a project to be implemented.

Project team A group of individuals working interdependently to achieve the project objective.

Proposal A document, usually prepared by a contractor, that outlines an approach to meeting a need or solving a problem for a potential customer.

R

Reporting period The time interval at which actual project performance will be compared to planned performance.

Request for proposal (RFP) A document, usually prepared by the customer, that defines a need or problem, requirements, and expectations.

Required completion time The time or date by which a project must be completed.

Resource leveling A method for developing a schedule that attempts to minimize the fluctuations in requirements for resources without extending the project schedule beyond the required completion time; resource smoothing.

Resource-limited scheduling A method for developing the shortest schedule when the number or amount of available resources is limited. This method will extend the project completion time if necessary in order to keep within the resource limits.

Responsibility matrix A table that lists the individuals or organizational units responsible for accomplishing each work item in a work breakdown structure.

Risk The possibility that an unwanted circumstance will occur that can result in some loss.

Risk assessment matrix A table that includes potential risks, their likelihood of occurrence, impact, and planned responses.

Risk management The identification, assessment, and response to project risks in order to minimize the likelihood and impact of the consequences of adverse events on the achievement of the project objective.

S

Schedule A timetable for a project plan.

Scope of work *See* Project scope.

Smoothing *See* Resource leveling.

Standard deviation A measure of the dispersion, or spread, of a distribution from its expected value; the square root of the variance.

Statement of work (SOW) A document outlining the tasks, or work elements, the customer wants the contractor to perform.

Successor event The event at the end of an activity (head of the arrow) in the activity-on-the-arrow form of network diagramming; finish event.

Systems development life cycle (SDLC) A project management planning tool consisting of a set of phases or steps to be completed over the course of development of an information system.

T

Team building Developing a group of individuals into a team to accomplish the project objective.

Teamwork The cooperative effort by members of the project team to achieve the project objective.

Time estimate *See* Duration estimate.

Total budgeted cost (TBC) The portion of the entire project budget that is allocated to complete all of the activities and work associated with a particular work package.

Total slack (TS) Float. If it's a positive value, it's the amount of time that the activities on a particular path can be delayed without jeopardizing completion of the project by its required completion time. If it's a negative value, it's the amount of time that the activities on a particular path must be accelerated in order to complete the project by its required completion time.

V

Variance A measure of the dispersion, or spread, of a distribution from its expected value.

W

Win ratio A measure of an organization's success in the number or dollar value of proposals that result in contractual agreements with customers.

Work breakdown structure (WBS) A hierarchical tree of work elements or items that will be accomplished or produced by the project team during the project.

Work items Individual pieces of a project in a work breakdown structure.

Work package The lowest-level item of any branch of a work breakdown structure.

Work scope *See* Project scope.

Index

A

B

C

G

H

I

J

L

M

N

O

P

R

S

T